THE
EFFECTIVE
TEACHER

THE
EFFECTIVE
TEACHER

STUDY GUIDE AND READINGS

LORIN W. ANDERSON

RANDOM HOUSE
NEW YORK

First Edition
987654321
Copyright © 1989 by Random House, Inc.

Library of Congress Cataloging-in-Publication Data

Anderson, Lorin W.
    The effective teacher.

    Bibliography: p.
    1. Teaching.   2. Classroom management.
3. Television in teacher training.   I. Title.
LB1025.2.A6955   1989   371.1'02   88–18414
ISBN 0–394–37886–5

Manufactured in the United States of America

Cover Design: Karin Batten
Text Design: Susan Phillips

PREFACE

In 1984, I was asked by Dr. John Mulhern, then dean of the College of Education, University of South Carolina, to develop a telecourse that emphasized the improvement of classroom teaching and was based on existing research. Being a firm believer in the wise use of knowledge derived from research to improve teaching, and also believing that the medium of television could be helpful in both "telling and showing" basic concepts and principles of effective teaching, I agreed to develop such a telecourse.

I began my efforts by contacting some fifteen recognized experts in the field of classroom teaching and school learning. I invited them to the university to talk with me about their work and to be interviewed while the television cameras were rolling. Most of them graciously accepted my invitation. Much of what is included in the telecourse I learned from them.

After they left Columbia, I wrote and asked them to suggest articles, book chapters, and scholarly papers that would be appropriate for inclusion in a book of readings to accompany the telecourse. Once again, the response was overwhelming. Some sixty potential readings were recommended.

As the development of the telecourse pro-

ceeded, I began to make selections from among the recommended readings, selections that supported and extended the content included in the various lessons and units. The thirty-three readings included in this anthology represent the final selections.

This volume begins with a study guide prepared for students enrolled in the telecourse. The study guide starts with an introduction and is organized around the five major units of the telecourse and the lessons within the units.

The readings that follow the study guide also are organized around the five major units. Within each unit, the readings are organized alphabetically by author. The study guide links the readings with specific lessons within the units.

In combination with the videotaped lessons, the readings add depth and detail to what can be "shown and told" in a 27-minute, 50-second time period. Independent of the accompanying videotaped lessons, the readings in this volume provide much food for thought concerning the improvement of teaching.

LWA
Columbia, South Carolina
December 1987

ACKNOWLEDGMENTS

Producing a television course is a challenging, time-consuming, frustrating, yet rewarding endeavor. Several years were devoted to the development of this particular course, and a number of people were involved in its evolution. A great deal of gratitude is owed them all. Special thanks go to Linda DuRant, the producer and director of the telecourse, for her insight, support, and technical competence; Sara Nalley, the host of the series, for her professionalism and for rewriting my jargon-filled, sometimes inaccurate, scripts; Sian Wetherill, Casey Reiling Schnepel, and Catherine Schachner for their patience and ability to produce under stressful conditions; Arlayne Ash and Carol Carlson of Richland County (South Carolina) School District One for their assistance in securing the teachers and students who agreed to be televised and interviewed; Susan Bridwell, Lynn Nerren, John Scruggs, and Sue Willis for their efforts in getting this book into production; Walt Lardner for the cartoons appearing in the televised lessons; Dan Greshel for the opening and closing graphics; Landry Layson for lighting design; Sam Glenn for the design of the set; the Richland County (South Carolina) School District One administrators and teachers who invited us into their classrooms and agreed to be interviewed on camera; the university researchers for subjecting themselves to hours of interviews—-specifically, Peter Airasian, Boston College; Rebecca Barr, National College of Education, Evanston, Illinois; Daniel Barron, University of South Carolina; David Berliner, then of the University of Arizona, now of Arizona State University; Virginia Biggy, University of Lowell, Massachusetts; Christopher Clark, Michigan State University; Carolyn Evertson, Vanderbilt University; Judith Green, Ohio State University; Asa Hilliard, Georgia State University; Philip Jackson, University of Chicago; David Johnson, University of Minnesota; Dorothy Strickland, Teachers College, Columbia University; Herbert Walberg, University of Illinois, Chicago; Margaret Wang, Temple University; Jean Akers, of Random House, for project direction; Carol Flechner for her impeccable responsibility and care in seeing the manuscript to finished product in every detail; Lane Akers for his publishing expertise, and for his interest and vision for the project and confidence in making this production a new venture into telecourse marketing for Random House; and, finally, the administrators at both South Carolina ETV and the University of South Carolina who provided the necessary financial support for the preparation and production of the course. Thank you all.

CONTENTS

READINGS

STUDY GUIDE

INTRODUCTION TO THE STUDY GUIDE

TO THE STUDENT

"A teacher affects eternity. He can never tell where his influence stops" (Henry Adams, 1918).

Welcome to *The Effective Teacher,* a graduate education television course. Whether you are a novice or have been teaching for decades, some of the ideas and information presented in this course should be of interest and use to you as you struggle to solve the problems confronting all teachers in today's school.

If this is your first telecourse, you may wish to consider several important points about the nature of this course.

- Although you will be watching television for only 12 or 13 hours, the information contained in these hours is "densely packed"—that is, a great deal of information is contained in a very short period of time (30-minute lessons).
- Because of the "packaging" of this information, be sure to watch each segment without interruption. Watching television for the purpose of learning is not like watching a situation comedy, an adventure series, or a sporting event. You will have to watch *actively* and avoid the temptation to fall into the passive, half-viewing approach you use with entertainment television.

- Also because of this "packaging," be sure to read the appropriate portions of the study guide *both before and after* you view that segment. Do not take notes as you watch. Rather, *after* viewing the segment *but before* reading over the study guide, jot down what you consider to be the major ideas presented in the segment that you observed.
- Although you, like most people who enroll in telecourses, are likely to be busy with other activities while enrolled, try to keep up with the assigned readings. These readings supplement as well as expand upon the information and ideas included in the televised lessons.
- The lessons are organized into units. The course consists of six units, the final unit of which summarizes the information and ideas presented in the previous five units and speculates on the future of effective teaching.
- Within each unit, attempt to integrate the information presented in the various lessons. Look for interrelationships. Look for opposing points of view. Pay attention to the overview of each unit presented in the study guide, and take time to respond to the questions asked in the unit "Self-Test."
- Finally, because the viewing time is only 12 or 13 hours, the unit assignments are an important part of your learning.. Take the time needed to prepare essays, pro-

posals, plans, or projects that both foster your learning and demonstrate the extent and quality of that learning.

GOALS AND OBJECTIVES

The purposes of this course can be stated in terms of two general goals and a related set of objectives. The goals are that students should (1) develop an understanding of the complexity of classroom teaching and school learning and, based on that understanding, (2) develop practices and strategies that enable them to continually evaluate and improve teaching and learning effectiveness.

The associated set of objectives are best presented on a unit-by-unit basis. Students should acquire important concepts and skills in the following areas:

- teachers' content, pedagogical, and personal knowledge (Lesson 1); organization constraints on teachers (Lesson 2); methods used to study teaching (Lesson 3); and varying conceptions of "good teaching" (Lesson 4).
- starting school (Lesson 5); establishing and maintaining meaningful and workable rules and routines (Lesson 6); alternative approaches to organizing classrooms (e.g., whole class, subgroups, individuals) (Lesson 7); and cooperative, competitive, and individualistic learning environments (Lesson 8)
- defining educational aims and purposes (Lesson 9); recognizing and attending to differences among learners (Lesson 10); teacher planning (Lesson 11); concerns for instructional time and opportunity to learn (Lessons 12 and 13); and using instructional support materials and educational technologies (Lessons 14 and 15)
- orienting students (Lesson 16); explaining

(Lesson 17); questioning (Lesson 18); using assignments (Lesson 19); and involving students in learning (Lesson 20)
- assessing students (Lesson 21); grading (Lesson 22); providing feedback and correction (Lesson 23); and evaluating teachers (Lesson 24)

As has been mentioned, the final two lessons are intended to summarize the major points made during the previous lessons ("What We Know") and to speculate as to what knowledge and practice is needed to improve teacher effectiveness ("Where Do We Go from Here?").

THE STRUCTURE OF THE TELEVISION LESSON

The structure of the lessons in this course can be simply understood. In each, there is an opening, a body, and a closing.

The Opening

Each lesson begins with one or more short scenes emphasizing a main point or common theme. Try to identify the lesson topic by determining the main point or common theme. The course host, Sara Nalley, then gives a brief introduction to the lesson, including a set of questions to be addressed. In most lessons, the end of the opening is signaled by a skit that highlights a major topic or concept included in the lesson whether by placing it in a nonschool setting or through the use of exaggeration.

The Body

The body of each lesson contains what is known (or believed to be known) about the lesson topic. Three key sets of "players" participate in the body. The basic knowledge in the form of research evidence or informed opinion is presented by *faculty members from several major research universities* who have specialized in research on classroom teaching and school learning. This knowledge is illustrated by a *variety of teachers and students in actual classrooms and schools.* Some of these illustrations are "shown" using videotapes of classroom activities. Other illustrations are "told" using teachers' and students' responses to questions asked during interviews. Finally, the *course host* introduces important concepts, provides transitions from one concept to another, and summarizes major points made during the lesson.

The Closing

The closing of most lessons includes a series of recommendations pertaining to the use of the information in improving the practice of teaching. These recommendations are typically few in number (usually from three to six) and are intended as guidelines, rather than rigid prescriptions, for enhancing the quality of classroom teaching. The recommendations are made by the course host, often illustrated by the classroom teachers, with supportive arguments offered by the university researchers.

The Set and the Apple. Wooden desks, chalkboards, and near-perfect cursive writing—the set for *The Effective Teacher.* This traditional set is intended to convey the long history of teaching. Although teachers come and go, teaching in schools and classrooms in its present form has survived for almost a century in this country. "New" knowledge and ideas are best understood within this rich historical tradition.

The apple is a traditional symbol of appreciation. Apples have been given to teachers to thank them for many things, often for simply being there. The emphasis in both the opening and closing of each lesson is on two hands holding the apple. In its most basic form,

education requires just three elements: a teacher, a learner, and knowledge to be shared.

THE STUDY GUIDE

Like the telecourse, this study guide is organized into units. At the beginning of each unit, an overview of the structure of the unit is presented. At the end of each unit, a self-test and one or more unit assignments are included. The purpose of the self-test is to permit you to test your knowledge and understanding of the basic concepts and principles included in the unit. The purpose of the unit assignments is to assess your ability to apply these concepts and generalizations. There are at least three audiences for whom the course is intended: practicing teachers, practicing administrators, and non-practicing teachers and administrators. As a consequence, most units have multiple assignments. Members of the audiences are to choose the unit assignment most appropriate, potentially useful, or both.

Sandwiched between the beginning and the end of each unit is information concerning each of the lessons contained within that unit. The format for the presentation of this information is virtually identical from lesson to lesson. Each lesson guide begins with a statement of the purpose of the lesson. Next, an overview of the lesson is presented, which provides an abstract of the lesson as presented on television. The basic concepts and principles included in the lesson are then discussed in the order in which they appear in the televised lesson. Finally, the readings associated with each lesson are identified and summarized briefly. (Additional readings may also be given.) Coupled with the information presented during the televised lesson, these readings should help to answer questions raised at the beginning of the lesson.

TEACHERS AND TEACHING

The lessons in this unit focus on teachers: who they are, where they work, how we study them, and what they do. Consider first the variety of teachers of which you are aware: religious teachers, teachers of cooking and music, ski instructors and tour guides, even animal trainers. All possess certain knowledge and skills, make a variety of decisions as to how to use that knowledge and those skills, and are able to transmit that knowledge and those skills to one or more people (or animals) called "students." Although this wide variety of teachers exists, this course focuses on only one category of teachers and, furthermore, on only a portion of the teachers in that category.

The structure of this first unit can best be portrayed as an inverted pyramid, one with a flat bottom as shown in Figure 1.1. The top of Figure 1.1 includes all teachers. Two "screens" are used to sort out particular groups of teachers from the rest. The first screen, labeled "Conditions and Constraints of Schools," implies that the teachers in our group work in elementary and secondary schools and teach groups of students housed in classrooms located within those schools. In a phrase, our teachers are schoolteachers.

The second screen, labeled "Criteria and Evidence of Teaching Quality," implies, first, that schoolteachers differ from one another in quality of their teaching (i.e., some are "better" teachers than others) and, second, that with proper criteria and credible evidence, we can identify those teachers whose teaching is of higher or, presumably, the highest quality. We shall refer to these teachers as "good" teachers.

The first lesson focuses on those individuals located at the top of the pyramid—that is, the universe of *all* teachers (although, even in this lesson, schoolteachers will be emphasized). In the second lesson, the conditions and constraints of the schools in which large numbers of these teachers teach are described (i.e., screen 1 in Figure 1.1). The third lesson addresses the question of how teachers and teaching are studied by others. The criteria used by these researchers and the evidence they gather to identify "good" teachers are identified (i.e., screen 2 in Figure 1.1). Finally, in the fourth

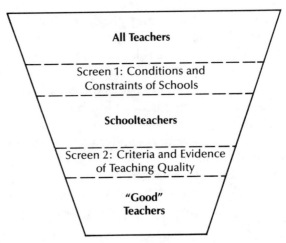

FIGURE 1.1 Teachers, Schoolteachers, and "Good" Teachers

lesson, some generalizations that apply to teachers labeled "good" are offered. Although these generalizations are few and broad, they form the basis for many of the lessons included in other units.

In many ways, the first screen limits, by definition, the population of teachers and administrators to whom this course is "targeted" or addressed. While at present the second screen also limits the population, the primary purpose of this course is to increase the number of teachers who are able to "pass through" this second screen. In order to accomplish this, the course presents both facts and informed opinion that schoolteachers and administrators can use as they seek to improve the quality of schooling offered to their students and as they struggle with many of the fundamental problems that confront today's teachers, principals, and superintendents. In simplest terms, the more the base of the pyramid expands, the greater the success of the course.

LESSON 1

WHAT IS A TEACHER?

PURPOSE OF THE LESSON

The purpose of the lesson is to address two questions. First, what do we mean when we call someone a teacher? Second, how do our perceptions of teachers reflect and perhaps determine their status in our society?

OVERVIEW OF THE LESSON

In this lesson, three views of teachers are presented. Dr. Philip Jackson argues that teachers are knowledgeable decision makers. They understand their students, are able to restructure a subject matter to make it "educationally digestible" for them, and, when teaching, "know when to do what."

Dr. David Berliner suggests that the metaphor "teacher as executive" is useful in thinking about teachers. He argues that this metaphor is both accurate, since teachers perform a variety of executive functions in their classrooms almost on a daily basis, and important, since the acceptance of this metaphor is likely to enhance the status of teachers.

Dr. Asa Hilliard asserts that teaching is essentially a human endeavor, involving "actual human contacts between a teacher and student." As a consequence, the nature of that relationship determines whether teachers are able to teach and students are willing to learn. The willingness of teachers to share their ideas, values, and feelings honestly and openly with their students contributes to the quality of this relationship.

Although on the surface these three views may be seen as conflicting ones (by reviving the old "cognitivist," "behaviorist," and "humanist" arguments), they are in fact compatible and complementary. This complementary nature is displayed in Figure 1.2.

One thing we do know about teachers is that they are very complex individuals. Attempts to define them in simple terms always sound trite (e.g., they know their subject and love children). But leaving such definitions to noneducators typically results in the use of metaphors that have low status in our society (e.g., kindly caretakers). As a consequence, coming to terms with the question "What is a teacher?" seems a necessary first step if teachers themselves are to increase their effectiveness and enhance their status.

BASIC CONCEPTS AND PRINCIPLES

Contradictory Common Sense

Common sense is *not* a well-ordered body of knowledge on how to behave under all circumstances. Rather, it is a complex fund of knowledge, much of which is contradictory (e.g., strike while the iron is hot versus patience is a virtue). While to "outsiders" teaching may seem to involve little more than "common sense," effective teaching requires the ability to make sense out of this massive amount of information in order to make a wide variety of decisions concerning "when to do what" (Jackson—Unit I, Reading 4).

Restructuring Knowledge

As students, teachers acquire bodies of knowledge that their teachers or they themselves structured in particular ways. As teachers, they need to *restructure* that knowledge in ways that facilitate its acquisition by their students. In order to properly restructure the knowledge,

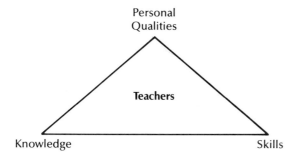

FIGURE 1.2   Personal Qualities, Knowledge, and Skills: Trademarks of People We Call Teachers

teachers need to understand both their subject areas and their students (Jackson—Unit I, Reading 4).

Presumption of a Shared Identity

Teachers often presume that their students are like them, that they and their students share a common language, a common set of experiences to call upon, and common physiological and emotional characteristics (e.g., fatigue, excitement). If, during a discussion, teachers want to know whether their students are bored, they simply ask themselves, "Am I bored?" (Jackson—Unit I, Reading 4).

Executive

An executive works to accomplish the goals of an organization and directly supervises one or more people in a formal organization; he or she plans, organizes, directs or leads, and controls (Berliner—Unit I, Reading 2).

Executive Functions of Teaching

The *Random House Dictionary of the English Language,* second edition (1987), defines "function" as "the kind of action or activity proper to a person, thing, or institution; the purpose for which something is designed and exists; role" (p. 775). The teacher shares several key functions with a business executive. These functions are (1) planning work, (2) communicating goals, (3) regulating the activities of the workplace, (4) creating a pleasant work environment, (5) educating new members of the work group, (6) relating work at the site to other units of the system, (7) supervising and working with other people, (8) motivating others, and (9) evaluating the performance of others (Berliner—Unit I, Reading 2).

Teacher-Student Relationships

Over a century ago, J. Currie (1869) suggested that the quality of the relationship between teacher and student has an impact on the student's willingness to participate in the classroom. In Currie's words, if a sound positive relationship exists between teacher and student, the student "will make great efforts to enter into the work of the teacher, both from his instinct of imitation, and the happiness he derives from [his relations with the teacher]" (p. 91).

Self-Disclosure

One of the keys to positive teacher-student relationships is the willingness of teachers to permit themselves to be seen as "real people" by their students—that is, people who can be trusted and whose values and knowledge are to be respected. Self-disclosure implies that teachers are willing to share their ideas, perceptions, and feelings with their students in an honest and forthright manner. Saying "I don't know" rather than feeling compelled to come up with an answer to a student's question because "I'm the teacher" is a simple example (Jourard, 1968).

Status of Teachers

Status refers to the social standing ascribed to teachers by members of society. Status influences the value we attach to particular occupations and, often, the money we pay them. The metaphors we use to describe occupations suggest the status we ascribe to them, and, unfortunately, "teacher as caretaker" suggests low status. Other metaphors are needed to raise the status of teachers in our society.

READING ASSIGNMENTS

Berliner, David C. *The Executive Functions of Teaching*. (Unit I, Reading 2)

Berliner defines an executive and describes ten functions performed by the typical business executive. Of these ten functions, only budgeting is not performed by the classroom teacher. In describing each of the remaining nine functions, Berliner uses existing research evidence to support his metaphor "teacher as executive." In addition, Berliner presents examples of the teaching activities associated with each of those functions. He concludes by suggesting that the "teacher as executive" metaphor is likely to enhance the status of teachers and the teaching profession.

Jackson, Philip W. *On Knowing How to Teach.* (Unit I, Reading 4)

Jackson begins with a fundamental question: Is there a little or a lot to know about teaching? He then presents the arguments of those who would suggest that teaching involves little in the way of formal knowledge. These arguments include "teaching as common sense," "teaching as 'show and tell,'" and the ability to teach knowing little, if anything, about the students being taught. Jackson presents a series of counterarguments for these contentions and suggests that the knowledge teachers need in order to teach well (1) is not the same for all teachers and (2) is best determined by the teachers themselves.

ADDITIONAL READINGS

Currie, J. (1869). *The Principles and Practices of Common-School Education*. Edinburgh: Thomas Laurie.

Jourard, S. M. (1968). *Disclosing Man to Himself*. Princeton, N.J.: Van Nostrand.

Smith, B. O. (1961). "A Concept of Teaching." In *Language and Concepts in Education*, edited by B. O. Smith and R. H. Ennis. Chicago: Rand McNally.

LESSON 2

SCHOOLTEACHER

PURPOSE OF THE LESSON

The purpose of the lesson is to address two questions. First, in what ways do schoolteachers differ from others who are referred to as teachers? Second, under what conditions and constraints do schoolteachers operate in their attempts to become more effective teachers?

OVERVIEW OF THE LESSON

Schoolteachers differ from many other types of teachers (e.g., piano teachers, tennis coaches, and priests and rabbis) in that they (1) receive formal instruction in pedagogy and (2) work in hierarchically bureaucratic organizations. Because they work in such organizations, teachers are typically "dealt a hand" and expected to "play that hand" the best they can. Included in the hand they are dealt are the (1) size and composition of their classes, (2) time at which the classes meet and the duration of the classes, (3) curricular goals, scope, and sequence, (4) textbooks, and (5) requirements to administer a series of district and statewide tests (i.e., "official" assessments).

Schoolteaching is a job. Because of the complexity of the job, however, people have difficulty determining exactly what kind of job it is. "Laborer," "craftsperson," "artist," and "professional" have all been used to describe the schoolteacher. The manner in which the job of teaching is perceived is important because perceptions determine in part the ways in which those holding the job are treated.

Based on what we now know about the job of schoolteaching, several recommendations can be offered concerning improving both the working conditions and effectiveness of school-teachers. First, educators—particularly school administrators—need to provide working conditions in which schoolteachers can be more effective. In order to do this, administrators must differentiate between those activities in which regulation is necessary (e.g., regularity of attendance, completion of various forms such as report cards) and those activities in which teacher autonomy and decision making are crucial (e.g., providing proper instruction for students reading two grade levels below the norm).

Second, teachers must learn to communicate about, and work together to solve, common educational problems. The development of a common language for discussing such problems and greater acceptance of the school's responsibility for solving them are necessary first steps in breaking away from the feelings of isolation and powerlessness experienced by many teachers today.

Third, teachers must work toward establishing themselves as professionals. In order to do so, however, they must (1) assume greater responsibility for ensuring the professionalism and competence of their colleagues and (2) continually inquire into "better ways" of teaching.

Fourth, and finally, the public and the higher-education community as well as school administrators must begin to respect teachers as knowledgeable professionals.

BASIC CONCEPTS AND PRINCIPLES

Official Assessment

Teachers are required to engage in "official" assessments, typically formal tests, solely because they are members of a bureaucratic organization. The results of such assessments, frequently placed in the students' "permanent files," are used primarily to classify students or place them into various state and federal programs. The results of such assessments are not frequently used by teachers to make decisions abut the effectiveness or efficiency of their teaching or instructional programs (Airasian—Unit V, Reading 1).

Teacher Isolation

There is ample evidence that teachers' classrooms are their "castles." Teachers rarely have time to consult with one another about instructional matters (e.g., difficulties that students are having across classes or subjects, plans for coordinating English and social-studies instruction). Common planning periods are uncommon (McLaughlin, Pfeifer, Swanson-Owens, and Yee—Unit I, Reading 5). A single adult is almost always present in a classroom (Anderson, Ryan, and Shapiro, 1988).

The Classification of Teachers

Because teaching is a job, teachers are perceived in different ways by various people. Laborers, craftspersons, artists, and professionals are four of the primary ways to classify teachers. Each classification has an impact on the perceptions people have of teachers as well as on the nature of the relationship between teachers and administrators. In this latter regard, different "types" of teachers require different "kinds" of administrative support (Mitchell and Kerchner—Unit I, Reading 6).

Colleagueality

Rather than work in isolation, teachers need to perceive themselves as members of a larger profession. Ninth-grade teachers, for example, must be knowledgeable of what other ninth-grade teachers are doing in their classrooms as well as what teachers at earlier and later grade levels are doing. What content and objectives are emphasized? What rules and routines are in place? What teaching methods are being used? What seems to "work," and what doesn't? The development of a common language to talk about instruction and instructional problems, and the availability of common planning periods for teachers of particular subject matters and range levels of students contribute to the development of colleagueality.

Inquiring Professional

An inquiring professional is a teacher who believes that it is necessary to ask questions and seek answers continually. Typically, research is one means of seeking such answers, either in the form of written formal reports or informal studies conducted by teachers within their own classrooms. The opposite of the inquiring professional is the dogmatic teacher, the teacher who has all the answers and never needs to ask questions, the teacher who does things in a particular way because "they have always been done that way" or "because someone told me to do it that way."

READING ASSIGNMENTS

Barr, Rebecca, and Dreeben, Robert, with Wiratchai, Nonglak. *How Schools Work.* (Unit I, Reading 1)

The authors assert that school systems are organizations consisting of several "nested" levels: districts, schools, classrooms, groups within classrooms, and individual students. An understanding of how schools work, then, requires that the events occurring at each of these levels be identified and the influence of the events at one level on events at other levels be examined. Furthermore, each level produces its own outcomes or values (e.g., resource acquisition, scheduling). While learning is a critically important value, particularly at the individual student level, other levels of the organization (e.g., district, school) have nothing directly to do with learning.

McLaughlin, Milbrey Wallin; Pfeifer, R. Scott; Swanson-Owens, Deborah; and Yee, Sylvia. *Why Teachers Won't Teach.* (Unit I, Reading 5)

McLaughlin and her colleagues contend that "in fundamental ways, the U.S. educational system is structured to guarantee the failure of teachers." Several organizational features "combine to minimize teachers' professional satisfaction and effectiveness." Among these features are (1) the composition of classes, (2) the lack of tools (i.e., teaching materials and equipment), (3) isolation, and (4) the lack of recognition from administrators and parents. McLaughlin and her colleagues conclude that teachers must be protected from distractions and disturbances, be provided with feedback concerning their performance, and engage in continuous professional development.

Mitchell, Douglas E., and Kerchner, Charles T. *Labor Relations and Teacher Policy.* (Unit I, Reading 6)

Mitchell and Kerchner describe the structure of the job of teaching. Every job is said to have some system of "task definition" and some sort of "oversight mechanism." In combination, variations in task definitions and oversight mechanisms produce four different work structures that define the job of teaching: labor, craft, art, and profession. Mitchell and Kerchner discuss ways in which contracts, the social system, and the political system have an impact on teacher work structures. Finally, the authors discuss the various administrative roles and responsibilities suggested by the different work structures: labor requires supervisors, craft requires managers, art requires leaders, and profession requires administrators.

ADDITIONAL READINGS

Anderson, L. W.; Ryan, D. W.; and Shapiro, B. (1988). *The Classroom Environment Study: Teaching for Learning.* Oxford, Eng.: Pergamon.

Lortie, D. C. (1975). *Schoolteacher.* Chicago: University of Chicago Press.

LESSON 3

RESEARCH ON TEACHING

PURPOSE OF THE LESSON

The purpose of the lesson is to address three questions. First, how do we study teachers and teaching? Second, how do we gain an understanding of teachers and teaching from the variety of research studies that have been, and are being, conducted? Third, what are some of the problems involved in using research evidence to improve teaching?

OVERVIEW OF THE LESSON

There are three primary ways of learning about teachers and teaching: you can look and listen, ask, and read. Direct observations of classrooms are like taking photographs or motion pictures of events. What is seen and ultimately recorded depends on the direction in which the camera is pointed and the lens used to observe and record. As a consequence, direct observations describe "selective slices" of classrooms as perceived by observers.

Questions are asked of both teachers and students in an attempt to understand their perspectives on classroom events and activities. Sometimes, the questions asked are included in an interview schedule. Other times, the questions are used to stimulate teachers or students to recall what transpires in the classroom as they watch a videotape or listen to an audiotape of a recent lesson.

Reading research studies is a time-consuming and often confusing endeavor. On most topics, there are many studies. They are frequently written in a technical manner and appear contradictory. In recent years, researchers have attempted to help practitioners by summarizing or synthesizing sets of studies conducted on a single topic.

While research on teaching is potentially useful in helping teachers to increase their effectiveness, such a use of research is not without its hazards. Research evidence primarily describes the nature of classroom teaching and school learning as it currently exists. This evidence is less helpful in understanding why teaching and learning are as they are or in prescribing precisely how teaching and learning should be altered if they are to improve. Educators who fail to grasp the distinction between description, explanation, and prescription are likely to misapply research findings.

Despite the problems inherent in conducting and using research to study and improve classroom teaching, research has great potential for helping us understand the nature of teaching and for increasing teaching effectiveness. If research is to be more beneficial than detrimental, however, we must attend to several cautions and concerns. First, research is not, nor should it be, directly translated into practice. Rather, research becomes one source of information to be used by practitioners (i.e., administrators and teachers) in their efforts at continued improvement.

Second, administrators and teachers must work toward understanding the full meaning and limitations of particular research findings before attempting to put them into practice. Application without sufficient comprehension will likely lead to problems. Third, administrators and teachers should be skeptical of people who attempt to convince them to change by informing them that "the research says . . . "

Research findings are not animate objects; their meaning and applicability are determined by those who read and consider them.

BASIC CONCEPTS AND PRINCIPLES

Direct Observation

In recent years, researchers have begun to study teaching by entering classrooms and recording as accurately as possible what they see and hear. Some of these researchers have used structured observation forms such as behavioral checklists to focus their attention on certain activities and events. Other researchers have recorded their observations on blank sheets of paper, relying on their knowledge of classrooms and skill in observation to determine what is recorded.

Stimulated Recall

In this technique, a teacher or student watches a videotape or listens to an audiotape of a recent lesson. From time to time, the tape is stopped (either at predetermined times or at times suggested by those viewing the tape). When the tape is stopped, the teacher or student is asked to put himself or herself back into that situation immediately prior to the stoppage of the tape and to try to recall what he or she was doing and thinking at the time. Typically, the teacher's or student's responses are recorded on audiotape and subsequently analyzed.

Triangulation

Triangulation is a "systematic comparison of alternative perceptions of the same (or similar) . . . events" (Morine-Dershimer, 1985). The comparison may involve the perceptions of observers, teachers, and students. Similarly, it may involve researchers who engaged in direct observation, researchers who interviewed the teachers and students, and researchers who used the stimulated-recall technique. Triangulation is used to increase the validity of findings from descriptive studies of classrooms.

Research Synthesis (Meta-analysis)

Researchers have begun to use statistics in their attempts to make sense of a variety of research findings on similar topics, variables, or relationships. One of the simplest approaches to synthesizing sets of findings is to total the number of studies that yield positive, negative, and neutral results. More sophisticated techniques include the computation of median correlation coefficients or mean effect sizes (i.e., the magnitude of the difference between two groups in terms of standard-deviation units) (Walberg—Unit I, Reading 7).

Practice versus Practitioners

Contrary to the popular belief that research is "translated into practice," research probably needs to be first and foremost "translated" so as to be comprehensible and credible to practitioners. Research, then, becomes one source of information that administrators and teachers can use in making educational and instructional decisions. As one source of information, research competes for the attention of practitioners with common sense, experiential knowledge (e.g., "I knew a student once who . . . "), and other sources of information.

READING ASSIGNMENTS

Clark, Christopher M. *Research into Practice: Cautions and Qualifications.* (Unit I, Reading 3)

Clark describes four attributes that researchers should possess in order to improve educational practice. Researchers need a more modest sense about what social science has to offer practice (humility). They need to understand that the main role of research and researchers is to serve teachers (service orientation); in this regard, research literature is portrayed as an encyclopedia that teachers can consult with their own questions in mind. Researchers have to learn to ask questions that are both intriguing and useful (creativity). Finally, both researchers and practitioners need to improve their "professional communication about professional matters."

Walberg, Herbert J. *Improving the Productivity of America's Schools.* (Unit I, Reading 7)

Walberg posits a model of educational productivity that includes nine variables arranged into three causal factors: aptitude (ability, development, and motivation); instruction (amount and quality); and environment (home, classroom, peers, and television). Some 3,000 studies were identified and the results examined in terms of three scientific canons: parsimony, replication, and generalizability. The results of the research synthesis provided a test of the validity of the model. Variables within each factor having large influences on student learning were found to exist. Examples include intelligence (aptitude), the use of reinforcement (instruction), and class morale (environment).

ADDITIONAL READINGS

Green, J. L., and Smith, D. (1983). "Teaching and Learning: A Linguistic Perspective." *The Elementary School Journal* 83:353–391.

Morine-Dershimer, G. (1985). *Talking, Listening, and Learning in Elementary Classrooms.* New York: Longman.

LESSON **4**

THE "GOOD" TEACHER

PURPOSE OF THE LESSON

The purpose of the lesson is to address two questions. First, what traits and behaviors combine to make "good" teachers? Second, what are some of the reasons that some teachers are better teachers than others?

OVERVIEW OF THE LESSON

Early attempts to identify good teachers focused on the traits that such teachers possessed, such as approachability, cheerfulness, dependability, enthusiasm, fairness, honesty, intelligence, morality, and patience (Charters and Waples, 1929). Two traits that have received increased attention in recent years are a "spirit of inquiry" and a "sense of efficacy" (a "can do" attitude). Unfortunately, reviews of research on the impact of such traits on teacher effectiveness concluded that "very little is known about the relation between teacher personality and teacher effectiveness" (Getzels and Jackson, 1963).

In the past quarter century, therefore, most studies have focused on teacher behaviors and teaching practices in an attempt to define good teachers. A composite definition of a good teacher can be inferred from the results of these studies. Good teachers clearly delineate goals or intended outcomes; they select or develop a curriculum (including assignments and tests) that is linked directly with these goals or intended outcomes; and they are able to "deliver" the identified curriculum to the students. Despite this composite definition, many teachers are not successful in one or more of these three key elements. First, some teachers have no explicit goals or fail to make their goals explicit to their students. Second, for some teachers, the curriculum is misaligned with the goals or the goals misaligned with the tests used to judge the success of both student learning and classroom teaching. Third, standardized approaches to instructional delivery are being advocated by many educators at the same time that researchers are suggesting the context-bound nature of effective teaching (i.e., behaviors and practices that are effective in one setting or situation may not be effective in others).

Presently, a certain consistency emerges from a careful consideration of existing research studies concerning the qualities and practices of effective teachers. Such teachers are more concerned with "ends" than with "means." They care more about the impact of their behavior on students than on how that behavior might look to an outside observer. They thrive on accomplishment—both their students' and, ultimately, their own as teachers. Because of this, these teachers develop a "sense of efficacy."

At the same time, effective teachers possess those characteristics that we have valued in teachers for generations: they know their subject well enough to teach it; they care about their students and treat them with respect; they are able to make wise and prudent decisions. Although some people are naturally predisposed toward these practices, the knowledge that has been gained through research enables us to develop strategies and techniques that permit the production of large numbers of more effective teachers.

BASIC CONCEPTS AND PRINCIPLES

Effective Teachers

"'Teacher effectiveness' will be used to refer to the results a teacher gets or to the amount of the progress the pupils make toward some specified goal of education. One implication of this definition is that teacher effectiveness must be defined, and can only be assessed, in terms of behaviors of pupils, not behaviors of teachers" (Medley, 1982). Teacher effectiveness can be contrasted with teacher performance and teacher competence. "'Teacher performance' refers to the behavior of a teacher while teaching a class" (Medley, 1982). Obviously, not all behaviors produce results. Finally, teacher competence is "the set of knowledges, abilities, and beliefs a teacher possesses and brings to the teaching situation. . . . The knowledges, skills, and beliefs in a teacher's repertoire will be referred to as 'competencies' that the teacher possesses" (Medley, 1982). An effective teacher is able to use the existing competencies to achieve the desired results.

Born versus Made

This commonly used dichotomy is, in fact, false. Clearly, some teachers may be predisposed toward cheerfulness, dependability, enthusiasm, and fairness. At the same time, however, virtually all teachers can be expected to acquire sufficient knowledge of the subject matters they are called upon to teach, to work toward a greater understanding of their students, and to develop a repertoire of useful pedagogical techniques and strategies.

Spirit of Inquiry

Teachers who possess this "spirit" are constantly asking questions and searching for answers to them. They are seeking to develop greater levels of understanding and to make changes when necessary, both within their classrooms and within themselves.

Sense of Efficacy

Teachers who possess this "sense" are said to have a "can do" attitude. They believe that they can make a difference in the lives of their students. Such teachers examine and take pride in the accomplishments of their students. They assume greater responsibility for these accomplishments (and, conversely, for the lack of accomplishments) rather than attributing them to the ability or home background of the students (Ashton and Webb, 1986).

Traits versus Behaviors

Traits can be defined as relatively permanent qualities or characteristics of individuals. Traits describe what teachers "are." In contrast with traits, behaviors are what teachers "do." While in the classroom, teachers behave in various, predictable ways. They explain, question, direct, supervise, praise, and reprimand as they attempt to "deliver a curriculum to children that is linked logically or empirically to the outcomes that are valued" (Berliner—see Lesson 1). While early studies attempted to identify critical traits of effective teachers, more recent studies have focused on the performance of teachers in and around the classroom.

Teaching by Rule versus Teaching by Making Decisions

A recent movement in teacher education and teacher evaluation has been the identification of a generic set of teacher behaviors that are to be exhibited by virtually all teachers at all grade levels and in all subject areas during every lesson. In essence, teachers are to learn a set of behavioral rules that they are to apply routinely. Critics of this movement do not deny the existence or utility of a generic set of teacher behaviors. Rather, they suggest that such behaviors should be part of teachers' repertoires and that decisions to use such behaviors should rest with the teachers themselves, depending on the settings and situations in which the teachers find themselves.

controversy? The Berliner, Jackson, and Walberg papers may be particularly useful in this regard.

READING ASSIGNMENTS

There are no new reading assignments for this lesson. Rather, reread several of the previously assigned readings as you begin to formulate your own position on several of the issues raised in this lesson. For example, how do you see the distinction among teacher competence, teacher performance, and teacher effectiveness? Do traits or behaviors contribute more to a teacher's effectiveness? Where do you stand on the "teaching by rule" and "teaching by making decisions"

ADDITIONAL READINGS

Ashton, P. T., and Webb, R. B. (1986). *Making a Difference: Teachers' Sense of Efficacy and Student Achievement.* New York: Longman.

Charters, W. W., and Waples, D. (1929). *The Commonwealth Teacher-Training Study.* Chicago: University of Chicago Press.

Getzels, J. W., and Jackson. P. W. (1963). "The Teacher's Personality and Characteristics." In *Handbook of Research on Teaching,* edited by N. L. Gage. Chicago: Rand McNally.

Medley, D. M. (1982). "Teacher Effectiveness." In *Encyclopedia of Educational Research,* 5th ed., edited by H. E. Mitzel. New York: The Free Press.

UNIT 1

ASSIGNMENTS

SELF-TEST

1. In which of these situations is the presumption of shared identity most likely to be valid?
   a. recent college graduates teaching elementary-school students
   b. recent college graduates teaching high-school students
   c. experienced teachers teaching elementary-school students
   d. experienced teachers teaching high-school students

2. Teachers' decisions concerning the pacing of instruction, the sequence of topics or units, and the use of instructional time are associated with which of these executive functions?
   a. regulating the activities of the workplace
   b. creating a pleasant work environment
   c. supervising and working with other people
   d. motivating those being supervised

3. Teachers have to find ways of getting students to put forth the time and effort needed to learn and learn well. Which of the following would a teacher endorsing a humanistic philosophy most likely use in this regard?
   a. provide incentives and rewards for students
   b. employ systematic classroom management techniques
   c. gain the commitment of the students
   d. distribute challenging and interesting assignments

4. Which of the following is an example of an "official" assessment?
   a. class projects
   b. homework assignments
   c. standardized tests
   d. quizzes

5. School principals who work to provide adequate support services for teachers, articulate a system of norms to guide teachers in their work, and implement a system of peer review probably view their teachers as
   a. artists.
   b. craftspersons.
   c. laborers.
   d. professionals.

6. School principals who are knowledgeable in the techniques of effective teaching and are able to assist teachers in applying these techniques probably view their teachers as
   a. artists.
   b. craftspersons.
   c. laborers.
   d. professionals.

7. By virtue of their employment in a bureaucratic organization, schoolteachers are basically "dealt a hand." All of these are likely to be found in that "hand" except
   a. the students they teach.
   b. the textbooks they use.
   c. the teaching schedules they follow.
   d. the instructional techniques they use.

8. *Inquiring professional* is to *dogmatic teacher* as
   a. *doubt* is to *certainty*.
   b. *professional* is to *laborer*.
   c. *expert* is to *novice*.
   d. *researcher* is to *practitioner*.

9. The systematic comparison of the ways in

which different people holding different viewpoints interpret the same or similar events is referred to as

a. stimulated recall.

b. triangulation.

c. research synthesis.

d. meta-analysis.

10. When both a researcher and a teacher sit together and watch a videotape of a recently taught lesson, then discuss various portions of that lesson, they are using a technique called

    a. stimulated recall.

    b. direct observation.

    c. interviewing.

    d. meta-analysis.

11. Which of the following most accurately describes the relationship between research and teaching?

    a. Research can be directly translated into teaching practices.

    b. Research has focused primarily on teachers rather than teaching.

    c. Research is one source of information for improving teaching.

    d. Research is basically unrelated to the improvement of teaching.

12. According to Medley, if you were interested in identifying an effective teacher, you would most likely

    a. interview teachers to determine their knowledge and values.

    b. observe teachers, using a behavioral checklist.

    c. examine the work and performance of the students.

    d. use stimulated recall to learn how teachers make decisions.

13. When confronted with a student who is having difficulty learning a particular concept or skill, a teacher with a sense of efficacy would most likely

    a. attribute the problem to the student's home background.

    b. arrange for the student to meet with a school counselor.

    c. plan an extra study session with the student.

    d. resign himself or herself to the fact that such a student cannot learn.

14. Which one of the following is a behavior?

    a. planning

    b. adaptability

    c. enthusiasm

    d. leadership

15. A series of behaviors is identified based on a review of existing research. These behaviors are then included on an observational instrument that is to be used by all teachers in a school district. During each observation, teachers are to exhibit as many of the behaviors as possible, and their performance is judged by comparison with the performance of all the other teachers in the district. Which of the following phrases describes the view of teaching underlying this practice?

    a. teacher competence

    b. teacher effectiveness

    c. teaching by rule

    d. teaching by decision making

UNIT ACTIVITY

Write a 1,500-word essay comparing and contrasting the points of view taken by the authors of two articles pertaining to the same topic, issue, or problem. For example, you could write an essay on the nature of teachers as portrayed by Berliner in "The Executive Functions of Teaching" and by Mitchell and Kerchner in "Labor Relations and Teacher Policy." Make certain that your essay is well organized, the comparisons are clearly stated, quotations from the two articles are used in support of your comparisons, and standard rules of English grammar and usage are followed throughout.

ANSWER KEY FOR SELF-TEST

1. b (Lesson 1)
2. a (Lesson 1)
3. c (Lesson 1)
4. c (Lesson 2)
5. d (Lesson 2)
6. b (Lesson 2)
7. d (Lesson 2)
8. a (Lesson 2)

9. b (Lesson 3)
10. a (Lesson 3)
11. c (Lesson 3)
12. c (Lesson 4)
13. c (Lesson 4)
14. a (Lesson 4)
15. c (Lesson 4)

SCHOOLS AND CLASSROOMS

The lessons in this unit focus on schools and classrooms: the importance of the start of school, the establishment of classroom rules and routines, the ways in which classrooms are organized, and the relationships among students that are permitted or prohibited, encouraged or discouraged. As was mentioned in the last unit, schoolteachers work in hierarchically structured bureaucratic organizations. However, these teachers work in isolation. Their "isolation booths" are their classrooms. Within them, teachers traditionally have reigned supreme.

Teachers have the freedom to organize their classrooms as they see fit—placing desks in rows or chairs in semicircles, setting up "stations" or learning centers. They have the freedom—within broad limits—to set rules governing appropriate behavior and to enforce those rules. They have the freedom to decide whether to teach to the whole class, form subgroups within the class, or permit students to work individually on self-paced instructional materials. The variety of physical arrangements and social configurations is evident to even the most naïve observer.

Regardless of how teachers organize their classrooms, they should be mindful of both management and instructional concerns. Seating arrangements, for example, may be made to minimize casual, potentially disruptive conversations between students; changes in seating patterns are often used to deal with behavioral problems. In describing the fears of middle-school youngsters, Delamont and Galton (1986), for example, state that the "biggest danger most pupils face is being forced to sit next to a child of the opposite sex and share a textbook" (p. 90).

On the other hand, seating arrangements also address instructional concerns of teachers. Teachers place students in rows so that all can see the chalkboard, in circles so that ideas and opinions can be exchanged, and around laboratory tables so that students have access to needed equipment.

Different ways of organizing classrooms place different demands on students, particularly social demands. Social demands have an impact on the ways in which students are expected to interact with one another and with the teacher and to participate in class activities. These demands are often contrasted with academic ones that pertain to acquisition of the subject-matter content (Erickson, 1982). While some social demands are relatively stable over lengthy periods of time, others change from week to week, day to day, or hour to hour.

For example, the way in which homework is to be completed, given to the teacher, graded, and returned to the students may be the same across an entire school year. The social demands relative to homework tend to remain stable. In contrast, students may be expected to pay attention to the teacher and not talk to other students on one day but to work together on a group project the next. Students may be expected to call out answers to questions during one portion of a lesson, take turns answering questions during a second portion, and raise their hands to answer questions during a third. In these examples, the social demands are shifting on a daily or hourly basis.

The lessons in this unit all deal with classroom organization and the social demands placed on students within classrooms. (Academic demands will be discussed in Units III and IV.) The lessons differ from one another in two respects. First, Lessons 5 and 6 are concerned with the long-term effects of the ways in which classrooms are organized at the beginning of the school year. In contrast, Lessons 7 and 8 deal primarily with ongoing organizational issues and problems. Second, Lessons 5 and 8 address the role of interpersonal relationships (e.g., teacher-student and student-student relationships) in organizing classrooms. But Lessons 6 and 7 are primarily concerned with techniques and methods of classroom organization. Table 2.1 illustrates the relationships among this unit's lessons.

TABLE 2.1 The Relationships among the Lessons in Unit II

	INTERPERSONAL RELATIONSHIPS	CLASSROOM ORGANIZATION
Long-Term Concerns	Lesson 5 Starting School	Lesson 6 Rules and Routines
Ongoing Concerns	Lesson 8 Learning Together	Lesson 7 Organizing Classrooms

REFERENCES

Delamont, S., and Galton, M. (1986). *Inside the Secondary Classroom.* New York: Routledge and Kegan Paul.

Erickson, F. (1982). "Classroom Discourse as Improvisation: Relationships between Academic Task Structure and Social Participation Structure in Lessons." In *Communicating in the Classroom,* edited by L. C. Wilkinson. New York: Academic Press.

LESSON 5

STARTING SCHOOL

PURPOSE OF THE LESSON

The purpose of the lesson is to address three questions. First, how important is the way the school year begins? Second, what happens in classrooms during the first week or two of school? Third, how can the start of school be orchestrated so that things run smoothly during the school year?

OVERVIEW OF THE LESSON

Teachers are confronted with a wide variety of young people at the beginning of each school year. Elementary-school teachers teaching in self-contained classrooms must develop an understanding of twenty-five or more "children" or "pupils." Secondary-school teachers typically must deal effectively with over one hundred "adolescents" or "students." Because classrooms usually contain a variety of young people, one of the first tasks that teachers must undertake is to transform "aggregates" into "groups." That is, they must turn the individuals assigned to them into a group with a common purpose.

Before such a transformation is possible, however, teachers must engage in what Dr. Peter Airasian terms "'sizing up' assessment." That is, teachers must gain an understanding of their students based on impressions formed prior to or early in the school year. The impressions formed prior to the school year come primarily from permanent records or recollections of students' siblings. Early in the school year, teachers form impressions based on the ways in which students respond to a teacher, other students, and academic and social demands. That is, first-grade students unable to recite the alphabet or count to ten may be labeled "low achievers" or "slow learners." Students who sit in the corner or cling to the teacher may be labeled "shy" or "insecure." Similarly, secondary-school students on the "lowest track" may be seen as being "hard to teach." Furthermore, those whose older siblings were "holy terrors" may be viewed with suspicion or trepidation.

Just as teachers "size up" their students, students "size up" their teachers. Students decide whether their teachers are to be trusted, are fair in their treatment of students, and are able to identify with what it means to be a student. Like the assessments made by teachers, the students' assessments are made early in the school year, primarily on initial impressions.

From the students' point of view, however, much of their time during the first week or two of school is spent learning how to "do school"— deciphering what they can do when, with whom, where, for how long, and for what purpose. That is, they learn what the classroom game is and how it is played. Once students understand the "game," most try to "play by the rules." In fact, they quickly learn how to signal to teachers that they know how to play the game but are incapable of playing it or unwilling to play it at a particular point in time. This student strategy is referred to as "mock participation."

Overall, then, both teachers and students start each school year by trying to make sense of the social situation so that they can live and work together in relative harmony for the next thirty-six weeks. Both parties engage in "sizing up" assessments as students learn how to "do school." Three recommendations can be offered to help teachers start the school year "right."

First, because of the importance of the first

few weeks of school, teachers should plan more carefully for this time period than for almost any other period of the school year. Second, teachers should give clear signals as to what is expected of students in terms of their behavior and participation as well as the amount and quality of their schoolwork. Third, teachers should refrain from making "snap judgments" about students during the first few weeks of school, judgments based primarily on initial, often fleeting, impressions.

BASIC CONCEPTS AND PRINCIPLES

Aggregate versus Group

Sociologically, an aggregate is defined as a collection of people who happen to be in the same place at the same time. In contrast, a group is defined as a collection of people who are in the same place at the same time for some common purpose. Thus, *purpose* differentiates an aggregate from a group.

"Sizing up" Assessments

In some respects, all assessments attempt to "size up" the situation. In contrast to other types of assessments, however, "sizing up" assessments are based on initial impressions and reactions rather than on data collected from assignments and tests. Thus, "sizing up" assessments are typically less reliable (but, unfortunately, stable over the school year) than are either "instructional" or "official" assessments (Airasian—Unit V, Reading 1).

"Doing School"

In today's society, people "do lunch" and, regrettably, "do drugs." It is not surprising, then, that they learn to "do school." "Doing school" means that students know the rules and expectations governing their relationships with other students and with the teacher and their participation in the activities of the classrooms. Some would argue that knowing how to "do school" is a necessary but not sufficient condition for learning the subject matter presented. Thus, learning to "do school" means that students are able to meet the social demands of the classroom, although not necessarily the academic demands.

Social-Participation Structure

The social-participation structure is the "patterned set of constraints on the allocation of interactional rights and obligations of various members of the interacting group" (Erickson—Unit II, Reading 2). Thus, the social-participation structure helps students determine what they can do when, with whom, where, for how long, and for what purpose.

Academic Task Structure

The academic task structure is the "patterned set of constraints provided by the logic of sequencing in the subject-matter content of the lesson" (Erickson—Unit II, Reading 2). Thus, the academic task structure is defined in part by the structure of the subject matter being taught and in part by the tasks and assignments given to students by the teachers.

Mock Participation

Students may understand the social participation structure and the associated rules for classroom participation but may be unable to participate (as when they do not know the answers to questions posed by teachers) or unwilling to do so (as when they find answering questions in the classroom socially embarrassing). In this situation, they engage in what Dr. Judith Green refers to as "mock participation." That is, students signal to their teachers that while they understand the "rules of the game," they do not wish to participate.

READING ASSIGNMENTS

Airasian, Peter W. *Classroom Assessment and Educational Improvement.* (Unit V, Reading 1)

Although assigned to Unit V, the first portion of this chapter provides a definition of assessment and a discussion of the role assessment plays in the classroom during the first few days of school. During this time, the teacher is constantly collecting information about individual students and entire classes of students that will enable him or her to make decisions: How fast can I move this group through the curriculum? Which students are likely to cause me trouble? Which students can I count on "in a pinch"? Unlike instructional and official assessments, "sizing up" assessments are impressionistic and rarely recorded. At the same time, however, they are stable over time.

Erickson, Frederick. *Classroom Discourse as Improvisation: Relationships between Academic Task Structure and Social Participation Structure in Lessons.* (Unit II, Reading 2)

Erickson differentiates between the academic task structure (the subject matter) and the social-participation structure (the social interactions and obligations) present in the classroom. The social-participation structure is signaled by patterns of verbal and nonverbal behavior, typically on the part of the teacher. These signals may be explicit, elliptic, or implicit. A student's communicative competence is his or her ability to "read" these signals. Lessons are defined as educational encounters between teachers and students that, although based on previously learned, normative "rules," provide opportunities for innovation through adapting to fortuitous circumstances.

LESSON 6

RULES AND ROUTINES

PURPOSE OF THE LESSON

The purpose of the lesson is to address three questions. First, what are the differences between rules and routines? Second, why are classroom rules and routines important? Third, how can classroom rules and routines be introduced and used effectively?

OVERVIEW OF THE LESSON

Think of a formal social setting—a business meeting perhaps. Most business meetings have agendas; in many, *Robert's Rules of Order* are followed. A person attending several such meetings quickly develops an understanding of what can and cannot be said or done by the various participants. This person learns the procedures that are followed so that the meetings can run smoothly and achieve their desired ends.

Classrooms are formal social settings. Observers of classrooms, particularly during the first week or two of school, have noticed the establishment of rules governing what class members can and cannot say and do, as well as the setting up of procedures (or routines) that are to be followed so that lessons can be taught efficiently and the desired learning can take place.

In general, rules are prohibitions on behavior. "No talking!" and "No getting out of your seats!" are rules frequently found in classrooms. Routines, on the other hand, are steps to be followed when students are performing activities that occur regularly in classrooms. "First, put your name and the date in the upper right hand corner of the paper. Second, number from one to twenty. Third, I will pronounce the

word, use it in a sentence and pronounce it again. Fourth, you will spell the word correctly on your paper, writing it legibly."

Classroom management routines pertain to gross motor behavior (e.g., procedures for leaving your seat to use the pencil sharpener) and crowd control (e.g., entering and leaving the classroom). Instructional routines, on the other hand, pertain to participation in classroom activities that are directly related to learning. Procedures for taking a spelling test (as illustrated above) and participating in class discussions and recitations are examples of instructional routines.

Rules and routines serve a variety of functions in the classroom. They help to bring order to a potentially chaotic situation, one in which the adult is hopelessly outnumbered and in which students compete with one another for that adult's attention and help. Rules and routines also permit the development of "shared control"—that is, classrooms in which both teacher and students are responsible for getting along and getting things done. The establishment of shared control fosters responsibility on the part of students and frees the teacher to spend more time on real learning.

Although the benefits of rules and routines are obvious, they can cease to be useful if they are applied rigidly without periodic evaluation of their efficiency and effectiveness. Fortunately, several recommendations can be offered concerning classroom rules and routines.

First, classroom rules should be few and enforceable. Second, the reasons for the rules should be made clear to the students. Third, the consequences of violating the rules also should be made clear. Fourth, teachers should periodically examine their routines and make adjustments as necessary. Fifth, essential routines should be established either early in the school year or as the need arises. Finally, both rules and routines must be maintained during the year if they are to be effective.

BASIC CONCEPTS AND PRINCIPLES

Rules

Rules are prohibitions on behavior. They may be explicit (i.e., students are informed of them in advance) or implicit (i.e., students learn about them by violating them). Because rules are prohibitions, they often are stated negatively (e.g., Do not chew gum in school; Do not cheat; Do not speak without permission). Rules can be—and sometimes are—stated positively (e.g., Behave honestly; Raise your hand if you wish to speak).

Routines

Routines are "fluid, paired, scripted segments of behavior that help movement toward a shared goal" (Leinhardt, Weidman, and Hammond—Unit II, Reading 4). In essence, routines convey sequences of behaviors that are expected to take place if frequently occurring classroom tasks are to be accomplished. Typically, teachers refer to what researchers term "routines" as "procedures"; for all practical purposes, these two terms are synonymous. In the videotaped lesson, two types of routines are considered: management and instructional. Gaea Leinhardt, C. Weidman, and K. M. Hammond describe three types of routines: management, support, and exchange. Support and exchange routines are both instructional routines. Exchange routines involve direct interchanges between teachers and students (e.g., calling on students in class). Support routines enable the exchange routines to occur efficiently; they include distributing papers, getting materials such as text-

books ready, and locating appropriate pages in the textbooks.

Shared Control

Shared control describes classrooms in which teachers and students understand and assume responsibility for the activities that occur within them. When shared control has been properly established, students can behave in an orderly, responsible manner without constantly consulting with the teacher about the appropriateness of each action. Explicit rules and routines, coupled with the delegation of responsibility and authority to students, are necessary for the establishment of shared control.

Classroom-Management Functions

Rules, routines, and shared control are all elements of successful classroom management. However, they must also be seen as means to ends. Classroom management itself is not a virtue. Effective classroom management achieves two primary purposes or functions. One major purpose is to establish a climate for learning. "A management system that interferes with student learning is unacceptable no matter what its other virtues might be" (Evertson and Emmer, 1982). A second major purpose is to "engage students in school work and keep them engaged" (Evertson and Emmer). Effective classroom management, then, must take into account both long-term concerns for student learning and short-term (almost immediate) concerns for student attention and work.

READING ASSIGNMENT

Leinhardt, Gaea; Weidman, C.; and Hammond, K. M. *Introduction and Integration of Classroom Routines by Expert Teachers.* (Unit II, Reading 4)

Leinhardt *et al.* studied routines established during the beginning of the school year by expert teachers. Their study was based on an analysis of teaching from a cognitive psychological perspective. Data were collected from observations and audiotapes of teachers' lessons, the use of the stimulated-recall technique, and interviews with teachers. Summaries of the results in terms of three types of routines—management, support, and exchange—are provided. More common routines are illustrated, including "cycle to correct," "I'll play dumb," "eyes to me," "distribute/collect," "wait to start," and "what to do when finished." Dysfunctional routines are also illustrated.

ADDITIONAL READING

Evertson, C. M., and Emmer, E. T. (1982). "Preventive Classroom Management." In *Helping Teachers Manage Classrooms,* edited by D. Duke. Alexandria, Va.: Association for Supervision and Curriculum Development.

LESSON **7**

ORGANIZING CLASSROOMS

PURPOSE OF THE LESSON

The purpose of the lesson is to address three questions. First, what options do teachers have in organizing their classrooms? Second, what are the strengths and weaknesses of forming within-class instructional groups? Third, why are concerns for climate and responsibility important?

OVERVIEW OF THE LESSON

The teacher's job within the classroom is difficult. Not only do teachers have to get to know their students and develop workable sets of rules and routines, but they must confront the fact that instruction and learning operate at two distinct levels: group and individual. Teachers have to design and execute *instruction* appropriate for groups of students. *Learning,* on the other hand, is an individual student activity. The extent to which students can benefit from instruction depends largely on what they bring to the classroom in the way of previous achievement, attitudes, work habits, social skills, and the like.

Teachers have a range of options as to how they intend to "deliver" the instruction to their students. They can lecture, engage in discussions, use audio-visual materials or computers, and permit students to work alone or in groups on a variety of reading, written, or laboratory assignments. To be effective, teachers need to understand the costs and benefits of the alternatives.

A major question teachers must address is whether or not to form groups of students within their classroom. Typically, secondary-school teachers do not form such groups because "students are already grouped by ability or interest before they appear in . . . class." Elementary-school teachers, on the other hand, partially rely on within-class groups. While the formation of groups of students may be appealing to teachers, several negative consequences are apparent. First, students placed in groups are often labeled (e.g., dull, bright), and the movement from group to group becomes difficult. Second, students may be placed in groups based on irrelevant issues or information. Third, low-achieving students, particularly in reading, may be hurt by grouping. Fourth, the formation of groups may result in overall classroom-management problems.

The formation of groups aside, one of the primary concerns of teachers in classrooms is the development of a general positive classroom climate. As Dr. Dorothy Strickland asserts, "Some classrooms seem to invite learning." In such classrooms, students tend to assume a greater responsibility for their own learning partly because of their commitment to the teacher and to their peers.

Researchers who had studied the problems and possibilities of organizing classrooms have offered several recommendations. First, the formation of within-class groups should depend on the purpose for which the groups were formed (not because the teacher likes such groups). Second, if used properly, grouping can have beneficial effects on individual students as well as on the overall classroom climate. "Proper use" implies that teachers must (1) give appropriate assignments, (2) establish rules concerning how students can have access to the teacher when he or she is working with another group, (3) consider the total length of time individual students will be working independently and without supervision, (4) determine the most appropriate order for working with the students in each group, (5) look at the overall seating arrangement in the classroom when groups are formed, and (6) consider the size of the "remainder" (i.e., the number of students remaining in the classroom when the teacher is working with a single group). Third, students in the lower groups may need "richer instruction" (e.g., more teacher contact, additional practice, stronger home-school support). Fourth, there are no right or wrong answers concerning the proper way to organize classrooms. Rather, teachers must take many factors into consideration as they make this difficult decision.

BASIC CONCEPTS AND PRINCIPLES

Instruction versus Learning

Usually, instruction is planned for groups of students (e.g., mixed fourth- and fifth-grade students, academically advanced high-school biology students). More specifically, instruction is targeted toward some idealized group (e.g., the "typical" student in a mixed fourth- and fifth-grade classroom, the most able students in an advanced biology class). But because students in all classes differ, they benefit differently from identical instruction. Thus, initial learning primarily depends on each student's capacity to benefit from the instruction as designed and presented. If most students are to learn what is expected, teachers should be sensitive to these differences and adjust their teaching as necessary.

Instructional Grouping

Because of differences among students in the same classroom, teachers must decide whether or not to form subgroups within the classroom so that teaching will be easier and students will be more likely to benefit from it. As Barr and Dreeben (1983) argue, the decision to form subgroups depends largely on the magnitude of

the ability or achievement differences among students and specifically on the number of very low-ability or low-achieving students in the classroom. Instructional grouping is more likely to occur in elementary than in secondary classrooms (presumably because students come to secondary classrooms "already grouped"). In this regard, it should be pointed out that differences among secondary-school students have been estimated to be ten to fifteen times as large as those among elementary-school students. Thus, even with the formation of four "tracks" or "levels" within a secondary grade level, the differences among students in a particular track or level are likely to be larger than those in a so-called "heterogeneous" first-grade classroom. Instructional grouping also is more likely to occur in reading than in any other subject area. Finally, instructional grouping is most often practiced by teachers who prefer grouping, the preferences based in part on past experiences.

Climate

The term "climate" refers to the perceptions that students and teachers have of the classroom. That is, climate does not exist in an objective sense; rather, it, like beauty, lies in the minds of the beholders. In the study of climate, students are typically asked questions concerning "the affective and social relations among the class members, the emphasis given to efficient completion of learning tasks, and the implicit and explicit system of rules and organization of the class" (Walberg, 1987). In general, classrooms that are "warm, yet businesslike" contain students with higher levels of academic achievement.

READING ASSIGNMENTS

Emmer, Edmund T., and Evertson, Carolyn M. *Synthesis of Research on Classroom Management.* (Unit II, Reading 1)

Emmer and Evertson begin their synthesis with Kounin's classic 1970 study. In general, one major finding has emerged from the studies conducted since that time. Students spend more time learning when they have continuous cues as to appropriate behavior and learning progress. These cues are present when (1) teachers are interacting with the students, (2) teachers are pacing the students, (3) the activity in which students are engaged provides the needed cues (e.g., when students are constructing something), or (4) teachers are able to insulate students from outside distractions. Consequences of student involvement include less disruptive behavior and higher achievement.

Slavin, Robert E. *Grouping for Instruction: Equity and Effectiveness.* (Unit II, Reading 5)

Slavin discusses two types of grouping arrangements: assigning students to different classes and assigning students to subgroups within the same class. Alternative approaches exist for both types. "Ability grouped class assignment," "regrouping for reading and/or mathematics," and the "Joplin Plan" (where cross-age homogeneous ability groups are formed) are examples of differential class assignment. "Mastery learning" and "cooperative learning" are examples of subgroup assignment. "Ability groups class assignment," the most common form of grouping, has repeatedly been found to be ineffective. Most of the other alternatives have produced positive results in terms of achievement and attitudes.

ADDITIONAL READINGS

Barr, R., and Dreeben, R. (1983). *How Schools Work.* Chicago: University of Chicago Press.

Kounin, J. S. (1970). *Discipline and Group Management in Schools.* New York: Holt, Rinehart and Winston.

Walberg, H. J. (1987). "Psychological Environment." In *The International Encyclopedia of Teaching and Teacher Education,* edited by M. J. Dunkin. Oxford, Eng.: Pergamon.

LESSON **8**

LEARNING TOGETHER

PURPOSE OF THE LESSON

The purpose of the lesson is to address four questions. First, what kinds of relationships among students can and do exist in classrooms? Second, how has the nature of these relationships changed over the years? Third, what are the advantages of emphasizing cooperative relationships among students? Fourth, what is the role of teachers in classrooms in which cooperative relationships are emphasized?

OVERVIEW OF THE LESSON

Most of the communication in classrooms flows from teacher to students. Less frequently, the direction of communication is from one or more students to teacher. Very rarely is communication among students encouraged or permitted. In fact, Dr. David Johnson (1981) refers to student-student interaction as the "neglected variable in education." For conversation among students to be productive rather than disruptive, however, classrooms and lessons must be structured in particular ways.

Three possible structures exist: competitive, individualistic, and cooperative. Cooperative structures were commonplace in American education until the late 1930s. Students were expected to work and learn together. From the late 1930s until the late 1960s, competitive structures reigned supreme. Students were expected to strive to be the best (i.e., highest-ranking) in the class or school. Most recently, individualistic structures have become popular: each student is expected to be the best that he or she can be. Johnson suggests that the time is right for a more balanced approach to structuring classrooms and lessons, an approach including competitive, individualistic, and cooperative structures.

If cooperative structures are to be workable, students must possess certain knowledge and skills. First, students need to understand the concept of "positive interdependence" (i.e., as a group they will sink or swim together). Second, students need to understand the concept of "individual accountability" (i.e., as members of a group they remain responsible for their own learning and the demonstration of that learning). Third, students need social skills (i.e., they must be able to carry on discussions, make group decisions, resolve conflicts, and the like).

Teachers must make a series of logistical decisions before cooperatively structured classrooms can be operative. They must decide on the size of the groups, how students will be assigned to groups, how the room is to be arranged, what materials are to be made available to groups, and what tasks to perform within the groups. Teachers who choose to structure their classrooms cooperatively must also realize that their own roles and responsibilities will change. After ensuring that students understand the task at hand and their individual and collective responsibilities, teachers supervise the group work, monitoring progress and providing assistance as necessary.

Because the research on the effectiveness of cooperatively structured classrooms and lessons is positive, teachers may be interested in moving toward such a structure in their own classroom. Several recommendations can be offered. First, teachers must be realistic about how much can be accomplished in short periods of time. Because most American students are not particularly good at collaborating with one another, "re-education" of students may be necessary. Second, teachers should provide classroom time for students to reflect on their successes and failures as groups. Third, teachers should not rely exclusively on cooperative structures. Some balance among competitive, individualistic, and cooperative structures is necessary to achieve maximum effectiveness.

BASIC CONCEPTS AND PRINCIPLES

Roger

Dr. Roger Johnson, Dr. David Johnson's brother, has collaborated with his brother on research on cooperative lesson structures and has co-written with him several articles (including one of the readings in this unit).

Competitively Structured Lessons

In lessons structured competitively, for some students to succeed others must fail. Success is defined by one's ranking or relative standing within the class or group. This ranking may be based on the number of answers given correctly, the number of "A" grades received on the report card, or the speed with which a task is completed.

Individualistically Structured Lessons

In lessons structured individualistically, for students to succeed they must achieve some preset standard of success. Success is defined by achieving some learning goal or mastering some objective. All students who achieve the standard receive a grade of "A" or "Pass."

Cooperatively Structured Lessons

In lessons structured cooperatively, for students to succeed all members of the group must succeed. Success is defined in terms of the welfare of the group combined with the level of individual learning. Some tasks are assigned in such a way that individual students only complete portions of the task and the overall task is completed when the "pieces" come together.

Teacher Responsibilities

The role and responsibilities of teachers change dramatically during cooperatively structured lessons. Teachers need to assign tasks that require or encourage cooperation. They need to remind students of "positive interdependence" and "individual accountability." They need to circulate and monitor the progress of the various groups. When necessary, they need to intervene in order to provide assistance with the acquisition of academic content and/or social skills. In other words, teachers become less directive, more supervisory.

READING ASSIGNMENT

Johnson, David W., and Johnson, Roger T. *Cooperative Learning.* (Unit II, Reading 3)

Teachers can structure their lessons in one of three ways: competitively, individualistically, or cooperatively. There are five key elements of cooperatively structured lessons: positive interdependence, face-to-face interaction, individual accountability, collaborative skills, and group processing. When lessons are structured cooperatively, the role of the teacher changes. Teachers should complete five sets of activities: clarifying the objectives, placing students in groups, explaining the elements of cooperation, monitoring the groups, and evaluating achievement and collaborative skills. Teacher professional support groups can help those who desire to structure at least some of their lessons cooperatively.

ADDITIONAL READINGS

Johnson, D. W. (1981). "Student-Student Interaction: The Neglected Variable in Education." *Educational Researcher* 10:5–10.

Slavin, R. E. (1983). "When Does Cooperative Learning Increase Student Achievement?" *Psychological Bulletin* 94:429–445.

Slavin, R. E. (1985). "Cooperative Learning: Applying Contact Theory in Desegregated Schools." *Journal of Social Issues* 41:45–62.

UNIT II

ASSIGNMENTS

SELF-TEST

1. For teachers to transform the aggregate they confront on the opening day of school into a workable social group, they must
   a. establish a common purpose for all students.
   b. "size up" the individual students in the class.
   c. develop an appropriate academic task structure.
   d. help individual students learn to "do school."

2. Which of the following is least likely to be used by a teacher making "sizing up" assessments?
   a. prior experience with older siblings
   b. initial responses or reactions in class
   c. a battery of tests given early in the year
   d. performance on the first homework assignment

3. Students learning to "do school" are most interested in determining the
   a. "whats" of the class.
   b. "hows" of the class.
   c. "whys" of the class.
   d. "whos" of the class.

4. The social-participation structure of the classroom imposes constraints on each student's
   a. academic knowledge and skills.
   b. performance on homework assignments.
   c. placement in a subgroup within the classroom.
   d. ability to speak in class.

5. *Rule* is to *routine* as
   a. *restrict* is to *enable*.
   b. *manage* is to *instruct*.
   c. *school* is to *classroom*.
   d. *management* is to *discipline*.

6. A teacher demonstrates to her chemistry students how she wants them to set up their equipment at the beginning of each laboratory period. This teacher is teaching a(n)
   a. exchange routine.
   b. management routine.
   c. rule.
   d. support routine.

7. All of the following are benefits of establishing "shared control" in the classroom *except* for
   a. students becoming more responsible.
   b. teachers spending more time teaching.
   c. rules being determined jointly by teachers and students.
   d. classrooms being more organized and behavior more orderly.

8. A primary function of effective classroom management is to
   a. maintain order at all costs.
   b. create an atmosphere conducive to learning.
   c. foster positive interpersonal relations.
   d. demonstrate to students "who's in charge."

9. *Instruction* is to *learning* as
   a. *teacher* is to *student*.
   b. *group* is to *student*.
   c. *teaching* is to *achievement*.
   d. *cause* is to *effect*.

10. When managing small groups of students within a classroom, a teacher must attend to all of these potential problems *except*
    a. the assignments given to the groups.
    b. the order in which he or she should work with the groups.

c. the size of the groups and the class "remainder."

d. the correct way to form groups.

11. In describing classrooms, the term "climate" refers to the
    a. physical environment.
    b. "objective" environment.
    c. psychological environment.
    d. physiological environment.

12. In a cooperative goal or lesson structure, students are graded on their performance
    a. relative to others in the class.
    b. relative to some preset mastery standard.
    c. as a member of a group within the class.
    d. on a graded series of tasks.

13. In an individualistic goal or lesson structure, students are graded on their performance
    a. relative to others in the class.
    b. relative to some preset mastery standard.
    c. as a member of a group within the class.
    d. on a graded series of tasks.

14. In a competitive goal or lesson structure, students are graded on their performance
    a. relative to others in the class.
    b. relative to some preset mastery standard.
    c. as a member of a group within the class.
    d. on a graded series of tasks.

15. Perhaps the biggest shift in teacher responsibilities when a cooperative goal or lesson structure is adopted is the shift from

a. telling to asking.
b. directing to supervising.
c. interacting to watching.
d. showing to telling.

UNIT ACTIVITIES

Complete one or both of the following activities.

1. Write a detailed plan for the first two or three weeks of the next school year. In your plan, discuss the rules and routines you would introduce and the way in which you would organize your classroom. Give a brief rationale for your choices.

2. Outline a talk you would give to your faculty or colleagues on incorporating the principles of cooperative learning in the classroom. Describe the strengths and weaknesses of cooperative learning and its appropriate place in an overall strategy of classroom organization.

ANSWER KEY FOR SELF-TEST

1. a (Lesson 5)
2. c (Lesson 5)
3. b (Lesson 5)
4. d (Lesson 5)
5. a (Lesson 6)
6. d (Lesson 6)
7. c (Lesson 6)
8. b (Lessons 6, 7)
9. b (Lesson 7)
10. d (Lesson 7)
11. c (Lesson 7)
12. c (Lesson 8)
13. b (Lesson 8)
14. a (Lesson 8)
15. b (Lesson 8)

UNIT **III**

CLASSROOM INSTRUCTION

The lessons in this unit focus on classroom instruction: the establishment of appropriate goals, the problems caused by differences among students, the importance of planning, the allocation and use of available time, the opportunity students have to learn what they are expected to learn, the use of instructional support materials, and the impact of educational technologies. Glaser (1976) has defined instruction as "the conditions which can be implemented to foster the acquisition of competence" (p. 1). In many ways, this simple definition "pulls together" the lessons included in Unit III.

Lesson 9 deals with the definition of "competence." The primary question raised in this lesson is, What's worth learning? Lesson 10 suggests that a variety of "conditions" may be necessary if all students in the same classroom are to acquire competence since students differ widely in terms of their prior experiences, achievements, and attitudes. Lesson 11 is concerned with the "can be implemented" phrase in Glaser's definition. Before appropriate conditions can be implemented, they must be planned. Finally, Lessons 12 through 15 are concerned with factors that can be manipulated to create conditions favorable to "foster[ing] the acquisition of competence." Among these factors are the productive use of classroom time (Lesson 12); the pace of instruction and the relationship of the content covered with the tests used to certify learning (Lesson 13); the availability and use of textbooks and workbooks (Lesson 14); and the availability and use of various educational technologies, such as television and computers (Lesson 15).

A more visual way of examining the relationships among the seven lessons in this unit is shown in Figure 3.1. As depicted in the figure, instruction is a bridge connecting the goals of schooling to the individual characteristics of the students who are enrolled in school.

To paraphrase Glaser, the primary purpose of instruction is to design a bridge (i.e., create conditions) so that when students cross that bridge they will achieve the goals of schooling (i.e., competence). But before such a bridge can be built, a blueprint must be prepared. The blueprint is a plan, and the process by which the blueprint is prepared is "planning." As the planner prepares the plan, he or she must be

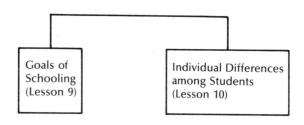

Blueprint

    Plans (Lesson 11)

Tools

    Time (Lesson 12)
    Opportunity to Learn (Lesson 13)
    Instructional Support Materials (Lesson 14)
    Educational Technologies (Lesson 15)

FIGURE 3.1   A Graphic Representation of the Structure of Unit III

aware of the tools that can be used to construct the bridge.

Two of the most important tools are time and materials. Time is necessary for any learning to occur—especially school learning, which requires contemplation, practice, or both. How that time is spent—the opportunities students have to profit from the available time—is related to goal attainment. How to allocate and make productive use of time are decisions that must be made by the instructional planner.

Materials are available both in traditional forms (e.g., textbooks) and in "new, improved" packages (e.g., television, computers). To choose new materials simply because they are "new" and "improved" is dangerous. Knowing when to rely on traditional forms and when to change to the "new" and "improved" is a vital skill of the instructional planner.

Just as classrooms must be organized if teaching and learning are to take place, instruction must be planned if the teaching and learning that do take place are to be effective. A lack of awareness of the student; inadequate time or the movement through a curriculum at too slow or rapid a pace; the inability or unwillingness to align goals, materials, and tests; the exclusive reliance on traditional materials at all costs or the rapid endorsement of new technologies without concern for their usefulness—all of these factors will contribute to a decrease in teaching and learning effectiveness.

REFERENCE

Glaser, R. (1976). "Components of a Psychology of Instruction: Towards a Science of Design." *Review of Educational Research* 46:1–24.

LESSON 9

WHAT'S WORTH LEARNING

PURPOSE OF THE LESSON

The purpose of the lesson is to address two questions. First, what are the purposes of schooling? Second, should there be a single set of purposes for all students?

OVERVIEW OF THE LESSON

Four general purposes of schooling are offered, two concerned with the betterment of society and two pertaining to the welfare of the individual. First, schooling is directly linked to the economic development of a state, region, or nation: the greater the number of educated people, the greater the economic development. Second (and somewhat related to the first), schooling helps students to develop the skills they need to succeed on the job and in the community. Third, schooling helps students develop the abilities and attitudes they need to continue to learn once they leave school. Truly educated people are usually able to adapt to the demands placed on them by the settings and situations in which they find themselves. Fourth, schooling helps students grow and develop, become "better" people. Although purposes vary, a statement of purpose is needed if we are to identify appropriate goals, objectives, curriculums, and instruction.

Regardless of stated or implied purposes, many people believe that schools are not accomplishing them. Schools do not help students function in real-life settings, and schools do not help students become self-sufficient. One reason that schools have been perceived negatively by the public is that educators may not be concerned primarily with the attainment of goals. Materials, activities, and test performance often take precedence over important goals perhaps because the former are more concrete and visible than the latter.

Should the same goals be set for all students? If similar goals are not set for all, then slower students tend to get a "watered down" curriculum. If, however, similar goals are set for all, then slower students must be given more time and extra help to achieve those goals. In other words, *unequal* treatment of students is needed if *equality* in the achievement of similar goals is to be attained.

At the least, goals provide direction or purpose for teachers. As such, teachers are advised to formulate worthwhile goals and use those goals wisely. When formulating goals, teachers should consider several issues. First, teachers must discover what the overall purpose of schooling is as defined by their school boards. Second, teachers must figure out how much time is needed for most students to reach the goals. Goals requiring one hour of instruction during an entire school year are probably not goals at all. To differentiate between "things that can be taught" (e.g., understanding mathematical concepts) and "things that must be fostered" (e.g., writing organized, meaningful paragraphs) is useful in this regard. Third, goals should require more of students than memorization of facts, rules, and generalizations. Memorization may aid in the attainment of goals, but they are not goals in and of themselves. Fourth, whether or not goals are included in a course or at a particular grade level should depend primarily on the importance of the goals in the lives of students and only secondarily on the difficulty students have in achieving those goals. Fifth, in today's educational climate, demonstrating that goals have been achieved has become more important than achieving the goals. Thus, an awareness of the ways in which students learn is needed by both teachers and students.

BASIC CONCEPTS AND PRINCIPLES

Goal

As defined in the *Random House Dictionary of the English Language,* second edition, a goal is "the result or achievement toward which effort is directed." To determine goals, then, teachers need to ask: What am I trying to achieve with these students? Why am I expending all of this effort? Typically, goals are broad-based achievements requiring the expenditure of effort over a long period of time (e.g., weeks, months, years). In order to achieve goals, students must master certain content and attain certain objectives.

The Goal of Teaching

In the words of Dr. Dorothy Strickland, our goal as teachers is to "produce youngsters who don't need us. Youngsters who can really get out there and get that information and use it and make it their own." Unfortunately, some goals make students more dependent rather than less dependent on their teachers.

The Relationship between Goals and Materials

Although many teachers of teachers suggest that goals precede the selection of materials, evidence indicates that materials are frequently selected independently of specific learning goals. As a consequence, teachers often are not aware of the specific goals they have for their students.

Equal versus Equitable

If students in the same class differ widely in knowledge and skills, equal treatment will increase those differences. Equitable treatment may require students to be treated differently; teachers must adjust to and accommodate initial differences so that similar ends are attained for virtually all students.

Taught versus Fostered

This distinction involves two factors. The first is time; the second, the role of the teacher. Things that can be taught can generally be taught in a relatively short period of time. In contrast, things that must be fostered require longer periods of time for students to learn. For those things that can be taught, the teacher typically assumes a direct role—he or she structures, supervises, demands, and asserts. In contrast, for those things that must be fostered, the teacher assumes an indirect role—he or she monitors progress, makes recommendations for improvement, and serves as a resource.

Importance versus Difficulty

Teachers often decide on what to teach based on the difficulty students may have in learning it. Simply stated, the importance of learning something should take precedence over the difficulty students may have in learning it.

Alignment

Alignment is defined as the relationship among goals, curriculum, and tests. Misalignment can cause a teacher to underestimate the effects of teaching. That is, no matter how good the teaching is, if the goals, curriculum, and tests are misaligned, the quality of that teaching will go unnoticed.

READING ASSIGNMENTS

Bruner, Jerome. *Models of the Learner.* (Unit III, Reading 3)

At the heart of the decision-making process concerning learning and learners, there must be a value judgment about how the mind should be cultivated and to what end. Five models of the learner are described: tabula rasa (we learn directly from experience); hypothesis generator (our models of the world help us to select the experiences from which we learn); nativism (innate mental powers enable us to organize our experiences); constructivism (learning consists of applying general rules to particulars); novice-to-expert (we learn from the experts). No single model is "right" or "best"; rather, each helps us to understand particular types of learning.

Jackson, Philip W. *The Mimetic and the Transformative: Alternative Outlooks on Teaching.* (Unit III, Reading 6)

Two different ways of thinking about and engaging in the practice of education are discussed: the mimetic and the transformative. Within the mimetic tradition, knowledge is transmitted from teachers to students by means of an imitative process. Teachers present new knowledge; students reproduce it. The aim is the acquisition of more knowledge. Within the transformative tradition, teachers attempt to change their students in fundamental ways. Teachers model and tell stories about the type of person they want students to become. The aim is the acquisition of different values, different ways of thinking. Although recently the influence of the mimetic tradition has been the greater, balance between the traditions would be beneficial.

LESSON **10**

INDIVIDUAL DIFFERENCES

PURPOSE OF THE LESSON

The purpose of the lesson is to address three questions. First, what is the extent of individual differences among students? Second, how do these differences influence teacher-student relationships in classrooms? Third, how can teachers successfully deal with differences among students?

OVERVIEW OF THE LESSON

Since children grow up in different homes, they develop differently. Children who come from homes in which books are read, conversations occur over dinner, and encouragement to try new and different things is the rule rather than the exception tend to be high achievers in school. Because of these different experiences, children enter schools with different aptitudes for learning.

Teachers can ignore individual differences by teaching and treating all students the same, arguing that such treatment provides students with "equal opportunities" for learning. However, when students with different aptitudes are exposed to uniform instruction, their aptitude differences are simply transformed into achievement differences.

Rather than ignoring them, individual differences can be acknowledged. But many who acknowledge individual differences tend to see such differences as unalterable. This perception often leads to a defeatist attitude on the part of those who teach students of "lower aptitude." The attitude is often expressed as "What do you expect me to do with these children?"

Traditionally, two approaches have been used to deal constructively with the problem of individual differences. First, students are placed in different curriculums, different courses, or different levels of the same course, based on their aptitude or prior achievement. Those in the lower levels are provided with remedial or compensatory instruction; those in the higher levels are provided with accelerated instruction and are enrolled in "academically advanced" or "advanced placement" courses.

Second, students are placed in the same curriculums and classrooms with teachers who provide "adaptive instruction" that accommodates individual differences. Adaptive instruction utilizes a wide variety of materials and activities so that all students succeed in achieving common objectives.

Proponents of adaptive instruction accept two basic assumptions concerning students. First, students learn in different ways (have different learning styles) or at different rates (i.e., faster or slower) or both. Consequently, instruction that is uniform in method, materials, and time is nonadaptive. Second, initial differences among students are alterable rather than stable. That is, instead of being permanent, aptitudes can be changed. As these aptitudes are changed, students adapt to varying classroom conditions. Ideally, adaptive instruction is no longer needed at this time.

Teachers implementing adaptive-instruction programs need to assume a role distinct from the traditional one. They need to be more aware of what individual students are thinking and doing; they need to try different things in an attempt to "reach" the students; they need to be willing to learn from their own teaching experiences (and mistakes) so that they can become increasingly effective in their classroom.

For those teachers confronted with the problems caused by individual differences, several recommendations can be offered. First, the teachers must never form fatalist attitudes toward those with lower aptitudes or lower prior achievement. Second, they should be aware that the stronger the relationship between aptitude and achievement (i.e., the higher the predictive validity of the aptitude test), the less adaptive the instruction that students receive. One of the things we know about education is that individual differences increase the longer students are in school. And, as Dr. Asa Hilliard contends, "it is the avowed intent of the pedagogue to undermine and to destroy predictive validity." Third, in talking about individual differences, teachers should emphasize differences in achievement rather than differences in ability. As educators, we know far more about what students have accomplished than about what they are capable of accomplishing. Fourth, teachers can communicate high expectations for all students, even when they hold low expectations for some students. Teachers who can convince their students that they can and will learn have served their profession well. Finally, teachers can develop techniques and methods that enable them to adapt their instruction to the individual student. Such techniques and methods would include (a) mechanisms for the continual monitoring of student learning, (b) multiple materials and resources that can be used to facilitate student learning, (c) the providing of additional time and help to those students who need it, and (c) the development of additional student responsibility for learning.

BASIC CONCEPTS AND PRINCIPLES

Nature versus Nurture

For decades, a debate has raged as to whether individual differences are genetic or environmentally caused. While this is an interesting academic question, the central issue confronting educators is, What can be done to help different students get the most out of school? Acceleration and adaptive instruction are two methods of effectively dealing with individual differences.

Acceleration

Acceleration is an approach to instruction in which students who are different academically are placed in different curriculums and different classrooms. Specifically, acceleration refers to the practice of placing academically advanced students in advanced courses. As such, acceleration requires a differentiated curriculum and, typically, the formation of homogeneously grouped classrooms. Those who advocate acceleration assume that individual differences among students are stable over time.

Adaptive Instruction

Adaptive instruction is an approach to instruction in which students who are different academically are placed in the same curriculum and same classroom. Successful adaptive-instruction programs share nine important characteristics.

1. Initial strengths and weaknesses of students are determined.
2. A system to continue monitoring and assessing students is implemented.
3. A variety of resources and materials is available and used.
4. Student progress is evaluated periodically.
5. Students' responsibility for their own work and progress is stressed.
6. Varying amounts of instructional time are made available.
7. Students have some choice as to the goals to be pursued and the materials to be used.
8. Teams of teachers are formed.
9. Students are permitted or required to help one another (peer assistance).

Those who advocate adaptive instruction assume that individual differences among students are alterable.

Ability versus Achievement

Generally, ability is defined as a relatively permanent abstract characteristic of students. Achievement, on the other hand, is more alterable (since it is directly related to the teaching that students have received) and more concrete. While information about student achievement can be used to improve instruction, information about student ability is most frequently used to predict achievement. In fact, errors of prediction are said to occur when achievement cannot be predicted perfectly from ability.

ADDITIONAL READINGS

Kulik, J. A., and Kulik, C. L. (1984). "Effects of Accelerated Instruction on Students." *Review of Educational Research* 54:409–425.

Wang, M., and Lindvall, C. M. (1984). "Individual Differences and School Learning Environments." In *Review of Research in Education*, vol. 11, edited by E. W. Gordon. Washington, D.C.: American Educational Research Association.

LESSON **11**

PLANS AND PLANNING

PURPOSE OF THE LESSON

The purpose of the lesson is to address three questions. First, what is the role of planning in teaching? Second, what kinds of planning do teachers do? Third, how can plans and the process of planning contribute to a teacher's effectiveness in the classroom?

OVERVIEW OF THE LESSON

Two definitions of planning are offered—one practical, the other psychological. Psychologically, planning is a process by which an individual visualizes the future and creates a framework to guide his or her action in that future.

Teachers plan in a variety of ways—by constructing yearly plans, term plans, unit plans, weekly plans, and daily (or lesson) plans. Teachers plan for several reasons: planning reduces anxiety and uncertainty; planning provides a learning experience for teachers; planning permits teachers to accommodate individual differences among students; planning gives structure and direction to teaching; finally, planning is required of some teachers.

Two styles of planning have been identified. Incremental planners plan for small portions of time, try out the plan, and make modifications as necessary. Comprehensive planners plan for entire units, providing them with some sense of the "big picture."

Novice and experienced teachers plan differently. Novice teachers usually write down very detailed plans and doggedly stay with them. Experienced teachers are more telegraphic in their planning and are more ready to depart from the plan if it appears not to be working or if a worthwhile digression seems appropriate. Furthermore, experienced teachers do not plan the way they were taught to plan when they were undergraduates. Rather, much of what they know about planning was acquired "on the job."

The subject matter being taught influences the ways in which teachers plan. For example, planning for mathematics lessons revolves around the textbook and teacher's guide. Planning for writing lessons, on the other hand, tends to require more originality and thought.

Fortunately, several recommendations can be offered to teachers intent on improving their planning. First, because of the many potential benefits, teachers should engage in planning. Second, to the extent possible, teachers should put their plans in writing. Third, teachers should develop an approach to planning that works for them. Fourth, teachers should plan both the content to be taught and the manner in which it is to be taught. Finally, teachers should stop periodically and ask themselves, "How's everything going?" And, if things are not going well, teachers should be willing and able to alter the plans—to be flexible and responsive to the reactions of their students.

BASIC CONCEPTS AND PRINCIPLES

Planning

Planning can be defined as a process in which teachers visualize the future and create a framework to guide their actions in that future. Planning also can be defined as what teachers do when they say they are planning. The process of planning, rather than the particular format of the plans, appears to be the key to success.

Types of Planning

The types of planning that teachers do are organized around either time or content. Yearly, term, weekly, and daily planning are time-based. Course, unit, and lesson planning are content-based. According to teachers, the most important types of planning are unit planning, weekly planning, and daily planning.

Incremental versus Comprehensive Planning

These two approaches to planning differ in scope. Incremental planning is a short-term endeavor in which modifications are made in the plan based on how things are going. Comprehensive planning is a long-term undertaking requiring the planner to see daily and weekly activities within the context of the "big picture." Often teachers move from one approach to the other during the course of the year.

The "Invisibility" of Planning

Unlike the behaviors and actions of teachers in the classroom, planning generally cannot be observed. As a consequence, it is sometimes neglected or "placed on the back burner." Nonetheless, teachers are aware of the importance of planning, as is evinced by their acceptance of research findings on planning.

The Right Approach to Planning

There is none. Rather, teachers should develop an approach that works for them. Furthermore, they should take time to plan, although several conditions hinder or detract from teacher planning—heavy course loads, years of teaching experience, and so forth.

Tuesday as the First Day of the Week

Because of the intrusions of the weekend, teachers can make Tuesday the first day of the week. Monday, then, becomes the review day, the testing day, the end-of-the-week day.

READING ASSIGNMENT

Clark, Christopher M., and Yinger, Robert J. *The Hidden World of Teaching: Implications of Research on Teacher Planning.* (Unit III, Reading 4)

Approaching the study of teaching from a cognitive information-processing perspective, Clark and Yinger seek to answer questions concerning how and why teachers plan as well as the consequences of that planning. Planning is defined as preparing a framework for guiding future action. Seven generalizations derived from their research are presented: planning (1) is plural, important, and invisible; (2) differs in practice from the way teachers are taught to plan; (3) has long-term effects when done early in the school year; (4) transforms curriculum into instruction; (5) can increase teacher efficiency and flexibility; (6) puts thought into action when communicated to students; and (7) aids in teacher development.

ADDITIONAL READING

Clark, C., and Peterson, P. (1986). "Teachers' Thought Processes." In *Handbook of Research on Training,* 3d ed., edited by M. C. Wittrock. New York: Macmillan.

LESSON **12**

TIME TO LEARN

PURPOSE OF THE LESSON

The purpose of the lesson is to address three questions. First, what do we know about how time is used in schools? Second, why are some educators concerned about an exclusive focus on time as a critical instructional variable? Third, what can administrators and teachers do to increase the productive use of school time?

OVERVIEW OF THE LESSON

Over the past several decades, the time that students have spent in school has remained fairly constant while the amount of knowledge and the number of skills to be taught have expanded exponentially. Advocates of several subject-matter areas have argued that their area is a "basic skill." In view of the amount of knowledge and the number of skills students *could* acquire, and the time available for them to acquire this knowledge and these skills, the most productive use of available time is critical.

Several variables associated with the use of time have been identified. Allocated time is the amount of time given over to instruction in a particular subject matter—how much time is scheduled for reading, mathematics, science, and other subject areas. In general, three factors guide teachers' decisions on allocating time to particular subjects (at the elementary-school level) or to specific topics within subject areas (at the secondary-school level): (1) the attitude of the teacher toward the subject or topic; (2) the teacher's perceptions of the difficulty that students will have learning the subject or topic; and (3) the time needed by the teacher to prepare for teaching the subject or topic.

Clearly, not all of the time allocated to a subject or topic is spent on instruction. Tardy students, the collection of lunch money, and announcements over the public address system all reduce the amount of time available for instruction. The amount of allocated time devoted to instruction is termed "instructional time."

And not all instructional time is learning time. While instructional time is under the control of administrators and teachers, learning time, engaged time, or time-on-task is primarily under the control of the students. Differences among allocated time, instructional time, and learning time provide us with different views of the school year.

As expected, the emphasis on time as an important educational variable has its critics. At least some work is assigned to students to keep them busy. In addition, some students work hard at looking as if they are paying attention, participating in class, and/or working on assignments.

Partly in response to these criticisms, researchers have emphasized the concept of academic learning time (ALT). ALT is that portion of allocated time during which students are successfully answering questions and completing assignments that are directly related to the content and objectives included on an end-of-unit or end-of-year test. Thus, ALT enables concerns about both the quantity and quality of instruction to be merged into a single variable. ALT also suggests that the proof of the teaching is in the learning.

Several recommendations can be derived from the research on the allocation and use of time. First, all school personnel must work together to guard against the erosion of school time. Second, in their classroom, teachers must plan for the most productive use of time for themselves and their students. Third, teachers should explore a variety of approaches as they search for ways to maximize the amount of time students are on task. Fourth, teachers should be aware of the concept of ALT as they select the assignments that they give to students.

BASIC CONCEPTS AND PRINCIPLES

Allocated Time

Allocated time is the amount of time scheduled for the teaching of particular subject areas or topics. The minimum amount of time spent on the teaching and learning of some subject areas or topics is determined at the district or state level. Although the responsibility for scheduling the time for other subject areas and topics is determined at the district or state level, the implementation rests primarily with the teacher or teachers.

Instructional Time

Instructional time is that portion of allocated classroom time during which academic (rather than procedural or disciplinary) matters are emphasized. Time spent distributing or collecting materials, moving students from one activity to another, or reinforcing appropriate or disciplining inappropriate classroom behavior is subtracted from allocated time to yield an estimate of instructional time.

Engaged Time or Time-on-Task

Engaged time or time-on-task is that portion of instructional time during which students are paying attention, participating in class, or working on assigned tasks. Either the percentage of

students observed to be on task or the percentage of time that the average student spends on task is used as an estimate of engaged time.

Academic Learning Time (ALT)

ALT is a composite of three variables. First, the student must be engaged in learning (be on task). Second, the student must be successful in the activity in which he or she is engaged (e.g., responding to questions, completing assignments). Third, that activity must be linked to success on some external criterion, such as an end-of-year achievement test. Unfortunately, ALT is often only a small portion of allocated time.

READING ASSIGNMENT

Berliner, David C. *Tempus Educare*. (Unit III, Reading 2)

The design and findings of the Beginning Teacher Evaluation Study (BTES) are reviewed. One basic assumption underlying the BTES is that teacher behavior does not influence student achievement directly. Rather, teacher behavior influences students' ALT, which, in turn, influences student achievement. ALT is that time during which students are engaged in learning appropriate curriculum content (i.e., content logically or empirically related to the outcomes being sought and measured and presented at a reasonable level of difficulty). ALT allows learning to be studied as it occurs, rather than having to wait until the end of the term or year.

ADDITIONAL READING

Smyth, W. J. (1987). "Time." In *The International Encyclopedia of Teaching and Teacher Education*, edited by M. J. Dunkin. Oxford, Eng.: Pergamon.

LESSON **13**

OPPORTUNITY TO LEARN

PURPOSE OF THE LESSON

The purpose of the lesson is to address three questions. First, what is meant by opportunity to learn? Second, what factors influence the extent to which students have opportunities to learn? Third, what can be done to increase students' opportunities to learn?

OVERVIEW OF THE LESSON

Common sense dictates that students have difficulty learning that which they have not had the opportunity to learn. At the same time, many of the items given to students on state or national tests violate this common-sense principle. In fact, opportunity to learn is much more than common sense—it is composed of several interrelated variables.

Content coverage, one component of opportunity to learn, refers to the total number of facts, concepts, principles, and skills to which students are exposed during a lengthy period of time (e.g., a semester, a year, several years).

Pacing, a second component of opportunity to learn, refers to the rate at which those facts, concepts, principles, and skills are covered on a daily or weekly basis. Four factors are related to the pacing of instruction. First, teachers adjust their pace partly in response to their students. If students need more time on a particular topic, for example, the pace for teaching that topic slows. Second, the pace of instruction is determined partly by a teacher's classroom style: some teachers are relaxed; others move at breakneck speed. Third, students exposed to difficult content tend to learn it at a rapid pace, with little time spent on the review of previously covered content. Some teachers assume that students exposed to easy content need to learn it slowly, with a lot of time spent on review. Fourth, time of year influences the pace of instruction. As teachers approach the end of the year, they tend either to speed up or slow down, based on their perceptions of the demands placed on students by teachers at the next higher grade level. Teachers' misconceptions of other teachers' demands on students may have negative consequences on students and their learning.

Classroom management is a third component of opportunity to learn. In Dr. David Berliner's words, "You don't have an opportunity to learn if you are in a chaotic classroom." The ways in which teachers schedule their time, make use of that time, and talk with and supervise students during the allocated time also influence the opportunities students have to learn.

The final component of opportunity to learn is the alignment of goals, curriculums, and tests. Because tests are the concrete representations of our more abstract goals, the curriculums to which students are exposed should be aligned with those tests if the actual amount of learning that occurred is to be estimated accurately. Misalignment of goals, curriculums, and tests will cause the amount learned by students to be underestimated.

Several recommendations can be given to educators interested in increasing students' opportunities to learn. First, administrators and teachers must be aware of how complex the concept of opportunity to learn is. Second, careful planning is necessary for students to have the opportunity to learn what they are expected to learn. Third, in general, much that is being taught can be taught at a more rapid pace. Fourth, as teachers teach, they should ask themselves periodically, "What have my students had the opportunity to learn?"

BASIC CONCEPTS AND PRINCIPLES

Content Coverage

Content coverage refers to the amount of knowledge and/or number of skills to which students are exposed over a lengthy period of time (e.g., a semester, a year). The more knowledge and skills taught during eighth-grade science, for example, the greater the content coverage. Content coverage, even when estimated simply by the number of pages in a textbook, is related to higher levels of achievement.

Pacing

Pacing refers to the rate at which content is covered per day or per week. One objective per day, ten pages per week, a chapter every two weeks are all estimates of pacing. Like content coverage, pacing tends to be related to higher levels of achievement. However, very rapid pacing may be as detrimental to achievement as very slow pacing.

Steering Group

A steering group is usually a small number of low-average students in a classroom whose reactions teachers use to make decisions such as when to move from one topic to another and when to go over the material one more time. That is, the steering group influences the pacing of instruction.

Teacher Behavior and Opportunity to Learn

Teachers can engage in at least three activities that are likely to increase students' opportunities to learn: (1) they can create classrooms conducive to studying and learning; (2) they can make optimal use of the time available for instruction; and (3) they can supervise students as the students work at their desks or tables.

Alignment

In an era in which test performance is emphasized and valued, students need an opportunity to obtain the knowledge and skills included in the major district, state, and national tests. For students to have such an opportunity to learn, the goals, curriculums, and tests must be in alignment. Some researchers have referred to alignment as "content overlap" (Leinhardt and Seewald, 1981). Misalignment (e.g., choosing a curriculum without considering its appropriateness for the previously identified goals and tests, or selecting tests that neither measure the goals nor match the adopted textbook series) will probably lead to underestimating the knowledge and skills acquired by the students.

READING ASSIGNMENT

Anderson, Lorin W. *Opportunity to Learn.* (Unit III, Reading 1)

Opportunity to learn has been defined in two related but distinct ways. First, it is the amount of time allocated to students for the learning of a task or tasks. Using this definition, opportunity to learn is identical to either allocated or instructional time. Second, it is the extent to which students have received instruction on the content and objectives included on an achievement test. Using this definition, opportunity to learn is identical to content overlap. Allocated time, measured in minutes, hours, or days, is only slightly related to student achievement. In contrast, content overlap, measured in terms of the percentage of items that students have had an opportunity to learn, is strongly related to achievement.

ADDITIONAL READINGS

Leinhardt, G., and Seewald, A. M. (1981). "Overlap: What's Tested, What's Taught?" *Journal of Educational Measurement* 18:85–96.

Barr, R. (1987). "Content Coverage." In *The International Encyclopedia of Teaching and Teacher Education,* edited by M. J. Dunkin. Oxford, Eng.: Pergamon.

LESSON **14**

INSTRUCTIONAL SUPPORT MATERIALS

PURPOSE OF THE LESSON

The purpose of the lesson is to address three questions. First, what are the functions of instructional support materials? Second, why do teachers rely so heavily on particular materials such as textbooks? Third, how can teachers use available materials more effectively?

OVERVIEW OF THE LESSON

There are times when students are expected to learn directly from a textbook or other curriculum materials. Most of the time, however, these materials are intended to provide "instructional support" (i.e., to provide an alternative explanation, different examples and illustrations, or opportunities for practice). When materials are used in this way, they are termed "instructional support materials."

Several factors account for the popularity of these materials. First, many teachers feel pressured to use "district-adopted" textbooks, particularly in the areas of reading, language arts, and mathematics. Second, many teachers teach different subjects or courses each day. Adequate preparation for all of these subjects or courses would be difficult without relying on published materials. Third, teachers unfamiliar with the subject or content being taught are likely to use the textbook and other published materials extensively, and novice teachers tend to be "textbook-bound." Fourth, in general, the published materials tend to be of reasonably high quality.

In selecting materials, teachers should keep in mind two questions: Will the use of these materials help students reach established goals and objectives? Is there a variety of materials that will enable different students to achieve these goals and objectives? If the answer to either question is no, teachers should modify and supplement the materials as needed.

At least three dangers can be associated with the use of instructional support materials. First, teachers can overrely on such materials, using them even when they know that the materials may be ineffective for students. Second, teachers can allow the materials to become the instructional program and, consequently, to define the goals of the program. Third, teachers can see materials as "perfect," thus requiring no alteration or expansion. But since most materials are mass-produced, they are likely to be imperfect for some students in some classrooms.

Three recommendations can be given to educators interested in making the best use of available instructional support materials. First, teachers must see instructional support materials for what they are: means to ends rather than ends in themselves. Second, once teachers are aware of their primary goals and objectives, they should search for a variety of materials to aid students in achieving those goals and objectives. Third, teachers should develop their expertise in creating, selecting, and using instructional support materials either through collaborative efforts with other teachers or by noting reactions and responses of students as they use particular instructional support materials.

BASIC CONCEPTS AND PRINCIPLES

Instruction versus Instructional Support Materials

The emphasis in this lesson is on the use of textbooks and other commercially available materials to support classroom teaching and school learning. This is not to say that some students don't learn directly from these materials. However, the pedagogical value of much of the written materials is questionable (Rothkopf, 1976). An introduction, an explanation, or a translation of the materials by teachers is usually necessary and almost always advantageous.

Materials-driven Instruction

Materials-driven instruction occurs when "getting through the book" becomes the primary goal of the teacher. It also occurs when the materials are accepted as a "given"—that is, when the teacher decides what activities are appropriate and what goals can be pursued given the available materials.

Approaches to Examining Instructional Support Materials

Since commercially available materials are mass-produced, modification is necessary if goals are to be achieved and differences among students are to be considered. Groups of teachers can meet and discuss specific instructional support materials (e.g., "This lesson really helped my students learn about addition"). Students can be an excellent gauge of the quality and appropriateness of materials. Their reactions while working on the materials (including the questions they raise) can be noted; specific questions about the materials can be asked.

READING ASSIGNMENT

Shannon, Patrick. *A Retrospective Look at Teachers' Reliance on Commercial Reading Materials.* (Unit III, Reading 7)

Articles pertaining to teachers' dependence on commercial reading materials over six decades are reviewed. During this period, writers in the field have both applauded and condemned teachers' use of commercial materials. Those in favor have argued that commercial materials help "[spread] the results of research." The majority of the writers, however, have opposed attempts to standardize reading instruction through the use of commercial materials. Despite this "highly vocal and severe criticism," such materials have been used and are currently being used in 90 to 95 percent of classrooms. Research is needed to understand why teachers rely so heavily on commercial materials.

ADDITIONAL READING

Rothkopf, E. Z. (1976). "Writing to Teach and Reading to Learn: A Perspective on the Psychology of Written Instruction." In *The Psychology of Teaching Methods,* edited by N. L. Gage and D. Berliner. Chicago: University of Chicago Press.

LESSON 15

EDUCATIONAL TECHNOLOGIES

PURPOSE OF THE LESSON

The purpose of the lesson is to address three questions. First, what is the current status of educational technologies? Second, what are the strengths and weaknesses of such technologies? Third, how can available technologies be used effectively and efficiently?

OVERVIEW OF THE LESSON

Two facts are known about the application of technology to education. Regardless of how well intentioned and potentially useful technological innovations are, they will be greeted with skepticism, criticism, and fear. Furthermore, it takes a long time for technological innovations to become a regular part of educational practice. Both of these facts apply to two of the more modern technologies: television and microcomputers.

Like everything else, television and microcomputers have weaknesses and strengths. Some programs and software emphasize rote memorization; some are more entertaining than educational. Sufficient programs often are not available. Consequently, access to the technologies becomes a reward rather than an integral part of the overall instructional program.

On the positive side, however, the various technologies provide unique and, ultimately, educational opportunities and experiences. For example, the technologies give students a common set of experiences that they normally would not have. Both television and microcomputers are "detached" from the realities of classroom life. As a result, they can be used to introduce important but sensitive topics. Furthermore,

students find technologies to be "fair": television does not hold grudges based on yesterday's performance; microcomputers do not attribute mental deficiencies to students who frequently make errors.

Despite these potential benefits, neither television nor the microcomputer is widely used in schools. Why? In many cases, it's simply a matter of insufficient funds. Also, because of the rapid development of these technologies, it is difficult to decide what and when to buy. Purchasing second-generation equipment just as the third generation is arriving on the market is expensive and frustrating. Finally, time and effort typically unavailable to administrators and teachers are needed to sort through the variety of hardware and software available before informed choices can be made.

Educational technologies must be incorporated into the overall educational program to be effective. The purpose of a particular videotape or computer diskette should be made clear to students when it is used. After its use, some type of summary is helpful. Finally, because the information included on a videotape or diskette is massive and densely packed, multiple uses are suggested.

Several recommendations concerning the availability and use of technologies in schools and classrooms can be given to administrators and teachers. First, both availability and use of these technologies must be increased. Second, because of the rapid advancement of these technologies and the wealth of information about them, for assistance teachers should rely on local experts such as library media specialists. Third, teachers and administrators need time to explore the available technologies and consider their appropriateness and utility. Fourth, the roles and responsibilities of students in terms of the various technologies must be clarified: "passive receptivity" must be replaced by "active participation" if students are to benefit from the technologies. Finally, careful planning and implementation strategies are needed for the technologies to be maximally effective.

BASIC CONCEPTS AND PRINCIPLES

Technology Phobia

Some people think that technologies will interfere with or inhibit learning. They claim that "calculators will lead to a generation of students unable to compute," "word processors will undermine the development of proper cursive writing skills," and "television viewing leads to blank expression and equally blank minds." Although there are educational goals for which the use of technologies is inappropriate, wise use of available technologies will prove extremely beneficial. The trick is to match goals with technologies and to balance the use and nonuse of technologies in the classroom.

Minimum Hardware Needed

The effectiveness of educational technologies depends to a large extent on the availability of the technological hardware. One microcomputer for 300 students or one small-screen television improperly placed in the classroom will cause more problems than it will solve. At the least, each classroom should include one television monitor, one videocassette recorder, and about six microcomputers.

Disks versus Tapes

The trend in most technologies is from tapes to disks. "Floppy disks" have replaced magnetic tapes in virtually all microcomputers. Similarly, in radio and television, compact disks (CDs) and videodisks have several advantages over tapes. First, they can store far more information. Second, information can be retrieved quicker and with greater precision. Third, the quality of reproduction is superior. Because of these advances, however, they are more expensive and require more time and effort on the part of educators to learn.

Means versus Ends

John Stuart Mill wrote in his *On Liberty* that the "greatest difficulty to be encountered does not lie in the appreciation of means toward an acknowledged end, but in the indifference of persons in general to the end itself." Technology is a means to an end. Just as the printing press has produced the Bible as well as pornography, educational technologies can be used well or poorly.

READING ASSIGNMENTS

Clark, Richard E. *Reconsidering Research on Learning from Media.* (Unit III, Reading 5)

Recent studies on the effects of television and computers on student achievement are reviewed. In general, few, if any, benefits can be attributed to the use of any one medium. Benefits attributed to media by some researchers could just as easily be attributed to variables such as differences in content or method, or the novelty effect. Media are best understood as delivery vehicles for instruction; they do not directly influence learning. However, certain elements of media (e.g., animated motion) in combination with certain characteristics of learners (e.g., beliefs and attitudes) might influence student learning.

Suppes, Patrick. *Historical Perspective on Educational Technology.* (Unit III, Reading 8)

Five technological innovations of the past are reviewed: written records, libraries, the printing press, mass schooling, and testing. Although each was severely attacked by critics, it has become an integral part of our educational system. For each innovation, however, changes have taken place and are likely to continue to take place. The emphasis in the libraries of tomorrow, for example, will probably be more on access and less on holdings. Four issues raised by computer-assisted instruction are identified and described: (1) individualization of instruction, (2) standardization of instruction, (3) complexity of instruction, and (4) freedom in education. Finally, problems and promises of educational technologies are discussed.

UNIT III

ASSIGNMENTS

SELF-TEST

1. For decades, "equal opportunity" has been a catch phrase in American education. Green contends, however, that "equal" is not necessarily "equitable." Which of the following equations best illustrates Green's contention?
   a. equal learners + equal treatment = equal learning
   b. equal learners + unequal treatment = unequal learning
   c. unequal learners + equal treatment = unequal learning
   d. unequal learners + unequal treatment = equal learning

2. An important distinction can be made between "things that can be taught" and "things that can be fostered." Which of the following can be fostered but not taught?
   a. learning the names of the various geometric figures
   b. learning the basic principles of Euclidean geometry
   c. learning the formulas for computing area, perimeter, and circumference
   d. learning the method of geometric proof

3. With respect to the relationship between goals and materials, the most reasonable statement concerning the current practice is that teachers
   a. select materials in line with their goals.
   b. base their goals on the materials that are available.
   c. are complacent concerning the relationship.
   d. are too busy to consider either goals or materials.

4. Alignment refers to the relationship of
   a. curriculums and tests.
   b. goals and curriculums.
   c. goals and tests.
   d. goals, curriculums, and tests.

5. Whether you attempt to deal with differences among students by means of adaptive or accelerated instruction depends in large part on your beliefs about differences among students. Which two of the following are the appropriate matches between the beliefs and the types of instruction?
   a. stable differences–adaptive instruction
   b. alterable differences—adaptive instruction
   c. alterable differences—accelerated instruction
   d. stable differences—accelerated instruction

6. *Ability* is to *achievement* as all of the following answers *except*
   a. *stable* is to *alterable*.
   b. *classification* is to *improvement*.
   c. *unknown* is to *known*.
   d. *adaptive* is to *accelerated*.

7. Which of the following is a content-based (rather than a time-based) element of planning?
   a. course
   b. day
   c. week
   d. term

8. Concerning teacher planning, *incremental* is to *comprehensive* as
   a. *today* is to *tomorrow*.
   b. *stability* is to *change*.
   c. *part* is to *whole*.
   d. *context* is to *isolation*.

9. Academic learning time (ALT) is unique among the components of instructional time in that ALT includes the time that students
   a. have an opportunity to learn.
   b. are engaged in learning.
   c. appear to be engaged in learning.
   d. are successful in their learning.

10. Which of the following would yield the maximum estimate of time (i.e., the largest number)?
    a. allocated time
    b. instructional time
    c. engaged time
    d. academic learning time

11. All of the following are associated with the pacing of instruction *except*
    a. the style of the teacher.
    b. the reactions of the students.
    c. the time of year.
    d. the subject being taught.

12. Pacing differs from content coverage primarily in the
    a. length of time being considered.
    b. correlation with achievement tests.
    c. role of the steering group.
    d. role of the teacher.

13. All of the following are associated with teachers' reliance on commercially produced materials *except*
    a. the pressure teachers feel to use them.
    b. the number of preparations teachers have.
    c. the number of years teachers have been teaching.
    d. the appropriateness of the materials for their particular students.

14. The emphasis on the word "support" in the discussion of both instructional support materials and educational technologies implies that
    a. neither existing materials nor technologies can stand alone.
    b. technologies and materials can be combined in useful ways.
    c. teachers are likely to be replaced with available materials and technologies.
    d. students are able to learn directly from available materials and technologies.

15. Based on recent studies of the effects of television and computers on student achievement, it seems reasonable to conclude that
    a. technology is universally beneficial.
    b. the benefits of technology depend on the way in which it is used.
    c. technology is a high-cost, nonproductive approach to teaching and learning.
    d. computers are more beneficial than television.

UNIT ACTIVITIES

Complete one or more of the following activities.

1. Estimate the opportunity that students in one of your classes will have to acquire the knowledge and skills included in a grade-appropriate state or national standardized test. Prepare a profile of the amount of time that you have spent in a particular week on whole-class instruction, small-group instruction, seat work, and management activities. Finally, discuss these results in terms of the concepts and principles presented in this unit.

2. Develop a plan for incorporating one of the modern educational technologies into the overall instructional program of your school or district. In your plan, indicate (a) the uses you would suggest for the technology, (b) the in-service training you would recommend for your faculty, and (c) the way you would ensure proper integration of the computer software or video material into the curriculum.

3. Define "alignment." Give three reasons why alignment is an important variable in determining teacher effectiveness. Indicate the steps that you, as a teacher or an administrator, would take to maximize alignment.

ANSWER KEY FOR SELF-TEST

1. c (Lesson 9)
2. d (Lesson 9)
3. b (Lesson 9)
4. d (Lessons 9, 14)
5. b, d (Lesson 10)
6. d (Lesson 10)
7. a (Lesson 11)
8. c (Lesson 11)
9. d (Lesson 12)
10. a (Lesson 12)
11. d (Lesson 13)
12. a (Lesson 13)
13. d (Lesson 14)
14. a (Lessons 14, 15)
15. b (Lesson 15)

UNIT IV

CLASSROOM TEACHING

The lessons in this unit focus on five key components of classroom teaching: orienting students, giving explanations, asking questions, assigning work, and involving students in learning. Combined, these components represent the primary functions (Rosenshine and Stevens, 1986) that teachers must perform or the major tasks (Anderson, 1986) that they must do if they are to be effective in the classroom.

Each task consists of a goal and a set of operations (techniques) to achieve that goal (Doyle, 1979). Teachers orient their students to make them aware of *what* they are expected to learn, *that* they are expected to learn, and *why* that learning is expected. Students' awareness of learning expectations, then, is the goal of orienting students. Teachers have several techniques (or, in Doyle's terms, operations) that they can use when working toward this goal: they can write objectives on the chalkboard; they can provide frequent opportunities for student success early in the term or year; in discussions with students, they can relate what students are learning to what students already know or to problems that students encounter or are likely to encounter.

Teachers explain to ensure student understanding of the content. Students' understanding of the content, then, is the goal of giving explanations. Again, teachers have several techniques that they can use in working toward this goal: they can provide concrete illustrations; they can use precise language; they can show students specific steps to follow to arrive at answers or to solve problems.

By asking questions, teachers are able to determine the extent to which their students have learned what they were expected to learn and have understood the explanations given. Questions also are asked for the purposes of classroom management (e.g., "Billy, what are you doing out of your seat?"). A variety of questioning techniques are available to teachers: they can direct questions to the whole class or to individual students; they can call on particular students or ask for volunteers; they can ask general or specific questions; they can ask questions that require a factual answer, a "thoughtful" answer, or an opinion.

Teachers assign work to provide opportunities for students to practice what they recently have been taught; to test the limits of students' newly acquired learning; or, less frequently, to ready students for upcoming lessons. Students' retention of what they have learned and their proficiency in applying that learning in new and different situations are the major goals of assigning work. (Work is also assigned because parents, school administrators, or both expect it to be assigned.) Teachers have a variety of asssignments at their disposal: workbooks, textbook exercises, reports, projects, and performances (e.g., pieces of music, gymnastic routines). Like questions, assignments can require simple recall of previously learned information or the creation of complex or novel answers, products, or performances. Whatever the assignment, students should be made aware of its purpose as well as the directions for its proper completion. As students work on these assign-

TABLE 4.1   Summary of Major Tasks of Classroom Teaching

TASK	MAJOR GOAL(S)	SELECTED TECHNIQUES ("OPERATIONS")
Orienting students	Students' awareness of learning expectations	• Write objectives on chalkboard • Provide opportunities for early learning success • Discuss relevance to previous experiences, future problems
Giving explanations	Students' understanding of content being presented	• Provide concrete illustrations • Use precise language • List specific steps to be followed
Asking questions	Teachers' awareness of students' understanding and learning	• Ask questions that require students to remember, "think," and express and defend opinions • Direct questions to whole class and to individual students • Call on specific students, and ask for volunteers
Assigning work	Students' retention of what they've learned; proficiency in their use of that learning in the future	• Give a variety of assignments directly related to desired learning outcomes • Clarify purposes and directions for proper completion of each assignment • Check students' work, providing additional explanations as needed
Involving students in learning	Students' spending of time and expending of effort needed to learn and learn well	• Indicate relevance of learning to students • Give enthusiastic explanations • Pose intriguing questions • Assign interesting, challenging work

ments in class, teachers can periodically check the students' work, providing explanations and asking questions as necessary.

As teachers orient their students, give explanations, ask questions, and assign work, they should keep in mind that the primary teaching task is to involve students in their own learning. Students' spending of time and expending of physical and mental effort needed to learn and learn well are the major goals associated with this task. Again, teachers can accomplish this task in a variety of ways: they can explain how the learning is relevant to the students' lives; they can give enthusiastic explanations; they can pose intriguing questions; they can assign interesting, challenging work.

In many ways, the five teaching tasks, sum-marized in Table 4.1, lie at the heart of teaching. For some educators, these tasks define teaching, since they describe what teachers actually do in their classrooms. For others, these tasks must be accomplished if teaching is to occur. These latter educators inextricably link teaching and learning: teachers "teach," students "student" (Fenstermacher, 1986), and only when both "teaching" and "studenting" are done well does learning take place.

REFERENCES

Anderson, L. W. (1986). "Research on Teaching and Educational Effectiveness." *NASSP Curriculum Report* 15, no. 4:1–6.

Doyle, W. (1979). "Classroom Tasks and Students' Abilities." In *Research on Teaching: Concepts, Findings, and Implications*, edited by P. L. Peterson and H. J. Walberg. Berkeley, Calif.: McCutchan.

Fenstermacher, G. D. (1986). "Philosophy of Research on Teaching: Three Aspects." In *Hand-book of Research on Teaching,* 3d ed., edited by M. C. Wittrock. New York: Macmillan.

Rosenshine, B. V., and Stevens, R. (1986). "Teaching Functions." In *Handbook of Research on Teaching,* 3d ed., edited by M. C. Wittrock. New York: Macmillan.

LESSON **16**

ORIENTING STUDENTS

PURPOSE OF THE LESSON

The purpose of this lesson is to address three questions. First, how do students make sense of all the activities that go on in a typical classroom? Second, to what extent are students aware of the purpose of the various activities? Third, what can teachers do to ensure that students are busy learning rather than just busy?

OVERVIEW OF THE LESSON

Several decades ago, Ralph Tyler asserted that learning depends on the student. Every day, students experience a variety of activities in their classrooms. They listen to lectures, engage in discussions, and work on assignments. Some students, particularly those who have learned well and rapidly in the past, can make sense of these activities automatically. They know intuitively what to listen for when the teacher is talking, when to participate in classroom discussion, and how assignments can be completed with ease and efficiency. Other students, however, need help understanding the various activities. Teachers have at least three tools at their disposal for assisting these students: they can present objectives, engage students in review, and communicate high expectations.

Objectives are statements of what students are expected to learn from an activity or activities within a set amount of time. These statements help students understand why they are doing what they are doing. Objectives are important for two reasons. First, it is impossible to talk about teacher effectiveness without statements of purpose or goals. Second, clear statements of objectives empower students to be-

come involved in their own learning. The statements give students direction, a sense of purpose.

Review is a second tool teachers possess for helping students make sense of classroom activities. Students recall previous learning experiences that are related to experiences soon to be encountered. Reviewing for a test, for example, assists students in remembering what they have been taught so that they may be prepared for the exam. Thus, review helps students make connections between the known and unknown or between the familiar and unfamiliar, thereby building confidence.

When connections cannot be made between the novel and the familiar, repetition, drill, and practice are necessary. Much of what very young students learn in schools consists of a set of arbitrary social conventions: learning the alphabet, learning how to count, and acquiring a basic sight vocabulary. Similar examples, such as learning technical terminology (e.g., iambic pentameter) and learning about historical facts (e.g., battles and generals), can be given for secondary-school students.

Contrary to popular opinion, review is not something teachers do *for* students. Rather, review is something students do *for* themselves *with* teachers. When teachers conduct a review, they help students to recall what has been taught and supposedly learned. When students review, teachers pose questions that probe their students' memory. While going over material is easier and less time-consuming than helping the students to go over material, this practice is also less effective.

The communication of high expectations is a third tool teachers have for orienting students. These expectations convey to students that they *can* and *will* learn the knowledge and skills needed or likely to be needed.

Like most of us, students tend to live up or down to the expectations others hold for them. Students for whom teachers hold low expectations encounter a different classroom than students for whom high expectations are held. Specifically, students for whom teachers hold low expectations are seated away from the teacher, are smiled at and called on infrequently, are praised for marginal and inadequate answers, and are often interrupted during their work.

Several recommendations can be offered to educators intent on effectively orienting their students. First, teachers should make explicit the objectives that students are working toward. Second, teachers should express their expectations to motivate students to do well. Third, review should be used to help students form associations between what they have learned and what they are expected to learn. Finally, teachers should develop or adopt into their daily or weekly practices strategies that incorporate concerns for objectives, review, and expectations.

BASIC CONCEPTS AND PRINCIPLES

Objectives

Objectives give purpose to activities and experiences. Too many objectives trivialize education; too few result in aimless attempts at learning. Without objectives, it is impossible to consider teacher effectiveness. Without objectives, students are unsure as to what they are expected to learn from all their attentiveness and work.

Objectives versus Materials

While most undergraduate teacher educators suggest that teachers should base their choice of materials in large part on their choice of objectives, available evidence indicates that this suggestion is often not followed. Instead, teachers tend to examine the materials that are available and to identify objectives that can be achieved given those materials. These objectives may not be communicated to the students.

Purposes of Review

Review helps students to (1) summarize what they already know (and may not know), (2) anticipate what they are expected to know, (3) connect what they know with what they are expected to know, and (4) build confidence in their knowledge.

"Apperceptive Mass"

"Apperceptive mass" is an age-old concept. In recent years, the term has been replaced by the word "schema." Both terms refer to the mental organization of the knowledge a person has acquired. Both imply that "new" learning must be connected to "old" learning if the new is to be meaningful and remembered for any period of time. Some educators suggest that the greater the number of connections, the more meaningful the learning.

The Good in Each Culture

Once we know what students are expected to learn, we can capitalize on the good in each culture or subculture to teach it. Using sports to teach arithmetic, bugs to teach biology, adolescent problems to teach social studies, and movies to introduce literature are examples of this technique.

Holding Expectations versus Communicating Expectations

While human nature indicates that we hold varying expectations of other people, a teacher must communicate high expectations for all his or her students. The explicit or implicit communication of low expectations to students results in negative classroom experiences for those students.

READING ASSIGNMENT

Good, Thomas. *Research on Classroom Teaching*. (Unit IV, Reading 6)

Two general areas of research on classroom teaching are reviewed: teacher expectations and teacher effectiveness. Teachers tend to behave differently toward high- and low-achieving students. These behaviors suggest that teachers are inclined to expect very little from those students they perceive as having limited ability. The expression of high expectations, then, is one component of teacher effectiveness. Other components are the (1) presentation of information actively and clearly, (2) academic task orientation of the classroom, (3) encouragement of student questions and other means of checking for student understanding, (4) provision of structure and feedback as necessary, and (5) creation of a nonevaluative, relaxed learning environment.

LESSON 17

PRESENTATIONS AND EXPLANATIONS

PURPOSE OF THE LESSON

The purpose of the lesson is to address three questions. First, why do teachers talk so much in the classroom? Second, what do they talk about? Third, how can teachers increase the clarity of their presentations and explanations?

OVERVIEW OF THE LESSON

As Arno Bellack and his colleagues have written in their now classic study *The Language of the Classroom* (1966): "Few classroom activities can be carried on without the use of language. Indeed, observation of what goes on in elementary and secondary schools reveals that classroom activities are carried on in large part by means of verbal interaction between students and teachers." Teachers talk a great deal in class because talking is the primary means of human communication and communication with groups virtually requires talking. In this latter vein, talking is often used by teachers for crowd control (e.g., "Sit down!").

Teachers spend much of their time talking *to* students rather than *with* them. Lectures (i.e., one-way communication) occur far more frequently in classrooms than do discussions (i.e., two-way communication). One reason for this is that discussions require teachers to relinquish at least partial control of their classroom— which is something they are reluctant to do.

Because of the large amount of time teachers spend talking in their classroom, a great deal of research on this has been conducted, yielding several findings. Perhaps the most important finding is that teachers can learn to increase the clarity of their presentations and explanations.

Based on this research, several recommendations can be offered to teachers intent on improving their verbal communication. First, teachers can provide students with mental "scaffolding" that can be used to better understand the information presented. "Advance organizers" are attempts to provide students with generalized concepts that can bring together seemingly diverse pieces of information.

Second, teachers can be precise in their explanations. Ambiguous expressions such as "a few" can be replaced by precise expressions such as "three."

Third, teachers can use examples and illustrations to make abstract ideas and points concrete. Stating a rule, giving an example, then restating the rule is one way of doing this.

Fourth, when teaching a strategy or technique, teachers can list the steps to be followed when students apply the strategy or technique. Key words such as "first," "second," "third," or "next" and "then" can be used to make students aware of the specific steps.

Fifth, teachers can use similes and metaphors in attempts to link novel ideas to more familiar ones.

Sixth, teachers can use verbal markers to indicate important elements or aspects of information that they are presenting to the students. Simple statements such as "Please note," "This is important," and "Pay particular attention" are examples of verbal markers.

Seventh, teachers can explicitly describe the relationships or associations between ideas being presented. Linking words such as "because" and "therefore" are useful in this regard.

Finally, open discussions among students can be productive provided that the "rules of the game" are made explicit and are agreed upon by all participants (including the teacher). Teachers must be able to reestablish control if such discussions are to function properly.

BASIC CONCEPTS AND PRINCIPLES

Law of Two-Thirds

Based on a number of observational studies of classrooms in the 1960s, Ned Flanders (1970) proposed the law of two-thirds, which states that two-thirds of the time spent in classrooms is spent talking; two-thirds of this talk is done by teachers; and two-thirds of the time that teachers talk, they talk *to* students (i.e., lecture) rather than *with* students (i.e., discuss).

Advance Organizers

Contradictory to common sense, when more generalized, abstract ideas are presented to students prior to a set of specific, concrete facts, these "advance organizers" facilitate the learning of those facts. Advance organizers provide the mental scaffolding students use to relate, retain, and recall the specific facts presented.

Precision versus Ambiguity

As suspected, precision assists communication and understanding. "A few" (rather than twelve), "someone" (rather than Aristotle), "et cetera" (because you ran out of examples), and "you know" (because you cannot get the point across) are ways of not being precise.

Examples and Illustrations

Examples and illustrations can be used to make the abstract concrete. Even with the simplest concepts (such as the number 2), a variety of examples and illustrations (such as two deer, two feet, and two flowers) help the students to comprehend the concept. The examples should differ in all characteristics except the one being

illustrated (e.g., "two-ness"). Furthermore, both examples and nonexamples (i.e., examples that do not illustrate the concept being taught or the point being made) are useful.

Verbal Markers

Students are exposed to a great deal of information in a single class period let alone an entire school day or school year. They must determine which facts, concepts, rules, and principles are the most important ones. Teachers can use verbal markers to single out important items for their students.

Metaphors and Similes

As schoolchildren, we learned that metaphors use "are" while similes use "are like." In either case, they serve the function of relating novel experiences to more familiar ones. Telling students that "geometric planes are like large blankets" and "friendly countries are families—they don't always get along" is a way of making new learning meaningful to students.

Relationships and Associations

Unlike advance organizers, metaphors, and similes, which emphasize connections between the novel and the familiar, relationships and associations emphasize the connectedness of new content being presented during the same lesson. If, for example, monarchies and autocracies are introduced to students in a single lesson, their similarities and differences could be discussed and emphasized. Words such as "because" and "therefore" form links between new concepts and pieces of information.

READING ASSIGNMENT

Cruickshank, Donald R. *Applying Research on Teacher Clarity*. (Unit IV, Reading 3)

Generalizations derived from research on teacher clarity are reviewed and implications for teacher education discussed. Clarity is a stable, multidimensional phenomenon for which certain behaviors are more important than others. Among these behaviors are providing students with opportunities to learn, using illustrations and examples, and logically organizing and reviewing the material to be learned. Several instruments are available for assessing teacher clarity (e.g., Clear Teacher Checklist, Teacher Clarity Observation Instrument). Furthermore, several programs exist for helping teachers improve the clarity of presentations and explanations.

ADDITIONAL READINGS

Bellack, A. A.; Kliebard, H. M.; Hyman, R. T.; and Smith, F. L., Jr. (1966). *The Language of the Classroom*. New York: Teachers College Press.

Flanders, N. A. (1970). *Analyzing Teacher Behavior*. Reading, Mass.: Addison-Wesley.

70 / STUDY GUIDE

LESSON **18**

ASKING QUESTIONS

PURPOSE OF THE LESSON

The purpose of the lesson is to address three questions. First, what kinds of questions are asked in the classroom, and to whom are they directed? Second, what problems are associated with the use of questions in the classroom? Third, how can teachers improve their questioning skills and techniques?

OVERVIEW OF THE LESSON

In contrast with questions asked in most out-of-school settings, teachers generally know the answers to the questions they pose. In the classroom, questions provide an opportunity for teachers to listen to their students and, based on what they hear, to gauge the knowledge and understanding these students possess.

Classroom questions differ from one another in at least two ways. They differ in their intended audience. Some questions are addressed to students to answer on a volunteer basis ("invitational" questions). Others are addressed to specific students ("targeted" questions).

Classroom questions also differ in the level of thinking required to answer them. Some questions require students to recall from memory specific facts, concepts, or rules they have recently been taught ("memory" questions). Others require students to "think about" what they are being asked, to search for connections in their memories in order to give correct, reasonable, or defensible answers ("beyond memory" questions). Still other questions have no correct answer; rather, they require students to express and defend their own opinions ("opinion" questions). Most questions asked by teachers are "memory" questions.

From a teacher's perspective, questions are useful in determining their students' knowledge and understanding. From a student's point of view, however, these questions are a form of public evaluation. To admit ignorance in public is socially embarrassing. To add to the student's problem, teachers may require the answer to be both correct and presented correctly (e.g., in a complete sentence). Furthermore, teachers may misinterpret the meaning of a correct response, an incorrect response, or no response to a question.

Based on research conducted on classroom questions, several recommendations can be offered to those interested in improving their questioning skills and techniques. First, teachers can increase the number of questions that require students to go "beyond their memories" or to express and defend their opinions. Second, teachers can increase slightly the time they wait for students to respond to a question. Third, teachers can ask questions that enable them to diagnose their students' misunderstandings and misinterpretations. Once diagnosed, teachers can help students overcome these learning problems. Fourth, teachers can provide opportunities for students to ask questions. The general question "Any questions?" rarely elicits student queries. Finally, teachers can arrange for private questioning of students. Because of the potential social embarrassment of giving incorrect or inadequate answers, some students may be unwilling to participate in the "question-answer" or recitation method of teaching.

BASIC CONCEPTS AND PRINCIPLES

Intended Audience

Teachers address some questions to the whole class and some to individual students. When questions are addressed to individual students, teachers may invite students to respond or may call on students. Thus, questions are addressed to different student audiences.

Higher-Order Questions

Higher-order questions cannot be answered by recalling from memory some particular fact, concept, or rule. Rather, such questions can be answered only after students have spent some time mentally sorting through what they know and understand about the issue being raised. Two types of higher-order questions are "beyond memory" questions and "opinion" questions. "Beyond memory" questions have correct answers, while "opinion" questions do not.

Wait Time

Once a teacher asks a question, there is some time (however brief) during which there is silence. This period of silence is referred to as "wait time." A wait time of three seconds (or slightly more) pays great dividends in terms of the quality of student responses.

READING ASSIGNMENTS

Gall, Meredith. *Synthesis of Research on Teachers' Questioning*. (Unit IV, Reading 5)

Academic questions asked by teachers can be placed into one of two categories: fact (requiring recall) and higher cognitive (requiring thinking). Although the type of questions asked should reflect the type of learning desired, Gall suggests a 60:20:20 ratio for fact, higher cognitive, and procedural (i.e., nonacademic) questions. Whether or not questions are effective in eliciting the desired responses depends on five factors: (1) practice and feedback, (2) cuing (i.e., focusing students' attention on particular information), (3) the similarity of instruction and testing, (4) the provision of structure and feedback as necessary, and (5) the creation of a nonevaluative, relaxed learning environment.

Tobin, Kenneth. *The Role of Wait Time in Higher Cognitive Level Learning*. (Unit IV, Reading 7)

"Wait time" is defined in several ways (e.g., pause after teacher question, pause after student question or response). Studies in which wait time was observed and in which wait time was manipulated are reviewed. In studies in which wait time was manipulated, teachers were instructed to extend wait time beyond three seconds (the "threshold" level). The cognitive level of questions increases as wait time increases. Both teachers and students tend to use the extra time to think about subsequent discourse. Extended wait-time classes are more conversational and result in greater student achievement. The sole negative finding is that teacher anxiety increases as wait time increases.

LESSON **19**

ASSIGNMENTS

PURPOSE OF THE LESSON

The purpose of the lesson is to address three questions. First, how much time do students spend working on assignments? Second, what functions do assignments serve in the instructional process? Third, what should teachers know and do about assignments to make them more useful and productive for students as well as for themselves?

OVERVIEW OF THE LESSON

Most lessons include two portions: the "teaching portion," in which students are instructed by the teacher as a total class or in small groups, and the "work portion," in which students are expected to work on assignments individually or cooperatively at their seats, desk, or tables. In some classes (e.g., home economics, individualized mathematics), the vast majority of time is spent on the work portion. In others (e.g., many high-school and college classes), almost all the time is spent on the teaching portion, with the work portion expected to be completed out of class or at home.

Students are given assignments for a variety of reasons. Some assignments are given simply to keep students busy and to "fill up" remaining class time. To both students and teachers, these assignments are known as "busy work." Other assignments give students opportunities to practice what they have been taught, give teachers opportunities to determine how well students have learned what they were expected to learn, and help students to develop proper work habits and to value academic work.

Although assignments can be valuable, they also can be problematic if they are not designed and presented properly. And many students may be more interested in completing assignments than in the quality of their work on them.

Fortunately, research on assignments has led to several recommendations for teachers and administrators, First, as students work on assignments, teachers should circulate among the students, providing assistance as necessary. Second, teachers should carefully design their assignments. Hastily prepared assignments are of questionable value; overly lengthy and repetitious assignments are likely to produce boredom on the part of students. Third, teachers can give different assignments to different students (or groups of students) in their classroom. Such "individualized" assignments can be used after common lectures or discussions. Fourth, teachers should periodically check on the accuracy as well as completeness of individual student's assignments. Spot checking may be needed if assignments are lengthy or complex. Fifth, teachers should consider assigning group projects. The Jigsaw technique is one approach to promoting group work. With this technique, each member of a group works on a portion of the assignment, but the group as a whole is responsible for the completion of the entire assignment. Sixth, students can be given a choice of assignments from time to time. Providing students with such a choice while holding them accountable for the completion and quality of their work helps them to develop a sense of responsibility.

BASIC CONCEPTS AND PRINCIPLES

Busy Work

Assignments given to students because time remains at the end of class or because other students have not finished their original assignments are termed "busy work." Students will tell researchers that "she just gave me this to keep me busy." Consequently, they quickly learn that the "reward" for completing one assignment is to receive yet another.

Finishing an Assignment versus Learning from an Assignment

Assignments are usually given for some purpose—preparation for a forthcoming lesson, practice of previously taught skills, or development of good work habits. Often, since students fail to grasp the reason that assignments are given, they are more interested in completing the assignments than in learning from them.

Circulate and Monitor

As students work on their assignments, teachers should circulate among them and monitor the quality of their work. Students are more likely to remain on task and put forth the effort needed to complete the assignments when teachers monitor their work. In addition, the problems students have in completing the assignments can be identified as teachers circulate and monitor. Once these problems are evident, teachers can provide the help necessary so that students can complete the assignments. If common problems or difficulties are noted, teachers can stop the individual seat work and direct their explanations to the whole class or to a group of students in the class.

Characteristics of "Good" Assignments

Assignments that are likely to produce the desired results for both teachers and students share several characteristics. First, the purpose of the assignments and directions for their completion have been made clear to students. Second, the assignments are of "reasonable length"—long enough so that students can suc-

cessfully complete them, yet short enough so that they are not perceived as "busy work." Third, assignments that require students to "make or do" things help keep students on task. These assignments possess what Kounin and Sherman (1979) refer to as "holding power"—that is, they keep students involved in task completion without much teacher intervention. Fourth, group techniques such as the Jigsaw are useful in promoting high levels of involvement and producing higher-order thinking skills (such as planning, problem analysis, and organization).

READING ASSIGNMENT

Anderson, Linda. *The Environment of Instruction: The Function of Seatwork in a Commercially Developed Curriculum.* (Unit IV, Reading 1)

Five times during the year, observers took extensive notes on what first-grade students did as they worked on reading assignments. Observers also talked informally with the students. In general, students were given the same types of assignments on almost a daily basis. These assignments were taken from commercial materials and emphasized discrete reading skills. Students stated being more concerned with completing the assignments than with mastering the skills. Teachers seldom stated the purpose of the assignments; students were praised for looking busy and finishing work, not for their level of mastery. Especially for low-achieving students, a combination of difficult assignments and an emphasis on completion may be detrimental.

ADDITIONAL READINGS

Kounin, J. S., and Sherman, L. W. (1979). "School Environments as Behavior Settings." *Theory into Practice* 18:145–149.

Lee, J. F., and Pruitt, K. W. (1979). "Homework Assignments: Classroom Games or Teaching Tools?" *The Clearing House* 53:31–35.

LESSON 20
INVOLVING STUDENTS IN LEARNING

PURPOSE OF THE LESSON

The purpose of the lesson is to address two questions. First, how important is the role of students in their own learning? Second, what can teachers do to help students become involved in learning and put forth the effort necessary to learn and learn well?

OVERVIEW OF THE LESSON

Too often, students are treated as though everything they experience is stored in their memories precisely as they experience it. But students selectively attend to certain experiences and interpret those experiences in terms of their unique previous experiences. Stated simply, students determine in great part what they actually learn. And while this learning takes time and effort, it does not have to be drudgery, nor does it have to be painful. In fact, when examined over several decades, there has been a definite trend toward making the conditions of learning less discomforting for the student.

Under certain circumstances, students are likely to volunteer to spend the necessary time and effort to learn. If the knowledge or skill to be acquired is seen as important or desirable, if students believe that they have a chance to acquire the knowledge or skill, or if the students have some choice in selecting the knowledge or skill to be acquired, they might spend more time learning.

Researchers often use time-on-task to indicate the involvement of students in learning. Time-on-task can be estimated with accuracy provided that (1) the rules for determining who is and is not on task are agreed upon, (2) the procedure for observing students is specified and followed, and (3) a sufficient number of observations of the students is made. Low time-on-task often indicates curricular, instructional, or management problems within a classroom. On the other hand, classrooms in which time-on-task is high are not necessarily free from such problems. If the content taught is overly simple or the activities in which students are engaged are unrelated to the desired learning, high levels of time-on-task are associated with less need for classroom management and discipline.

Based on research conducted over the past twenty years, several factors associated with high levels of time-on-task have been identified. First, teachers should present students with clear learning goals, goals students believe to be important and see themselves as capable of achieving. In this regard, peers can often help students see the importance of achieving certain goals. Second, teachers should create a classroom in which students have greater responsibility for their own behavior as well as their own learning. In such classrooms, students have some choice either in the goals they pursue or in the activities they perform in order to accomplish specified goals. Third, teachers should provide incentives to students for learning (e.g., if you master this material, we will take Friday off), assign tasks that students are likely to accomplish and thus succeed at, reinforce task-oriented behaviors, and provide feedback as to the adequacy of student learning. All of these techniques will probably result in higher levels of student involvement in learning.

BASIC CONCEPTS AND PRINCIPLES
"Painless Pedagogy"

This term, coined by Dr. Philip Jackson, refers to the long-term trend in education toward making the conditions of learning pleasurable for the student. Coupled with the trend toward increased self-determination on the part of students (e.g., the increased number of elective courses), painless pedagogy represents a noteworthy change in educational philosophy over the past several decades.

Student Involvement in Learning and Time-on-Task

Student achievement depends on the degree to which students become and remain involved in learning. Stated negatively, students have absolute veto power in matters of their own learning. Time-on-task is one indicator of student involvement in learning—a quantitative one. There also is a qualitative aspect of student involvement—the degree or level of concentration—that is far more difficult to estimate. Time-on-task provides an estimate of the amount or proportion of time that students spend in learning. If the goal or assignment is inappropriate or if students feign their involvement in learning, the estimate will be a poor one. On the other hand, with proper observational rules and procedures, useful estimates of time-on-task are possible.

Correlates of Time-on-Task

Students are more likely to spend their time-on-task when the tasks are chosen at appropriate levels of difficulty, the tasks are communicated clearly to the students, the information that students need to complete the tasks successfully is continuously available, the students' work on the tasks is monitored by the teacher or someone else, the students' task orientation and effort are reinforced, and the students are given feedback as to the accuracy or quality of their work with suggestions for improvement offered as needed.

READING ASSIGNMENTS

Anderson, Lorin W. *Attention, Tasks and Time.* (Unit IV, Reading 2)

The relationships of attention, tasks, time, and learning are examined from two perspectives: historical and modern. Several generalizations have stood the test of time. Attention is critical for learning (although automaticity can reduce the need for concentration). To be effective, teachers must direct their students' attention to important tasks and help students maintain that attention for lengthy periods of time. Several suggestions as to how teachers can gain, direct, and sustain their students' attention are offered. Without equal concern for attention and tasks, time becomes a "psychologically empty quantitative concept" unlikely to produce desired learning results.

Doyle, Walter. *Academic Work.* (Unit IV, Reading 4)

The curriculum is composed of a collection of academic tasks (i.e., learning goals that students are expected to achieve and the methods or techniques to achieve them). Memory, procedure, comprehension, and opinion tasks are common in schools. Suggestions for the improvement of instruction depend in great part on the type of task students are asked to accomplish. Although research on cognitive psychology provides insights into the improvement of instruction, the complexities of the classroom also must be considered. Careful attention should be given to the preparation of instructional materials, student accountability for task accomplishment, and the provision of direct instruction (e.g., instruction in which the teacher is actively involved in "showing and telling" students what they need to know and do to achieve the learning goal or objective).

UNIT **IV**

ASSIGNMENTS

SELF-TEST

1. The most important aspect of objectives is that they
   a. are stated in behavioral terms.
   b. give purpose to activities and experiences.
   c. are less specific than educational goals.
   d. should be based on available materials.

2. Which of the following concerning review is *false*?
   a. Review helps students build confidence in their own learning.
   b. Review allows students to summarize what they already know.
   c. Review enables students to listen passively to what has been taught.
   d. Review permits students to anticipate what they soon will be learning.

3. Expectations are important in education, but *only* if they are
   a. positive.
   b. negative.
   c. communicated to students.
   d. held by teachers.

4. "Please write this down" is an example of a(n)
   a. advance organizer.
   b. metaphor or simile.
   c. example or illustration.
   d. verbal marker.

5. "Have you ever wondered about truth? How do we know that Columbus discovered America? Are we sure that groundhogs are able to forecast the arrival of spring? Is something true because we read it in the newspaper or in the Bible? Rachel, how do you know that something is true?" This dialogue between a teacher and her students is an example of the use of
   a. an advance organizer.
   b. a metaphor.
   c. relationships and associations.
   d. verbal markers.

6. "There are three important features that make a plane figure a square. First, the figure must have four sides. Second, all sides must be equal. Third, the adjacent sides must be perpendicular." This dialogue is a good example of
   a. examples and illustrations.
   b. relationships and associations.
   c. advance organizers.
   d. precision.

7. "Tanya, why do you think there are more single-parent families today than there have been in the past?" Which of these options best describes this question?
   a. an invitational recall question
   b. a targeted recall question
   c. an invitational "beyond memory" question
   d. a targeted "beyond memory" question

8. "Who remembers the capital of Bolivia?" (Teacher pauses, calls on Simon, who has raised his hand.) Which of these options best describes this question?
   a. an invitational recall question
   b. a targeted recall question
   c. an invitational "beyond memory" question
   d. a targeted "beyond memory" question

9. Based on recent research, what is the minimum time that teachers must wait for students' answers after asking questions if higher-level thinking is the goal?
   a. 1.5 seconds
   b. 3 seconds
   c. 5 seconds
   d. 10 seconds

10. From a teaching-learning perspective, which of these is *not* a characteristic of "good" assignments?
    a. assignments with "holding power"
    b. assignments that "fill up" the available classroom time
    c. assignments that require students to work together to complete
    d. assignments for which purpose and directions are given

11. Student responsibility for the completion of assignments is likely to be enhanced when
    a. students are given assignments to keep them busy.
    b. students can choose some of their assignments.
    c. teachers circulate among students, monitoring their work.
    d. teachers give different assignments to different students.

12. When students fail to understand the purpose for which an assignment is given, they are likely to be more concerned with
    a. keeping busy than with completing the assignment.
    b. completing the assignment than with learning from the assignment.
    c. keeping busy than with learning from the assignment.
    d. developing good study habits than with proper preparation.

13. "Painless pedagogy" implies that
    a. prospective teachers require fewer education courses.
    b. the basic principles of teaching are more easily learned.
    c. the content being learned is reduced to simplest terms.
    d. the conditions of learning are less discomforting.

14. Which of the following best describes the relationships between time-on-task and student involvement in learning?
    a. Student involvement is an estimate of time-on-task.
    b. Time-on-task is an estimate of student involvement.
    c. These two concepts are independent.
    d. These two concepts are synonymous.

15. Both internal and external factors are associated with students' involvement in their own learning. Which of the following is an *internal* factor?
    a. perceived chance of success
    b. difficulty of assigned work
    c. reinforcement for on-task behavior
    d. provision of feedback concerning adequacy of performance

UNIT ACTIVITIES

Complete one or more of the following activities.

1. Prepare a plan for a single lesson in which you emphasize one or more of the following elements:
    a. orienting students
    b. presentation and explanations
    c. asking questions
    d. assignments
    e. involving students in learning
    After you have devised your plan, try it out. And after you have tried it out, write your reactions to its successes and failures.

2. Observe a teacher during a single lesson or class period. During the observation, note the ways in which the teacher
    a. orients students
    b. makes presentations and gives explanations to students
    c. asks questions
    d. gives assignments
    e. involves students in learning
    Following the observation, prepare an outline that you would use in conducting a postobservation conference with the teacher.

3. Visit a local school. Talk with several teachers and the school principal concerning their views on

a. orienting students
b. presentation and explanations
c. asking questions
d. assignments
e. involving students in learning

Based on your findings, which of these elements appears to be (1) most important, (2) least important, and (3) most problematic from the perspective of those interviewed?

ANSWER KEY FOR SELF-TEST

1. b (Lesson 16)
2. c (Lesson 16)
3. c (Lesson 16)
4. d (Lesson 17)
5. a (Lesson 17)
6. d (Lesson 17)
7. d (Lesson 18)
8. a (Lesson 18)
9. b (Lesson 18)
10. b (Lesson 19)
11. b (Lesson 19)
12. b (Lesson 19)
13. d (Lesson 20)
14. b (Lesson 20)
15. a (Lesson 20)

UNIT **V**

ASSESSING AND EVALUATING

Much teaching comes down to trial, error, and revision, the reason being that while teaching is generally a group activity (with teachers attempting to target their efforts toward the largest number of students in the group), learning is an individual matter. No matter how well planned or well executed, a single act of teaching is unlikely to reach all students in a classroom in the same way. The lessons in this unit focus on the ways in which teachers identify errors, whom they blame for those errors (the students or themselves), and what they do to overcome those errors in the present and prevent them from occurring in the future. The structure of Unit V is shown in Table 5.1.

As shown in the table, teachers should ask two questions when errors are detected: Whose fault is it? What should I do about it?

Before these questions can be asked, however, the errors must be detected. Detection of errors and "nonerrors" (i.e., "good and proper" learning) is the topic of Lesson 21. In this lesson, appropriate ways of detecting these errors are discussed under the general rubric of assessment. Traditionally, students making the most errors have been labeled "low achievers." Conversely, those making the least errors have been labeled "high achievers." Beyond simply locating these errors and classifying students based on the number of errors made, assessment can aid in understanding the nature of the errors being made and, consequently, the students.

Examing the horizontal dimension of Table

5.1, we see that teachers, like most of us, tend to ascribe responsibility for errors. They begin by asking, Whose fault is it? Frequently, the fault is ascribed to the students. Increasing numbers of teachers, however, at least ponder their role in producing the errors. Regardless of where the fault lies, teachers have two choices in dealing with the errors (see the vertical dimension of Table 5.1). They can either judge the students or themselves, or they can work to overcome those errors. Prior to deciding whether to judge or help, however, teachers are wise to ensure that they understand how well students are learning (Lesson 21).

Lesson 22 includes the problems involved in judging (or grading) students based on the number of types of errors made. The criteria used to judge students, the evidence needed to

TABLE 5.1 The Relationships among the Lessons in Unit V

	STUDENTS	TEACHERS
Understanding	Lesson 21 Assessing Students	
Judging	Lesson 22 Grading Students	Lesson 24 Evaluating Teachers and Teaching
Helping	Lesson 23 Feedback and Correctives	Lesson 24 Evaluating Teachers and Teaching

judge them, and the comparisons to be made when judging are addressed. Grading students is also examined from the students' perspective. Determining what they, as students, need to do in order to receive acceptable grades (the so-called "performance-grade exchange") is an important aspect of school life for most students.

Lesson 23 is concerned with the use of assessment data to help students improve their learning, rather than to judge them on the basis of what they have and have not learned. When data as to their strengths and weaknesses are presented to students, they begin to understand what they have learned and what they have failed to learn. The next step is to help them correct their errors so that these errors do not accumulate and interfere with future learning.

Finally, Lesson 24 addresses the problems associated with teacher evaluation. At the very least, teacher evaluation assumes that a portion of the "fault" for errors resides in teachers. At the same time, however, the question of what should be done with the information collected remains unanswered. The information can be used to judge teachers—that is, to determine which teachers should be hired, fired, or promoted. Or the information can be used to help teachers acquire the knowledge and skills they need to overcome their deficiencies and/or to improve their teaching expertise.

LESSON 21

ASSESSING STUDENTS

PURPOSE OF THE LESSON

The purpose of the lesson is to address three questions. First, what is known about the quizzes and tests that teachers administer to their students? Second, how do teachers use the information that these tests and quizzes provide? Third, how can teachers improve the way in which they assess their students?

OVERVIEW OF THE LESSON

Assessment is the process of gathering information about a person, usually for the purpose of making a decision about that person. Before teachers can engage in assessment, they must know two things: What decisions do I need to make? What information do I need in order to make these decisions? Traditionally, the decisions concerned the sorting and classification of students, and the information pertaining to these decisions was taken from standardized tests.

Recently, some educators have argued that the primary purpose of assessment should be the improvement of teaching and learning. That is, assessment should be geared toward gaining an understanding of students so that they can receive more appropriate instruction and, ultimately, learn more. Assessment for the purpose of improving teaching and learning is termed "instructional" assessment. Assessment for the purpose of sorting and classifying students is referred to as "official" assessment. Because of these two vastly different purposes, it is not surprising that teachers find little instructional value in official assessment.

Over the past two decades, greater emphasis has been placed on the results of official assessment. District, state, and national tests have become common; test results for particular school, districts, or states regularly appear in newspapers and magazines. Because of this emphasis on test results, our educational system has become "test-driven"—that is, the knowledge and skills included in the curriculum and emphasized in the classroom are those that appear on the end-of-term or end-of-year tests. Consequently, states and school districts must assume greater responsibility for the kind and quality of instruction students need in order to do well on these tests.

Good instructional assessment possesses four characteristics. First, good assessment is integrated with, rather than separate from, the instructional process. Second, it is continuous and ongoing rather than one time only or sporadic. Third, it is collaborative—it involves the impressions of people from a variety of perspectives. Fourth, it aids in instructional decision making because it is diagnostic as well as descriptive—that is, it provides information about where the teaching and learning problems may lie.

Sound, well-constructed teacher-made tests are a first step toward good instructional assessment. Unlike some commercially prepared curriculum-embedded tests, teacher-made tests can be directly targeted toward the curriculum as taught (i.e., the instruction provided by the teacher) rather than the curriculum as intended.

For certain learning outcomes (e.g., writing, reference skills), assessment over time is needed. An assessment made early in the term or year can provide base-line data on students. The results of similar assessments made throughout the year can be compared with one another as well as with the base-line data to indicate changes in the knowledge acquired or skills being taught.

Five recommendations can be offered to educators intent on improving the ways in which they assess students and use the results. First, teachers should focus their assessment efforts on important learning goals, not just those that are easily measurable. Second, teachers should develop tests and other devices that allow assessment of student learning over extended periods of time—topics, units, even years. Third, in light of the emphasis on standardized tests, educators should provide students with practice in taking such tests. Fourth, since there are no right or wrong approaches to assessment, educators must determine for themselves an approach. In developing this approach, however, teachers should strive for valid, reliable, and useful information. Finally, information gained from assessments should be used to inform, not dictate, instructional decisions. We can ill afford to abandon the judgment role of the educator.

BASIC CONCEPTS AND PRINCIPLES

Assessment

Assessment is the process by which information about a person is gathered. Typically, the information is used to make a decision about that person. To aid in making this decision, the assessment usually includes information about the environment. For example, knowing something of the instructional program as well as something about the student enables a teacher to make relatively informed decisions about a student.

"Official" versus "Instructional" Assessment

Two major types of assessment are "official" and "instructional" (with "sizing up" being a third—see Unit II). The primary goal of official assessment—which occurs solely because of federal, state, district, or school mandates or regulations—is to sort and classify students (e.g., to identify academically talented students, to place students in a remedial program). The goals of instructional assessment—which occurs because the teacher needs or wants the information to make decisions—are to understand students and improve the quality of instruction they receive.

"Test-driven" Educational Systems

Curriculum (an organized set of formal educational intentions), instruction (the ways in which the curriculum is delivered to students), and assessment (the gathering of information on actual learning of students relative to educational intentions) are three components of an educational system. Any of these components can "drive" the system. Historically, educators and philosphers supported the "curriculum-driven" system. That is, they believed that the system should be developed around "formal educational intentions." More recently, however, the test-driven system has been developed. That is, test results have become the "bottom line" of education. Consequently, the remaining components of the system have had to be shifted in order to align with the content and objectives included on the tests.

Characteristics of Good Instructional Assessment

Four characteristics of good instructional assessment have been identified.

1. It is integrated with the instructional process. Sound, well-constructed teacher-made tests can promote such integration.
2. It is continuous and ongoing rather than one time only or sporadic. Time sampling (i.e., repeated assessment using the same or similar tasks or instruments) is one approach to continuous assessment.

3. It is collaborative. Good decision making is impossible when it is based on a single piece of information or a single viewpoint. Multiple sources of information and multiple perspectives contribute to informed professional decision making.

4. It aids in instructional decision making. More than simply allowing teachers to assign grades to students, it provides them with information as to "what to do next" and "how to improve the instructional process" for individual students as well as groups of students.

READING ASSIGNMENTS

Airasian, Peter W. *Classroom Assessment and Educational Improvement.* (Unit V, Reading 1)

Assessments made by teachers are an important and undervalued resource in our quest for educational excellence. Three types of assessment are discussed: sizing up, instructional, and official. Sizing-up assessments are made early in the school year; instructional assessments are made continuously during the school year; and official assessments are made as required by policies or regulations. In instructional assessment, teachers rely heavily on observations, questions, assignments, and teacher-made tests. In combination, these assessments correlate highly with students' performance on standardized tests (i.e., official assessments). And because of the error inherent in any one type of assessment, the use of multiple assessments is recommended.

Stiggins, Richard J.; Conklin, Nancy Faires; and Bridgeford, Nancy J. *Classroom Assessment: A Key to Effective Education.* (Unit V, Reading 6)

Most people think that educational measurement is a means of documenting student achievement by using paper-and-pencil tests for the purposes of public accountability. Consequently, we know little about the nature, role, or quality of school assessments developed and used by classroom teachers. Available research indicates that teachers have little training in assessment and that what they do have is narrow in focus. Furthermore, when measuring achievement, many teachers rely on short, easy-to-score objective tests. The majority of questions on these tests requires students to recall verbatim recently taught factual knowledge. Implications of this research for teachers and teacher educators are presented.

LESSON **22**

GRADING STUDENTS

PURPOSE OF THE LESSON

The purpose of the lesson is to address three questions. First, what is known about grading students? Second, what options do teachers have in grading students? Third, what can teachers do to develop meaningful and fair approaches to grading students?

OVERVIEW OF THE LESSON

Although many teachers find grading students complex, ambiguous, and distressing, teachers are responsible for grading. Grades are a "fact of life." Consequently, students learn early the importance of grades and soon become interested in negotiating a "performance-grade exchange" with teachers. That is, students want to know what they need to do in order to get a grade that is acceptable to them (and their parents). Armed with this knowledge, they set out to perform according to those specifications.

Teachers must answer several questions as they design and implement defensible grading systems. Two of the more important questions are, What do good grades represent (e.g., hard work, high achievement, great improvement, good behavior)? What comparisons need to be made in order to assign proper grades to students (e.g., comparisons with other students, comparisons with the teacher's standards)?

Grading students is more difficult when students work in groups. Teachers can randomly select the paper of one student in each group and assign all students in the group the grade given to that paper. Individual testing of students in the groups is another alternative.

Educators must remember that the primary function of grading is to differentiate among students in terms of their learning, performance, skills, effort, or whatever the grading criteria may be. In other words, grading students is impossible without some identifiable gradations of learning, performance, and so on. As a consequence, every grading system is going to have its "winners" and "losers."

Three of the most important elements of a defensible grading system are the criteria on which students are to be evaluated (i.e., what those good grades represent), the quality of the evidence gathered relative to those criteria, and the standards used to judge the evidence in terms of the criteria and ultimately to assign the grade (i.e., what comparisons need to be made). The second of these elements—appropriate evidence—is often overlooked. Such evidence should be valid (i.e., clearly related to the criteria) and reliable (i.e., indicative of consistent performance) so that an accurate description of the student is possible. If improvement in learning is a criterion, then it is necessary to collect evidence at several points in time.

Three recommendations can be offered to educators intent on improving the way in which students are graded. First, although there are no correct ways to assign grades to students, teachers should strive to develop grading systems in which (a) the grading criteria and standards are explicit (i.e., known by the students), (b) the grading procedures are uniformly applied (i.e., the system is fair), and (c) the grade assigned conveys some meaning to the student in terms of his or her learning or achievement. Second, in determining appropriate criteria and standards, teachers should consider the content and objectives being taught, the students being taught, and the tests and other information sources used to assess the students. Grades, then, reflect not only the learning of the student, but also the circumstances under which he or she was expected to learn and the ways in which he or she was to demonstrate that learning. Third, whatever criteria and standards are used for grading, students should be aware of them. While criteria and standards determine the validity of the grading system, the procedures used to inform students and assign them grades determine its fairness.

BASIC CONCEPTS AND PRINCIPLES

"Performance-Grade Exchange"

"Performance-grade exchange," a phrase coined by Doyle (1979), has great significance for those interested in understanding the student perspective in schools and classrooms. Although many educators would like students to be intrinsically motivated (i.e., to learn for the sake of learning), most students become aware early that grades are important in their lives. Consequently, they attempt to negotiate with their teachers precisely what they need to do in order to receive acceptable grades. Rather than bemoan the fact that grades are more important to many students than is learning, educators would be wise to find ways in which the performance needed to receive particular grades is directly linked with the desired learning. In this way, the "performance-grade exchange" would be replaced with the more desirable "learning-grade exchange."

Norm-referenced versus Criterion-referenced Grading

Two general approaches to grading students exist. Both involve comparisons of students' performance with some external standards. In norm-referenced grading, these standards are based on the learning or performance of other students in the class or school. Grades designate "much above average," "above average," "average," "below average," and "much below average" performance. Traditionally, this approach has been known as "grading on the curve." The "curve" is the normal "bell-shaped" distribution of student achievement. In criterion-referenced grading, these standards represent the expectation of the teacher (or teachers) as to what constitutes "excellent," "good," "fair," "poor," or "very poor" learning. In most criterion-referenced grading systems, these standards are set a priori—that is, before teachers know how well a particular group or class of students has learned or can perform.

Criteria versus Standards

Criteria are the specific qualities or performance dimensions on which the grading system is based. Typical grading criteria include achievement, motivation (effort), or conduct (behavior). Standards are based on answers to the question, How much is enough? That is, how much motivation is needed to assign an "A"? How little motivation is needed to assign an "F"? Thus, criteria are qualitative, while standards are quantitative.

Components of a Defensible Grading System

Since there are no "right" grading systems, the best that educators can hope for is defensible grading systems. Such systems have (1) explicit criteria and standards, (2) procedures that are uniformly applied to all students, and (3) evidence that can be tied directly to the criteria and standards. Thus, explicitness, fairness, and meaningfulness become the criteria for judging a grading system.

READING ASSIGNMENT

Kubiszyn, Tom, and Borich, Gary. *Marks and Marking Systems*. (Unit V, Reading 4)

Marks are defined as cumulative grades that reflect achievement over a period of time (e.g., nine weeks). Marks are intended to provide feedback about academic performance. Marking systems differ in the types of comparisons made (e.g., with other students, with established standards) and the type of symbols used (e.g., letters, numbers). All grading systems have both advantages and disadvantages. Consequently, the choice of system rests with teachers and administrators. Once a system has been established, the rationale for the choice of that system and the meaning of various marks should be communicated clearly to all involved in its implementation.

ADDITIONAL READINGS

Doyle, W. (1979). "Classroom Tasks and Students' Abilities." In *Research on Teaching: Concepts, Findings, and Implications*, edited by P. L. Peterson and H. J. Walberg. Berkeley, Calif.: McCutchan.

Livingston, S. A., and Zieky, M. J. (1977). *Manual for Setting Standards on the Basic Skills Assessment Tests*. Princeton, N.J.: Educational Testing Service.

LESSON 23

FEEDBACK AND CORRECTIVES

PURPOSE OF THE LESSON

The purpose of the lesson is to address three questions. First, how important is it for students to be aware of what they have and have not learned? Second, what must teachers and students do to correct identified learning errors and misunderstandings? Third, what role do feedback and correctives play in the teaching-learning process?

OVERVIEW OF THE LESSON

In simplest terms, feedback is "knowledge of results." When students are given feedback, they know whether their responses are right or wrong, appropriate or inappropriate. In numerous studies, few psychological variables have been positively related to student achievement. But one variable that has consistently been related to achievement is knowledge of results.

Feedback is a component of "reinforcement," a larger psychological construct. As defined by Bates (1987), reinforcement is "the process of increasing the frequency of occurrence of a low-frequency behavior or maintaining the frequency of occurrence of a high-frequency behavior." That is, reinforcement is used to get students to "work a little harder" or "do a little better" on the one hand, or to "keep up the good work" on the other. Common reinforcers used by teachers are praise, gold stars (or "smile faces"), grades, or enjoyable activities (e.g., "When you correctly solve all of these problems, you can read your favorite book, talk quietly for a few minutes, or rest").

Feedback can be given to answers to questions, completed assignments, or unit tests; it

can be positive or negative. All of these types of feedback are important.

Although teachers sometimes find it difficult to provide negative feedback, students need to know when their answers are wrong or their performance unacceptable. If errors and misunderstandings are allowed to go unmentioned, they might accumulate and interfere with future learning. Effective negative feedback, however, must address the behavior or performance of the student, not the student himself or herself. "This essay is unacceptable" is negative feedback; "You are a lousy writer" is an *ad hominem* attack.

Students also benefit from understanding the nature of their mistakes (e.g., "This essay is unacceptable *because* . . ."). If the particular mistakes and the reasons for the mistakes are known, students can work to overcome them and teachers can provide additional instruction directed toward correcting those mistakes. Thus, "correctives" is the general term used to designate instruction targeted toward the errors made by students, while "correction" is the process by which students overcome those errors. While teachers should provide "correctives," only students can engage in "correction."

Although daily assignments and unit tests can be used to identify problems in learning, most teachers use these devices primarily to assign grades to students. Consequently, the potential diagnostic value of these assignments and tests is lost. Specific feedback on written assignments and tests is particularly important because students as well as teachers attach so much value to these assignments and tests (see Lesson 22).

Several recommendations can be given to those educators intent on improving the quality of their feedback and correctives. First, feedback given to students must be precise and must focus on the behavior or performance of the student, not on the student himself or herself. Second, teachers can design daily assignments and unit tests so that useful information on both learning and failing to learn can be obtained. Third, teachers can examine students' performance on assignments and tests in terms of the errors and misunderstandings evinced by large numbers of students. Finally, teachers must encourage students to engage in correction. Teachers cannot correct errors and misunderstandings for their students; rather, students must correct them. In this regard, students can be encouraged to help one another; individual students should be encouraged to revise papers, reports, or projects so that these assignments meet or surpass the standards of excellence established for them.

BASIC CONCEPTS AND PRINCIPLES

Feedback

Feedback is provided so that students are aware of the correctness or adequacy of their behaviors or performances. Positive feedback ("You are correct") is reinforcing; negative feedback ("You are incorrect") is reinforcing when students are helped to correct their errors and misunderstandings.

Feedback on Oral Responses and Written Work

Teachers provide feedback constantly. When students respond to questions in class, teachers inform students about whether the answers are correct, incorrect, or partially correct. Likewise, when students complete assignments and tests, teachers inform students about which portions of the assignments and tests are ac-

ceptable, unacceptable, or partially acceptable. Some teachers favor minute-by-minute feedback; others favor "long-term" feedback. Both types of feedback are important.

Positive versus Negative Feedback

While teachers find it easy to tell students that the students are right, few teachers enjoy telling students that the students are wrong. When, for example, questions asked in the classroom are answered incorrectly, teachers are more likely to redirect the questions to other students or to probe the same student for a different answer than they arc to say that the answer is wrong (Anderson, Ryan, and Shapiro, 1988). Most students probably learn early in their schooling that redirecting and probing signal that the answer is wrong. Both positive and negative feedback are important in facilitating learning. Effective negative feedback, however, must emphasize the inaccuracy of the performance, not the inadequacy of the performer.

Correctives versus Correction

A "corrective" is something that teachers do for students; "correction" is something that students do for themselves. Correctives are alternative methods or materials that teachers can use to help students overcome identified errors and misunderstandings. But if they are to be effective, correctives must address specific errors and misunderstandings and then be utilized by students.

READING ASSIGNMENT

Guskey, Thomas R. *Feedback, Correctives, and Enrichment*. (Unit V, Reading 3)

Feedback, correctives, and enrichment are essential components of any instructional program intent on promoting mastery by students. Two types of feedback are needed: information about the learning of individual students and information about the quality of instruction provided. Based on this feedback, various types of corrective activities can be recommended. For these activities to be effective, they must be linked with specific learning problems and managed successfully by the teacher. Because of individual differences among students, enrichment activities must be provided to those students who do not require corrective instruction. Appropriate types of enrichment activities are discussed.

ADDITIONAL READINGS

Anderson, L. W.; Ryan, D. W.; and Shapiro, B. J. (1988). *The IEA Classroom Environment Study: Teaching for Learning*. Oxford, Eng.: Pergamon.

Bates, J. A. (1987). "Reinforcement." In *International Encyclopedia of Teaching and Teacher Education*, edited by M. J. Dunkin. Oxford, Eng.: Pergamon.

Hilliard, A. G., III (1983). "Integrating Testing, Teaching, and Learning." Unpublished manuscript. Atlanta: Georgia State University.

LESSON **24**

EVALUATING TEACHERS AND TEACHING

PURPOSE OF THE LESSON

The purpose of the lesson is to address two questions. First, what is the current status of teacher evaluation? Second, what can be done to improve the quality of teacher evaluation as it is currently practiced?

OVERVIEW OF THE LESSON

Although teacher evaluation is not new, several changes have taken place during the past two decades. Previously, teachers were evaluated before they were offered a job. Once on the job, it was assumed that those selected would teach in an acceptable and approprite manner. Furthermore, teachers were judged primarily on the qualities and traits that they possessed, rather than on their teaching ability or practices. Application files and interviews—not in-class observations—provided the information used in the evaluation.

On the one hand, evaluating teachers on the basis of what they do rather than who they are seems a reasonable shift in focus. On the other hand, this shift has been accompanied by at least two problems. First, many of the observational instruments used to evaluate teachers were never intended to be used for that purpose. Second, the number of observations made of any teacher is too small to yield reliable information about that teacher's classroom behavior and teaching practices.

The problems of teacher evaluation are further complicated because there are two competing aims and motives for conducting teacher evaluation: accountability and improvement. Some want to evaluate teachers in order to

"identify the incompetent teachers" or to provide an "objective means" for the awarding of "merit pay"; others want the results of these evaluations to lead to improvement on the part of all teachers. These two purposes are referred to as "summative evaluation" and "formative evaluation," respectively. While administrators must assume the primary responsibility for summative evaluation, teachers—individually and collectively—must assume the primary responsibility for formative evaluation. Even though administrators are ultimately responsible for accountability-type decisions, they should consult with experts in teaching and learning prior to making those decisions.

Student achievement data are sometimes mentioned in the context of teacher evaluation. Those who support the use of such data believe that higher student achievement means better teaching. Because of a number of problems with student achievement, such data should be used cautiously in summative teacher evaluation. On the other hand, student achievement data may be useful in formative teacher evaluation.

While many teachers find teacher evaluations unpleasant or undesirable, at least two benefits are associated with sound, well-developed teacher-evaluation programs. First, administrators and teachers begin to share a common language about teaching. Second, the quality of the relationships between teachers and administrators improves.

Several recommendations can be offered to those educators interested in designing and implementing a workable teacher-evaluation program. First, those concerned with the program (e.g., administrators, teachers) should be aware of and agree on the criteria used to evaluate teachers. Second, those responsible for evaluating should be knowledgeable about the principles and practices of effective teaching. Third, those being evaluated and those doing the evaluating should have opportunities to engage in a face-to-face discussion of the results of the evaluation. Fourth, when the results of the evaluation are unsatisfactory to the teacher, he or she should have the opportunity to prepare a written statement. Fifth, teachers should self-evaluate. Such self-evaluation should be clearly linked to the learning and performance of their students.

BASIC CONCEPTS AND PRINCIPLES

Traits versus Behaviors

Traits are relatively permanent characteristics or qualities of teachers. In contrast, behaviors are verbal interactions and physical actions of teachers in classrooms. Charters and Waples (1929) identified eighty-three teacher traits, many of which are routinely used to describe teachers today. Some of the traits are attractive personal appearance, dependability, enthusiasm, honesty, loyalty, patience, and sobriety. Also in 1929, A. S. Barr published his classic study of teachers, which included both traits and behaviors. In terms of behavior, Barr painstakingly identified expressions that contrasted good and poor teachers. Poor teachers said things like "Are you working hard?" "Everyone sit up straight, please," and "Oh, dear, don't you know that?" Good teachers said things like "Are you satisfied with that statement?" "Don't be too easily discouraged," and "Come on, you know."

Accountability versus Improvement

Historically, teacher evaluation has been used for purposes of accountability (i.e., to decide who should be hired, fired, or promoted). Thus, the phrase "teacher evaluation" has acquired

negative connotations. Recently, teacher evaluation has been suggested as a means of teacher improvement. These are two distinct purposes for teacher evaluation. Consequently, different groups of educators should assume the primary responsibility for each. Specifically, administrators should be responsible for evaluation conducted for the purposes of improvement. Typically, evaluation for the purposes of accountability is termed "summative evaluation," while that for the purposes of improvement is termed "formative evaluation."

Evaluator Qualifications and Training

Regardless of the type of teacher-evaluation program being used, someone has to gather the appropriate evidence and make the overall decisions (e.g., Should we terminate this teacher? In what areas does this teacher seem to need the most improvement?). Perhaps the best we can hope for in terms of teacher evaluation is "informed professional judgment." Because of the human element in evaluation and the import of decisions made about teachers, the qualifications and training of evaluators are critical to a successful teacher-evaluation system.

READING ASSIGNMENTS

Darling-Hammond, Linda; Wise, Arthur E.; and Pease, Sara R. *Teacher Evaluation in the Organizational Context: A Review of the Literature.* (Unit V, Reading 2)

The public has come to believe that the key to educational improvement lies in upgrading the quality of teachers. Changes in teacher evaluation have resulted from this belief. Four basic purposes of teacher evaluation are presented: individual and organizational improvement and individual and organizational accountability. Often, multiple purposes must be included in a single evaluation system for it to be acceptable and defensible. Once purposes have been decided upon, appropriate models and methods must be determined. Because schools are social organizations, teacher-evaluation systems do not always operate as designed. In view of this, four minimal conditions for the successful operation of a teacher-evaluation system are described.

Medley, Donald; Soar, Robert; and Coker, Homer. *The Minimum Conditions for Valid Evaluation of Teacher Performance*. (Unit V, Reading 5)

A four-step procedure for valid evaluation of teacher performance is described and defended. First, the tasks to be performed must be defined and agreed upon. Second, a record must be made of the teacher's performance of these tasks. The record must be as accurate and objective as possible. No "expert" judgment should enter into the record. Third, the record must be scored—

that is, numbers must be assigned to the portions of the record pertaining to the various tasks. Fourth, the scores must be evaluated. Standards can be set to aid in this evaluation. A critique of the use of rating scales in teacher evaluation concludes the paper.

ADDITIONAL READINGS

Barr, A. S. (1929). *Characteristic Differences of Good and Poor Teachers*. Bloomington, Ill.: Public School Publishing Company.

Charters, W. W., and Waples, D. (1929). *The Commonwealth Teacher-Training Study*. Chicago: University of Chicago Press.

UNIT **V**

ASSIGNMENTS

SELF-TEST

1. *Assessment* is to *evaluation* as
   a. *test* is to *observation*.
   b. *test* is to *judgment*.
   c. *information* is to *observation*.
   d. *information* is to *judgment*.
2. Which of the following is most likely a form of official assessment?
   a. observations and questions
   b. assignments
   c. teacher-made tests
   d. standardized tests
3. A "test-driven" educational system implies that
   a. tests must be used to determine the effectiveness of teaching.
   b. instructional objectives have taken precedence over the tests given.
   c. tests determine the instructional goals and objectives.
   d. the system has been "tried out" before being used in schools.
4. Which of the following is *not* a characteristic of good instructional assessment?
   a. It is a part of the entire instructional process.
   b. It takes place on a regular basis throughout the term or year.
   c. It involves several sources of information.
   d. It results in the sorting and classification of students.
5. Augustus attempts to determine the minimum amount of work his teacher will accept and still give him a passing grade. Augustus's motive is best understood within the context of

   a. a norm-referenced grading system.
   b. a criterion-referenced grading system.
   c. the performance-grade exchange.
   d. the explicit grading standards set by the teacher.
6. *Excellent* is to *much above average* as
   a. *criterion* is to *standard*.
   b. *standard* is to *criterion*.
   c. *criterion-referenced* is to *norm-referenced*.
   d. *norm-referenced* is to *criterion-referenced*.
7. *Criterion* is to *standard* as
   a. *test* is to *test*.
   b. *relative* is to *absolute*.
   c. *kind* is to *amount*.
   d. *criterion-referenced* is to *norm-referenced*.
8. All of the following are elements of a defensible grading system *except*
   a. comprehensiveness.
   b. explicitness.
   c. fairness.
   d. meaningfulness.
9. *Correctives* is to *correction* as
   a. *feedback* is to *reinforcement*.
   b. *reinforcement* is to *feedback*.
   c. *teacher* is to *student*.
   d. *student* is to *teacher*.
10. Which of the following is an example of negative feedback?
   a. "No, Billy, the answer is not 42.8."
   b. "If you answered incorrectly, write the correct answer five times."
   c. "Wrong, Gerard! You are always wrong!"
   d. "Freda, can you help Paul with his answer?"

11. If the results of assignments and tests are to be of *diagnostic* value, the results must help us to understand
    a. what errors were made.
    b. why the errors were made.
    c. how the errors were made.
    d. who made the errors.
12. All of the following are problems with the use of classroom observation in teacher evaluation *except*
    a. the qualifications and training of observers.
    b. the instruments used to record the observations.
    c. the number of times each teacher is observed.
    d. the emphasis on what teachers do, not who they are.
13. Which of the following phrases describes a teacher trait?
    a. giving directions
    b. asking questions
    c. supervising seat work
    d. interest in students
14. Student achievement data are used most appropriately for which of the following types of teacher evaluation?
    a. accountability
    b. improvement
    c. self-evaluation
    d. summative evaluation
15. *Summative evaluation* is to *administrators* as
    a. *formative evaluation* is to *teachers.*
    b. *formative evaluation* is to *students.*
    c. *improvement* is to *accountability.*
    d. *accountability* is to *improvement.*

UNIT ACTIVITIES

Complete one or more of the following activities.

1. For a particular quiz or unit test, devise a set of materials and activities that students could use to correct the errors and misunderstandings that they may make on the quiz or test. In addition, devise a strategy that you could use to motivate students to spend the time and effort needed to correct those errors and misunderstandings.
2. Choose a system for grading students with which you are familiar. Write a critique of the system. In your critique, identify
    a. the major strengths of the system
    b. the major weaknesses of the system
    c. changes in the system needed to improve it
3. Choose a system for evaluating teachers with which you are familiar. Write a critique of the system. In your critique, identify
    a. the major strengths of the system
    b. the major weaknesses of the system
    c. changes in the system needed to improve it

ANSWER KEY FOR SELF-TEST

1. d (Lessons 21, 22)
2. d (Lesson 21)
3. c (Lesson 21)
4. d (Lesson 21)
5. c (Lesson 22)
6. c (Lesson 22)
7. c (Lesson 22)
8. a (Lesson 22)
9. c (Lesson 23)
10. a (Lesson 23)
11. b (Lesson 23)
12. d (Lesson 24)
13. d (Lesson 24)
14. c (Lesson 24)
15. a (Lesson 24)

POSTSCRIPT

The Effective Teacher has attempted to raise long-standing, important questions and to provide information that teachers and administrators can use to find answers.

The final two lessons of *The Effective Teacher* are intended to end the telecourse. In this postscript, the main points of each of these lessons are summarized.

LESSON 25

WHAT WE KNOW

Two related yet distinct questions can be asked. First, what is an effective teacher? Second, what makes a teacher effective? The answer to the first question is straightforward: an effective teacher produces effects or outcomes, accomplishes what he or she sets out to accomplish. The answer to the second question is more complex and tentative. Nonetheless, the following seven characteristics combine in some way to produce effective teachers.

1. They have clear aims, purposes, goals, or objectives that guide their teaching.
2. They use their resources (e.g., time, instructional support materials, educational technologies, the students themselves) wisely.
3. They monitor the extent to which they are achieving their goals and make changes as needed to increase the likelihood that their goals will be reached.
4. They understand the importance of the teacher-student relationship in enhancing the learning of the student as well as the teaching of the teacher.
5. They create "workable" classrooms— classrooms that are inviting, task-oriented, friendly, and productive.
6. They make sound, defensible decisions concerning a variety of classroom and student matters.
7. They are students themselves; they read, listen, inquire, and strive for improvement.

LESSON 26

WHERE DO WE GO FROM HERE?

For more than half a century, critics have assailed American schools. Some criticisms have been ignored. Others have provided the impetus for changes in curriculum (e.g., modern math), instruction (e.g., individualized instruction), and teacher preparation (e.g., the Holmes group). Despite these changes, however, the criticism continues. How can this be? One answer is that few of these changes have addressed three issues central to substantial improvements in teaching and learning: the enhancement of the school as a workplace, the professionalization of teaching, and the recognition of the central role of students in their own learning. We must attend to these three issues as we answer the question, Where do we go from here?

We need to create conditions in schools that foster success and facilitate growth of those who work in them. We need to concern ourselves with "teacher induction"—that is, helping young teachers make the transition from school to work. Administrators and teachers need to see themselves as members of a social organization: the school. Concerns for the health of that organization must be raised and addressed.

We need to develop the profession of teaching. We need to attend to the qualifications of those who enter the field. We need to resist attempts to mandate apparently simple answers to complex questions. We need to strive for moderation in a world of extremes. We need to continue to add to our knowledge and enhance our skills by attending conferences, reading current literature, and trying out new ideas in the classroom.

Finally, we need to acknowledge and act on the central role of students in their own learning. We need to develop strategies that require students to assume at least some responsibility for their own learning. We need to allow students to work together on projects and to assist one another as learning difficulties are experienced. We need to find ways to give us a more complete understanding of what is going on in our students' heads.

Although we know a great deal about effective teaching and the conditions that foster it, we still have much to learn. Dr. Wilson Riles, former California state superintendent of education, maintains that excellence is a journey, not a destination. To increase our effectiveness, we must continue on that journey.

READINGS

TEACHERS AND TEACHING

1. HOW SCHOOLS WORK

Rebecca Barr and Robert Dreeben, with Nonglak Wiratchai

Over the past quarter century, the civil rights movement, the Great Society programs, and the more recent rise of public sentiment for accountability, minimum competency, and free choice have all indicated deficiencies in how well the schools perform and have sought remedies for them through legislation, judicial action, and other political means. Yet it is a remarkable commentary on the state of our knowledge about education that despite the staggering sums invested and the massive efforts to improve and reform the schools, we do not have a clear conception of how they work. . . . Like any organization that tries to produce something of value, schools attract, allocate, and mobilize resources; and while we know a lot about how the amounts of different sorts of resources are associated with learning—the value that schools are supposed to produce—we do not know much about how the different parts of an educational system contribute or about how resources are actually used to produce the value.

. . . [W]hen school systems are analyzed in the fashion we describe here, some extraordinarily large educational effects appear in places where they have not hitherto been sought. For example, in the past, where comparisons between school characteristics have shown exceedingly modest effects upon learning, and comparisons between classrooms both modest and inconsistent ones, we have found strikingly large effects on learning that originate in activities taking place in the suborganization of classrooms: in reading groups. Our evidence suggests that the differences between groups that account for so much learning get averaged out in classroom and school comparisons and as a result the productive

events taking place inside schools become obscured. Does this mean, then, that classrooms produce only trivial effects? Not at all. Classroom characteristics might not affect individual learning directly, but rather influence the formation of instructional groups. Group arrangements, not learning, may then be thought of as the value produced by classrooms.

. . . Past work has been largely preoccupied with trying to account for differences in individual learning by associating them with district, school, and classroom characteristics. But this general strategy does not address the question of workings directly. Rather, such familiar measures as per pupil expenditure, class size, teacher experience and credentials, the availability of laboratories and libraries—the staples of educational effectiveness research—are little more than remote proxies for the productive activities taking place in educational institutions. How much money there is is one question; how it is spent, quite another. The library may have thousands of volumes; but are they checked out and read? Some teachers may be verbally facile but so inept at managing a class that not enough time is left for them to turn their verbal intelligence into sound instruction. Teachers in the early primary grades usually divide their classes into reading groups; but knowing that students are assigned to a group does not indicate the nature of the group instruction they receive. In all these cases, the productive events that constitute schooling escape both conceptualization and consideration.

Our formulation begins with the idea that school systems are organizations that like others can be readily subject to sociological analysis. In all organizations labor is divided, which means that different activities are carried out in the different parts and that the parts are connected to each other in a coherent way. The parts of school systems are very familiar. They consist of a central administration with jurisdiction over a school district as well as local administrations situated in each school with responsibility for what happens therein. The business of schooling, mainly instruction, takes place in classrooms run by teachers; and teachers preside not only over classes but over parts of them as well when they rely upon grouped forms of instruction. . . . [T]he work that gets done in district offices, schools, classes, and instructional groups is different in character[;] . . . these separate jurisdictions are locations for carrying on different sorts of activities. Indeed, this proposition is true for teachers as classroom instructors and as group instructors in that teachers do different things in organizing a class from what they do while instructing subgroups within it. Part of the answer to our question of how schools work, then, is to be found by identifying the distinct events happening at each level of school system organization.

A second part of the answer can be found by discovering how the events characteristic of one level influence those taking place at another. It would be a strange organization indeed if the parts were hermetically sealed off from each other; if, for example, what the principal did had no bearing on what teachers did and if what teachers did made no difference for what students did and learned. Yet it is precisely the failure to come up with satisfactory answers to these questions that has caused so much grief in our understanding of educational effects. The answer must come from identifying correctly what the activities are and from being able to trace their antecedents and effects across pathways that connect one level to another.

The third part of the answer pertains not so much to what to look for as it does to how to look for it. School systems, like other forms of social existence, are characterized by variability. We can learn about their workings by attending to the different ways that comparable parts act: different schools in the same system, different classes in the same school, different groups in the same class. What can vary in these levels of school organization is the way in which resources are allocated, transformed, and used. A particular resource, like books, may be purchased by the district office. All fourth grade mathematics texts, for example, can then be distributed to each elementary school, thence to be stocked in each fourth grade class. Thus, a simple process of resource transmission takes place. From there, teachers in the same school may use the text in almost identical ways or in vastly different ways depending on how they organize their instructional programs. The program itself determines the instructional use, and hence the meaning, of the resource. Accordingly, insofar as the school is no more than a transmission belt for transporting books from the district office to the classroom, school-by-school comparisons will show similar activities. Class-by-class comparisons in textbook use, however, might show sharp contrasts. Depending upon the nature of those class contrasts, they may average out to show no school differences or bunch up to show marked school differences. In either case, it is the comparison of events at the same level—school and class in these examples—that tells us what is going on. We will try to discover how schools work, then, by identifying the ways in which resources are used at each level of school system organization, by tracing the effects of events from one level to another, and by comparing events both within and between parts of the organization. . . .

LEVELS OF ORGANIZATION

. . . [S]chool systems characteristically contain a managerial component responsible for centralized financial, personnel, procurement, plant maintenance, and supervisory functions applicable to all their constituent elements. This component is also engaged in direct dealings with agencies of the federal and state governments as well as with locally based interest groups and units of municipal government. Activities occurring at this managerial level have *nothing directly* to do with running schools or teaching students but rather are concerned with the acquisition of resources, with general supervision, and with the maintenance of relations with the surrounding community including suppliers of labor. We refer to this as the *district* level of organization; its jurisdiction includes all schools in the district.

Even though districts are divided into levels (elementary and secondary) related to the ages of students, and some are also divided into geographical areas as well as functional units, we are primarily concerned—at the next lower hierarchical level— with *schools*. Contrary to conventional belief, schools are not organizational units of instruction. They are structures akin to switching yards where children within a given age range and from a designated geographical area are assigned to teachers who bring them into contact with approved learning materials, specified as being appropriate to age or ability, during certain allotted periods of time. Schools deal in potentialities; they assemble a supply of teachers, of students, and of resources over a given period of time. Their central activities are the assignment of children to specific teachers, the allocation of learning materials to classrooms, the arrangement of a schedule so that all children in the school can be allotted an appropriate amount of time to spend on subjects in the curriculum, and the integration of grades so that work completed in one represents adequate preparation for the next.

These activities are the primary responsibility of school principals; they are core functions peculiar to the school level of organization. This is so because decisions affecting the fate of all classrooms in a school are not likely to be left to individuals (teachers) who have in mind primarily classroom interests rather than whole school interests and whose self-interest puts them in a poor position to settle disputes among equals. Nor are they likely to be left to district-wide administrators, whose locations can be too remote and jurisdictions too widespread to allow them to make informed decisions about local school events.

While these decisions constitute the peculiar core activities of school level administration, they by no means exhaust the responsibilities of school administrators, which frequently include such matters as planning curriculum; establishing disciplinary standards; and making school policies for homework, decorum in public places, and the like. But while such concerns are frequently characteristic of school administration, they are not peculiar to it because district-wide administrators and teachers also participate in them at the school level in fulfilling responsibilities within their own respective jurisdictions.

While instruction is not the business of the school, it is the business of *classrooms* and of teachers responsible for the direct engagement of students in learning activities. Aggregations of children are assigned to specific teachers who direct their activities and bring them into immediate contact with various sorts of learning materials. These activities are more than potentialities because children's active engagement working with teachers and materials is what enables them to learn.

Because classes contain diverse aggregations of children, it is not automatic that the instruction appropriate for one member of the aggregation will be appropriate for another. Hence, teachers in the lower grades characteristically create an additional level of suborganization to manage activities not easily handled in a grouping as large as the class. For example, in primary grade reading, there are suborganizations called *instructional groups* that represent still another level of organizational differentiation.

Finally, there are *individual students*. It is only individuals who work on tasks, and it is only they who learn; so that while work tasks might be set for all students in the class or in a group, the individual members vary in how much work they do and in how much they learn.

We argue here not only that school systems can be described by their constituent organizational levels, but that the events, activities, and organizational forms found at each level should be seen as addressing distinct as well as partially overlapping agendas. Districts, schools, classes, and instructional groups are structurally differentiated from each other; and what is more they make different contributions to the overall operation of the school system. . . .

LINKAGES BETWEEN LEVELS

If organizational levels are as distinct as this analysis suggests, how is it possible to think about a coherent production process for the whole school district organization? How should the connections between levels be formulated? We contend that each level of a school system has its own core productive agenda even though certain activities are performed at more than one level. That is, productive events of differing character occur at each level to effect outcomes that are themselves characteristic of each level. For example, a school outcome becomes a productive condition in classes yielding in turn a class outcome; the class outcome in turn becomes a productive element for instructional groups yielding a group outcome; and so on. We see, then, a set of nested hierarchical layers, each having a conditional and contributory relation to events and outcomes occurring at adjacent ones.

Consider an example of how levels of organization are connected to each other to constitute school production. As we observed earlier, classroom characteristics do not directly affect individual learning; they influence the formation of instructional groups. This might seem to be a strange statement since everyone knows that classroom teachers are responsible for instructing all children in a class. However, the teacher's job, we maintain, is first to transform an aggregation of children into an arrangement suitable for establishing an instructional program. In first grade reading, this usually means creating instructional reading groups. Hence, before any instruction takes place, decisions are made about how to arrange the class; whether to teach everyone together in one group, as in recitation; whether to establish subgroups in which only some children work intensively with the teacher while the others proceed by themselves with little supervision; whether to set everyone to work independently at their desks to perform at their own rate such more or less individualized tasks as are contained in workbooks.

The results of these classroom decisions are not instructional, nor do they appear as individual learning. They are alternative grouping arrangements which should be thought of as class outcomes, or values. We must draw a distinction between what teachers do in organizing classes *for* instruction and the instruction they actually provide for the groupings of children that make up classroom organization. Down the road, those grouping arrangements influence individual learning through a chain of connections consisting of instructional activities. Individual learning, however, is not itself a class outcome. As our story unfolds, we will show how class grouping arrangements determine certain characteristics of the groups composing them, in particular the level of children's ability characteristic of each classroom group. As it turns out, this level of ability is a direct determinant of certain instructional activities under-

taken by teachers, who treat differently composed groups in different ways. One form this treatment takes is the amount of material covered, which we construe as an outcome, or value, created by instructional groups. (Note again: individual learning is not a group outcome any more than it is a class outcome.) Then, depending on how much material children cover over a given span of time, in combination with their own characteristics, they learn proportionally more or less. In sum, group arrangements are the value created at the class level, coverage the value at the group level, and learning the value at the individual level. Note particularly that the activities and outcomes characteristic of each level are qualitatively distinct—grouping, coverage, learning—and that they are linked together in a coherent manner.

. . . An implication of this analysis is that we can take any single educationally relevant resource and trace its manifestations across several hierarchical levels of school system organization. . . . [T]o illustrate the logic of the formulation, we will consider here the resource of time.

A school district administration makes three kinds of decisions about time. The first reveals its responsibilities of law enforcement to the state: the schools must remain open for a stipulated number of days to qualify for state aid. While this enforcement of state law places an outside limit on time available for teaching, it does not bear directly on teaching, instruction, or learning. Furthermore, when the length of the academic year is combined with a determination about the length of the school day, the second type of district decision is made: how much time teachers (and other employees) will work as part of a contractual agreement with suppliers of labor. The third type of decision pertains to when the schools will start and finish each academic year, open and close each day, and recess for vacations, decisions that determine when and whether parents can leave the household for work and arrange for the care of very young children. Basic time considerations, then, at the district level of organization are tied up with law enforcement, labor contracts, and the integration of the school system with households in the community; and district outcomes can be defined in these terms.

School systems, of course, do not hire teachers

in general, but teachers who instruct in particular subjects in secondary schools and in a variety of basic skills in elementary schools. Hiring teachers by subject and skill presumes that curricular priorities have been established, which means that decisions have been made about how much time will be devoted to each segment of the curriculum: to English, mathematics, science, foreign languages, and so on, in secondary schools; to reading, arithmetic, science, social studies, and so on, in elementary schools. At the level of schools, these decisions become manifest in the time schedule, a formal statement written in fine-grained time units of how much time will be devoted to each subject matter and to extracurricular pursuits.

The school schedule is really a political document that acknowledges the influences of administrative directives and the preferences of teachers and parents expressing varying views about the welfare of the student body, of individual students, and of different types of students. It embodies past decisions about how much ordinary instruction there will be, in which subjects, at which more or less desirable times, and in which more or less desirable places. It expresses how segregated or desegregated classes will be in response to higher level administrative directives as well as the integration of the handicapped in regular and special classes. These resultant priorities conventionally expressed in the time schedule are an outcome of school level organization.

The curricular priorities expressed in the school time schedule represent temporal constraints upon the work of teachers in classrooms. While in secondary schools the order of classes throughout the day is established by the schedule itself, in elementary schools the teachers themselves arrange activities within the confines of daily time allotments, deciding which activities come earliest in the day, which next, and which last, with some flexibility about how long each successive activity will last. In addition to determining which activities take place during the "better" and "worse" times of the day, teachers also establish, within school guidelines and across parts of the curriculum (reading, arithmetic, science), how long instruction will last in each of a variety of classroom formats (whole class, grouped, individual instruction) and how much time gets

wasted through interruptions, poor planning, and transitions between activities. At the classroom level, then, teachers allocate time in ways that bear directly upon instruction by determining the amount of time that students will have available for productive work in various subject areas.

Finally, given the time that teachers make available for productive work, students then decide how much of that time to use and to waste, and in so doing influence the amount they will learn.

What we have done here is to trace the allocation of time through the layers of school system organization to show how it takes on different manifestations as district, school, class, and individual phenomena. We have also shown how the nature of time at one level becomes a time condition for events occurring at the next lower level.

What our formulation does is very simple. It locates productive activities at all levels of the school system that in more common but less precise parlance are known as administration and teaching. It also states that productive activities specific to levels produce outcomes specific to levels. Accordingly, we distinguish carefully between the productive processes that constitute the working of school organization from the outcomes, or values, produced by those processes. They are not the same thing, although they have commonly been confused in discussions about educational effects. The distinction between production and value not only is important conceptually, but provides a principle that ties the parts of the levels of school organization into a coherent pattern.

The formulation also carries us some distance in thinking about how the effectiveness of schools should be viewed. The common practice of using individual achievement (or aggregations of individual achievement) as a primary index to gauge whether schools are productive is of limited value because there are other outcomes that are the direct result of productive processes occurring at higher levels of school system organization. There is no question that achievement is an important outcome at the individual level; it may or may not be an important outcome at other levels, as our previous analyses of time and grouping indicate. Perhaps, for example, the properly understood outcome of instructional groups is a group-specific rate of covering learning materials or the amount of time a teacher makes available for instruction, outcomes that when considered at the individual level are properly construed as conditions of learning. An important class level outcome may be the creation of an appropriate grouping arrangement or the establishment of a productive time schedule, both of which are conditions bearing on the nature of group instruction. . . .

Similarly, at the school level, the important outcomes may be the allocation of time to curricular areas that makes enough time available for basic skill subjects, an assignment of teachers to classes that makes the most appropriate use of their talents or that provides equitable work loads, or the appropriate coordination of skill subjects from year to year so that children are prepared for the work of the succeeding grade. At the district level, perhaps negotiating labor contracts that satisfy employees, administrators, and the taxpayers, or having a satisfactory book and materials procurement policy represents a significant outcome. . . .

THE ORGANIZATIONAL LEVELS OF SCHOOL SYSTEMS

The formulation of production rests upon a satisfactory understanding of how the labor of school systems is divided among its levels. Most research on educational effects, whether of the production, attainment, or instructional variety, focuses on a single level of analysis, usually the individual level. People naturally differ about what is appropriate, and most acknowledge that different problems require different levels of analysis. But while there is no argument against doing what is appropriate, the preoccupation with one level or another obscures the possibility that productive events occur over several levels.

Some investigators are patently aware that the events that constitute schooling occur in different places; that some contributions come from principals, some from teachers, and others from students themselves. To accommodate these differently located influences, everything is expressed at the level of the individual student, with the result that school or class events become dissolved into individual experiences. In the process the character of produc-

tive processes taking place in schools and classes—expressed in school and class terms—is lost. Others argue that school organization is loosely coupled so that the connections between levels tend toward randomness. In both ways, we lose our grip on the events that constitute school production and that influence its outcomes.

Our work is based on the general presupposition that when labor is divided, there is a reason for it; and that when people set about accomplishing distinct tasks in different parts of an organization, one should pay attention to what they do and to how the parts fit together. We are building upon the familiar insight of Parsons[1] that organizations have qualitatively distinct levels of a technical, managerial, and institutional kind, each having an agenda of its own to work out and each being tied through interchanges to the adjacent one. Our point is not to affirm the particular utility of his three types but rather to show how the typology itself draws attention to the importance of identifying the special contribution of each level to the organization's total operation. "There has been a tendency," he observed, "to neglect the importance of what in some sense are qualitative breaks in the continuity of the line structure" (1963, p. 59).

A major implication of this perspective is to attend to the particular nature of events that occur at the district, school, class, group, and individual student level of school system organization. By further implication, it means raising the possibility that each level of organization produces its own outcomes, or values, which in turn have meaningful connections to events that occur elsewhere. This view acknowledges that learning is a critically important value of school production, particularly at the level of individual students, but it questions deeply the prevailing assumption that it is necessarily an important outcome at any other level of school system organization. Nevertheless, the productive events and outcomes at these other levels might have a strong impact on learning through a series of hierarchical connections.

[1 T. Parsons, "Some Ingredients of a General Theory of Formal Organization," in *Structure and Process in Modern Societies,* edited by T. Parsons (Glencoe, Ill.: Free Press, 1963), pp. 59–96.]

2. THE EXECUTIVE FUNCTIONS OF TEACHING

David C. Berliner

THE CLASSROOM WORKPLACE

Classrooms are workplaces; complex and dynamic workplaces that require management by an executive of considerable talent. Teachers are not usually thought of as executives. But it's time they became universally recognized as such. That recognition will help achieve the pay increases and prestige the profession so desperately needs, as well as make teachers more effective.

I've long been aware of the intense managerial demands on teachers. But the close parallels of teaching to good corporate management didn't strike me until recently. While attending a meeting on reading instruction at a prominent hotel, I discovered during a break that a business management seminar conducted by the American Management Association was underway in an adjoining room. The speaker was saying: "One of the most crucial skills in management is to state your objectives. You have to have clearly stated objectives to know where you are going, to tell if you are on track, and to evaluate your performance and that of others." That sounded very familiar to an educator. I stayed to listen.

This group of managers spent an hour on the topic of management by objectives. The instructors quoted Mager and Popham, familiar names to educators. Their second topic was the use of time. They called this the greatest single management problem. The third topic was motivation. They discussed positive reinforcement, the negative effects of criticism and punishment, the benefits of contracts, and the positive effects of high expectations. The next topic was evaluation. I felt right at home. The parallels between the training of these executives and some of the knowledge and skills needed to run an elementary school classroom seemed obvious.

Could the concepts and principles of executive training be useful to teachers? I began to look at the research on management to find out.

HOW DO WE DEFINE MANAGEMENT?

Just what constitutes executive behavior? In the book *Executive,* Jean-Jacques Serven-Schreiber is quoted as saying, "Management is, all things considered, the most creative of all arts. It is the art of arts because it is the organizer of talent." Peter Drucker tells executives, "Your job is not to tell someone what to do, it is to enable him or her to perform well." Both statements are compatible with what a teacher tries to do.

In the early 1960s, Douglas McGregor changed the beliefs of American corporations about the mediocre nature of the majority of workers with Theory Y, a set of concepts about the inherent potential of all people. The following parts of Theory Y can be applied to the management of students.

- The expenditure of physical and mental effort in work is as natural as play or rest. The average human being does not inherently dislike work.
- External control and the threat of punishment are not the only means for bringing about effort toward organizational objectives. People will exercise self-direction in the service of objectives to which they are committed.
- Commitment to objectives results from the rewards associated with their achievement. The most significant of such rewards, such as the satisfaction of ego and self-actualization needs, can be direct products of effort directed toward organizational objectives.
- The average human being learns, under proper conditions, not only to accept but to seek responsibility.
- The capacity to exercise a relatively high degree of imagination, ingenuity, and creativity in the solution of organizational problems is widely, not narrowly, distributed in the population.
- The intellectual potential of the average human being is only partially utilized.

The concepts in Theory Y are used intuitively by many good teachers in developing management practices in classrooms.

What other parallels are there with the role of the classroom teacher?

Drucker says, "The first criterion in identifying those people within an organization who have management responsibility is not command over people. It is responsibility for contribution."

E. F. Huse defines an executive as one who works to accomplish the goals of an organization and who directly supervises one or more people in a formal organization; plans, organizes, directs or leads, and controls. The results of a study of 160 private sector managers by Huse in 1979 show that teachers even have a working style similar to an executive's. Huse found that executives had "little time alone to think. On the average, during the four weeks of the study, they were alone only nine times for a half-hour or more without interruptions. True breaks were seldom taken. Coffee was drunk during meetings and lunch time was almost always devoted to formal or informal meetings."

M. L. Kastens, in another study in 1980, said of business what is true of classrooms: "Let us have some plain talk about management. Management is 'running the place.' More elegantly, management is the assembly, disposition, and exploitation of resources to produce a new value." In the new style of corporate management, less emphasis is on raw materials and manufacturing and more is on managing and using the resources of personnel in such a way as to create something of value that did not exist before. The more new value created by the commitment of a given store of resources, the better the management.

All teachers manage when they add value, that is when they produce changes in the knowledge, skills, and attitudes of their students in an acceptable way, using available resources.

WHAT ARE THE EXECUTIVE FUNCTIONS OF TEACHING?

In running a classroom or a corporation, the person in charge of the workplace must perform nine executive functions: *planning; communicating goals; regulating the activities of the workplace; creating a pleasant environment for work; educating new members of the work group; relating the work of the site to other units in the system; supervising and working with other people; motivating those being supervised;* and *evaluating the performance of those being supervised.*

Motivating students and evaluating student performance are two functions well known to teachers, and for the most part teachers understand what makes those functions important. But observations

by myself and others suggest that too often teachers are not aware of their other executive functions and as a result disregard these important powers. In addition, teacher training institutions at the present time do little to alert teachers to their executive function or to help teachers see themselves as executives whose every managerial act is guided by a set of flexible operating principles.

Let's take a look at the executive functions of teachers and the educational research concerning how teachers carry out these functions.

PLANNING OF WORK

Teachers, like all executives, engage in planning. And most teachers plan on five levels: First there is the yearly plan wherein the general framework of that which will be covered is outlined; second, slightly more focused, is the term plan; third is the monthly plan wherein basic units of instruction are specified and such things as movies and field trips are scheduled; fourth is the weekly plan, a more detailed description of what will occur, including the time allocations for activities. Finally there is the daily plan with its schedule and its requirements for special materials or human resources. Researchers agree that the plans made by teachers early in the year have a profound effect on teaching and learning during the course of the year.

Among the many planning decisions that teachers must make, four in particular determine what is learned in classrooms. These are decisions about *choosing content, scheduling time, forming groups,* and *choosing activity structures.* These factors affect behavior, attitude, and achievement.

Choosing Content

Chief state school officers, superintendents of schools, school board members, and principals often believe that they know what is taught in the nation's classrooms. They do not. The final arbiter of what is taught is the classroom teacher. If teachers use this executive function wisely, curriculum goals are likely to be met. If teachers aren't aware of the importance of this function, the results could be disastrous. For example, in the Beginning Teacher Evaluation Study my colleagues and I observed one elementary school teacher for more than 90 days.

During that period of time she taught nothing about fractions, despite the fact that the topic was mandated by the state for instruction at that grade. When asked why she did not teach any fractions she said, "I don't like fractions!" That's a human response illustrating the power that teachers have in deciding the content of the curriculum and the failure of our educational system to provide training in how to use their executive functions of choosing how a student will use his or her time. As executives, they need to make sure that these decisions reflect the goals of the district. Unless the congruence between what is tested is high, schools and teachers will appear to be failures. What we have learned from a Michigan State teaching research team is that the perceived *effort* required to teach a subject matter area, the perceived *difficulty* of the subject matter area for students, and the teachers' *personal feelings of enjoyment* while teaching a subject matter area influence the teachers' choice of content. One striking example illustrates this point. An elementary school teacher who enjoyed teaching science taught 28 times more science than one who said she did not.

Buchanan and Schmidt of the Institute for Research on Teaching summarized the evidence about the powerful effects of content selection: "During the school day, elementary school teachers can be a law unto themselves, favoring certain subjects at their discretion. . . . Responsibility in content decision-making requires that teachers examine their own conduct, its mainsprings, and potential effects on what is taught."

Scheduling Time

Elementary teachers, more than others, decide how to allocate that most precious of scarce resources—time—to subject matter areas. Studies of teachers find incredible variation in the time allocations that are made by different teachers. While observing fifth-grade teachers, we noticed that one teacher allotted only 68 minutes a day for instruction in reading and language arts, while another teacher allotted 137 minutes a day. One second-grade teacher allocated 16 minutes a day to instruction in mathematics, another teacher in the same grade, same school, spent 51 minutes a day on mathematics.

Another time-management issue has to do with the way time within a curriculum area is scheduled.

One of our fifth-grade teachers, observed for 87 days, managed to allocate 5,646 minutes to comprehension activities such as drawing inferences, identifying main ideas, and paraphrasing. Another fifth-grade teacher, observed for 97 days, allocated 917 minutes to those activities.

Of course student needs account for some variation. However, the time allocated to particular content areas of the curriculum is causally related to achievement in those content areas. This is as true of achievement in music, art, and physical education as it is of science, mathematics, and reading.

Forming Groups

Like other executives who are responsible for supervising more than just a few people, teachers form work groups. These decisions too are powerful variables that affect student achievement and student attitude. Studies show that the range of ability among the members of the work group affects the achievement of some of the members of the group but not others; that status assignments made at the beginning of kindergarten are sometimes still in force years later; that once students are grouped, the group can become the unit for planning instruction, and not the student; and that the plans teachers make for high and low groups differ.

Moreover, research shows that students are well aware of classroom groups and have no difficulty describing the nature of the differential treatment of individuals and groups in classrooms. The evidence suggests that the assignment of students to work groups can be like a life-long sentence and always results in students in different groups learning different things while in school. The biggest question teachers face in making these decisions is: on *what* grounds? These executive decisions should be made cautiously, skillfully, and reevaluated regularly.

Choosing Activity Structures

The building blocks of the curriculum are found in the activity or task structures, such as reading circle or seatwork, recitation, or learning. The activity structures determine teacher behavior, as well as student behavior, attitudes and achievement. For example, researcher S. T. Bossert found that teachers who rely on lecturing "establish fewer close social ties with their students than teachers who primarily utilize small group and individualized projects. Recitation places teachers at the center of control. It forces them to rely on equitable, impersonal sanctions (usually short verbal desists) and on the authority of an office rather than on more personalized influence mechanisms. By contrast, small group and individualized instruction increases opportunities for teachers to covertly bend classroom rules to handle individual problems and facilitates teacher involvement in, rather than simply teacher direction of, the activity."

In a recent study in which I was involved, we coded 1,200 activity structures in 75 classrooms from kindergarten to sixth grade. We tried to determine for each activity structure how long it lasted; the number of students in the activity; whether the group remained stable over the time it was together or whether students moved in and out of the group; and the percent of time students were attending to the activity at hand. We also tried to describe the role of the teacher in each activity structure, asking what teachers do differently in, for instance, silent reading versus reading circle, and whether or not there was an opportunity for teachers to evaluate students in the activity structure. We also analyzed each activity structure in terms of feedback from teachers to students and whether or not such feedback could be immediate or had to be delayed.

What was most intriguing about this project was the discovery that teachers—who make choices about activity structures every day—were unable to compare the relative costs and benefits of one form of instruction over another for different pedagogical purposes or for different kinds of students. Teacher training institutions haven't trained teachers to be successful managers in this area yet they must make choices like these every day. This probably accounts for the reason that many teachers seem to adhere to a few familiar activity structures and do not often change classroom routines.

The responsibility for making reasonable decisions about instruction does not end at the planning stage. Teachers, of course, must make decisions during interactive instruction. During the lesson, teachers use information about students' participation and involvement for self-evaluation about how good or poorly the lesson is going. It is estimated that the number of nontrivial decisions that teachers

make is at least 10 per hour in the complex and dynamic environment of an interactive lesson. The sensitivity of teachers to those important dimensions is remarkable.

P. W. Marland says teachers' interactive classroom behavior is often guided by five teaching principles. Teachers use the *compensation* principle to favor the shy, the quiet, the dull, or the culturally different. They follow the principle of *strategic leniency* so that they ignore some inappropriate behavior. (One teacher being observed said the best advice she ever got was to "*see* but don't *notice* everything.") Another guiding principle used is *power sharing*, whereby the teacher selectively reinforces students in order to enlist their aid in sharing responsibility. In a fourth principle Marland called *progressive checking*, the teacher makes a special effort to check the problems and progress of low ability students. Teachers follow the principle of *suppressing emotions* because they feel emotion during teaching could lead to a higher level of emotionality among the students, which creates management problems. Thus, interactive teaching makes considerable cognitive demands on the teacher.

I've spent a disproportionate amount of space on planning and decision-making to demonstrate the complexity of the job and to recognize the power of the variables a teacher commands.

COMMUNICATING GOALS

Just as executives do, teachers as managers communicate their goals to those they supervise in two important ways: by tightly structuring lessons and by communicating to students high expectations for performance. Both affect student achievement and performance and can be taught to teachers.

Structuring Lessons

The importance of this variable was demonstrated during a study of more and less effective teachers. While analyzing reading and mathematics lessons, we found that with some teachers students did not have a clue about why the lesson was occurring, where it fit in the scheme of things, or what they needed to focus on for success at the task. Almost invariably, those students had lower academic achievement. Students pay more attention when the teacher spends time discussing the goals or structures of the lesson and giving directions about what students are to do. Further, both success rate and attention improve when teachers spend more time structuring the lesson and giving directions.

Structuring is especially important in classes where seatwork is used frequently, and consequently children work alone a good deal of the time. Children who do not have a clear handle on what they are to do easily find ways to do nothing.

Structuring is sometimes overdone. Researchers have found classrooms in which the directions given for worksheet assignments actually lasted longer than the amount of time needed by most of the children to finish.

Communicating Expectations

We all know that if teachers set high but attainable goals for performance, performance usually increases. Conversely, if they set low goals, performance usually decreases.

We must also be aware of the differential treatment accorded to high and low ability students. Thomas Good summarized the research this way. "The students perceived to be low performers are most often seated farther away from the teacher; treated as groups, not individuals; smiled at less; made eye contact with less; called on less to answer questions; are given less time to answer those questions; have their answers followed up less frequently; are praised more often for marginal and inadequate answers; are praised less frequently for successful public responses; and are interrupted in their work more often. This kind of treatment influences their performance in predictable ways."

Such expectations are not restricted to classrooms. They can also permeate a school. Several studies have shown that children have better academic success in schools where the teachers expressed expectations that a high proportion of the children would do well in national examinations.

A school's high overall expectations influenced not only academic performance but student success in other areas as well. Schools that expect children to take care of their own belongings and to be responsible for their own actions had better behavior, better attendance, and less delinquency. Schools

that give children posts or tasks of responsibility got better pupil behavior.

Some teachers use these powerful variables of communicating goals to the benefit of their students. Those who do not can learn this executive skill.

REGULATING THE ACTIVITIES OF THE WORKPLACE

The person who runs the classroom—the executive in charge—regulates the activities of the classroom. It is true, of course, that what happens in classes is somewhat affected by what happens within schools, within districts, and within states because classes are nested in larger systems. But it is also true that elementary classes appear to be only "loosely coupled systems" in which the teacher is subject to the bare minimum or organizational control from the superintendent or principal. Control of many factors known to affect student achievement and student attitude resides with the teacher. At least six of these factors are worth a closer look.

Pacing the Learners

The pacing variable is powerful. The more a teacher covers, the more students seem to learn—hardly shocking news. But pacing differences among classes are worth noting. One teacher adjusts the pace in the workplace and covers half the text in a semester; another finishes it all. One teacher has 20 practice problems covered in a lesson, another covers 10. One teacher has students who develop a sight vocabulary of 100 words before Christmas, another teacher's students learn only 50. One study found that 80 percent of the variance in measures of basal reading achievement could be accounted for by the pace of instruction.

Sequencing Events

Some sequences of events, some standard routines, seem to be more conducive to learning than others. We have learned, for example, that the sequencing of positive and negative examples has an effect on retention in concept teaching. Another way of sequencing such as "rule-example-rule" may have value when principles are to be learned. For example, in a study of math instruction, Good and Grouws have shown the positive effects of an instructional sequence in mathematics that starts each day with a review and then moves to new material followed by a stage of prompted practice, then seatwork, and a homework assignment. Special reviews are recommended weekly and monthly. Mathematics achievement in classes where teachers use this pattern exceeds the achievement of students in classes that do not.

Sequencing is not a well understood variable in schools, but it affects achievement and is worth more attention than we give it.

Monitoring Success Rate

Just as executives need to monitor employee productivity, teachers must monitor pupil success at learning. The Beginning Teacher Evaluation Study provides evidence about the relationship between high success rates and achievement. For younger students and for the academically least able, almost errorless performance during learning tasks results in higher test performance and greater student satisfaction. A number of studies conclude that during the initial phases of learning, during recitation or small group work, student success rate in reading should be at about the 70 to 80 percent level.

When students are reviewing or practicing as in seatwork, engaging in drill activities, or working on homework, student responses should be rapid, smooth, and almost always correct. Jere Brophy's comments about the monitoring of success rate are relevant: "Bear in mind that we are talking about independent seatwork and homework assignments that students must be able to progress through on their own, and that these assignments demand application of hierarchically organized knowledge and skills that must be not merely learned but *mastered* to the point of overlearning if they are going to be retained and applied to still more complex material. Confusion about what to do or lack of even a single important concept or skill will frustrate students' progress, and lead to both management and instructional problems for teachers. Yet, this happens frequently. Observational study suggests that, to the extent that students are given inappropriate tasks, the tasks are much more likely to be too difficult than too easy."

Some findings from the Beginning Teacher Eval-

uation Study support Brophy's assertion. Students were coded in some classes as making almost 100 percent errors in their workbooks or during their group work as much as 14 percent of the time. That is, students in some classes were observed to experience total failure in their learning activities for many consecutive minutes of the school day.

Controlling Time

There must be a thousand management books on controlling time. But few relate to education. Time must be controlled once it is allocated or it is lost. And it is easy to lose. For example, transition times—the time between activities (the start-up time and time needed to put things away)—can mount up rapidly. In one of the classes we studied where the school day was around 300 minutes, we found 76 minutes lost to transition. A fourth of the day lost to commuting!

The management of classroom time has been affected by law and governmental regulations. Recent changes in the law have resulted in a return of children with special needs into regular classrooms. This has caused time management problems of an enormous magnitude. And the "pull out" program has also required time management capabilities that would tax any manager of any workplace. It's hard to manage when those you supervise enter and leave classes at odd times on an odd schedule to visit reading specialists, speech pathologists, school psychologists, and others.

Another cause of time loss is a lack of coordination between the teachers and other members of the school. In one school we recorded more than 30 P.A. system announcements in one day!

Simple management hints make a big difference in controlling time. One teacher began writing the language arts assignments of her different reading groups on the board at the start of recess. The first student into the classroom after recess starts work and no one waits until the last student wanders in for oral instructions. Savings of six minutes a day in this class occurred with that simple advice. This is not trivial. That adds about 180 student-learning minutes a day. It provides a half-hour more of instruction a week, and, potentially, it adds 18 hours of instructional time per year.

Fortunately, techniques for managing time effectively are becoming available in education. Several excellent manuals for elementary teachers provide dozens of helpful hints on management. One district which emphasized time management techniques to reduce the amount of time spent on noninstructional activities estimated that it added the equivalent of 10 to 16 days of instructional time per school year. If purchased, that time would be worth two to three million dollars!

Running an Orderly and Academically Focused Workplace

The research on effective schools is amazingly congruent. There is always higher achievement in schools with an orderly, safe environment, a businesslike manner among the teachers, and a school-wide system that reflects thoughtfulness in developing academic programs, focuses on achievement, holds students accountable for achievement, and rewards achievement. Where order and focus are missing, achievement is lower.

Such findings, of course, can lead to over-control and a strict academic focus that denies the arts a place in the curriculum or produces student anxiety. But it is clear that a lack of order and a lack of an academic focus can lead to low achievement. It's part of a teacher's role as executive to balance forces (to know, for example, that playfulness and order are not incompatible, and that students need a well-rounded curriculum) and to convince others of the necessity for that balance.

Preventing or Controlling Behavior Problems

As an observer of thousands of classrooms, I've found that there are really very few totally out-of-control classes—though the media would sometimes have us believe otherwise. In many classes, however, behavior problems occur frequently enough to cause teacher stress, loss of time, and a break in the orderliness and flow of classroom life.

Jacob Kounin helped us understand how to keep classrooms free from behavior problems. His concepts are worth noting. *Withitness* describes how effective managers nip behavioral problems in the bud; *overlappingness* describes how effective class-room managers handle more than one thing at a time. He also described the need for *signals* for

academic work; the effects on student behavior of *momentum* and *smoothness* in lessons; and the positive effects of *group alerting, accountability,* and *variety* in teaching. W. R. Borg and F. R. Ascione developed these concepts into teacher training materials. Their work provides clear evidence that the students in classes where teachers had been taught management skills were markedly more on task and showed less deviant behavior.

Regulation of the workplace requires the simultaneous intelligent handling of such variables as pacing, sequencing, success rate, and time as well as the ability to create an orderly and academically focused workplace and the ability to prevent or control behavior problems. It takes an extraordinary executive to do a good job of attending to all these things at once.

CREATING A PLEASANT ENVIRONMENT FOR WORK

Every executive needs to create a convivial atmosphere for work. This means a workplace characterized by politeness, cooperation, mutual respect, shared responsibility, humor, and a number of other social dimensions that we value. Teachers have long known and practiced this managerial function and a number of studies have shown that the most effective classrooms are pleasant places to be.

In the last few years, teachers have worked to enhance the relationships among members of different social classes, races, sexes, or different ability groups. There is evidence that the nonsexist, multicultural components of curriculum have led to success in creating more cooperation and interdependency among the students.

EDUCATING NEW MEMBERS OF THE WORK GROUP

This executive function is performed very systematically in most business settings but is virtually ignored in education. When new students enter a classroom, they enter a new culture and they need to be socialized to that culture. That does not happen in a day or even a month. Teachers need to deal with a new student in three ways. First they must make an assessment of ability, one of the strongest indicators of achievement and a necessary condition for any diagnostic-prescriptive model of instruction. When a student enters a class in, say, February, the teacher needs as much information as possible to make that assessment.

A second issue is also an assessment issue; does the student know how to think about the tasks that are required for success in a particular class? Without such awareness, real learning may not occur.

A third step involves the teaching of rules. Most rule-setting takes place during the first few days of the school year. Because families move, many schools have large turnover rates. Who is responsible for communicating the rules to the new members of the class? Furthermore, rules may be communicated in subtle ways. And the tacit dimension of the rule structures may require considerable time to learn.

RELATING THE WORK OF THE SITE TO OTHER UNITS IN THE SYSTEM

All workplaces that exist in organizations are nested within other structures of the system. They affect and are affected by what happens elsewhere. In education, this function takes on meaning in two ways. First, a teacher needs to find ways to have the classroom processes match the priorities of the school and district.

Second, teachers must match the present curriculum followed by students with the previous and the subsequent curriculum. This is a difficulty that shows up during interviews with classroom teachers. Many have little knowledge about what is taught in the grades below and above them. Sometimes within one district or one school curriculum areas are repeated or completely missed. This occurs when management of the workplace is done independent of the system.

SUPERVISING AND WORKING WITH OTHER PEOPLE

This common executive function, stressed heavily in business schools, is not well-addressed in most teacher-preparation programs. Usually without any formal training, teachers must learn ways to either govern or share responsibility with such diverse visitors to the classroom as: parent volunteers, paraprofessionals, tutors, school psychologists, itinerant music and art teachers, reading specialists, speech pathologists, school nurses, probation officers, and others. Because teachers are the executives charged with the responsibility to run the workplace, those teachers who have mastered the problems that accompany the supervision of others enjoy fewer classroom interruptions, smoother schedules and more cooperation with those involved.

OTHER EXECUTIVE FUNCTIONS

Two other executive functions that teachers share with other managers are *motivating those being supervised* and *evaluating the performance of those being supervised*. In my years of working with teachers, I've found that by and large they are aware of these two functions and strive to perform them successfully. In addition, teacher trainers and school administrators acknowledge the importance of these functions and pay attention to them in preservice and inservice training.

The fulfillment of these nine executive functions is essential for effective teaching—though not sufficient in itself. There is no doubt that subject area knowledge is of great importance. And in all this, we must acknowledge that there is art as well as technique in effective teaching, and that we must respect the practitioner for it. As Peter Drucker says, "There is 'management science' and there is 'art in management.' . . . In every practice, it is the practitioner rather than the scholar who develops the discipline, who finds and tests new knowledge, and who teaches and sets the example. In every practice, it is the practitioner who leads the profession and who has responsibility for the advancement of its capacity to perform and its ethics."

At a time when new definitions of the teaching profession are sought, it will be teachers, the practitioners, who will establish them, through their art and their executive skills.

3. RESEARCH INTO PRACTICE
Cautions and Qualifications

Christopher M. Clark

. . . This chapter is addressed to both teachers and educational researchers. The message is an optimistic one, namely, that research on teaching and school learning can be even more useful to practicing teachers than it has been in the past. To realize this desirable state I believe that teachers and researchers must begin to think more flexibly and creatively about the nature and roles of educational research, the needs of the practical world of schools and classrooms, and new ways in which their two communities can communicate in mutually helpful ways. The chapter is divided into four sections, each headed by an exhortation: Let's get humble! Let's demand service! Let's get creative! and Let's get communicating! I hope that this chapter will serve as a constructive step in encouraging more use of educational research in the service of teaching.

LET'S GET HUMBLE!

Like many virtues, humility is a great deal easier to prescribe than to practice. As John Wesley said, "It is difficult to be humble. Even if you aim at humility, there is no guarantee that when you have attained the state you will not be proud of the feat." When I call for humility in connection with educational research and teaching what I am urging is a more modest sense of proportion about the size and scope of what social science has to offer practice. In research proposals and in the introductions to text-books educational researchers often claim that the fundamental bedrock of effective teaching is, or should be, empirical research. "Research based" is a much sought-after prefix for texts, curricula, and teacher education programs, not unlike the Good Housekeeping Seal of Approval. The old saying, "To the carpenter, the world is made of wood," can also be applied to some educational researchers who tend to value teaching to the extent that it reflects their own research.

But, in my view, teaching is not primarily an applied science. Rather, teaching is a complex social, personal, political, and interactive human process.

Empirical research on teaching and learning can be one element of what teachers take into account in their planning and teaching, but only one of many. Research can *inform* practice, but research—because of self-imposed constraints—can be much too narrow or highly constrained to literally serve as a *foundation* for practice.

One approach that I believe would help us to be more appropriately humble about the role of research in informing practice is to take some of the mystery out of the research process. People have a tendency to be somewhat awed by very complex research designs, analysis methods, and jargon-laden reports of results. Sometimes the complexity is necessary and the special technical terms crucial for precise expression of meaning. But meaning is obscured and potential usefulness to teachers reduced by unnecessarily complex designs and excessive use of technical terminology.

It helps me to reduce the mystery surrounding research in education when I remind myself that, when you boil them down, all research reports consist of descriptions of researcher's experiences and ideas. These experiences and ideas may be expressed in numbers or in words, more or less clearly, but there is always a person or group of persons behind the words and numbers. And these persons, the researchers, are not inaccessible beings set apart and somehow quite different from the other members of the community of educators. On the whole, they are quite willing to return telephone calls, respond to letters, and come to conferences to talk, to listen, to learn, and to teach. So perhaps one of the most valuable resources we have as a profession is access to dedicated and intelligent people who have spent years thinking about, observing, and writing about topics and situations that are of importance to educators.

At the same time it is important to remember that the world's foremost expert on a particular classroom or school setting is the teacher in that setting. The experience and expertise of a teacher may sometimes be enhanced or helpfully focussed by drawing on the experiences of others outside the classroom. But, in the final analysis, teachers are the planners, decision makers, and actors who have the most intimate knowledge of and greatest influence in their classrooms. Teaching, like research, can be a constructively humbling experience.

LET'S DEMAND SERVICE!

The idea that the main role of research and researchers is to *serve* teachers is new and has not yet swept through the profession like wildfire. The concept of service is not well developed in our profession. But for teachers to be able to make more appropriate use of research and researchers' experience, a richer, more positive conception of service must emerge. Part of this new notion of service will have to be worked out in practice between individual researchers and teachers. What I have to offer to this process is a list of four ways in which research on teaching, and the researchers themselves, might serve teachers. The four modes of service are: information, inspiration, vision, and support.

Information

The most typical way in which research has served the practice of teaching is by providing information. The journals are full of descriptions of how teaching and learning worked under various conditions and in various settings. Most of this information is presented at a general level, having been derived from the averaging of many observations of many individuals or classes. And most of the information found in the research literature pertains to specific questions or hypotheses formed by the researchers. From a social science point of view this is good, reliable information. But precise answers to researchers' questions are unlikely to be of service to teachers. And general principles and average trends are as likely to misinform as to inform a particular classroom teacher dealing with a particular individual child.

So, in terms of information, the vast bulk of the research literature will be of little practical use to any particular teacher. This is not to say that such research should be stopped. Rather, we should treat the research literature on, say, literacy as a kind of encyclopedia that we consult for information as we

need it, with our own specific questions in mind and with a clear sense of the applicability of that information to our particular situation.

Inspiration

A second way in which research can serve practice is to provide inspiration. By inspiration I mean a picture of how schooling could be different, could be better, could become the world we imagined when we first signed on to become teachers. As the literary critic and historian Walter Pater wrote 100 years ago: "We need some imaginative stimulus, some not impossible ideal such as may shape vague hope, and transform it into effective desire, to carry us year after year, without disgust, through the routine-work which is so large a part of life" (*Marius the Epicurean,* Chap. 25). I certainly need such a guiding pillar of cloud by day and pillar of fire by night to get me through the school year, and I think that research is one possible source of such inspiration.

My favorite example of an inspiring bit of research is the book *In the Early World* by Elwyn S. Richardson (1964). It was published in 1964 as Educational Research Series No. 42, by the New Zealand Council of Educational Research, so it certainly qualifies as research. (Sadly, I've heard that the book is now out of print.) The book is about learning to be literate in poetry, science, art, and community building in a two-room country school in New Zealand. The report spans a five-year period of life at Oruaiti School and is rich with the words and artifacts produced by the children and the stories behind the artifacts. *In the Early World* is the most vivid example of complete integration of learning with life, art with science, and people with people that I have ever read.

Now, the point of this example is not to urge you to recreate or to imitate the Oruaiti School of 20 years ago in the Utah or Michigan of today. No, the inspiration for me comes from knowing and being able to visualize a time and place in which, with simple materials, ordinary children, and a bit of imagination and risk-taking one teacher was able to foster the kinds of integrated learning experience that I value. Knowing that it is possible, knowing that it *did* happen, seeing the beautiful evidence in the haiku from which the book borrows its title, all of these help me to search for that extra spark, that constructive riskiness in my own teaching.

The blue heron stands in the early world,
Looking like a freezing blue cloud in the morning.

—Irene

Vision

Research can serve to broaden and sharpen our vision of the world of schooling by offering us concepts, models, and theories through which we can see our familiar surroundings in new ways. I believe that professional boredom and burnout result, in part, from the feeling that one is trapped in a thoroughly predictable situation that is unlikely to change. But, even in such situations, it is possible to see the situation differently, with the help of an outsider's point of view. When anthropologists work in their own culture, as when ethnographers of education study American public school classrooms, one of their biggest challenges is to "make the familiar strange," to see with new eyes what they have learned to take for granted. When research provides tools for seeing the practical setting of the classroom in new ways, researchers are indeed serving practice.

An example of research in the service of vision comes from my own work with Susan Florio-Ruane on school writing. One analysis of a year-long descriptive study of the teaching of writing in elementary and middle school involved categorizing writing assignments on the basis of their forms and functions (Florio & Clark, 1982). Each of the major occasions for writing observed were sorted into one of four function categories: (1) writing to participate in community, (2) writing to know oneself and others, (3) writing to occupy free time, and (4) writing to demonstrate academic competence. And each function category was described in terms of its initiator, composer, writer, audience, format, fate, and evaluation. The importance of this example is not that the researchers' analysis is elegant, logical, and supported by data, or that the study was published in the journal *Research in the Teaching of English*. No, its importance lies in the fact that this descriptive framework helped at least one teacher to see his own classroom differently as an environment for writing. He used the form and function categories from our research to examine the oppor-

tunities that his own students had to write, to plan for changes in his curriculum, and to ask more penetrating questions about writing activity ideas that came his way. In short, this teacher used research to come to a new vision of what his teaching was and could be.

Support

Finally, research can serve practicing teachers by providing them with support for what they are already doing well. All too often, in my opinion, research in education is seen exclusively as a force for change. Usually, a call for change implies that what has gone before is faulty, inefficient, or inadequate to the task. Yet we know that American public schools are among the best in the world, and that truly terrible, damaging, and incompetent teaching is rare.

At the same time, teaching is an isolating and potentially lonely profession in which individual teachers rarely have the time or opportunity to learn about and discuss how their own teaching compares with others'. While research reports are certainly not a substitute for professional dialogue among teachers, research on teaching can provide both evidence for and explanation why good teaching works as it does.

In this connection, I think of an example from research on teacher planning. A number of studies of planning for the teaching of writing (reviewed in Clark, 1983) have confirmed that experienced teachers do not follow the so-called "rational model" of planning typically prescribed in teacher education programs (i.e., define learning objectives, generate alternatives, choose the optimum alternative, teach, and evaluate). Rather, teachers typically start with an idea for a writing activity, which they elaborate and adapt to their own classroom situations. Further, this research has documented the elaborate interconnections among different levels of teacher planning (e.g., yearly, term, unit, weekly, and daily planning). This line of research can be taken as supportive of teachers in at least two ways. First, it offers support to those teachers who do their planning in ways that are apparently adaptive to the complexity and constraints of the real classroom, but who might also feel guilty for not following the model that they were trained to use as undergraduates. Second, this research is a step toward acknowledging some of the invisible and unappreciated demands of the teaching profession and toward describing aspects of teaching that are truly professional in the sense that the work of designers, physicians, and lawyers is professional.

So, when I say, "Let's demand service!" what I am calling for is a combination of information, inspiration, vision, and support. Part of the responsibility for serving teachers rests with researchers; in the ways that they design their studies, share what they have learned, and call on practicing teachers to cooperate in the process. And part of the responsibility lies with teachers, who can begin to seek and also call for more relevant information, as well as inspiration, vision, and support from the research community.

LET'S GET CREATIVE!

When I call for more creativity in this context, I am calling for better ways to use the resources already available in the service of teaching. I am reminded of the brother of a neighbor of mine who worked for Libby Foods. For years he saw Libby discarding tons and tons of pumpkin seeds as a waste product of the processing of pie filling. After much stove-top experimentation he invented a snack food of processed pumpkin seeds that is now being marketed nationally. I'd like to apply that same kind of creativity to the research literature that we already have on the shelf to try to realize more of the potential that is there but is currently wasted.

Briefly, my proposition is that there are six different but related kinds of products of research on teaching that can be used to enrich the practice of teaching. The six classes of research outcomes are: (1) observed relationships among variables, (2) concepts, (3) theoretical models, (4) questions, (5) methods of inquiry, and (6) case studies. My hope is that by thinking more broadly and divergently about what research on teaching has to offer we might improve both the research on teaching enterprise and the practice of teaching itself. At the very least, both communities may come to believe that the grounds on which they could meet are larger in area and more varied and interesting in terrain than is typically thought. I will now discuss briefly each of the six classes of outcome of research on teaching, giving examples as I proceed.

Observed Relationships among Variables

Classically, the fruits of the research process are expressed as "findings and implications." The findings part of this dyad consist of brief summary descriptions of the observed relationships among variables studied, while the implications are inferences drawn by the researchers that typically go beyond the data. To oversimplify, findings are observed facts about the world and implications are what the investigator believes these facts suggest about how practitioners should behave in situations similar to the experimental one. The facts that many researchers on teaching pursue consist of causal statements about the relationship between particular teacher behaviors and measured student achievement. Still other kinds of facts about teaching have been pursued by researchers on teacher thinking who have sought to describe how teachers plan, process information, and make decisions (see Clark & Peterson, 1984). Both behaviorally and cognitively oriented research have played important roles in establishing research on teaching as a distinct and even thriving field, but the direct translation of findings and implications into prescriptions for teaching and teacher education has not worked well, for all of the reasons articulated by Cronbach (1975), Fenstermacher (1979), Phillips (1980), Floden and Feiman (1981), and Eisner (1984). In my judgement, the findings of research on teaching that describe observed relationships among teacher and student visible or cognitive behaviors are the least likely to be directly useful in the classroom.

However, I do have a suggestion that might yield additional mileage from reexamination of this research. I have long believed that ineffective teaching—poor teaching, if you will—is due less to the absence of particular effective strategies and teacher behaviors than it is a consequence of the presence of things that teachers sometimes do that sabotage what could otherwise be good teaching. When, for example, students are faced with double binds and mixed messages about competition and cooperation, meritocracy and egalitarianism, equality of opportunity and self-fulfilling prophecies about the normal distribution of achievement, even technically excellent teaching may have mediocre effects. What I propose is to rephrase the big question of researchers on teaching effectiveness from "What kind of teaching (or teacher thinking) works best in almost all situations? (a discouraging question to pursue) to "What have some teachers done sometimes that have fouled things up?" Taking this perspective, could a reexamination of the literature of research on teaching yield ideas about what some of these avoidable impediments to good teaching and school learning are? And would it not make sense to include attention to these empirically observed impediments and pitfalls in our teacher preparation and professional development program? (Remember that the Ten Commandments have stood up for so long, in part, because they constitute a short list largely about what we should *not* do, rather than detailed prescription of what we should do. Perhaps proscriptions are more generalizable than prescriptions.)

The researchers who did the original work may have to be the ones who lead the search for evidence of impediments to good teaching, because explicit attention is seldom given to this side of teaching effectiveness when a study is first reported. Such evidence is more often present in the parts of the story that are left out of journal articles and technical reports or in sometimes speculative explanations of surprising or seemingly paradoxical findings. To illustrate from my own work, I was part of a team that did a laboratory study of teacher planning and teaching effectiveness in 1974 (Peterson, Marx, & Clark, 1978). One of our surprising findings was that among 12 teachers who thought aloud while planning there was a significant negative correlation between the number of planning statements they made and their students' postteaching achievement scores. Paradoxically, more planning was associated with lower achievement, and that is where we left matters in 1978. Now, with several years of hindsight, I believe that there is a more satisfying and logical explanation for this anomaly: the teachers with the largest number of planning statements were those who focussed their attention almost exclusively on reading and reviewing content to be taught, giving little or no planning time to the process of instruction. These teachers (legitimately) used their planning time as a study and curriculum review session and emerged with increased knowledge of their subject matter, but without a well-thought-out plan for instruction. This leads me to make a practical suggestion: that teachers and prospective teachers should pay attention to how they spend their planning time and what the balance is between attention to subject matter and attention to instructional process.

Novices, especially, should be cautioned that planning for teaching is different from studying for a test (even though there is sometimes a testlike quality to observed sessions of practice teaching).

Concepts

A second category of outcomes of research on teaching is concepts. By concepts I mean verbal labels for phenomena that researchers have found useful in describing the dynamics of the classroom, aspects of teaching and school learning, and curriculum. From the researchers' point of view, concepts about teaching are seen as a means to the end of defining variables and subsequently measuring strength and direction of relationships among those variables. But my claim is that concepts themselves, when they are usefully descriptive of teaching, can be seen as valuable products of research on teaching. Examples of concepts of this kind include academic learning time (Fisher et al., 1980), academic work (Doyle, 1983), wait time (Rowe, 1974), the steering group (Lundgren, 1972), withitness (Kounin, 1970), incremental planning (Clark & Yinger, 1979), and the occasion for writing (Clark & Florio, 1982). There are many more concepts of this kind that originated in research on teaching that are not obvious to the naive observer of the practice of teaching and that should be a part of the conceptual vocabulary of teachers. Concepts help us to organize, make sense of, communicate about, and reflect on our experiences. A teacher education or professional development program that equips its graduates with some of the means to make meaning, communicate, and reflect is on the right track.

Theoretical Models

A third kind of product of research on teaching that has potential application in teacher education is the theoretical model. By this I mean verbal or graphic representations of the relationships among concepts in teaching-learning situations. Theoretical models can serve all of the functions that I have attributed to concepts, and they also provide a more comprehensive framework for thinking about and perceiving classrooms in their complexity. Examples of theoretical models and constructs that could serve these purposes include the Carroll Model of School Learning (Carroll, 1963), Shavelson and Stern's (1981) and Peterson and Clark's (1978) models of teacher interactive decision making, Yinger's (1977) process model of teacher planning, and the participation structure model of the classroom (Phillips, 1972; Shultz, Florio, & Erickson, 1982). It is important, I believe, that abstractions of the kind that these models represent be taken as heuristic and suggestive rather than as prescriptions for "the correct way to think about teaching." Indeed, their principal value to educators may be that exposure to multiple theoretical models could encourage teachers to examine, make explicit, and refine their own implicit theories.

Questions

The fourth product of research on teaching on my list is questions. Here I commend to you both questions that are posed at the outset of a study and used to guide inquiry (typically called *research questions*) and also questions that are raised later when researchers are trying to make sense of the data and when calling for additional research. A teacher can learn a great deal about how to think about what is problematic in teaching by learning what the challenging and partially answered questions are that thoughtful researchers are asking. Even (or perhaps especially) when questions seem to have no definitive answer, they can serve to orient professional reflection. Similarly, researchers could learn a great deal from taking the concerns and dilemmas of practicing teachers into account as they frame the questions that guide their research. Examples of generative questions that are being addressed by researchers on teaching include: Why is writing so difficult to teach? What are the possibilities and limitations of small-group cooperative learning? What makes some schools more effective than others? What roles do textbooks play in school learning? How can individual differences in student aptitudes for learning be accommodated? What roles do teacher planning, judgement, and decision making play in classroom instruction? How do teachers' implicit theories affect their perceptions and behavior?

Methods of Inquiry

Fifth, research on teaching can be a source of methods of inquiry by inventing, demonstrating,

and discovering the limitations of various techniques and tools for describing and understanding teaching. Teacher educators and teachers need ways of seeing, describing, and analyzing the complexities of teaching that go beyond what one can do with unstructured live observations. Researchers have developed many category systems for counting and rating the quality of teacher-student interaction (Simon & Boyer, 1970), including some that focus on dyadic interaction between the teacher and particular students (e.g., Brophy & Good, 1974). The technology of microteaching was originally developed to meet the needs of researchers on teaching and has been adopted as a useful part of many teacher preparations programs. More recently, researchers studying teachers' thought processes have employed stimulated recall, think aloud procedures, and structured journal writing to make visible the formerly hidden world of teaching. And practitioners of the ethnography of classrooms have provided us with clear examples of what their methodology can accomplish as well as improved guidelines for how to pursue this kind of inquiry and what some of its limitations are. All of these methods of inquiry offer interesting possibilities for adaptation in teacher preparation and professional development programs if an important goal of continuing education is to equip teachers to be reflective, analytic, and constructively critical of their own teaching.

Case Studies

Sixth, and finally, research on teaching has recently been producing case studies—rich and thick descriptions of classroom events ranging in duration from a few moments to an entire school year. Case studies can serve a number of valuable purposes for teachers, including illustration of concepts and theoretical models in context, providing opportunities to analyze and reflect on real classroom events from a variety of disciplinary points of view and illustrating how the perspective held by the researchers shapes and limits the form and content of the resulting case study. At Michigan State University my colleagues Robert Floden, Susan Florio-Ruane, and I have been using case studies from research on teaching to serve these purposes in our undergraduate and graduate education courses in educational psychology, the philosophy of education, and language arts methods.

In summary, I believe that research on teaching has a great deal to offer to the practice of teaching if we think more broadly than we are accustomed to about what research actually produces. Observed relationships among operationally defined variables in a particular study may be the primary product of research for the audience of other researchers. But teachers can and should be helped to become reflective and autonomous professionals by sharing with them the concepts, models, questions, methods of inquiry, and case studies that research on teaching also produces. Teachers, so prepared, must still face complex and demanding problem-solving situations in their own classrooms, and research on teaching probably will not make the process of teaching simpler. But creative use of the unexploited outcomes of research on teaching can be used to make teaching more appropriately complex.

LET'S GET COMMUNICATING!

My fourth and final exhortation, "Let's get communicating!," concerns the conditions for and methods of discourse between researchers and teachers and among teachers themselves. My claim is that neither teachers nor researchers are very adept at professional communication about professional matters. I suspect that none of us is fully satisfied by the traditional media of journal articles, textbooks, half-day in-service workshops, or evening and summer courses at the local university. Even when done well, these traditional approaches to professional communication fall short of genuine service to teachers.

For the past three years I have been working in a nontraditional format for professional communication called the Michigan State University Written Literacy Forum. The Forum is a collaborative effort by teachers and researchers aimed at developing effective means of bringing research on the teaching of writing into practice. Founded in September, 1981, the Forum has conducted inquiry into the relationship between written literacy research and practice through two kinds of activity: (1) Forum deliberations, in which the nine members (five teachers and four researchers) discussed and analyzed key issues in the teaching of writing, and (2) planning, delivery, and reflection on in-service workshops on writing instruction. In both of these

major activities we drew from the substantial data base (Clark & Florio, et al., 1982) collected in the Michigan State University Written Literacy Project (in which all initial Forum members were participants), research literature on writing instruction, and extensive field experiences of the teachers and researchers themselves. By these means we sought to develop thoroughly grounded and practical ways of bringing the fruits of research on writing into action in the classroom.

The Written Literacy Forum was created as one possible answer to the challenge of bringing research and practice together. In creating it we attempted to modify the traditional culture of research that defines teachers as "subjects," researchers as "data analysts," and teacher educators as "change agents." Each participant in the Written Literacy Forum takes on all of these roles and more. New social, methodological, and theoretical forms developed as we collectively reflected on the teaching and learning of writing in schools. The Forum extends the conventional boundaries of teaching, research, and teacher education. In the affirmative social context of the Forum, trust and dialogue arose, yielding not only increased knowledge about the process of writing instruction but insight as well into the process of professional development as it is experienced by practitioners and researchers alike.

One example of the influence of Forum deliberations on our research agenda evolved from discussions by Forum teachers of the practical problem of when and how to provide constructive feedback to students during the composition process. This issue appeared to be a substantial problem for teachers from the primary grades through high school. Cases in which this problem was seen as serious were contrasted with situations in which providing constructive feedback was not problematic. These discussions, and the insights and questions that they stimulated, led to the drafting of a preliminary model of the process of school writing instruction that emphasizes social and contextual influences on the teaching of writing. This preliminary model is being elaborated and tested in the current work of the Forum.

Forum deliberations have also influenced the practice of teaching. One example involves a primary-grade teacher and Forum member who reports that she has dramatically increased the number of opportunities for her students to do writing for audiences other than herself. This teacher attributes her decision to promote writing for audiences outside the classroom to her participation in Forum discussions of two issues: the fundamental function of writing as a medium that can bridge time and distance and the importance of writing activities feeling meaningful and consequential to authors. (Our earlier research on written literacy indicated that activities that seemed to students to have no purpose beyond pleasing the teacher were difficult to manage and rarely produced good writing.) The importance of this change in a teacher's practice lies not in the particulars of how she teaches differently. Rather, it is more significant that she has internalized a new question to pursue as she builds her own writing curriculum: How can I make this activity more meaningful and consequential for the young author?

My experience during the first three years of the Written Literacy Forum suggests that professional communication can be raised to new levels of usefulness when we invest the time and energy it takes to make it happen. Writing was a good choice of focus for our deliberations because it is a richly problematic part of the curriculum. But I see no reason why the Forum concept would not work equally well if the focus were other than writing. The general point holds: bringing the fruits of research into practice seems to require an intermediate step in which intelligent practitioners, through deliberation, make the important connections and adaptations themselves. As a researcher I may be able to facilitate this process a bit, but I certainly cannot expect to force my models on unwilling teachers. Face-to-face communication among teachers and between teachers and researchers is crucial to bringing research into practice.

CONCLUSION

In conclusion, teachers and researchers must cooperate if research on teaching is to be of real service to teaching. We need to get humble, to demand service, to get creative, and to communicate. Pursuing these four exhortations will look quite different in different professional settings. Unless we all take care to pursue each of them, research and practice will continue to go their separate ways.

REFERENCES

Baker, E. L. (1984). Can educational research inform educational practice? Yes! *Phi Delta Kappan, 65* (March), 453–455.

Brophy, J. E., & Good, T. L. (1974). *Teacher-student relationships: Causes and consequences.* New York: Holt, Rinehart and Winston.

Carroll, J. B. (1963). A model of school learning. *Teachers College Record, 64,* 723–733.

Clark, C. M. (1983). Research on teacher planning: An inventory of the knowledge base. In D. C. Smith (Ed.), *Essential knowledge for beginning educators,* 5–15. Washington, D.C.: American Association of Colleges for Teacher Education. . . .

Clark, C. M., & Florio[, S.] (1982). *Understanding writing in school: A descriptive case study of writing and its instruction in two classrooms.* Research Series No. 104. East Lansing: Michigan State University, Institute for Research on Teaching.

Clark, C. M., & Peterson, P. L. (1984). *Teachers' thought processes.* Occasional Paper No. 72, East Lansing: Michigan State University, Institute for Research on Teaching.

Clark, C. M., & Yinger, R. J. (1979). *Three studies of teacher planning.* Research Series No. 55. East Lansing: Michigan State University, Institute for Research on Teaching.

Cronbach, L. J. (1975). Beyond the two disciplines of scientific psychology. *American Psychologist, 30,* 116–126.

Doyle, W. (1983). Academic work. *Review of Educational Research, 53,* 159–199.

Eisner, E. W. (1984). Can educational research inform educational practice? *Phi Delta Kappan, 65* (March), 447–452.

Fenstermacher, G. D. (1979). A philosophical consideration of recent research on teacher effectiveness. In L. S. Schulman (Ed.), *Review of research in education,* 157–185. Itasca, Ill.: Peacock.

Fisher, C. W., et al. (1980). Teaching behaviors, academic learning time, and student achievement: An overview. In C. Denham & A. Lieberman (Eds.), *Time to learn,* 7–32. Washington, D.C.: National Institute of Education.

Floden, R. E., & Feiman, S. (1981). Should teachers be taught to be rational? *Journal of Education for Teachers, 7,* 274–283.

Florio, S., & Clark, C. M. (1982). The functions of writing in an elementary classroom. *Research in the Teaching of English, 16,* 115–130.

Kounin, J. (1970). *Discipline and group management in classrooms.* New York: Holt, Rinehart and Winston.

Lundgren, U. P. (1972). *Frame factors and the teaching process.* Stockholm: Almquist & Wiksell.

Peterson, P. L., & Clark, C. M. (1978). Teachers' reports of their cognitive processes during teaching. *American Educational Research Journal, 15,* 555–565.

Peterson, P. L., Marx, R. W., & Clark, C. M. (1978). Teacher planning, teacher behavior, and student achievement. *American Educational Research Journal, 15,* 417–432.

Phillips, D. C. (1980). What do the researchers and the practitioners have to offer each other? *Educational Researcher, 9,* 17–24.

Philips, S. U. (1972). Participation structures and communicative competence: Warm Springs children in community and classroom. In C. B. Cazden, V. John, & D. Hymes (Eds.), *Functions of language in the classrooms,* 370–394. New York: Teachers College Press.

Richardson, E. S. (1964). *In the early world.* Wellington, New Zealand: New Zealand Council of Educational Research.

Rowe, M. B. (1974). Wait time and rewards as instructional variables, their influence on language, logic, and fate control: Part one—Wait time. *Journal of Research in Science Teaching, 11,* 81–94.

Shavelson, R. J., & Stern, P. (1981). Research on teachers' pedagogical thoughts, judgements, decisions, and behavior. *Review of Educational Research, 51,* 455–498.

Shultz, J., Florio, S., & Erickson, F. (1982). Where's the floor? Aspects of the cultural organization of social relationships in communication at home and at school. In P. Gilmore & A. Glatthorn (Eds.), *Children in and out of school: Ethnography and education,* 88–123. Washington, D.C.: Center for Applied Linguistics.

Simon, A., & Boyer, E. G. (Eds.) (1970). Mirrors for behavior II: An anthology of observational instruments. *Classroom Interaction Newsletter,* special edition.

Yinger, R. J. (1977). *A study of teacher planning: Description and theory development using ethnographic and information processing methods.* Ph.D. diss., Michigan State University.

Work on this chapter was sponsored by the Institute for Research on Teaching, College of Education, Michigan State University. The Institute for Research on Teaching is funded primarily by the Program for Teaching and Instruction of the National Institute of Education, United States Department of Education. The opinions expressed in this publication do not necessarily reflect the position, policy, or endorsement of the National Institute of Education. (Contract No. 400–81–0014)

4. ON KNOWING HOW TO TEACH

Philip W. Jackson

What must teachers know about teaching? What knowledge is essential to their work? Is there a lot to learn or just a little? Is it easy or difficult? How is such knowledge generated and confirmed? Indeed, dare we even call it knowledge in the strict sense of the term? Is not much of what guides the actions of teachers nothing more than opinion, not to say out-and-out guesswork? But even if that were so, what of the remainder? If *any* of what teachers claim to know about teaching qualifies as knowledge (and who dares deny that some does?), what can be said of its adequacy? How complete is it? Does much remain to be discovered or do the best of today's teachers already know most of what there is to learn? . . .

This spate of questions, to which others of a similar nature could easily be added, has to do with the form and content of what shall be referred to here as the epistemic demands of teaching. . . . More specifically, the questions raised at the start of this chapter refer to the epistemic demands of teaching *as a method*, a way of doing things, rather than to an additional set of demands, also epistemic in kind, that arise from the teacher's need to master the material being taught. The two kinds of knowledge—of methods and of instructional content—are related, of course, as common sense suggests they would be, but they are by no means synonymous, as soon will become clear.

Questions having to do with methodological know-how, as opposed to knowledge of subject matter, may not always be uppermost in the minds of teachers as they go about their work, but they are seldom overlooked entirely. More than that, every teacher must surely have answered, at least partially and provisionally, the most pivotal of those questions: what do teachers need to know in order to teach? This has to be true, for without having done so they would be stalled in their tracks at the start and the activity called teaching could not even get underway. . . .

In America today, as is abundantly evident, nearly everyone goes to school from age five or so onward. From the very first day of that experience our store of knowledge about teachers and their work begins to build. By the time our schooling is complete, the tally of our face-to-face encounters with teachers runs into the thousands. That extended acquaintance, whose product makes up something that might be called "school sense," leaves many people believing that they too, though not teachers themselves ("mind you," they might add), have a pretty good idea of what the job entails in the way of knowledge and skill. They may even go so far as to claim that they could teach quite well themselves, if they but tried.

Moreover, although formal schooling is obviously the chief source of such notions, it is by no means the only one. Teaching, as we all discover while still very young, is not confined to schools. We encounter it in all kinds of settings—at home, on the street, in churches and synagogues, in doctors' offices, and on the playground, to name but a few. As a consequence, our cumulative knowledge of what it takes to be a teacher is derived from many different kinds of experiences with teachers of many different sorts. . . .

However, despite the ubiquity of teaching as an activity, there is no uniformity of opinion about it. Thus, though almost everyone might think he or she has the answer to most of the questions raised at the start of this chapter, it would be quite wide of the mark to say that everyone agrees on what those answers should be. On the contrary, when it comes to teaching and what it entails, disagreement, rather than agreement, turns out to be rife.

In response to our opening questions, some people contend there is a lot to know about teaching; others say, very little. Some argue that whatever there is to know is easily learned; others say the task is very difficult. Teaching can be learned only on the job, according to some people; there is much to be learned beforehand, according to others. And so it goes. Sharp differences of opinion crop up almost invariably wherever teaching is discussed, from the family dinner-table to the public forum. . . .

[A VARIETY OF TEACHERS]

Among the first things to note is how many kinds of teachers there are. Leaving aside the large number of nonprofessional teachers (most parents, for example), we are still left with an impressive variety of types, the major ones well-known.

To start, we are all familiar with the practice of classifying teachers according to the level of schooling at which they work. Preschool, elementary, high school, and college teachers (the last-named being called professors by many) comprise the most widely used categories of all. We are also used to hearing teachers referred to by the subjects they teach. Teachers of voice, physics, home economics, Latin, physical education, and countless other subjects are familar enough to most of us. A complete list of such descriptive titles would contain almost as many entries as there are divisions within the domain of human knowledge.

Then there are many people, both within and outside the categories that have been named, who do not always call themselves teachers but who are so all the same. These include tutors, masters, coaches, trainers, counselors, lecturers, public speakers, professional consultants, and discussion leaders. A special subgroup is comprised of priests, preachers, and rabbis in their instructional roles, not to mention gurus and sundry other holy men. Also to be included are alpine guides, animal trainers, tour directors, certain TV performers, and recreational advisers at seaside resorts.

The duties of many of these people go far beyond teaching, true enough, but their work remains pedagogical in character all the same. So the variety of people properly called teachers, *professional* teachers to be more precise, is very great indeed. Examples range from TV's Julia Child to the professor of neurosurgery at the nearby medical school, from the lady who teaches flower arranging at the local "Y" on Saturday afternoons to the Visiting Fellow in the Department of Paleontology at Harvard. . . .

With such differences in mind, let us now ask: can anything be said about the epistemic demands of teaching based solely on what we know to be true about how people become various kinds of teachers in our society today and how they have done so in the past? Common knowledge about such matters provides us with two interrelated observations, each bearing directly on the set of questions with which we began.

The first is that formal instruction in pedagogy *per se* largely, but not exclusively, confined to persons training to become either elementary or secondary school teachers. Not only is this true today, but it has been so for some time, perhaps for as long as there has been such instruction.

Students preparing to teach at the college level and beyond seldom enroll in education courses of any sort along the way. Nor are most of them given instruction within the confines of their own academic departments on how to teach the subject matter in which they are specializing. The same is true for many, if not most, teachers who work in settings other than schools. They too are unlikely to have studied teaching methods in any formal way.

Julia Child, for example has probably never taken a course on how to give cooking lessons, much less one on teaching in general. Nor is she at all unusual in this regard. She is just like the neurosurgeon at the medical school, who in all probability has never formally studied the pedagogy of his or her craft either. The same is probably true of the lady who teaches flower arranging at the local "Y" and the Visiting Fellow in the Department of Paleontology at Harvard. . . .

The second observation about how teachers typically are trained, or not trained, in their craft calls attention to the fact that even for elementary and secondary teachers formal training in pedagogy is a relatively new requirement. Until quite recently—within the last hundred years or so—there were very few teacher training institutions as we know them today. Even books on pedagogy were not all that numerous. In generations past people undertook to become teachers of the young solely on the strength of what they themselves had learned in school, often before completing the equivalent of today's twelfth grade, and without benefit of anything approaching the kind of training for the task undertaken in a modern teachers' college or even the kind provided in many of today's liberal arts colleges. . . .

. . . [T]he norm has now become a training course in a college or university, typically requiring several years to complete. However, in the case of teaching, unlike most other professions, the old pattern still prevails here and there. In our independent schools in particular—both parochial and secular—one can still find a sizable number of elementary and secondary teachers who have had no official work in education. . . . [Their mere existence] poses a continuing challenge to all mandates governing what courses public school teachers must take in order to be certified. Moreover, . . . many of the schools continuing to hire teachers without formal training in pedagogy are considered to be among the very best in the country.

Thus all claims about what teachers need to know in order to do their work are confronted at the start with a double paradox. They first must take into account the somewhat puzzling fact that the most prestigious class of teachers in our society—those working in colleges and universities—devote less time to the formal study of teaching than do their less respected colleagues who work in elementary and secondary schools. . . . [In addition,] those who argue on behalf of requiring teachers to take some education courses before they begin to teach must also confront the . . . fact that even at lower levels of schooling some elementary and secondary teachers—often in the best of schools at that—seem to get along quite well without any formal training at all. . . .

From the standpoint of teacher education in general, the harshest interpretation of the facts cited is that they add up to a sweeping indictment of the entire enterprise. "How can such programs be worth much," the interpreter of those facts well might ask, "when it is precisely the teachers who work in some of our very best schools and who teach the most advanced and complicated subjects in our colleges and universities who seem to get along quite well without them? . . .

As a comment upon the epistemic demands of teaching, that line of thought has several important shortcomings. The first is that it addresses those demands indirectly at best. From the observation that many teachers seem to get along quite well without formal training, the conclusion is drawn that all or most other teachers might do so as well. But the fact that some teachers can go without formal training says nothing about what teachers in general need to know. It certainly does not prove that there is little to learn about how to teach. All it asserts directly is that apparently not everyone needs to take courses on the subject of teaching (and perhaps read books about it) in order to perform reasonably well in the classroom. Which teachers can safely go without such training and which others cannot is a question the facts themselves do not address. Also they leave the door wide open to the possibility of learning through direct experience, informal interchange with teaching colleagues, and so forth. Of course, the people making use of such facts usually are doing so to denigrate the notion of teachers' needing to know much of anything beyond the actual subject matter they teach. Consequently, the facts are intended to *insinuate* that there really *is* little to learn about teaching. Like all insinuations, however, they stop short of saying what those who employ them want others to conclude. . . .

The second shortcoming of such observations is that they ignore the phenomenon of *unsuccessful* teaching and why it happens. The question here is, if learning how to teach is really as simple as the evidence seems to imply, why do people fail at it? There are many ways of answering that question without introducing epistemic notions—for example, it may be that unsuccessful teachers suffer from some kind of emotional deficit—but until the phenomenon is addressed head-on and the epistemic alternative discarded, there remains the strong possibility, vexing to those who think there is little to learn about teaching, that many such teachers are best explained as simply lacking in know-how.

These and other weaknesses aside, we still must deal with the facts on which the criticism rests. To avoid interpreting them in a way that is highly critical of teacher education programs and, indirectly, of the teachers who pass through them, we must seek other interpretations. A favorite interpretation among those teacher educators who bother to address the question makes use of the idea that there are compensatory qualities of one sort or another enabling teachers with little training, or even none at all, to make up for their deficiency.

John Dewey, for one, favored this view. He acknowledged that there are some teachers who, as he put it, "violate every law known to and laid down by pedagogical science."[1] What makes such teachers effective? They are so, explained Dewey, because "[t]hey are themselves so full of the science of inquiry, so sensitive to every sign of its presence and absence, that no matter what they do, nor how they do it, they succeed in awakening and inspiring like alert and intense mental activity in those with whom they come in contact."[2] Thus, Dewey posited a superabundant "spirit of inquiry" that was capable of making up for a lack of pedagogical knowledge. . . . What this line of reasoning reduces to is the contention that there are, in a word, "born" teachers, whose abilities are such that they either instinctively behave correctly when placed in a teaching situation or, as Dewey puts it, behave in such a way as to compensate for whatever else they might be doing that could be judged wrong. . . .

The chief difficulty with all such *post hoc* theories lies in their circularity. We begin with the observation that some teachers seem to be doing quite well without training, and we proceed to explain that "anomaly" by ascribing to such persons some special powers or gifts. . . .

Another difficulty with these compensatory theories is that they usually are designed to deal with special cases, whereas the phenomenon of teachers without formal training, at least in colleges and universities, is the rule rather than the exception. Unless we are prepared to entertain the possibility that *all* such teachers, or nearly so, are blessed with one or more of those special talents believed to overcome a lack of training, theories of the kind suggested will not cover sufficient ground to do the job required.

The most serious difficulty of all, however, is that all such theories beg the question: Are there truly, as Dewey claimed, "laws known to and laid down by pedagogical science"? If so, what might they be? Indeed, is there any such thing as a "pedagogical science"? Dewey must have believed there was, or he would not have used the term as

---

[1] Reginald D. Archambault, *John Dewey on Education* (New York: Random House, 1964), 330.
[2] *Ibid.*

he did. But was he correct? We certainly don't find the expression in wide use today. Why not? The most sensible explanation I can think of is that the term is pretentious when used to describe what we today can say with confidence about how to teach. . . .

[TEACHING AS "COMMON SENSE"]

Let's begin afresh by granting one of the underlying assumptions of many people who belittle the importance of pedagogical training: that the knowledge teaching calls for draws heavily on common sense. Let's agree that it does. That may seem like too great a concession to make to the foes of the entire concept of pedagogical knowledge, but we quickly see it is not when we consider that the same could be said of most other human activities as well. Indeed when we stop to think of it, we quickly realize that common sense, roughly defined as knowledge picked up in the course of living, is crucial to the performance of everything we do.

Not only does it serve as a guide to action in all our endeavors, it also provides, through the medium of language, the concepts and categories that make reality intelligible. It gives meaning to experience. It speaks authoritatively in both descriptive and prescriptive terms, telling us not only what *is* but also what *ought to be* with respect to all manner of things and situations.[3] Given its vital role in human affairs in general, we should hardly be surprised to find common sense crucial for teaching as well.

What does common sense say to teachers? What does it tell them to do? . . . Much that it provides bears upon the professional activities of teachers in no uncertain terms. It tells teachers things like, "That's what a person looks like who wants to say something," "There's a look of surprise," "That's an expression of disbelief," "There's a nod of understanding," and so forth. It further tells teachers, along with the rest of us, to speak in a clear voice, to write legibly, to listen when others are speaking, to ask questions when puzzled, to smile when pleased, to frown when displeased, and much, much

more about how to "read" the behavioral cues of others and how to respond to them in a manner that is at once understandable and socially acceptable.

Common sense also speaks in sterner tones from time to time. As the voice of conscience, it tells teachers to keep their promises to students; to be considerate of those who are having difficulty with the material being taught; to express thankfulness for cooperativeness and other expressions of goodwill; to be truthful; to persist in the face of adversity; to avoid behaving in a way that might corrupt the morals of youth; and, again, much, much more about how to govern one's actions, not simply in the interest of communicating with others and being understood by them, but also as a way of contributing to loftier goals like justice, harmony, and humaneness.

Having gone only this far in explicating what common sense might be thought to include and how its various components might contribute to a teacher's performance, we are prepared to draw two conclusions. The first is that common sense, as here defined, is absolutely essential to the teacher's work and is so in a nontrivial way. Any lingering doubt about that proposition present at the start should by now be gone. The actions of teachers, like those of everyone else, are constantly responsive to that vast and largely unarticulated network of shared understanding that comprises much of what people mean when they talk of common sense. . . .

But it should also be clear from the examples given thus far that, costly or not, the dictates of common sense are not always obeyed. This is the second conclusion pressing for recognition. Most of us know to bundle up when cold, to ask questions when puzzled, to persist in the face of adversity, and to do most of the other things that common sense tells us. The truth is, however, that we do not consistently act on that knowledge.

Why not? For a variety of reasons. Sometimes we are forcibly prevented from doing so. Sometimes we just plain forget. Sometimes we willfully and even perversely disregard what common sense tells us to do. . . .

There is an additional point that must be inserted here. It is that common sense, when it speaks imperatively, is not always of one voice. It tells us to be prudent and cautious, but it also advises us to

---

[3]For a provocative discussion of the complexity of common sense, see Clifford Geertz, "Common sense as a cultural system," *The Antioch Review* 33, number 1 (Spring 1975): 5–26.

strike while the iron is hot. It tells us to be gentle in our dealings with the young, but it also warns us not to spare the rod, for fear of spoiling the child.

This contradictory nature of common sense means that the simple formula of listening to its dictates and doing what they say will clearly not do. What teachers (and everyone else as well) often need is some way of deciding *which* voice of common sense to heed.

Can common sense itself deliver us from such dilemmas? It's hard to see how it can. What seems to be needed in all such situations is something more on the order of "good" sense, as opposed to "common" sense. . . .

The near universality of the experience of going to school would seem to put our memories of school life in the same class of mental "stuff" as that containing most of what goes by the name of common sense. But even if that should turn out to be an unacceptable argument, it is perfectly clear that the knowledge culled from prior experience in school is there as a potential resource to be drawn upon by all who face the demands of teaching.

What does that knowledge provide the would-be teacher? It provides him or her with some notion, vague though it may be, of how to do many of the things teachers do—how to use blackboards, assign homework, correct papers, construct tests, conduct exams, give grades, lead discussions, deliver lectures, monitor seatwork, pass out materials, and more. . . . In short, it provides a set of norms for the would-be teacher, a veritable scrapbook of memories about how teachers in the past have acted and, therefore, how one might oneself act in a similar situation.

At this point, advocates of today's teacher training programs, and perhaps all fair-minded critics of those programs, might well object that many of our most enduring memories of our schooldays are based on experiences with "old-fashioned" teachers or teachers of poor quality and are therefore not fit to be used as guides by anyone teaching today. They doubtless have a point. But two observations must be made in response.

The first is that a poor or old-fashioned guide is still a guide, like it or not. The primary question being addressed here is not: Where might untrained teachers turn for the *best* advice on how to teach? Rather, it is: Where might they turn for any advice at all? Professional educators may complain to their hearts' content about the quality of the average teacher, past or present; but there can be no doubt that everyone who undertakes to teach anything comes equipped, for better or for worse, with a built-in encyclopedia of pedagogical information contributed by teachers he or she has known in the past. Whether that encyclopedia should be consulted or ignored is a question totally distinct from the sheer fact of its existence.

The second, and more important, observation is that in all likelihood much of what the experts would consider to be poor teaching, and therefore not to be tapped from the storehouse of memory, we recognize as such without the aid of expert opinion. Most people do not remember simply that teacher X did this and teacher Y that. They also recall liking teacher X and disliking teacher Y. They remember that X made the subject interesting and Y made it dull, X was fair and Y unfair, and so on. . . .

Summarizing what has been said so far about the contribution of past experience in school to pedagogical know-how, we would begin by pointing out that to teach as one remembers having been taught is an option open to everyone. Teachers who lack formal training, such as those working in colleges and universities, may have no other option to consider. Even those who have been systematically introduced to other possibilities may still prefer the way they remember having been taught themselves. Nonetheless, whether they use it or not, the way of teaching prescribed by their "school" sense (the latter a sub-division of "common" sense) remains a resource to be drawn upon by all teachers, trained and untrained alike.

Thus it turns out that common sense alone, broadened to include the outcome of having witnessed many teachers in action from childhood onward, equips our would-be teacher with a lot of what he or she needs to know in order to do what the job demands. Indeed, if anything, it tells the teacher *more* than he or she needs to know about certain aspects of the work, in that the teacher is confronted with not one but two or more common-sensical ways of behaving. Given this abundance of advice issuing from common sense alone, we might well ask whether anything else at all is needed when it comes to what teachers must know. Why, in short, look elsewhere?

As a prelude to addressing that question, two reminders are in order. We first must recall that our concern throughout this chapter is with the *epistemic* demands of teaching. . . . This means that even if we were to discover that all of teaching calls for little more than the application of common sense we would still not be allowed to conclude that everyone who possesses common sense is capable of being a teacher. That conclusion would be questionable for the simple reason that it overlooks the possibility of there being other qualities that teachers must possess, beyond knowledge *per se*, if they are to do their job well.

We must also recall that an additional epistemic demand of teaching, beyond the purely pedagogical, was acknowledged at the start. This was the teacher's need to have mastered the material to be taught, a demand said to be related to his or her knowledge of how to teach that material, but not identical with it. . . . The central question is whether the knowledge of any teachable subject or skill, from astrophysics to basket weaving, entails a certain amount of pedagogical knowledge as well. In other words, if a person knows something, does he or she automatically know how to teach it? . . .

Most people would answer yes to this question, but not with equal assuredness and not all for the same reason. Some would do so because for them school teaching is essentially a game of show and tell. In this view, to know something or to know how to do something is tantamount to knowing how to teach that something. All the knowledgeable person need do, this line of reasoning concludes, is to pass the word along, show-and-tell style.

The chemist who knows the formula for some chemical compound need only display that piece of knowledge in the presence of his or her students in order to teach it to them. (For the slow learners in the class the formula might have to be repeated a few times, granted, but the basic principle remains the same.) The tennis instructor need only grasp the racquet properly and show the position of his grip for the attentive novice to see at once how it is done. . . .

From this perspective, every kernel of knowledge and every unit of skill might be said to contain within itself a pedagogical imperative of the sort that says, "Tell me or show me to someone else if you want to pass me along." Such a conception of

the teacher's task is appealingly simple; that much must be granted. Moreover, it is basically correct. Many teachers are indeed "show-ers" and "tell-ers" a good portion of the time. . . .

Usually, however, teaching involves much more than either showing or telling in the narrow sense of either term, which is to say simply demonstrating a skill or reciting an assortment of facts. The process of learning calls for more than that too. Typically, students are called upon to do much more than merely parrot back what the teacher says or mindlessly mimic what he or she does.

Beyond memorization lie other forms of learning, most of which depend upon the creation of conditions of conscious consent that go by names like understanding, appreciation, comprehension, realization, and the like. To establish these conditions teachers are constantly required to give reasons, to explain, to justify, and, generally, to provide rational support for what is being taught. Thus, the trouble with the show-and-tell conception of how knowledge guides pedagogy is not so much that it is wrong as that it does not go far enough. . . .

To correct these shortcomings we first need to recognize that facts seldom exist in isolation, nor do we usually present them to students in that way. They are parts of large wholes, or rather more grandly, they are elements within enveloping frameworks of epistemic significance. Physical skills too, particularly those taught in school, exhibit the same kind of relatedness. Typically, they are shown to be linked, one to the next, in some overall strategy or plan of action. . . .

. . . Each discernible structure of knowledge or repertoire of skillful performance is laid out according to a plan of some sort whose gross outline and features are generally familiar to people considered to be experts in that particular domain. . . . [I]n many fields of knowledge there is no single, universally agreed upon "structure" at all. Instead, there are alternative ways, some hotly contested, of bringing order to what is known. The competition among such organizational schemes is clearly evident in school and college textbooks in many subjects.

What this means pedagogically is that teachers are often faced with a choice of frameworks within which to couch their efforts. (This point is very much like the one made earlier about the plethora of advice issuing from common sense.) Thus the simple dictum: "Teach what you know" is made complicated by the fact that what one knows usually can be presented to students in a variety of different ways.

A recognition of this condition would seem to move us very close to a type of know-how that is both central to the teacher's work and unequivocally pedagogical in nature: *the knowledge of how to organize knowledge for teaching purposes*. If that organization is in any way different from the way knowledge is organized for *other* purposes—that is, for handy reference by people who are already experts on the subject or skill in question—it would seem like a piece of pedagogical know-how teachers could not do without.

The proposition that knowledge need be specifically arranged for teaching purposes seems sufficiently incontrovertible to be considered a truism. . . . [In fact,] many of the principles we encounter are sufficiently a part of almost everyone's way of looking at things to make them as common-sensical as they are pedagogical.

One such principle, for example, would be to proceed from the easy to the difficult. Another, related to the first but not precisely the same, would be to move from the simple to the complex. A third, useful when narrating events that can be arranged chronologically, would be to start at the beginning and continue on to the end. A fourth would be to move deductively, from the logically prior to the subsequent. . . .

The listing of such pedagogical rules of thumb appears to return us to our earlier observation that common sense contains most of what people need to know when called upon to teach something to someone. If following such rules is all there is to it, it begins to look as though the critic's view was right after all. Even when we move from common sense in general to pedagogical principles in particular, teaching continues to look as easy as rolling off a log. . . .

By this time it will have occurred to some readers that nothing has been said to this point about one very important element in all teaching situations, namely, the person or persons being taught. Here surely is a source of information for making pedagogical decisions that must be fully as important as the material being taught. . . .

Though that conclusion *sounds* sensible enough, it turns out to be false. The truth is that many teachers seem to get along quite well without knowing much at all (in the extreme case, nothing!) about the students they teach. . . .

One group of teachers who characteristically get along with very little information about the students they teach are those who do their teaching via television or radio. They do so, it seems, by substituting three key assumptions for what other teachers and common sense itself might deem it essential to know. . . .

The first of these assumptions, rarely necessary in most teaching situations, is that there actually are students witnessing the teacher's actions or at least listening to his words. This assumption, which is absolutely crucial for all radio and television teachers who are not working with a live audience, we will call *the presumption of a public*. . . .

The second assumption that teachers of invisible audiences have to make in order to give sense to what they are doing is that some if not all of their students are in need, in purely epistemic terms, of whatever it is that is being taught. For short, let's call this the *presumption of ignorance*. . . . For the presumption of ignorance to work all that need be assumed is a gap of understanding or skill, capable of being filled at least in part by what the teacher does or directs his or her students to do. . . .

The third assumption is more difficult to describe than the first two. It has to do with the similarity between the teacher and his or her students. For this reason I call it *the presumption of shared identity*[.] . . . One aspect of what is shared with students, or is assumed to be by most teachers, is summed up by the expression: "our common cultural heritage." What that heritage contains is rather difficult to say with precision, but certain of its contents are clear enough. It includes a common language and a large part of the kind of commonsense knowledge about which much has already been said. It includes a knowledge of cultural heroes, popular tastes, and everyday customs and conventions, all of which enable people to feel at home and to behave understandably within a specific cultural context.

Another aspect of the presumption of shared identity has to do with psychological functioning.

Acting on this presumption, teachers take for granted that their students are like themselves in the way their minds work, in the way they think and feel, in what makes them laugh and cry, and so forth. This includes an assumed similarity in physiological terms as well, in such things as the factors that create fatigue, how much stress can be tolerated, the conditions that bring on excitement or boredom, and so forth. . . .

Such an assumption effectively frees the teacher of the need to inquire into the nature of his or her students as a guide to making pedagogical moves. It enable[s] him or her to teach, almost literally, with eyes closed. Should a question arise, for example, about whether students might find a particular piece of instructional sequence interesting or boring, the teacher need search no further than the boundaries of his or her own consciousness for an answer. Does he find the material interesting? . . .

There is one more requirement for the teacher who lacks direct knowledge of his or her students, either by choice or because it is unattainable. . . . [T]he teacher must . . . have some indication of how long instruction should continue in both the short-term and the long-term sense. What he or she needs, in other words, are ways of knowing when to terminate instruction, without relying on information from students to make that decision. The requirement, in short, is for an *a priori* set of exit rules.

In many teaching situations this is quite possible to do without establishing such rules in advance. Instead, the teacher may rely upon more naturally occurring signs that it is time to stop work. For example, the teacher might keep an eye out for signs of fatigue among her students. Alternatively, she might monitor her own feelings of stress and strain for signs of when to call it quits for the day. Instead of deciding in advance how many teaching sessions to have, she might choose to continue teaching until her own knowledge runs out, until she can truthfully face her students and say, "Now I have taught you all I know," or something to that effect.

In reality, of course, teachers seldom go that far. Nor do they wait until fatigue shows among their students to terminate individual lessons. Instead, whether forced to do so or not, they commonly settle upon a more or less standard and somewhat arbitrary unit of time as the length of a single teaching session or "lesson," and they space such units with considerable precision and regularity within large blocks of time. The result is the familiar: "Typing I will be taught on Tuesdays and Thursdays from 4:30 to 6:00 PM in Room 109." They also commonly establish in advance (or have it established for them) the overall duration of instruction, either tying it to a particular date—for example, "classes will end on June 12"—or limiting it to a specific number of sessions, as in "ten easy lessons." . . .

[THE PROBLEM OF "SHARED IDENTITY"]

The enumeration of situations calling for "pedagogical" knowledge, as opposed to common sense plus what might simply be called erudition, gives rise to an important question about the presumption of shared identity. Quite simply, it is: Can such a presumption *ever* be validly held? Is it true that no two people are exactly alike? That being so, doesn't everyone who presumes a shared identity · with others—teachers no less than anyone else—run the risk of being in error at least part of the time? Therefore, why presume a shared identity to start with? Why not begin with the assumption that the teacher and her students do *not* fully share the same outlook on life or the same psycholgical makeup or the same anything else and move forward from there?

The answer, it seems, is that some form of the presumption of shared identity must remain unquestioned, at least temporarily, for social interaction to become a possibility. That is, if I believe the objects before me do not even share my humanness, if they are mannequins, let's say, or some lower form of life, I may proceed to act upon them, moving them about, shouting commands at them, and so forth. But I do so in a manner quite unlike that of most human interactions. Consequently, the question is rarely whether the presumption of shared identity is valid or invalid. Rather it is: To what *extent* is it valid? What are its limits? . . . Most teachers are adults; most students, children. It follows, therefore, that some knowledge of what children are like, what things appeal to them, what the limits of their understanding might be, and so forth comprises the major epistemic ingredients of what teachers of the young must know.

Where does such knowledge come from? How is it acquired? . . . The answer seems to be that some people gain an understanding of children in the course of living that others never do. Jobs as baby-sitters and camp counselors must certainly play a role for some. So too must experience with younger brothers and sisters. But however it comes about, it turns out that some adults are more comfortable in the presence of children and enjoy their company more than do others.

For such persons the usual kinds of introduction to the world of childhood provided by most teacher training programs would probably add very little to what they already know. This is not to say they have nothing to learn from developmental and cognitive psychologists like Vigotsky and Piaget. The point is simply that such knowledge is not likely to make them feel more at ease with children than they already feel.

Teachers and students differ in more than age, of course, and sometimes these other dimensions of dissimilarity turn out to be very significant as well, more so at times than age itself. Differences in social class, for instance, are widely acknowledged to be a hindrance in the communication between teachers and students. So too are differences covered by the standard variables of race, ethnicity, sex, and physical handicaps.

A teacher's failure to take such differences into account can be the source of difficulty in many a tale of pedagogical woe. But as the same time, this is not invariably true. Differences between teachers and students in any or all of the aforementioned variables are often irrelevant to what the teacher decides to do. The question of whether they are or are not relevant seems to depend chiefly on what is being taught. . . .

Given what has been said in the closing section of this chapter, it is easy to see why teachers of the very young are more likely to be "child-centered"

than "subject-centered." The latter point of view gains sympathizers as we move up the grades. However, it should also be clear at this point that the debate is focused on what is really a false issue.

First, the expression "student-centered" should replace "child-centered" so that the issue is broadened to cover all of teaching.[4] Second, the question that really needs careful examination and perhaps public discussion as well is: When is it appropriate and necessary for teachers to be sensitive to the students' characteristics and when not? The two extreme answers—always and never—can be eliminated at the start.

Finally, we must ask where this discussion of the epistemic demands of teaching has taken us with respect to questions having to do with the usefulness of methods courses and other practical experiences— such as classroom observations and student teaching—that comprise a large part of the curriculum of many teaching training programs. In the light of what has been said in this chapter, are such courses and training experiences largely a waste of time, as critics have sometimes charged?

There is certainly no way of answering that question without a look at each program; however, it should be clear from what has been said that many teachers might gain much from those portions of their training curriculum that help them think about how particular materials and skills might best be arranged and presented for pedagogical purposes. Critics who claim that all such knowledge is simply a matter of common sense are surely wrong. At the same time, the fact that such courses *could* be useful does not make them so. In the final analysis, teachers themselves must judge.

---

[4]All, that is, save for a rather exotic group of teachers who work exclusively with animals. It is not entirely clear what to call animals who are being trained or taught by humans, if indeed they require any special name at all. To refer to them as "students" seems a bit odd, yet in a sense that is what they are. "Subjects," the terms scientists use to refer to animals (and often humans as well) when reporting on their experiments, sounds a bit more appropriate, even though regal in tone. Perhaps the absence of any special designation suggests there need be none.

5. WHY TEACHERS WON'T TEACH

Milbrey Wallin McLaughlin, R. Scott Pfeifer, Deborah Swanson-Owens, and Sylvia Yee

Eric Cullins, a white male teacher in his early thirties, said he wanted to be a teacher because he felt that children "deserved more than they were getting in school." After three years in the classroom, however, he is no longer certain that he has the "emotional stamina it takes to keep up with this environment, because there's so much strife and frustration." He says he often has days when teaching is like "pushing toothpicks into cement." At times he's so tired that, during his lunch break, all he can do is "stare and chew." Ultimately, he expects to have to move on because, as he puts it, "I can't give what it takes to be an elementary teacher for 20 years—I'd go mad."

Those who would reform education no longer ask why Johnny can't read. The question they ponder is why Johnny's teacher can't or won't teach.

Policy makers and practitioners alike recognize that issues associated with teacher quality go far beyond the low scores of many recruits on competency tests or scattered examples of incompetence in the classroom. The issues most central to the health of the teaching profession and to the long-range quality of U.S. education have to do with the fact that competent teachers—indeed, some of our most talented teachers—believe that they can't, and thus won't, teach. Teachers who won't teach either leave the profession completely or resign themselves to going through the motions of educating children.

Teachers who won't teach are symptoms of an ailing educational system. In fundamental ways, the U.S. educational system is structured to guarantee the failure of teachers. Ironically, a teacher can experience professional success, in terms of fostering student learning, but still feel a profound sense of personal failure because the process of teaching is frustrating, unrewarding, and intolerably difficult. It is this inability to fulfill the aspirations with which they entered teaching that drives many talented individuals from the profession and fosters dull cynicism in a great many of those who remain. Drawing on our ongoing study of teachers' incentives, rewards, and working environment, we intend in this article to explore a broad range of organizational features that combine to minimize teachers' professional satisfaction and effectiveness.[1]

Several of the teachers we interviewed said that they entered teaching "accidentally" or because it seemed the "only option"—but these individuals were the exceptions. Most of the 85 teachers in our sample said that they entered the profession because they wanted to help children learn. Indeed, the vast majority said that they had "always wanted to teach"; these teachers also expressed a strong sense of mission.

We found, as have other researchers, that the dominant motivation and source of reward for teachers lies in promoting students' growth and development.[2] The thing that makes teaching meaningful and worthwhile is watching students learn and "working with their wonder." If it weren't for the natural responsiveness of children, one teacher said, "I would have walked away a long time ago, sold stockings at Macy's, and made the same amount of money."

Having a positive impact on students' lives yields the psychic rewards that teachers seek and need in order to sustain their efforts. Time and again, teachers in our sample told us that their inability to serve students—to meet their varied needs effectively—is a source of frustration that leads to dissatisfaction with themselves and strong feelings of failure.

SET UP FOR FAILURE

Our research has furnished abundant examples of school conditions that prevent teachers from obtaining the rewards that initially drew them to teaching. After four years of substitute teaching and two years of full-time teaching on a permanent contract, one middle school teacher described her professional life this way:

> Things are set up these days so that teachers never feel they can do a good job. The classes are too large, the materials aren't there, and the students

come to school with incredible needs that teachers can't meet. We are constantly pushed. We are constantly told by the superintendent that teachers have to do this, and we are constantly told by parents that teachers have to do that. Everyone expects the schools to take care of social problems. I think that schools could be a very progressive force—but not with the resources they currently have. I feel angry; I feel depressed; I feel frustrated. It is a very difficult situation for those teachers who care.

A successful and energetic middle school teacher in another urban district asserted that "the structure of the schools is insane." A veteran teacher with 30 years of classroom experience said that "teachers are set up to experience constant failure," becuse so much of their time and energy is spent attending to noninstructional responsibilities or to controlling a disinterested (but conscripted) clientele. An equally dedicated elementary teacher said that the hardest thing about teaching is having "lots of little things over which teachers have no control," such as the number of youngsters with problems, the amount of paperwork, and the number of interruptions.

These comments are typical of teachers in all kinds of school settings, from wealthy suburbs and middle-income areas to inner cities. Even more disturbing is the fact that the most effective teachers feel these frustrations and the concomitant sense of failure most acutely. Not surprisingly, many of these able and dedicated individuals decide after a time that—in one way or another—they will no longer teach.

THE CONSEQUENCES

As we have said, the conditions under which teachers carry out their responsibilities are often set up in such a way as to deny teachers a sense of efficacy, success, and self-worth. In such situations, even the most dedicated teachers experience personal failure.

As is true of religious vocations,[3] individuals enter teaching with a strong service ethic and a dedication to helping others. For such individuals, self-esteem comes from the belief that they are performing capably a task that they value, and satisfaction comes from the feeling that they are using their abilities appropriately and effectively.

Frustration and a sense of failure are the outcomes when these conditions are not met. Our research on teachers supports the major finding of other studies of service-oriented professionals: inadequate opportunities for psychological or personal success inevitably weaken commitment to and acceptance of the organization.[4]

Incongruity between an individual's motivation and abilities and his or her conditions of work creates a situation structured for psychological failure. Many U.S. teachers, especially the most competent ones, show signs of this sense of failure. Teachers often attempt to minimize their feelings of failure by acting in ways that are educationally counterproductive, such as:

- withdrawing emotionally from the classroom or becoming apathetic,
- placing increased value on material rewards,
- becoming hostile toward school officials,
- working for promotion to other positions that afford them better prospects, or
- leaving the profession altogether.[5]

Such responses by teachers are not belligerent posturings. Rather, they represent rational and adaptive responses to a workplace over which teachers have little control.

Unfortunately, many of the current reform efforts aimed at improving the quality of teachers fail to consider the configuration of conditions that leads even the most dedicated teachers to experience demoralization and a sense of personal failure. Indeed, some of the organizational and environmental features that contribute most prominently to this sense of failure are also basic aspects of the current system of education in the U.S. Teachers in our sample identified the following factors, which interact to deny them the rewards they prize.

Class Composition

Problems related to the composition of classes— particularly class size and the increased academic and emotional needs of students—head the list as a source of teacher dissatisfaction and concern. Changes in the student population, coupled with the public's expectations that teachers will meet the needs of individual students, create classroom conditions that many teachers perceive as incompatible with effective instruction.

Asked what they would change in order to become more effective, these teachers most often said that they would decrease the number of students in any given class. Many teachers told us that the hardest part of teaching is the stress of trying to deal with 25 to 35 students at any given time, since effective teaching requires that they be able to identify each student's needs and tailor their own responses accordingly. A majority of these teachers said they felt they had failed, because they had not been able to reach every student.

Although large classes keep teachers from feeling successful, class size is less important than class composition in this regard. The difficulty of trying to reach a large number of students is compounded when a classroom contains students who function at a wide range of academic levels. One high school teacher said that her biology and physiology classes typically include learning-disabled students who have been assigned to these courses for administrative reasons that have nothing to do with their ability to cope with the textbook or course content.

Meanwhile, most of the teachers in our sample said that the increase in single-parent and dual-career families has forced them to take on a bigger parenting role, as well. For example, one elementary teacher told us she feels that she must "mother" her students, since many of them don't receive the kind of parental attention and support they need to approach their studies with interest and confidence. A high school teacher described the situation as a Catch-22: teaching students in classroom settings presupposes that they possess certain attitudes about learning; but, if students lack those attitudes, teachers cannot do anything about it because such students are not disposed to learn attitudes (or anything else) in classroom settings. One teacher in an urban elementary school told us that she spends the first instructional hour of each school day feeding children whose parents did not get them to school on time to take advantage of the breakfast that the school provides.

In sum, many teachers work with large classes whose members exhibit a wide range of academic abilities and come from a variety of family backgrounds. Such teachers are often diverted from engaging in the kinds of activities that drew them to teaching. But they experience a sense of dissatisfaction at their inability to reach each student effectively—and they experience a deep sense of failure when youngsters "slip through their fingers."

Working without Tools

Al White has been a middle school teacher for seven years, but only in the last two years has he had any stability in his work environment. By *stability*, White means having his own classroom, access to clerical help, and textbooks, paper, and pencils for his students. He describes his early teaching experiences thus:

> As a beginning teacher, I taught history and math. I received a set of math books—in February! I never did get history books. Instead, every night I wrote history and mimeographed it. My total supplies that year consisted of chalk. Paper came from a publisher. . . . [I] dug through his trash cans.

Noting that land mines had been placed in his path as a teacher, White concluded, "Don't criticize me for not being able to run with the ball."

Without the necessary tools, teachers are handicapped. Yet approximately half of the teachers we interviewed rated their teaching materials as "poor" or "barely adequate."

A high school biology teacher told us that "the least rewarding aspect [of teaching] is the fact that there's so little science equipment." Her 31 students had only 12 microscopes to share among them. "This kills their enthusiasm," she said. "They have to sit and wait, or I've got to find something else for them to do. And the lesson loses a lot." When a lesson involves dissection, this same science teacher "prays they won't all come to class, since I have only six dissecting pans." She added, "Those are the things that make you not want to come to work." Not surprisingly, she also said that she would not become a teacher, if she had the choice to make over again.

The teachers in our sample gave us many reasons for materials being in short supply. An elementary teacher in a bilingual program, for example, said that her school expects the district's bilingual education department to provide bilingual teaching materials, while that department argues that the school should provide them. In the meantime, her class has too few workbooks; therefore, she has to improvise and produce all the instructional materials herself.

A teacher in another school speculated that "most good teachers spend their own money on their classes." She said that she spends about $400 annually on supplemental materials, rewards for her students, and registration fees for professional conferences.

Administrative Actions

Every day, administrative decisions undermine teachers' feelings of competence and efficacy. Uniformly and bitterly, the teachers in our sample complained about a lack of clear and consistent policies on discipline and attendance designed to support their efforts in the classroom.

In one school, the principal required teachers to complete a great deal of paperwork for each disciplinary referral; administrative action was initiated on a given case only after three referrals. "The policy is written in such a way that the burden—including parent contact—falls on the teacher," according to one faculty member in that school. "And, by the time any administrative action takes place, you really have a problem. It reduces the administrators' workload, but it certainly increases ours."

Other administrative decisions thwart teachers in their role as classroom managers and undercut their expertise. When students' test scores are not returned to teachers until late spring, prescribing appropriate instruction becomes more difficult. Midyear shifts in the composition of classes erode the continuity of lesson plans. Classes composed of two grade levels, established to meet guidelines for racial balance, frustrate teachers' instructional efforts. Failure to process orders quickly for classroom materials disrupts instruction. When extracurricular activities, such as band trips or cheerleading practices, are scheduled during the school day, the quality of instruction suffers.

However, assigning teachers to courses outside their areas of interest and competence is the administrative action most damaging to teachers' self-esteem and satisfaction. Administrative decisions such as these can actually create incompetence. The

outcome is a "demoralized teaching force, because it is being asked to do things that are not smart at all."[6]

Isolation

Reflection and the professional growth that accompanies it are the hallmarks of a professional.[7] Teachers' feelings of efficacy and satisfaction are undermined by the absence of opportunities to reflect on their performance, to examine new or alternative practices, or to consider feedback regarding their effectiveness. The classroom door provides a measure of autonomy for teachers, but it also fosters isolation, limits feedback about performance, and promotes staleness.

One teacher complained, "There's not a lot of communication in this business to tell you what kind of a job you are doing. The only feedback you get is from your individual students. You don't really hear anything from the administration, fellow teachers, or even parents."

Furthermore, teachers in many schools have no common preparation periods or other free intervals for collegial exchanges. A high school teacher told us that, at her school, many teachers even work with students through the lunch hour.

Like other professionals, teachers view competence as an ongoing developmental process, not a static state. They need and miss the stimulation and new ideas that interactions with colleagues provide. By the same token, insufficient opportunities to receive feedback and collegial support contribute to teachers' uncertainties and concerns about the extent to which they are using their capabilities effectively. In the words of one teacher, the lack of opportunities for interaction with colleagues "makes teaching seem less like a profession and more like a job."

Nobody Says Thanks

Lack of recognition was a recurring theme in our interviews with teachers. They told us that their work is difficult and important to the society but that—both from within the educational system and from outside it—they get the message that they are unimportant.

Perhaps one of the most pathological symptoms

of teaching today is that many practitioners are apologetic about, instead of proud of, what they do for a living.[8] Teachers in our sample pointed to unswept classroom floors and the decrepit buildings in which they worked, as evidence that the society does not see their work as significant. Of course, low pay is a major indicator of lack of respect for educators. At the building level, teachers see incessant paperwork, parental complaints, and their own lack of involvement in decision making as signals that they lack importance and value. Virtually every teacher in our sample said that teachers do not receive the respect that they need and deserve.

"In general, recognition [for one's work as a teacher] is so infrequent," noted a dedicated teacher of high school English. "Nobody says thank you," declared another. Service-oriented professionals are probably more selfless than individuals in other kinds of occupations, but they need recognition for their contributions and accomplishments at least as much as do individuals in other walks of life—and probably more. Being valued by the society is one of the psychic rewards that attracted them to teaching in the first place. When recognition and respect are not forthcoming, many teachers—especially the most talented and most dedicated members of the corps—conclude that teaching is "just not worth the effort."

First Years on the Job

Teaching is an occupation in which important learning takes place on the job. Most new teachers frame their goals for the first year or two in terms of "survival" and are profoundly concerned about proving their competence. Yet new teachers often receive difficult teaching assignments; they are also more likely than their experienced colleagues to be assigned to teach courses for which they lack background and training.

One teacher in our sample started his professional life as a substitute. He was laid off twice during his first few years of full-time teaching. He was also forced to teach outside his area of specialization, and he had no textbooks from which to teach. Said he, "You can only learn to be a teacher if you have a supportive, nurturing environment. If you are a soldier in a war zone, you don't plant a garden. If you do, the garden doesn't do very well."

Kathy Reed, another respondent in our sample, always wanted to be an English teacher. She "waited it out" as a paralegal worker during those years when a surplus made jobs for teachers almost impossible to find. Having served as a temporary teacher for the last four years, she now feels that the most difficult thing for her is not knowing from one year to the next whether she is going to have a job.

Because she is a new teacher and because she has a master's degree in special education, Reed is assigned to teach an excessively high proportion of the special education students who are mainstreamed at her grade level. While her colleagues each receive a maximum of three handicapped students, she is assigned from nine to 17 of them. She is bitter about this imbalance in the placement of handicapped students, because it has a negative impact on her effectiveness.

Reed's experience is not unusual. New teachers are often given those students or courses with which experienced teachers do not wish to deal. Instead of giving beginning teachers a nurturing environment in which to grow, we throw them into a war zone where both the demands and the mortality rate are excessively high. It is really not surprising that almost one-third of teachers leave the profession within their first five years of teaching.[9]

The conditions that negatively affect the effectiveness and the success of veteran teachers are even more devastating to young recruits. Beginning teachers strongly desire interactions with colleagues, the support of their principals, teaching assignments that are consistent with their competencies, a stable work environment, and access to the tools of their trade.

POLICY IMPLICATIONS

The workplace of teaching is a fragile environment, where mutually reinforcing organizational arrangements combine to produce conditions that work against success—and thus against the retention of talented and committed teachers. Theodore Sizer put it well: "Excellent teachers are strong, proud people," he said, and "strong, proud people only take jobs which entrust them with important things and which are structured in such a way that success is reasonably possible."[10] Revitalization of the teaching profession can occur only if the conditions of teaching are structured and managed to yield the professional success and personal job satisfaction that will bind effective teachers to the profession.

Reforms will undoubtedly fall short of their intended effects if they merely tinker with current organizational arrangements in education. Unfortunately, many of the current proposals aimed at improving teacher quality—merit pay, career ladders, competency tests—seem to do just that. Whatever their strengths, such single-issue solutions (which are uniformly applied across a broad set of problems) ignore the complexities inherent in the issue of teacher quality. Clearly, just increasing teachers' salaries will not alter the basic conditions that prevent teachers from teaching. Just decreasing class sizes will not keep effective teachers from leaving the profession, if they continually confront parental apathy or intrusion. Just increasing opportunities for professional development will do little to make teachers effective, if a building administrator fails to protect them from unnecessary interruptions and paperwork or fails to manage the school in a fashion that supports instructional efforts.

A comprehensive agenda of reform is necessary to structure the teaching profession for success. Efforts to improve teachers' working conditions should focus especially on five areas.

Parental Support

The attitudes of parents do much to shape the structure of the workplace for teachers. Indeed, teachers find the current lack of parental support discouraging.

That lack of support springs in large part from the fact that schools still operate as though a two-parent family, including a mother who does not work outside the home, were the mode. Full-time homemakers have time to attend conferences during the school day, to supervise their children after school, and to help them with homework. But teachers in diverse settings, from wealthy suburbs to the inner city, have come to realize that home/school partnerships based on this family model are now outdated. In many cases, today's dual-career

or single parents are "just too tired" to take an active role in their youngsters' education.

By failing to address this erosion in the relationship between home and school, policy makers ignore an important means of increasing teachers' effectiveness and job satisfaction. Yet no simple, across-the-board method exists for increasing parental involvement in their children's education. Therefore, policies must be tailored to the needs of individual school communities.

In one inner-city elementary school in Los Angeles that serves many immigrants from Southeast Asia, for example, the staff realized that parents lacked the most basic skills. Some mothers did not even know how to hold a pencil to write. So the staff arranged daytime and evening classes to teach parents how to help their children with schoolwork. Early outcomes of that program have been encouraging.

Meanwhile, the Oakland (California) School District drew up a contract with parents, in which the parents promised to supervise their children's homework each night. This program has been a positive and highly visible response to the problem of lack of parental involvement. More important, the existence of such a program acknowledges the critical importance of rebuilding the home/school partnership.

Buffering Teachers

The principal as an instructional leader is not a novel idea. But an even more venerable idea is that of the principal as a buffer who protects teachers and their classrooms from distractions and disturbances. Teachers tend to take it for granted when they are spared needless interruptions, when their paperwork is kept to a minimum, and when they receive adequate disciplinary support, because these conditions form the bedrock on which effective practice is built. When such buffering is absent, however, even the most carefully planned lesson can crumble.

District-level administrators and school board members also play an important buffering role through their policies that set limits on class size and that establish budgets for instructional materials. Decreasing class size may not raise standardized test scores in any given classroom, but our data suggest that this action will have a powerful impact on teachers' perceptions of their own effectiveness. Smaller classes put teachers in closer contact with their students and enable them to reap in full measure the psychic rewards that brought them into teaching. It is hard to catch the "light of learning in a child's eyes" when the child is one of 35 students crowding a classroom.

The wisdom of providing teachers with adequate instructional materials is self-evident. No rational person would ask an architect to create a set of plans without paper, pencil, reference books, and drafting table—nor would a carpenter be expected to build a house without a hammer and saw. Yet, in many ways, this is exactly what we expect of teachers. Giving teachers adequate instructional materials enables them to fully use their talents.

Feedback

Our efforts to construct a workplace that will promote the effectiveness and satisfaction of teachers should also include serious consideration of the nature and extent of feedback that teachers receive about their performance in the classroom. The teachers in our sample said that their performance suffers becasue they lack routine, constructive feedback. Collegial feedback could help teachers solve recurrent problems and reduce their uncertainty about whether or not they are attaining their instructional goals.

Administrators can take three steps to help teachers break out of the isolation that characterizes the teaching profession. First, they can obtain training in supervision for themselves and for their teachers, so that both groups have better observation and communication skills. Second, they can work with teachers to develop a common language that will enable both administrators and teachers to approach instructional improvement as a joint activity in problem solving. Third, administrators can make certain that teachers have time to engage in collegial interactions during the school day.

Increasing the quality and the quantity of feedback to teachers achieves several goals. First, teachers broaden their repertoire of instructional strategies, which increases their effectiveness. Second, the investment of district resources in this enterprise sends a clear signal to teachers that their work has

worth. Third, good teachers receive the recognition that is often lacking. Fourth, effective performance is maintained and burnout is avoided.

Professional Development

The diversity of the sources that our respondents identified as contributing to their effectiveness as teachers and the variable effect these sources had at different career stages suggest that school districts should revise their approach to professional development. Rather than lodge the responsibility for professional development entirely with the individual teacher or entirely with the school district, a joint effort seems appropriate. The outcome should be a merging of organizational and personal goals.

Teacher's needs for professional development vary according to their skills, their teaching assignments, and their experience. Guiding individual teachers to appropriate workshops, grant-funded projects, professional conferences, and graduate programs is an activity that school districts rarely approach in any systematic way. Management development programs in the private sector, by contrast, treat such activity as an integral part of the personnel function.

New Teachers' Needs

Finally, districts across the U.S. will be hiring large numbers of new teachers during the coming decade. In California alone, school officials estimate that 110,000 new teachers will be needed by 1990. Therefore, it is particularly important at this time that school districts carefully reassess the ways in which they structure the early years of a teacher's career.

Teachers whose initial assignments are frustrating or stressful seem more likely to experience decreased commitment, confidence, and satisfaction in later years than those whose initial assignments are supportive and satisfying. Thus all the strategies designed to restructure the workplace for teachers are even more important in the case of the beginning teacher.

Organizational responses that structure the teaching workplace for success will help new teachers avoid future frustration and failure. New teachers need fewer, not more, responsibilities. They require released time for additional training and for careful planning. Mentor relationships that provide feedback on performance and that encourage experimentation are necessary in order to break the pattern of teacher isolation.

Although no school district we studied approached the critical needs of new teachers in a comprehensive fashion, several promising strategies were evident. In one school, new teachers receive funds to support their instructional needs that are double the discretionary budget of experienced teachers. Several districts hold special workshops for new teachers on lesson planning and disciplinary techniques. But such responses, standing alone, are not sufficient to fully revitalize the teaching profession. A more comprehensive approach to addressing the developmental needs of new teachers—an approach that assumes that new teachers require socialization and training beyond that provided by their teacher education programs—will begin to produce teachers who are set up for success, not failure, later in their careers.

Without such an approach, and without sufficient attention to conditions of the workplace, the U.S. system of education risks producing yet another cadre of individuals who entered teaching with a strong desire to serve students—but who find, after exposure to the working conditions of their profession, that they can't and won't teach.

[NOTES]

1. This article uses the findings of an ongoing study of the sources of teacher effectiveness and satisfaction, sponsored by the Walter S. Johnson Foundation and conducted by Milbrey McLaughlin, Annette Lareau, Scott Pfeifer, Deborah Swanson-Owens, and Sylvia Yee of the Stanford University School of Education. The research team conducted hourlong interviews with 85 teachers representing five school districts in the San Francisco Bay Area. The teachers in the sample had differing levels of teaching experience. They came from elementary, junior high, and secondary schools located in both high- and low-income areas.

2. See, for example, Dan C. Lortie, *Schoolteacher: A Sociological Study* (Chicago: University of Chicago Press, 1975).

3. Douglas T. Hall and Benjamin Schneider, *Organizational Climates and Careers: The Work Lives of Priests* (New York: Seminar Press, 1973).

4. Ibid.; and Chris Argyris, *Personality and Organization* (New York: Harper, 1957).

5. See, for example, Theodore R. Sizer, *Horace's Compromise: The Dilemma of the American High School* (Boston: Houghton Mifflin, 1984); John I. Goodlad, *A Place Called School* (New York: McGraw-Hill, 1984); and Argyris (which presents the model for this analysis).

6. Theodore R. Sizer, testimony before the California Commission on the Teaching Profession, 23 May 1985, Chapman College, Orange, Calif.

7. Donald A. Schon, *The Reflective Practitioner* (New York: Basic Books, 1983).

8. Ibid.

9. Phillip C. Schlechty and Victor Vance, "Recruitment, Selection, and Retention: The Shape of the Teaching Force," *Elementary School Journal*, vol. 83, 1983, pp. 469–87.

10. Sizer, testimony before the California Commission on the Teaching Profession. . . .

6. LABOR RELATIONS AND TEACHER POLICY
Douglas E. Mitchell and Charles T. Kerchner

. . . This chapter explores the policy framework within which labor relations are conducted. Recent debate over labor relations policy, though intense, has been extremely limited. Most discussions have focused on the economic and political effects of teacher bargaining, but little attention has been given to the impacts of labor policy on the definition of teaching work. Managers have naively assumed that their interests are best protected by legally narrowing the scope of permissible bargaining (Kerchner, 1978). And teachers have tended to insist that virtually any expansion of their powers is a step toward liberation from arbitrary, insensitive, or irresponsible control over their work (see Mitchell, 1979). Both groups have neglected the redefinition of education implied in the selection of one labor policy over another. . . .

THE STRUCTURE OF TEACHING WORK

The activities of teachers can be compared with those of other workers along two dimensions. First, every job has some system of "task definition" to specify the particular activities workers are expected to perform. And second, all have some sort of "oversight mechanism" for monitoring the performance of these tasks. . . .

Task Definition

There are two basic approaches to task definition. Some jobs are structured primarily through "rationalization." That is, specific tasks are preplanned (by either managers or the workers themselves) and then undertaken as a matter of routine enactment of standard operating procedures. Automobile assembly and building construction are typical examples of this approach to task definition. In other job settings, however, tasks are primarily adaptive—requiring accommodation to unexpected or unpredictable elements within the work situation. In this case, the task definitions cannot be embodied in a preplanned program. Instead, the emphasis must be on responding to conditions arising on the job, exercising proper judgment regarding what is needed, and maintaining intellectual and technical flexibility. Newspaper editors, firemen, and emergency room doctors all rely on this type of task definition.

Oversight Mechanisms

Monitoring or overseeing work performance is also typically structured in one of two basic ways. Some workers are subjected to direct oversight through close supervision (such as assembly line workers) or through stringent reporting requirements (such as policemen). For other workers (such as architects or accountants) oversight is indirect. Preparation and skill—that is, the *ability* to perform the work—are the prime considerations. In the first case, the work itself is "inspected." In the second, the work often goes unexamined while workers are certified or "licensed" to perform the work on their own.

The criteria used to evaluate these two different types of work are quite different. Licensed workers are expected to have at their disposal a set [of] learned techniques for performing needed tasks, and they are held accountable for the care and precision with which they apply the appropriate techniques. Where work is inspected rather than licensed, however, a worker's cooperativeness, dedication, and overall level of effort are most important. If special skills or techniques are required, managers are expected to guide workers in their application through direct supervision and critical review.

As indicated in Figure [1], four distinctive work structures are created when the basic task definition systems and oversight mechanisms are combined. "Labor" (upper-left cell of Figure [1]) is the term which best describes those work settings where tasks are rationally planned and oversight is undertaken by direct supervision. As used here, the word "labor" has a special meaning. All jobs involve labor to the extent that they all require an expenditure of effort directed at task accomplishment. . . . Laboring is not distinguished by its association with "low-level" jobs but rather by the rationalized and preplanned character of tasks and direct inspection of how those tasks are performed. While low-level jobs (such as those of sanitation or assembly line workers) are more frequently subjected to routinization and close supervision, there is no intrinsic reason why high-status jobs cannot also be so structured. . . .

Loyalty and insubordination are the most important concepts in evaluating laboring work. It is very important for laborers to give allegiance to the organization for which they work and to respond energetically and promptly to directions given by superiors. This need for loyalty arises because laborers are not expected to take personal responsibility for the overall purposes toward which their efforts are being directed. As Frederick Taylor's *Principles of Scientific Management* (1911) makes abundantly clear, it is the manager, not the laborer, who must decide when, how, and for what purposes work effort should be directed. The worst offense of a laborer is insubordination to a supervisor—not inadequate results. Laborers need to do what they are told to do, when they are told to do it. If the result is unproductive, it is the manager's, not the worker's, fault.

Craft workers (upper-right cell of Figure [1])

Oversight and Monitoring Mechanisms

	Direct/ Inspection	Indirect/ Licensure
	Activity Monitoring	Technique Monitoring
Rationalized **Preplanned** **Programs** **Routinized**	Labor (Loyalty) insubordination as basis of evaluation)	Craft (Precision/ incompetence as basis of evaluation)
Adaptive **Situation** **Responsive** **Flexible**	Art (Sensitivity/ frivolousness as basis of evaluation)	Profession (Responsibility/ malpractice as basis of evaluation)

(Left axis label: Task Definition Approaches)

FIGURE [1]   Task Definition and Oversight Structures

differ from labor workers. These workers are generally freed from direct supervision but held responsible for selecting and applying appropriate specialized techniques in order to realize the specific objectives of their work. In place of direct supervision, craft workers are licensed, certified, or otherwise explicitly identified as having special abilities. Managers (or clients in the case of craft workers who operate on a direct contract basis) establish the overall objectives of the work, but once craft specialists take an assignment, they are expected to carry it out without needing detailed instructions or close supervision. Licensure is a matter of public policy in many craft areas because incompetent or unscrupulous craft workers are difficult for unskilled clients to recognize. . . .

Craft work (typified in tool making, routine computer programming, or electronic instrument repair) is evaluated on the basis of precision and competence. Craft workers are judged on how adequately they execute required tasks. They are even expected to risk insubordination toward their superiors in order to competently apply the techniques of their craft. While laborers are only expected to follow orders, craft workers are deemed incompetent if they are unable to recognize which tech-

niques to use in the performance of particular tasks.

Rationalization and planning are important in both labor and craft work structures, but they take very different forms. For laboring work, rationalization is conventional and refers to *standardization* of procedures or *specificity* of managerial directions. For craft workers, however, rationalization is technical and refers to the *appropriateness* of the methods being used. For laborers, standard operating procedures are right because they are standardized. For craft workers, by contrast, they become standarized because they are technically correct (Gouldner, 1954, pp. 223–224). . . .

Professional workers (lower-right cell of Figure [1]), like craft workers, are expected to possess a set of specialized techniques. Where professional work differs from craftsmanship, however, is in the way tasks are defined. While both craft and professional workers perform specialized tasks, professionals are expected to analyze or diagnose situational factors and adapt their working strategies to the true needs (not just the expressed wishes) of their clients. A craft worker has to know whether a particular task *can* be performed and how to perform it. But a professional is responsible for deciding whether the task *should* be performed. As craft workers, surgeons must know how to operate; as professionals, they must know whether an operation is needed.

Responsibility and malpractice are the key elements in evaluating professional work. Professionals (e.g., surgeons or architects) are expected to consider the implications of choosing a particular course of action, resisting interference and pressure from superiors or outsiders and accepting personal responsibility for the outcome. Thus, while the worst criticism to be leveled at a craft worker is incompetence, malpractice is the appropriate label for inadequate professional work. Malpractice differs from incompetence in two important ways. First, even if the execution of a task is completely competent, a professional worker is guilty of malpractice if it can be shown that the task was unnecessary or inappropriate to a particular case. Second, in a case of malpractice the judgments of professional *peers,* rather than those supervisors or other superiors, are recognized as the basis for determining whether the work was properly executed.

We have given the label "art" (lower-left cell of Figure [1]) to work characterized by both adaptive task definitions and direct monitoring of workers' activities. Although artistic work may require a high level of technical skill, the social organization of this type of work is not based on the possession of particular skills. Art is recognized in the products produced and by the quality of the artists' engagement in their work. When necessary for their work, artists are expected to rise above the limits of specific techniques or established conventions and to develop novel, unconventional, or unexpected techniques. Like professional workers, artists are expected to be flexible and adaptive in defining their work responsibilities. Like laborers, however, artists are not licensed. They are monitored and evaluated directly—by assessing whether their work is engaging, exciting, and creative.

Actors and musicians are prototypical artists. Key concepts in the evaluation of their work are sensitivity and frivolousness. Whereas the professional is required to be responsible, the craft worker to be competent, and the laborer to be loyal, the artist in an organizational setting is called upon to be sensitive to the need for integrity, creativity, and spontaneity. They are frequently granted a great deal of autonomy

in order to allow for the exercise of this artistic sensitivity. There is no such thing as malpractice for the artist—only the frivolous use of talent or refusal to enter fully into the creative process. Genuine art work requires dedicated and serious effort. Loyalty to preplanned institutional programs, a basic requirement in laboring work settings, is often the enemy of great art.

The works of solitary artists (such as novelists or painters) are evaluated through inspection and critical review by individual consumers or by editors, juries, and reviewers in journals and newspapers. Organized artistic ventures, such as designing buildings or performing plays, are closer in form to teaching. Here the creation of an artistic masterpiece depends on adequate coordination or direction as well as sensitive review and critical evaluation.

The work structures presented in Figure [1] are "ideal types" in the sense in which Weber (1947) used that phrase. Real jobs will always involve a mixture of labor, craft, art, and professional work activities. . . . When, for example, teachers are on lunchroom duty or are asked to report student attendance to the school office, they are performing tasks which closely fit the ideal definition of labor. No special skills are presumed, no advanced training for this work is offered, and the work is expected to be performed in strict accordance with preplanned guidelines. These tasks are generally defined and supervised in ways quite different from such craft or artistic tasks as planning curricula, leading discussions, or evaluating student achievements. . . .

THE IMPACT OF LABOR RELATIONS ON TEACHER WORK STRUCTURES

. . . Labor contracts themselves are more ambiguous than they appear. Very similar contract clauses—on evaluation procedures, for example—can have quite different impacts in different places. In part, this is due to the interdependence of work rules and the grievance mechanisms specified within a contract. "One is meaningless without the other," one Illinois labor leader told us. "You can have all the work rules you want, but without the means to grieve violations, those rules mean exactly what management wants them to mean." On the other hand, he continued, "the right to grieve an empty contract doesn't mean much either." The impact of a contract clause can be understood only when the ability to use it is considered. . . .

Labor relations in education are . . . influenced by school district policies. Teacher labor relations evolve through three distinct phases or "generations" separated by two periods of over political conflict (Mitchell et al., 1981). Before the first conflict period, first-generation labor relations are characterized by an acceptance of the proposition that ultimate authority in all school policy matters rests with the board. "Meet and confer" sessions between a teacher committee and the school board may occur, but the board is recognized as having unilateral authority. First-generation labor relations end with the onset of a political struggle over the legitimacy of teachers' rights to organize and deal collectively with school systems. A second generation begins when the teacher organization is accepted as a legitimate interpreter of teacher interests. During this period labor relations are based on bilateral "good faith bargaining." Teacher interests are accepted as legitimate, but as inimical to those of management. During this period teacher "wins" are seen as management "losses." As the second-generation relationship matures, overt conflict generally subsides as each side develops ways of accommodating the essential interests of the other. In doing so, however, they tend to isolate school board and citizen groups from the process.

A second districtwide controversy erupts when disagreements over the propriety of teacher organizations' power and influence over matters of personnel and policy become politicized. The third generation in labor relations—which arises only after there has been an overt political rejection of the second-generation arrangement—involves teachers in the creation of "negotiated policy" for the school district. School boards and managers eventually come to recognize that working conditions for teachers are inextricably bound up with major educational policy decisions and that both are being hammered out at the bargaining table (Eberts and Pierce, 1980).

Unfortunately, except for the question of managerial authority, the significance of labor relations policy disputes is frequently unrecognized by the participants (McDonnell and Pascal, 1979, p. 80). The process tends to be seen as one of conflict management or coalition building rather than institutional policymaking. Settling the contract peacefully is frequently more important to both sides than the educational effects of the agreement. . . .

How Labor Relations Support the Laboring Work Structure

Both rationalization (preplanning and routinization of activities) and inspection (close monitoring of teacher work performance) tend to be supported by the evolution of formal labor relations. Rationalization is encouraged as teachers attempt to protect themselves. Closer inspection is stimulated by management efforts to define and enforce their rights in responses to unionization.

While craft, professional, and artistic conceptions are abundant in the literature on teaching work, the labor definition is most compatible with collective bargaining. A craft conception, which encourages rationalization through improved techniques rather than standardization of practice, is most popular with the school administrations we studied. Traditionally, managers have believed that teacher training assures the development of needed skills and that certification means that teachers possess them. Recently, however, widespread doubt about the efficacy of specific techniques, combined with a lack of confidence in teacher dedication, has encouraged managers to feel that school programs—not individual teachers' skills—are what counts. Nationwide concern about student achievement has created a suspicion that

> Incompetent teachers wind up in the classroom because the state sets *virtually no standard of performance*. Most candidates become teachers after obtaining state certification, which simply means that the college student passed the required number of education courses at an accredited college or university. (*New York Times,* July 3, 1979, Section C, p. 4) . . .

The Mechanisms for Rationalization and Inspection

. . . [C]ontract language, social relationship changes, and new political decision-making mechanisms within the school each contribute to the rationalization of teaching tasks and encourage increased inspection of teacher job performance.

The Contract. . . . [T]hree aspects of typical teacher contracts encourage rationalization of the work. First, by specifying hours and duties, contracts encourage the general industrial-society drift from "mission-bounded" work to "time-bounded" work. . . . Whereas the "school day" has always been time-bounded, the teacher's day has been ambiguous. Classes begin and end at set hours, but an undefined duty extends beyond those hours for grading and preparing lessons and nonclass interactions with students and parents. Through collective bargaining, teachers have asked that previously undefined hours and duty requirements be specified—when teachers are to be on campus and when they are to be available for after-school activities, meetings with parents, open houses, and the like.

In addition to specifying hours and duties, contracts formalize the distinction between teachers' "regular" and "extra" duties. Regular duties are largely limited to classroom instruction while extra duties cover most extra-curricular and student supervision responsibilities. Also by contract, many teachers have been relieved of onerous lunchroom and playground supervision duties. By making this separation obvious, contracts encourage teachers to narrow their sense of responsibility for outcomes and concentrate on explicitly stated (i.e., rationalized) tasks. . . .

The propensity for negotiators to develop elaborate procedural rules to cover all adjustments in teacher job definitions and assignments represents a third source of work rationalization. By expanding requirements for notification, consultation, and review of work assignments (through layoff and transfer policies, curriculum planning councils, etc.) contracts encourage planning and rationalization for every aspect of a teacher's job.

. . . Three elements found in most contracts support increased inspection of teacher job performance.

First, because arbitration proceedings require school site managers to show a contractual basis for their orders and to show that they have enforced the same work rules for all employees, grievance clauses encourage inspection of teacher job performance.

. . . Second, managers are motivated to inspect teacher job performance because contract administration requires standardization of practice in all buildings and classrooms (Gonder, 1981, p. 41). As principals come to accept their role as contract administrators, they also tend to adopt a diminished definition of management, confining their oversight to those work rules explicitly set forth in the contract.

Third, evaluation clauses found in many contracts encourage inspection by linking evaluation more closely with teacher discipline and discharge. Quite apart from the matter of difficulty in dismissing teachers, collective contracts have changed the definition of legitimate causes for dismissal. Judgments of technical competence or personal adequacy by superiors have been largely replaced by a factual assessment of whether a teacher did or did not follow rules. For example, in the celebrated case of Cyril Lang, an English teacher in Rockville, Maryland, a suspension for misconduct and insubordination was ordered because Lang exposed tenth-graders to Aristotle's *Poetics* and Machiavelli's *The Prince*— books not on the approved reading list. To school officials, the issue was not learning but whether rules were followed. As superintendent Edward Andrews said, "I don't know whether Lang is right or wrong about the books, but in a public school system, you have to have reasonable procedures to determine what is to be used and the superintendent has to uphold them" (*Time,* 1980, p. 77). . . .

The Social Organization. . . . [C]hanges in the social organization of the school have also contributed to the rationalization and inspection of teacher's work. In some respects these social system changes are more dramatic than those resulting from written contracts. As one national teacher organization staff member told us, "Schools changed a lot when senior teachers shifted from bringing the younger ones into line with what principals wanted to adopting the ideology that any grievant is right."

Most school districts now contain two distinct social organizations—each competing from the loyalty and cooperation of teachers. The administrative organization, led by the superintendent, wants teachers to adopt district goals as their own and to pursue those goals diligently. The teacher organization, led by the union president or staff executive, needs teachers to be willing to challenge the legitimacy of management directives and perhaps even withdraw services if a suitable accommodation to their demands is not forthcoming. The integration of these two social systems is accomplished largely by rationalizing each of them—that is, by circumscribing the powers of each system and emphasizing the importance of formal "official" interpretations of all rules and organizational practices. . . .

While competition for teacher loyalty encourages rationalization, the need for both social systems to demonstrate their vitality and power increases the level of inspection. Administrators feel a great need to show that they are willing and able to monitor and enforce the rules governing teacher behavior. At the same time, although they often do not recognize it, teacher organizations need to call attention to the behavior of their members. As teachers try to show that they are serious about demands for improved working conditions, they invariably go out of their way to attract attention to their work. . . .

Rationalization of teaching work is further encouraged by surprisingly strong pressures for the homogenization of teacher job definitions. Both teachers and administrators have generally come to believe that collective bargaining requires identical working conditions for all teachers. Teachers tend to be suspicious that administrators only try to differentiate work roles in order to control teachers rather than to improve education. Moreover, the political structure of teacher organizations and the dynamics of collective bargaining make the homogenization of teacher work roles attractive. . . .

The overall impact of these various changes in the social system of the school can be summarized in terms of changes in the roles of two groups of key actors: principals and teacher organization leaders. For school principals, collective bargaining has meant giving greater attention to two concepts that have recently been receiving increased attention in both professional and scholarly circles: *management* and *supervision*. Widespread use of "management by objectives" (MBO) techniques and recent enthusiasm for "clinical supervision" are only the most obvious indicators of this new emphasis on the principal as manager and supervisor. As managers, principals are expected to help rationalize the teaching process. As supervisors they are asked to increase the level of inspection in the system. . . .

The Political System. . . . Achieving a satisfactory contract settlement in education depends heavily on the ability of each side to form and sustain strong political support coalitions. While solidarity within labor and management groups is necessary for effective bargaining, attracting and holding the support of politically active citizens is also a critical element. Since teachers rarely have powerful economic sanctions to use against school managers and managers have political survival or personal pride—not economic benefit—at stake in trying to resist teacher demands, political support from citizens (especially in the matter of voting for school board members) sets the overall direction in labor relations as in other areas of school policy (Lutz and Iannaccone, 1978).

Enhancing the importance of the political coalitions with citizens is a weakening of what Meyer and Rowan (1978) have called "the logic of confidence." They argue that schools have traditionally operated on the basis of "ritual" classifications rather than closely inspected work performances. For example, special requirements for certifying mathematics teachers are scrupulously followed—but then almost no attention is paid to what they actually do once certified. . . . Ritual classification is applied to both students and teachers. It enables schools to assure themselves of at least the appearance of success by simply declaring that teachers are fully certified or that students have "passed" from one classification to another. . . .

There are two other aspects of school politics which interact with labor relations to encourage the adoption of a laboring conception of teaching. One is the emergence of teacher organizations as lobbyists and major political contributors at the state and federal levels. Teachers rank among the largest political contributors in some states. . . .

In appealing to state and federal policymakers for support, teachers have endorsed the belief that education can be rationalized and controlled through program structures, funding categories, and procedural regulations. While this belief, taken by itself, would tend to support the craft rather than the labor paradigm, it has interacted with a second factor—a widespread demand for accountability and assessment underlying the "politics of evaluation" which has dominated most recent state and federal initiatives (House, 1974). The interaction between teacher power and evaluation politics has led to a climate in which state and federal policy frequently encourages compliance rather than excellence, maintenance of effort rather than appropriateness of service, and following guidelines rather than responding to needs. . . .

POLICY IMPLICATIONS

. . . [P]olicymakers can provide . . . support through a wide range of . . . policy actions. Two important policy areas currently receiving widespread attention are: (1) school finance and budget policies and the related market or pseudo-market mechanisms aimed at controlling when and how educational services are purchased and (2) staff development policies aimed at influencing the work orientations of principals and other middle managers.

School Finance and the Educational Marketplace. Current public interest in educational vouchers, tuition tax credits, and support for private or parochial school systems reflects serious interest in the role of market forces in shaping the delivery of educational services. These forces interact strongly with school tax and budget policies, which are also being debated and implemented at all governmental levels. Thus, for example, the development of block grants interacts with other mechanisms for raising

and allocating resources to alter both the level of funding and the patterns of expenditure in most school districts. Debate over the desirability of strengthening the role of the marketplace in education is both intense and confusing. The most serious confusion in the debate springs from a general failure to recognize that there are many different types of market mechanisms. The market for professional services (such as medical care or legal assistance) is very different from that associated with the purchase of relatively low technology products (such as staple foodstuffs or furniture), high technology products (such as home appliances or automobiles), or artistic objects (such as records, high-fashion clothing, or Broadway plays).

As indicated in Figure [2], each of the four basic work structures is most compatible with one particular type of market mechanism. Each also presumes a very different basis for choice on the part of consumers. Products created through labor, for example, are best suited to a classical "commodity" market system. In a commodity market, consumers assume that quality is generally standardized; they make choices based primarily on the *price* charged for the good (or services) being purchased.

Commodity markets are not, however, best suited to the distribution of high-technology craft-based products. Craft-based production presents high risks to both investors and consumers. Investors seek a

	Labor	Craft	Profession	Art
Market and Pseudo-market Control Through: (Market Choice Based on)	Free trade (Price)	Competitive commerce (Value)	Established clientele (Trust)	Personal patronage (Taste)
Fiscal Allocation Mechanisms:	Block grants to local districts	Categorical aids to specific programs	Categorical aids to specialist groups	Block grants to individual schools

Work Structure to Be Supported

FIGURE [2] Non-Labor Relations Policy Strategies Related to Marketing and Financing Educational Services

market mechanism that will protect the large capital investments needed to sustain a craft industry. Consumers seek a market where *value* rather than price forms the basis for decisions to buy. Autos and home appliances illustrate these problems clearly. In these industries brand names, a small number of large-scale producers (i.e., oligopolies), and consumer research and education systems play a prominent role in marketing. It is appropriate to say, therefore, that craft industries involve "competitive commerce" rather than commodity markets. Competitive commerce markets are characterized by intense product differentiation efforts and value-oriented advertising rather than simple price competition. The "human capital" approach to analyzing educational productivity reflects an adoption of this perspective.

Professional markets are even less competitive than craft markets. In this case, constraint on competition springs from the fact that consumers select professional services on the basis of whether they feel they can *trust* the professionals. That is, professional markets create "established clienteles" which are carefully cultivated by professional workers and are even passed from one professional to another through various systems of referrals. Prestige private schools clearly illustrate this market mechanism in education. The impact of school quality on neighborhood housing values reflects a similar market process for public school services.

Art markets are controlled by choices based on *taste*. Whatever one may think of designer blue jeans or Broadway musicals, it is clear that such art products acquire their worth to consumers through critical review and acclaim, not through any calculation of the labor costs of producing them. Thus art consumers develop a market structure organized around the personal patronage of recognized art producers and dealers. Art markets are also highly fragmented and pluralistic. One consumer's masterpiece is another's kitsch. To sell an art product one must locate consumers who have the appropriate inclinations and tastes. In public education, this type of market structure is implicit in the fact that parents express great concern over which teachers their children will receive. The artistic (taste) rather than craft (value) basis to this concern is reflected in the fact that parents with very similar educational values

will still demand that their children be placed with *different* teachers.

At present, education, like other governmental services, has a rather weak market system. To be sure, homes are frequently purchased on the basis of the school systems which serve them, and private education is frequently purchased by those who can afford it. Financial support for education, however, is largely controlled through legislative tax and budget decisions which have a powerful but indirect impact on educational market processes and work structures. . . .

Management Staff Development Options. Figure [3] outlines alternative staff development and training approaches that can be used to help principals and other middle managers support particular teaching work structures. As the arrows on this figure suggest, the relationships between managerial style and work structure fall along a continuum. Laboring work structures call for an emphasis on *direct control* of teacher work activities. The more the work is structured along artistic lines, however, the more managers must concentrate on stimulation, encouragement, or *socialization*.

When teaching is conceptualized as a laboring activity, the word "supervisor" captures the essence of the principal's work role. Supervision involves direct oversight of teacher work performance. To be effective, principals must learn to concentrate on consistency and stability in the interpretation and application of work rules. If they allow work expectations to vary greatly from day to day or from school to school, teachers can be expected to become confused and resentful of supervision.

"Manager" describes the principals' role when teaching is seen as a skilled craft. Management by principals is improved if they are trained in skillful definition of work goals and careful coordination of work activities to reach those goals. Thus, management training for principals must include thorough grounding in the techniques of effective teaching and knowledge of how to assist teachers in applying these techniques in the classroom.

For teachers to work as professionals, principals need to view themselves as "administrators." Effective administration involves the maintenance of adequate support services (such as budget making, food services, transportation, etc.) and the articulation of a system of ethical norms which are

Work Structure to Be Supported

	Labor	Craft	Profession	Art
Encourage Principals to Be:	Supervisors	Managers	Administrators	Leaders
(Emphasizing)	(Consistency and stability)	(Skill and coordination)	(Ethics and support services)	(Sensitivity and spontaneity)
Enhance the Quality and Importance of:	Direct oversight	Technique application	Peer review	Critical review

———— More Emphasis on Socialization ————→

←———— More Emphasis on Direct Control ————

FIGURE [3]   Non-Labor Relations Policy Strategies Related to Staff Development for Principals and Middle Managers

expected to guide professionals in the conduct of their work. Principals expected to support a professional work structure need to understand the details of support service operations and to know how to keep these support services functioning efficiently. Rather than personally evaluating teacher job performance, principals being asked to adopt this view of teaching need to be trained to organize and implement a system of *peer* review. Professional teachers need to believe that they have a formal responsibility for evaluation of their peers in order to prevent malpractice and secure public respect for the profession.

In order for teaching to be seen as an art, principals need to see themselves primarily as "leaders." They must learn how to encourage sensitivity and spontaneous creativity among teachers and will need to express these qualities in their own work. Leadership in the art of teaching means providing effective critical reviews of teacher performance. Quality art is stimulated and improved when talented performances are given critical acclaim and when uninspired work is explicitly recognized as such. Criticism is a particularly difficult social process to institutionalize. A delicate balance must be maintained between the need for public reviews, which help to define the meaning of good art for everyone, and private criticism, which helps the individual performer to recognize strengths and weaknesses. In the fine arts (music, drama, painting, etc.) public criticism is

usually undertaken by individuals not directly involved in the creation of the art products. Private criticism is undertaken by directors, teachers, and fellow performers in order to improve the product, but usually without an attempt being made to influence public acceptance of it. School principals, unfortunately, have been cast in a role which requires them to both nurture public support and stimulate teacher excellence. It is important for them to learn, therefore, to distinguish help for individual teachers from efforts aimed at shaping the overall quality of school programs. For the artistic teacher, principals must learn to become connoisseurs of live performances and critics of artistic technique. For the public the principal is a reviewer and critical evaluator— one who defines "good taste" in educational services.

CONCLUSION

. . . [W]e have argued that labor, craft, professional, and artistic work structures rely on different approaches to task definition and worker oversight. We have described the ways in which teacher organizations and collective bargaining encourage the adoption of a laboring conception of teaching work. And we have indicated how this tendency toward a laboring paradigm can be either strengthened or ameliorated by key public policy choices.

In closing we want to underscore two obvious

facts about the relationship between making policy and educating children. First, policymakers may influence teachers, but they do not control the learning process. If policies are based on an inadequate understanding of learning processes, education will be hampered rather than facilitated. Policies that encourage laboring behavior will not help children who need the services of craft, professional, or artistic teachers. Second, policy analyses such as the one presented here can help to clarify what *will* happen if different policy decisions are taken, but they cannot determine what *ought* to happen in society. If policymakers encourage craftsmanship among teachers when the public is seeking a more artistic approach to education, the result will be deflection of effort rather than realization of the public interest. In short, policy analysis is no substitute for either a knowledge of how children learn or an understanding of the goals of public education. In the final analysis, no policy can be better than the statesmanship of political leaders or the wisdom of educational scholars.

Our analysis suggests that careful attention to the implicit assumptions and natural consequences of specific choices is necessary if policymakers are to avoid damaging the capacity of the schools to educate or breaking the fragile link between public goals and the intrinsic character of teaching and learning processes. Care must be taken to ensure that policies do not become mutually contradictory and self-destructive. Supporting a proper balance of labor, craft, art, and professional work structures requires that tough-minded and careful political choices be made.

REFERENCES

Eberts, R. W. and Pierce, L. C. *The effect of collective bargaining in public schools.* Eugene, OR: University of Oregon, College of Education, 1980.

Gonder, P. O. *Collective bargaining problems and solutions.* Arlington, VA: American Assn. of School Administrators, 1981.

Gouldner, A. *Patterns of industrial bureaucracy.* New York: Free Press, 1954.

House, E. R. *The politics of educational evaluation.* Berkeley, CA: McCutchan Publishing Company, 1974.

Kerchner, C. T. From scopes to scope: The genetic mutation of the school control issue. *Educational Administration Quarterly,* 1978, *14,* 64–79.

Lutz, F. W. and Iannaccone, L. *Public participation in local school districts.* Lexington, MA: Lexington Books, D. C. Heath, 1978.

McDonnell, L. and Pascal, A. *Organized teachers in American schools.* Santa Monica, CA: Rand Corporation, 1979.

Meyer, J. W. and Rowan, B. The structure of educational organizations. In M. W. Meyer and Associates, *Environments and organizations.* San Francisco: Jossey-Bass, 1978, pp. 79–109.

Mitchell, D. E. The impact of collective bargaining on public and client interests in education. *Teachers College Record,* 1979, *4,* 695–717.

Mitchell, D. E., Kerchner, C. T., Erck, W., and Pryor, G. The impact of collective bargaining on school management and policy. *American Journal of Education,* 1981, *89,* 147–188.

Taylor, F. W. *Principles of scientific management.* New York: Harper, 1911.

Time. How to protect tender minds. *Time,* December 15, 1980, *116*(24), 77.

Weber, M. *The theory of social and economic organization.* New York: Oxford University Press, 1947. Translation by A. M. Henderson and T. Parsons.

This research is, in part, supported by National Institute of Education Grant No. NIE-G-79-0036. Exploratory research on the same subject was aided by a grant from the Eli Lilly Endowment to Charles Kerchner. However, the conclusions reached and the opinions offered do not necessarily reflect those of the Institute, the Endowment, or the staffs of either organization.

7. IMPROVING THE PRODUCTIVITY OF AMERICA'S SCHOOLS
Herbert J. Walberg

Education may be our largest enterprise in terms of the numbers of people involved, the value of human time required, and the capital and operating expenditures budgeted. The value of education invested in the American labor force, for example, is now $815 billion compared to $65 billion in 1900 (Walberg, 1983).

In the last few decades, moreover, spending on

schools and colleges accelerated: it rose from $11 billion to $200 billion per year; from 3.4 to 6.8 percent of the gross national product. During the past half century, the inflation-adjusted annual cost of public-school education rose about five-fold from $490 to $2,500 per student (Walberg, 1984).

EDUCATION: A DECLINING INDUSTRY?

Even though costs have risen, the National Commission on Excellence in Education (1983) and other groups report that students appear to be learning less. For example, comparisons made a decade or two ago showed that American students did relatively poorly. Although comparing achievements of U.S. students with those from countries with more homogenous populations, national ministries of education, and centralized control can be misleading, the differences are striking enough to compel attention to our assumptions and practices.

Recent studies provide a grim picture of U.S. achievement even in the elementary grades. Stevenson (1983) found that in mathematics, U.S. students fell farther behind the Japanese and Taiwanese at each grade level; and, by 5th grade, the worst Asian classes in his large sample exceeded the best American class. My research and observations in elementary science classes in Japan corroborate his findings. Recent achievement comparisons in high school mathematics also showed that American high school students score on average at the first or second percentile of Japanese norms (Walberg, 1983; Walberg, Harnish, and Tsai, 1984).

Thus, by measurable standards, U.S. educational productivity has not kept up even with that of U.S. smokestack industries such as steel, automobiles, and consumer electronics—which themselves are declining as world-class competitors in quality and costs. Of course, neither the costs of educational inputs, including human effort, nor the value of outputs relevant to immediate and long-term goals are well measured. For that reason it is difficult to arrive at definitive conclusions about the causal relations of educational investments, services, and values beyond the narrow areas indicated by objective achievement tests and reports of attitudes and behavior. Nevertheless, since 1975 my colleagues and I have tried to develop a comprehensive frame-

work for the analysis of productivity and test it out in a variety of classroom studies in the U.S. and other countries.

RESEARCH APPROACH

Following the lead of early agricultural experimentation, much educational research focuses on the relation of single causes and effects. Education, however, obviously involves many means and ends, each with an explicit or implicit cost or value. The promotion of efficiency requires the specification and measurement of the chief causes, means, or "factors" of production.

Experiments and statistical studies of productivity data together with cost and value estimates have enabled a wide variety of industries to increase the value of their output while simultaneously reducing costs, thereby raising human welfare. Although such thinking may seem alien to some educators, the public ranks research on educational productivity higher in priority than scientific investigation in most other natural and social sciences (Gallup, 1983; Walberg, 1983); and we educators may do well to think more explicitly and unsentimentally about our business and to try to found it on the emerging consensus of scientific evidence.

It should also be said, however, that we are far from being able to estimate explicit costs and values. The prior problem, now being solved, is estimating the magnitude of effects of educational inputs on outputs, which primarily involves causal rather than value questions.

A THEORY OF EDUCATIONAL PRODUCTIVITY

Nine factors require optimization to increase affective, behavioral, and cognitive learning (see Figure 1). Potent, consistent, and widely generalizable, these nine factors fall into three groups:

Student aptitude includes:
1. Ability or prior achievement, as measured by the usual standardized tests
2. Development, as indexed by chronological age or stage of maturation, and

FIGURE 1   Causal Influences on Student Learning

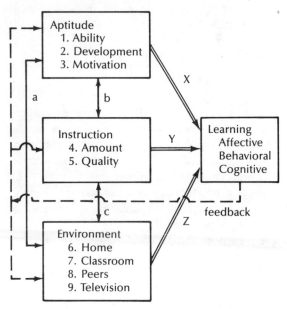

Aptitude, instruction, and the psychological environment are major direct causes of learning (shown as double arrows X, Y, and Z). They also influence one another (shown as arrows a, b, and c), and are in turn influenced by feedback on the amount of learning that takes place (shown as broken arrows).

3. Motivation, or self-concept, as indicated by personality tests or the student's willingness to persevere intensively on learning tasks.
   Instruction includes:
4. The amount of time students engage in learning and
5. The quality of the instructional experience, including psychological and curricular aspects.
   Four environmental factors also consistently affect learning: the educationally stimulating, psychological climates of
6. The home,
7. The classroom social group,
8. The peer group outside the school, and
9. Use of out-of-school time (specifically, the amount of leisure-time television viewing).

The first five aspects of student aptitude and instruction are prominent in the educational models of Benjamin Bloom, Jerome Bruner, John Carrol, Robert Glaser, and others (see Walberg, 1984, for

a comparative analysis); each appears necessary for learning in school; without at least a small amount of each, the student can learn little. Large amounts of instruction and high degrees of ability, for example, may count for little if students are unmotivated or instruction is unsuitable.

These five essential factors, however, are only partly alterable by educators since, for example, the curriculum in terms of lengths of time devoted to various subjects and activities is partly determined by diverse economic, political, and social forces. Ability and motivation, moreover, are influenced by parents, by prior learning, and by the students themselves. Thus educators are unlikely to raise achievement substantially by their own efforts alone.

Three of the remaining factors—the psychological climate of the classroom group; enduring affection and academic stimulation from adults at home; and an out-of-school peer group with learning interests, goals, and activities—influence learning in two ways: students learn from them directly, and these factors indirectly benefit learning by raising student ability, motivation, and responsiveness to instruction. In addition, about ten (not the more typical 30) weekly hours of television time seems optimal for learning; more hours than this displace homework and other educationally and developmentally constructive activities outside school.

As Figure 1 shows, the major causal influences flow from aptitudes, instruction, and the psychological environment to learning. In addition, however, these factors also influence one another, and are influenced in turn by how much students learn, since those who begin well learn faster (Walberg, 1984a).

Other factors influence learning in school but are less directly linked to academic learning. For example, class size, financial expenditures per student, and private governance (independent or sectarian in contrast to public control of schools) correlate only weakly with learning, especially if the initial abilities of students are considered. Thus, improvements in the more direct and more alterable factors hold the best hope for increasing educational productivity (Walberg and Shanahan, 1983).

APPLIED RESEARCH

Unlike other national studies of education that have relied on hearings and testimony, our investigations of educational productivity followed applied research in the natural sciences in several respects (Walberg, 1983a). The theory of educational productivity (discussed above) which guided the inquiry (Walberg, 1981) is sufficiently explicit to test; and, using large bodies of national and international data, a wide variety of empirical studies of it was conducted.

We published about two dozen of these empirical studies in research journals of the American Educational Research Association and the American Psychological Association that require review by referees as in other scientific disciplines. Only after extensive observation and some modifications of the theory (notably the addition of television and peer group to the list of major factors) were the implications drawn in professional and policy journals such as *Educational Leadership* and *Daedalus*. Like other explicit scientific theories, however, the theory of educational productivity should be considered open to disproof in part or whole by empirical contradiction.

In our investigations, we tried to follow three scientific canons—parsimony, replication, and generalizability. Parsimony means that the theory converges on the least number of factors that powerfully and consistently predict or explain cognitive, affective, and behavioral learning.

In this regard, the theory is reductionist and psychological: it fundamentally assumes that academic learning is an individual affective, behavioral, and cognitive activity that mainly takes place in the social context of the classroom group as well as in the home and peer groups. This is not to deny the influence of Washington, the statehouse, the community, the superintendent, and principal but to encourage examination of their effects on the nine factors directly impinging on individual students.

Thus, from our view, school and district economic, political, and sociological characteristics are less relevant to learning because their influences are less alterable, direct, and observable. They are not substitutes for the nine factors, but more distant forces that can support or interfere with them.

More and less productive classes, moreover, may be expected in the same school; and it is somewhat misleading to characterize a whole school or district as effective—just as it is less accurate to speak of the optimal condition for plant growth as being the average annual rainfall in a state rather than the amount of moisture reaching the roots of a single plant.

The educational productivity theory itself is admittedly simplified because learning is clearly affected by school and district characteristics as well as by many economic, sociological, and political forces at the school, community, state, and national levels. Yet these characteristics and forces—such as the sex, ethnicity, and socioeconomic status of the student, the size and expenditure levels of schools and district, and their political and sociological organization—are less alterable in a democratic, pluralistic society; are less consistently and powerfully linked to learning; and appear to operate mainly through the nine factors in the determination of achievement. Thus, we offer our theory not as a threat to those concerned about these other factors but as a friendly, collegial invitation to demonstrate their effects on the nine factors or directly on the outcomes of schooling.

The canon of *replication,* means that the findings in similarly designed studies should reproduce one another fairly closely. For example, reinforcement or reward of learning has been implemented in various forms such as candy, tokens, symbols, and social recognition; it can be and usually is operationally defined in various studies. The question is whether these forms are the same or different in their effects.

To answer this question, the various implementations or strategies grouped under the same category may be more finely categorized and empirically compared in their effects on learning to see if their magnitudes are the same or different. Simple rather than complicated, detailed classifications usually serve to summarize the findings; and these relatively simple findings suggest educational implications that are convenient and practical to implement.

Generalizability means that studies should yield similar results in national and international samples of students of different characteristics such as sex and age, in different subjects such as civics and science, and using different research methods such as surveys, case studies, and experiments (Walberg, 1983a). For example, the effects of mastery learning on different types of students and in different school subjects and grade levels may be estimated to determine the extent of their generality.

What has been empirically found in thousands of studies is that generally the results are surprisingly robust. Echoing the folk adage, what's good for the goose is good for the gander.

But there are exceptions to the results reported below. The more powerful factors appear to benefit all students in all conditions; but some students appear to benefit somewhat more than others under some conditions. In addition, some studies report larger effects than the averages given below; others, of course, report smaller effects than the average. The cited research should be consulted for details.

METHODS OF RESEARCH

Since our concern was productivity, we hoped that our own research would efficiently capitalize on previous inquiry; and, under the support of the National Institute of Education and the National Science Foundation, our team of investigators started by compiling reviews of the 1970s on the productive factors in learning (Walberg, Schiller, and Haertel, 1979; Waxman and Walberg, 1982). Next, quantitative syntheses of all available studies of productive factors were conducted; syntheses of nearly 3,000 investigations—summarized below—were compiled (see Walberg, 1984c, for a more detailed account). Case studies of Japanese and American classes were carried out to compare educational productivity in the two countries (Schiller and Walberg, 1982; Walberg, 1983).

The productive factors were further probed for their significance in promoting learning in three large sets of statistical data on elementary and high school students—the National Assessment of Educational Progress, High School and Beyond, and the International Study of Educational Achievement (Walberg, 1984c; Walberg and Shanahan, 1983; and Walberg, Harnisch, and Tsai, 1984). Finally, large-scale studies were made of the most effective ways of assisting educators to bring about constructive changes in schools (Walberg and Genova, 1982).

RESULTS

Collectively the various studies suggest that the three groups of previously-defined nine factors are powerful and consistent in influencing learning. Syntheses

Aptitude	Effect	Size
Ability		
IQ	.71	XXXXXXX
IQ (Science)	.48	XXXXX
Development		
Piagetian Stage	.47	XXXXX
Pia. Stage (Science)	.40	XXXX
Motivation		
Motivation	.34	XXX
Self-Concept	.18	XX

Note: The X symbols represent the sizes of the correlation coefficients in numbers of tenths.

FIGURE 2 Influences of Aptitudes on Learning

of about 3,000 studies suggest that these generalizable factors are the chief influences on cognitive, affective, and behavioral learning (see Figures 2 through 4). Many aspects of these factors can be altered or influenced by educators.

The first five essential factors appear to substitute, compensate, or trade-off for one another at diminishing rates of return. Immense quantities of time, for example, may be required for a moderate amount of learning if motivation, ability, or instructional quality is minimal. Thus, no single essential factor overwhelms the others; all appear important.

Although the other factors are consistent correlates of academic learning, they may directly supplement as well as indirectly influence the essential classroom factors. In either case, the powerful influences of out-of-school factors, especially the home environment, must be considered.

For example, the 12 years of 180 six-hour days in elementary and secondary school add up to only about 13 percent of the waking, potentially-educative time during the first 18 years of life. If a large fraction of the student's waking time nominally under the control of parents that is spent outside school were to be spent in academically-stimulating conditions in the home and peer group, then the total amount of the student's total learning time would be dramatically raised beyond the 13 percent of the time in conventional American schools.

For instance, the mere four or five hours per week high school students typically devote to home-

Method	Effect	Size
Reinforcement	1.17	XXXXXXXXXXX
Acceleration	1.00	XXXXXXXXXX
Reading Training	.97	XXXXXXXXXX
Cues and Feedback	.97	XXXXXXXXXX
Science Mastery Learning	.81	XXXXXXXX
Cooperative Learning	.76	XXXXXXXX
Reading Experiments	.60	XXXXX
Personalized Instruction	.57	XXXXX
Adaptive Instruction	.45	XXXXX
Tutoring	.40	XXXX
Individualized Science	.35	XXXX
Higher-Order Questions	.34	XXX
Diagnostic Prescriptive Methods	.33	XXX
Individualized Instruction	.32	XXX
Individualized Mathematics	.32	XXX
New Science Curricula	.31	XXX
Teacher Expectations	.28	XXX
Computer Assisted Instruction	.24	XX
Sequenced Lessons	.24	XX
Advance Organizers	.23	XX
New Mathematics Curricula	.18	XX
Inquiry Biology	.16	XX
Homogeneous Groups	.10	X
Class Size	.09	X
Programmed Instruction	− .03	− .
Mainstreaming	− .12	− X.
Instructional Time	.38	XXXX

Note: The X symbols represent the sizes of effects in tenths of standard deviations.

FIGURE 3   Instructional Quality and Time Effects on Learning

work might be supplemented by some of the 28 hours per week they spend viewing television (Walberg and Shanahan, 1983). Europeans and Japanese believe homework helps learning; empirical results of American research summarized below support their belief.

SPECIFIC EFFECTS

Figures 2 through 4 show the numerical results of syntheses of several thousand studies of academic learning conducted during the past half century. Interested readers and those who wish technical details may examine the findings and methods reported in the compilations of these syntheses (cited in the references), which, in turn, contain references to the original studies. (In several instances, separate estimates of correlations and effects are available for science and mathematics because the National Science Foundation awarded grants for special syn-

thesis projects on these two subjects. The tables contain both effects and correlations, and the correlations assume a one-standard deviation rise in the independent variable).

Method	Effect	[Size]
Graded Homework	.79	XXXXXXX
Class Morale	.60	XXXXX
Home Interventions	.50	XXXXX
Home Environment	.37	XXXX
Assigned Homework	.28	XXX
Socioeconomic Status	.25	XXX
Peer Group	.24	XX
Television	− .05	X.

Note: The X symbols represent the sizes of effects in tenths of standard deviations or correlations.

FIGURE 4   Home, Peer, Class Morale, and Media Effects

STUDENT APTITUDE

Figure 2 shows that IQ is a strong correlate of general academic learning but only a moderately strong correlate of science learning. A student's Piagetian stage of development correlates moderately with both general and science learning. By comparison, motivation and self-concept are weaker correlates.

Student aptitudes as a set may be less alterable than instruction. Yet positive home environments and good instruction affect them (Figure 1); and, since they are powerful correlates of learning, they deserve inclusion in theories of educational productivity.

THE LARGEST INSTRUCTIONAL EFFECTS

Figure 3 shows the effects of various aspects and methods of instruction. Of all the factors in the table, the psychological components of mastery learning rank first and fourth in their effects on educational outcomes: Skinnerian reinforcement or reward for correct performance has the largest overall average effect—1.17 standard deviations; instructional cues, engagement, and corrective feedback have effects equal to approximately one standard deviation. Separate syntheses of mastery programs in science show an average effect of .8.

Acceleration programs, ranked second in effect, provide advanced activities to elementary and high school students with outstanding test scores. Students in these programs gain much more than comparable control groups.

Reading training, ranked third in instructional impact, refers to programs that coach learners in adjusting reading speed and techniques to purposes such as skimming, comprehension, and finding answers to questions. The usual learning criterion in evaluating these programs is learner adaptability to purpose.

OTHER LARGE EFFECTS

Several other instructional programs and methods have strong effects ranging from .3 to .8. These include cooperative-team learning in which some autonomy over the means and pace of learning is delegated to students who help each other in small groups.

Personalized and adaptive instruction, tutoring, and diagnostic-prescriptive methods also have strong effects. Personalized learning, sometimes called "the Keller Plan," is similar to mastery learning in mainly eliminating lectures and recitations but guiding each student by entry tests and written lessons plus individual help. Adaptive instruction uses similar techniques plus work in small groups and differentiated staffing to increase learning.

Tutoring and lesson prescriptions based on diagnosed individual needs are similar ways to adapt instruction to learners rather than batch-processing them. These related methods may attain their success by helping students to concentrate on the specific goals they individually need to achieve, or by freeing them from the pervasive seatwork and recitation in groups that may suit only the middle third of the students.

MODERATE AND SMALL EFFECTS OF INSTRUCTION

Although many schools no longer use the science and mathematics curricula created in the decade after Sputnik in 1957, several syntheses of their evaluations show that they had moderate effects on learning.

High teacher expectations for student performance also have a moderate effect, on average, as do advance organizers, which are "cognitive maps" showing the relationship of material to be learned in a lesson to concepts learned in previous lessons.

Some highly touted programs have had small and even negative effects on average (shown in the lower part of Figure 3). Reduced class size, for example, has small positive effects but is expensive and draws money and effort away from factors with large effects.

(Japanese school classes often run three times the current U.S. average of 17 students per class; yet they consistently rank highest among nations compared in mathematics and science achievement. With fixed or declining budgets for U.S. education, we may face the trade-off of sharply increasing teachers' salaries and incentives—which may help the morale and productivity of a smaller, elite workforce—*versus* keeping class sizes far smaller than the averages of the first seven decades of American education in this century.)

The effect reported for computer-assisted instruction is deceptively small. Most of the research was conducted with drill-and-practice or "page-turning" programs rather than the more psychologically sophisticated ones now being developed. Because future programs will be able to adapt to learner interests and abilities, they are likely to show large effects (Walberg, 1983). (However, educators may have to wait a decade or two before such effects are demonstrated. Accumulating closets full of unused or usable computers today may deter valid and efficient use of much better ones later.)

QUANTITY AND INSTRUCTION

Instructional time, as shown in the last line of Figure 3, has an overall correlation of about .4 with learning outcomes. It is neither the chief determinant nor a weak correlate of learning; like the other essential factors, time appears to be a necessary ingredient but insufficient by itself to produce learning.

For at least two reasons, time is a particularly interesting factor: first, several national reports have called attention to the need for lengthening the school day and year to the levels of other countries, particularly Japan and Western Europe (National Commission, 1983; Walberg, 1983).

Second, time is the only factor that can be roughly measured on a ratio scale with equal intervals between scale points and a true zero point. Perhaps because it can be measured on an absolute scale resembling capital and labor inputs to production processes in agriculture and industry, time has shown diminishing returns (Frederick and Walberg, 1980): equal additions of time, with other factors held fixed, yield ever smaller gains in learning, which suggests that neither time alone nor any other factor by itself can solve the productivity problem.

It is also reasonable to think that zero time results in zero learning no matter what the level of the other factors, and, to generalize, that each of the other essential factors, if well measured, would prove necessary but insufficient by itself and would show diminishing returns—thus the possible danger of concentrating on any one factor alone.

Since the other factors are not measured as universally and precisely as time, this remains a matter of speculation. But it can be concluded that learning is produced jointly by several factors rather than any one by itself. A preliminary estimate suggests that optimizing all of the factors simultaneously is associated with an effect of about 3.7, which is about three times the 1.2 effect of the most powerful factor, reinforcement, by itself and nearly 15 times the effect of socioeconomic status (Horn and Walberg, 1984).

ENVIRONMENTS

Figure 4 shows the major results of syntheses of the supportive or supplementary factors. Ignored in several national reports and in instructional theories, these factors have strong influences on learning. The psychological morale or climate of the classroom group, for example, strongly predicts end-of-course measures of affective, behavioral, and cognitive learning. Morale refers to the cohesiveness, satisfaction, goal direction, and related social-psychological properties or climate of the classroom group perceived by students. By comparison, the influence of the peer-group outside of school is moderate and comparable to the influence of the student's socioeconomic status (SES).

As also shown in Figure 4, homework that is graded or commented upon has three times the effect of SES. By comparison, homework that is merely assigned has an effect comparable to SES. More than about 12 per weekly hours of leisure-time television viewing, perhaps because it displaces more educationally-constructive home activities, has a weak negative or deleterious influence on school learning.

In addition to increasing supervised homework and reducing television viewing, school-parent programs to improve academic conditions in the home have an outstanding record of success in promoting achievement. What might be called "the alterable curriculum of the home" is twice as predictive of academic learning as is family SES.

This curriculum refers to informed parent-child conversations about school and everyday events; encouragement and discussion of leisure reading; monitoring and joint critical analysis of television viewing and peer activities; deferral of immediate gratifications to accomplish long-term human-capital goals; expressions of affection and interest in the child's academic and other progress as a person; and perhaps, among such unremitting efforts, smiles, laughter, caprice, and serendipity.

Cooperative efforts by parents and educators to modify these alterable academic conditions in the home have strong, beneficial effects on learning. In 29 controlled studies of the past decade, 91 percent of the comparisons favored children in such programs over nonparticipant control groups. Although the average effect was twice that of SES, some programs had effects ten times as large; and the programs appear to benefit older as well as younger students.

Since few of the programs lasted more than a semester, the potential for those sustained over the years of schooling is great. On the other hand, it should be recognized that educators cannot carry out these programs by themselves; they require the concerted cooperation of parents, students, and other agents in the community.

AUTONOMOUS LEARNING

If education proceeds by fads rather than cumulative research, it will fail to make the great advances in productivity that have characterized agriculture and industry in this century. Syntheses of research on the effects of open education illustrate the dangers of basing conclusions, policies, and practices on single studies no matter how large or widely publicized. They also illustrate the strengths of replication and improved methods of synthesis, and a shortcoming of some of the research discussed above that employs grades and standardized achievement as the only outcome of education.

Open education has been dismissed by many educators, but syntheses of research now illuminate its beneficial effects. From the start, open educators tried to encourage educational outcomes that reflect teacher, parent, student, and school board goals such as cooperation, critical thinking, self-reliance, constructive attitudes, life-long learning, and other objectives that technically oriented psychometrists seldom measure. Raven's (1981) summary of surveys in Western countries, including England and the United States, shows that, when given a choice, educators, parents, and students rank these goals above standardized test scores and school marks.

Moreover, a synthesis of the relation between grades and adult success shows their slight association (Samson and others, 1984). Thirty-three post-1949 studies of the college and professional-school grades of physicians, engineers, civil servants, teachers, and other groups show an average correlation of .155 of these educational outcomes with life-success indicators such as income; self-rated happiness; work performance and output indexes; and self-, peer-, and supervisor-ratings of occupational effectiveness.

These results should challenge educators and researchers to seek a balance between continuing autonomy, motivation, responsibility, and skills to learn new tasks as an individual or group member on one hand and memorization of teacher-chosen, textbook knowledge that may soon be obsolete or forgotten on the other. Perhaps since Socrates, however, these views have remained so polarized that educators find it difficult to stand firmly on the high middle ground of balanced or cooperative teacher-student determination of the goals, means, and evaluation of learning.

Progressive education, the Dalton and Winnetka plans, team teaching, and the ungraded school, and other innovations in this century—all held forth this or a similar ideal but drifted into authoritarianism, permissiveness, or confusion. They were difficult to sustain as idealized.

Although open education, like its precursors, faded from view, it was more massively researched by dozens of investigators whose work goes little noted. Perhaps the syntheses of this research may be useful to educators who want to base practice on synthesized knowledge rather than on fads, or to those who will evaluate future descendants of open education.

Hedges, Giaconia, and Gage (1981) synthesized 153 studies of open education, including 90 dissertations. The average effect was near zero for achievement, locus of control, self-concept, and anxiety (which suggests no difference between open and control classes on this criteria). About .2 for adjustment, attitude toward schools and teachers, curiosity, and general mental ability; and about a moderate .3 for cooperativeness, creativity, and independence. Thus, students in open classes do no worse in standardized achievement and slightly to moderately better on several outcomes that educators, parents and students hold to be of great value.

Unfortunately, the negative conclusion of Bennett's (1976) single study—introduced by a prominent psychologist, published by Harvard University Press, publicized by *The New York Times* and by experts that take the press as their source—trumpeted the failure of open education, even though the conclusion of the study was later retracted (Aitkin, Bennett, and Hesketh, 1981) because of obvious statistical flaws in the original analysis (Aitkin, Anderson, and Hinde, 1981).

Giaconia and Hedges (1982) took another recent and constructive step in the synthesis of open education research. From their prior synthesis, they identified the studies with the largest positive and negative effects on several outcomes to differentiate more and less effective program features. They found that programs that are more effective in producing the nonachievement outcomes—attitude, creativity, and self-concept—sacrificed academic achievement on standardized measures.

These programs were characterized by emphasis on the role of the child in learning, use of diagnostic rather than norm-referenced evaluation, individualized instruction, and manipulative materials but not three other components sometimes thought essential to open programs—multi-age grouping, open space, and team teaching. Giaconia and Hedges speculate that children in the most extreme open programs may do somewhat less well on conventional achievement tests because they have little experience with them. At any rate, it appears from the two most comprehensive syntheses of effects that open classes on average enhance several nonstandard outcomes without detracting from academic achievement unless they are radically extreme.

CAVEATS AND CONCLUSIONS

Research workers and educators should retain both openmindedness and skepticism about educational productivity and syntheses of research. Yet the present does seem a period of quiet accomplishment. In a short time, research synthesis and other comprehensive approaches helped sort what is known from what needs to be known about some important means and ends of education.

Agriculture, engineering, and medicine made great strides in improving human welfare as doubts arose about traditional, natural, and mystical practices, as the widened measurement of results intensified, as experimental findings were synthesized, and as their theoretical and practical implications were coordinated and vigorously implemented and evaluated. Education is no less open to humanistic and scientific inquiry and no lower in priority since half the workers in modern nations are in knowledge industries, and the value of investments in people is now more apparent than ever (Walberg, 1983). Although more and better research is required, synthesis points the way toward improvements that seem likely to increase teaching effectiveness and educational productivity.

In addition, we educators can learn more from our past successes and failures in using scarce resources, especially human time, to meet competing goals. Recent national reports may rightly call for more emphasis on academic subject matter, and the National Commission on Excellence (1983) seems right in emphasizing the need for more time in school. But students should also be employing more time in academic pursuits outside the school and using both in-school and out-of-school time more efficiently.

Synthesis of educational and psychological research in ordinary schools shows that improving the amount and quality of instruction can result in vastly more effective and efficient academic learning. Educators can do even more by also enlisting families as partners and engaging them directly and indirectly in their efforts.

The present overview of a vast amount of research cannot substitute for selectively reading some of the several dozen syntheses and thousands of studies conducted in the past half century. Since many details are omitted here, reading the original material might promote a more complete and critical understanding of specific factors and methods. For example, although the factors that have large effects are robustly positive, exceptional conditions can reduce their effectiveness.

Finally, educational costs and goals beyond immediate measurement are worth remembering. But great accomplishments also result from sustained hard work, supportive parents, and world-class standards and instruction. Psychological studies of the lives of eminent painters, writers, musicians, philosophers, scientists, and religious and political leaders of past centuries as well as prize-winning adolescents of today reveal early, intense, and sustained concentration as well as parents and teachers who sacrificed much to help them.

World-class performance may require 70 hours of effective instruction and practice per week for a decade (Walberg, 1983). It may take considerably more—or perhaps less. The fact that we cannot say shows how much more we need to know about investing in students—and how much more seriously educators and their allies might take the idea of improving their productivity.

REFERENCES

Aitkin, M.; Anderson, D.; and Hinde, J. "Modeling of Data on Teaching Styles (with Discussion)." *Journal of the Royal Statistical Society, Series A* 144 (1981): 419–461.

Aitkin, M.; Bennett, S.N.; and Hesketh, J. "Teaching Styles and Pupil Progress: A Re-Analysis." *British Journal of Educational Psychology* 51 (1984), in press.

Bennett, S.N. *Teaching Styles and Pupil Progress.* London: Open Books, 1976.

Gallup, G.H. "The 15th Annual Gallup Poll of the Public's Attitudes Toward the Schools." *Phi Delta Kappan* 65, 1 (1983): 33–47.

Giaconia, R.M., and Hedges, L.V. *Identifying Features of Open Education.* Stanford, Calif.: Stanford Center for Educational Research, 1982.

Hedges, L.V.; Giaconia, R.M.; and Gage, N.L. *Meta-Analysis of the Effects of Open and Traditional Instruction.* Stanford, Calif.: Stanford University Program on Teaching Effectiveness, 1981.

Horn, A., and Walberg, H.J. "Achievement and Attitude as Functions of Quantity and Quality of Instruction." *Journal of Educational Research* (1984), in press.

National Commission on Excellence in Education. *A Nation at Risk.* Washington, D.C.: U.S. Government Printing Office, 1983.

Raven, J. "The Most Important Problem in Education is to Come to Terms With Values." *Oxford Review of Education* 7 (1981): 253–272.

Samson, G.; Crane, M.F.; Weinstein, T.; and Walberg, H.J. "Academic and Occupational Performance: A Quantitative Synthesis." *American Educational Research Journal* (1984), in press.

Schiller, D.P., and Walberg, H.J. "Japan: The Learning Society." *Educational Leadership* 39 (March 1982): 411–413.

Stevenson, H. *Comparisons of Japanese, Taiwanese, and American Mathematics Achievement.* Stanford, Calif.: Center for Advanced Study in the Behavioral Sciences, 1983.

Walberg, H.J. "A Psychological Theory of Educational Productivity." In *Psychology and Education.* Edited by F.H. Farley and N. Gordon. Berkeley, Calif.: McCutchan, 1981.

Walberg, H.J. "Scientific Literacy and Economic Productivity in International Perspective." *Daedalus* 112 (1983): 1–28.

Walberg, H.J. "Families as Partners in Educational Productivity," *Phil Delta Kappan* (1984a), in press.

Walberg, H.J. "Quantification Reconsidered." In *Review of Research in Education.* Edited by E. Gordon. Washington, D.C.: American Educational Research Association, 1984b.

Walberg, H.J. "Synthesis of Research on Teaching." In *Handbook of Research on Teaching.* Edited by M.C. Wittrock. Washington, D.C.: American Educational Research Association, 1984c.

Walberg, H.J., and Genova, W.J. "Staff, School, and Workshop Influences on Knowledge Use in Educational Improvement Efforts." *Journal of Educational Research* 72 (1982): 69–80.

Walberg, H.J.; Harnisch, D.; and Tsai, S.L. "High School Productivity in Twelve Countries." *Journal of Educational Research* (1984), in press.

Walberg, H.J.; Schiller, D.P.; and Haertel, G.D. "The Quiet Revolution in Educational Research." *Phi Delta Kappan* 61, 3 (1979): 179–182.

Walberg, H.J., and Shanahan, T. "High School Effects on Individual Students." *Educational Researcher* 12, 7 (1983): 4–9.

Waxman, H.C., and Walberg, H.J. "The Relation of Teaching and Learning: A Review of Reviews." *Contemporary Education Review* 2 (1982): 103–120.

SCHOOLS AND CLASSROOMS

1. SYNTHESIS OF RESEARCH ON CLASSROOM MANAGEMENT

Edmund T. Emmer and Carolyn M. Evertson

Effective classroom management consists of teacher behaviors that produce high levels of student involvement in classroom activities, minimal amounts of student behaviors that interfere with the teacher's or other students' work, and efficient use of instructional time. These criteria have the advantage of being directly observable.

Classroom management should be viewed as one major dimension of effective teaching, rather than synonymous with it. Teachers also provide instruction, evaluate students, choose curriculum, promote self-adjustment, and influence student attitudes. Hence, effective teaching encompasses varying degrees of different tasks. But the centrality of classroom management to the teacher's role, as well as its relationship with learning, make it worth our while to inquire further about teacher behaviors that produce well-managed classrooms.

The "modern" era of research on classroom management began with Kounin's (1970) study of 49 first- and second-grade classrooms. Each class was videotaped for a full day. The behavior of selected children was coded for work involvement and deviancy every 12 seconds during student recitation and seatwork. Teacher behaviors were scored on the following variables.

"With-itness": the degree to which a teacher communicates awareness of student behavior; measured by computing the ratio of the number of times the teachers "desisted" (stopped) deviant behavior appropriately (caught the right student before the behavior spread or became more serious) to the total number of desist attempts.

Overlapping: teacher's ability to attend to more than one event or issue at a time. Such events occur when the teacher is busy in a recitation or involved with a group of children and deviant behavior or an interruption occurs. A high overlapping score means the teacher is able to handle simultaneous events smoothly, without becoming totally diverted by deviancy or "glued" to one activity.

Smoothness and momentum: aspects of the teacher's movement through different activities. Smoothness in moving through a lesson means not interrupting seatwork or an instructional sequence with irrelevant or tangential information, and not becoming diverted by behaviors or events that are not interfering in any noticeable manner. Momentum refers to avoiding behavior that slows down a lesson. Such behavior includes dwelling on a topic beyond what is necessary for the children's understanding, and focusing on a smaller subpart of an activity or instruction when it might have been dealt with as a whole. Although smoothness and momentum are conceptually different, they are highly correlated.

Group alerting: the teacher's attempts to keep children attentive when not reciting, that is, "on their toes" and with the group. The teacher can alert students by choosing reciters randomly, creating suspense, using chorus responses, or signaling children that they may be called on. Negative alerting is indicated by focusing on one reciter, choosing reciters before asking the question, or using a fixed sequence to call on students.

Accountability: how well the teacher monitors and maintains student performance during recitations. Accountability behaviors include requiring children to show work or recite as a group, calling for hands to show readiness to perform, or circulating to check students' work.

Valence and challenge arousal: the ratio of times the teacher uses a motivational comment (for example, "You'll enjoy the next problem") during a transition, compared to the total number of transitions.

Seatwork variety and challenge and *recitation variety and challenge:* the degree to which the child is presented with varied activities or task demands during a given time unit. A high score means relatively frequent shifts in activity focus or higher intellectual challenge as opposed to just listening, copying, or rote responding.

Kounin used each of the teacher variables as predictors with each of two student behaviors (work involvement and freedom from deviancy) in both recitation and seatwork activities. The results for work involvement and freedom from deviancy in recitation were similar. Correlations between these variables and with-itness, smoothness and momentum, and group alerting were high or moderate. Correlations with accountability, overlapping, and valence and challenge arousal were moderate. There were no significant correlations for seatwork variety or recitation variety.

The results for student involvement and freedom from deviancy during seatwork showed a different pattern, in part, from the results for recitation. With-itness and momentum/smoothness were moderately predictive of freedom from deviancy. The best predictor of involvement in seatwork was seatwork variety and challenge, at a moderately high level $r = .516$). It should be noted, however, that in an earlier videotape study using third- to fifth-grade classes, Kounin found a *negative* correlation between seatwork variety and challenge and involvement in seatwork.

Kounin's results were striking. Overall, he was able to predict management effectiveness at a high level with a set of relatively independent variables. This is evidenced by multiple correlations between the teacher variables and each of the student behaviors. The multiple correlations ranged from a low of .686 for involvement in seatwork to a high of .812 for involvement in recitation; the correlations for deviancy were in between. In addition, the teacher variables were carefully defined and described. Thus, considerable potential exists for translating the results into inservice and preservice teacher preparation programs.

We should note some cautions. The results are correlational; thus, we cannot be sure that the teacher variables caused the students' behaviors. It may be that when students are more work involved, it is easier for teachers to exhibit "with-it" behavior, that is, to make accurate and prompt desists. Other uncertainties are whether the results can be reproduced and whether they can be generalized to other settings, times of the year, or grade levels. Even accepting these results, how did the teachers and students develop the relationships and the patterns of behavior observed in the study? Subsequent research has shed light on some of these points.

LESSON FORMATS AND MANAGEMENT

Different lesson formats, such as small group recitations or seatwork, require different types of student and teacher behaviors. Lesson formats also elicit varying levels of student involvement. For example, Good and Beckerman (1978) observed greater amounts of pupil time-on-task in teacher-led large and small group activities than in either whole class or individual seatwork activities. Gump's analysis (1969) of a third-grade classroom obtained basically the same result: externally paced group activities had the highest pupil involvement (92 percent), followed by total class activities (81 percent), and self-paced activities (73 percent). Findings from the Beginning Teacher Evaluation Study, described later, also indicated higher student engagement rates in group settings than in independent seatwork. Teachers react differently to inappropriate behavior in varying lesson formats. Solomon and Kendall (1975) found higher rates of discipline and criticism in traditional versus open classrooms, without an observed difference in child misbehavior. A comparison of teacher "desist" statements in several third- and fourth-grade classrooms showed higher rates in recitation activities than in other activities such as seatwork or free-time (Bossert, 1977). These findings indicate that teachers are more sensitive to student misbehavior in certain settings and lesson formats than in others, and that student involvement is influenced by the type of activity.

The student or teacher behavior differences between lesson formats may result from the stronger signals or cues for attentive pupil behavior inherent in certain lesson formats. Kounin and Gump (1974), using videotapes of 596 lessons, contrasted those having high, average, and low pupil involvement. They found that the more successful lessons provided continuous cues for appropriate behavior and insulated students from external intrusions. For example, an individual construction activity has continuous cues because each step leads to the next. It is insulated because the student's progress is not dependent on the behavior of others. Low involvement occurred when lessons featured varying input from other children (such as role play) or [in] lessons with high intrusiveness (such as gross motor activity).

This study's results provide an explanation for the studies reporting higher levels of pupil involvement in teacher-led groups compared to seatwork. In the former, the teacher generally supplies a continuous set of signals for behavior, and can "steer" the group toward involvement. In seatwork, teacher control over cues is lessened. Consequently, unless the task is very highly structured, the student's attention is more easily diverted. The Kounin and Gump study also provides a basis for understanding teachers' greater sensitivity to inappropriate behavior during recitation formats: teachers are probably trying to maintain continuous cues for appropriate behavior in recitation.

VARIABLES ENHANCING MANAGEMENT

One of the most extensive studies of teaching in recent years has been the Beginning Teacher Evaluation Study (BTES). The major focus of this research was on identifying teaching behaviors that promoted pupil learning, but the aspect we are most concerned with here focused on identifying teacher behaviors associated with high student involvement. The BTES extensively observed numerous second- and fifth-grade classrooms. Analyses of interactive teaching behaviors and their relationships with student engagement rates showed that higher amounts of teacher academic feedback and more substantive academic interaction were associated with higher student engagement (Filby, 1978). More substantive instruction during seatwork was positively associated

with student engagement, but discipline-related feedback was negatively related to engagement rate. In mathematics, high engagement was also associated with high teacher structuring.

Teacher stimulus control has been consistently related to greater student on-task behavior in numerous studies. Krantz and Scarth (1979) found consistent positive effects of prompting (task-relevant questions) on the task persistence of nursery school children. Transitions between instructional activities have higher rates of pupil off-task behavior than the activities themselves, but when teachers *structure* the transitions (for example, by providing directions or close monitoring and feedback), then the off-task rates are significantly reduced (Arlin, 1979). Also, teacher inattention to students resulting from a long contact with another student in a group results in higher off-task rates (Scott and Bushell, 1974). Teachers can use questioning and signals more frequently to produce higher on-task rates (Carnine, 1974; Carnine and Fink, 1978).

We shall give Kounin the last word. In a study comparing pairs of high task involvement and low task involvement lessons taught by the same teachers who used the same lesson formats, Kounin and Doyle (1975) found that the most important predictor of involvement was the degree of continuity of the lesson's signal system. In teacher-led activities (teacher reading, teacher demonstration) higher task involvement occurred when long periods of student talk (recitations) were avoided. In other words, the teacher retained control over pacing. In student-paced (individual construction) lessons, higher involvement was produced by lessons that were more tightly programmed in a step-by-step manner.

The research reviewed in this section indicates that more effective management is associated with a more substantive and structured focus, by high rates of academic feedback, and by maintaining continuous signals for appropriate behavior. The latter feature may be accomplished differently, depending on the type of classroom activity.

CONSEQUENCES

Researchers, particularly in behavior modification, have extensively studied incentive systems and other types of consequences, such as response cost. They have conducted much of this research using one or two teachers and a few students, often out of the regular classroom setting. Nonetheless, there is an impressive accumulation of evidence regarding the effectiveness of providing incentives contingent on acceptable performance. Researchers have conducted several carefully designed field experiments in regular classroom settings using adequate samples of teachers and students at different grade levels. In these studies (Benowitz and Busse, 1976; Breuning, 1978; Rosenfeld, 1972), improved achievement has occurred as a result of the use of some system of consequences. Improved student achievement is likely the result, at least in part, of increased task engagement although other factors may be involved. For example, establishing a system of consequences contingent on certain behavior or performance requires clear identification of the acceptable performance, and the resulting improved goal clarity itself may increase achievement or engagement (Rosswork, 1977).

Contingency management is frequently used to reduce disruptive behavior or to increase on-task behavior in school settings, and the literature abounds with positive results. An examination of this research indicates that systems of consequences usually have several components. First, the desired behaviors are clearly identified. Second, students are given feedback about their behavior. Third, consequences that are rewarding are used consistently (and predictably), and are contingent on performance of the desired behavior. The elimination of undesirable behavior may occur when the newly acquired appropriate behavior takes place. Undesirable behavior can also be treated by using a response cost system in conjunction with an incentive system. When such a system is used, the undesirable behavior is clearly specified, students are given feedback, and punishment (such as loss of tokens, points, or privileges) is made contingent on inappropriate behavior.

The use of consequences is common in schools. Good grades, points, awards, treats, sports letters, and privileges have powerful rewarding properties. The behavior modification literature provides evidence of their usefulness for management when used systematically.

BEGINNING THE SCHOOL YEAR

All classroom management systems, good, poor, or in-between, have a beginning. The way in which teachers structure the first part of the year has consequences for their classroom management throughout the year. The research literature on the beginning of the year is not extensive, but existing studies attest to its importance.

A major management task at the beginning of the year is teaching children the rules and procedures of the classroom. In the elementary grades the teacher, in effect, socializes the children into the setting (Tikunoff and others, 1978). In an extensive study of 28 third-grade teachers (Emmer and others, 1980; Evertson and Anderson, 1979) more effective managers spent considerable time during the first several weeks helping students learn how to behave in their classrooms. They had carefully thought out procedures for getting assistance, contacting the teacher, lining up, turning work in, and standards for conduct during seatwork, group work, and whole class activities. Thus, these teachers knew what children needed to function in the classroom setting and in its activities, and they proceeded to teach these "survival" skills as part of the content at the beginning of the year. Better managers were also more careful monitors of student behavior and dealt with inappropriate behavior, when it occurred, more quickly than did less effective managers. The usefulness of this type of with-itness at the beginning of the year, before a pattern of inappropriate behavior becomes established, is evident. Better managers also had stronger instructional skills, such as clarity in directions and presentation, and stronger communication skills, such as listening and expressing feelings.

At the junior high level, similar differences between more and less effective managers have been found, although with some differences in emphasis associated with the older students. In a study comparing a group of beginning teachers to a group of "best" teachers, chosen from nominations by students, Moskowitz and Hayman (1976) found several differences in teacher behavior. Compared to new teachers, best teachers focused more on setting expectations and establishing appropriate behavior on the first day. They also used and accepted student ideas more, joked more, and contrary to the advice "Don't smile until Christmas," they smiled more. (The "best" teachers also turned out to be better managers, based on on-task student behavior rates.) In a study of junior high school mathematics and English teachers, subgroups of more and less effective managers were identified based on year-long criteria (Emmer and Evertson, 1980). Better managers set clear expectations for behavior, academic work standards, and classroom procedures during the first several class meetings, although they did not need as much time for these tasks as did elementary teachers. Better managers also were good monitors and dealt with inappropriate behavior promptly. Less effective managers' problems began early in the year, although not immediately. During the first week of school, off-task and disruptive behavior rates were low and not different in the more and less effective managers' classes. However, during the second and third weeks, such behaviors became significantly more frequent in the less effective managers' classes, but not in the more effective managers' classes. Management in lower ability track classes and in highly heterogeneous classes was also examined. Both instructional contexts present additional management problems for teachers. In lower track classes, teachers frequently encounter uncooperative students and higher off-task rates. Evidence (Evertson, 1980) indicates better management results from shorter, more frequent recitation-seatwork cycles embedded within each class period. High heterogeneity of students' entering ability levels had a negative impact on the management effectiveness of teachers who were poorer managers, whereas better managers were able to assimilate the heterogeneity into their management systems (Sanford, 1980). Better managers at the junior high level in heterogeneous classes obtained more information regarding student performance to diagnose pupil differences, seated lower achieving students nearer the teacher, and provided them with supplementary instruction. The better managers also had stronger accountability systems, enabling them to keep track of student progress.

OTHER LINES OF INQUIRY

Teacher planning and decision making influence management strategies and, ultimately, student behavior. However, the processes by which those links are established, and their nature, are not well researched. We know that student involvement is a highly salient cue for teachers when they choose curriculum (Taylor, 1970) and make judgments about how well their instruction is progressing (Peterson and Clark, 1978). Teachers' estimates of their ability to control classrooms are reduced by lower student ability levels, and are affected by the nature of classroom activities (Cooper and others, 1979). Research on teacher thinking and decision making is increasing (see reviews by Clark and Yinger, 1979; and Borko and others, 1979) and will improve our understanding of their relationship to management practices.

School level management and its effects at the classroom level deserve further research. Duke and Perry (1979) present data indicating wide variation in control or discipline problems across California high schools, with only a few reporting major schoolwide problems. Several studies point to important school level effects (Brookover and others, 1978; Rutter and others, 1979), but we are still unclear about the processes by which such effects are spread to teachers and classrooms. Significant elementary school management variables appear to be administrative leadership in instruction, coordination of programs, and setting and maintaining academic standards (Wellisch and others, 1978). The influence of schoolwide policies and rules at the individual classroom level is not clear. Many schools have schoolwide rules, but their effects have not been researched, and Duke (1978) has hypothesized several negative effects resulting from schoolwide attempts to control student behavior.

The influence students exert over the management of a classroom is another budding line of inquiry. Anyone who has read "The Child as Terrorist: Seven Cases" (Rader, 1975) cannot help but contemplate the impact one such child might have on a classroom. There is extensive evidence that adult responses to children are highly influenced by the nature of the child's behavior (Bates, 1976; Bell, 1968; Friedrich, 1976; Humphries and others, 1978) and that a unidirectional model of influence from adult to child is overly simple. Studies of pupil effects on teachers have confirmed that students exert influence and some control over classroom events (Fiedler, 1975; Klein, 1971; Sherman and Carmier, 1974). The extent of student influence and its effects on such variables as teachers' decisions about instruction, choice of activities, and how the influence process occurs need research.

REFERENCES

Arlin, M. "Teacher Transitions Can Disrupt Time Flow in Classrooms." *American Educational Research Journal* 16 (1979): 42–56.

Bates, J. E. "Effects of Children's Nonverbal Behavior upon Adults." *Child Development* 47 (1976): 1079–1088.

Bell, R. Q. "A Reinterpretation of the Direction of Effects in Studies of Socialization." *Psychological Review* 75 (1968): 81–95.

Benowitz, M. L., and Busse, T. V. "Effects of Material Incentives on Classroom Learning over a Four-Week Period." *Journal of Educational Psychology* 68 (1976): 57–62.

Borko, H.; Cone, R.; Russo, N. A.; and Shavelson, R. J. "Teachers' Decision Making." In *Research on Teaching,* pp. 136–160. Edited by P. L. Peterson and H. J. Walberg. Berkeley: McCutchan Publishing Corp., 1979.

Bossert, S. T. "Tasks, Group Management and Teacher Control Behavior: A Study of Classroom Organization and Teacher Style." *School Review* 85 (1977): 552–565.

Breuning, S. E. "Precision Teaching in the High School Classroom: A Necessary Step towards Maximizing Teacher Effectiveness and Student Performance." *American Educational Research Journal* 15 (1978): 125–140.

Brookover, W.; Schweitzer, J.; Sneider, J.; Beady, C.; Flood, P.; and Wisenbaker, J. "Elementary School Social Climate and School Achievement." *American Educational Research Journal* 15 (1978): 301–318.

Carnine, D. W. "Effects of Two Teacher-Presentation Rates on Off-Task Behavior, Answering Correctly, and Participation." *Journal of Applied Behavior Analysis* 9 (1974): 199–206.

Carnine, D. W., and Fink, W. T. "Increasing the Rate of Presentation and Use of Signals in Elementary Classroom Teachers." *Journal of Applied Behavior Analysis* 11 (1978): 35–46.

Clark, C., and Yinger, R. "Teachers' Thinking." In *Research on Teaching,* pp. 231–263. Edited by P. L. Peterson and H. J. Walberg. Berkeley: McCutchan Publishing Corp., 1979.

Cooper, H. M.; Burger, J. M.; and Seymour, G. E. "Classroom Context and Student Ability as Influences on Teacher Perceptions of Classroom Control." *American Educational Research Journal* 16 (1979): 189–193.

Duke, D. L. "Looking at the School as a Rule-governed Organization." *Journal of Research and Development in Education* 11 (1978): 116–126.

Duke, D., ed. *Classroom Management.* Seventy-Eighth Yearbook of the National Society for the Study of Education, Part II. Chicago: The University of Chicago Press, 1979.

Duke, D. L., and Perry C. "What Happened to the High School Discipline Crisis?" *Urban Education* 14 (1979): 182–204.

Emmer, E., and Evertson, C. *Effective Classroom Management at the Beginning of the Year in Junior High School Classrooms.* Austin, Texas: The Research and Development Center for Teacher Education, The University of Texas, Report No. 6107, 1980.

Emmer, E. T.; Evertson, C. M.; and Anderson, L. M. "Effective Management at the Beginning of the School Year." *Elementary School Journal* 80 (1980): 219–231.

Evertson, C. M. "Differences in Instructional Activities in High and Low Achieving Junior High Classes." Paper presented at the annual meeting of the American Educational Research Association, Boston, 1980.

Evertson, C. M., and Anderson, L. M. "Beginning School." *Educational Horizons* 57 (1979): 164–168.

Fiedler, M. L. "Bidirectionality of Influence in Classroom Interaction." *Journal of Educational Psychology* 67 (1975): 735–744.

Filby, N. N. "How Teachers Produce 'Academic Learning Time': Instructional Variables Related to Student Engagement." Paper presented at the annual meeting of the American Educational Research Association, Toronto, 1978.

Friedrich, W. N., and Boriskin, J. A. "The Role of the Child in Abuse: A Review of the Literature." *American Journal of Orthopsychiatry* 46 (1976): 580–590.

Good, T. L., and Beckerman, T. M. "Time-on-Task: A Naturalistic Study in Sixth-Grade Classrooms." *The Elementary School Journal* 78 (1978): 193–201.

Gump, P. V. "Intra-setting Analysis: The Third Grade Classroom as a Special but Instructive Case." In *Naturalistic Viewpoints in Psychological Research,* pp. 200–220. Edited by E. Williams and H. Rausch. New York: Holt, Rinehart & Winston, 1969.

Humphries, T.; Kinsborne, M.; and Swanson, J. "Stimulant Effects on Cooperation and Social Interaction between Hyperactive Children and Their Mothers." *Journal of Child Psychology and Psychiatry* 19 (1978): 13–22.

Klein, S. "Student Influence on Teachers' Behavior." *American Educational Research Journal* 8 (1971): 403–422.

Kounin, J. S. *Discipline and Group Management in Classrooms.* New York: Holt, Rinehart & Winston, 1970.

Kounin, J. S., and Doyle, P. H. "Degree of Continuity of a Lesson's Signal System and the Task Involvement of Children." *Journal of Educational Psychology* 67 (1975): 159–164.

Kounin, J. S., and Gump, P. V. "Signal Systems of Lesson Settings and the Task-related Behavior of Preschool Children." *Journal of Educational Psychology* 66 (1974): 554–562.

Krantz, M., and Scarth, L. "Task Persistence and Adult Assistance in the Preschool." *Child Development* 50 (1979): 578–581.

Moskowitz, G., and Hayman, M. L. "Success Strategies of Inner-City Teachers: A Year Long Study." *Journal of Educational Research* 69 (1976): 283–289.

Peterson, P., and Clark, C. "Teachers' Reports of Their Cognitive Processes during Teaching." *American Educational Research Journal* 15 (1978): 555–566.

Rader, H. "The Child as Terrorist: Seven Cases." *School Review* 84 (1975): 5–41.

Rosenfeld, G. W. "Some Effects of Reinforcement on Achievement and Behavior in a Regular Classroom." *Journal of Educational Psychology* 63 (1972): 189–193.

Rosswork, S. G. "Goal Setting: The Effects on an Academic Task with Varying Magnitudes of Incentive." *Journal of Educational Psychology* 69 (1977): 710–715.

Rutter, M.; Maughan, B.; Mortimore, P.; and Ouston, J. *15,000 Hours: Secondary Schools and Their Effects on Children.* Cambridge, Mass.: Harvard University Press, 1979.

Sanford, J. *Comparison of Heterogeneous and Homogeneous Junior High Classes.* Austin, Texas: Research and Development Center for Teacher Education, The University of Texas, Report No. 6108, 1980.

Scott, J., and Bushell, D. "The Length of Teacher Contacts and Students' Off-Task Behavior." *Journal of Applied Behavior Analysis* 7 (1974): 39–44.

Sherman, T., and Carmier, W. "An Investigation of the Influence of Student Behavior on Teacher Behavior." *Journal of Applied Behavior Analysis* 7 (1974): 11–21.

Solomon, D., and Kendall, A. J. "Teachers' Perceptions of and Reactions to Misbehavior in Traditional and Open Classrooms." *Journal of Educational Psychology* 67 (1975): 528–530.

Taylor, P. H. *How Teachers Plan Their Courses.* Slough, England: National Foundation for Educational Research in England and Wales, 1970.

Tikunoff, W. J.; Ward, B.; and Dasho, S. Volume A: *Three Case Studies* (Report A78–7). San Francisco: Far West Laboratory for Educational Research and Development, 1978.

Wellisch, J. B.; MacQueen, A. H.; Carriere, R. A.; and Duck, G. A. "School Management and Organization in Successful Schools." *Sociology of Education* 51 (1978): 211–226.

2. CLASSROOM DISCOURSE AS IMPROVISATION
Relationships between Academic Task Structure and Social Participation Structure in Lessons

Frederick Erickson

Talk among teachers and students in lessons—talk that is not only intelligible but situationally appropriate and effective—can be seen as the collective improvisation of meaning and social organization from moment to moment. How this improvisation happens, and what the pedagogical significance of improvisation may be, are the topics of this chapter. . . .

LEARNING TASK ENVIRONMENTS

Teachers and students engaged in doing a lesson together can be seen as drawing on two sets of procedural knowledge simultaneously; knowledge of the academic task structure and of the social participation structure. The academic task structure (ATS)[1] can be thought of as a patterned set of constraints provided by the logic of sequencing in the subject-matter content of the lesson. The social participation structure (SPS) can be thought of as a patterned set of constraints on the allocation of interactional rights and obligations of various members of the interacting group (see Erickson & Shultz, 1977, 1981; Shultz, Florio, & Erickson, in press).

The academic task structure governs the logical sequencing of instructional "moves" by the teacher

---

[1] It should be noted that this is a much more specific sense of the term than that used by Bossert (1979), whose "Task Activity Structure" is a much more general notion of task, and derives from a very different theoretical frame of reference.

and students. Consider, for example, the following problem in addition:

$$
\begin{array}{r}
14 \\
+\ 8 \\
\hline
22
\end{array}
$$

In solving this equation in "old math" style (and in teaching the steps in its solution) it is necessary to begin (a) with the rightmost column (the "1s"); (b) add the numbers in that column; (c) since the sum of that column is greater than 10, "carry" the 10 units into the column next to the left (the "10s" column); and (d) add the two 10s in that column. The sequence of steps is constrained by the logic of computation; one does not know that two 10s must be added in the "10s" column until one has first added the numbers in the "1s" column. Thus the steps in adding stand in "adjacency pair" relationship to one another that are analogous to the adjacency pair relationships in conversation that have been discussed by conversational analysts (Sacks, Schegloff, & Jefferson, 1974), for example, question-answer sequences. Both in conversation and in computation these are invariant relationships of series position, hierarchically and sequentially ordered.

There are at least four definable aspects of academic task environment in a lesson: (a) the logic of subject matter sequencing; (b) the information content of the various sequential steps; (c) the "meta-content" cues toward steps and strategies for completing the task; and (d) the physical materials through which tasks and task components are manifested and with which tasks are accomplished. These four aspects together manifest the academic task structure of the lesson as a learning environment.

The social participation structure governs the sequencing and articulation of interaction; it involves multiple dimensions of interactional partnership according to which interactional work is divided up in sets of articulated communicative roles, for example, listener roles in relation to speaker roles.[2] Considered as a whole pattern, a participation structure can be thought of as the configuration of all the roles of all the partners in an interactional event (see the discussion in Erickson & Shultz, 1977, 1981). Some aspects of these role relationships involve

patterns in the ways interactional partners exchange turns at speaking, tie pairs of turns together semantically in question-answer sequences, and coordinate listening behavior in relation to speaking behavior.

Paralleling the four aspects of the academic task environment of a lesson are four definable aspects of the social task environment: (a) the social gatekeeping of access to people and other information sources during the lesson; (b) the allocation of communicative rights and obligations among the various interactional partners in the event; (c) the sequencing and timing of successive functional "slots" in the interaction; and (d) the simultaneous actions of all those engaged in interaction during the lesson. Taken together, these four aspects manifest the social participation structure of the lesson as a learning environment.

Aspects of social participation have been studied by conversational analysts and by ethnographers of communication (e.g., Sacks et al., 1974, on turn allocation; Schegloff, 1968, on question-answer sequences; and Duncan & Fiske, 1977, Erickson, 1979, and Kendon, 1967, on listener-speaker coordination).

All this work presumes a definition of the social in Weber's terms as action taken in account of the actions of others (Weber, [1922] 1978). Social action is distinguished from asocial behavior in that it is articulated with and oriented to what others are doing in the scene as well as to what others may be doing outside the immediate scene at hand. Occasions of social interactions are in Goffman's terms encounters; focused gatherings in which the focus is on what others are doing there (Goffman, 1961). The boundary between the encounter and the world outside it is not impermeable; outside influences do impinge on it. But the action inside the encounter takes on, to some extent, a life of its own. It is, in part at least, immediately social. . . .

In encounters, the actions of the various interactional partners are articulated in immediately social ways both sequentially and simultaneously. Reciprocal actions are articulated sequentially, for example, in question-answer pairs, in which the question asked by one conversational partner obliges an answer by another in the next successive "slot" in the conversation. Complementary actions are articulated simultaneously, for example, in listener responses such as nods that may occur in the same

---

[2] Role here refers to a set of rights and obligations vis à vis others.

moment as the speaker's speech. In short, action that is immediately social is seen as radically cooperative and interdependent.

Sequential and simultaneous aspects of the social organization of interaction in classrooms have been considered recently by a number of researchers, notably, Bremme and Erickson (1977), Erickson and Mohatt (1982), Gumperz and Cook-Gumperz (1979). Mehan (1979), . . . Michaels & Cook-Gumperz (1979), Shultz *et al.* (in press), Sinclair and Coulthard (1975), and Wilkinson, Clevenger, and Dollaghan (1981). Only the authors of the most recent work have begun to consider the social and academic aspects of lesson tasks together (see Au, 1980; Collins & Michaels, 1980; . . . Griffin, Cole, & Newman, in preparation; Mehan & Griffin, 1980). This is necessary, as I have argued elsewhere (Erickson, 1980), if we are to develop an interactional theory of cognitive learning and teaching in social occasions (such as lessons) that are interactional learning environments.

Some earlier classroom research has emphasized the cognitive task environment of lessons (Smith, n.d.; Taba, 1964), while ignoring the social task environment. One notable attempt was made by Bellack, Kliebard, Hyman, and Smith (1966) to combine aspects of social and academic organization in the study of lessons. But in the years since then, sociolinguistically oriented researchers have studied mainly the social participation structure of lessons, whereas curriculum researchers and cognitive psychologists have concerned themselves primarily with the academic task structure of lessons. It is necessary to consider both aspects of organization as mutually constitutive. As Mehan puts it succinctly, for a student to give a right answer in a lesson, the answer must be "right" both in academic content and in social form (Mehan, 1979, p. 1). . . .

TIME AND SEQUENCE IN THE COORDINATION OF SOCIAL INTERACTION

If face-to-face interaction is a radically cooperative enterprise, "locally" produced in terms of locally situated actions and their significance, then interactional partners must have means available for establishing and maintaining interdependence in their collective action. These means appear to be patterns of timing and sequencing in the performance of

verbal and nonverbal behavior. The patterns function as a signal system—a social steering mechanism—by which interactional partners are able to tell each other what is happening from moment to moment. I will begin this discussion by considering different functions and behavioral manifestations of coordination signals and then will discuss the organization of these signals in the real-time duration of interaction.

The signals are both explicit and implicit. They may communicate information about a moment that is past, this moment now, and/or the moment coming next. Explicit signals can be found in the literal meaning (referential content) of talk. The last sentence of the previous paragraph is an instance of this in written discourse; it points the expectations of the reader to what is coming next in the text.

In lessons some of this orienting is done explicitly in talk. Often that talk has to do with subject matter content and the ATS. Consider the addition problem discussed earlier. If the teacher were demonstrating the solution of this problem to the class, the lesson discourse might go something like this as the teacher pointed to the various numbers and columns on a chalkboard:

1. TEACHER: *What's four plus eight?* (pointing to the "1s" column)
2. CLASS: *Twelve.*
3. TEACHER: *Right, so we write the two here* (Teacher does so) *and then what?*
4. CLASS: (no answer)
5. TEACHER: *What did I say last time?* (i.e., in the previous problem)
6. CLASS: *Carry.*
7. TEACHER: *Carry the 10 over to the 10s column and add the two 10s there . . . so the answer is . . .*
8. CLASS: *Twenty-two.*
9. TEACHER: *Very good. Now "seven plus five"* (Teacher moves on to the next problem).

The question in turn 1, *What's four plus eight?* (even if not accompanied by the nonverbal action of pointing to the chalkboard), explicitly identifies and focuses attention on the step in the academic task structure that is being done in this moment now. In addition, the question form also signals that an answer is due in the moment coming next; hence the question not only allows the class to identify what is happening in the current moment but to anticipate, through prospective interpretation, what should happen in the moment to come. Turn 5 explicitly points to the need for retrospective interpretation by the class, asking for recall of what was taught about "carrying" in the previous problem.

Signals pointing to a particular sequential stage in the lesson can be even more explicitly formulated than in the previous illustration. For example, the teacher could have preceded the question in turn 1 with the statement, *Let's begin by adding the numbers in the '1s' column.* This would have pointed explicitly to the sequential stage in the ATS itself, before getting into the computational operation necessary at that stage. Explicit formulations of this type may occur at the very beginning of the lesson, as in the following hypothetical example: *Now we will have our spelling test. First take out a sheet of paper, write your name in the upper right hand corner, and then I will begin to read the words you are to spell.* (This is the same sort of function performed by the sentence at the end of the first paragraph of this section, *I will begin this discussion by considering different functions and behavioral manifestations of coordination signals and then will discuss the organization of these signals in the real-time duration of interaction.*)

The same kind of orientation to sequence position in a lesson can also be signaled through ellipsis. Elliptic signals can be used successfully because of familiarity with sequential routines of classroom procedure. An example is found in Turn 9 of the previous illustration. There one word plus a pause, *Now . . .* can function as a formulation of sequential position that is equivalent to the whole phrase, *Let's begin by adding the numbers in the '1s' column.* Through ellipsis, the first word of Turn 3, *Right,* points retrospectively to the correctness of the answer in Turn 2. The semantic pointing is elliptic, but is still explicitly communicated in the lexical item, *Right.*

Pointing to sequence position is also done more implicitly. This function can be accomplished both by words and syntax, and by paralinguistic and nonverbal cues. An example of a lexical cue is found in Turn 3, in which the word *Right* functions explicitly to signal that the previous answer was correct. It also functions implicitly to signal prospectively that, since the previous answer was correct, the teacher is about to move on to something

new in the next moment. A syntactic cue accomplishes a similar prospective pointing function at the end of Turn 7, in which a pause interrupts the completion of the verb phrase: *so the answer is . . . .*[3]

Implicit prospective and retrospective pointing can also be done by so-called "suprasegmental" patterns of nonverbal and paralinguistic behavior; so-called because they are sustained across smaller phonological and syntactic units in the speech stream. Changes in postural position and interpersonal distance often mark the ending of one discourse unit and the beginning of another (see Erickson, 1975; Scheflen, 1973; and the analysis of postural positioning in classroom lessons by McDermott, 1976). Changes in pitch register and in speech prosody (pitch, stress, volume stress, tempo) can also signal the completion of one connected series of discourse "chunks," as in the successively falling pitch levels in the "listing intonation" found in this hypothetical example:

TEACHER: What did the ancient Greeks consider to be the essential material elements?
CLASS: E^{arth} A^{ir} F^{ire} Wa$_{ter}$

Here not only does the final pitch fall at the end of "water" signal the end of the list, but the slight rise of pitch in "air" and "fire" signals the end point is yet to come.

Gumperz (1977) uses the term contextualization *cues* to refer to all the surface-structural means by which communicative intent and interpretive form are signaled. Contextualization cueing procedures are learned and their usage is shared within speech communities. Cues of this general class point to various contexts of interpretation, not only to the aspects of sequential context discussed here, but to other aspects of context as well. These include keying of irony, sincerity, politeness, and framing as speaking activities of particular connected sets of communicative functions; for example, chatting about the weather, changing the subject, ordering a meal in a restaurant. (See Goffman, 1974, and Tannen, 1979, on the notions of keying and framing. See

[3]The aspects of sequence-position signaling discussed so far have all been noted by other researchers, notably Sacks *et al.* (1974); Schegloff (1968) (see the discussion in Mehan and Wood, 1975), and in applications of speech act theory to lesson discourse, as in Sinclair and Coulthard (1975).

also Schank & Abelson, 1977, for a more idealized notion of frame, plan, and expectation.) Tannen and Gumperz assume that context is not merely given in the scene of action. The scene is too complex and broad to be informative by itself. Specific features of context must be pointed to continually and sustained through communicative behavior. The cues are manifested across many levels of organization of speech and nonverbal behavior, in syntax, lexicon, stylistic register of speech, in speech prosody, in body motion, gaze, postural position, and interpersonal distance.

The ability to "read" the signal system of contextualization cues is a crucial aspect of what Hymes (1974) terms communicative competence, that is, contextualization cueing and the inferential processes by which the cues are read are a fundamental requisite for performing communication that is not only intelligible, but appropriate and effective in its use.

The particular aspects of contextualization cueing that I want to emphasize here are those of (*a*) pointing to the sequentially functional place of the moment at hand and the next moment to come and (*b*) pointing to the location in real time of the moments now and next.

We have been reviewing the importance, for interactional partnership, of all the participants in an interactional event being able to point one another to the sequentially functional "slots" in interaction as it unfolds. This is important both at the level of the immediately adjacent slots, such as those of noun phrase and verb phrase within a sentence, or in question and answer pairs across turns at speaking. It is also important to know where one is in the sequence of larger "chunks," the connected sets of functional slots at hierarchically higher levels of sequential organization; for example, knowing when one has come to the end of a "topically relevant set" of semantically tied question and answer pairs within a lesson, knowing the preparatory phase of the lesson is ending and the instrumentally focused phase of the lesson is about to begin (see Erickson & Shultz, 1977, 1981), or knowing that the point of instructional climax—the "punch line" in the academic task structure—has arrived (see Shultz *et al.*, in press).

These matters of sequencing in the ordering of sequential, functional slots and chunks define the time of "now" and "next moment" in a special sense; that of strategic time, in contrast to that of clock time (see the discussion in Erickson, 1981).

The ancient Greeks made a distinction between strategic and clock time. The former was termed kairos; the right time, the appropriate time. This is the time of human history, seasons, and weather. The latter kind of time was termed chronos; the time of literal duration, mechanically measurable. The anthropologist Hall makes a similar distinction between kinds of time, terming kairos as formal time and chronos as technical time (Hall, 1959).

In face-to-face interaction, both kairos and chronos must be clear to the interactional partners if they are to be able to coordinate their action socially, taking account of one another's actions simultaneously and sequentially. The partners must be able to anticipate that a functionally significant slot is about to be arrived at in the next moment; they must also be able to anticipate the actual point in real time in which that next functional moment can appropriately happen. This is done through contextualization cues of a special sort, which form patterns of what can be called verbal and nonverbal prosody. Points of emphasis in the speech stream—shifts in pitch, volume, and tempo, the onset and offset of syntactic junctions—appear at regularly periodic intervals. Points of emphasis in the stream of nonverbal behavior [co-occur] with those of the speech stream, or substitute for the verbal channel in marking the "next" rhythmic interval in the series. These points of emphasis occur in the change of direction of motion in hand gesture, in nodding, in the onset or offset of gaze involvement, and in changes of postural position and interpersonal distance. Taken together across the verbal and nonverbal channels, these points of emphasis outline an interactional rhythm that is almost, but not quite, metronomic.

In short, the same communicative means are used to delineate the semantic content with its sequential slots of kairos organization, and the rhythmic form, consisting of regular periods of chronos organization. Points in real time, as well as points of series position in a sequence relationship, are essential to the "context" of practical action and decision making that is being created and sustained in the conjointly articulated verbal and nonverbal behavior of the interactional partners. The maintenance of predictable patterns of convergence between kairos organization and chronos organization can thus be seen as fundamentally constitutive of the social coordination of face-to-face interaction, in Weber's ([1922], 1978) sense of the term. . . .

IMPROVISATION AS STRATEGICALLY ADAPTIVE ACTION IN LESSONS

Although the predictability of kairos and chronos defines the potential opportunities for social action by a teacher and students in a lesson, the actual opportunities arise not only in the times and functional places that can be formally modeled, but in points of fortuitous happening that are not amenable to formal modeling. This is because school lessons, considered as environments for learning and teaching, are social occasions that are distinctively characterized by fortuity. Considered in terms of the ethnography of speaking, lessons stand at a midpoint on the continuum between highly ritualized, formulaic speech events, in which all the functional slots and their formal contents are prespecified, and highly spontaneous speech events, in which neither the successive slots nor their content is prespecified. Considered in terms of social theory and socialization theory, school lessons are of special interest because they are anomalous in the paradigms at either theoretical extreme; that of social or psychological determinism on the one hand, and that of radical contextualism on the other hand. I will first discuss the special character of lessons as social occasions and then discuss the implications of this for social theory and socialization theory.

Lessons are first of all occasions for learning and teaching. What this means for the smooth and felicitous conduct of interaction is that lessons are especially tricky local places, since they are situations in which it is certain that mistakes will be made and correction and assistance will be provided. Indeed, mistakes and hesitations by students and adaptive responses by teachers are the lesson's raison d'être.

Mistakes are inevitable, since the students are learners; learning is by definition the acquisition of mastery, not the possession of it. The opportunity to learn is the opportunity to make mistakes. Moreover, student mistakes provide the teacher with the opportunity to teach. The student's level of mastery

is revealed by the level of difficulty in academic task at which mistakes are made. Having identified the student's level of mastery, the teacher should be able to adjust the learning environment of the lesson to accommodate the student; this is in the "folk" language of teacher education called "meeting the student where (s)he is." (On this point, see also the discussion in Mehan, 1979, pp. 122–124.)

Adjustments can be made across both dimensions of the lesson as learning environment—the Academic Task Structure (ATS) and the Social Participation Structure (SPS)—or across either dimension separately. The ATS can be simplified by lowering the level of difficulty of a given question or set of questions. The SPS too can be simplified through reallocation of rights toward speaking and listening. . . . [N]ot only can the overall cognitive task of the lesson be made easier for a child by simplifying the ATS as well as the SPS, but that changes in social participation structure can also provide the teacher with opportunities to diagnose more fully the learning capacity of the child. Changing the SPS so as to allow the child to answer along with another child, or with the teacher, gives the teacher observational access to what Vygotsky (1978) terms the child's zone of proximal development—the range across which the child can perform successfully with help, as contrasted to the point at which the child's mastery stops when the child is performing the learning task alone.

Direct questions in lessons, then, are a way for the teacher to gain insight into what the individual child does or does not know. Admittedly, this central tenet of pedagogy is not universally shared among humans. There are sociocultural groups in which teaching is done without any direct questioning of learners (see the discussion of Native American learning and teaching styles in Erickson & Mohatt, in press; and Philips, 1972). Still, for Western Europeans and Americans, existence of the interactional lesson as a speech event presupposes that it is necessary for the teacher to ask direct questions of individual children because it is not certain whether the child knows the old information being reviewed, or the new information about to be taught.

The paradox is that various kinds of student mistakes in answering—even though some of them are essential as opportunities for teaching and learning—can play havoc with the maintenance of a coherent academic and social task structure in the lesson. Content mistakes in the ATS can cause troubles in the maintenance of the SPS, as in the case of a hesitation by a student that breaks the interactional rhythm. Mistakes of academic content that are correct in social form (SPS) can also cause trouble in the ATS, as in the case of a student providing a wrong answer that violates the expectations of the teacher and other students as to the logically sequential flow of ideas in the lesson, even though the answer is given in the socially "right" time and does not distort the smooth rhythmic flow of alternation between question and answer. Conversely, mistakes in terms of SPS can damage the ATS, as in the case of a student giving the academically "right" answer in the socially "wrong" time. Because of this, lessons are speech events characterized by the presence of frequent cognitive and interactional troubles and repair work.

When school lessons are compared with other speech events, according to the comparative frame of the "ethnography of speaking model" of Hymes (1964, 1974), it is apparent that lessons stand at a midpoint between formal ritual and informal spontaneity. In the most highly stylized speech the sequence of turns at speaking is prespecified, as is the allocation of turns among the various partners, the semantic content of each turn, and the appropriate nonverbal actions accompanying speech. Consider the following example of dialogue from the Roman Catholic mass:

PEOPLE: (rise as Celebrant turns to face them)
CELEBRANT: *The Lord be with you.* (hands open, arms extended)
PEOPLE: *And also with you.*
CELEBRANT: *Lift up your hearts.*
PEOPLE: *We lift them to the Lord.*

In contrast, the dialogue between an evangelical Protestant minister and congregation during the sermon is organized more loosely. Alternation of turns is not prespecified, the content of the minister's turns is not fully prespecified, although formulaic reiteration of what has just been said often occurs. The content of the turns for members of the congregation is not prespecified, although the optional "fillers" of the response slot (e.g., *Amen, That's right, Thank you Jesus, shout, break into song*) is narrower in range than is the range of options available to the preacher (see the discussion in Rosenberg, 1975).

The organization of speaking in a Quaker meeting (see Bauman, 1974) is even more loosely constrained in terms of turn allocation, turn sequence, and turn content. This organization is by no means random, however. Indeed, the principle that a speaker self-selects a turn, and the absence of a leader-follower relationship between audience and speaker are both features of interactional organization consistent with a more general social organizational principle underlying the whole of Quaker polity, the principle of the absolute equality of all individuals before God and one another.

Ordinary middle-class conversation among Americans (as discussed in Sacks *et al.*, 1974) is even more loosely constrained than a Quaker meeting. Speakers in ordinary conversation can designate next speakers as well as self-select their own turn. The range of topics is wider than in a Quaker meeting; for instance, a dirty joke told in ordinary conversation would be inappropriate in a Quaker meeting. Still, even in ordinary conversation the underlying order is not random, as the analysis by Sacks *et al.* suggests. What is distinctive about ordinary conversation, in contrast to the other examples, is the radically "local" nature of the order. The principles of order apply to the immediate moment—to adjacency pairs such as this turn–next turn. This is a very general kind of rule; indeed a better term is operating principle or maxim, to use Grice's term (1975). The Gricean conversational maxim "be relevant" is advice that must be taken largely in terms of local context, within the conversation itself.

The generality of underlying operating principles and the locality of relevance for their application is what distinguishes speech events such as the Roman Catholic mass from speech events such as ordinary conversation. The mass as an encounter is radically nonlocal in its openness to influence from the outside, both across space and across time. In its Latin version, the sequence and content of the sample of dialogue previously presented has existed virtually unchanged for 1700 years. The usage began within the Christian congregation at Rome (which switched from Greek to Latin as its liturgical language ca. A.D. 300. Since then the Roman usage has spread throughout the world. . . .

The school lesson, as a speech event, stands

somewhere between the Roman mass and the evangelical sermon with audience participation. Some aspects of the academic task structure of a lesson are, like the mass, more predetermined than is the content of the evangelical preacher's sermon; the constraints on the content of student responses are narrower than those placed on the responses of the audience to the evangelical preacher. Yet the social participation structure of the lesson resembles the evangelical sermon more than it does the mass, in that the alternation of turn-taking is not fully prespecified, and in that the content of what is said by teacher and student is not fully prespecified, although much of it is influenced by cultural norms that stand, as it were, outside the situation of use. The lesson in its academic task structure is like the sermon in that it is conducted according to a moderately specified plan. Similar to a Quaker meeting and ordinary conversation, the lesson also is organized around operating principles that are quite general in reference. In consequence the lesson is moderately open to fortuitous happenings and it includes principles of both nonlocal and local organization in the production of interaction. . . .

Turning now to consider the lesson in terms of theories of society and of socialization, it is extremely important to keep hold of the notion of the school lesson as an encounter, that is, a partially bounded social occasion, influenced by cultural norms and having within its own frame something of a life of its own.

Such a view of the lesson avoids the extremes of social or psychological determinism on the one hand, and radical contextualism on the other.[4] Functionally determinist theories of society, culture, and education, such as those of Durkheim, leave no room for human choice. The model is of an oversocialized individual who has learned to play every social scene as if it were the Roman mass. (In Durkheim's model, the individual has learned to want this.) A similarly oversocialized model of the individual can be seen in psychologically determinist theories, whether they be Skinnerian or Freudian. (In Freud's model, the individual resists the socialization, but is overcome by it.) Both the psychological and the

sociocultural determinists locate the major causes of individual action outside the immediate scene of action. They presuppose an individual who is almost totally preprogrammed by prior experience; in Garfinkel's term, a "cultural dope" who operates as a robot (Garfinkel, 1967). Socialization is a one-way process in a world without freedom.

At the other extreme is the position of radical contextualism. Here the immediately local circumstances of production (e.g., this turn, next turn) are focused on so narrowly as to exclude the relevance, if not the possibility, of nonlocal influences, for example, culturally learned standards of expectation and performance, constraints from the wider society on the choices possible in the scene of action. There is no need for socialization in this theory. Virtually everything can be explained in terms of making sense in the immediate momentary scene of action. Taken to its logical conclusion, this theoretical position leads to solipsism. There is no oppression in such a world, but there is no freedom either, for there is neither an individual nor a society, only the interaction of the moment; there are no opportunities for choices that have consequences beyond the moment and the immediate scene.

Each extreme is untenable as grounds for a theory of education, which must presuppose at least three levels of organization—general society and culture, specific situations, and specific individuals—and some processes of relationship among the levels, one of which is socialization of the individual. What is argued for here is a middle way between the two extremes: a way that preserves the integrity of each level of organization in its own right and that enables us to view socialization as a two-way process.

This leaves us a place for a theory of school lessons as educational encounters; partially bounded situations in which teachers and students follow previously learned, culturally normative "rules," and also innovate by making new kinds of sense together in adapting to the fortuitous circumstances of the moment. Students are seen as active participants in this process, not simply as the passive recipients of external shaping. Teachers and students are seen as engaged in praxis, improvising situational variations within and around socioculturally prescribed thematic material and occasionally, within the process of improvisation, discovering new possibilities for learning and for social life. . . .

---

[4]In the following discussion I am indebted to comments by Jenny Cook-Gumperz and by Hugh Mehan. See also his discussion in Mehan [1979], pp. 126–130, and in Mehan and Griffin, 1980.

REFERENCES

Au, K. Hu-pei. Participation structures in a reading lesson with Hawaiian children: Analysis of a culturally appropriate instructional event. *Anthropology and Education Quarterly,* 1980, *11* (2), 91–115.

Bauman, R. Speaking in the light: The role of the Quaker minister. In R. Bauman & J. Scherzer (Eds.), *Explorations in the ethnography of speaking.* Cambridge, Mass.: Cambridge University Press, 1974.

Bellack, A., Kliebard, H., Hyman, R., & Smith, F. *The language of the classroom.* New York: Teachers College Press, 1966.

Bossert, S. T. *Tasks and social relationships in classrooms.* Cambridge, Mass.: Cambridge University Press, 1979.

Brazelton, T. B., Koslowski, B., & Main, M. The origins of reciprocity: The early mother-infant interaction. In M. Lewis & L. Rosenblum (Eds.), *The effects of the infant on its caregiver.* New York: John Wiley & Sons, 1974.

Bremme, D. W., & Erickson, F. Relationships among verbal and nonverbal classroom behaviors. *Theory into Practice,* 1977, *16* (3), 153–161.

Byers, P. *From biological rhythm to cultural pattern: A study of minimal units.* Unpublished doctoral dissertation, Columbia University, 1972. (Ann Arbor: University Microfilms, No. 73–9004).

Cazden, C., Carrasco, R., Maldonado-Guzmán, A., & Erickson, F. The contribution of ethnographic research to bicultural bilingual education. In J. Alatis (Ed.), *Current issues in bilingual education.* Washington, D.C.: Georgetown University Press, 1980.

Collins, J., & Michaels, S. The importance of conversational discourse strategies in the acquisition of literacy. *Proceedings of the Sixth Annual Meetings of the Berkeley Linguistic Society,* Berkeley, California, 1980.

Condon, W. Neonate movement is synchronized with adult speech: Interactional participation and language acquisition. *Science,* 1974, *183,* 99–101.

Duncan, S., & Fiske, D. *Face to face interaction: Research, methods, and theory.* Hillsdale, N.J.: Lawrence Erlbaum, 1977.

Erickson, F. Gatekeeping and the melting pot: Interaction in counseling encounters. *Harvard Educational Review,* 1975, *45* (1), 44–70.

Erickson, F. Talking down: Some cultural sources of miscommunication in inter-racial interviews. In A. Wolfgang (Ed.), *Research in nonverbal communication.* New York: Academic Press, 1979.

Erickson, F. *Stories of cognitive learning in learning environments: A neglected area in the anthropology of education.* Paper presented at the symposium "The Anthropology of Learning" at the Annual Meeting of the American Anthropological Association, Washington, D.C., December 1980.

Erickson, F. Timing and context in everyday discourse. In W. P. Dickson (Ed.), *Children's oral communication skills.* New York: Academic Press, 1981.

Erickson, F., Cazden, C., Carrasco, R., & Maldonado-Guzmán, A. *Social and cultural organization of interaction in classrooms of bilingual children.* Second Year Interim Report to National Institute of Education, Teaching and Learning Division, Project #NIE C–0099, 1980.

Erickson, F., & Mohatt, G. The cultural organization of participation structures in two classrooms of Indian students. In G. Spindler (Ed.), *Doing the ethnography of schooling.* New York: Holt, Rinehart, and Winston, 1982.

Erickson, F., & Shultz, J. When is a context?: Some issues and methods in the analysis of social competence. *The Quarterly Newsletter of the Institute for Comparative Human Development,* 1977, *1* (2), 5–10. Also reprinted in J. Green & C. Wallat (Eds.), *Ethnography and language in educational settings.* Norwood, N.J.: Ablex, 1981.

Erickson F., & Shultz, J. *The counselor as gatekeeper: Social interaction in interviews.* New York: Academic Press, 1982.

Garfinkel, H. *Studies in ethnomethodology.* New York: Prentice-Hall, 1967.

Goffman, E. *Encounters: Two studies in the sociology of interaction.* Indianapolis: Bobbs-Merrill, 1961.

Goffman, E. *Frame analysis.* New York: Harper Colophon Books, 1974.

Grice, H. P. Logic and conversation. In P. Cole & J. L. Morgan (Eds.), *Syntax and semantics III: Speech acts.* New York: Academic Press, 1975

Griffin, P., Cole, M., & Newman, D. Locating tasks in psychology and education. In R. O. Freedle (Ed.), *Discourse Processes,* in preparation.

Gumperz, J. J. Sociocultural knowledge in conversational inference. In M. Saville-Troike (Ed.), *Linguistics and anthropology* (Georgetown University Roundtable on Languages and Linguistics). Washington, D.C.: Georgetown University Press, 1977.

Gumperz, J. J., & Cook-Gumperz, J. *Beyond ethnography: Some uses of sociolinguistics for understanding classroom environments.* Paper presented at the annual meeting of the American Educational Research Association, San Francisco, April 1979.

Hall, E. T. *The silent language.* New York: Fawcett, 1959.

Hymes, D. Introduction: Toward ethnographies of communication. In J. Gumperz & D. Hymes (Eds.), The ethnography of communication. *American Anthropologist,* 1964, *55* (5, Pt.2), 1–34.

Hymes, D. Studying the interaction of language and social life. In D. Hymes, *Foundations in sociolinguistics: An ethnographic approach.* Philadelphia: University of Pennsylvania Press, 1974.

Kendon, A. Some functions of gaze direction in face to face interaction. *Acta Psychologica,* 1967, *26,* 22–63.

McDermott, R. P. *Kids make sense: An ethnographic account of the interactional management of success and failure in one first grade classroom.* Unpublished doctoral dissertation, Stanford University, 1976.

Mehan, H. *Learning lessons: Social organization in the classroom.* Cambridge: Harvard University Press, 1979.

Mehan, H., & Griffin, P. Socialization: The view from classroom interactions. *Sociological Inquiry,* 1980, *50* (3–4), 357–392.

Mehan, H., & Wood, H. *The reality of ethnomethodology.* New York: John Wiley and Sons, 1975.

Michaels, S., & Cook-Gumperz, J. A study of sharing time with first grade students: Discourse narratives in the classroom. *Proceedings of the Fifth Annual Meetings of the Berkeley Linguistic Society.* 1979.

Philips, S. Participant structures and communicative competence: Warm Springs children in community and classroom. In C. Cazden, V. John, & D. Hymes (Eds.), *Functions of language in the classroom.* New York: Teachers College Press, 1972.

Rosenberg, B. A. Oral sermons and oral narrative. In D. Ben-Amos & K. S. Goldstein (Eds.), *Folklore: Performance and Communication.* The Hague: Mouton, 1975.

Sacks, H., Schegloff, E., & Jefferson, G. A simplest systematics for the organization of turn-taking for conversation. *Language,* 1974, *50,* 696–735.

Schank, R. C., & Abelson, N. P. *Scripts, plans, goals, and understanding: An inquiry into human knowledge structures.* Hillsdale, N.J.: Lawrence Erlbaum, 1977.

Scheflen, A. E. *Communicational structure: Analysis of a psychotherapy transaction* (Formerly Stream and structure in psychotherapy). Bloomington: University of Indiana Press, 1973.

Schegloff, E. A. Sequencing in conversational openings. *American Anthropologist,* 1968, *70,* 1075–1095.

Scollon, R. The rhythmic integration of ordinary talk. In *Georgetown University Roundtable on Languages and Linguistics.* Washington, D.C.: Georgetown University Press, 1981.

Shultz, J., Florio, S., & Erickson, F. Where's the floor?: Aspects of the cultural organization of social relationships in communication at home and at school. In P. Gilmore & A. Glatthorn (Eds.), *Ethnography and education: Children in and out of school.* Washington, D.C.: Center for Applied Linguistics, in press.

Sinclair, J. M., & Coulthard, R. M. *Toward an analysis of discourse: The English used by teachers and pupils.* Oxford: Oxford University Press, 1975.

Smith, B. Othanel, and others. *A study of the logic of teaching.* U.S. Department of Health, Education, and Welfare: Cooperative Research Project No. 258 (7257). Urbana, Ill.: Bureau of Educational Research, College of Education, University of Illinois, n.d.

Stern, D., & Gibbon, J. Temporal expectancies of social behaviors in mother-infant play. In E. Thoman (Ed.), *Origins of the infant's social responsiveness.* Hillsdale, N.J.: Lawrence Erlbaum, 1979.

Taba, H. *Thinking in elementary school children.* U.S. Department of Health, Education, and Welfare: Cooperative Research Project No. 1574. San Francisco: San Francisco State College, 1964.

Tannen, D. What's in a frame?: Surface evidence for underlying expectations. In R. O. Freedle (Ed.), *New directions in discourse processing* (Advances in Discourse Processes: Vol. 2). Norwood, N.J.: Ablex, 1979.

Vygotsky, L. L. *Mind in society: The development of higher psychological processes.* M. Cole., V. J. Steiner, S. Scribner, & E. Souberman (Eds.). Cambridge: Harvard University Press, 1978.

Weber, M. *Wirtschaft und gesellschaft* (Vol. 1). Tübingen, 1922, pp. 1–14. Translated as The nature of social activity. In W. C. Runciman (Ed.), *Weber: Selections in translation.* Cambridge, England: Cambridge University Press, 1978. Pp. 7–32.

Wilkinson, L. C., Clevenger, M., & Dollaghan, C. Communication in small instructional groups: A sociolinguistic approach. In W. P. Dickson (Ed.), *Children's oral communication skills.* New York: Academic Press, 1981.

3. COOPERATIVE LEARNING

David W. Johnson and Roger T. Johnson

INTRODUCTION

In a Minnesota 5th-grade classroom, the teacher assigns her students a set of math story problems to solve. She assigns her students to groups of three, ensuring that there is a high-, medium-, and low-performing math student and both male and female students in each group. The **instructional task** is to solve each story problem correctly and to understand the correct process for doing so. Each group is given a set of story problems (one copy for each student) and a set of three "role" cards. Each group member is assigned one of the roles. The **reader** reads the problem aloud to the group. The **checker** makes sure that all members can explain how to solve each problem correctly. The **encourager** in a friendly way encourages all members of the group to participate in the discussion, sharing their ideas and feelings.

Within this lesson **positive interdependence** is structured by the group agreeing on (1) the answer and (2) the process for solving each problem. Since the group certifies that each member (1) has the correct answer written on his or her answer sheet and (2) can correctly explain how to solve each problem, **individual accountability** is structured by having the teacher pick one answer sheet at random to score for the group and to ask randomly one group member to explain how to solve one of the problems. The **collaborative skills** emphasized in the lesson are checking and encouraging. Finally, at the end of the period the groups *process* their functioning by answering two questions: (1) What is something each member did that was helpful for the group and (2) What is something each member could do to make the group even better tomorrow?

The above teacher is one of the thousands of teachers we have trained over the past 15 years to use cooperative learning procedures. There are at least two major approaches to implementing cooperative learning: Conceptual applications and direct applications. A **conceptual application** involves providing teachers with a conceptual framework consisting of general procedures and principles as

to the nature of cooperative learning and how it may be used. Teachers then take their existing lessons, materials, and curricula and adapt them to include cooperative learning. Lessons are uniquely tailored by the teachers to their instructional needs, circumstances, subject areas, and students. Cooperative learning can thus be used in any subject area with any age student. A **direct application** involves providing teachers with specific procedures and curriculum packages to be used in detailed and preset ways.

This article describes our conceptual application of cooperative learning, the nature of our cooperative learning procedures, and our approach for training teachers to utilize cooperative learning. The key messages of this article are:

1. Whenever a learning task is assigned, a clear goal structure should be given so that students know what behaviors are appropriate. There are three goal structures: Cooperative, competitive, and individualistic.

2. Cooperative, competitive, and individualistic learning are all important and should be used, but the dominant goal structure in any class should be cooperative. The procedures for using all three goal structures in an integrated and coordinated way and the circumstances under which each should be used are detailed in Johnson and R. Johnson (1987a).

3. Any lesson can be taught cooperatively. Any curriculum unit can be organized around cooperative lessons. All it takes is a teacher who is skilled in modifying existing curriculum and lessons from competitive or individualistic to cooperative.

4. The basic elements of cooperative learning are positive interdependence, face-to-face interaction, individual accountability, collaborative skills, and group processing.

5. The relative superiority of cooperative over competitive and individualistic learning in promoting high achievement and cognitive and social development has been demonstrated

by hundreds of research studies (Johnson & Johnson, 1988). Many teachers, administrators, students, and parents are unaware of the amount of evidence available.

6. The teacher's role in structuring learning situations cooperatively involves clearly specifying the objectives for the lesson, placing students in productive learning groups and providing appropriate materials, clearly explaining the cooperative goal structure, monitoring students as they work, and evaluating students' performance. The students should always be aware that they "sink or swim together" in a cooperative learning situation.

7. For cooperative learning groups to be productive, students must be able to engage in the needed collaborative skills. Teaching cooperative skills can be done simultaneously with teaching academic material.

8. An extension of cooperative learning is the use of structured academic controversies in which conflict between intellectual conclusions and positions is orchestrated by the teacher (Johnson & Johnson, 1987b; Johnson, Johnson, & Smith, 1986). There are many powerful instructional outcomes that result. Constructive controversy, however, is effective only when the overall context of instruction is cooperative.

9. The implementation of cooperative learning needs to be coupled with the implementation of professional support groups among teachers (Johnson, Johnson, & Holubec, 1986). Both the success of implementation efforts and the quality of life within most schools depend on teachers and other staff members cooperating with each other. Collegial relationships take as careful structuring and monitoring as do cooperative learning groups.

TYPES OF INTERDEPENDENCE

An essential instructional skill that all teachers need is knowing how and when to structure students' learning goals competitively, individualistically, and cooperatively. By structuring positive, negative, or no interdependence, teachers can influence the pattern of interaction among students and the instruc-

tional outcomes that result (Deutsch, 1962; Johnson & Johnson, 1987a, 1988; Johnson, Johnson, & Holubec, 1986).

Each time teachers prepare for a lesson, they must make decisions about the teaching strategies they will use. Teachers may structure academic lessons so that students are (a) in a win-lose struggle to see who is best, (b) learning individually on their own without interacting with classmates, or (c) learning in pairs or small groups helping each other master the assigned material. When lessons are structured competitively, students work against each other to achieve a goal that only one or a few students can attain. Students are graded on a curve, which requires them to work faster and more accurately than their peers. In a **competitive** learning situation, students' goal achievements are negatively correlated; when one student achieves his or her goal, all others with whom he or she is competitively linked fail to achieve their goals. Students seek outcomes that are personally beneficial but also are detrimental to the others with whom they are competitively linked. They either study hard to do better than their classmates or they take it easy because they do not believe they have a chance to win. In a competitively structured class, students would be given the task of completing the assignments faster and more accurately than the other students in the class. They would be warned to work by themselves, without discussing the assignments with other students, and to seek help from the teacher if they needed it.

Teachers can structure lessons individualistically so that students work by themselves to accomplish learning goals unrelated to those of their classmates. Individual goals are assigned each day, students' efforts are evaluated on a fixed set of standards, and rewards are given accordingly. Each student has a set of materials and works at his or her own speed, ignoring the other students in the class. In an **individualistic** learning situation, students' goal achievements are independent; the goal achievement of one student is unrelated to the goal achievement of others. Students seek outcomes that are personally beneficial and they ignore as irrelevant the goal achievements of their classmates. In a class structured individualistically, students would be given the task of completing the assignments correctly to reach a preset criteria of excellence. Students would be told to work by themselves, without disturbing their neighbors, and to seek help and assistance from the teacher.

For the past 45 years competitive and individualistic goal structures have dominated American education. Students usually come to school with competitive expectations and pressures from their parents. Many teachers have tried to reduce classroom competition by switching from a norm-referenced to a criteria-referenced evaluation system. In both competitive and individualistic learning situations teachers try to keep students away from each other. "Do not copy!" "Move your desks apart!" "I want to see how well you can do, not your neighbor!" are all phrases that teachers commonly use in their classrooms. Students are repeatedly told, "Do not care about the other students in this class. Take care of yourself!" When a classroom is dominated by competition, students often experience classroom life as a "rat race" with the psychology of the 100-yard dash. When a classroom is dominated by individualistic efforts, students will concentrate on isolating themselves from each other, ignoring others, and focusing only on their own work. Many students begin to compete within individualistic situations, even though the structure does not require it.

There is a third option. Teachers can structure lessons cooperatively so that students work together to accomplish shared goals. Students are assigned to small groups and instructed to learn the assigned material and to make sure that the other members of the group also master the assignment. Individual performance is checked regularly to ensure all students are learning. A criteria-referenced evaluation system is used. In a **cooperative** learning situation, students' goal achievements are positively correlated; students perceive that they can reach their learning goals if and only if the other students in the learning group also reach their goals. Thus, students seek outcomes that are beneficial to all those with whom they are cooperatively linked. Students discuss material with each other, help one another understand it, and encourage each other to work hard. In a cooperatively structured class, heterogeneous small groups made up of one high, one medium, and one low ability student would be formed. The students are given three tasks: to learn the assigned material, to make sure that the other

members of their group have learned the assigned material, and to make sure that everyone in the class has learned the assigned material. While the students work on assignments, they discuss the material with the other members of their group, explaining how to complete the work, listening to each other's explanations, encouraging each other to try to understand the solutions, and providing academic help and assistance. When everyone in the group has mastered the material, they go look for another group to help until everyone in the class understands how to complete the assignments.

Cooperative learning is the most important of the three ways of structuring learning situations, yet it is currently the least used. In most schools, class sessions are structured cooperatively only for 7 to 20 percent of the time (Johnson & Johnson, 1983a). The research indicates, however, that cooperative learning should be used whenever teachers want students to learn more, like school better, like each other better, have higher self-esteem, and learn more effective social skills.

BASIC ELEMENTS OF COOPERATIVE LEARNING

There are many ways in which cooperative learning may be used in class. Learning basic facts, understanding concepts, higher level reasoning, problem solving, and applying may all be best done in cooperative learning groups (Johnson & Johnson, 1988; Johnson, Maruyama, Johnson, Nelson, & Skon, 1981). The more conceptual the task, the more problem solving that is required, and the more creative the answers need to be, the greater the superiority of cooperative over competitive and individualistic learning. Cooperative learning is indicated whenever the learning goals are highly important, the task is complex or conceptual, problem solving is desired, divergent thinking or creativity is desired, quality of performance is expected, higher level reasoning strategies and critical thinking are needed, long-term retention is desired, or when the social development of students is one of the major instructional goals.

In most cases teachers may modify their existing curriculum to include cooperative learning. Whenever they do so, however, certain elements are essential. The five basic elements that need to be included for a lesson to be cooperative are:

1. **Positive interdependence** is the perception that one is linked with others in a way that one cannot succeed unless the other members of the group succeed (and vice versa) and, therefore, that their work benefits one and one's work benefits them. It is a sense of common fate and mutual causation or, in other words, that they "sink or swim together." Positive interdependence may be structured through common goals or rewards, being dependent on each other's resources, assigning specific roles to each member, or a division of labor.

2. **Face-to-face interaction** exists when students orally explain to each other how to solve problems, discuss with each other the nature of the concepts being learned, teach one's knowledge to classmates, and explain to each other the connections between present and past learning. There are cognitive activities and interpersonal dynamics that only occur when students get involved in explaining how [to answer the] assignments to each other. This face-to-face interaction is **promotive** in the sense that students help, assist, encourage, and support each other's efforts to learn.

3. **Individual accountability** exists when the performance of each individual student is assessed and the results given back to the group and the individual. It is important that the group knows who needs more assistance in completing the assignment. It is also important that group members know that they cannot "hitch-hike" on the work of others, that is, they must personally learn the assigned material. The intent of ensuring that each student believes he or she will be held accountable for learning the assigned material is to increase each student's sense of **personal responsibility** to the group and class. Common ways to structure individual accountability include (a) giving an individual test to each student and (b) randomly selecting one student's product to represent the entire group.

4. **Collaborative skills** include the leadership, decision-making, trust-building, communica-

tion, and conflict-management skills required for the students to work together productively. Groups cannot function effectively if students do not have and use the needed collaborative skills. These skills have to be taught just as purposefully and precisely as academic skills. Many students have never been required to collaborate in learning situations and, therefore, lack the needed social skills for doing so. Procedures and strategies for teaching students social skills may be found in Johnson (1986, 1987), Johnson and F. Johnson (1987), and Johnson, Johnson, and Holubec (1986).

5. **Group processing** occurs when groups discuss how well they are achieving their goals and maintaining effective working relationships among members. Groups need to describe what member actions are helpful and unhelpful and make decisions about what behaviors to continue or change. Such processing (a) enables learning groups to focus on group maintenance, (b) facilitates the learning of collaborative skills, (c) ensures that members receive feedback on their participation, and (d) reminds students to practice collaborative skills consistently. Some of the keys to successful processing are allowing sufficient time for it to take place, making it specific rather than vague, maintaining student involvement in processing, reminding students to use their collaborative skills while they process, and ensuring that clear expectations as to the purpose of processing have been communicated (Johnson & Johnson, 1984, 1987a).

OUTCOMES OF COOPERATION

Hundreds of research studies have validated the efficacy of cooperative learning. We have reviewed these studies a number of times (Johnson & Johnson, 1974, 1988; Johnson, Johnson, & Maruyama, 1983; Johnson, Maruyama, Johnson, Nelson, & Skon, 1981). We have also conducted an extensive program of research (Johnson & Johnson, 1983a). **Cooperative learning experiences, compared with competitive and individualistic ones, promote higher achievement, greater motivation, more positive**

interpersonal relations among students, more positive attitudes toward the subject area and teacher, greater self-esteem and psychological health, more accurate perspective taking, and greater social skills. With the amount of research evidence available, it is surprising that classroom practice is so oriented toward individualistic and competitive learning. It is time for the discrepancy to be reduced between what research indicates is effective in teaching and what teachers actually do.

THE TEACHER'S ROLE

Within cooperative learning situations, the teacher is both an academic expert **and** a classroom manager to promote effective group functioning. The teacher structures the learning groups; teaches the academic concepts, principles, and strategies that the students are to master and apply; and then monitors the functioning of the learning groups and intervenes to (a) teach collaborative skills and (b) provide assistance in academic learning when it is needed. Students are taught to look to their peers for assistance, feedback, reinforcement, and support. Students are expected to interact with each other, share ideas and materials, support and encourage academic achievement, orally explain and elaborate the concepts and strategies being learned, and hold each other accountable for learning. A criteria-referenced evaluation system is used.

Implementing cooperative learning involves a structured, but complex, process. Teachers are encouraged to start small by taking one class and using cooperative learning procedures until the process feels comfortable to them and then expanding into other classes. When structuring lessons cooperatively, teachers must complete the following five sets of activities (Johnson & Johnson, 1984, 1987a; Johnson, Johnson, & Holubec, 1987):

1. Clearly specifying the objectives for the lesson.
2. Making a number of decisions about placing students in learning groups before the lesson is taught.
3. Clearly explaining the task, the positive interdependence, and the learning activity to the students.

4. Monitoring the effectiveness of cooperative learning groups and intervening to provide task assistance (such as answering questions and teaching task skills) or to increase students' interpersonal and group skills.
5. Evaluating the students' achievement and helping students discuss how well they collaborated with each other.

The following discussion elaborates on these activities and details a procedure for structuring cooperative learning. Specific examples of lessons may be found in Chasnoff (1979), Lyons (1980), Roy (1982), R. Johnson and Johnson (1984), and D. W. Johnson, Johnson, & Holubec, (1987). Two films are also available that demonstrate the use of cooperative learning procedures (*Belonging, Circles of Learning*). More complete descriptions of how to structure cooperative learning may be found in *Cooperation in the Classroom* (Johnson & Johnson, 1984), *Learning Together and Alone: Cooperative, Competitive, and Individualistic Learning* (Johnson & Johnson, 1987a), and *Circles of Learning, Revised Edition* (Johnson, Johnson, & Holubec, 1986).

Objectives

Two types of objectives need to be specified before the lesson begins: (1) an academic objective specified at the correct level for the students and matched to the right level of instruction, and (2) a collaborative skills objective detailing what interpersonal and small group skills are going to be emphasized during the lesson. A common error many teachers make is to specify only academic objectives and to ignore the collaborative skills objectives needed to train students to cooperate with each other.

Decisions

Deciding on the Size of Group. Cooperative learning groups tend to range in size from two to six. When students are inexperienced in working cooperatively, when time is short, and when materials are scarce, the size of the group should be two to three. When students become more experienced and skillful, they will be able to manage groups of four or five members. Cooperative learning groups need to be small enough so that every student has to participate actively. A common mistake is to have students work in groups of four, five, and six before the students have the skills to do so competently.

Assigning Students to Groups. Teachers may wish to assign students to ability heterogeneous or homogeneous learning groups. When working on a specific skill, procedure or set of facts, homogeneous groups may be useful. When working on problem-solving tasks and on learning basic concepts heterogeneous groups may be most appropriate. When in doubt, teachers should use heterogeneous groups where students of different achievement levels in math, ethnic backgrounds, sexes, and social classes work together. Teachers will want to take special care in building a group where students who have special learning problems in math or who are isolated from their peers will be accepted and encouraged to achieve. Random assignment of students to groups is often effective.

Planning How Long Groups Will Work Together. The third decision teachers make is how long to keep groups together. Some teachers assign students to groups that last a whole semester or even a whole academic year. Other teachers like to keep a learning group together only long enough to complete a unit or chapter. In some students student attendance is so unpredictable that teachers form new groups every day. Sooner or later, however, every math student should work with every other classmate. Usually it is preferable to keep groups together for at least two or three weeks.

Arranging the Room. Members of a learning group should sit close enough to each other that they can share materials and talk to each other quietly and maintain eye contact with all group members. Circles are usually best. The teacher should have clear access lanes to every group. Common mistakes that teachers make in arranging a room are to (1) place students at a rectangular table where they cannot have eye contact with all other members or (2) move several desks together, which may place students too far apart to communicate quietly with each other and share materials.

Planning Materials. Instructional materials need to be distributed among group members so that all students participate and achieve. Especially when students are inexperienced in cooperating, teachers will want to distribute materials in ways planned to communicate that the assignment is a joint (not an individual) effort and that students are in a "sink or swim together" learning situation. Materials can be arranged like a jigsaw puzzle so that each student has part of the materials needed to complete the task. The steps for structuring a jigsaw lesson are to (1) distribute a set of materials to each group, divide the materials into four parts, and give each member one part; (2) assign students the individual tasks of learning and becoming an expert on their part of the material and planning how to teach the material to the other group members; (3) [have] each student meet with a member of another learning group who is learning the same section of the materials and [confer] about how [best to] teach the section to other group members (expert pairs); and (4) have the groups meet and the members teach their area of expertise to the other group members so that all students learn all the assigned material. An alternative to a jigsaw is giving one copy of the materials to a group to ensure that the students will have to work together.

Assigning Roles. Cooperative interdependence may also be arranged through the assignment of complementary and interconnected roles to group members. Such roles include a **summarizer** (who restates the group's major conclusions or answers), a **checker** (who ensures that all members can explain how to arrive at an answer or conclusion), an **accuracy coach** (who corrects any mistakes in another member's explanations or summaries), and a **relater** (who asks other members to [relate] current concepts and strategies to material studied previously). Assigning students such roles is an effective method of teaching them cooperative skills and fostering interdependence.

Explaining the Academic Task and Cooperative Goal Structure

Explaining the Academic Task. Teachers clearly explain the academic task so that students are clear about the assignment and understand the objectives of the lesson. Direct teaching of concepts, principles, and strategies may take place at this point. Teachers may wish to answer any questions students have about the concepts or facts they are to learn or apply in the lesson.

Structuring Positive Goal Interdependence. Teachers communicate to students that they have a group goal and must work collaboratively. This may be done by asking the group to produce a single product or report [or] arrive at consensus concerning how assigned problems are solved, providing group rewards, giving bonus points if all members of a group reach a preset criteri[on] of excellence, or picking a student at random to represent the group and explain its conclusions to the class. In a cooperative learning group, students are responsible for learning the assigned material, making sure that all other group members learn the assigned material, and making sure that all other class members learn the assigned material, in that order.

Structuring Individual Accountability. The purpose of the learning group is to maximize the learning of each member. Lessons need to be structured so that the level of each student's learning is assessed and that groups provide members with the encouragement and assistance needed to maximize performance. Individual accountability may be structured by having each student individually tested or randomly choosing the work of one member to represent the group as a whole.

Structuring Intergroup Cooperation. The positive outcomes found with a cooperative learning group can be extended throughout a whole class by structuring intergroup cooperation. Bonus points may be given as all members of a class reach a preset criteri[on] of excellence. When a group finishes its work, the teacher should encourage the members to go help other groups complete the assignment.

Explaining Criteria for Success. Evaluations within cooperatively structured lessons need to be criteria-referenced. At the beginning of the lesson teachers need to explain clearly the criteria by which students' work will be evaluated.

Specifying Desired Behaviors. The word cooperative has many different connotations and uses. Teachers will need to define cooperation operationally by specifying the behaviors that are appropriate and desirable within the learning groups. Beginning behaviors are "stay with your group," "use quiet voices," and "take turns." When groups begin to function effectively, expected behaviors may include having each member explain how to get an answer and asking each member to relate what is being learned to previous learning.

Monitoring and Intervening

Monitoring Students' Behavior. The teacher's job begins in earnest when the cooperative learning groups begin working. Much of the teacher's time is spent observing group members to see what problems they are having completing the assignment and working cooperatively. Many teachers also use student observers to gather information on the appropriateness of activities within each group.

Providing Academic Assistance. In monitoring the learning groups as they work, teachers will wish to clarify instructions, review important math concepts and strategies, answer questions, and teach academic skills as necessary.

Intervening to Teach Cooperative Skills. While monitoring the learning groups, teachers often find students who do not have the necessary cooperative skills and groups where members are having problems in collaborating. In these cases, the teacher should intervene to suggest more effective procedures for working together and more effective behaviors in which students should engage. Basic interpersonal and small group skills may be directly taught (Johnson, 1986, 1987; Johnson & F. Johnson, 1987).

Providing Closure to Lesson. At the end of each lesson, students [should] be able to summarize what they have learned. Teachers may wish to summarize the major points in the lesson, ask students to recall ideas or give examples, and answer any final questions students have.

Evaluation and Processing

Evaluating Students' Learning. Students' work is evaluated, their learning assessed, and feedback is given as to how their work compares with the criteria of excellence. Qualitative as well as quantitative aspects of performance should be addressed.

Assessing How Well the Group Functioned. The learning groups assess how well they worked together and plan how to improve their effectiveness in the future. Our two favorite questions for doing so are: "What actions helped the group work productively? What actions could be added to make the group even more productive tomorrow?" A common error of many teachers is to provide too brief a time for students to process the quality of their collaboration.

Teacher's Role Summary

Implementing cooperative learning is not easy. It can take years to become an expert. Teachers may wish to start small by taking one subject area or one class and us[ing] cooperative learning procedures they feel comfortable teaching cooperatively, and then expand[ing] into other subject areas or other classes. In order to implement cooperatively learning successfully, teachers will need to teach students the interpersonal and small group skills required to collaborate, structure and orchestrate academic disagreements and conflicts among students, and form collaborative relations with other teachers.

TEACHING STUDENTS COLLABORATIVE SKILLS

Students who have never been taught how to work effectively with others cannot be expected to do so. Thus, the first experience of many teachers who structure cooperative learning is that their students cannot collaborate with each other. Yet it is within cooperative situations, where there is a task to complete, that social skills become most relevant and should ideally be taught. All students need to become skillful in communicating, building and maintaining trust, providing leadership, and managing conflicts (Johnson, 1986, 1987; Johnson & F. Johnson, 1987). Teaching collaborative skills becomes an important prerequisite for academic learning since achievement will improve as students become more effective in working with each other.

There are two reasons why collaborative skills are directly taught in classrooms where teachers are serious about utilizing cooperative learning. The first is that interpersonal and small group skills are the engine that powers cooperative learning groups. For cooperative learning groups to be productive, students must be able to engage in the needed collaborative skills. Without good leadership, effective communication, the building and maintenance of trust, and the constructive resolution of conflicts, cooperative learning groups will not maximize their productivity and effectiveness.

Second, collaborative skills in and of themselves are important instructional outcomes that relate to future career and life success. The importance of cooperative learning procedures goes beyond achievement, positive relationships among diverse students, high self-esteem, and many other important outcomes. The ability of all students to work cooperatively with others is the keystone to building and maintaining stable marriages, families, careers, and friendships. Schooling is future oriented in the sense that the instruction taking place is primarily aimed at preparing students for career and adult responsibilities. The assumption is made that students will be able to apply successfully what they learn in school to career, family, community, and society settings. Being able to perform technical skills such as reading, speaking, listening, writing, computing, and problem solving are valuable but of little use if the person cannot apply technical skills in cooperative interaction with other people in career, family, and community settings. It does no good to train an engineer or secretary, for example, if the person cannot work effectively with other people and contribute what he or she knows to joint efforts and thereby maintain a job as an engineer or secretary after [he or she has] finished school. Without some skill in cooperating effectively, it would be difficult (if not impossible) to maintain a marriage, hold a job, or be part of a community, society, and world. Schools have long been places that have promoted unrealistic expectations of what career, family, and community life may be like. Most careers do not expect people to sit in rows and compete with colleagues without interacting with them. The quality of the American work force and the growth of American productivity [depend] largely on how well citizens can work cooperatively. Teamwork, communication, effective coordination, and divisions of labor characterize most real life settings. It may be time for schools to more realistically reflect the reality of adult life. Learning how to work cooperatively with others, knowing how to function as part of a team, may be one of the most important outcomes of schooling.

The interpersonal and small groups skills students need to master in order to work cooperatively with peers are detailed elsewhere in *Reaching Out: Interpersonal Effectiveness and Self-Actualization* (Johnson, 1986), *Human Relations and Your Career* (Johnson, 1987), and *Joining Together: Group Theory and Group Skills* (Johnson & F. Johnson, 1987). The procedures for teaching students collaborative skills while simultaneously working on academic learning are discussed in *Circles of Learning* (Johnson, Johnson, and Holubec, 1986).

STRUCTURING ACADEMIC CONTROVERSIES

Within cooperative groups students often disagree as to what answers to assignments should be and how the group should function in order to maximize members' learning. Conflict is an inherent part of learning as old conclusions and conceptions are challenged and modified to take into account new information and broader perspectives. **Controversy** is a type of academic conflict that exists when one student's ideas, information, conclusions, theories, and opinions are incompatible with those of another, and the two seek to reach an agreement. When students become experienced in working cooperatively, and when teachers wish to increase students' emotional involvement in learning and motivation to achieve, teachers may structure controversy into cooperative learning groups by structuring five phases (Johnson & Johnson, 1987b; Johnson, Johnson, & Smith, 1986):

1. Assigning students to groups of four[;] dividing the group into two pairs. One pair is given the pro position and the other pair is given the con position on an issue being studied. Each pair prepares [its] position.
2. Each pair presenting its position.
3. Students arguing the two positions.
4. Pairs reversing perspectives and arguing the opposition position.
5. Reaching a decision and coming to a consensus on a position that is supported by facts and logic and can be defended by each group member.

TEACHER PROFESSIONAL SUPPORT GROUPS

Teachers will not become proficient in using cooperative learning procedures by attending a workshop or from reading this book. Teachers become proficient and competent from **doing.** Expertise in cooperative learning is reached when teachers routinely structure lessons cooperatively without conscious planning or thought. This requires using cooperative learning for several years while receiving in-classroom help and assistance. In order to ensure such a (1) sustained use of cooperative learning strategies and (2) support system, teachers must belong to a professional support group that provides continuous, immediate in-class assistance in perfecting teachers' competencies. Ongoing training over a period of years needs to be provided when individual teachers want and need it. Experts who can provide support and assistance have to be on call to demonstrate, coteach, problem solve, and provide help when it is needed and wanted.

This means that teachers and other staff members must be structured into professional support groups aimed at teaching each other how to use cooperative learning strategies effectively and how to use all three goal structures in an integrated and coordinated way. The implementation of cooperative learning needs to be coupled with the implementation of professional support groups among teachers. Both the success of implementation efforts and the quality of life within most schools depend on teachers and other staff members cooperating with each other. Collegial relationships take as careful structuring and monitoring as does cooperative learning.

SUMMARY

Whenever a learning task is assigned, a clear cooperative, competitive, or individualistic goal structure should be given, so that students know how to behave appropriately. While all three goal structures are important and should be used, the dominant goal structure in any class should be cooperative. Any lesson with any age student in any subject area may be taught cooperatively. All it takes is a teacher who is skilled in translating the old competitive and individualistic lesson into cooperative ones. In order to be cooperative, a lesson must include positive interdependence, face-to-face interaction among students, individual accountability, the use of collaborative skills, and the processing of how well the learning groups functioned. When done correctly, cooperative learning tends to promote higher achievement, greater motivation, more positive relationships among students, more positive attitudes toward the subject area and the teacher, greater self-esteem and psychological health, greater social skills, and many other important instructional outcomes. The teacher's role in structuring learning situations cooperatively involves clearly specifying the objectives for the lesson, placing students in learning groups and providing appropriate materials, clearly explaining the cooperative goal structure and learning task, monitoring students as they work, and evaluating students' performance. For cooperative learning groups to be productive, students must be able to engage in the needed leadership, communication, trust-building, and conflict resolution skills. Teaching students the required interpersonal and small group skills can be done simultaneously with teaching academic material. When cooperative groups are functioning at a high level, controversies occur where students disagree as to the answers and conclusions that may be derived from their knowledge and reasoning. Such academic controversies are powerful learning opportunities and the specific procedures are available for structuring cooperative learning groups to ensure that academic conflicts occur and are constructively managed. In order to sustain the long-term implementation and in-classroom help and assistance needed to gain expertise in cooperative learning, teachers need professional support groups made up of colleagues who are also committed to mastering cooperative learning. Good collegial relationships take as careful structuring and monitoring as do cooperative learning groups.

REFERENCES

Chasnoff, R. (Ed.) (1979). *Structuring cooperative learning in the classroom: The 1979 handbook.* Edina, MN: Interaction Book Company.

Deutsch, M. (1962). Cooperation and trust: Some theoretical notes. In M. Jones (Ed.), *Nebraska symposium on motivation* (pp. 275–320). Lincoln, NE: University of Nebraska Press.

Johnson, D. W. (1986). *Reaching out: Interpersonal effectiveness and self-actualization* (3rd ed.). Englewood Cliffs, NJ: Prentice-Hall.

Johnson, D. W. (1987). *Human relations and your career: A guide to interpersonal skills* (2nd ed.). Englewood Cliffs, NJ: Prentice-Hall.

Johnson, D. W., & Johnson F. (1987). *Joining together: Group theory and group skills* (3rd ed.). Englewood Cliffs, NJ: Prentice-Hall.

Johnson, D. W., & Johnson, R. T. (1974). Instructional goal structure: Cooperative, competitive, or individualistic? *Review of Educational Research, 44,* 213–240.

Johnson, D. W., & Johnson, R. T. (1980). *Belonging* (16mm film). Edina, MN: Interaction Book Company.

Johnson, D. W., & Johnson, R. T. (1983a). The socialization and achievement crisis: Are cooperative learning experiences the solution? In L. Bickman (Ed.), *Applied social psychology annual 4* (pp. 119–164). Beverly Hills, CA: Sage Publications.

Johnson, D. W., & Johnson, R. T. (1983b). *Circles of learning* (16mm film). Edina, MN: Interaction Book Company.

Johnson, D. W., & Johnson, R. T. (1984). *Cooperation in the classroom.* Edina, MN: Interaction Book Company.

Johnson, D. W., & Johnson, R. T. (1987a). *Learning together and alone: Cooperative, competitive and individualistic learning* (2nd ed.). Englewood Cliffs, NJ: Prentice-Hall.

Johnson, D. W., & Johnson, R. T. (1987b). *Creative conflict.* Edina, MN: Interaction Book Company.

Johnson, D. W., & Johnson, R. T. (1988). *Cooperation and competition.* Hillsdale, NJ: Lawrence Erlbaum.

Johnson. D. W., Johnson, R. T., & Holubec, E. (Eds.) (1986). *Circles of learning: Cooperation in the classroom* (Revised ed.). Edina, MN: Interaction Book Company.

Johnson, D. W., Johnson. R.T., & Maruyama, G. (1983). Interdependence and interpersonal attraction among heterogeneous and homogeneous individuals: A theoretical formulation and a meta-analysis of the research. *Review of Educational Research, 53,* 5–54.

Johnson, D. W., Johnson, R. T., & Smith, K. (1986). Academic conflict among students: Controversy and learning. In R. Feldman, *Social psychological applications to education.* Cambridge, MA: Cambridge University Press.

Johnson, D. W., Maruyama, G., Johnson, R. T., Nelson, D., & Skon, L. (1981). Effects of cooperative, competitive, and individualistic goal structures on achievement: A meta-analysis. *Psychological Bulletin, 89,* 47–62.

Johnson, R. T., & Johnson, D. W. (Eds.) (1984). *Structuring cooperative learning: Lesson plans for teachers.* Edina, MN: Interaction Book Company.

Johnson, R. T., Johnson, D. W., & Holubec, E. (Eds.) (1987). *Structuring cooperative learning: Lesson plans for teachers.* Edina, MN: Interaction Book Company.

Lyons, V. (Ed.) (1980). *Structuring cooperative learning in the classroom: The 1980 handbook.* Edina, MN: Interaction Book Company.

Roy, P. (Ed.) (1982). *Structuring cooperative learning in the classroom: The 1982 handbook.* Edina, MN: Interaction Book Company.

4. INTRODUCTION AND INTEGRATION OF CLASSROOM ROUTINES BY EXPERT TEACHERS

Gaea Leinhardt, C. Weidman, and K. M. Hammond

The purpose of this research was to learn how successful teachers establish the instructional structure in their classrooms at the beginning of the year and maintain it throughout the year. The presence of functioning activity structures and efficient supporting routines is one benchmark of a successful mathematics teacher (Leinhardt 1983). Activity structures are goal directed segments of teacher and student behavior that involve teachers and students in particular actions, for example, lesson presentation or boardwork. Routines are small cooperative scripts of behavior, used to support several activity structures, for example, choral response, or paper passing out. These structures and their supporting routines permit instruction to take place in a focused, predictable, and fluid way. Activity structures help to pattern and make predictable the normal flow of a lesson. Routines free up cognitive processing space for both teachers and students by making automatic a subset of the cognitive processing tasks that would confront teachers and students if the problems for which these are solutions had to be solved anew each time. For routines to become established they must be taught and rehearsed. . . .

THEORETICAL BACKGROUND

In the current study we examined the behavior of expert teachers during the first few days of school and at midyear. (Experts were identified by their students' unusual academic successes and by convergent nomination from principals and supervisors.) Further, we discuss the establishment of routines and patterns of behavior as a way of helping to reduce the cognitive demands for both students and teachers when content information is to be transmitted.

Studies of the beginning of the school year have

noted the significance of the first few days in establishing rules and norms and in setting the tone for the year. The research in education has emphasized the development of rules and management routines in the context of contrasting successful and unsuccessful managers. It is important to distinguish between rules and routines. Although some rules are also routines, most rules are statements of what is not permitted or are explicit or implicit constraints. Routines, on the other hand, are fluid, paired, scripted segments of behavior that help movement toward a *shared goal*. Routines can have explicit descriptors, can be modeled or, more commonly, can simply evolve through a shared exchange of cues.

In studying how expert teachers go about establishing effective routines we have found it useful to break apart the math lesson into repeatable goal directed segments that are very similar to what Bossert (1978) calls activity structures and which can be modeled using the planning and script analyses from cognitive psychology. An activity structure perspective allowed us to examine the recurrent activities within a given lesson as they were shaped by the teacher and students. Berliner, King, Rubin, and Fisher (1981) specified the features which defined a number of common activity structures which increased student opportunity to learn.

There now exists a substantial number of studies that directly address the issues of how teachers establish themselves with their students in the first few days or weeks of school (Ball 1980; Buckley and Cooper 1978; Clark and Elmore 1979; Cornbleth, Korth, and Dorow 1983; Edelshy, Draper and Smith 1983; Emmer, Evertson and Anderson 1980; Evertson and Anderson 1979; Pittman 1983; Sanford and Evertson 1980; Tikunoff and Ward 1978; McDermott 1977). The studies fall into two basic categories—those that address the issues of management and control, growing quite directly from process product research, and those that grow out of the ethnography of human relations and negoti-

---

Editor's Note: This is the first article in a series on Personal Practical Knowledge edited by Jean Clandinin and Miriam Ben-Peretz.

ations. For the most part, the studies focus on management of students or rules for conduct.[1]

In studying the development of classroom routines, we are more interested in the system of exchanges that are set up in order for instruction to take place than in the system of rules to limit behavior, although rules may be used to help establish routines (Good 1983; Good and Hinkel 1982). Because the precise analytic framework for studies of teachers that goes beyond a list of their action types has not been developed fully, the field still searches for a metaphor—teacher as decision maker, problem solver, executive, etc. The metaphor helps both reader and author fill in the empty pieces of conceptualization. For this particular study we use the notion of teacher as choreographer or lead dancer. Verbal and movement behaviors must be assembled so they can be danced out. Selecting the steps to be combined and rehearsing them becomes a task of the teacher with the participation of the students.

Further, we assume that students have a well

developed school schema in place by fourth grade. Second graders have a school schema to a lesser extent. This schema is much more than a rule list. It anticipates the information that will come from other students, the teachers, parents, principal, lunch aide, etc. in the first few days of school. If no information is forthcoming, the student puts information in from previous experience, including the information of how to interpret no information.

A Perspective

In cognitive psychology, the work on planning shows how one can move through a sequence of actions and decisions efficiently. Thus, one can build a skeletal sequence of actions that has embedded in it the schemata for collecting information, storing it, and then using it in a different (later) location in the sequence (Greeno, Glaser, and Newell 1983; Hayes-Roth and Hayes-Roth 1978; Joyce 1978–1979; Sacerdoti 1977; Stefik 1980; Leinhardt and Greeno 1986). In order to do this not only must the teacher's repertoire contain action and content schemata, but the teacher/student team must also have a set of established routines to facilitate information collection, storage, and retrieval. The combination of these elements constitutes a lesson agenda or plan.

Teachers who function well have agendas (Leinhardt 1983; Leinhardt and Greeno 1986). Agendas consist of the working lesson plans and they contain major segments within each lesson that can be modeled, for example, homework check, presentation, and guided practice. An agenda is not the lesson plan. However, it contains the topic of the lesson and all of the goals and supporting actions that permit a teacher to execute a segment of instruction. Elsewhere we have described in some depth the content of these agendas (Leinhardt 1983; Leinhardt and Greeno 1986). For the purpose of this study, planning nets (Greeno, Riley, and Gelman 1984) are used to represent segments of the agenda. Plans, or agendas in the psychological sense, can be considered ways of systematically ordering action strings, each of which calls up a familiar knowledge schema that enables the action to take place (Hayes-Roth and Hayes-Roth 1978). In a socially dynamic setting, planning must incorporate estimates of what the other members of the group will do. Planning

---

[1] There is considerable diversity in methodology from retrospective interviews conducted seven weeks after school starts (Clark and Elmore 1979) to daily observational logs collected for the entire school day (Tikunoff and Ward 1978; Buckley and Cooper 1978). It seems fairly clear that in order to get a good picture of the emergence of the educational dance of the school, interviews and observations must be conducted before and during the first few days of school. A consistent finding is that for good teachers, the regulation system is in place very, very quickly (Edelsky, Draper, and Smith 1983; Pittman 1983; Emmer, Evertson, and Anderson 1979). This is true whether the research is addressing the issue of teacher as manager (Emmer, Evertson, and Anderson 1980) or teacher as negotiator (Cornbleth, Korth, and Dorow 1983), or teacher as rule establisher (Tikunoff and Ward 1978; Buckley and Cooper 1978). In some contrast to the Buckley and Cooper findings that teachers determine all the rules, several researchers find considerable negotiation which influences the way a classroom emerges (see especially Ball 1980; Cornbleth, Korth, and Dorow 1983; and Edelsky, Draper, and Smith 1983; McDermott 1973). Perhaps it is really a matter of semantics as there is no question of where the *power* is in the system, just some question as to its use. We consider that the effective teacher at the beginning of the year has an objective of setting up an efficient and smoothly running classroom where instruction, not management, is the major thrust. The first few days involve explicit statements of the teacher's expectations (Buckley and Cooper 1978; Clark and Elmore 1979; Emmer, Evertson, and Anderson 1980; Evertson and Anderson 1979) and rehearsals of the routines. As the expectations and routines become internalized, the teacher can call up these routines with minimal cues to the students. By mapping the routines as they are explicitly stated at the beginning of the year onto the midyear version, we can specify how these routines serve to reduce the processing load carried by teacher and student.

in this context is further facilitated if the execution can draw upon shared action schemata, namely routines. The instruction to "pass your papers in" results in all actors understanding the expected actions and executing them in a routine way.

Using planning nets to analyze some of the activity segments of expert teachers, we have focused on the presentation segment of a lesson. Lesson presentation integrates several sub-segments, each of which has its own planning net. The planning net is the formal representation of a plan or agenda segment. (Planning nets have nodes and links. The nodes can be either goals or actions. Actions represent bundles of knowledge that can have pre-,

post- and co-requisite states [goals] attached. Links connect goals and actions.)

Figure 1 . . . starts with oral presentation. Presentation of lesson material is accomplished by achieving several goal states. Goals appear in hexagons (nodes), and actions in rectangles. In Figure 1, the first goal state is to have the *terms defined*. One action, which has as its consequence the definition of terms, is for the teacher to state the definition. A second action, which has as an indirect consequence achieving that goal, is to call on a student; but calling the student also has the consequence that the student is then in the goal state of being a responder who states the definition. A test

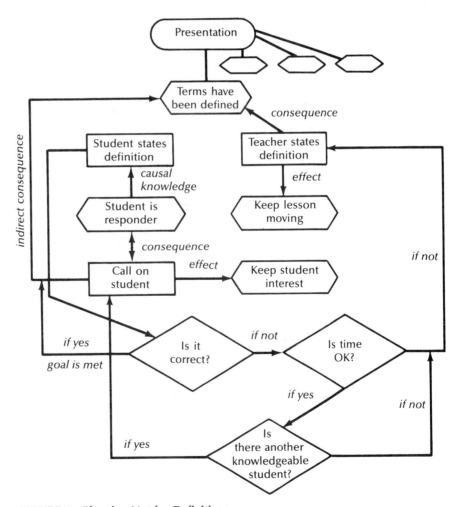

FIGURE 1   **Planning Net for Definitions**

for correctness is attached to the terminal student action. The point of this elaboration of a small bit of teacher action is both to display the complexity of a simple action and to locate the role and consequence of student/teacher routines. If the routine for selecting a student and having the student respond is not clearly established, the lesson can falter or even fail.

In examining a planning net for a lesson segment, we can see the function of a routine. Routines can be thought of as pieces of socially scripted behavior or they can be shown in their role as supporting actions for achieving some goal. For example, one of the first goals in this lesson is to define the terms of the algorithm. In Figure 1 this goal state is shown as the consequence of two actions: the teacher stating the definitions or the student(s) stating them. The effect (link) of having the teacher state the definitions is that the lesson moves along quickly. The effect of having the student(s) state the definitions is that student interest is maintained. However, in order for the teacher to get the student to respond, the teacher relinquishes control of a portion of the lesson, as can be seen by the absence of direct connections between the teacher's actions and student actions in Figure 1. Student response *routines* are what allow this segment of the lesson to proceed successfully. . . .

During a lesson, teachers are often in a position in which they have to surrender control of the execution of a portion of a plan. Whenever a teacher calls on a student s/he runs the risk that the student's verbal productions or actions may not produce exactly what is needed. The probability of achieving the goal is reduced by some amount. The student's potential action is linked to a goal in the teacher's plan by the teacher's causal knowledge. One might ask why the teacher gives up this control. The answer lies with another goal—that of keeping students active, interested participants in their own learning. . . .

METHODS AND DATA SOURCE

Six expert mathematics teachers were identified by examining student achievement growth scores over a five year period. These teachers' growth scores were consistently in the top 20% of the districts' distribution.[2] The teachers taught in the following grades: three teachers in fourth, one teacher in fourth and fifth, one teacher in second and third, and one teacher in first. All of the teachers taught in self-contained classrooms (including one open classroom) and two taught math to a second class. When a teacher taught an additional math class, we only focused on one class for the analysis. Median class size was 28. The classrooms all served middle to lower middle class families. One was all white; one was all black; and four were integrated. The classrooms were distributed across five schools in a major metropolitan area.

The following types of data were collected for each teacher: observational logs, four of which covered the beginning school days and an average of 20 additional ones; an average of eight math class videotapes with corresponding stimulated recalls, an average of 10 additional ones; audiotapes of classes on different days; and extensive interviews on the teacher's class planning (17), math subject matter knowledge (4), perceptions of students (1), and general educational orientation. Data were collected over two academic years: midyear of year one, the first four days of year two, and midyear of year two. The audiotapes of observations, interviews, and stimulated recalls were transcribed. The transcribed data and videotapes were analyzed to identify the activity structures and supporting routines that were used in each lesson.

A matrix mapping the relationship between routines and activity structures was developed, both for individual teachers and across the sample of teachers. We were then able to identify the introduction of the routines in the first four days and describe the actions of each teacher as the routines were established. The final step was to find the attachments

---

[2]In this context, expertise is based on the assessment of the product of the teacher's behaviors. However, expertise is not unidimensional and, in fact, all of our teachers showed skills and weaknesses in varying degrees in varying circumstances. The notion is that instruction is a domain of compensating factors. While failure in some areas does produce class failure, weakness in one area (subject matter knowledge, for example) can be compensated for in others—lesson presentation skill, for example. In our case, most of the teachers were outstanding managers, but at least two were not; these two, however, had unusual command of the subject matter.

linking the teacher's actions to the routine. These linkages occurred as explicit directions, cues, reinforcers, the use of a child as a model, or as emergent repetitions.

We categorized each linkage as conveying either the procedure for doing a routine, the goal or purpose of a routine, or both. If a teacher explained or taught how to do something, it was considered procedural (for example, "pass papers to the person in front, then pass center, I will collect"; or, "when you are finished, turn your paper over, fold your hands and look up"). If a teacher gave the objective, but not procedure, it was considered goal based (for example, "let me know when you're finished and then keep busy"). In some cases, the teacher gave both the procedure and the goal.[3] Each routine was coded as *management, support* or *exchange*.[4] Interobserver agreement on the identification and categorizing of routines was 95%.

Management routines can be thought of as housekeeping, discipline, maintenance, and people-moving tasks; for example, hanging up coats, never interrupting, lining up (to change classes or go to the bathroom). Management routines provide a classroom superstructure within which the social environment and behaviors are clearly defined and well known. Failure of management routines results in a sense of disorder or lack of discipline. Typically, "open" classrooms have fewer of these routines routinized than do other classrooms. Thus, open classroom teachers may state goals and leave the particular action procedure to the student, perhaps because they tend to have fewer instances of whole-class movement. When whole-class movement is required or when record keeping is required, standardization is introduced.

Support routines define and specify the behaviors and actions necessary for a learning-teaching exchange to take place; in other words, they are set-ups for this exchange. Examples are distribution and collection of papers; getting materials ready (books, pencils, crayons); specifying where an action is to occur (at the board, at student's seat, at teacher's desk); locating pages and lines in texts. Failure in these routines leads to a sense that the teacher is not "with it" or well prepared, or that students are having (or giving) a hard time. Failure also leads to loss of time.

Exchange routines specify the interactive behaviors that permit the teaching-learning exchange to occur. They are largely language contacts between teachers and students. More specifically, the preferred types of communication between students and teacher are modeled or defined and are often activity-structure specific. Examples are: choral exchanges, teacher travels and checks student's work, and teacher calls on a series of individual students until she gets the correct answer. Failure in these routines leads to the appearance that teachers are talking to themselves, with students not listening or at least not responding *or* vice versa. To use our metaphor for teaching—the first type of routine gives broad stage directions; the second, the steps to the dance; and the third, the *pas de deux*. . . .

Management/Support/Exchange Summary

Figure [2] shows the cumulative count of the introduction and use in midyear of routines in each of the three categories—management, support and exchange. The counts are cumulative numbers of routines from Day One to Day Four. Retention of each type of routine at midyear is indicated. Most

---

[3]We were primarily interested in analyzing the routines used in a functioning mathematics class; therefore, our method of establishing the specific time and activity structure when routines were presented becomes important. During the first four days we observed all of the teachers for an entire day. During the day, there are many routines that may be used or introduced in nonmath classes and that are later used in the math class itself (such as pencil sharpening). We observed, however, some routines that are not used in math class (hanging up coats, for example) and these were not counted.

[4]The system used to identify routines present at the beginning of school and at midyear consisted of three major phases. The first phase (coding) was the coding of routines that occurred in the first four days. In this stage, researchers read the observational logs of each teacher in the first four days. Routines and rules as well as activity structures were noted in the margin and then mapped onto a matrix developed for coding routines across activity structures. The observational logs were read a second time and the method for introducing each routine was added to the matrix. In the second phase (sorting), routines were sorted by type—management, support, and exchange. The routine was then sorted by its main function. Two researchers sorted these routines. One chose the type while the other either agreed or disagreed. The assignment was made by consensus. In the third phase (checking), videotapes or transcripts were watched to see if coded routines from the beginning of school were observable in midyear. A checklist was compiled on which the researcher noted whether or not the routine was present on any of the days that were videotaped, or in transcribed notes.

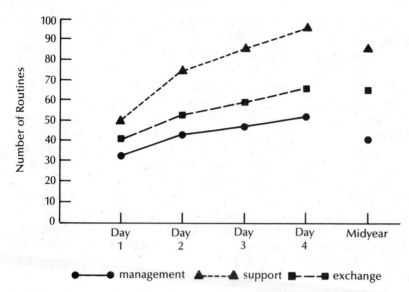

FIGURE [2]   Cumulative Introduction of Routines and Their Midyear Retention

routines are introduced in the first day with gradually less acute slopes (which means fewer new routines are added) towards day four. The introduction of exchange routines appears to be the most evenly distributed across the first four days.

Management. . . . During the first four days, teachers' use of different types of management routines varied from a low of two to a high of fifteen. Recall that management routines refer to those routines that involve student movement and non-academic interactions. The first and second grade teachers introduced the most management routines (fifteen each) but retained lower percentages. The best manager in the fourth grade group used a greater number of management routines than any other fourth grade teacher; in addition, she used them in consistently more powerful and complex combinations than any other teacher. There was crispness in her execution of the management routines as well as complexity that resulted from frequent combination of routines into strings. The most frequently used management routines were used by four or more teachers—pencil sharpening (4), line up (6), "don't interrupt" (4), and no talking (4). With the exception of "don't interrupt," all these important management routines were still present in midyear. "Don't interrupt" may have

disappeared because interruptions had disappeared. . . .

Support. The teachers introduced a great variety of support routines, 44 different ones in all. Teachers used support routines to facilitate instructional actions. However, only twelve of the support routines were used by three or more teachers. An implication of this relatively limited overlap of specific routines may be that support routines reflect a teacher's personal style. Thus, a teacher has to spend considerable time at the beginning of the year teaching idiosyncratic procedures to the students. The most important support routines were used by four or more teachers—take out/put away (6), paper format (6), teacher collects/distributes (6), student collects/distributes (4), wait to start (5), open/turn to/look at/close (5), keep busy when assigned work is finished (4). In general, these routines continued to be used throughout the year. . . .

Exchange. Teachers introduced slightly more exchange routines (32) than management routines (25) and fewer than support (44). Exchange routines facilitated communication between teacher and student. The first and second grade teachers tended to use fewer exchange routines and to introduce them later in the first week of school. However, only two exchange routines were introduced on the fourth day. The most important exchange routines were used by four or more teachers—hand raising as a signal (5), call until a student gives a correct answer (5), individual exchange (6), travel/check (6), and choral exchange (6). Two versions of an attention getting routine ("eyes on me" and "pay attention") were used by three teachers, the two primary teachers and the best manager in the fourth grade. All of these important routines were still present in mid-year. . . . Unlike the other routines, exchange routines were not explicitly taught, they were just done and maintained by constant use. Having a large repertoire of exchange routines adds variety, flexibility and interest to the overall conversation of the classroom. There is a sense of spontaneity and the variety livens up the discourse. Of course, having too many exchange routines could lead to confusion about the purpose of the talk, but we never saw that happen. . . .

Some Routines in Detail

What follows is a more detailed description to exemplify how routines can function in enhancing instruction, including three exchange routines (cycle to correct; play dumb; and "eyes to me") and two support routines (collect/distribute and wait behaviors). The teachers used multiple versions of both of these support routines. A description of the use of games by one teacher is presented to highlight how routines can be combined. Finally, we discuss the use of routines that do not enhance instruction, which we call dysfunctional routines.

Cycle to correct (or call 'til correct) is a routine used in presentation, shared presentation, review and guided practice. Essentially, it involves the teacher calling on students in rapid succession until the correct answer is given or in some cases, until the teacher gives it. A certain speed is required so that students do not forget the initial question. Cycle to correct serves to get the correct answer stated and keeps students' attention high. . . .

A second exchange routine was "I'll play dumb." This involved the teacher pretending not to understand how to do something or why one way was right and another wrong. While this particular routine was unique to [one teacher], other teachers also developed less routinized styles that permitted or

invited discussion. Essentially, [this teacher's] routine involved putting an erroneous or ambiguous piece of information on the board and proceeding as if it were totally correct. For example, she drew a circle, divided it into six unequal parts, and started to talk about one-sixth. The students "explained" her error to her. At other times, she said, "I don't understand . . . why the three has more value than the nine" (this on day two in a lesson on place value). When this routine was used, it always occurred during a shared presentation and included both a cycle to correct (or complete) and her conversation routine. She simply introduced this routine by "doing it" and reinforcing the correct style of response, but she never explained that she would try to fool the class. "I'll play dumb" had the risk of leading the class off on a discussion that neither got the point across nor saved any time. Its advantage was that it represented a clear invitation to discussion.

Another exchange routine, "eyes to me," was one of several attentional cues and/or begin exchange cues. It was slightly different from the notion of teacher points/student looks (at a problem on the board) because it was the cue for the beginning of a teacher/student interaction. The students learned that their attention was to be focused on the teacher and what she was saying, not on a problem or a chart which was being described. The routine was modeled in the first day by all teachers but with corrections for non-compliance. Several teachers said things like "I know you are ready," or "I need you to look at me," etc., but most just stated the request and corrected non-compliance. "Eyes to me" became a shorthand for returning control to the teacher. In general, it was not a disciplinary routine, but rather it signaled a switch in attention.

Distribute/collect was, as its name implies, the set of routines used by teachers to pass out material or to retrieve it. Each teacher had several such routines; all taught at least one or two of them on the first day. The routine was used in at least six activity structures by most teachers: presentation, guided practice, transition, test, check and monitored practice. It was introduced by demonstration, verbal explanation, and modeling. Some examples of the specifics of distribution were: pass to head of column and pass back; walk to each child and give child paper; go to a location and get a paper. Collect had a similar array. The routine was primarily a time saver and permitted the overlapping of activity structures without transition breaks (monitored practice with homework distribution at the end, for example). Failure to have at least one and preferably several such routines is one of the most common problems facing novices and produces tremendous delays.

Wait to start and what to do when finished were routines that often covered the beginning and end of an activity. The wait to start routine allowed the teachers to control the pacing of events. The teachers often handed out a paper, told the students to wait before working, went over directions plus an example, and finally had the students begin working. Wait to start frequently occurred at the beginning of a drill, a test or a timed practice. What to do when your work was finished covered the time when some students finished the assigned task before the class ended. All the teachers had a version of this, which sometimes included explicit directions about things students might do when finished. However, often teachers merely reminded students of appropriate tasks, directing their reminders to students who were talking or doing nothing. In addition, most students knew that an excess of unfinished work from other classes could be completed at this time. What to do when finished occurred most frequently in a monitored practice and occasionally during a test.

Games Using Routines

Games to facilitate instruction were used occasionally by most teachers[.] [One teacher] used games regularly to keep the interest and pace high. In addition, the first games she used were excellent examples of how routines taught in isolation could be combined to facilitate complex and sophisticated strings of action. As early as the first day [she] used a simple and familiar game, Simon Says, as a teaching device. This game served two purposes. It required the children to listen carefully to what she, in the role of Simon, said and it also required them to copy her actions.

After [she] had rehearsed a number of routines with her class, she combined them into more sophisticated games to enhance learning. At the end of math class on the second day, [she] introduced a game into the oral guided practice. The game had two forms: in the first, the students who stood up could sit when they answered an addition problem correctly; in the second, a number relay game, a student could tag another student if s/he answered the problem correctly. In both game forms [she] asked the child to answer one of the addition problems they had just practiced.

If we break these two game forms up into their composite element, we find that [she] had incorporated a number of routines in each. For the first game form, an important routine was [her] technique for having children get out of their desks. The repeated practice meant that even in the excitement of a game, students' exits from their desks took place smoothly. The second routine involved individual students' responses to the problem given by [the teacher]. When the students did not follow directions in the first try of the game, [she] first reminded them to listen to directions. [She] then used the signaling technique she modeled for teaching the children during the first few days—she got their attention, explained the directions, and asked them to show her if they understood by putting their hands on their heads. They started the game again. Everyone followed the rules until near the end of the game when one boy forgot to sit. [She] reminded him to follow directions, asked everyone to stand, and repeated the game. By the third round everyone played the game smoothly.

The second form of the game followed a segment in which [she] added new math facts to the list to practice as well as a routine of one student choosing another. The verbal pattern was [teacher] gave a problem, Child A responded, [teacher] evaluated, Child A chose Child B, etc. The game continued until everyone had a turn to answer a problem. Throughout the first four days, [she] continued to use games both to teach and to create a brief interlude between traditional lessons. Her games were more sophisticated by midyear, serving primarily as a way of practicing facts and previously learned material. The routines used first separately, and then together in games included: move from seat (in/out); hands to head; individual response; call on another child; listen; and "eyes on me." The presence of these routines permitted the "game" to be played very early on in the year.

Dysfunctional Routines

Dysfunctional routines are scripted pieces of behavior that do not enhance management or teaching in the classroom. Dysfunctional routines are, unfortunately, learned as completely as functional ones. These were not simply repeated events that we did not personally like; rather they were segments that tended to compete with or destroy some other clearly valued goal such as learning. One example of this occurred in [one teacher's] class. As early as the middle of the morning of the first day of school. She stopped the class and gave a lengthy lecture on bad behavior. These lectures frequently focused on the inappropriateness of certain behavior or responses or on the need to strive for higher levels of behavior or achievement. The lectures were lengthy, impassioned, and equally likely to have an individual or group target. The students responded to these explosive bursts of verbal anger by sitting in sullen silence. When the lesson resumed, there was no observable change in class behavior—only a loss of time.

Dysfunctional routines also developed in [another teacher's] room, but in a somewhat different way. Because she neither modeled nor reinforced routines that she set up on the first day (for example, pencil sharpening should occur first thing in the morning), the children took advantage of her flexibility and developed boredom-break activities. They used pencil sharpening, bathroom trips and the like as a means to break up the lengthy practice periods or as a way of socializing. These dysfunctional routines tended to be individual in use and type.

SUMMARY AND CONCLUSIONS

. . . In summary, this research was designed to identify the content and configuration of activity structures and routines in effective teachers' classrooms; to trace the origins of routines at the beginning of school; and to identify the mechanisms used by effective teachers in teaching their students about the routines that will be used throughout the year. We found that activity structures emerged slowly at the beginning of the year. They were quite primitive on the first day, evolved gradually over days two and three, and were clearly discernible by day four.

By midyear, activity structures were noticeable features of lessons and the teachers used the routines taught during the first days flexibly within a variety of activity structures. Unlike the slow emergence of activity structures, teachers introduced routines early with frequent rehearsal, gradually moving toward efficiency in cuing them. . . .

There are several implications of this research for the training of teachers. Student teachers working in a master teacher's room need to recognize existing routines and to understand their function. When a student teacher is actually responsible for managing the class, it is important that s/he either explicitly modify the master teacher's routines or use them as they exist, so that the students do not perceive the changes or modifications as disintegrations. Practice in recognizing and modifying routines can help teachers when they are required to develop their own routines. Novice teachers need to be prepared to develop and maintain routines that serve a variety of functions so that teaching can occur. If they either change the form or cues without warning, or they do not require completely correct execution in the beginning, multiple inconsistent versions develop. We can see this inconsistency in our weak manager who tended to introduce a routine and then to compromise it almost immediately; this meant that not only was the original use of the routine unavailable but composite use (the ability to combine routines to play games, for example) was also unavailable. When only fragments of routines are taught or when established routines are allowed to disintegrate, the students do not respond quickly or consistently to cues. As a result, time and fluidity are lost and the cognitive burden is increased for both the teacher and students.

REFERENCES

Ball, Stephen J. Initial encounters in the classroom and the process of establishment. In *Pupil strategies: Explorations in the sociology of the school,* edited by Peter Woods. Croom Helm: London, 1980.

Berliner, D. C., King, M., Rubin, J., and Fisher, C. W. *Describing classroom activities.* Unpublished manuscript. Far West Laboratory for Educational Research and Development, San Francisco, 1981.

Bossert, Steven T. *Activity structures and student outcomes.* Prepared for the National Institute of Education's Conference on School Organization and Effects, January 1978.

Buckley, P. K., and Cooper, J. M. *An ethnographic study of an elementary school teacher's establishment and maintenance of group norms.* Paper presented at the Annual Meeting of the American Educational Research Association, Toronto, 1978.

Clark, C. M., and Elmore, J. L. *Teacher planning in the first weeks of school.* Research Series No. 56. The Institute for Research on Teaching, October 1979.

Cornbleth, C., Korth, W., and Dorow, E. B. *Creating the curriculum: Beginning the year in a middle school.* Paper presented at the Annual Meeting of the American Educational Research Association, Montreal, April 1983.

Edelsky, C., Draper, K., and Smith, K. Hookin' 'em in at the start of school in a "whole language" classroom. *Anthropology & Education Quarterly* 14 (1983): 257–281.

Emmer, E., Evertson, C., and Anderson, L. Effective management at the beginning of the school year. *Elementary School Journal* 80 (1980): 219–231.

Evertson, C., and Anderson, L. Beginning school. *Educational Horizons* 57 (1979): 164–168.

Good, T. *Classroom research: A decade of progress.* Invited address presented at the Annual Meeting of the American Educational Research Association, Montreal, [April] 1983.

Good, T., and Hinkel, G. *Schooling in America: Some descriptive and explanatory statements.* Paper presented for the National Commission on Excellence in Education, 1982.

Green, Judith L. Research on teaching as a linguistic process: A state of the art. In *Review of Research in Education* (Vol. 10, pp. 151–252), edited by E. W. Gordon. American Educational Research Association: Washington, DC, 1983.

Greeno, J., Glaser, R., and Newell, A. *Summary: Research on cognition and behavior relevant to education in mathematics, science and technology.* Research paper submitted to the National Science Board Commission on Precollege Education in Mathematics, Science and Technology by the Federation of Behavioral Psychological and Cognitive Sciences, April 1983.

Greeno, J., Riley, M., and Gelman, R. Conceptual competence and children's counting. *Cognitive Psychology* 16 (1984): 94–143.

Grice, H. P. Logic and conversation. In *Syntax and semantics, Vol. 3: Speech acts* (pp. 41–58). New York: Seminar Press, 1975.

Hayes-Roth, B., and Hayes-Roth, F. *Cognitive processes in planning.* (R-2366-ONR). A report prepared for the Office of Naval Research, December 1978.

Joyce, B. Toward a theory of information processing in teaching. *Education Research Quarterly* 3 (1978–1979): 66–77.

Leinhardt, G. *Routines in expert math teachers' thoughts and actions.* Paper presented at the annual meeting of the American Educational Research Association, Montreal, April 1983.

Leinhardt, G., and Greeno, J. G. The cognitive skill of teaching. *Journal of Educational Psychology* 78 (April 1986): 75–95.

McDermott, R. P. Social relations as contexts for learning in school. *Harvard Educational Review* 47 (May 1977): 198–213.

Pittman, S. I. *A cognitive ethnography and quantification of a first grade teacher's selections of strategies to manage students.* Paper presented at the Annual Meeting of the Southwest Educational Research Association, Houston, January 1983.

Rommetveit, R. *Words, meanings and messages.* New York: Academic Press, 1968.

Rommetveit, R. Language games, syntactic structures and hermeneutics. In *The context of social psychology,* edited by J. Israel and H. Tagfel. New York: Academic Press, 1972.

Sacerdoti, E. D. *A structure for plans and behavior.* New York: Elsevier-North Holland, 1977.

Sandford, J. P., and Evertson, C. M. *Beginning the school year at a low SES junior high: Three case studies.* R&D report No. 6104, February 1980.

Schank, R., and Abelson, R. *Scripts, plans, goals and understanding.* Hillsdale, NJ: Lawrence Erlbaum Associates, 1977.

Stefik, M. J. *Planning with constraints.* Unpublished doctoral dissertation. Stanford University, California, 1980.

Tikunoff, W. J., and Ward, B. A. *A naturalistic study of the initiation of students into three classroom social systems.* Paper presented by Symposium on Socialization of Students to Classroom Instructional Styles: Three Perspectives, American Educational Research Association, Toronto, 1978.

AUTHOR'S NOTES

The research reported herein was supported by the Learning Research and Development Center, supported in part by funds from the National Institute of Education (NIE), United States Department of Education. The opinions expressed do not necessarily reflect the position or policy of NIE, and no official endorsement should be inferred.

The authors wish to acknowledge the extensive conceptual help of Cheryl Figura, Sharon Lesgold and Joyce Fienberg, the massive transcription and manuscript help of Patricia Flannagan and Jean Steppe. In addition, the authors wish to thank the reviewers and editors of *Curriculum Inquiry* for their careful and insightful comments.

Requests for reprints should be sent to Gaea Leinhardt, University of Pittsburgh, Learning Research and Development Center, 3939 O'Hara Street, Pittsburgh, PA 15260.

5. GROUPING FOR INSTRUCTION
Equity and Effectiveness[*]

Robert E. Slavin

One of the oldest debates in education concerns the problem of grouping students for instruction. The problem is that students differ in knowledge, skills, developmental stage, and learning rate. How can schools and classrooms be organized to provide appropriate levels and rates of instruction for all students?

The issue of grouping has taken on a new importance in recent years, particularly as it pertains to desegregation. The most common form of grouping is ability grouped class assignment, where students are assigned to ability-homogeneous classes or tracks according to some general measure of ability or achievement. For example, an elementary school might have a high fourth grade, an average fourth grade, and a low fourth grade. A high school might have college preparatory, general, and vocational tracks. This form of ability grouping often creates racially identifiable classes or tracks (e.g., McPartland, 1968), and has therefore been a major issue in lawsuits in which the plaintiffs argue that tracking is used as a means of resegregating ostensibly desegregated schools (e.g., *Hobson v. Hansen,* 1967). In one recent case in South Carolina, an administrative law judge ruled that since ability grouped class assignment concentrated black students in low ability classes and had no educational justification, the district was compelled to abandon the practice or lose its federal funds (*U.S. Depart-*

ment of Education v. Dillon County School District No. 1, 1986).

What is the evidence concerning the achievement effects of ability grouped class assignment, and what alternative means of grouping students for instruction might plausibly be used to accommodate student heterogeneity? This article briefly reviews the research on these questions from the standpoint of both instructional effectiveness and potential segregative impact of alternative means of grouping students.

WHY GROUP?

Grouping of students for instruction is done for many reasons, but most grouping plans exist to deal with one central fact of mass education: That students differ in knowledge, skills, and learning rate. If a teacher is to present a lesson to a class, then it seems intuitively obvious that the lesson should be neither too easy nor too difficult for the students. If the class is highly heterogeneous, then one lesson will of necessity be easier than would be optimal for some students, and more difficult than would be optimal for others. For the sake of instructional efficiency, it seems that students should be grouped so that they will all be able to profit from one lesson.

Yet virtually every means of grouping students by ability or performance level has its own drawbacks, which may be serious enough to offset any advantages. Grouping by age is so common now that we take it for granted, yet this was itself an

[* Paper written under funding from the Office of Educational Research and Improvement, U.S. Department of Education, 1986, No. OERI-G-86-0006.]

innovation of the 19th century (Goodlad and Anderson, 1963). Various ability grouping plans may stigmatize low achievers and put them into classes or groups for which teachers have low expectations, or lead to the creation of academic elites (Persell, 1977; Oakes, 1985). As noted earlier, ability grouping plans often result in racially or ethnically identifiable tracks or groups, undermining the goals of desegregation (McPartland, 1968). Methods of dealing with student heterogeneity within the classroom, such as use of reading or math groups, mastery learning, and cooperative learning, create problems in terms of management of multiple groups and reductions in direct instruction received by individual students.

TYPES OF GROUPING

The principal types of grouping arrangements fall into two major categories: between-class and within-class. Between-class plans are school-level arrangements by which students are assigned to classes. Within-class grouping arrangements may attempt to reduce the heterogeneity of instructional groups, as in the use of within-class ability grouping or mastery learning. Finally, cooperative learning is a within-class grouping strategy which uses heterogeneous rather than homogeneous subgroups. The following sections define the various grouping plans, and briefly present the research that has been done on each.

BETWEEN-CLASS ABILITY GROUPING

Perhaps the most controversial form of grouping is assignment of students to groups according to ability or performance. Arguments about the desirability of between-class ability grouping have raged from the 1920's (e.g., Miller & Otto, 1930) to the present (e.g., Good and Marshall, 1984; Kulik & Kulik, 1982, 1984; Oakes, 1985; Persell, 1977). Over this time period, the same essential arguments have been advanced on both sides. Proponents have argued that ability grouping lets high achievers move rapidly and gives low achievers attainable goals and extra help. Opponents have countered that ability grouping is unfair to low achievers, citing problems of poor peer models, low teacher expectations, concentration of minority students in low tracks, and slow instructional pace.

Recently, I reviewed research on ability grouping in elementary schools (Slavin, 1986), and found that ability grouping is not a single practice, but has many fundamentally different forms which have different educational as well as psychological effects. The most important forms of between-class ability grouping are discussed in the following sections.

Ability Grouped Class Assignment

In many elementary schools, students are assigned to self-contained classes on the basis of a general achievement or ability measure. As noted earlier, this might produce, for example, a high-achieving fourth grade class, an average achieving class, and a low-achieving class, with students assigned to classes according to some combination of a composite achievement measure, IQ scores, and/or teacher judgment. Students remain with the same ability-grouped classes for all academic subjects. In secondary schools, students are usually assigned to tracks, such as college preparatory, general, and vocational.

The achievement effects of ability grouped class assignment (in comparison to heterogeneous grouping) are essentially zero at the elementary level (Slavin, 1986), and very slight at the secondary level. (Kulik & Kulik, 1982). There is some evidence that high achievers may gain from ability grouping at the expense of low achievers, but most studies find no such trend. Overall, the effects of ability grouping cluster closely around zero for students of all achievement levels.

One probable reason that ability grouped class assignment has little effect on student achievement is that this plan typically has only a limited impact on the heterogeneity of the class. For example, Goodlad (1960) estimated that dividing a group of elementary students into two ability groups on the basis of IQ reduced total variability in each class by only seven percent. With three groups, heterogeneity was reduced by seventeen percent, still not likely to be enough to have a measurable impact. Even though a student's performance in any one subject is correlated with performance in other subjects, this correlation is far from perfect. This means that grouping students on any one criterion is sure to leave substantial heterogeneity in any specific skill domain. On the other hand, assigning students to "high" and "low" ability classes may have a stigmatizing effect on low achievers and may evoke low expectations for student achievement and behavior, and reduce student self-esteem even if the grouping has a minimal impact on class heterogeneity. Thus, ability grouped class assignment may be enough to produce psychological drawbacks (see Rosenbaum 1980) but does not do enough to reap the potential educational benefits of reducing student heterogeneity in any particular skill.

If ability grouped class assignment produces few if any learning benefits, is detrimental to self-esteem, and has a segregative impact in desegregated schools, then its continued use can hardly be recommended. Yet the problem of student heterogeneity must be addressed in some way. The following sections discuss alternative between- and within-class grouping plans which may be able to adapt instruction to students' needs more effectively and equitably than ability-grouped class assignment.

Regrouping for Reading and/or Mathematics

One commonly used ability grouping arrangement in elementary schools involves having students remain in heterogeneous classes most of the day but regrouping for selected subjects. For example, three fourth grade classes in a school might have reading scheduled at the same time. At reading time, students might leave their heterogeneous homerooms and go to a class organized according to reading levels.

There are three important advantages of regrouping for selected subjects over ability grouped class assignment. First, students remain in a heterogeneous setting most of the day, so they are likely to identify with that group, reducing the labeling effects and racial identifiability of all-day grouping. Second, students are grouped solely on the basis of their achievement in reading or mathematics, not general achievement or ability level, so a meaningful reduction in heterogeneity in the skill being taught is possible. Third, regrouping plans tend to be more flexible than ability grouped class assignment, because changing students between reading or mathematics classes is less disruptive than changing basic class assignments. For this reason, any errors in

assignment can be easily remedied, and any changes in student performance level can be accommodated with a change in grouping.

Research on regrouping plans indicates that they can be instructionally effective if two conditions are fulfilled: Instructional level and pace must be completely adapted to student performance level, and the regrouping must be done for only one or two subjects (reading and/or mathematics only) so that students stay in heterogeneous placements most of the day (Slavin, 1986). On the other hand, when regrouping has been done without adapting the pace or level of instruction or in more than two different subjects, no benefits for regrouping have been found.

Joplin Plan

One interesting form of regrouping once common in elementary schools is the Joplin Plan (Floyd, 1954), in which students are regrouped for reading without regard for grade levels. That is, a reading class at the fourth grade, first semester level might contain some third, some fourth, and some fifth graders. One important consequence of this grouping plan is that it allows for the reduction or elimination of within-class grouping for reading, as students in each reading class may all be at the same reading level. This allows teachers to spend more of the reading class time doing direct instruction, reducing the time during which students must do unsupervised followup seatwork.

Achievement effects of the Joplin Plan and closely related forms of nongraded plans (Goodlad and Anderson, 1963) have been quite positive overall. There are two particular advantages of the Joplin Plan with respect to equity issues. One is that by grouping across grade lines, each regrouped reading class is likely to be about as racially integrated as the total school. Second, by reducing or eliminating the use of reading groups within the class, total time for direct instruction is increased and equalized for all students.

Summary and Conclusions: Between-Class Ability Grouping

Evidence from studies of various forms of between-class ability grouping indicates that achievement effects depend on the types of programs evaluated.

In general, ability grouping plans are beneficial for student achievement when they incorporate the following features (adapted from Slavin, 1986):

1. Students remain in heterogeneous classes most of the day and are regrouped by performance level only in such subjects as reading and mathematics in which reducing heterogeneity is particularly important.
2. The grouping plan reduces heterogeneity in the specific skill being taught.
3. Group assignments are flexible and are frequently reassessed.
4. Teachers adapt their level and pace of instruction in regrouped classes to accommodate students' levels of readiness and learning rates.

The between-class grouping plan that most completely incorporates the four principles listed above is the Joplin Plan, in which students remain in heterogeneous classes except for reading, are grouped strictly according to reading level, and are constantly re-evaluated, and in which all achievement levels are accommodated. Evidence on the Joplin Plan supports the effectiveness of this arrangement and of within-grade regrouping plans and nongraded plans which most resemble it. In contrast, ability grouped class assignment does not meet the four criteria; it segregates students all day, groups students on the basis of general ability or achievement rather than skill in a specific subject, and tends to be highly inflexible. Teachers may or may not adjust their level and pace of instruction to adapt to students' needs in this plan.

WITHIN-CLASS ABILITY GROUPING

Within-class ability grouping is the practice of assigning students to homogeneous subgroups for instruction within the class. In general, each subgroup receives instruction at its own level and is allowed to progress at its own rate. Within-class ability grouping is virtually universal in elementary reading instruction and is common in elementary mathematics (Hallinan & Sorenson, 1983; Barr & Dreeben, 1983).

Within-class grouping plans generally conform to the four requirements for effective ability grouping proposed earlier. They involve only reading and/or mathematics, leaving students in relatively hetero-

geneous classes the rest of the school day. They group students in specific rather than general skills, and at least in principle within-class groupings are easy to change. Most teachers do adapt their level and pace of instruction to meet students' needs (Barr & Dreeben, 1983). However, within-class ability grouping introduces a problem not characteristic of between-class grouping plans. This is the problem of management of multiple groups. When the teacher is instructing one reading group, for example, the remaining students must work independently on seatwork activities, which may be of questionable value (see Anderson, Brubaker, Alleman-Brooks, & Duffy, 1985). Supervising multiple groups and transitions between them are major classroom management problems (Anderson, Evertson, & Brophy, 1979).

Methodologically adequate research on within-class ability grouping has unfortunately been limited to the study of mathematics grouping, perhaps because few reading teachers would be willing to participate in an experiment in which they had to teach heterogeneous classes without breaking students into reading groups. However, the research on within-class grouping in mathematics supports this practice. Every one of eight studies of within-class ability grouping in mathematics identified in my review (Slavin, 1986) favored the grouped treatment. Effects of within-class grouping were somewhat higher for low achievers than for average and high achievers. There was some trend for effects to be more positive when the number of ability groups was two or three rather than four.

Effects of within-class grouping on mathematics achievement cannot be assumed to hold for reading. In mathematics, there is a need for students to work problems independently, so there is an appropriate place for independent seatwork. A corresponding need for independent seatwork time is less compelling in reading. However, the universality of within-class grouping in reading provides at least some indication that this form of within-class ability grouping is also instructionally necessary.

MASTERY LEARNING

Mastery learning (Bloom, 1976; Block & Burns, 1976) exists in three principal forms. In grouped-based mastery learning, students receive a lesson as a whole class and then take a formative test. Those whose test scores exceed a preset mastery criterion (e.g., 80%) then do enrichment activities while those who do not achieve this criterion receive corrective instruction. Group-based forms of mastery learning are by far the most commonly used in elementary and secondary schools. Mastery learning can also be implemented in an individualized, or continuous-progress form. Finally, the Keller Plan is a form of mastery learning in which students take as much time as they need to pass a series of tests covering the content of a course, using self-study materials, peer tutoring, and/or lectures to prepare to take the tests. The Keller Plan is used almost exclusively at the college level, as it does not fit well within time-driven elementary and secondary programs. Since individualized and Keller Plan forms of mastery learning are rarely seen in elementary and secondary schools, this section only considers research on group-based forms of mastery learning.

I recently completed a review of research on group-based mastery learning at the elementary and secondary levels (Slavin, 1987). I found that in studies of at least four week's duration which compared mastery learning to control groups, effects of mastery learning on standardized measures of reading and math achievement were essentially zero. On experimenter-made measures, effects were more positive, but these measures were usually more closely related to the objectives studied by the mastery learning classes than by the control classes. However, mastery learning does tend to reduce the achievement gap between the highest and lowest achievers, and provides a means of focusing teachers and students to a well-defined set of objectives, and for these reasons this strategy may be desirable for certain uses. Also, several school district evaluations of mastery learning show promise for the method (see, for example, Levine & Stark, 1982), although these studies rarely use control groups and confound the use of mastery learning per se with changes in curricula, other teaching methods, promotion policies, and alignment of curriculum with outcome measures.

COOPERATIVE LEARNING

Cooperative learning (Sharan, 1980; Slavin, 1983a, b) refers to various instructional methods in which students work in small, heterogeneous learning groups toward some sort of group goal. Cooperative learning differs from within-class ability grouping not only in that cooperative learning groups are small and heterogeneous, but also in that these groups are expected to engage in a great deal of task-focused interaction, such as studying together or completing group assignments. In a sense, cooperative learning views student heterogeneity as a resource to be taken advantage of rather than as a problem to be solved; in their cooperative groups, students are expected to share a broad range of perspectives and understandings to help one another master academic content.

Cooperative learning methods vary considerably in their basic structures. Some, such as Jigsaw Teaching (Aronson, Blaney, Stephen, Sikes, and Snapp, 1978) and Group Investigation (Sharan & Sharan, 1976) assign students specific tasks within a larger group task. In others (e.g., Johnson & Johnson, 1975) students work together to complete a common group worksheet or other group product. A third category consists of methods in which students study together and are rewarded on the basis of the achievement of all group members (e.g., DeVries & Slavin, 1978; Slavin, 1983c). For example, in Student Teams Achievement Divisions, or STAD, students are assigned to four-member heterogeneous teams. The teacher presents a lesson and then students study worksheets together in their teams, attempting to make certain that all team members have mastered the material. Finally, the students are individually quizzed, and teams are rewarded with certificates or other recognition on the basis of the average of their members' quiz scores.

The idea behind cooperative learning is that if students are rewarded based on the performance of a group or team, they will be motivated to help and encourage one another to achieve (Slavin, 1983a, b). In a heterogenous learning group, it is expected that students among themselves will be able to solve problems or organize material presented by the teacher and to transmit the group's understanding to each individual.

Research on cooperative learning in elementary and secondary schools has found that the effects of this grouping strategy depend on how it is organized. Instructionally effective cooperative learning methods provide group rewards based on the individual learning of all group members. Student Teams Achievement Divisions (Slavin, 1983c), Teams-Games-Tournaments (DeVries & Slavin, 1978), Team Assisted Individualization (Slavin, 1985a), Cooperative Integrated Reading and Composition (Madden, Slavin, & Stevens, 1986; Stevens, Madden, Slavin, & Farnish, 1987), and related methods all provide group rewards based on the sum or average of individual student learning performances. This means that if students wish to succeed as a group, they must focus their efforts on ensuring that every group member has mastered the material being studied. Studies of these methods have consistently found that they increase student achievement in a variety of subject areas and grade levels from 3–12. In contrast, methodologically adequate studies of cooperative learning methods in which students complete a single group worksheet or other product (e.g., Johnson, Johnson, & Scott, 1978) have not found positive achievement effects. In addition to effects on academic achievement, cooperative learning methods have had positive effects on several important non-cognitive outcomes, in particular race relations and self-esteem (Slavin, 1983a). For example, in one study junior high school students who experienced STAD for a semester in just one subject, English, not only had more close and reciprocated friendships outside of their own racial group than did control students at the end of the study, but they still had more cross-racial friendships in the next school year, when they were no longer in the same classes (see Slavin, 1985b).

COMBINING COOPERATIVE LEARNING AND WITHIN-CLASS ABILITY GROUPING

The most effective forms of cooperative learning for enhancing students' basic skills are two complex methods which combine cooperative learning with within-class ability grouping. These are Team Assisted Individualization (TAI) in mathematics (Slavin, 1985a; Slavin, Leavey, and Madden, 1986), and Cooperative Integrated Reading and Composition (CIRC) in reading, writing, and language arts (Madden et al., 1986; Stevens et al., 1987). In TAI, students work in mixed-ability teams on material appropriate to their levels of math skills. Teammates check one another's work and help one another with

problems. In the meantime, the teacher calls up groups of students from among the various teams who are working at the same point in the curriculum. For example, the teacher might call up a decimals group for a lesson on that subject. These students would leave their teams while their teammates continue working on self-instructional materials back at the team table. Following the lesson, the students would return to their team areas, and the teacher might call up the fractions group for a lesson, and so on.

The achievement effects of TAI have been extraordinary; in six evaluations, TAI students have gained an average of twice as many grade equivalents as control students in mathematics computations (Slavin, 1985). For example, in one study in inner-city Wilmington, Delaware, intermediate schools, TAI students gained an average of 1.65 grade equivalents in eighteen weeks, while control students gained 0.61 (Slavin & Karweit, 1985). Further, positive effects of TAI have been found on race relations and on attitudes toward mainstreamed peers (Slavin, 1985a).

Effects of CIRC have been equally positive. In CIRC, students work in mixed-ability teams on a series of reading activities, including reading aloud to one another and completing activities relating to story structure, reading comprehension, decoding, vocabulary, and spelling. In writing, they engage in peer response groups in a writing process model. Effects of the CIRC model have been found on standardized tests of reading comprehension, language expression, and language mechanics; in a 24-week study (Stevens et al., 1987), CIRC students gained 64% of a grade equivalent more than control students on these variables. Further, significant effects were found on oral reading measures and on ratings of writing samples. Positive effects were found not only for the samples as a whole, but also specifically for students receiving remedial reading . . . and special education services (Madden, Stevens, & Slavin, 1986).

DISCUSSION

Much of the debate about ability grouping over the past half century has revolved around the question of whether or not instruction must be adapted to students' individual needs. Proponents of ability grouping have always justified this practice on the basis that it gives all students instruction appropriate to their level of readiness. Yet accepting the idea that students need to have material taught at their level in certain subjects, such as mathematics and reading, does not force us to any particular form of instructional grouping. This review shows that there are many means of accommodating student differences. The most common of these, ability grouped class assignment, has been repeatedly found to be ineffective for increasing student achievement and to have the greatest potential segregative effect of all grouping plans. Yet there are several alternative means of grouping students for instruction which have considerably better evidence of effectiveness and less segregative potential, in particular the Joplin Plan, within-class ability grouping, and cooperative learning. In particular, cooperative learning methods have an *integrative* effect in having students of different ethnic backgrounds work together cooperatively on a routine basis; studies of cooperative learning in desegregated schools regularly find positive effects of these methods on intergroup relations (Slavin, 1985b).

Earlier reviewers of research on instructional grouping (e.g., Borg, 1965; Esposito, 1973; NEA, 1968; Passow, 1962) generally concluded that research on ability grouping was a hopeless muddle. However, these reviewers often failed to make critical distinctions between different types of grouping plans, combining studies of programs for the gifted with comprehensive between-class ability grouping plans, regrouping for selected subjects, and within-class ability grouping. Yet when the research on these different plans is separated, the picture becomes relatively clear. Ability grouping plans such as the Joplin Plan and certain forms of nongraded and regrouping plans can be instructionally effective. They all meet a set of criteria proposed earlier in this paper: they leave students in heterogeneous classes most of the school day, regroup only for reading and/or mathematics according to student performance in these skills, can flexibly change student placements, and tend to adapt completely the level and pace of instruction to the needs and preparedness of the regrouped classes. Within-class ability grouping in mathematics also meets these criteria, and has also been consistently found

to increase student achievement. Cooperative learning programs, particularly those which combine the use of cooperative, heterogeneous work groups with homogeneous instructional groups, have been found to have a strong positive effect on student achievement. On the other hand, wholesale between-class grouping plans, such as ability grouped class assignment, have not been found to be beneficial for student achievement. Considering evidence on all kinds of grouping plans, it can be concluded that grouping can be a useful tool in elementary school organization, but it is a tool that must be used sparingly, precisely, and planfully if it is to have a positive effect on student achievement.

The conclusions drawn in this article will be discomfiting both to those who believe that ability grouping is always appropriate and to those who believe that it is never appropriate. Yet the "always-never" debate has been in progress for decades, and most schools today are using the most pernicious form of ability grouping, ability grouped class assignment. Hopefully, this article will serve to point the way to broader use of forms of grouping which maintain heterogeneous classes but group for specific purposes and brief periods, toward broader use of grouping strategies with little or no potential segregative impact, and toward broader use of cooperative learning methods which view student heterogeneity as a resource rather than a liability.

REFERENCES

Anderson, L. M., Brubaker, N. L., Alleman-Brooks, J., & Duffy, G. G. (1985). A qualitative study of seatwork in first grade classrooms. *Elementary School Journal, 86,* 123–140.

Aronson, E., Blaney, N., Stephen, C., Sikes, J., & Snapp, M. (1978). *The jigsaw classroom.* Beverly Hills, CA: Sage.

Barr, R., & Dreeben, R. (1983). *How schools work.* Chicago: University of Chicago Press.

Block, J. H., and Burns, R. B. (1976). Mastery learning. In L. S. Shulman (ed.), *Review of Research in Education* (vol. 4). Tasca, Ill.: F. E. Peacock, Inc.

Bloom, B. S. (1976). *Human characteristics and school learning.* New York: McGraw-Hill.

Borg, W. P. (1965). Ability grouping in the public schools: A field study. *Journal of Experimental Education, 34,* 1–97.

Devries, D. L., & Slavin, R. E. (1978). Teams-Games-Tournament (TGT): Review of ten classroom experiments. *Journal of Research and Development in Education, 12,* 28–38.

Esposito, D. (1973). Homogeneous and heterogeneous ability grouping: Principal findings and implications for evaluating and designing more effective educational environments. *Review of Educational Research, 43,* 163–179.

Floyd, C. (1954). Meeting children's reading needs in the middle grades: A preliminary report. *Elementary School Journal, 55,* 99–103.

Good T., & Marshall, S. (1984). Do students learn more in heterogeneous or homogeneous groups? In P. Peterson & L. Cherry Wilkinson, *Student diversity and the organization, process, and use of instructional groups in the classroom.* New York: Academic Press.

Goodlad, J. I., & Anderson, R. H. (1963). *The nongraded elementary school.* (Rev. Ed.) New York: Harcourt, Brace, & World.

Hallinan, M., & Sorenson, A. (1983). The formation and stability of instructional groups. *American Sociological Review, 48,* 839–851.

Hobson v. Hansen, 269 F. Supp. 401 (1967).

Johnson, D., & Johnson, R. (1975). *Learning together and alone.* Englewood Cliffs, N.J.: Prentice-Hall.

Johnson. D. W., Johnson, R. T., & Scott, L. (1978). The effects of cooperative and individualized instruction on student attitudes and achievement. *Journal of Social Psychology, 104,* 207–216.

Kulik, C.-L., & Kulik, J. (1982). Effects of ability grouping on secondary school students: A meta-analysis of evaluation findings. *American Educational Research Journal, 19,* 415–428.

Kulik, C.-L., & Kulik, J .A. (1984, August). *Effects of ability grouping on elementary school pupils: A meta-analysis.* Paper presented at the annual convention of the American Psychological Association, Toronto.

Levine, D. V., & Stark, J. (1982). Instructional and organizational arrangements that improve achievement in inner-city schools. *Educational Leadership, 39,* 41–46.

Madden, N. A., Slavin, R. E., & Stevens, R. J. (1986). *Cooperative Integrated Reading and Composition: Teacher's Manual.* Baltimore, Md.: Johns Hopkins University, Center for Research on Elementary and Middle Schools.

Maden, N. A., Stevens, R. J., & Slavin, R. E. (1986). *Reading and writing in the mainstream: A cooperative learning approach.* (Technical Report No. 5). Baltimore, Md.: Johns Hopkins University, Center for Research on Elementary and Middle Schools.

McPartland, J. (1968). *The segregated student in desegregated schools: Sources of influence on Negro secondary students.* Baltimore, Md.: Johns Hopkins University, Center for Social Organization of Schools.

Miller, W. S., & Otto, H. J. (1930). Analysis of experimental studies in homogeneous grouping. *Journal of Educational Research, 21,* 95–102.

National Education Association (1968). *Ability grouping research summary.* Washington, D.C.: National Education Association.

Oakes, J. (1985). *Keeping track: How schools structure inequality.* New Haven, Conn.: Yale University Press.

Passow, A. H. (1962). The maze of research on ability grouping. *Educational Forum, 25,* 281–288.

Persell, C. (1977). *Education and inequality: The roots and results of stratification in America's schools.* New York: Free Press.

Rosenbaum, J. (1980). Social implications of educational grouping. *Review of Research in Education, 8,* 361–401.

Sharan, S. (1980). Cooperative learning in small groups: Recent methods and effects on achievement, attitudes, and ethnic relations. *Review of Educational Research, 50,* 241–271.

Sharan, S., & Sharan, Y. (1976). *Small-group teaching.* Englewood Cliffs, N.J.: Educational Technology Publications.

Slavin, R. E. (1983a). *Cooperative learning.* New York: Longman.

Slavin, R. E. (1983b). When does cooperative learning increase student achievement? *Psychological Bulletin, 94* 429–445.

Slavin, R. E. (1983c). *Student team learning.* Washington, D.C.: National Education Association.

Slavin, R. E. (1985a). Team-assisted individualization: Combining cooperative learning and individualized instruction in mathematics. In R. E. Slavin, S. Sharan, S. Kagan, R. Hertz-Lazarowitz, C. Webb, & R. Schmuck (Eds.), *Learning to cooperate, cooperating to learn.* New York: Plenum. 177–209.

Slavin, R. E. (1985b). Cooperative learning: Applying contact theory in desegregated schools. *Journal of Social Issues, 41,* 45–62.

Slavin, R. E. (1986). *Ability grouping and student achievement in elementary schools: A best evidence synthesis.* (Technical Report No. 1). Baltimore, Md.: Johns Hopkins University, Center for Research on Elementary and Middle Schools.

Slavin, R. E. (1987). *Mastery learning reconsidered.* (Technical Report No. 6). Baltimore, Md.: Johns Hopkins University, Center for Research on Elementary and Middle Schools.

Slavin, R. E., & Karweit, N. L. (1985). Effects of whole-class, ability grouped and individualized instruction on mathematics achievement. *American Educational Research Journal, 32,* 351–367.

Stevens, R. J., Madden, N. A., Slavin, R. E., & Farnish, A. M. (1986). *Cooperative Integrated Reading and Composition: Two field experiments.* (Technical Report No. 7). Baltimore, Md.: Johns Hopkins University, Center for Research on Elementary and Middle Schools.

U.S. Department of Education v. Dillon County School District No. 1 (1986). Initial decision in compliance proceeding under Title VI of the Civil Rights Act of 1964, 42 U.S.C. Sec. 200d *et seg.*

CLASSROOM INSTRUCTION

1. OPPORTUNITY TO LEARN

Lorin W. Anderson

Opportunity to learn as an important variable influencing, and possibly explaining, the effectiveness of classroom instruction was introduced into the educational literature during the decade of the 1960s. Carroll (1963) included opportunity to learn as one of five central variables in his model of school learning (see *Carroll Model of School Learning*). Opportunity to learn was also examined in a major international study of mathematics achievement described in two volumes edited by Torsten Husén (1967). Despite the use of the same variable label, however, Carroll's opportunity to learn and Husén's opportunity to learn are conceptually distinct. The purposes of this entry are to (a) describe the conceptual distinctions, (b) explore the ways in which opportunity to learn has been measured, (c) summarize briefly the research evidence concerning opportunity to learn, and (d) speculate on the future of opportunity to learn as a key variable in classroom instructional research and practice.

1. CONCEPTUAL DISTINCTIONS

Carroll (1963) defined opportunity to learn as the amount of time allocated to the learner for the learning of a given task. If, for example, the task assigned to a learner is to understand the concept of noun, opportunity to learn is simply the amount of time the learner has available to learn what a noun is.

In Carroll's model, opportunity to learn is contrasted with the amount of time the learner needs to spend in order to learn. This latter variable is primarily dependent on the learner's aptitude for the

task. Thus, while teachers have virtually no control over the time needed for learning, they do have some control over opportunity to learn.

Carroll also contrasted opportunity to learn with the amount of time the learner actually spends actively engaged in the process of learning. This latter variable, frequently referred to as engaged time, active learning time, or time-on-task (see *Time and School Learning*) is believed to be influenced by the perseverance of the learner, the quality of the instruction, and opportunity to learn. In this context opportunity to learn places an upper bound on engaged time.

In contrast with Carroll, Husén (1967) defines opportunity to learn in terms of the relationship between the content taught to the students and the content tested by the achievement test. Thus opportunity to learn from the Husén perspective is best understood as the match between what is taught and what is tested. Put simply, the greater the match, the greater the opportunity to learn.

Two major distinctions exist between Carroll's and Husén's conceptualizations of opportunity to learn. First, while Carroll's conceptualization clearly suggests that opportunity to learn is an instructional variable (one under the direct influence of administrators and teachers), Husén's conceptualization implies that opportunity to learn is mainly a measurement variable (one akin to content validity).

Second, Carroll's opportunity to learn is a continuous variable while Husén's opportunity to learn is essentially a dichotomous variable. The issue from Carroll's perspective is how much time a learner has available to learn a particular task. The issue from Husén's perspective is whether or not a learner (or particular groups of learners) [has] been provided with any instruction relative to the content included on the achievement test(s).

The distinctions between the two conceptualizations have been noted by several researchers since the early 1960s. Poyner et al. (1977), for example, included two opportunity to learn variables in their *Instructional Dimensions Study*. One variable, which they termed "quantitative," is identical to Carroll's opportunity to learn. The other variable, termed "qualitative," is the same as Husén's opportunity to learn.

Increasingly, researchers have begun to use labels other than opportunity to learn to highlight these conceptual distinctions. Allocated time (Wiley and Harnischfeger 1974, Fisher et al. 1980) has replaced Carroll's opportunity to learn. Content coverage (Cooley and Leinhardt 1980) and, perhaps most appropriately, content overlap (Leinhardt and Seewald 1981) have replaced Husén's opportunity to learn. Since the labels "allocated time" and "content overlap" seem to capture best the conceptual distinctions mentioned earlier, these labels will be used in place of opportunity to learn in subsequent sections of this article.

2. ALLOCATED TIME: MEASUREMENT AND RESEARCH

One of the reasons Carroll placed time in such a central position in his model of school learning was the properties of time as a metric. Time is relatively easy to measure, has an absolute zero point, and is expressed in commonly understood and equal units (e.g., seconds, minutes, hours, days, and years). These three properties make it quite easy to conduct research on allocated time.

In fact, research has been conducted using several of the time units. Carroll's (1974, 1975) research has focused primarily on the number of years students have studied a particular subject matter. In the earlier study the subject areas were reading and mathematics. Several successive levels of the Comprehensive Tests of Basic Skills (CTBS) were equated for the purpose of examining student progress from ages 6 to 17. Using a memory test as a measure of mathematics aptitude, a vocabulary test as a measure of reading aptitude, and grade level as an indicator

of opportunity to learn, Carroll was able to partially test his model of school learning. The fit of the data to the model was quite good, providing strong support for the inclusion of opportunity to learn (defined in terms of number of years of schooling) in the model.

Carroll's (1975) second study provided additional support for the importance of opportunity to learn as measured by the number of years of schooling. In this study Carroll reported the results of an international study of the teaching of French as a second language. Eight countries participated in the study. One of the variables examined in relationship to differences in student achievement among the various countries was the number of years during which students received instruction relating to the learning of French. Of all the instructional variables included in the study, this opportunity to learn variable was most clearly related to between-country differences in the learning of French.

Quite clearly the number of years of instruction is the most global indicator of allocated time. Wiley and Harnischfeger (1974) studied a slightly less global indicator, average daily attendance. This is defined as the proportion of students who are able, because of their attendance, to receive *any* instruction on a typical school day. In one sense, then, average daily attendance can be viewed as the number of days per year on which students received instruction pertaining to a variety of subject areas. Wiley and Harnischfeger found a small, but statistically significant relationship between average daily attendance and student achievement differences between schools.

The Beginning Teacher Evaluation Study (Fisher et al. 1980) brought the unit of allocated time to the level of hours and minutes. In addition, estimates of allocated time were based on classroom observations rather than written records (as was the case in both the Carroll, and Wiley and Harnischfeger research). One of the most intriguing aspects of the study was the great differences in the amount of time allocated to particular subject areas and to specific topics within various subject areas. For example, in an early study report, Dishaw (1977) reported large differences in the amount of time per day devoted to the teaching of reading in 25 second grade classrooms (age 7). While the most reading-oriented teacher spent 127 minutes per day teaching reading, the least reading-oriented teacher spent only 34 minutes. If this difference remains consistent over a 180-day school year, the first group of students would receive an additional 279 hours of reading instruction in the second grade. Similar differences were found for second grade mathematics and for fifth grade (age 10) reading and mathematics. As in the case of the Wiley and Harnischfeger (1974) study, these differences in allocated time were slightly but statistically significantly assoicated with achievement differences between classes.

One final point needs to be raised before moving on the content overlap. In the Beginning Teacher Evaluation Study, engaged time or time-on-task was more highly related to achievement than was allocated time. This finding is in line with the predictions that can be made based on Carroll's model. In Carroll's model engaged time or time-on-task is hypothesized to directly influence learning. Allocated time, on the other hand, is expected to have only an indirect influence on learning. The direct influence of allocated time is on engaged time or time-on-task, not on learning.

In summary, then, allocated time, expressed either in years, days, or minutes, is related to student achievement. This relationship tends to be stronger for years than for either days or minutes. This stronger relationship for more global indicators of allocated time makes sense from two perspectives. First, more global indicators allow for cumulative effects of learning (or failure to learn). That is, three years of French instruction is one more than two years. This is not necessarily true of minutes of instruction where the differences found by Dishaw in second grade reading instruction can be compensated for by differences in first or third grade reading instruction.

Second, fairly global indicators of allocated time are more likely to be related to fairly global indicators of achievement. The more specific the indicator of allocated time, the more likely that content overlap interferes with the allocated time-achievement relationship.

3. CONTENT OVERLAP

Content overlap has been measured in several ways. In the Husén (1967) study and in a subsequent study by Comber and Keeves (1973) content overlap was

estimated in the following manner. Each teacher was asked to examine each item on the international achievement test. For each item the teacher was to estimate the percentage of students in his or her class who received instruction relating to the content or skill tested. The teacher then selected one of three percentage categories for each item: less than 25 percent, 25 to 75 percent, and more than 75 percent. The ratings were scaled by assigning the midpoint of each category to each estimate. For each teacher a content overlap score was computed by summing the values of the midpoints corresponding to the responses made to each item.

Borg (1979) asked teachers to examine each test item and indicate on a five-point scale the degree to which they had emphasized the content or skill tested. For each item, teachers were to choose from among the following five response options: "E—teacher emphasized content related to the given item; DC—teacher definitely covered content, PC—teacher probably covered content; DR—teacher did not remember whether content was covered; NC—teacher did not cover content" (Borg 1979 p. 638). Each response option was assigned a numerical value from 5 (E) to 1 (NC). These numerical values were summed to arrive at a content overlap score. Borg (1979) contends that his procedure for estimating content overlap "is likely to produce more accurate teacher estimates than would be obtained by asking what percentage of pupils had an opportunity to learn each concept, as was done in previous studies" (p. 638). No evidence is presented to support this contention, however.

Despite the differences in procedures, both Husén and Borg used teachers to provide the estimates of content overlap. Other researchers, however, have relied on an examination of the curriculum to yield such estimates. The techniques used in these studies are quite similar. For example, Jenkins and Pany (1978) examined the overlap of five standardized achievement tests and seven commercial reading series. Their focus was on word recognition of first and second grade students (age 6 and 7). Two sets of word lists were formed. The first set of word lists consisted of all words included on the word recognition subtest of each standardized achievement test. The second set of word lists consisted of all words included in each of the seven commercial reading series. Each time a word included on an achievement test was also included in a reading series, one point was assigned. In this way, each achievement test was assigned an overlap score with each of the seven reading series. Armbruster et al. (1977) used a similar technique in exploring content overlap in terms of reading comprehension. Sixteen categories of reading comprehension were identified to aid in the analysis. Similarly, Porter et al. (1978) and Schmidt (1978) developed a taxonomy for classifying the content included in mathematics curricula and on standardized mathematics achievement tests.

Despite the differences in measuring content overlap, the results are quite similar. Jenkins and Pany (1978) did not examine differences in achievement test scores. Instead, they considered each "match" as one correct item, computed a raw score on each of the five tests for a hypothetical "average" student, and transformed these average raw scores to grade equivalent scores. The grade equivalent scores for the average first grade student studying the various curricula were estimated to range from less than 1.0 to approximately 2.3 for five tests. For the average second grade student the grade equivalent scores were estimated to range from less than 1.0 to approximately 3.5. The Jenkins and Pany results suggest that differences in content overlap can result in achievement differences as large as 1.5 grade levels in grade 1 and 2.5 grade levels in grade 2.

Both the Husén study and the Borg study included actual student achievement as the dependent variable. Since the Husén study predates the Borg study it will be discussed first. Furthermore, since the Husén study was in many ways the first study of opportunity to learn, the results will be discussed in some detail. In the Husén study the results pertaining to content overlap were analyzed both within countries and between countries. Median within-country correlations between content overlap and student achievement in mathematics were computed separately for each of four samples: (a) a sample of 13-year-old students, (b) a sample of students enrolled in the grade in which the majority of 13-year-olds are enrolled, (c) a sample of students enrolled in one or more mathematics courses during their final year in secondary school, and (d) a sample of students not enrolled in a mathematics course during their final secondary year. Since students in this last sample would not have had any opportunity to learn mathematics during their final secondary year, this sample is not relevant to the present discussion.

The median within-country correlations for the

three samples of interest ranged from 0.10 to 0.18. These relatively low correlations were attributed in part to the homogeneity of teachers' ratings within certain countries. That is, the countries with the lowest correlations were those countries in which the teachers had the least influence on the content actually covered in a given year.

When the data were analyzed between countries the results were quite different. For the three samples of interest the correlations between content overlap and student achievement ranged from 0.64 to 0.81. This difference in within-country and between-country results led to the conclusion that "a considerable amount of the variation between countries in mathematics scores can be attributed to the differences between students' opportunities to learn the material which was tested" (Husén 1967 pp. 168–69).

The results of Borg's (1979) study generally supported the results of the Husén study while at the same time identifying conditions under which the content overlap–student achievement relationship would be more and less likely to hold. Perhaps the conditions affecting the relationship are more informative than the magnitude of the relationship itself. Borg found that the magnitude of the content overlap–student achievement relationship depended on (a) the nature of the material being learned, (b) the type of achievement test administered (i.e., multiple choice, essay), and (c) the type of students being taught (i.e., white, minority). For example, for white students learning particular types of material tested by a multiple-choice test, the correlation between content overlap and student achievement was approximately 0.40. Furthermore, the magnitude of this relationship did not depend greatly on student ability or socioeconomic status.

In summary, then, content overlap has been found to be significantly associated with student achievement in several studies. The magnitude of the relationship depends on several factors including, but not limited to, the amount of variation in content taught, the type of material being taught, the students being taught, and the test used to assess learning.

4. A COMPARISON OF ALLOCATED TIME AND CONTENT OVERLAP

Only a few studies have examined allocated time and content overlap. One of the largest studies to investigate both was the Instructional Dimensions Study (Poyner et al. 1977), a study involving approximately 4,500 students and 350 teachers. Students in both first and third grades (ages 6 and 8) were included in the study. Both reading and mathematics achievement of the students were examined. Although results pertaining to several subsamples were presented, only the results pertaining to four samples will be discussed. These four samples are: (a) total sample of first grade reading students, (b) total sample of first grade mathematics students, (c) total sample of third grade reading students, and (d) total sample of third grade mathematics students.

In all four samples the correlation between allocated time and content overlap was quite small, ranging from 0.03 to 0.18. Thus, empirically speaking, the two conceptualizations of opportunity to learn are quite independent. Furthermore, in all four samples, the content overlap–student achievement relationship was stronger than the allocated time–student achievement relationship. The correlations between content overlap and student achievement ranged from 0.31 to 0.44. In contrast, the correlations between allocated time and student achievement ranged from -0.11 to 0.12.

The magnitude of the correlations found in the Instructional Dimensions Study parallel those found in studies examining either allocated time (e.g., Fisher et al. 1980) or content overlap (e.g., Borg 1979) separately. In general, then, it appears that content overlap is more strongly related to achievement than is allocated time. Of course, this conclusion is based on studies conducted within a single academic year. If multiyear studies are considered, the importance of allocated time may increase while that of content overlap may decrease. This latter conclusion is based primarily on the quasilongitudinal research conducted by Carroll (1974, 1975).

5. THE FUTURE OF OPPORTUNITY TO LEARN

Based on the information presented in this entry two generalizations concerning the future of opportunity to learn can be proffered. First, opportunity to learn will emerge as a key extraneous variable in future instructional research. Second, a composite "opportunity to learn" variable will be formed from the present, conceptually distinct variables of allocated time and content overlap. Each of these generalizations will be briefly discussed.

If differences in curricula, instructional programs, or teaching are to be examined validly, differences in opportunity to learn must be controlled or estimated. In this context opportunity to learn is best considered an extraneous variable. The potential impact of opportunity to learn as an extraneous variable has been addressed from both the allocated time and content overlap perspective.

Walker and Schaffarzick (1974) reviewed some 23 studies on the basis of curriculum type and resultant student achievement. They concluded that the extent to which the innovative curriculum was superior depended on the nature of the achievement test administered. Students studying an innovative curriculum displayed higher achievement gains only when the content tested matched the innovative curriculum more than the traditional curriculum. In those cases in which the content tested more closely matched the traditional curriculum, students studying the traditional curriculum outperformed their innovative curriculum counterparts.

In a reaction to the results of a large-scale study conducted by Bennett (1976), Gray and Satterly (1978) suggested that the differences in the effectiveness of formal and informal teachers described by Bennett can be attributed to time allocations. "Formal teachers not only allocate more time to the basic skills but also ensure (because they believe such skills are overridingly important) that their pupils [spend more time] by maintaining stricter discipline and by being less tolerant of what they perceive as pupil 'time-wasting' " (Gray and Satterly 1978 p. 141). Both of these reviews (i.e., the Walker and Schaffarzick, and the Gray and Satterly) clearly indicate the potential confounding of opportunity to learn with curriculum, instructional, or teaching variables.

Finally, despite the different conceptualizations of opportunity to learn some merger of the two conceptualizations seems worthwhile. Such a merger could conceivably result in a more powerful variable if the merger could maintain the strengths of both conceptualizations. This new conceptualization would focus on the amount of time allocated to the teaching of content underlying each of the items included on the achievement test.

A modification of Borg's approach could be used to measure this new variable. Each teacher would be given a copy of the test and asked to indicate the number of lessons (or class periods) spent teaching the content tested by each item. The length of each lesson (or class period) also could be ascertained by asking the teacher. The total number of hours and minutes spent teaching content directly related to the achievement test could be estimated by multiplying the total number of lessons by the number or minutes per lesson. Other measurement approaches, some of which involve direct observation of teachers, also could be used in this regard.

A single conceptualization of opportunity to learn coupled with the inclusion of the variable in classroom instructional research on a regular basis could have profound effects on our understanding of life in classrooms. This entry has provided some insights to guide researchers and practitioners in this direction.

BIBLIOGRAPHY

Armbruster B B, Stevens R J, Rosenshine B 1977 *Analyzing Content Coverage and Emphasis: A Study of Three Curricula and Two Tests*. Technical Report No. 26. Center for the Study of Reading, University of Illinois, Urbana, Illinois

Bennett N 1976 *Teaching Styles and Pupil Progress*. Open Books, London

Borg W R 1979 Teacher coverage of academic content and pupil achievement. *J. Educ. Psychol.* 71: 635–45

Carroll J B 1963 A model of school learning. *Teach. Coll. Rec.* 64: 723–33

Carroll J B 1974 Fitting a model of school learning to aptitude and achievement data over grade levels. In: Green D R (ed.) 1974 *The Aptitude–Achievement Distinction: Proceedings of the 2nd CTB/McGraw-Hill Conference on Issues in Educational Measurement, Carmel, California, 1973*. CTB/McGraw-Hill, Monterey, California

Carroll J B 1975 *The Teaching of French as a Foreign Language in Eight Countries*. Wiley, New York

Comber L C, Keeves J P 1973 *Science Education in Nineteen Countries: An Empirical Study*. Wiley, New York

Cooley W W, Leinhardt G 1980 The instructional dimensions study. *Educ. Eval. Policy Anal.* 2: 7–25

Dishaw M 1977 *Descriptions of Allocated Time to Content Areas for the A-B Period*. Beginning Teacher Evaluation Study (BTES) Technical Note Series, Technical Note N-2a. Far West Laboratory for Educational Research and Development, San Francisco, California

Fisher C W et al. 1980 Teaching behaviors, academic learning time, and student achievement. In: Denham C, Lieberman A (eds.) 1980 *Time to Learn*. National Institute of Education, Washington, DC

Gray J, Satterly D 1978 Time to learn? *Educ. Res.* 20: 137–41

Husén T (ed.) 1967 *International Study of Achievement in Mathematics: A Comparison of Twelve Countries*. Wiley, New York

Jenkins J R, Pany D 1978 Curriculum biases in reading achievement tests. *J. Read. Behav.* 10: 345–57

Leinhardt G, Seewald A M 1981 Overlap: What's tested, what's taught? *J. Educ. Meas.* 18: 85–96

Porter A C, Schmidt W H, Floden R E, Freeman D J 1978 *Impact on What? The Importance of Content Covered*. Educational Resources Information Centers (ERIC), National Institute of Education, Washington, DC ERIC Document No. ED 155 215

Poyner H et al. 1977 *Final Report on the Instructional Dimensions Study*. National Institute of Education, Washington, DC

Schmidt W H 1978 *Measuring the Content of Instruction*. Educational Resources Information Centers (ERIC), National Institute of Education, Washington, DC. ERIC Document No. 171 783

Walker D F, Schaffarzick J 1974 Comparing curricula. *Rev. Educ. Res.* 44: 83–111

Wiley D E, Harnischfeger A 1974 Explosion of a myth: Quantity of schooling and exposure to instruction, major educational vehicles. *Educ. Res.* 4: 7–12

2. TEMPUS EDUCARE

David C. Berliner

Since the early 1970s, the Beginning Teacher Evaluation Study (BTES) has promoted inquiry into teaching and learning in the elementary school. The design of the study was influenced by the research literature and those methodological paradigms for research that were available in the middle of the 1970s, and it was these factors that led to an investigation of various aspects of instructional time.

Three measures of time—allocated time (the time a teacher provides for instruction in a particular content area), engaged time (the time a student is attending to instruction in a particular content area), and academic learning time (the time a student is engaged with instructional materials or activities that are at an easy level of difficulty for that student)—were considered to be important variables through which teacher behavior and classroom characteristics influence student achievement. This chapter opens with an explanation of how the inquiry into use of instructional time began. It goes on to investigate the three measures of time considered important in the educational process and concludes with a summary of why the three time variables deserve the attention of those who study classroom teaching and learning.

THE BTES DESIGN

Many flaws in design and logic are apparent in the literature on teaching and learning in the elementary schools. Nevertheless, a cluster of variables that related consistently to achievement did emerge.[1] They are called direct instructional variables.

- One variable was the goal-setting or structuring behavior provided by the teacher. Teachers identified as being effective in eliciting achievement from their students made more verbal statements directing students to the tasks in which they should be engaged.[2] They clearly informed students what they should be doing, where to do it, and for how long, which ensured that students did not lose time because they were confused or because they were waiting for decisions to be made.
- Another variable was absence from school. Absence of either teacher or student was usually negatively related to student achievement, indicating that the time spent in school contributes to achievement. Additional data support the belief that instructional time is an important predictor of student achievement in academic areas.[3]
- The focus of the time spent in the classroom also emerged as an important variable. An academic focus was found to result in consistently higher achievement. When, on the other hand, large amounts of time were spent in telling stories or in art, music, or play activities, as opposed to reading and mathematics activities, correlations with achievement were found to be negative.
- As for coverage of content, this was also considered to be a positive predictor of achievement. Particularly in mathematics, the more content that was covered, the greater the achievement.
- The importance of monitoring by the teacher was another variable that emerged as significant. When monitoring was carefully done, the teacher was able to keep children engaged in their assigned tasks and correlation with achievement was positive.
- Yet another variable that demonstrated a positive relation with achievement outcomes was the type of question asked by teachers. Factual, concrete questions were associated with higher achievement in the elementary grades than evaluative, abstract ones.
- The type of feedback that teachers provide to students also seemed to be important. Feedback that was academic in nature correlated positively with achievement.
- And, finally, the classroom environment was found to be important. A classroom environment characterized as warm, democratic, and convivial showed up as a positive predictor of achievement.

The conclusion reached after reviewing the literature was a simple one: Elementary school teachers who find ways to put students into contact with the academic curriculum and to keep them in contact with that curriculum while maintaining a convivial classroom atmosphere are successful in promoting achievement in reading and mathematics. It was this simple summary statement that led us to design the BTES study so that the student and curricular materials were focal points in collecting and analyzing data.

MODIFYING THE PARADIGMS

Research on teaching had not received much attention before 1960. By 1975, however, a number of team and individual research efforts had been completed or were under way, almost all of which were cast in the form of process-product analyses. This means that teacher behavior and classroom characteristics were observed and subsequently related to measures of student achievement and attitude. Correlation was the most frequently used statistic in such studies. It was expected that the BTES would reflect this traditional approach. As the study progressed and the research literature was examined, however, the investigators became increasingly dissatisfied with the process-product approach since it appeared that certain illogical elements were inherent in the design of a process-product study of classroom teaching. For example, how could the number or percentage of teacher verbal communications coded as praise statements in November influence results on achievement test items given in May? Without imposing strict experimental controls, how can one evaluate the effects of teachers' questioning behavior in a particular subject area when one teacher devotes five hours a week to that area and another teacher devotes one and one-half hours per week to the same area? How could anyone expect to discover a relationship between a variable such as time spent lecturing on ecology and achievement test items that measure dictionary usage? The latter occurs when investigators use instruments that code teacher behavior of various sorts and correlate that behavior with broad-spectrum tests of reading achievement.

At first it appeared that correlational approaches using the process-product research paradigm were inherently deficient. Some of our colleagues argued that only by recourse to true experiments could the situation be remedied. But true experimental designs used in the investigation of teaching and learning in classrooms also have certain flaws. The most serious of these are that such designs do not reflect the complexities of the classroom, with its myriad interactions; they do not reflect the dynamic quality of the classroom, with its ever-changing events; nor can they, typically, develop an appropriate time perspective since the acquisition of knowledge in the classroom is best conceived of as a multiyear process.[4] Thus, experimental designs that reflect the process-product framework often suffer from problems of ecological validity.[5]

If correlational studies were to be conducted in natural classroom environments, which would appear to give them more potential external validity, then the logical and hypothetical causal flow of events in the process-product model needed to be modified. Researchers on the Beginning Teacher Evaluation Study proposed a simple modification of the process-product approach to the study of classroom learning. This modification is based on the belief that what a teacher does at any one moment while working in a circumscribed content area affects a student primarily at only that particular moment and in that particular content area. The link between teacher behavior and student achievement is, therefore, the ongoing student behavior in the classroom learning situation. The logic continues in this way. What a teacher does to foster learning in a particular content area becomes important only if a student is engaged with *appropriate* curriculum content. Appropriate curriculum content is defined as curriculum that is logically related to the criterion and is at an easy level of difficulty for a particular student. Thus, a second-grade student engaged in the task of decoding blends in reading, either by means of a workbook or by watching the teacher at the chalkboard, is engaging in processes that can lead to proficiency in decoding blends if the task requires a low rate of error on the part of the student. The variable used in BTES research is the accrued engaged time in a particular content area using materials that are not difficult for the student. This complex variable is called Academic Learning Time (ALT). Although the relationship is probably not linear, the accrual of ALT is expected to be a strong positive correlate of achievement.

It was originally believed that engagement with curriculum materials of an intermediate level of difficulty would lead to greater achievement. The data, however, show that young children trying to learn in traditional classroom settings need to work on academic tasks that give rise to low error rates. A low error rate occurs when about 20 percent or fewer errors are noted for a student engaged with workbook pages, tests, or classroom exercises. When a student's responses are not overt, an observer must estimate the level of difficulty of the activities in which the student is engaged.

Certainly trying to keep students engaged for too long with too many easy tasks will not improve academic performance. Engagement is likely to drop off, and content coverage will be reduced. Knowing when to move a student to new materials and activities is a complex diagnostic decision that teachers must make. That must always be kept in mind. Still, for the conception of classroom learning proposed here, it is when teachers put students into contact with academic materials and activities that are relatively easy that learning is hypothesized to take place.

This variable of ALT, which is measured in real time, has some roots in the works of Carroll, of Bloom, of Harnischfeger and Wiley, and of others.[6] The effort to develop a variable focusing on students' use of time and the curriculum, simultaneously, comes from the earlier literature, as has already been discussed. The concern for the easy level of difficulty, where low error rates are noted or inferred, has some roots in the literature of instructional design, particularly that concerned with programmed instruction. Investigating the relations of ALT to teacher behavior and to student achievement requires, as was noted, that a change be made in the process-product research paradigm. This modification is shown in Figure [1].

In this conception of research on teaching, the content area the student is working on must be specified precisely, the task engagement of the student must be judged, the level of difficulty of the task must be rated, and time must be measured. The constructed variable of ALT, then, stands between measures of teaching and measures of student achievement. A design for research using this approach requires the construction of two correlational matrices. The first is used to study how teacher behavior and classroom characteristics affect ALT. The second is used to study how ALT and achievement are related.

Essential to this conception of how teachers influence student achievement is the variable of engaged time. The upper limit on measures of engaged time in classrooms, for a particular content area, is the time the teacher has allocated for instruction in that area. The remainder of this chapter is concerned with allocated time, engaged time, and

ALT in different content areas. The thesis is that the marked variability in allocated time, engaged time, and ALT, between and within classes, is the most potent explanatory variable to account for variability in student achievement—after initial aptitude has been removed as a predictor variable. A corollary of this thesis is that interactive teaching behavior (praise, questioning, use of organizers, feedback, and so forth) can only be understood through its effect on ALT. In this conception of classroom learning, interactive teaching behavior or teaching skills are not thought to be directly linked to achievement.

A STUDY OF INSTRUCTIONAL TIME

Allocated time, engaged time, and ALT were studied during a recent school year in twenty-five second-grade and twenty-five fifth-grade classes in California. Teachers were trained in log-keeping procedures so that the daily time allocations for selected students could be recorded within particular content areas of reading and mathematics. In addition, a trained observer was present approximately one day a week for over twenty weeks of the school year. The observer recorded engaged time and provided data to compute estimates of ALT, as well as providing data about a number of other facets of classroom life.[7] Selections from this larger data set are used to illustrate some of the within- and between-class variability in allocated time, engaged time, and ALT.[8]

Allocated Time

Table [1] presents allocated time in content areas of second-grade mathematics and Table [2] presents allocated time for content areas of fifth-grade read-

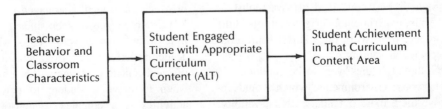

FIGURE [1]   Simple Flow of Events That Influence Achievement in a Particular Curriculum Content Area

TABLE [1]   Time (in Minutes) Spent in Content Area of Mathematics and Related Variables for Students in Four Second-Grade Classes

CONTENT AREAS AND RELATED VARIABLES	TIME (IN MINUTES)			
	CLASS 5	CLASS 21	CLASS 8	CLASS 13
Content areas of the curriculum				
Computation				
Addition and subtraction, no regrouping, short form	835	420	1,839	540
Addition and subtraction, no regrouping, instructional algorithm	172	177	131	596
Addition and subtraction, with regrouping, short form	0	357	246	736
Addition and subtraction, with regrouping, instructional algorithm	43	464	138	723
Speed tests	232	31	71	100
Other computation	0	3	68	15
Concepts-applications				
Computational transfer	453	185	580	130
Place value and numerals	416	352	684	692
Word problems	109	226	416	132
Money	98	9	228	315
Linear measurement	29	130	107	400
Fractions	0	21	63	399
Developmental activities	0	76	111	40
Other concepts or applications	145	237	54	309
Related variables				
Total time in minutes	2,530	2,687	4,736	5,127
Number of days data collected	93	83	94	96
Average time per day in minutes	27	32	50	53
Percent of time students engaged	71	62	61	78
Engaged minutes per day	19	20	31	41
Percent of time students are in material of easy difficulty level	67	59	65	55
Academic learning time per day in minutes	13	12	20	23
Engaged hours per 150 days in school year	48	50	78	103
Academic learning time in hours per 150-day school year	33	30	50	58

SOURCE: Marilyn Dishaw, *Descriptions of Allocated Time to Content Areas for the A-B Period,* Technical Note IV-11a; *id., Descriptions of Allocated Time to Content Areas for the B-C Period,* Technical Note IV-11b; and Nikola N. Filby and Richard N. Marliave, *Descriptions of Distributions of ALT within and across Classes during the A-B Period,* Technical Note IV-1a—all publications of the Beginning Teacher Evaluation Study (San Francisco: Far West Laboratory for Educational Research and Development, 1977).

ing. These data were obtained from teachers' logs over an average of ninety days of instruction from October to May of the school year. The logs were filled out daily for six students in each of the classrooms. Within each grade level the students were of comparable ability levels in reading and mathematics, both within and across classes.[9] The data from the six students who were studied inten-sively in each class will be used to generalize about the whole class.

With the data from both second-grade mathematics and fifth-grade reading, one can notice widespread variation in how teachers spend their time. Different philosophies of education yield different beliefs about what is important for students to learn. These beliefs, along with the teacher's likes and

TABLE [2]   Time (in Minutes) Spent in Content Area of Reading and Related Variables for Students in Four Fifth-Grade Classes

CONTENT AREAS AND RELATED VARIABLES	TIME (IN MINUTES)			
	CLASS 1	CLASS 3	CLASS 11	CLASS 25
Content areas of the curriculum				
Word structure				
Root words and affixes	250	112	126	103
Syllables	67	60	102	212
Word meaning				
Synonyms	95	152	10	119
Pronoun reference	0	0	9	56
Other word meaning	558	949	1,042	615
Comprehension				
Verbatim (no rephrasing)	206	329	188	325
Translations (paraphrase)	122	151	1,649	383
Inference-synthesis	235	252	1,432	306
Identifying main items	153	243	943	326
Evaluation of fact and opinion	5	0	66	56
Other comprehension	196	325	1,368	239
Reading practice				
Oral reading	604	63	885	305
Silent reading	1,083	724	956	3,640
Reading in content areas	505	256	400	284
Related reading				
Spelling	694	847	664	1,415
Grammar	242	183	859	413
Creative writing	56	343	98	573
Study skills	472	669	270	171
Other	207	687	1,317	426
Related variables				
Total time in minutes	5,749	6,344	12,383	9,965
Number of days data collected	97	96	87	74
Average time per day in minutes	59	66	142	135
Percent of time students engaged	82	77	84	75
Engaged minutes per day	48	51	119	101
Percent of time students are in material of easy difficulty level	51	61	47	58
Academic learning time per day in minutes	24	31	56	59
Engaged hours per 150 days in school year	120	128	298	283
Academic learning time in hours per 150-day school year	60	78	140	148

SOURCE: Dishaw, *Descriptions of Allocated Time to Content Areas for the A-B Period; id., Descriptions of Allocated Time to Content Areas for the B-C Period;* and Filby and Marliave, *Descriptions of Distributions of ALT within and across Classes during the A-B Period.*

dislikes for teaching certain areas, result in some interesting differences in the *functional* curriculum of a class. For example, from Table [1] it can be seen that students in class 13 had an average of 400 minutes each to learn the concepts and operations involved in linear measurement, while students in class 5 had an average of 29 minutes each to learn those operations and concepts. Class 21 received very little time in the content area of fractions and in the content area of money, while class 13 received markedly more time in these areas. From Table [2] it can be seen that class 11 spent dramatically more time on comprehension in reading than any of the other three fifth-grade classes. In class 25 silent reading and spelling were emphasized, to judge from the dramatically greater allocation of time to those content areas, in contrast to the average amount of time each student of classes 1, 3, and 11 received. And oral reading hardly seemed to be of interest to the teacher of class 3; at least that could be inferred if the data from class 3 were compared with the data from the other fifth-grade classes.

These rather significant differences in the functional classroom curriculum should, from all we know about learning, result in considerable differences in achievement. If students in these second-grade classrooms were tested at the end of the year on linear measurement, one might wager that students in class 13 would demonstrate better performance than students in class 5. If the fifth-grade classes were part of some end-of-year statewide testing program where drawing inferences from paragraphs of prose was tested, as it often is, one might well expect that students in class 11 would show superior performance when contrasted with similar students in the other fifth-grade classes.

The broad-spectrum standardized achievement test may be a social indicator from which state or national policy can be illuminated. But as long as teachers have the freedom to choose what areas they will emphasize in their classrooms, these tests can never be used as fair measures of a teacher's effectiveness. It simply is not fair to teachers to evaluate their students in areas that the teacher did not cover or emphasize. On the other hand, it may not be fair to students and their parents to let teachers arbitrarily choose what is to be taught. Tighter control of the functional curriculum of the classroom may be desirable. This problem is recognized by many, and has led some curriculum developers to insist upon stringent control of teacher behavior in order to implement the program that they would promote.[10]

Another interesting aspect of allocated time is the average daily time devoted to mathematics and reading. States and school districts usually insist upon a certain minimum number of minutes per day or hours per week for certain subject matters. Let us suppose, by law, that forty minutes a day is the minimum amount of time to be devoted to mathematics in the second grade within a particular school district. Let us also suppose that this mathematics

time begins at 11:15, after a recess, and that the time period devoted to mathematics ends at noon. The teacher, principal, and superintendent may well feel that the state minimum requirements are being met and exceeded. But careful observation will reveal otherwise. A ten-minute delay in the start of work, called transition time in the Beginning Teacher Evaluation Study, may occur before the mathematics curriculum is really in effect. Toward the end of the allocated time students are putting workbooks, contracts, and Cuisenaire rods away, getting lunches out, and lining up for dismissal at noontime. Another ten minutes may be lost. Functional time for mathematics is now twenty-five minutes, which is 60 percent under the legal requirements.

The data presented in Table [1] reflect the difficulty of managing time in the classroom. Classes 5 and 21 have, on the average, a daily allocation totaling about thirty minutes per day for mathematics, while classes 8 and 13 show, on the average, an allocation of over fifty minutes per day for mathematics. From other data collected as part of this study, we estimated that the students in class 5 and class 21 spend an average of 42.5 minutes per day in transitions from activity to activity, while students in classes 8 and 13 spend about half that time, approximately 22 minutes per day, in transitions. The average number of minutes per day devoted to fifth-grade reading, as presented in Table [2], shows similar variability. Teachers in classes 11 and 25 allocated over 100 percent more total time to reading than teachers in classes 1 and 3. Other data from our full fifth-grade sample reveal that the teachers with the lower rate of allocated time had a higher than average amount of class time spent in transitions and the management of behavioral problems. What this indicates is that the time allocated for academic instruction in a school day can easily slip away when a teacher cannot keep transitional time and behavioral problems to a minimum. Any sensible manager knows that. Somehow, in some classes, there is a casualness about classroom management that results in considerable inefficiency.

This brief examination of selected data presenting estimates of time allocated in the classroom shows clearly that some teachers spend considerably more time instructing in particular content areas than other teachers, and some teachers allocate considerably more total time for instruction than other teachers. These differences, put into experimental terminology, represent clear differences in the type and in the duration of treatment. One can expect, therefore, considerable variability on the outcome measures used to assess these vastly different treatments.

Engaged Time

Tables [1]and [2] also present data on the average percentage of time students are engaged in reading or mathematics instruction. These data are from observer records, and not from teacher logs. Previous work revealed that teachers can keep accurate records of allocated time, but that classroom observers were necessary to obtain accurate records of engaged time.[11] In examining these data it appears that the percentage of time students are engaged is relatively high. This is an artifact of the observational system that was in use. The system required that transition time and other classroom phenomena be coded as separate events. Thus, the data on engagement rates are for the time spent in mathematics and reading, after a class has settled down and before the class starts to put away their work. If engagement were coded for the entire time block denoted by teachers as mathematics or reading time, the engaged time rates would be considerably lower because most of the class is not engaged during transitions. Still, variation among classes is noted for an important variable. The engagement rates in the four second-grade classes vary from 61 percent to 78 percent during mathematics instruction. In the four fifth-grade classes engagement rates vary from 75 percent to 84 percent during reading instruction. These ranges were much larger in the total sample of classes studied.

The average number of minutes per day allocated for instruction, multiplied by the engagement rate, provides liberal estimates of the number of engaged minutes per day for each student. These data are found in Tables [1] and [2]. In the second-grade data for mathematics, at the lower end of the range, 20 minutes of engaged time per day is noted. At the higher end of the range, 40 minutes per day is noted. For fifth-grade reading, the range in the four classes is between 48 and 119 minutes of engaged time per day. These are dramatic differences of 100 percent or more in the amount of engaged time students allot to learn mathematics and reading. For reasons that we do not yet fully understand, some combination of teacher behavior and students' socialization to school interacts to produce classes where most of the children are attending to their work most of the time. And these same factors sometimes result in classes where less than half of the children are attending to their work during the time allocated for instruction.

In most districts we may assume that a school year is about 180 days. This figure must be reduced by absences of teachers and students, strikes, busing difficulties, the difficulties of instructing before Christmas and Easter breaks, testing at the beginning and end of the school year, and other factors. A reasonable estimate of the "functional" school year may be about 150 days. Accumulating the engaged minutes per day over these 150 days gives an estimate of the engaged instructional time allotted by students to the academic curriculum during the entire school year. Tables [1] and [2] present these data for the four classes in each grade level. Between 50 and 100 hours per year of active student involvement in classroom instruction in mathematics is noted in the four second-grade classes. In the four fifth-grade classes, with more mature and more independent learners, between 120 and 298 cumulative hours per school year are noted for all areas of reading. When these and other data collected as part of the study are examined, it is evident that many second-grade classes have cumulative engaged time, in *both* reading and mathematics, of under 100 hours for the entire school year. In the fifth grade, these data provide considerably higher estimates of engaged time for the school year.

As these data come to light, some important questions must be asked. For example, what should be expected in the way of engaged time for thirty students and one teacher, working together throughout the school year? What are the expectations for instructional time held by parents and school board members as they make policy to educate the young of a community? Because these new estimates of classroom allocated and engaged time do not conform to the prevailing beliefs that exist among the people who manage and support education, either those beliefs must be changed, or instructional practices must be altered.

Academic Learning Time

As noted above, academic learning time is the research variable of most interest in the Beginning Teacher Evaluation Study. One component of ALT is the level of difficulty of the material that is attended to by a student. It is the belief of the investigators that learning occurs primarily with materials that are at an easy level of difficulty. Materials that are too hard for a student do not add much to his acquisition of the concepts, skills, and operations that are required at a particular grade level. Nor do they allow for practice, repetition, and overlearning. These are important concerns if retention is to be maximized. Tables [1] and [2] present information on the percentage of time that students are working with relatively easy material. These data are ratings made by observers in classrooms. As shown in Table [1], for second-grade mathematics the range is between 55 percent and 67 percent. In fifth-grade reading the range is between 47 percent and 61 percent. Multiplying the engaged minutes per day by the percentage of time students are assigned work that yields low error rates provides an estimate of ALT per day. These data are also provided in the tables.

As noted above, the typical academic school year of 180 days may be considered to be a functional school year of 150 days. The last line in Tables [1] and [2] presents academic learning time, in hours, for a school year of 150 days. In these four classes, at each grade level, differences of many hundreds of percent in accumulated ALT are noted. In second-grade mathematics, the range is from 30 hours per school year to 58 hours per school year. In fifth-grade reading, the range is from 60 hours per school year to 148 hours per school year. In the total sample studied the range of ALT is considerably larger. It should also be noted that all of the elementary school teachers in this sample were volunteers. These data, if they could be obtained from a nonvolunteer sample, would most likely show even more between-class variability.

If academic learning time is the key to acquiring the knowledge and skill required to master the curriculum of a particular grade level, for a particular content area, one can see that the school year does not contain as much ALT as might be desired. If our concerns about instruction are correct, there are many classes where there is not sufficient time for students to master the curriculum that has been chosen for them.

IN SUMMARY

Descriptive data on allocated time, engaged time, and academic learning time have been presented.

Data from four second-grade and four fifth-grade classes were chosen to reflect differences in the variables of interest. If the type of treatment and the duration of treatment are crucial variables in the determination of what is learned and how much is learned, then between-class differences in allocated time in content areas, and in total allocated time per day or per school year, become important operationally defined behavioral indicators of the instructional treatment. If learning is likely to occur only when students attend to the instruction offered them, then between-class differences in engaged time become an important operationally defined behavioral indicator of the effective stimulus situation, as opposed to the nominal stimulus situation. And, finally, if learning primarily takes place when students are engaged with materials and activities that are of an easy level of difficulty for that particular student, then ALT becomes an important operationally defined behavioral indicator of student learning. The construct of ALT has an intriguing virtue. One does not need to wait until the end of the school year to decide if learning has taken place. One can study learning *as it happens* if the construct of ALT is accepted as it has been defined. In the conception of instruction that has guided the research that has been conducted and on which this chapter is based, ALT and learning are synonymous.

The commonsense logic of the above statements is appealing. Even without data relating allocated time, engaged time, and ALT to achievement, these descriptive data have a certain obvious validity, and they can, moreover, lead teachers and supervisors of teachers to examine classroom processes in ways that logically relate to student achievement. Without turning classes into authoritarian factories of learning, many teachers can improve their effectiveness by attending to these variables and reorganizing classroom practices to maximize teaching time and learning time—resources over which they have considerable personal control.

NOTES

1. David C. Berliner and Barak V. Rosenshine, "The Acquisition of Knowledge in the Classroom," in *Schooling and the Acquisition of Knowledge,* ed. Richard C. Anderson, Rand J. Spiro, and William E. Montague (Hillsdale, N.J.: Erlbaum, 1977), 375–396; Barak V. Rosenshine and David C. Berliner, "Academic Engaged Time," *British Journal of Teacher Education* 4 (1978): 3–16.

2. W. J. Tikunoff, David C. Berliner, and R. C. Rist, *An Ethnographic Study of the Forty Classrooms of the Beginning Teacher Evaluation Study Known Sample,* Technical Report No. 75-10-5 (San Francisco: Far West Laboratory for Educational Research and Development, 1975).

3. David E. Wiley and Annegret Harnischfeger, "Explosion of a Myth: Quantity of Schooling and Exposure to Instruction, Major Educational Vehicles," *Educational Researcher* 3 (1974): 7–12; Jane A. Stallings and David H. Koskowitz, *Follow Through Classroom Observation Evaluation, 1972–73* (Menlo Park, Calif.: Stanford Research Institute, 1974).

4. Charles W. Fisher and David C. Berliner, *Quasi-clinical Inquiry in Research on Classroom Teaching and Learning,* Technical Report VI-2, Beginning Teacher Evaluation Study (San Francisco: Far West Laboratory for Educational Research and Development, 1977).

5. Glenn H. Bracht and Gene V. Glass, "The External Validity of Experiments," *American Educational Research Journal* 5 (1968): 437–479.

6. John B. Carroll, "A Model of School Learning," *Teachers College Record* 64 (1963): 723–733; Benjamin S. Bloom, *Human Characteristics and School Learning* (New York: McGraw-Hill, 1976); Annegret Harnischfeger and David E. Wiley, "Teaching-Learning Processes in Elementary School: A Synoptic View," *Curriculum Inquiry* 6 (1976): 5–43.

7. Beginning Teacher Evaluation Study, *Proposal for Phase III-B of the Beginning Teacher Evaluation Study, July 1, 1976–June 30, 1977* (San Francisco: Far West Laboratory for Educational Research and Development, 1976).

8. Marilyn Dishaw, *Descriptions of Allocated Time to Content Areas for the A-B Period,* Technical Note IV-11a, Beginning Teacher Evaluation Study (San Francisco: Far West Laboratory for Educational Research and Development, 1977); *id., Descriptions of Allocated Time to Content Areas for the B-C Period,* Technical Note IV-11b, Beginning Teacher Evaluation Study (San Francisco: Far West Laboratory for Educational Research and Development, 1977); Nikola N. Filby and Richard N. Marliave, *Descriptions of Distributions of ALT within and across Classes during the A-B Period,* Technical Note IV-1a, Beginning Teacher Evaluation Study (San Francisco: Far West Laboratory for Educational Research and Development, 1977).

9. Leonard S. Cahen, *Selection of Second- and Fifth-Grade Target Students for Phase III-B,* Technical Note III-1, Part 2, Beginning Teacher Evaluation Study (San Francisco: Far West Laboratory for Educational Research and Development, 1977).

10. Wesley C. Becker and Siegfried Engelmann, "The Direct Instruction Model," in *Encouraging Change in America's Schools: A Decade of Experimentation,* ed. Ray Rhine (New York: Academic Press, 1978).

11. Richard N. Marliave, Charles W. Fisher, and Nikola N. Filby, "Alternative Procedures for Collecting Instructional Time Data: When Can You Ask the Teacher and When Must You Observe for Yourself?" paper presented at the annual meeting of the American Educational Research Association, New York, 1977.

The ideas and data presented in this chapter emerged from work performed while conducting the Beginning Teacher Evaluation Study. That study was funded by the National Institute of Education and administered by the California Commission for Teacher Preparation and Licensing. The research was conducted by the Far West Laboratory for Educational Research and Development. The study represents a joint effort on the part of David C. Berliner, Leonard S. Cahen, Nikola N. Filby, Charles W. Fisher, Richard N. Marliave, Marilyn Dishaw, and Jeffry E. Moore.

3. MODELS OF THE LEARNER

Jerome Bruner

Topics, including the topics of keynote addresses to learned societies, have a hermeneutic history. The hermeneutic history of a topic, we are cautioned, must be taken into account if we are fully to interpret its meaning. The topic of my paper, Models of the Learner, is no exception. It has such a history and has a proximal origin in a set of exchanges—first as a conversation and then as the topic of a more formal learned discussion.

Let me set forth the beginning narrative of that hermeneutic circle (or spiral) and continue it in the discussion that follows. The setting was an international conference in the not very Orwellian summer of 1984, a conference ostensibly on the vexed subject of how to improve the quality of education. Sponsored jointly by the Van Leer Jerusalem Foundation and the Aspen Institute, it took place in a handsome mansion overlooking one of the scenic lakes on the outskirts of Berlin—a mansion that had been reconstructed on the ruins of the residence of the infamous Goebbels, Hitler's Minister of Culture, or was he the Minister of Propaganda? The participants were appropriately distinguished: some Deans of famous faculties of education, more than a sprinkling of great names in what everybody would agree is educational research, and a handful of psychologists and associated behavioral scientists whose work bore that tangential relation to the process of education that excites the optimism of educators with respect to the relevance of "pure" research. We were perhaps two dozen in number, and it was a convivial company.

After a day and a half of discussion on topics of great generality, all conducted at a level of striking knowledgeability, someone proposed that we could really not get to the heart of the matter unless we had more clearly in mind some working model of what a learner was, how he or she operated, and above all, what we thought to be an adequate learning environment for our putative learner. It was proposed to the plenary session that we give over the next morning to these issues.

I was among those asked to prepare some sort of statement on the matter. The discussion that ensued was lively. What it left behind in my mind and what several of us discussed later was the flat-footed impossibility of ever settling institutional questions of education without first making a decision—yes, a political decision—on the nature of learning and learners. Yet for all that, the decision about learning and learners was perforce a decision about an ideal, about how we conceived what a learner *should* be in order to assure that a society of a particularly valued kind could be safeguarded. There is no completely naturalistic way of resolving the question about what model of the learner we want to enshrine at the center of our practice of education. For there are many ways to learn and many ways of encouraging different forms of learning with different ends in view. At the heart of the decision process there must be a value judgment about how the mind should be cultivated and to what end.

While I wish to consider alternate models of the learner, I have no illusion that I can do so just in the spirit of a naturalist or as a student of the learning process. In fact, models of the learner that are on offer in the psychological literature, in the cognitive sciences, or in AI are themselves constructions based on a selection not simply of data, but of the conditions under which learning is studied. As I tried to say a few years ago, it is possible to construct not only experimental studies but "real life" situations that make people (or pigeons, for that matter) look stupid or clever, generative or passive, combinatorial or rote (Bruner, 1982). Then the theoretical model that is constructed becomes, as it were, the text of the culture, and life is made to imitate text in the same subtle ways in which, in another closely related domain, life imitates art.

Please do not interpret what I am saying in the relativistic sense that all theories or models of the learner are equally true or even equally right. Rather, what I wish to say is that any model of learning is right or wrong for a given set of stipulated conditions, including the nature of the tasks one has in mind, the form of the intention one creates in the learner, the generality of specificity of the learning to be accomplished, and the semiotics of the learning situation itself—what it means to the learner.

This is *not* to say that a new or different model of the learner is needed for every task or situation in which learning takes place. To put it in the current jargon, it is absurd to insist that each and every theory of learning is utterly domain specific, that nothing general can be said about learners or learning or learning environments. You do not quite need a different model of a learner to talk about learning how to play chess, learning how to play the flute, learning mathematics, and learning to read the sprung rhymes in the verse of Gerard Manley Hopkins. Even if I do have to say it in folk psychology rather than in programming talk, all of them will involve attention and memory and courage and even, *pace* AI, some heuristics for maintaining frustration tolerance. The issue, as we shall see yet again, is that learning is indeed context sensitive, but that human beings, given their peculiarly human competence, are capable of adapting their approach to the demands of different contexts. But I am tipping my hand, for it is only later that I wanted to talk about a general model of a learner as one equipped to discriminate and deal differentially with a wide variety of possible worlds exhibiting different conditions, yet worlds in which one can cope.

Let me now take a fast gallop through the landscape we surveyed that day from the phoenix nest on the site of Goebbels' house in the exurbs of Berlin when we got down to our formal discussion of "models of the learner."

MODELS OF THE LEARNER

Tabula Rasa

The first, and perhaps the most ancient is really based on the Aristotelian notion of *mimesis*. In its 18th century version, it rested on the premise that experience writes on the wax tablet of the mind. One learns from experience (rather than through divine revelation or through received texts). Or as Locke put it, nothing gets into the mind save through the senses—but as Leibniz countered, nothing except mind itself. This view takes as a central premise that such order as there is in mind is a reflection of the order that exists in the world, and that is why the concept of association is always so central to empiricist theories. Things that are together in space and time in the world succeed, under the sway of this principle, in being together in the mind. I need not go into the troubles of empiricism. They have been raked over historically by everybody from Aristotle (whose *sensus communis* was something of a constructivist takeover bid) through the School-men, from Kant through Wittgenstein and Chomsky. I want, rather, to take it as a given, a cultural text in Geertz's sense, to be examined for its cultural significance in shaping our practices. I want to note only that, given belief in associationist empiricism, we adopted ideas about learning procedures to fit and constructed learning environments that in fact made people look like little empiricists—averting our eyes from all instances where it didn't, as for example in the acquiring of a language. And when we were forced to look at that, we concocted Augustinian theories about it and devised nonsense syllable research in support of them.

The formula for success in empiricism is to have experience.

Hypothesis Generator

There is a class of learner models that represents a reaction against the rather passive view of empiricist, *tabula rasa* notions. They have in common a notion of intentionality at their center. The learner, rather than being the creature of experience, selects that which is to enter. The principle of selection varies from theory to theory: from the *sensus communis* of Aristotle and the *vis integretiva* of Aquinas that sorted the associated input of experience in the light of the principles of reason, to the principles of wish-fulfillment and ego defense of Freud that permitted us to experience (or interpret) only those parts of experience that were adequate compromises between the demands of conflicting needs. What exactly generates hypotheses or programs the filter, which selects and organizes what gets through the senses into the mind, varied widely and was always seriously underdefined. Even such towering learning theorists as Edward Tolman, Lev Vygotsky, and John Dewey, all of whom took the view that experience came shaped by hypotheses rather than by the world, were grandly vague in their specification of how hypotheses came into being—though Dewey and Vygotsky gave special pride of place to the role of language as a hypothesis-generator, a place that promised more than it delivered.

It was never altogether clear how to extrapolate an educational posture from hypothesis theories, save in one respect. Emphasis was on an active curiosity guided by self-directed project—a feature of Progressivism in America and in the unrealized pedagogy of Vygotsky's followers in the Soviet Union, unrealized save in the discipline of "defectology."

The formula for success in learning, according to the hypothesis formulation, is to have a good theory.

Nativism

At least three forms of muted nativism have shaped our models of the learner. One derives from Immanuel Kant. A second comes from Gestalt theory. The third, derivative of Descartes, is still with us in Chomsky's theory of mind. In a deep historical sense, they are all inheritors of the tradition of Platonism. All share one central concept: Mind is inherently or innately shaped by a set of underlying categories, hypotheses, forms of organizing experience. The task of the learner is to work his or her way through the cluttered surface structure of sense to an underlying or ideal or deep organization that provides a richer or righter or more predictive or more generalizable representation of reality. Where evolutionism entered this view (as with ethnologists and, in a shriller form, in sociobiology) it is assumed that the fit between the categories or hypotheses of mind and the world that they represent is a product of natural selection.

For all their disagreements on details, Nativist theories have one big thing in common: The opportunity to use and exercise the innate powers of mind is all. That is the formula for success as well.

Constructivism

Probably the most powerful expression of this view comes from Jean Piaget, although a more rigorous and considered expression of it can be found in the writings of the philosopher Nelson Goodman. The tenet of Piaget's constructivism is that the world is not found, but made, and made according to a set of structural rules that are imposed on the flow of experience. By structural rules it is intended to emphasize that knowledge is not local but derived from a structure of the whole—that local operations reflect universal operations of the system as a whole. Learning is bound within the limits of the rules of the system; it consists of realizations of the general rules in application to particulars. Development consists of a series of stage-like progressions, stage change consisting of a change in the rules of the system and later rule systems absorbing earlier ones as special cases. The learning dynamic of the system at any stage is provided by an unstable equilibrium or dialectic between assimilating experience to the rules and accommodating the rules to experience. When the equilibrium becomes unstable enough, the structure changes.

The constructivist model of the learner places strong emphasis on self-propelled operations on the world as the way to mastery—a pretty wide-band conception. Its formula for success is that nothing succeeds like a theoretical system, and one succeeds supremely only by going to a higher system that subsumes it.

Novice-to-Expert

This view of the learner has so recently emerged that it is hard to characterize. It is very practical, in some respects highly anti-theoretical. It operates within domains, almost at times denying the utility of a general theory—or perhaps that is a sign of its immaturity. It begins with the premise that if you want to find out about learning, ask first about what is to be learned, find an expert who does it well, and then look at the novice and figure out how he or she can get there. To aid in this task, simulate the novice's performance and the expert's in a computer program, and see what transformations and heuristics will get you from the one to the other. You may even be helped by studying and simulating some typical mid-stages. Such generality as may be present in learning different tasks will eventually show up in the simulations. The immediate challenge is to get the novice to be an expert as quickly and as painlessly as possible, and never mind high theory.

The formula for success is "be specific and be explicit." Or, a computer programmer is a better friend than a philosopher of mind. Or, it is more important to get through the keyhole than to see the sky. Or, and perhaps more seriously, subordinate the learner to the steps he must take to attain expertise.

In sketching these views about the model of the learner, I have omitted an important issue, one that had better be treated independently of each, for it is curiously extrinsic to all of them. It is the issue of the carrot and the stick—the role of motivation in learning. It has been a source of embarrassment in the history of the subject from the Stoics to Skinner. Let me state its dilemma in the starkest way. How can knowing something be affected by whether the knowledge gained leads to reward or to punishment? If the theory of reinforcement related to the acquisition of knowledge, God would not have had to expel poor Adam and Eve from the garden for eating of the tree of knowledge. He would have arranged, Huck Finn style, for them to have developed a very bad stomach ache from the consumption of green apples. Instead, He knew that knowledge, once attained, is irreversible and for better or for worse. And so, if I may be Miltonian, he had to condemn them to a new of life where that knowledge could be put to use.

It is the use of knowledge rather than knowledge itself that is affected by the nature of its consequences. Use implies performance; performance entails action. The carrot and the stick are instruments for affecting action, not thought. Thus the degree to which models of the learner feature reinforcement is the degree to which they concentrate on the behavior of the learner rather than on his or her mind. It is not surprising, then, that even in the heyday of the Empiricists (who thought of themselves as philosophers of mind) virtually nothing was said about carrots and sticks. Indeed, as Crane Brinton reminded us a generation ago in his classic *Anatomy of Revolution,* the precepts of Empiricism (particularly in John Locke) were designed to justify man's freedom from the authority of King and Clergy. He was, in this new dispensation, his own knowledge getter. Thus Jonathan Edwards could preach to his flock in Northampton on the frontier of the Massachusetts Bay Colony in the late 17th century that they too, like Isaac Newton, could by their own efforts of mind unlock the secrets of God.

It is interesting, then, that most theories depicted the learner, either implicitly or explicitly, as self-motivated—at least while they concentrated on learning as a means of acquiring knowledge. Indeed, we can say that the carrot and the stick—reinforcement—have to do not with learning but with morality: how one acts on the basis of what one knows. Even then, the connection between reward and punishment on the one side and virtuous action on the other remains as obscure as ever. The debate over the effectiveness of, say, prisons rages as incoherently as ever. And the thought controls imposed by dictators are much more concerned with censorship and other means of stopping the flow of information than they are with tinkering with schedules of reinforcement.

A MODEL OF MODELS

I have already tipped my hand, as I confessed in passing. There is no reason, save ideology and the exercise of political control, to opt for a single model of the learner. We *do* learn from experience, when that is all we have to go on. On occasion we act like induction machines, though it is rarely so dark out that we can't do better than that. Indeed, given half a chance, we generate hypotheses that take us way beyond the information given—often with good effect, and always with some risk, which requires courage and the buffering of a support system. There is every reason to believe that a nervous system evolved in nature and more latterly and swiftly in culture endows us with a set of useful presuppositions about both nature and culture. How else can we account for the swift mastery of language and other symbolic forms to which we take so easily and with insufficient knowledge for proper induction? How can we doubt that a culture that regulates its moods and acts according to such abstract inventions as interest rates, social slights, gross national products, and loyalty to Alma Mater is made up of people who not only construct the world in which they live but share it as an ontological given? It is even true that if you want to be a postman or a trust officer, you would do well to look closely at how they go about their business and then try to simulate them as a clever clone, hopefully keeping your tongue in your cheek and your powder dry the while.

What it amounts to, as I have already hinted, is treating all models of the learner as stipulative, and then inquiring into the conditions under which they might be effective or useful or comforting. If you genuinely believe that it improves a nation's confidence in its control over things to keep children in schools for a good part of the day, then do so. Or if you think formal schooling is structurally inevitable in a society with more disensus than consensus, again keep them in school. These are reasons of politics, and they plainly have a place in any debate, for education is political too. But if you see children learning mathematics by rote, you can also say (this time on more naturalistic yet practical grounds) that somebody got confused about models and slipped in an empiricist one in place of a constructionist one. In a word, the best approach to models of the learner is a relfective one that permits you to "go meta," to inquire whether the script being imposed on the learner is there for the reason that was intended or for some other reason.

There is not *one* kind of learning. It was the vanity of a preceding generation to think that the battle over learning theories would eventuate in one winning over all the others. Any learner has a host of learning strategies at command. The salvation is in learning how to go about learning before getting irreversibly beyond the point of no return. We would do well to equip learners with a menu of their possibilities and, in the course of their education, to arm them with procedures and sensibilities that would make it possible for them to use the menu wisely.

Here the hermeneutic circle ends. You cannot improve the state of education without a model of the learner. Yet the model of the learner is not fixed but various. A choice of one reflects many political, practical, and cultural issues. Perhaps the best choice is not a choice of one, but an appreciation of the variety that is possible. The appreciation of that variety is what makes the practice of education something more than a scripted exercise in cultural rigidity.

4. THE HIDDEN WORLD OF TEACHING
Implications of Research on Teacher Planning[1]

Christopher M. Clark and Robert J. Yinger[2]

. . . Our orientation to research on teaching (one that is shared by many of the projects at the Institute for Research on Teaching) is called the cognitive information-processing approach (Clark, 1979; National Institute of Education, [Reference] Note 4). This research centers upon the basic psychological processes thought to occur in a teacher's mind that organize and direct his or her behavior both prior to and during interactive teaching. Given the complexity of the teaching situation, the implied model of teaching in our research is that the teacher, like any other intelligent and rational agent, deals with this complexity by simplifying it in some rational and adaptive way. In the language of cognitive psychology, the teacher enters a complex *task environment* and simplifies it by defining part of it as the *problem space* within which he or she will work. The judgment and decision-making processes that affect how a teacher simplifies and organizes a classroom are central to our interests. These basic processes have been investigated in the psychology laboratory, but have not been thoroughly studied in realistic and complex school settings.

The basic psychological processes of teacher judgment and decision-making do not operate in a vacuum. Researchers using the cognitive information-processing approach must attend to the psychological, ecological, and social contexts in which basic processes are embedded. The psychological context for teacher judgment and decision-making is made up of the teacher's implicit theories, beliefs, and values about teaching and learning. The ecological context includes all of the resources, external circumstances, administrative requirements, and the like that limit, facilitate, and shape teacher and student thought and action. And the social context refers to the collective and interactive properties of the classroom group both internally and as it relates to larger communities.

In looking for naturally-occurring circumstances in which teacher judgment and decision-making might be seen in action, we have been led to investigate teacher planning. The various kinds of planning that are undertaken by teachers provide opportunities to study how teachers' thoughts are translated into action in the classroom, in particular, how teacher actions reflect the psychological, ecological, and social contexts for decision-making.

Having stated our purpose and laid out some of the assumptions that guide our inquiry, in the remainder of this paper we address three topics:

1. the issue of how basic descriptive research on teaching can inform practice;
2. a brief overview of our research[;] . . .
3. seven findings from our research and our ideas about what they imply for practice. . . .

[1][Research Series No. 77 (East Lansing, Mich.: The Institute for Research on Teaching, 1980).] An earlier version of this paper was presented at the annual meeting of the American Educational Research Association, Boston, 1980.

[2]Christopher M. Clark is the coordinator of IRT's Teacher Planning Project and a professor of educational psychology at MSU. Robert J. Yinger is a senior researcher with the Teacher Planning Project and a professor of educational psychology at The University of Cincinnati. The authors wish to express their appreciation to Robert Katterns, who read and commented on a draft of this paper, and to Patricia Marshall for assistance in manuscript preparation.

WHAT ROLE FOR DESCRIPTIVE RESEARCH?

Descriptive research on teaching, including our work on teacher planning, is not a search for general laws. The principal goal of descriptive research is understanding why a particular teaching situation is the way that it is, rather than prediction or control. Understanding is pursued through careful and complete description of teaching-learning situations, in terms that make sense to the participants. Descriptive research is not intended to be the handmaiden of correlational and experimental work, as has been suggested by Rosenshine and Furst (1973). Descriptive research is not a search for "variables" to be manipulated in subsequent experimental studies. Rather, it is an attempt to find out both what is going on out there and how it works in particular situations.

One might argue against this approach by stating that what "is" in teaching is not necessarily what "should be." We are not in opposition to this position. However, we believe that it is important to examine and describe the behavior of experienced and successful practitioners who have developed methods and strategies for functioning effectively in the teaching environment. Furthermore, our stance is that models of teaching based on what is *possible* in the classroom will in the long run be more effective than models borrowed from other fields (e.g., medicine, counseling, cybernetics) that are too difficult and complex or simply inappropriate for most classroom teachers to implement.

Like Good and Power (1976), we hold that classroom research need not yield rigorous prescriptions in order to be of value to teachers and teacher educators:

We suspect that the generalizations derived from classroom research and theory have a different role from those of the natural sciences. They function not as predictors of future events but as guidelines for understanding particular situations and contexts. Thus, at best, generalizations about teaching derived from research act as guides to assessing the likely consequences of alternative strategies in complex educational situations. Such generalizations must necessarily be indeterminate since they cannot predict precisely what will happen in a particular case. But this does not decrease their *value for the teacher;* he is not interested in establishing general laws.

Theories can be of value in specifying those dimensions which are relevant to an understanding of classroom phenomena, can extend the range of hypotheses (alternative strategies) considered, and sensitize the teacher to the possible consequences of his actions (p. 47).

Theories, findings, and concepts derived from classroom research constitute a vital part of the raw material that teachers may use to describe, understand, and influence events in their own unique classroom situations. We hold that teachers should be helped to think from theory and research but not be controlled by them. Or, in Philip Jackson's words:

Customarily, we speak of putting theory *into* practice. But that is not what we do at all. We put theory, or whatever you want to call the ideas we transmit, into *practitioners,* where it may serve a wide variety of functions, only one of which is the actual guidance of their actions (Jackson, [Reference] Note 5, p. 36).

The particular example of "theory into practitioners" that we address in this paper is the connection between, on the one hand, descriptive research on teacher planning and classroom behavior and, on the other, the practices of teaching and teacher education. . . .

TEACHER PLANNING

The mention of teacher planning brings to mind thoughts and images of outlines, plan books, objectives, textbooks, syllabi, and a variety of related products and activities. To accommodate this richness and variety, we have defined teacher planning very broadly to include any activity of a teacher that is concerned with organizing his or her school-related activities, or the activities of students, other teachers, aides, parent volunteers, and so on.

Planning may be formal, as when a teacher prepares a lesson plan or outline of a unit in science, or informal, including the usually invisible thinking that a teacher does while shopping, driving home from work, or eating lunch. As long as what a teacher is doing *aids in preparing a framework for guiding future action*, it counts as planning.

By defining teacher planning as we have, several important aspects of planning activity come to light.

First, planning is regarded as a process strongly oriented toward action rather than, for instance, knowledge acquisition or self-development; such action will most likely be visible to, and may involve, other persons (e.g., team teachers, aides, reading specialists).

Second, the fact that planning is concerned with future action introduces the problems of uncertainty and unpredictability. Our knowledge of the future is scanty and the complexity of social interaction makes prediction in the classroom especially difficult. Planning thus requires making judgments and decisions using incomplete information. Prediction is as important in planning as careful organization of content, materials, and the like is.

The third aspect of planning activity embedded in our definition relates to how planning is accomplished. The process of preparing a framework for future action is accomplished through teacher thinking, decision-making, and judgment. Planning, when it is done well, requires significant intellectual effort, drawing on practical and theoretical knowledge and experience, and involves a wide range of mental activities, including predicting, guessing, weighing, restructuring, and visualizing.

RESEARCH ON PLANNING

. . . Teacher planning is a complex professional activity that takes many forms. As such, teacher planning constitutes a large and potentially rich research domain. One way to represent this domain is proposed in Figure 1, which we have used to generate research questions about influences on teacher planning, the process of planning, the products of the planning process, and about the eventual effects of teacher planning on students and on teachers themselves.

One important research topic is the factors that influence teacher planning. How do teacher characteristics, student characteristics, curriculum characteristics, and environmental factors combine to affect planning? The overt and covert processes that occur during planning is another potential research topic. The effects of planning on the subsequent classroom interaction and on more long term outcomes are two other important research topics within this domain. In addition to addressing these topics

individually, one could begin to explore the relationships between several topics. For instance, how do characteristics of teachers, students, curricula, and the environment affect the process of teacher planning for instruction? Or how do variations in planning processes affect subsequent classroom interaction?

To guide our inquiry we have grouped research questions under three major headings: the how of teacher planning, the why of teacher planning, and the relationship between teacher planning and teaching effectiveness.

The How of Teacher Planning. To answer the question "How do teachers plan?" we require descriptions of both observable teacher behavior and of teacher thought processes while planning. We are interested in the amount and distribution of time spent planning, settings in which planning takes place, the types of planning engaged in (with regard both to scope of the plan—yearly, daily, and so on—and to the differences between planning lessons for the first time compared with revision and adaptation of previously taught material), variety of the forms that plans take, resources used by teachers, sources of ideas, and differences in the focus of planning (e.g., focus on teacher verbal behavior compared with focus on student activity or teacher physical movement).

In exploring the psychology of planning, we need to know more about the pyschological processes that teachers use while planning. How do judgment, visualization, memory, and tolerance of uncertainty contribute to teacher planning? How do teachers vary in the number and variety of factors taken into account during planning? What roles do student characteristics play in teacher planning? Sociological factors such as teacher role definition, institutional press, peer expectations, and administrative regulations can also be hypothesized to shape and limit teacher planning behavior.

The Why of Teacher Planning. In addressing the question "Why do teachers plan?" we are interested both in teachers' motives and goals (internal influences on teacher planning) and in external factors that influence teacher planning. Hypotheses we have entertained concerning teacher motives and goals for planning include the reduction of anxiety, insuring equitable treatment of all students, composition of a smooth script for action, increased subject-

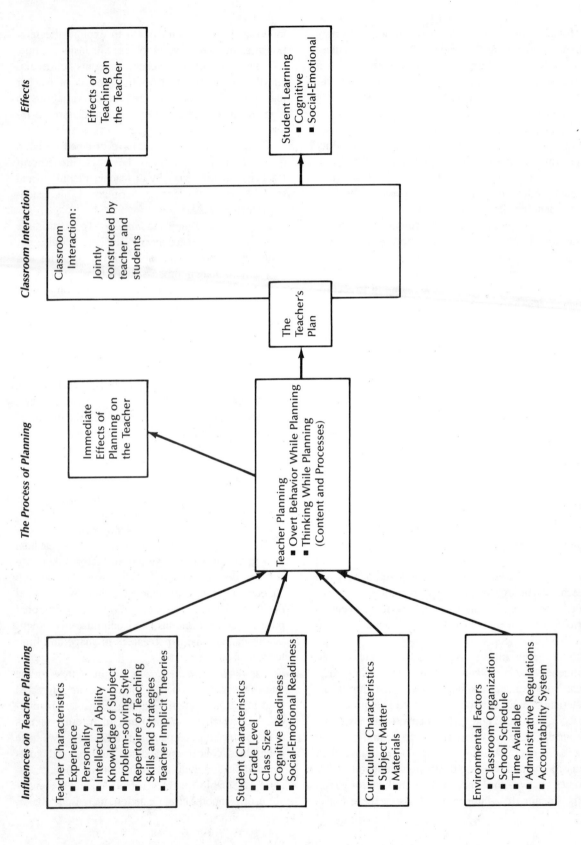

FIGURE 1   A Model for Research on Teacher Planning for Instruction

matter mastery, conformity to teacher role expectations, and compensation for the isolation of the self-contained classroom. What other motives and goals may lie behind teacher planning? What individual differences exist in the mixed and relative emphasis of these motivations for planning?

Among external influences on teacher planning we have considered curriculum materials, classroom and school organization, administrative requirements, accountability systems, and preservice and inservice training. In what ways do these and other factors external to the teacher influence the amount and kinds of teacher planning? What are the consequences of not planning or of poor planning? And how do the forces that influence and motivate teacher planning interact as the school year progresses and the social system of the classroom develops?

Teacher Planning and Teaching Effectiveness. In this third focus of our research we are concerned both with teacher effectiveness in planning as an end in itself, and with the effects of teacher-planned classroom behavior on student outcomes. What criteria do teachers use for judging the completeness of a plan? What are the differences, in the eyes of teachers, between good plans and adequate plans? What is important to know before entering the classroom? What part do teacher expectations about students play? What is the relationship of a plan to subsequent interactive teacher thoughts and actions, and, through teacher actions, to effects on students? . . .

Research Findings and Implications

Our program of research on teacher planning is quite young. Since 1977, we have done five small studies of teacher planning in elementary and middle school grades and reviewed the handful of other studies of planning done elsewhere (Clark & Yinger, [Reference Notes 2 and 3]; Clark & Elmore, [Reference] Note 1). We are by no means ready to recommend a particular way of planning as superior, but we do have some preliminary findings that will be useful for thinking about effective teaching and how to encourage and support it. . . .

Finding 1. Planning is plural, important, and invisible. In our surveys, interviews, and observation, teachers all agreed that they do a great deal of different types of planning. Planning is *plural,*

planning is *important* to them, and planning is generally *invisible* to everyone else. Our survey results show that elementary-school teachers spend an average of about 12 hours per week planning for instruction, including five hours per week planning for reading and language arts, 2.25 hours per week for math, 1.7 hours per week for social studies, and 1.4 hours per week for science. In addition to lesson planning, the teachers listed daily planning, weekly planning, term planning, unit planning, yearly planning, and planning for special events (e.g., school open house, parent conferences) as different types or varieties of teacher planning. All these types of planning are important to teachers (although teachers most frequently said that *weekly* planning was of primary importance), and they all take time. If this set of findings is true, what lessons can be drawn from them?

First, in preservice preparation, teacher educators should pay more attention to the many different types of planning. The emphasis in most undergraduate training programs is on lesson planning and, perhaps, unit planning. But prospective teachers need to experience the full range of teacher planning and the challenge of making the many tradeoffs, adjustments, and fine tunings of their plans that are inevitably necessary in the partially unpredictable world of the classroom.

For experienced practicing teachers, our first finding implies that administrators should allow more time and provide more support for teacher planning. Planning is the lifeblood of enthusiastic and well organized teaching, and most of it seems to be coming out of the hides of teachers. Some inservice days or half-days should be set aside for individual and group teacher planning instead of for lectures from visiting experts. And, most of all, uninterrupted planning must be recognized as a legitimate and respected way to spend "company time." If planning is truly at the core of teachers' professional lives, then it should receive a higher priority for support than it typically does. This issue is one on which teachers, administrators, and union officials can all join hands in mutual self-interest. More time and support for planning will pay dividends in more effective and better organized teaching, higher morale, and better use of expensive curriculum resources and materials.

Finding 2. Planning in practice differs from

traditional prescriptions for planning. Our second finding is that experienced teachers do not follow the so-called Tyler or linear model of planning in which the planner begins with a specific learning objective, generates alternative ways to meet that objective, and chooses the best alternative. This is the way that teachers are taught to plan, but it simply does not describe what actually takes place. In our experience, teachers typically begin with an idea for an activity. This idea is elaborated and adapted to fit the time available, student and teacher interests, resources on hand, and so forth. It is only at this late point in the planning process that teachers are comfortable with predicting what specific skills and processes their students may learn by doing this activity. There is much more emphasis on smooth execution of the process and on full participation by all students than there is on mastery of behavioral objectives. And it is practically unheard of for a teacher to spend time developing several different activities for the sake of choosing the "best" one and rejecting the others.

If this finding is true, what can be learned from it? One implication is that there are legitimately different approaches to planning for teaching. Toomey's research (1978) also supports this point. The approach that we have just described as typical of experienced practicing teachers seems to fit well with the demands and constraints of life in classrooms. Teacher planning is preparation for organizing and carrying off a complex series of social interactions, replete with uncertainty. We believe that the demands of the art and science of teaching have shaped teacher planning to produce a variation that is adaptive. Rather than try to impose a single logical (but possibly impractical) model of planning on teachers, we should acknowledge, support, and teach prospective teachers that there is more than one way to plan, that planning should be compatible with the situation in which it occurs, and that the sun does not rise and set on behavioral objectives.

Finding 3. Planning during the first weeks of school has long-term effects. Part of one of our studies of teacher planning involved interviewing five elementary school teachers and observing in their classrooms during the first weeks of school (Clark & Elmore, [Reference] Note 1). In brief, we learned that teacher planning is particularly important during the first few weeks of the school year. During September, a framework of rules, routines, schedules, expectations, and groupings of students is established that has far-reaching effects for the remainder of the school year. In addition to allocating time for and planning instruction in the various subject matters, teachers are concerned with planning for the physical environment of the classroom, assessment of students' knowledge and abilities, and with establishing a workable and constructive social system to serve as a foundation for instructional activities. Schedules, routines, new curricular materials, and groupings are pilot tested and adjusted during the first few weeks until, in early October, a reasonably workable system emerges. With minor modifications, this system characterizes the remainder of the school year. Other descriptive research supports this picture of the first weeks of school (e.g., Schultz & Florio, 1979; Yinger, [Reference] Note 3; Buckley & Copper, [Reference] Note [6]; Tickunoff & Ward, [Reference] Note [7]; Anderson & Evertson, [Reference] Note [8]).

If planning in the first weeks of school is so important, what does this mean for the teaching profession? One implication for teacher educators has to do with the practicum experience timing for student teachers. Typically, student teachers enter the classroom after "things have settled down." This prevents them from observing and partaking in the first weeks of planning, which may largely determine the character of the classroom. The typical practicum experience provides some training in operating the classroom system in a steady state, after almost all of the structural properties of the classroom have crystalized. How much more challenging and professionally relevant it would be to train prospective teachers in planning, organizing, and getting the year off to a good start. In cases in which actual field experience in planning and organizing the first weeks of school is not possible for preservice candidates, simulation exercises could be developed that provide some training and practice in this important domain of professional activity.

Practice in planning and organizing the first weeks of school becomes especially important if the notion that the school and its programs should reflect and be responsive to the values, cultural background, and social milieu of the community of which it is a part is taken seriously. This suggests that new teachers at a school should spend at least some part of the late summer getting to know the community, visiting the homes of their prospective students, and grounding their instructional and social system decisions in the reality of the larger community in which their students live.

Another suggestion that follows from what we have learned about planning during the first weeks of school is addressed to school administrators. Limited time, interruptions, and unexpected schedule changes are difficult enough to cope with during the later parts of the school year. But, during the first weeks of school, these constraints and intrusions can easily make a shambles of teacher planning and classroom organization. Administrators should protect their teachers as much as possible from changes and demands that, while seemingly trivial, might upset the delicate balance that teachers are trying to establish in September. Postpone that open house, minimize public address system announcements, and please don't change the times for lunch or special area classes.

Finding time for careful planning is always a challenge, but it is especially so at the beginning of the year. Is there any way to bring teachers back on the payroll sooner than the typical two or three days before the students arrive? Even one more day, devoted mainly to planning, would help a great deal in making the most of a very difficult time. Teachers and students are likely to reap the dividends of such an investment for the whole school year.

Finding 4. Teacher planning transforms curriculum into instruction. One of the last questions on our Teacher Planning Survey is "what purposes does planning serve for you?" We received many fascinating answers to this question that suggest a strong link between planning and curriculum. For example, teachers reported that they plan in order to learn the subject matter themselves, to prepare or acquire needed curricular materials, and to make decisions about the content, pace, sequence, completeness, and clarity of the curricular materials they have to work with. The most frequently mentioned resources used in teacher planning were teacher's guides, teacher's editions of student textbooks, and student texts themselves. In short, much of teacher planning for instruction is an attempt to answer the two-part question "What do I have to work with and how can I best present it to my students?"

In our interview study, all five teachers happened

to be implementing at least one new curriculum at the beginning of the interview period. Two of the teachers delayed their implementation of a new math curriculum for up to five weeks because they were awaiting an inservice workshop on how to use the new curriculum. The other three teachers began to use their new curricula very conservatively, following the teacher's guide meticulously and with almost no adaptation of the curriculum to the uniqueness of their students and classrooms. Given the circumstances of no prior experience with the curricula and a sense of urgency about getting started on academic activities, these teachers behaved in a reasonable way. But the situation could have been considerably improved if the new curricula had been comprehensively introduced, "walked through," and analyzed by the teachers during the previous spring. The teachers would have been able to adapt the new curricula to the characteristics of their students and other circumstances peculiar to their classrooms rather than sit and wait or implement without adaptation [3]

Finding 5. Routines can increase teacher efficiency and flexibility. The complexity and unpredictability that characterize the teaching environment impose many demands on the teacher, and it is therefore necessary to find methods to decrease the amount of information to be processed at any one time. One method we found teachers use to cope with these demands is to develop routines. The routinization of action fixes certain aspects of behavior and thus reduces the amount of information that must be evaluated, decided upon, and manipulated. Since most planning must necessarily take place on the teacher's time—before and after school and in the evenings or on weekends—and since planning competes with other activities for this time, the use of routines reduces the time and energy expended for planning, thus freeing time and energy for other activities.

Often the word "routine" carries with it a negative

---

[3]This recommendation is consistent with the research and writings of teacher educator and curriculum theorist Miriam Ben-Peretz (1975) of the University of Hiafa, Israel. She argues that teachers should be trained and supported to analyze, take apart, reorganize, and reassemble curriculum materials, both to permit adaptation to fit their own unique circumstances and to give them a feeling of curriculum ownership, rather than the feeling that they are mere technicians executing someone else's plan.

connotation of inflexibility. Our findings suggest that routines can be effectively used in the classroom to improve and simplify both planning and teaching. Routines can simplify the planning task by reducing the need to plan each new activity from "square one." Routines can increase the effectiveness of in-class time by increasing the stability of activities and reducing time lost to interruptions. They can also increase student time on task by increasing the predictability of activities and possibly reducing the students' anxiety about what will happen next and what will be expected of them. It is likely that routines are a common tool of experienced teachers, but few educators encourage their use to preservice teachers. We suggest that teacher educators should make students aware of the potential benefits of using routines, while at the same time warning of the dangers of rigidly relying upon them.

Finding 6. Communicating plans puts thought into action. Our research on teacher planning has made us think about the link between the plan and the subsequent classroom interaction. This link seems to be the teacher's communication of the plan to his or her students. No matter how elaborate and complete a plan may be, it cannot be carried out successfully unless the students are brought rather fully into the knowledge of what to do and how to do it, and brought to a commitment to cooperate in the process. Planning itself is given inadequate attention in preservice and inservice teacher preparation, but usually is addressed at some level; communication of plans to students is almost never addressed. Yet success or failure of this link between thought and action can make a substantial difference between whether a plan is merely a grandiose entry in a plan book, or becomes the description of a lesson or activity well executed.

Communication of teacher plans (or the absence of communication) is particularly important at times of transition between activities and subject matters. And communication of a plan need not be simply oral. Part of this communication can take the form of materials organized by the teacher, diagrams, routine configurations such as reading groups, and even pantomime. But the essence of our recommendation is that the more imaginative the thought invested in communication of teacher plans to students, the more likely those plans are to come to fruition without undue confusion, delay, or backtracking. Training exercises could be created for

both experienced teachers and preservice candidates in which they create and practice delivering the communication of a plan in several different ways, and obtain feedback on the clarity, motivational quality, and completeness of these communications. (Incidentally, we have noticed that teachers in a team-teaching situation are usually more explicit in communicating their plans than teachers in self-contained classrooms. This is probably because team teaching often requires more precise coordination and timing in order to orchestrate the activities of the teachers and students.)

Although we believe that communication of the plan is important, we do not want to leave the impression that the criterion for good planning is that the teaching match the planning exactly. On the contrary, our research indicates that many experienced teachers create elaborate plans, communicate them clearly and completely, and then feel free to depart from them if a better idea or opportunity unexpectedly presents itself. Planning is important in getting off to a good start, but these teachers do not become slaves to their own plans. They stay alert for ways to build on a good start that incorporates students' interests, needs, and moods. These same people, reflecting back to their first year or two of teaching, told us that they were then much more likely to be slaves to their plans and miss unpredictable or unexpected learning opportunities as a result.

Finding 7. Teacher reflection aids teacher development. In two of our studies we asked teachers to keep a journal or diary describing their thinking and planning on a day-to-day basis. We also met with these teachers each week to go over their journal entries and have them explain and elaborate them where appropriate. While we learned many important and interesting things about their planning from these journals and conversations, this last finding has to do with the apparent effects on the teachers of keeping a reflective planning journal.

The process of journal keeping was a powerful experience for the teachers who undertook it. They reported that they learned a great deal about their own thinking and teaching. Until asked to keep a detailed report of their planning, they did not realize how much thought and energy they put into planning for instruction. In a sense, they were newly appreciating themselves as professionals. Until this time, the teachers' activities that are most like those of physicians, lawyers, and other professionals were largely hidden from view. Their morale seemed to improve as they became aware of this and other things. But more importantly, these teachers became researchers on their own teaching—alert to the many opportunities teachers have to take responsibility for their own continued professional development . . . and to gradually and systematically improve the effectiveness of their teaching and the quality of life in their classrooms.

Certainly not every teacher would respond so dramatically to the experience of reflective journal keeping. But journal keeping, peer interviewing, and other techniques for helping teachers to reflect systematically on *what* they and their students are doing and *why* they are doing it constitute potentially powerful and inexpensive components of an inservice professional development program.

CONCLUSION

We have only begun to answer the many questions that we and others have raised about the hidden world of teaching: about the how, the what, and the why of teacher planning, and about the relationships between planning and action in the classroom. This is our first derivation of implications for teaching and teacher education. We are at once confident that these suggestions make sense to practitioners and aware that these ideas will be challenging to implement. Obviously more research is indicated—not only basic research of the sort that we have begun, but also research in the context of teacher education and applied action research of the sort that a principal, a faculty, or a single teacher can use to explore, reflect on, and improve the quality of thought and action in schools. We are in no immediate danger of exhausting the secrets of the hidden world of teaching.

REFERENCE NOTES

1. Clark, C. M., & Elmore, J. L. *Teacher planning in the first weeks of school* (Research Series No. 56). East Lansing, Michigan: Institute for Research on Teaching, Michigan State University, 1979.
2. Clark, C. M., & Yinger, R. J. *Three studies of teacher planning* (Research Series No. 55). East Lansing, Michigan: Institute for Research on Teaching, Michigan State University, 1979.
3. Yinger, R. J. *A study of teacher planning: Description and theory development using ethnographic and information processing methods.* Unpublished doctoral dissertation, Michigan State University, 1977.
4. National Institute of Education. *Teaching as clinical information processing.* Report of Panel 6, National Conference on Studies in Teaching, Washington, D.C., 1975.
5. Jackson, P. W. *How to talk to teachers: Lessons from William James.* University of Chicago, unpublished manuscript (no date).
6. Buckley, P. K., & Cooper, J. M. *An ethnographic study of an elementary school teacher's establishment and maintenance of group norms.* Paper presented to the American Educational Research Association, Toronto, 1978.
7. Tikunoff, W. J., & Ward, B. A. *A naturalistic study of the initiation of students into three classroom social systems.* San Francisco: Far West Laboratory for Educational Research and Development, Report A-78-11, 1978.
8. Anderson, L. M., & Evertson, C. M. *Classroom organization at the beginning of school: Two case studies.* Paper presented to the American Association of Colleges for Teacher Education, Chicago, 1978.

REFERENCES

Ben-Peretz, M. The concept of curriculum potential. *Curriculum Theory Network*, 1975, *5* (2), 151–159.

Clark, C. M. Five faces of research on teaching. *Educational Leadership*, 1979, *37*, 29–32. (Also available as IRT Occasional Paper No. 24. East Lansing, Michigan: Institute for Research on Teaching, Michigan State University, 1979.)

Clark, C. M., & Yinger, R. J. Research on teacher thinking. *Curriculum Inquiry*, 1977, *7* (4), 279–304.

Good, T. L., & Power, C. N. Designing successful classroom environments for different types of students. *Journal of Curriculum Studies*, 1976, *8*, 45–60.

Jackson, P. W. *The way teaching is.* Washington, D.C.: National Education Association, 1966.

Rosenshine, B., & Furst, N. The use of direct observation to study teaching. In R. M. W. Travers (Ed.), *Second handbook of research on teaching.* Chicago: Rand McNally, 1973, 122–183.

Shultz, J., & Florio, S. Stop and freeze: The negotiation of social and physical space in a kindergarten/first grade classroom. *Anthropology and Education Quarterly*, 1979, *10*, 166–181. (Also available as IRT Occasional Paper No. 26. East Lansing, Michigan:

Institute for Research on Teaching, Michigan State University, 1979).

Toomey, R. What can we recommend to teachers about instructional planning? *The South Pacific Journal of Teacher Education*, 1978, *6*, 215–219.

Yinger, R. J. A study of teacher planning. *The Elementary School Journal*, 1980, *80* (3), 107–127.

Yinger, R. J. Routines in teacher planning. *Theory into Practice*, 1979, *18*, 163–169.

This work is sponsored in part by the Institute for Research on Teaching, College of Education, Michigan State University. The Institute for Research on Teaching is funded primarily by the Program for Teaching and Instruction of the National Institute of Education, United States Department of Health, Education, and Welfare. The opinions expressed in this publication do not necessarily reflect the position, policy, or endorsement of the National Institute of Education. (Contract No. 400-76-0073.)

5. RECONSIDERING RESEARCH ON LEARNING FROM MEDIA
Richard E. Clark

Studies of the influence of media on learning have been a fixed feature of educational research since Thorndike (1912) recommended pictures as a labor-saving device in instruction. Most of this research is buttressed by the hope that learning will be enhanced with the proper mix of medium, student, subject matter content, and learning task. A typical study compares the relative achievement of groups who have received similar subject matter from different media. This research has led to so-called "media selection" schemes or models (e.g., Reiser & Gagne, 1982). These models generally promise to incorporate existing research and practice into procedures for selecting the best medium or mix of media to deliver instruction. Most of these models base many of their prescriptions on presumed learning benefits from media (Jamison, Suppes, & Welles, 1974).

However, this article will argue that most current summaries and meta-analyses of media comparison studies clearly suggest that media do not influence learning under any conditions. Even in the few cases where dramatic changes in achievement or ability have followed the introduction of a medium, as was the case with television in El Salvador (Schramm, 1977), it was not the medium that caused the change but rather a curricular reform that acompanied the change. The best current evidence is that media are mere vehicles that deliver instruction but do not influence student achievement any more than the truck that delivers our groceries causes changes in our nutrition. Basically, the choice of vehicle might influence the cost or extent of distributing instruction, but only the content of the vehicle can influence achievement. While research often shows a slight learning advantage for newer media over more conventional instructional vehicles, this advantage will be shown to be vulnerable to compelling rival hypotheses. Among these rival explanations is evidence of artifact and confounding in existing studies and biased editorial decisions which may favor research showing larger effect sizes for newer media. After summarizing evidence from current meta-analyses of media research, I will discuss advantages and problems with current "media attribute" and "symbol system" theories and will conclude by suggesting tentative solutions to past problems and future directions for research involving media.

MEDIA COMPARISON STUDIES

In the 1960s, Lumsdaine (1963) and others (e.g., Mielke, 1968) argued that gross media comparison and selection studies might not pay off. They implied that media, when viewed as collections of mechanical instruments, such as television and computers, were sample delivery devices. Nevertheless, earlier reviewers also held the door open to learning effects from media by attributing much of the lack of significance in prior research to poor design and lack of adequate models or theory.

Lumsdaine (1963) dealt primarily with adequate studies that had used defensible methodology, and had found significant differences between treatments. With the benefit of hindsight it is not surprising that most of the studies he selected for review employed media as simple vehicles for instructional methods, such as text organization, size of step in programming, cueing, repeated exposures, and prompting. These studies compared the effects of, for example, different step size in programmed instruction via television. It was step size (and other methods), not television (or other media), which were the focus of these studies. This is an example of what Salomon and Clark (1977) called research *with* media. In these studies media are mere conveyances for the treatments being examined and are not the focus of the study, though the results are often mistakenly interpreted as suggesting benefits for various media. An example of instructional research with media would be a study which contrasted a logically organized audiotutorial lesson on photosynthesis with a randomly sequenced presentation of the same frames (cf. Clark & Snow, 1975; Salomon & Clark, 1977, for a review of similar studies). Perhaps as a result of this confusion, Lumsdaine (1963) reached few conclusions beyond the suggestion that media might reduce the cost of instruction when many students are served because "the cost of perfecting it can be prorated in terms of a denominator representing thousands of students" (p. 670).

A decade later, Glaser and Cooley (1973) and Levie and Dickie (1973) were cautious about media comparison studies, which apparently were still being conducted in large numbers. Glaser and Cooley (1973) recommended using any acceptable medium as "a vehicle for making available to schools what psychologists have learned about learning" (p. 855). Levie and Dickie (1973) noted that most media comparison studies to that date had been fruitless and suggested that learning objectives can be attained through "instruction presented by any of a variety of different media" (p. 859). At that time televised education was still a lively topic and studies of computerized instruction were just beginning to appear.

During the past decade, television research seems to have diminished considerably, but computer learning studies are now popular. This current research belongs to the familiar but generally fruitless media comparison approach or is concerned with different contents or methods being presented via different media (e.g., science teaching via computers). Generally, each new medium seems to attract its own set of advocates who make claims for improved learning and stimulate research questions which are similar to those asked about the previously popular medium. Most of the radio research approaches

suggested in the 1950s (e.g., Hovland, Lumsdaine, & Sheffield, 1949) were very similar to those employed by the television movement of the 1960s (e.g., Schramm, 1977) and to the more recent reports of the computer-assisted instruction studies of the 1970s and 1980s (e.g., Dixon & Judd, 1977). It seems that similar research questions have resulted in similar and ambiguous data. Media comparison studies, regardless of the media employed, tend to result in "no significant difference" conclusions (Mielke, 1968). These findings were incorrectly offered as evidence that different media were "equally effective" as conventional means in promoting learning. No significant difference results simply suggest that changes in the outcome scores (e.g., learning) did not result from any systematic differences in the treatments compared.

Occasionally a study would find evidence for one or another medium. When this happens, Mielke (1968) has suggested that the active ingredient might be some uncontrolled aspect of the content or instructional strategy rather than the medium. When we investigate these positive studies, we find that the treatments are confounded. The evidence for this confounding may be found in the current meta-analyses of media comparison studies. The next section argues that it is the uncontrolled effects of novelty and instructional method which account for the existing evidence for the effects of various media on learning gains.

REVIEWS AND META-ANALYSES OF MEDIA RESEARCH

One of the most interesting trends in the past decade has been a significant increase in the number of excellent reviews and meta-analyses of research comparing the learning advantage of various media. The results of these overviews of past comparison studies seem to be reasonably unambiguous and unanimous. Taken together, they provide strong evidence that media comparison studies that find causal connections between media and achievement are confounded.

Size of Effect of Media Treatments

A recent series of meta-analyses of media comparison studies [has] been conducted by James Kulik and his colleagues at the University of Michigan

(Cohen, Ebling & Kulik, 1981; C. Kulik, Kulik, & Cohen, 1980; J. Kulik, Bangert, & Williams, 1983; J. Kulik, Kulik, & Cohen, 1979). These reviews employ the relatively new technology of meta-analysis (Glass, 1976), which provides more precise estimates of the effect size of various media treatments than were possible a few years ago. Previous reviews dealing primarily with "box score" sums of significant findings for media versus conventional instructional delivery were sometimes misleading. Effect size estimates often were expressed in portions of standard score advantages for one or another type of treatment. This discussion will express effects in one of two ways: (a) the number of standard deviations separating experimental and control groups, and (b) as improvements in percentile scores on a final examination.

Box Scores versus Effect Size

An illustration of the advantage of meta-analytical effect size descriptions of past research over "box scores" is available in a recent review of Postleth-wait's audiotutorial instruction studies (J. Kulik, Kulik, & Cohen, 1979). The authors found 42 adequate studies, of which 29 favored audiotutorial instruction and only 13 favored conventional instruction. Of those 42, only 15 reported significant differences, but 11 of the 15 favored audiotutorial and only 4 favored conventional instruction. This type of box score analysis would strongly favor the learning benefits of the auditutorial approach over more conventional means, whereas effect size estimates of [these] data show only .2 standard deviations differences in the final exam scores of audiotutorial and conventional treatments. Kulik and his colleagues reported that this difference was equivalent to approximately 1.6 points on a 100-point final examination. This small effect is not instructionally significant and could easily be due to confounding.

The most common sources of confounding in media research seem to be the uncontrolled effects of (a) instructional method or content differences between treatments that are compared, and (b) a novelty effect for newer media, which tends to disappear over time.

Uncontrolled Method and Content Effects

In effect size analyses, all adequate studies are surveyed. They involve a great variety of subject matter content, learning task types, and grade levels. The most common result of this type of survey is a small and positive effect for newer media over more conventional instructional delivery devices. However, when studies are subjected to meta-analysis, our first source of rival hypotheses, medium and method confusion, shows up.

The positive effect for media more or less disappears when the same instructor produces all treatments (C. Kulik, Kulik, & Cohen, 1980). Different teams of instructional designers or different teachers probably give different content and instructional methods to the treatments that are compared. If this is the case, we do not know whether to attribute the advantage to the medium or to the differences between content and method and the media being compared. However, if the effect for media tends to disappear when the same instructor or team designs contrasting treatments, we have reason to believe that the lack of difference is due to greater control of nonmedium variables. It was Mielke (1968) who reminded us that when examining the effects of different media, only the media being compared can be different. All other aspects of the treatments, including the subject matter content and method of instruction, must be identical.

Meta-analytic Evidence for Method and Content Confounding

In meta-analyses of college-level computerized versus conventional courses, an effect size of .51 results when different faculty teach the compared course (C. Kulik, Kulik, & Cohen, 1980). This effect reduces to .13 when one instructor plans and teaches both experimental and control courses. Presumably, the weak but positive finding for college use of computers over conventional media is due to systematic but uncontrolled differences in content and/or method, contributed unintentionally by different teachers or designers.

Time savings with computers. Another instance of this artifact may be found in studies that demonstrate considerable time savings due to certain media. Comparisons of computer and conventional instruction often show 30 to 50 percent reductions in time to complete lessons for the computer groups (C. Kulik, Kulik, & Cohen, 1980; Kulik, Bangert, & Williams, 1983). A plausible rival hypothesis here is the possible effects of the greater effort invested in newer media programs than in conventional presentations of the same material. Comparing this increased effort invested in computer instruction to that afforded conventional instruction might be likened to sponsoring a race between a precision engineered racer and the family car. The difference in effort presumably involves more instructional design and development, which results in more effective instructional methods for the students in computer treatments. Presumably, the students in other treatments would fare as well if given the advantage of this additional design effort, which produces more effective presentations requiring less time to complete.

Exchanging Method for Media in Instructional Research

There is evidence in these meta-analyses that it is the method of instruction that leads more directly and powerfully to learning. Glaser (1976) defines instructional methods as "the conditions which can be implemented to foster the acquisition of competence" (p. 1). It seems not to be media but variables such as instructional methods that foster learning. For example, instructional programs such as the Keller (1968) personalized system of instruction (PSI) and programmed instruction (PI) contain methods which seek to add structure, shorter steps, reduced verbal loads, and self-pacing to lessons. Each, however, is typically associated with a different medium. The PSI (Keller plan) approach is usually presented by text, and PI is often the preferred approach of those who design computer-assisted instruction. When studies of PI via text and via computer-assisted instruction are compared for their effect size they are similar. Both seem to show about a .2 standard deviation final examination advantage over conventional instruction (C. Kulik, Kulik, & Cohen, 1980). A compelling hypothesis to explain this similarity might be that most computerized instruction is merely the presentation of PI or PSI via a computer.

When computer and PI effects are compared with the use of visuals in televised or audiotutorial laboratories, the PI and computer studies show about a 30 percent larger effect size. The largest effect size however, is reserved for the PSI approach. The description of this instructional program tends to focus on its essential methods rather than on a medium. Perhaps as a result, it typically results in a .5 standard deviation effect size when compared with conventional, computer, PI, or visual instruction (C. Kulik, Kulik, & Cohen, 1980). This would indicate that when we begin to separate method from medium we may begin to explain more significant amounts of learning variance.

UNCONTROLLED NOVELTY EFFECTS WITH NEWER MEDIA

A second, though probably less important, source of confounding is the increased effort and attention research subjects tend to give to media that are novel to them. The increased attention paid by students sometimes results in increased effort or persistence, which yields achievement gains. If they are due to a novelty effect, these gains tend to diminish as students become more familiar with the new medium. This was the case in reviews of computer-assisted instruction at the secondary school level (grades 6 to 12) (Kulik, Bangert, & Williams, 1983). An average effect size of .32 (e.g., a rise in exam scores from the 50th to the 63rd percentile) for computer courses tended to dissipate significantly in longer duration studies. In studies lasting 4 weeks or less, computer effects were .56 standard deviations. This reduced to .3 in studies lasting 5 to 8 weeks and further reduced to the familiar .2 effect after 8 weeks of data collection. Cohen (1977) describes an effect size of .2 as "weak" and notes that it accounts for less than 1 percent of the variance in a comparison. Cohen, Ebling, and Kulik (1981) report a similar phenomenon in their review of visual-based instruction (e.g., film, television, pictures). Although the reduction in effect size for longer duration studies approached significance (about .065 alpha), there were a number of comparisons of methods mixed with different visual media, which makes interpretation difficult.

In their review of computer use in college, C. Kulik, Kulik, and Cohen (1980) did not find any evidence for this novelty effect. In their comparison of studies of 1 or 2 hours duration with those which held weekly sessions for an entire semester, the effect sizes were roughly the same. Computers are less novel experiences for college subjects than for secondary school students.

EDITORIAL DECISIONS AND DISTORTION OF EFFECT ESTIMATES

There is also some evidence for the hypothesis that journal editors typically select research that finds stronger effects for newer media. Kulik, Bangert, and Williams (1983) reported .21 and .3 effect sizes for unpublished and dissertation studies respectively. Published studies averaged effect sizes of .47 standard deviations, which is considerably larger. J. Kulik, Kulik, and Cohen (1979) found similar evidence in an analysis of audiotutorial instruction studies. Published studies showed a 3.8 percent final examination advantage for audiotutorial methods over conventional instruction (.31 standard deviations), but this reduced to a .6 percent advantage for the same method in unpublished studies.

A Research Caution

Based on this consistent evidence, it seems reasonable to advise strongly against future media comparison research. Five decades of research suggest that there are no learning benefits to be gained from employing different media in instruction, regardless of their obviously attractive features or advertised superiority. All existing surveys of this research indicate that confounding has contributed to the studies attributing learning benefits to one medium over another and that the great majority of these comparison studies clearly indicate no significant differences.

This situation is analogous to the problems encountered in research on teaching. In that area, the teach*er* was constantly confused with teach*ing*. Improvements in research findings result when specific teaching behaviors compete to influence learning rather than different types of teachers (Rosenshine, 1971). Where learning benefits are at issue, therefore, it is the method, aptitude, and task variables of instruction that should be investigated. Studies comparing the relative achievement advantages of one medium over another will inevitably confound medium with method of instruction.

RECENT DIRECTIONS: MEDIA ATTRIBUTE RESEARCH EXAMINED

During the 1970s a new type of question was suggested, which seemed to eliminate many of the conceptual problems in the media comparison question. Instead of focusing on media per se, it was recommended (Clark, 1975; Levie & Dickie, 1973; Salomon, 1974b; 1979) that we study "attributes" of media and their influence on the way that information is processed in learning. In this view, many media possess attributes such as the capacity to slow the motion of objects or "zoom" into details of a stimulus field or to "unwrap" a three-dimensional object into its two-dimensional form. These attributes were thought to cultivate cognitive skills when modeled by learners, so that, for example, a child with low cue attending ability might learn the cognitive skill of "zooming" into stimulus details (Salomon, 1974a), or novice chess players might increase their skills in recognizing potential moves and configurations of chess pieces through animated modeling of moves and patterns (Blake, 1977). Because this type of question dealt with the way that information is selected and transformed in the acquisition of generalizable cognitive skills, many believed that the possibility of a coherent theory dealing with media attributes was forthcoming (Olson, 1972; Schramm, 1977). In addition, it was exciting to imagine that these media attributes might result in unique cognitive skills because they promised to teach mental transformations which had not heretofore been experienced.

The promise of the media attributes approach is based on at least three expectations: (a) that the attributes were an integral part of media and would provide a connection between instructional uses of media and learning; (b) that attributes would provide for the cultivation of cognitive skills for learners who needed them; and (c) that identified attributes would provide unique independent variables for instructional theories that specified causal relationships between attribute modeling and learning—finally the evidence for a connection between media and learning. While the final point is most important, it now appears that the media attribute question has many of the problems that plagued the media comparison issue. Generally, the evidence suggests that only the second expectation has been fulfilled, which implies that media attribute research may contribute to instructional design but not to theory development.

Media Attributes and Media

The first expectation was that these media attributes would somehow represent the psychologically relevant aspects of media. Few of the originators of the media attribute construct (Olson & Bruner, 1974; Salomon 1974b) claimed that they were more then "correlated" with different media. Since they were not exclusive to any specific media and were only associated with them by habit or convenience, they were not "media" variables any more than the specific subject matter content of a book is part of the definition of "book." In fact, the early discussions of the construct most often referred to "symbol systems" or symbolic "elements" of instruction. All instructional messages were coded in some symbolic representational system, the argument went, and symbols vary in the cognitive transformation they allow us to perform on the information we select from our environment. Some symbolic elements (animated arrows, zooming) permit us to cultivate cognitive skills. However, many different media could present a given attribute so there was no necessary correspondence between attributes and media. Media are mere vehicles for attributes so it is misleading to call them *media* attributes.

Attributes and the Cultivation of Cognitive Skills

The second expectation of the attribute approach was more realistic. While Mielke (1980) is correct that very few of the skill cultivating attributes have been found and validated, there is positive evidence for Salomons's (1979) claim that "the coding elements of a . . . symbol system can be made to cultivate the mastery of specific mental skills by either activating or overtly supplanting the skills" (p. 216). (Much of the research buttressing this claim is presented in Salomon, 1979, and will not be reviewed in detail here.) The problem lies not in the fact that symbol systems can be made to cultivate skills but in whether these symbolic elements or attributes are exclusive or necessary to learning. If the attributes identified to date are useful in instruction they are valuable. However, theory development depends on the discovery of basic or necessary processes of instruction and learning. It is to this point, the third expectation of media attribute theories, that the discussion turns next.

Attributes as Causal Factors in Learning

There is recent evidence that attributes of symbol systems are occasionally sufficient but not necessary

contributors to learning. In science, sufficient conditions are those events which were adequate to produce some outcome in a past instance. There is no guarantee, however, that sufficient conditions will ever produce the outcome again because the variable that caused the outcome was merely correlated with the condition. For example, a lecture might be sufficient to produce the desired level of achievement in one instance but fail in another. Severing the optic nerve is sufficient to cause blindness but will not explain the cause of all cases of blindness. This issue is related to the problem of external validity. While it is often useful instructionally to know about sufficient conditions for producing desirable levels of achievement, our theories seek necessary conditions. Without necessary conditions we run the risk of failing to replicate achievement gains when we change the context, times, or student clients for instruction. Instructional theory (Shuell, 1980) seeks generalizations concerning the necessary instructional methods required to foster cognitive processes. To illustrate this point, the discussion turns next to research evidence for the skill-cultivating function of symbol system attributes.

The Research Evidence

In the zooming study mentioned earlier, students who had difficulty attending to cues in a visual field learned the skill by seeing it modeled in a film where they saw a camera "zoom" from a wide field to close-up shots of many different details (Salomon, 1974a). Here, an analysis of the task suggested that effective cue attending required an attention-directing strategy which began with a view of the entire stimulus and then narrowed the stimulus field until a single, identifiable cue remained. For those students with low cue-attending skill (the requisite cognitive skill to perform the task) Salomon (1974b) reasoned that the required instructional method would be modeling. In this case, the construction of the model followed an analysis of the symbol systems, which allowed this particular method to be coded for delivery to the students. While the zooming treatment he used was available in many media (e.g., film, television, video disc) the students seemed to model the zooming and used it as a cognitive skill which allowed them to attend to cues.

However, in a partial replication of this study, Bovy (1983) found that a treatment which used an "irising" attribute to provide practice in cue-attending was as effective as Salomon's zooming in cultivating the skill during practice. Irising consisted of slowly enclosing cues in a circular, gradually enlarging, darkened border similar to the effect created by an iris which regulates the amount of light permitted through a camera lens. More important, however, was her finding that a treatment that merely isolated cues with a static close-up of a successive details singled out by the zooming and irising was *even more effective at cultivating cue-attending skill than either zooming or irising*. It may be that only the efficient isolation of relevant cues is necessary for this task.

In a similar study, Blake (1977) taught chess moves to high or low visual ability undergraduates through a standard narration and (a) still pictures, (b) animated arrows with the pictures, or (c) a motion film from which the still pictures were taken. Therefore the recommendation is to exercise caution in future research on symbolic elements of media. While all three conditions worked for the higher ability students, low visualizers learned the chess moves equally well from the arrow and the motion treatments which were significantly better for them than the static pictures. Here, as in the Salomon (1974a) study, we presume that the modeled chess moves compensated for the low ability student's lack of spatial visualization. Unlike Salomon, Blake's subjects profited from two different operational definitions of the necessary model, animated arrows and moving chess pieces. Different stimulus arrangements resulted in similar performances but, we might expect, led to nominally different cognitive processes being modeled. The necessary process for learning chess moves, the visualizing of the entire move allowed each piece, could therefore be operationalized in any of various sufficient conditions for successful performance.

Summary

It seems reasonable to assume, therefore, that media are delivery vehicles for instruction and do not directly influence learning. However, certain elements of different media, such as animated motion or zooming, might serve as sufficient conditions to facilitate the learning of students who lack the skill being modeled. Symbolic elements such as zooming are not media (we can have a film or television program which does not contain zooming) but allow us to create sufficient conditions to teach required cognitive skills. The determination of necessary conditions is a fruitful approach when analyzing all instructional problems, and it is the foundation of all instructional theories. Once described, the necessary cognitive operation is a specification or recipe for an instructional method.

Of course, this point of view takes us a great distance from traditional conceptions of the role of media in instruction and learning. It suggests that systems of symbols that are correlated only with familiar media may sometimes serve as sufficient (but never necessary) conditions for learning from instruction. They accomplish this by providing operational vehicles for methods that reflect the cognitive processes necessary to perform successfully a given learning task. Generally, treatments such as zooming or animated arrows are but two of the many nominally different treatments which would result in the same performance. Just as some form of medium is required to deliver instruction, some form of a symbol system must be employed to construct a treatment. Similarly, as the medium does not influence learning, neither is the symbolic element chosen to construct the treatment the most direct influence on learning. We can employ a great variety of media and possibly, a similar variety of symbol systems to achieve the same performance. However, we cannot vary the requirement that the method somehow model the crucial cognitive process required for the successful performance of the task. It is the critical features of the necessary cognitive process which underlie the construction of successful instructional methods and the development of instructional theory (Clark, 1982). These cognitive process features must be translated into a symbol system understandable to the learner and then delivered through a convenient medium. The cognitive feature in the chess study was the simulation of the beginning and ending points of the moves of the various chess pieces. In the cue-attending studies by Salomon and Bovy, the cognitive features were probably the isolation of relevant cues. It is the external modeling of these features in a compatible symbol system that is necessary for learning. It is therefore not the medium or the symbol system that yields the required performance. When a chosen symbol system is shaped to represent the critical features of the task and other things are equal, learning will occur. When a medium delivers a symbol system containing this necessary arrangement of features, learning will occur also but will not be due to either the medium or the symbol system.

Of course, there are instructional problems other than learning that may be influenced by media (e.g., costs, distribution, the adequacy of different vehicles to carry different symbol systems, equity of access to instruction). While space prevents a complete discussion of these more promising areas, what follows is a brief overview of studies that deal with research on our beliefs and attributions concerning media. It should be noted that these new questions differ from traditional media research in that there are no media variables in the studies—only variables having to do with our attributions or beliefs about media. This is a subtle but important difference, as we shall see.

PROMISING RESEARCH: BELIEFS AND ATTRIBUTIONS ABOUT MEDIA

The fact that we learn (through education and experience) to prefer some media or to attribute varying levels of difficulty, entertainment value, or enjoyment to media might influence instructionally relevant outcomes. Several studies have fruitfully explored the attribution question.

Perceived Learning Demands of Media and Learning Strategies

Presumably, differences in the qualities attributed to different media may influence learning-related behaviors of students. Ksobiech (1976) and Salomon (1981) have reported studies where student beliefs about the different demands placed on them by different media influenced their approach to learning tasks. Ksobiech (1976) told 60 undergraduates that televised and textual lessons were to be (a) evaluated, (b) entertainment, or (c) the subject of a test. The test group performed best on a subsequent test with the evaluation group scoring next best and the entertainment group demonstrating the poorest performance. Also in this study some subjects were allowed to push a button and receive more video or more narrative content (verbal information) about the lessons. The test subjects consistently chose

more verbal information presumably because they believed that it was a surer route to the factual information they needed to succeed at the test. Also, the subjects who believed that a test awaited them persisted longer than the other groups.

Salomon (1981) has recently suggested a model for conceptualizing these differences in persistence which result from different media attributions. His model suggests precise relationships between the perceived "difficulty" of different media, the self-efficacy of students, and the resulting effort they will invest in learning from a given medium. Again, it is the students' perception or attributions of the medium and their own abilities that are thought to be causally connected to the effort they invest, not the medium per se. It is typical, Salomon reports, for students to attribute great difficulty to learning from computers but to think of television as "shallow" and "easy."

Enjoyment, Achievement, and Choice of Media

In related studies, Saracho (1982), Machula (1978–1979) and Clark (1982) reported studies where preferences and achievement from media were antagonistic. In a year-long study involving over 250 third- to sixth-grade students. Saracho (1982) found that those assigned to computer-assisted instruction in basic skills liked the computer less but learned more in the computer condition than from other media. Similarly, Machula (1978–1979) instructed 114 undergraduates via television, voice recording, and printed text. Students liked the television less but learned significantly more from it than from the voice recording, which they liked more.

Clark (1982) has reviewed similar studies and has suggested that by mistake students choose those media carrying methods that inadvertently result in less learning for them. Students incorrectly assess the extent to which the instructional method carried by the medium will allow them the most efficient use of their effort. Strong interactions with general abilities are often found in this research. Higher ability students seem to like methods and media that they perceive as more structured and directive because they think they will have to invest less efort to achieve success. However, these more structured methods prevent the higher ability student from employing their own considerable skills and yield less effort than the less directive methods and media.

Lower ability students typically seem to like less structured and more discovery-oriented methods and media. They seem to want to avoid investing the effort required by the more structured approaches to achieve the same disappointing results. These more unstructured approaches offer relative anonymity and the chance to invest less effort for the less able student who, on the other hand, actually needs the greater structure of the methods they like less. While medium and method are not the same experience, the methods conveyed by the media in studies such as these probably account for different levels of achievement while subject attributions about media influence their preferences.

Attitudes toward Computers

Hess and Tenezakis (1973) explored the affective responses of predominantly Mexican-American, low SES seventh, eighth and ninth graders to remedial mathematics presented by computer or teacher. Among a number of interesting findings was an unanticipated attribution of more fairness to the computer than to the teacher. It seems that these subjects felt that the computer treated them more equitably (kept promises, did not make decisions based on their heritage) than some of the teachers. They consistently trusted the computer more but also found the computer to be less "flexible" and unresponsive to student desires to change the course or content of their instruction. Stimmel, Connor, McCaskill and Durrett (1981) found strong negative affect toward computers and computer instruction among a large group of preservice teachers. These same teacher trainees had similar reactions to mathematics and science teaching, and they may have associated computers with these disciplines.

CONCLUSIONS

One might reasonably wonder why media are still advocated for their ability to increase learning when research clearly indicates that such benefits are not forthcoming. Of course such conclusions are disseminated slowly and must compete with the advertising budgets of the multimillion dollar industry which has a vested interest in selling these machines for instruction. In many ways the problem is anal-

ogous to one that occurs in the pharmaceutical industry. There we find arguments concerning the relative effectiveness of different media (tablets, capsules, liquid suspensions) and different brand names carrying the same generic drug to users.

An equal contributor to this disparity between research and practice is the high expectation we have for technology of all kinds. Other machine-based technologies similar to the newer electronic media have revolutionized industry and we have had understandable hopes that they would also benefit instruction. And, there is the fact that many educators and researchers are reserved about the effectiveness of our system of formal education. As environments for learning, media seem to offer alternative and more effective features than those available from the conventional teacher in the conventional classroom. Tobias (1982) for example, has provided evidence that we can help overcome student anxiety by allowing anxious students the chance to replay a recording of a lesson. This quality of "reviewability" is commonly thought to distinguish some of the newer media from the conventional teacher's lecture. It is important to note however, that teachers are entirely capable of reviewing material for anxious students (and probably do so often). It is what the teacher does—the teaching—that influences learning. Most of the methods carried by newer media can also be carried or performed by teachers. Dixon and Judd (1977), for example, compared teacher and computer use of "branching" rules in instruction and found no differences in student achievement attributable to these two "media."

The point is made, therefore, that all current reviews of media comparison studies suggest that we will not find learning differences that can be unambiguously attributed to any medium of instruction. It seems that existing research is vulnerable to rival hypotheses concerning the uncontrolled effects of instructional method and novelty.

More recent evidence questions the evidence for the media-based attempts to determine the components of effective instructional methods. These symbol system or media attribute theories seem to be useful for instructional design but of limited utility in explicating the necessary conditions that must be met by effective methods. Future research should therefore focus on necessary characteristics of instructional methods and other variables (task, learner aptitude, and attributions), which are more fruitful sources for understanding achievement increases. Recent studies dealing with learner attributions and beliefs about the instructional and entertainment qualities of different media seem particularly attractive as research directions. There are no media variables in attribution research, however. Independent variables are concerned with learner beliefs, and outcome measures are typically some measure of learner persistence at a task. It seems reasonable to recommend, therefore, that researchers refrain from producing additional studies exploring the relationship between media and learning unless a novel theory is suggested.

REFERENCES

Blake, T. Motion in instructional media: Some subject-display mode interactions. *Perceptual and Motor Skills*, 1977, *44*, 975–985.

Bovy, R. A. *Defining the psychologically active features of instructional treatments designed to facilitate cue attendance*. Paper presented at the annual meeting of the American Educational Research Association, Montreal, April 1983.

Clark, R. E. Constructing a taxonomy of media attributes for research purposes. *AV Communication Review*, 1975, *23*(2), 197–215.

Clark, R. E. Antagonism between achievement and enjoyment in ATI studies. *The Educational Psychologist*, 1982, *17*(2), 92–101.

Clark, R. E., & Snow, R. E. Alternative designs for instructional technology research. *AV Communication Review*, 1975, *23*(4), 373–394.

Cohen, J. *Statistical power analysis for the behavioral sciences* (Rev. ed.). New York: Academic Press, 1977.

Cohen, P., Ebling, B., & Kulik, J. A meta-analysis of outcome studies of visual based instruction. *Educational Communication and Technology Journal*, 1981, *29*(1), 26–36.

Dixon, P., & Judd, W. A comparison of computer managed instruction and lecture mode for teaching basic statistics. *Journal of Computer Based Instruction*, 1977, *4*(1), 22–25.

Glaser, R. Components of a psychology of instruction: Towards a science of design. *Review of Educational Research*, 1976, *46*(1), 1–24.

Glaser, R., & Cooley, W. W. Instrumentation for teaching and instructional management. In R. Travers (Ed.), *Second handbook of research on teaching*. Chicago: Rand McNally College Publishing, 1973.

Glass, G. V. Primary, secondary and meta-analysis of research. *Educational Researcher*, 1976, *5*(10), 3–8.

Hess, R., & Tenezakis, M. The computer as a socializing agent: Some socioaffective outcomes of CAI. *AV Communication Review*, 1973, *21*(3), 311–325.

Hovland, C., Lumsdaine, A. A., & Sheffield, F. *Experiments on mass communication*. Princeton, N.J.: Princeton University Press, 1949.

Jamison, D., Suppes, P., & Welles, S. The effectiveness of alternative instructional media: A survey. *Review of Educational Research*, 1974, *44*, 1–68.

Keller, F. Good-bye teacher. *Journal of Applied Behavior Analysis*, 1968, *1*, 79–89.

Ksobiech, K. The importance of perceived task and type of presentation in student response to instructional television. *Audio Visual Communication Review*, 1976, *24*(4), 401–411.

Kulik, C., Kulik, J., & Cohen, P. Instructional technology and college teaching. *Teaching of Psychology*, 1980, *7*(4), 199–205.

Kulik, J., Bangert, R., & Williams, G. Effects of computer-based teaching on secondary school students. *Journal of Educational Psychology*, 1983, *75*, 19–26.

Kulik, J., Kulik, C., & Cohen, P. Research on audio-tutorial instruction: A meta-analysis of comparative studies. *Research in Higher Education*, 1979, *11*(4), 321–341.

Levie, W. H., & Dickie, K. The analysis and application of media. In R. Travers (Ed.), *The second handbook of research on teaching*. Chicago: Rand McNally, 1973.

Lumsdaine, A. Instruments and media of instruction. In N. Gage (Ed.), *Handbook of research on teaching*. Chicago: Rand McNally, 1963.

Machula, R. Media and affect: A comparison of videotape audiotape and print. *Journal of Educational Technology Systems*, 1978–1979, *7*(2), 167–185.

Mielke, K. Questioning the questions of ETV research. *Educational Broadcasting Review*, 1968, *2*, 6–15.

Mielke, K. Commentary. *Educational Communications and Technology Journal*, 1980, *28*(1), 66–69.

Olson, D. On a theory of instruction: Why different forms of instruction result in similar knowledge. *Interchange*, 1972, *3*(1) 9–24.

Olson, D., & Bruner, J. Learning through experience and learning through media. In D. Olson (Ed.), *Media and symbols: The forms of expression, communication, and education* (73rd Yearbook of the NSSE). Chicago: University of Chicago Press, 1974.

Reiser, R., & Gagne, R. Characteristics of media selection

models. *Review of Educational Research*, 1982, *52*(4), 499–512.

Rosenshine, B. *Teacher behaviors and student achievement*. London: National Foundation for Educational Research in England and Wales, 1971.

Salomon, G. Internalization of filmic schematic operations in interaction with learners' aptitudes. *Journal of Educational Psychology*, 1974, *66*, 499–511.(a)

Salomon, G. What is learned and how it is taught: The interaction between media, message, task and learner. In D. Olson (Ed.), *Media and symbols: The forms of expression, communication, and education* (73rd Yearbook of the NSSE). Chicago: University of Chicago Press, 1974.(b)

Salomon, G. *Interaction of media, cognition and learning*. San Francisco: Jossey Bass, 1979.

Salomon, G. *Communication and education*. Beverly Hills, Calif.: Sage, 1981.

Salomon, G., & Clark, R. E. Reexamining the methodology of research on media and technology in edu-

cation, *Review of Educational Research*, 1977, *47*, 99–120.

Saracho, O. N. The effect of a computer assisted instruction program on basic skills achievement and attitude toward instruction of Spanish speaking migrant children. *American Educational Research Journal*, 1982, *19*(2), 201–219.

Schramm, W. *Big media little media*. Beverly Hills, Calif: Sage, 1977.

Shuell, T. J. Learning theory, instructional theory and adaption. In R. E. Snow, P. Federico, & W. Montigue (Eds.), *Aptitude, learning and instruction* (Vol. 2). Hillsdale, N.J.: Lawrence Erlbaum, 1980.

Stimmel, T., Connor, J., McCaskill, E., & Durrett, H. J. Teacher resistance to computer assisted instruction. *Behavior Research Methods and Instrumentation*. 1981, *13*(2), 128–130.

Thorndike, E. L. *Education*. New York: Macmillan, 1912.

Tobias, S. When do instructional methods make a difference? *Educational Researcher*, 1982, *11*(4), 4–9.

6. THE MIMETIC AND THE TRANSFORMATIVE
Alternative Outlooks on Teaching

Philip W. Jackson

The Greek Sophist Protagoras allegedly claimed that on every subject two opposite statements could be made, each as defensible as the other. Whether or not he was right in a universal sense is something for logicians and rhetoricians to decide. However, insofar as the affairs of everyday life are concerned, he seems to have hit upon a fundamental truth, for we encounter daily all manner of "opposite statements," each with its share of supporters and critics.

As might be expected, education as a field of study is no exception to the rule. There, too, differing outlooks, poles apart at first glance, are as common as elsewhere. Who, for example, is unfamiliar with the many verbal exchanges that have taken place over the years between "traditional" educators on the one side and their "progressive" opponents on the other, debates in which the merits of "child-centered" practices are pitted against those considered more "subject-centered"?

This . . . chapter introduces a dichotomy that encompasses the differences just named as well as others less familiar, though it is not usually talked

about in the terms I will employ here. Indeed, the names of the two outlooks to be discussed have been purposely chosen so as to be *un*familiar to most followers of today's educational discussions and debates. My reason for this is not to introduce novelty for its own sake, much less to add glitter by using a pair of fancy terms. Instead, it is to avoid becoming prematurely embroiled in the well-known controversies associated with phrases like "child-centered" and "subject-centered," controversies that too often degenerate into mud-slinging contests which reduce the terms themselves to little more than slogans and epithets. A similar fate may well await the pair of terms to be introduced here. But for the time being the fact that they are rather new, or at least newly employed within an educational context, should prevent that.

In brief, I contend in this chapter that two distinguishably different ways of thinking about education and of translating that thought into practice undergird most of the differences of opinion that have circulated within educational circles over the past two or three centuries. Framed within an argument, which is how they are usually encountered, each of these two outlooks seeks to legitimate its own vision of how education should be conducted. It does so by promoting certain goals and practices, making them seem proper and just, while ignoring others or calling them into question. . . .

What shall we name these two points of view? As the chapter title already reveals, I recommend they be called the "mimetic" and the "transformative." I also propose we think of them not simply as two viewpoints on educational matters but as two traditions within the domain of educational thought and practice. Why *traditions*? Because each has a long and respectable history going back at least several hundred years and possibly beyond. Also, each is more than an intellectual argument. Each provokes feelings of partisanship and loyalty toward a particular point of view; each also entails commitment to a set of related practices. In short, each comprises what might be called (following Wittgenstein[1]) a "form of life," a relatively coherent and unified way of thinking, feeling, and acting within a particular domain—in this instance, the sphere of education. The term "traditions" stands for that complexity. Its use reminds us that each outlook stretches back in time, and that each has a "lived" dimension that makes it something much more than a polemical argument.

THE MIMETIC TRADITION

We turn to the "mimetic" tradition first not because it is any older or any more important than the one called "transformative," but principally because it is the easier of the two to describe. In addition, it is closer to what most people today seem to think education is all about. Thus, presenting it first has the advantage of beginning with the more familiar and moving to the less familiar. Third, it is more harmonious with all that is thought of as "scientific" and "rigorous" within ecucation than is its competitor. To all who rank that pair of adjectives highly, as I reservedly do myself, therein lies an additional reason for putting it first.

This tradition is named "mimetic" (the root term is the Greek word *mimesis*, from which we get "mime" and "mimic") because it gives a central place to the transmission of factual and procedural knowledge from one person to another, through an essentially *imitative* process. If I had to substitute another equally unfamiliar word in its place, with which to engage in educational debate, I would choose "epistemic"—yet another derived from the Greek, this from *episteme*, meaning knowledge. The first term stresses the *process* by which knowledge is commonly transmitted, the second puts its emphasis on the *content* of the transaction. Thus we have the "mimetic" or the "epistemic" tradition; I prefer the former if for no other reason than that it places the emphasis where I believe it belongs, on the importance of *method* within this tradition.

The conception of knowledge at the heart of the mimetic tradition is familiar to most of us, though its properties may not always be fully understood even by teachers committed to this outlook on teaching. For this reason it seems essential to say something about its properties.

First of all, knowledge of a "mimetic" variety, whose transmission entails mimetic procedures, is by definition identifiable in advance of its transmission. This makes it secondhand knowledge, so to speak, not in the pejorative sense of that term, but simply in that it has to have belonged to someone first before it can belong to anyone else. In short, it is knowledge "presented" to a learner, rather than "discovered" by him or her.[2]

Such knowledge can be "passed" from one person to another or from a text to a person; we can thus see it as "detachable" from persons *per se*, in two ways. It is detachable in the first place in that it can be preserved in books and films and the like, so that it can "outlive" all who originally possessed it. It is detachable, secondly, in the sense that it can be forgotten by those who once knew it. Though it can

---

[1] Ludwig Wittgenstein, *Philosophical Investigations* (Oxford: Basil Blackwell, 1968), p. 9e.

[2] Aristotle once remarked that "All instruction given or received by way of argument proceeds from pre-existent knowledge." (*Posterior Analytic*, Book I, 71a) By this he meant that we must begin with major and minor premises whose truth is beyond dispute before we can move to a novel conclusion. This is not quite the same as claiming that all knowledge is secondhand, but it does call attention to how much of the "known" is properly described as having been "transmitted" or "passed along" to students from teachers or teacher surrogates, such as textbooks or computers.

be "possessed," it can also be "dispossessed" through memory loss. Moreover, it can be "unpossessed" in the sense of never having been "possessed" in the first place. A correlate of its detachability is that it can be "shown" or displayed by its possessor, a condition that partially accounts for our occasional reference to it as "objective" knowledge.

A crucial property of mimetic knowledge is its reproducibility. It is this property that allows us to say it is "transmitted" from teacher to student or from text to student. Yet when we speak of it that way we usually have in mind a very special kind of process. It does not entail handing over a bundle of some sort as in an actual "exchange" or "giving." Rather, it is more like the transmission of a spoken message from one person to another or the spread of bacteria from a cold-sufferer to a new victim. In all such instances both parties wind up possessing what was formerly possessed by only one of them. What has been transmitted has actually been "mirrored" or "reproduced" without its ever having been relinquished in the process.

The knowledge involved in all transmissions within the mimetic tradition has an additional property worth noting: It can be judged right or wrong, accurate or inaccurate, correct or incorrect on the basis of a comparison with the teacher's own knowledge or with some other model as found in a textbook or other instructional materials. Not only do judgments of this sort yield a measure of the success of teaching within this tradition, they also are the chief criterion by which learning is measured.

My final remark about knowledge as conceived within the mimetic tradition may already be obvious from what has been said. It is that mimetic knowledge is by no means limited to "bookish" learning, knowledge expressible in words alone. Though much of it takes that form, it also includes the acquisition of physical and motor skills, knowledge to be *performed* in one way or another, usually without any verbal accompaniment whatsoever. "Knowing that" and "knowing how" is the way the distinction is sometimes expressed.[3]

Here then are the central epistemological assumptions associated with the mimetic tradition. The key idea is that some kind of knowledge or

skill can be doubly possessed, first by the teacher alone (or the writer of the textbook or the computer program), then by his or her student. In more epigrammatic terms, the slogan for this tradition might well be: "What the teacher (or textbook or computer) knows, that shall the student come to know."

How might the goal of this tradition be achieved? In essence, the procedure for transmitting mimetic knowledge consists of five steps, the fourth of which divides in two alternate routes, "a" or "b," dependent on the presence or absence of student error. The series is as follows:

Step One: *Test.* Some form of inquiry, either formal or informal, is initiated to discover whether the student(s) in question already knows the material or can perform the skill in question. This step is properly omitted if the student's lack of knowledge or skill can be safely assumed.

Step Two: *Present.* Finding the student ignorant of what is to be learned, or assuming him or her to be so, the teacher "presents" the material, either discursively—with or without the support of visual aids—or by modeling or demonstrating a skillful performance or some aspect thereof.

Step Three: *Perform/Evaluate.* The student, who presumably has been attentive during the presentation, is invited or required to repeat what he or she has just witnessed, read, or heard. The teacher (or some surrogate device, such as a test scoring machine) monitors the student's performance, making a judgment and sometimes generating a numerical tally of its accuracy or correctness.

Step Four (A): (Correct performance) *Reward/Fix.* Discovering the performance to be reasonably accurate (within limits usually set in advance), the teacher (or surrogate device) comments favorably on what the student has done and, when deemed necessary, prescribes one or more repetitions in order to habituate or "fix" the material in the student's repertoire of things known or skills mastered.

Step Four (B): (Incorrect performance) *Enter Remedial Loop.* Discovering the student's performance to be wrong (again within limits usually established in advance), the teacher (or surrogate) initiates a remedial procedure designed to correct the error in question. Commonly this procedure begins with a diagnosis of the student's difficulty followed by the selection of an appropriate corrective strategy.

[3] For a well-known discussion of that distinction, see Gilbert Ryle, *The Concept of Mind* (New York: Barnes and Noble, 1949).

Step Five: *Advance*. After the unit of knowledge or skill has been "fixed" (all appropriate corrections having been made and drills undertaken), the teacher and student advance to the next unit of "fresh" instruction, returning to Step One, if deemed necessary by the teacher, and repeating the moves in sequential order. The sequence of steps is repeated until the student has mastered all the prescribed knowledge or until all efforts to attain a prescribed level of mastery have been exhausted.

In skeletal form, this is the way instruction proceeds within the mimetic tradition. Readers familiar with cybernetic models will readily recognize the five steps outlined as an instance of what is commonly referred to as a "feedback loop" mechanism, an algorithmic device equipped with "internal guidance circuitry."[4]

Which teachers teach this way? Almost all do so on occasion, yet not all spend an equal amount of time at it. Some teachers work within the mimetic tradition only on weekends, figuratively speaking, about as often as a "do-it-yourself-er" might wield a hammer or turn a wrench. Others employ the same techniques routinely on a day-to-day basis, as might a professional carpenter or mechanic.

Which do which? That question will be treated at some length later in this chapter, where I will take up the relationship between the two traditions. For now it will suffice to observe in passing what is perhaps obvious, that teachers intent upon the transmission of factual information, plus those seeking to teach specific psychomotor skills, would more likely use mimetic procedures than would those whose conception of teaching involved educational goals less clearly epistemic in nature.

What might the latter category of goals include? To answer that question we must turn to the second of the two dominant outlooks within educational thought and practice, which I have chosen to call:

THE TRANSFORMATIVE TRADITION

The adjective "transformative" describes what this tradition deems successful teaching to be capable of accomplishing: a transformation of one kind or another in the person being taught—a qualitative change often of dramatic proportion, a metamorphosis, so to speak. Such changes would include all those traits of character and of personality most highly prized by the society at large (aside from those having to do solely with the possession of knowledge *per se*). They also would include the eradication or remediation of a corresponding set of undesirable traits. In either case, the transformations aimed for within this tradition are typically conceived of as being more deeply integrated and ingrained within the psychological makeup of the student—and therefore as perhaps more enduring—than are those sought within the mimetic or epistemic outlook, whose dominant metaphor is one of "adding on" to what already exists (new knowledge, new skills, etc.) rather than modifying the would-be learner in some more fundamental way.

What traits and qualities have teachers working within the transformative tradition sought to modify? Our answer depends on when and where we look. Several centuries ago, for example, when the mission of schools was primarily religious, what was being sought was nothing other than students' salvation through preparing them for Bible reading and other religiously oriented activities. Such remains the goal of much religious instruction today, though the form of its expression may have changed somewhat.

Over the years, as schooling became more widespread and more secular in orientation, educators began to abandon the goal of piety *per se*, and focused instead upon effecting "transformation" of character, morals, and virtue. Many continue to speak that way today, though it is more common to name "attitudes," "values," and "interests" as the psychological traits many of today's teachers seek to modify.

However one describes the changes sought within the transformative tradition, it is interesting that this undertaking is usually treated as more exalted or noble than the more mimetic type of teaching. Why this should be so is not readily apparent, but the different degrees of seriousness attached to the two traditions are apparent in the metaphors associated with each of them.

As I have already said, within the mimetic tradition knowledge is conceived of as something akin to material goods. Like a person materially

---

[4] See, for example, G. A. Miller, E. Galanter, and K. H. Pribham, *Plans and the Structure of Behavior* (New York: Holt, 1960).

wealthy, the possessor of knowledge may be considered "richer" than his ignorant neighbor. Yet, like the materially rich and poor, the two remain fundamentally equal as human beings. This metaphor of knowledge as coins in one's purse is consonant with the concomitant belief that is "detachable" from its owner, capable of being "shown," "lost," and so forth. A related metaphor, one often used to lampoon the mimetic tradition, depicts the learner as a kind of vessel into which knowledge is "poured" or "stored." What is important about all such metaphors is that the vessel in question remains essentially unchanged, with or without its "contents."

The root image within the transformative tradition is entirely different. It is much closer to that of a potter working with clay than it is to someone using the potter's handiwork as a container for whatever contents such a vessel might hold. The potter, as we know, not only leaves her imprint on the vessel itself in the form of a signature of some kind, she actually molds and shapes the object as she creates it. All who later work with the finished product have a different relationship to it entirely. They may fill it or empty it to their hearts' content. They may even break it if they wish. But all such actions accept the object in question as a "given," something whose essence is fundamentally sacrosanct.

The metaphor of teacher-as-artist or teacher-as-creator gives the transformative tradition an air of profundity and drama, perhaps even spirituality, that is largely lacking within the mimetic tradition, whose root metaphor of mere addition of knowledge or skill is much more prosaic. But metaphors, as we know, are mere figures of speech. No matter how flattering they might be, they don't tell us whether such flattery is deserved. They leave us to ask whether teachers working within the transformative tradition actually succeed in doing what they and others sometimes boast they can do. And that's not all they leave unanswered. Beyond the question of whether transformative changes due to pedagogical interventions really occur at all there awaits the more practical question of *how* they happen. What do teachers do to bring them about? As we might guess, it is easier to answer the former question than the latter. . . .

As most teachers will readily testify, the answer to that question will disappoint all who seek overnight to become [such] teachers[.] . . . It seems there *are* no formulas for accomplishing these most impressive if not miraculous feats of pedagogical skill. There are neither simple instructions for the neophyte nor complicated ones for the seasoned teacher. There is not even an epigram or two to keep in mind as guides for how to proceed, nothing analogous to the ancient "advice" that tells us to feed a cold and starve a fever.

And yet that last point is not quite as accurate as were the two that came before it. For if we look carefully at what such teachers do and listen to what others say about their influence, we begin to see that they *do* have some characteristic ways of working after all, "modes of operation" that, even if they can't be reduced to recipes and formulas, are worth noting all the same. The three of these modes most readily identifiable seem to me to be:

1. *Personal modeling.* Of the many attributes associated with transformative teaching, the most crucial ones seem to concern the teacher as a person. For it is essential to success within that tradition that teachers who are trying to bring about transformative changes personify the very qualities they seek to engender in their students. To the best of their ability they must be living exemplars of certain virtues or values or attitudes. The fulfillment of that requirement achieves its apex in great historical figures, like Socrates and Christ, who epitomize such a personal model; but most teachers already know that no attitude, interest, or value can be taught except by the teacher who himself or herself believes in, cares for, or cherishes whatever it is that he or she holds out for emulation.

2. *"Soft" suasion.* Among teachers working toward transformative ends, the "showing" and "telling" so central to the mimetic tradition (actions contained in Step Two: *Present* of the methodological paradigm outlined above) are replaced by less emphatic assertions and by an altogether milder form of pedagogical authority. The teaching style is rather more forensic and rhetorical than it is one of proof and demonstration. Often the authority of the teacher is so diminished by the introduction of a questioning mode within this tradition that there occurs a kind of role reversal, almost as though the student were teaching the teacher. This shift makes the transformative teacher look humbler than his or her mimetic counterpart, but it is by no means clear that such an appearance is a trustworthy indicator of the teacher's true temperament.

3. *Use of narrative*. Within the transformative tradition "stories" of one kind or another, which would include parables, myths, and other forms of narrative, play a large role. Why this should be so is not immediately clear, but it becomes so as we consider what is common to the transformations that the schools seek to effect. The common element, it turns out, is their moral nature. Virtues, character traits, interests, attitudes, values—as educational goals all of them fall within the moral realm of the "right" or "proper" or "just." Now when we ask about the function or purpose of narrative, one answer (some might say the only one) is: to moralize.[5] Narratives present us with stories about how to live (or how not to live) our lives. Again, Socrates and Christ come readily to mind as exemplars of the teacher-as-storyteller as well as the teacher about whom stories are told. . . .

Within the mimetic tradition the teacher occupies the role of expert in two distinct ways. He or she supposedly is in command of a specifiable body of knowledge or set of skills whose properties we have already commented upon. Such knowledge constitutes what we might call *substantive* expertise. At the same time the teacher is thought to possess the know-how whereby a significant portion of his or her substantive knowledge may be "transmitted" to students. The latter body of knowledge, whose paradigmatic contours have also been sketched, constitutes what we might call the teacher's *methodological* expertise. The students, by way of contrast, might be described as doubly ignorant. They neither know what the teacher knows, substantively speaking, nor do they know how to teach it in methodological terms. This dual condition of ignorance places them below the teacher epistemologically no matter where they stand regarding other social attributes and statuses.

Within the transformative tradition, the superiority of the teacher's knowledge, whether substantive or methodological, is not nearly so clear-cut. Nor is the teacher's status in general vis-à-vis his or her students. Instead, the overall relationship between the two is often vexingly ambiguous if not downright upsetting to some students; it can even become so at times to teachers themselves. Nowhere are many of these ambiguities portrayed more dramatically than in the early Socratic dialogues of Plato.[6] In the person of Socrates we witness perhaps the most famous of all transformative teachers in action. He is also a teacher whose actions are often as puzzling as they are edifying. . . .

The way out of these difficulties is to deny neither the moral and philosophical dimensions of teaching nor the prosaic nature of much that teachers actually do. Rather it requires that we acknowledge the compatibility of both viewpoints, seeing them as complementary rather than mutually exclusive. In short, nothing save a kind of conceptual narrow-mindedness keeps us from a vision of teaching as both a noble and a prosaic undertaking. Erasmus approached that insight several centuries ago when he remarked that "In the opinion of fools [teaching] is a humble task, but in fact it is in the noblest of occupations."[7] Had he been a trifle more charitable he might have added that the fools were not totally wrong. Their trouble was that they were only half right.

Teachers themselves often overlook the moral dimensions of their work, but that failing must be treated as a problem to be solved, rather than as evidence of the amorality of teaching itself. There is no doubt that one can teach without giving thought to the transformative significance of what he or she is doing. But whether it should be so performed is another question entirely. Moreover, though the teacher may pay no attention whatsoever to such matters, we must ask if they are thereby eliminated as a class of outcomes. The well-known phenomenon of *unintended consequences*, sometimes referred to as "incidental learnings" when they take place within the context of a classroom, leads us to suspect that the delivery of moral messages and actions of transformative significance may often take place whether the teacher intends them to or not. Indeed, it is far more interesting to ask whether such outcomes are inevitable, which is equivalent to asking whether all teachers are ultimately working

[5]See Hayden White, "The value of narrativity in the representation of reality," in W. J. T. Mitchell (ed.), *On Narrative* (Chicago: University of Chicago Press, 1981), 1–24. Also, John Gardner, *On Moral Fiction* (New York: Basic Books, 1978). Gardner points out that "the effect of great fiction is to temper real experience, modify prejudice, humanize." (p. 114)

[6]See Edith Hamilton and Huntington Cairns (eds.), *The Collected Dialogues of Plato* (Princeton, New Jersey: Princeton University Press, 1961). See especially the *Charmides, Laches, Euthydemus, Protagoras, Gorgias*, and *Meno*.

[7]Claude M. Fuess and Emory S. Basford (eds.), *Unseen Harvests: A Treasury of Teaching* (New York: Macmillan, 1947): v.

within the transformative tradition whether they realize it or not. . . .

I can answer the question of how these two traditions relate in the real world by observing initially that they don't get sorted out very clearly at all. There are few, if any, instances of either purely mimetic or purely transformative teaching, a fact that poses an important theoretical problem to which we shall return.

The closest approximation to an unadulterated version of transformative teaching in action that I can think of is probably to be found in the office of a psychotherapist or psychoanalyst where the focus of the therapeutic session (which is, after all, a form of pedagogy) is exclusively on matters related to the patient's personal thoughts and feelings. Certain kinds of religious counseling probably come a close second, for there too the goal is often exclusively one of alleviating discomfort of one kind or another. In both instances the "teacher" does not aim to transmit any subject matter in particular, at least none that could have been objectively defined in advance. Instead, what he or she seeks is an altered condition on the part of the "student"—in a word, a transformation.

Teaching that is solely mimetic in orientation may be as rare as that which is solely transformative, for transformative outcomes may occur whether they are intended or not.[8] At the same time, I can more easily imagine the former than the latter. The examples of close to pure mimetic teaching that come most readily to mind all include rudimentary skill instruction, such as dancing lessons or the teaching of typing, but lectures whose content was intended to be purely informational might come just as close to being as exclusively mimetic as teaching ever gets. . . .

The malleability of teaching, its capacity to be skewed, as it were, in either direction, toward dominance by either more mimetic or more transformative sets of concerns, leads us to ask in which direction the profession as a whole seems to be moving these days. . . .

My own reading of the direction in which teaching seems to be headed is more of an hypothesis than it is a conclusion about which I feel quite confident. At the same time I would describe it as more than a guess. Teaching within our own country and possibly within the Western world at large seems to be moving in the direction of becoming increasingly mimetic in its orientation and, correspondingly, less transformative. Moreover, I suspect the drift in this direction has been going on for generations, if not centuries.

What are the signs that the influence of the mimetic tradition is on the increase and the transformative one in decline? A few seem fairly obvious to me, others are less so. Among the former, I am most struck by the gradual turning away of educators in general from that broad set of transformative goals that over the years have been called character, moral development, deportment, good conduct, and citizenship. This is not to say that all such terms have disappeared completely from the lexicon of educators. Indeed, a few of them seem to be enjoying something of a revival these days.[9] However, it seems to me incontrovertible that today's public schools are far less engaged in trying to shape and mold what today might be called the personality of their students than was true a generation or two ago. In current discussions of what our schools are all about talk of morality and character has been replaced by notions like mastery, basic skills, competency, and accountability. That shift in the language of educational goals and purposes is the most clear-cut sign of the move toward the mimetic tradition.

A far more subtle sign, though no less telling perhaps, is the gradual emergence and the ultimate hegemony of a "scientific spirit" within the educational community at large, particularly among its leadership, whether in universities or in high administrative positions. Educational research in general and the educational testing movement in particular are two of the more obvious expressions of that spirit. Each in its way constitutes a challenge to the transformative tradition through its endorsement of

---

[8]Some mimetic outcomes may be unintended. Consider the fact that students are sometimes able to imitate their teachers exactly, without the latter intending that to happen. Commonly, however, memory residue that is not "officially" sanctioned as a goal or objective within the mimetic lesson plan is not counted as "outcome."

[9]Moral development, in particular, seems to be back in vogue of late as the result of the studies of Kohlberg and his followers at Harvard. The "value clarifications" movement, spurred by the late Louis Raths, is another attempt to revitalize the interest of educators in what are essentially transformative ends.

greater precision, objectivity, and reliability in the conduct of educational affairs.

As evidence of the power and pervasiveness of this "scientific" outlook within the educational research community in particular, witness the fact that most research on teaching focuses on the teaching of those school subjects most infused with a mimetic outlook—reading skills, mathematics and the sciences. Also note that achievement test scores have become *the* outcome variable by which to measure teaching effectiveness and the quality of schools in general, not only for researchers and many school administrators but for the public at large. . . .

[W]ithin that vast assortment of studies several trends bearing upon the two traditions of teaching are clearly discernible. The first is that those teaching situations that get studied the most are ones in which mimetic goals predominate. I have already commented upon this regarding psychological research in education. The conditions responsible for this hold with equal force for educational research in general. There too is a strong tendency to study educational outcomes that are readily measurable by a written test of some kind—most commonly a standardized achievement test. What this means in terms of the curricular focus of such studies is that school subjects like math and science and reading get investigated far more often than do social studies or art or music. Moreover, even within those subjects most frequently studied the focus of the investigation is almost always upon *epistemic* outcomes rather than *transformative* ones—on the acquisition of scientific *knowledge* rather than the development of a scientific *attitude*, on the growth of reading *skills* rather than the cultivation of a love for literature.

A second characteristic of research on teaching too dominant to be called a mere trend is that most of its studies are normative rather than descriptive; that is, they are designed to come up with better ways of teaching rather than simply to describe or to understand what teachers do and why they do it.[10] This state of affairs is perfectly natural in an applied field like education. Indeed, one might reasonably wonder why a person would want to undertake a purely descriptive study of teaching at all without the ulterior motive of unearthing something about the process that might possibly be improved.

But even though it may seem like the most natural thing in the world to do, searching for better ways of teaching through the instrumentality of research is not the value-neutral process that some researchers claim. Nor is it simply a way of serving the teaching profession by lending it a helping hand, as it is also sometimes portrayed.

For one thing, most such research concentrates almost exclusively on the observable aspects of teaching—on what teachers *do* and, moreover on what they can be seen to do fairly regularly and repeatedly. (Long stretches of observation are prohibitively time-consuming and expensive from the standpoint of both data collection and analysis, and also intrusive and disruptive of classroom routines.) Thus, the bulk of such research leans strongly in the direction of subsuming all of teaching under the single category of technique.

For another, the possibility of discovering the secret of good teaching through research means at least hypothetically that the researchers will possess that knowledge before teachers themselves will. Thus, they will be in a position to control and benefit from its release. This position of epistemic superiority need not be abused, of course, but there is always the danger it could be. Should that happen, as has been known in the past, the situation becomes one of "experts" controlling teachers from above as would a puppetmaster, talking down to them, doing all the things that William James warned against (and was partially guilty of himself, as we have already seen).

As should by now be clear, a purely technological conception of teaching, teaching-by-the-numbers we

---

[10][For] a somewhat different distinction between "normative" and "descriptive" research on teaching see Karen Kepler Zumwalt, "Research on teaching: policy implications for teacher education," in Ann Lieberman and Milbrey W. McLaughlin (eds.), *Policy Making in Education*, Eighty-first Yearbook of the National Society for the Study of Education, Part 1 (Chicago: University of Chicago Press, 1982), 215–248. Zumwalt points out that descriptive research can also be normative in the sense of its being used as the basis for prescriptive statements about how to teach. Her point is that all research yielding prescriptions about how to teach falls within what she calls "a technological orientation." The difficulty I have with this is that it seems to conjoin methodological and purposive categories. What she calls "process-product" research is also in my terms "descriptive" provided all it seeks to do is to describe. When research seeks to establish norms for action I look upon it as no longer descriptive, no matter what its methodology.

might call it, is far more likely to take root within the mimetic tradition, with its emphasis on both methodological and epistemological concerns, than it is within the transformative tradition, where both the method and content of teaching are much more vaguely defined. However, although it may more easily take root there, a technological and a mimetic orientation toward teaching are not one and the same; nor does *taking root* mean that it will necessarily *take over* in the sense of becoming the dominant perspective within that tradition. Whether that will happen, or indeed has already happened, is a question to be examined and not treated as a foregone conclusion. . . .

Those who see the growth of mimetic teaching as regrettable do so, by linking it to the technological side of that tradition, by seeing in it all that is undesirable about the gradual encroachment of technology. In its extreme form the vision is one of widespread dehumanization, Orwellian in scope. "Bureautechnocracy" is the term given it by one pair of authors who explain the term as

> *a pattern of social management wherein the hierarchized, pyramidal, depersonalized model of human organization (bureaucracy) is linked with standardized, rationalized means (technology) with the overall aim of achieving control, flexibility, and efficiency in reaching some commercial or social objective.*[11]

There is an additional worry sometimes voiced in connection with the mimetic tradition in particular, though it can cover certain aspects of the transformative tradition as well. It is that students are differentially exposed to the two traditions on the basis of social class membership, a fact that itself constitutes a form of social injustice. What this charge declares in detail is that those practices most closely associated with the mimetic tradition—an emphasis on memorization, short answer tests, copying, drill, and recitation—are especially favored in schools and classrooms whose students come from predominantly if not exclusively poor and working-class families in underprivileged environments. Interestingly enough, though some of today's critics fail to recognize it, this situation appears to be at least a century or two old. One finds it lampooned in Dickens' *Hard Times* and commented upon in historical documents such as Matthew Arnold's reports on British school practices in the mid- to late-nineteenth century[12] and John Locke's plans for "pauper schools" more than a century earlier.[13]

Moreover, the charge goes beyond the accusation of differential exposure to the two traditions on the basis of social class. Not only are children from poor and working-class families the objects of more mimetically oriented practices, so critics inform, but they are often exposed to the worst of those practices. It is not just that they are asked to memorize more facts and copy material from textbooks that is troublesome, but that the facts they are asked to memorize and the material they are required to copy are themselves inferior, intellectually speaking, when compared with equivalent exercises in schools and classrooms that serve pupils from more affluent families.

The same criticism applies, as has already been suggested, to differences in the more transformatively oriented practices. Not only are they emphasized less in schools serving children from poor and working-class families, we are told, but when they are employed the focus is on the development of character traits such as docility and punctuality rather than those of inquisitiveness and intellectual agressiveness.[14]

Why children of the poor should receive more than their share of mimetic teaching—and perhaps an inferior brand of it as well—is not hard to figure out once we begin to consider the constellation of conditions surrounding their education—the deprivations they suffer in other spheres as well, their widely publicized "learning difficulties," public attitudes concerning the "place" of the poor within our society, what they are said to "need," and so forth. What all these add up to is the belief that such children need more "drill and practice" than

---

[11]Charles A. Tesconi, Jr., and Van Cleve Morris, *The Anti-Man Culture: Bureautechnocracy and the Schools* (Urbana, Illinois: University of Illinois Press, 1972), 7. (Italics in original.)

[12]Fred G. Walcott, *The Origins of Culture and Anarchy: Matthew Arnold and Popular Education in England* (Toronto: University of Toronto Press, 1970), 13.

[13]See Robert Herbert Quick, *Essays on Educational Reformers* (New York: D. Appleton and Company, 1899), 219ff.

[14]Some evidence that this may be so appears in John Goodlad's *A Place Called School* (New York: McGraw-Hill, 1984). See also the companion volume by Jeannie Oakes, *Keeping Track* (New Haven: Yale University Press, 1985).

do those coming from more privileged homes, that they need more in the way of "the basics," that they need more practical training, which means courses that are more vocationally oriented and purport to develop so-called "marketable skills," and so on.

Such "needs" seem to square with the mimetic tradition's emphasis on the primacy of knowledge and its transmission. They also go well with that tradition's focus on method and technique. Small wonder that programs like "mastery learning," written systems of individualizing instruction, and other "by-the-numbers" schemes for regularizing and automating instruction—routines that are essentially mimetic in nature—are so often first tried out and adopted in schools serving children of the poor. That's where they are so obviously needed, or so common sense encourages us to believe.

Here then are the two extremes within the gradual encroachment of the mimetic tradition: a kind of naive optimism on the one hand and a "gloom-and-doom" perspective on the other. Must we choose between them? I think not, or rather I hope not; yet my own optimism is tempered by two reservations. The first derives from my conviction that some worries that beset upholders of the transformative traditions are truly worth worrying about. Though I

can't accept the lugubrious vision that teaching will be reduced to nothing but technique, leaving teachers to behave like a bunch of automatons controlled "from above," neither can I sanguinely dismiss such a prospect as being downright silly. I feel similarly about worries over the preponderance of mimetic procedures in schools and classrooms serving large numbers of children of the poor. Such fears may be exaggerated, but they seem to me worthy of investigation all the same.

The other consideration that undermines my middle-of-the-road optimism, making it rather weaker than I would like, is my inability to see how an effective synthesis between the two traditions can be achieved. In short, I fear that as polarities of educational thought the mimetic and the transformative will be with us for a long time to come, perhaps forever. Moreover, a certain amount of tension and strife between the two traditions may turn out to be inevitable. How to keep the tension within tolerable limits and therefore productive rather than destructive and, at the same time, how to avoid the attraction of extremes within each tradition are questions I cannot answer except by advocating the continued exercise of intelligence and goodwill in the search for answers. . . .

7. A RETROSPECTIVE LOOK AT TEACHERS' RELIANCE ON COMMERCIAL READING MATERIALS

Patrick Shannon

Language Arts (1975–present) and its predecessors, *Elementary English* (1947–1975) and *The Elementary English Review* (1924–1947) have provided writers with a forum for interpretation of reading research for sixty years. During that time, prominent reading researchers have argued many important issues. For example, William S. Gray (1926), Arthur I. Gates (1936), and David H. Russell (1957) discussed pressing reading research concerns; Emmett Betts (1939) and E. W. Dolch (1936) discussed vocabulary load for beginning reading, and Nila Banton Smith (1960) reviewed the past and future trends in commercial materials. More recently, Harry Singer (1970) presented reading research that should

have made a difference, but did not; P. David Pearson (1976) interpreted a psycholinguistic perspective; Robert Tierney (1980) suggested that there is a contract between a writer and a reader; and Dolores Durkin (1981) evaluated the new interest in reading comprehension.

That such prominent reading researchers are represented in *Language Arts* makes it even more curious that its authors have not squarely addressed reasons for elementary teachers' dependence on commercial materials when they instruct students in reading. Since this behavior has long been recognized as a problem (Huey 1908, p. 9), and it seems to be at the root of many questionable instructional practices (Duffy 1982; Durkin 1978), *Language Arts*, which encourages interpretation and theoretical arguments, would seem a logical place to find a discussion of this issue. The purpose of this article is to review *Language Arts'* treatment of the relationship between elementary teachers and commercial reading materials.

1924–1934

Three main themes can be found in the relevant articles across the six decades that *The Elementary English Review, Elementary English*, then *Language Arts* have been published: analyses of the content of commercial materials, arguments concerning appropriate reading methodology, and descriptions of teachers' use of the materials. Analysis of content was the predominant issue for the first decade (Burris 1927; Gray 1926, 1933; Ide and Oberg 1931; Kibbe 1927; Smith 1927). Gray (1926) presented five reading problems that challenge attention, and devoted one to the content of commercial materials. He cautioned that the content should reflect students' interests and abilities. The commercial readers' content, he maintained, was markedly different from the survey results on children's interests. Kibbe (1931) and Smith (1927) presented classification schemes for the content of the most widely used commercial materials of the day. Gray (1933) characterized the seriousness of these analyses when he discussed a report from the Commission of Seven on Higher Education in California.

> "There exists in embryo the conflicting interests that will later manifest themselves in blocs, strikes, and even in religious and racial persecution" unless the school can reveal to those future citizens their common heritage and "can imbue them with a reverence for the common humanity that underlies all apparent differences." Such statements suggest the vital function that reading materials must serve today. (p. 162)

For this decade, authors who presented arguments concerning appropriate methodology were in favor of teaching reading as a meaning-getting process and against alphabetic phonics (Gray 1926; Zirbes 1926; Huber 1928). Zirbes (1926) characterized the arguments and demonstrated the close association between methodological change and commercial materials.

> In the process of change from the strict alphabetic method which at the time seemed to be the only reasonable way, to the multiplicity of commercialized methods and systems of yesterday and today, there has been much wasted effort but no small amount of true progress. . . . Investigation and experiment have not settled every issue, but they are chiefly responsible for the changed order and for a reading program characterized by broad aims, vigorous emphasis from the beginning on reading as a thought-getting process, and the subordination of mechanics to meaning. (p. 126)

Burris (1927) and Donovan (1928) presented the third theme, descriptions of teachers' use of commercial materials. They did so, however, in very different ways. Burris (1927) reported that "the textbook has offered the easy road and many times the fatal one . . . the textbook selections have been taken day after day with no thought of their lasting effect upon the minds and ideals of the pupils, to say nothing of the development of life attitudes and skills in reading" (p. 150). On the other hand, Donovan (1928) was appalled when reporting the results of a survey concerning the effect of scientific investigation on classroom reading instruction.

> In these places we find teachers instructing children as they themselves were taught, absolutely ignorant and oblivious that science had discovered for us truths and that little children are entitled to the benefit of these discoveries (p. 107). . . . One of the most potent factors in the spreading of the results of research is through a well prepared set of readers and their manuals. (p. 106)

1934–1944

Durrell (1936) and Gates (1936) remarked upon the paucity of research concerning commercial materials and their use. Their primary concern was the adaptation of materials to provide proper instruction and to match the interests of students. Pratt and Meighen (1937) and Meighen and Barth (1938) characterized what came to be the traditional analysis of commercial materials in *Language Arts*. These writers analyzed the stories according to various criteria and more often than not they found the content lacking.

A second type of content analyses dealt with the concept and vocabulary load for beginning readers (Betts 1939; Dolch 1936; Gates 1936; Sims 1938). Discussion centered on two issues: the number of "reappearances" necessary to learn a new word, and classification systems for the vocabularies and concepts in contemporary commercial materials. This second type of content analysis culminated with Spache's (1941) elaborate system for selecting commercial materials for primary grades.

Boney (1938, 1939) addressed the use of commercial materials in elementary classrooms. His article took sharp exception to William S. Gray's wholehearted endorsement of commercial materials in the 36th Yearbook (1937). He found Gray's remarks unfortunate for three reasons: other books had better content, readers were expensive ($1.37 per pupil in 1934), and use of the readers did not ensure thoughtful instruction. After defending individualized reading with test scores from his school district in New Jersey, Boney (1938) offered two reasons for the longevity of commercial materials.

> There are teachers and administrators who do not know how to rely entirely upon extensive reading for developing the reading skills. . . . And lastly, the publishing of a popular set of basal readers is, perhaps, the most lucrative pedagogical business. Estimates by bookmen of the royalties of popular sets are from ten to five hundred thousands of dollars. It is hard for those who receive these sums to give a true evaluation of set[s] of books. (p. 137)

Betts (1943) took the opposite perspective. From a survey of fifty teachers, he concluded that ninety-six percent of the elementary teachers use commercial materials, and sixty-six percent of them use one reader for their entire class. Betts (1943) paraphrased Donovan (1928) in his conclusion.

> In general, it appears that systematic reading instruction on a differentiated basis must be achieved, for the time being through carefully prepared teacher's manuals for basal materials. (p. 59)

1944–1954

Grouping for instruction and thoughtful use of commercial materials were the predominant themes for the third decade. Several writers implored ele-

mentary teachers to use more than one reader in their classrooms (McCullough 1954; Murphy 1948; Wilson 1947). Wilson (1947) found that even newly graduated teachers did not group their students. Murphy (1948) used personal anecdotes to describe his eventual rejection of commercial materials as the foundation of appropriate reading instruction. Abraham (1954) was pessimistic in his criticism of contemporary practices in reading instruction. He maintained that reading instruction would not change because teachers cling irrationally to their past experience and to commercial materials.

In the thirtieth anniversary issue of *Elementary English*, noted reading researchers discussed the unsolved problems in reading. Betts (1954) devoted one of his twenty-two unsolved problems to the evaluation of contemporary commercial reading systems. Dolch (1954) wrote against attempts to standardize reading instruction through commercial materials and called for the primacy of the teacher variable in the equation for sound reading instruction. Gates (1954), Russell (1954), Harris (1954), Strang (1954), and Witty (1954) paid little attention to commercial materials and their use. In the closing article, Yockum (1954) characterized the group's attitude toward commercial materials. They wished to find out "how to develop a program balanced between basal, curricular, recretory, and corrective reading so that it will meet the varying needs of children and lead to improved reading habits and interests among the next generation of adults" (p. 430).

1954–1964

The predominant themes reoccurred and received further definition in the fourth decade. Again, content analysis was the primary issue (Larrick 1956; Newton 1963; Smith 1960; Smith 1962; Store and Bartschi 1963). Smith (1960) and Smith (1962) reminded *Language Arts* readers that commercial materials did not reflect students' interests. Larrick (1956) suggested that many parents were aware of the shortcomings of commercial materials and questioned their use in elementary schools. Newton (1963) defended the content of commercial primers because the concept load was consistent with contemporary theories in developmental psychology and the vocabulary repetition was required according to linguistic principles. Stone and Bartschi (1963) continued the work of Betts (1939), Dolch (1936), and others through the classification of vocabularies from commercial materials.

As it had in previous decades (Betts 1943; Yoakam 1954; Zirbes 1926), the argument concerning methodology centered on commercial materials (Artley 1961; Betts 1961; Frame 1964; Russell 1957). That is, commercial materials were the vehicle by which the various methods were explained. When a particular method was endorsed, commercial materials were promoted simultaneously. For example, Russell (1957), when reviewing Daniels and Diack's *Progress in Reading*, endorsed the "phonic word method" and the commercially available *Royal Road Readers* by the same authors. Betts (1961) and Artley (1961) were a bit more subtle, but not less emphatic. Both suggested the best method for reading instruction was commercial readers supplemented with outside reading. Frame (1964), attempting to substantiate the translation of Betts' and Artley's suggestions into classroom practice, found that teachers' lack of knowledge inhibited the use of supplemental materials.

The use of commercial materials was touched upon by many authors, but it was the sole subject of only two articles. Dickhart (1958) suggested methods to break the rigidity of reading programs by putting the commercial readers and workbooks aside. Staiger (1958) surveyed 474 school districts from 48 states and Hawaii to determine "How Are Basal Readers Used?" He found that ninety-nine percent of the schools adopted commercial readers and that sixty-seven percent of that group used a single reader in each classroom. Moreover, ninety-nine percent of the respondents related that commercial teacher's manuals directed reading instruction in elementary classrooms.

1964–1974

Although there was an increase in the number of articles published concerning commercial reading materials during the fifth decade, the three themes were readily apparent. Identification of appropriate methodology became the predominant theme as the result of the First Grade Studies commissioned by

the United States Office of Education (Bond 1966; Fry 1966; Hammill and Mattleman 1969; Rutherford 1971; Sheldon and Lashinger 1968, 1969, 1970; Smith 1973). During the First Grade Studies, various methods for teaching reading were tested against the "traditional" commercial reader approach. The overall conclusion, according to Rutherford (1971), was that the teacher, and not the materials or method, made the difference in successful reading instruction. A separate group of articles compared individualized reading favorably with the use of commercial materials (Abbott 1972; Huser 1967; Johnson 1965; Veatch 1967). Huser (1967) and Johnson (1965) substantiated their arguments by finding no significant differences in achievement scores between participants in individualized and commercial reader programs. Stewart (1966a, 1966b) and Hardin and Corbin (1973) offered an additional methodological issue when they studied the efficacy of workbooks in elementary reading instruction. Finally, Smtih (1972) and Williams (1970) continued the confusion between materials and methods with their advocacy of commercial materials as an appropriate method for teaching reading in the intermediate grades.

Content analysis of commercial materials continued to be a popular type of article. Several writers analyzed the story content in various, but traditional ways (Moir and Curtis 1968; Rose et al. 1972; Smith 1968; Wiberg and Trost 1970). Collier (1967) and Foerster (1973) criticized the racial and social stereotypes in the contemporary commercial materials and found them unsuitable for minority students. Criscuolo (1968) and Moore (1972) reported that commercial reading series were used successfully with minority children when they were supplemented with additional texts. Maki and Kinnunen (1969) continued the classification of vocabularies approach to content analysis.

The work of Austin and Morrison (1963) and Barton and Wilder (1964) inspired several discussions concerning teachers' use of commercial materials during reading instruction (Callaway et al. 1972a, 1972b; Gutknecht 1973; Harris 1969; Lerner 1967). Lerner (1967) saw the irony of the situation: "Without judging the value of the basal reader as a tool for reading instruction, it is interesting to note the discrepancy between the highly vocal and severe criticism of the basal reader and the widespread acceptance and use of it in 90 to 95 percent of the classrooms throughout the country" (p. 238). After duplicating Austin and Morrison's findings in Georgia (Callaway et al. 1972a), Callaway et al. (1972b) rejected all nontextbook curricula for language arts because teachers would not use them. They suggested five curricular designs based on commercial readers. Articles of this sort led Gutknecht (1973) to conclude that "to a certain degree, educators have abrogated their responsibilities so that publishers by default have dictated the methods and materials to be used in teaching reading" (p. 80).

In his review of reading research that should have made a difference, Singer (1970) contradicted Betts' (1943) and Donovan's (1928) claim that commercial materials were a progressive force in classroom reading instruction. He stated that scientific research did not improve classroom reading instruction because commercial publishers were reluctant to alter their materials.

1974–1982

In the sixth decade of publication, the three themes continued. Content analysis, however, waned a good deal. Johnson (1974) and Rodenborn and Washburn (1974) disagreed over the appropriateness of the content of commercial readers in traditional content analysis studies. Schnell and Sweeny (1975) criticized the sex bias in the stories. Conspicuously absent were studies classifying the vocabularies of beginning commercial readers.

Commercial readers were still closely associated with discussions concerning appropriate instruction. Hill and Methot (1974) argued the merits of individualized reading over the Sullivan Reading Program. Neufeld (1975) and Winkeljohann (1980) carried on Betts' (1961) and Artley's (1961) search for the best eclectic reading program based on commercial materials. Cook (1976) described the appropriate integration of commercial kits into commercial reading programs. Singer (1977) revised the accepted conclusion of the First Grade Studies from "it's the teacher who makes the difference" to it is the teachers who can make the difference in a systematic and synchronized reading program. He described three attempts to influence teachers' use of commercial materials through the intervention of reading researchers.

The predominant theme during the sixth decade was the use of commercial materials and the assumptions on which they were designed (Artley 1980; Goodman 1974, 1979; Klein 1975; Roehler and Duffy 1982; Rouch et al. 1975). Each writer suggested that commercial materials controlled classroom reading instruction to various extents. Rouch et al. (1975) criticized teachers' pacing of reading instruction and suggested that teachers appeared more interested in covering materials than providing appropriate instruction. Roehler and Duffy (1982) echoed this concern in light of the current enthusiasm for "direct instruction." Klein (1975), Goodman (1974, 1979), and Artley (1980) were explicit in their criticism of the control ideology implicit in current commercial reading materials.

> "There are three educational elements in the reading instruction process." That was the assertion, and the speaker was a reading authority . . . three elements; went the assertion—curriculum, which you buy in the form of textbooks, basal series, what not; methodology, which you buy in the form of teacher's manuals and related instructional guides; and organization, which you cannot buy. (Klein 1975, p. 351)
> Literacy in this competency-based highly structured, empty technology is reduced to a tight sequence of arbitrary skills. The teacher becomes a technician, part of a "delivery system." (Goodman 1979, p. 663)
> Without realizing what would ultimately take place we have been walking the road of performance objectives, mastery reading, and back to basics under the false assumption that if readers demonstrate the mastery of skills, ipso facto, they will be effective readers. (Artley 1980, p. 549)

DISCUSSION

Language Arts' messages to its readers were mixed concerning the relationship between elementary teachers and commercial reading materials. Many authors found the materials lacking interesting content, criticized some uses of the readers, and offered alternatives to commercial programs. A few authors considered the use of commercial materials beyond teachers' control; they blamed the conflict of interest between reading researchers and commercial publishers (Boney 1938) and administrators' acceptance of control ideologies (Klein 1975; Goodman 1979). The overwhelming majority of authors implied that the problem was well within teachers' control. This implication is evident in the numerous articles which attempted to cajole teachers from dependence on commercial materials with descriptions of appropriate behavior. These authors appear to have assumed that if teachers would just put forth the effort, then reading instruction based on commercial materials would disappear.

However, many articles condoned the use of commercial materials and contradicted the criticism offered in the rest of *Language Arts*. For example, Betts (1943), Donovan (1928), Gray (1926), and Smith (1972) suggested commercial reading materials as appropriate instruction. Other authors may have unwittingly encouraged teachers to use commercial materials. In most articles which compared methodologies, the authors found no significant difference between the "traditional" commercial reader and experimental methods. Teachers, upon reading these articles, might have asked themselves, "Why should I switch from the commercial reader if the experimental method is not superior?"

CONCLUSION

Although teachers' dependence on commercial reading materials has been a concern of *Language Arts'* authors for sixty years, they have avoided a direct investigation of why teachers are so dependent. To date, these authors have attempted to change teachers' behavior without first understanding why the behavior is present. Investigations of why teachers use commercial reading materials must go beyond the notion implicit in many *Language Arts* articles that teachers use the materials because it is an easy way to conduct school. Profitable investigations will examine teachers' training, reading methodology textbooks, Western Society's penchant for technology, and administrators' requests for standard instruction as well as teachers' subjective reasons. I hope a review of *Language Arts* on its seventieth anniversary will show four themes in its treatment of teachers' reliance on commercial reading materials: analyses of content, arguments concerning appropriate methodology, descriptions of teachers' use of the materials, and most important, discussions

of why teachers are dependent on commercial reading materials.

REFERENCES

Abbott, J. "Fifteen Reasons Why Personalized Reading Instruction Does Not Work." *Elementary English* 49 (1972): 33–36.

Abraham, W. "A New Look at Reading." *Elementary English* 31 (1954): 139–143.

Artley, A. "An Eclectic Approach to Reading." *Elementary English* 38 (1961): 320–327.

Artley, A. "Reading: Skills or Competences?" *Language Arts* 57 (1980): 546–549.

Austin, M. and Morrison, C. *The First R.* New York, NY: Wiley, 1963.

Barton, A. and Wilder, D. "Research and Practice in the Teaching of Reading." In *Innovations in Education*, edited by M. Miles. New York, NY: Teachers College Press, 1964.

Betts, E. "A Study of the Vocabularies of First Grade Basal Readers." *Elementary English Review* 16 (1939): 65–69.

Betts, E. "Systematic Sequences in Reading." *Elementary English Review* 20 (1943): 54–59.

Betts, E. "Unsolved Problems in Reading." *Elementary English* 31 (1954): 325–329.

Betts, E. "How Well Are We Teaching Reading." *Elementary English* 38 (1961): 377–381.

Bond, G. "First Grade Reading Studies: An Overview." *Elementary English* 43 (1966): 464–470.

Boney, C. "Basal Readers." *Elementary English Review* 15 (1938): 133–137.

Boney, C. "Teaching Children to Read as They Learned to Talk." *Elementary English Review* 16 (1939): 139–141, 156.

Burris, M. "Vitalizing Reading through Organization." *Elementary English Review* (1927): 150–152.

Callaway, A. and Jarvis, O. "Programs and Materials Used in Reading Instruction: A Survey." *Elementary English* 49 (1972a): 578–581.

Callaway, A.; McDaniel, H.; and Mason, G. "Five Methods of Teaching Language Arts: A Comparison." *Elementary English* 49 (1972b): 1240–1245.

Collier, M. "An Evaluation of Multi-Ethnic Basal Readers." *Elementary English* 44 (1967): 152–157.

Cook, J. "If It's SRA, It Must Be Friday." *Language Arts* 53 (1976): 385–386, 391.

Criscuolo, N. "How Effective Are Basal Readers with Culturally Disadvantaged Children." *Elementary English* 45 (1968): 364–365.

Dickhart, A. "Breaking the Lock-Step in Reading." *Elementary English* 35 (1958): 54–56.

Dolch, E. "How Much Word Knowledge Do Children Bring to Grade One?" *Elementary English Review* 13 (1936): 177–183.

Dolch, E. "Unsolved Problems in Reading." *Elementary English* 31 (1954): 329–331.

Donovan, H. "Use of Research in the Teaching of Reading." *Elementary English Review* 5 (1928): 104–107.

Duffy, G. "Commentary: Response to Borko, Shevelson, and Stern: There's More to Instructional Decision-Making in Reading Than the Empty Classroom." *Reading Research Quarterly* 17 (1982): 295–300.

Durkin, D. "What Classroom Observation Reveals about Reading Comprehension Instruction." *Reading Research Quarterly* 14 (1978): 481–533.

Durkin, D. "What Is the Value of the New Interest in Reading Comprehension?" *Language Arts* 58 (1981): 23–43.

Durrell, D. "Research Problems in Reading in the Elementary School." *Elementary English Review* 13 (1936): 101–106, 111; 149–156; 184–193.

Foerster, L. "Personalizing Reading Instruction." *Elementary English* 50 (1973): 461–463.

Frame, N. "The Availability of Reading Materials for Teachers and Pupils at the Primary Level." *Elementary English* 41 (1964): 262–268.

Fry, E. "Comparing the Diacritical Marking System, ITA, and a Basal Reading Series." *Elementary English* 43 (1966): 607–611.

Gates, A. "Needed Research in Elementary School Reading." *Elementary English Review* 13 (1936): 306–310.

Gates, A. "Unsolved Problems in Reading." *Elementary English* 31 (1954): 331–334.

Goodman, K. "Effective Teachers of Reading Know Language and Children." *Elementary English* 51 (1974): 823–828.

Goodman, K. "The Know-More and the Know-Nothing Movements in Reading: A Personal Response." *Language Arts* 56 (1979): 657–663.

Gray, W. "Reading: Problems that Challenge Attention." *Elementary English Review* 3 (1926): 105–107.

Gray, W. "New Issues in Teaching Reading." *Elementary English Review* 10 (1933): 162–164.

Gutknecht, B. "How Do You Teach Reading?" *Elementary English* 50 (1973): 77–80.

Hammill, D. and Mattleman, M. "An Evaluation of a Programmed Reading Approach in the Primary Grades." *Elementary English* 46 (1969): 310–311.

Hardin, W. and Corbin, D. "Motivation and the Lowly Workbook." *Elementary English* 50 (1973): 563–564.

Harris, A. "Key Factors in a Successful Reading Program." *Elementary English* 46 (1969): 69–76.

Harris, A. "Unsolved Problems in Reading." *Elementary English* 31 (1954): 416–418.

Hill, C. and Methot, K. "Making an Important Transition." *Elementary English* 51 (1974): 842–845.

Huber, M. "Teaching Beginners to Read." *Elementary English Review* 5 (1928): 116–118.

Huey, E. B. *The Psychology and Pedagogy of Reading.* Boston: MIT Press, 1968.

Huser, M. "Reading and More Reading." *Elementary English* 44 (1967): 378–382, 385.

Ide, A. and Oberg, W. "The Content of Present Day School Readers." *Elementary English Review* 8 (1931): 64–68.

Johnson, J. "Wanted: Reality Oriented Reading Materials." *Elementary English* 51 (1974): 557–558.

Johnson, R. "Individualized and Basal Primary Reading Programs." *Elementary English* 42 (1965): 902–904, 915.

Kibbe, D. "Duplicate Materials in Elementary Readers." *Elementary English Review* 4 (1927): 35–41.

Klein, M. "The Reading Program and Classroom Management: Panacea or Perversion?" *Elementary English* 52 (1975): 351–355.

Larrick, N. "What Parents Think about Children's Reading." *Elementary English* 33 (1956): 206–209.

Lerner, J. "A New Focus in Reading Research: The Decision-Making Process." *Elementary English* 44 (1967): 236–242, 251.

Maki, V. and Kinnunen, S. "A Comparison of Sentence Length and Frequency of Word Repetition in McGuffey's First Reader and a Modern First Reader." *Elementary English* 46 (1969): 313–317.

McCullough, C. "Groping or Grouping?" *Elementary English* 31 (1954): 136–138.

Meighen, M. and Barth, E. "Geographic Materials in Third Grade Readers." *Elementary English Review* 15 (1939): 299–301.

Moir, H. and Curtis, W. "Basals and Bluebirds." *Elementary English* 45 (1968): 623–629.

Moore, M. "A Multi-Approach to Beginning Reading in the Urban Schools." *Elementary English* 49 (1972): 44–49.

Murphy, G. "Reading Materials—1948." *Elementary English* 25 (1948): 469–477.

Neufeld, K. "A Kaleidoscopic Reading Organization Plan." *Elementary English* 52 (1975): 673–675.

Newton, E. "The Basal Primer May Be Deceptively Easy." *Elementary English* 40 (1963): 273–274.

Pearson, P. D. "A Psycholinguistic Model of Reading." *Language Arts* 53 (1976): 309–314.

Pratt, M. and Meighen, M. "What Beginning Readers Read." *Elementary English Review* 14 (1937): 125–128, 151.

Rodenbom, L. and Washburn, E. "Some Implications of

the New Basal Readers." *Elementary English* 51 (1974): 885–888.

Roehler, L. and Duffy, G. "Matching Direct Instruction to Reading Outcomes." *Language Arts* 59 (1982): 476–480.

Rose, C.; Zimet, S.; and Blom, G. "Content Counts: Children Have Preferences in Reading Textbook Stories." *Elementary English* 49 (1972): 14–19.

Rouch, R.; Chandler, J.; and Fleetwood, L. "Teaching Books or Teaching Children. *Language Arts* 52 (1975): 709–792, 835.

Russell, D. "Unsolved Problems in Reading." *Elementary English* 31 (1954): 334–338.

Russell, D. "Progress in Reading: A Special Review." *Elementary English* 34 (1957): 242–244.

Rutherford, W. "The Success Ingredient in Reading Instruction." *Elementary English* 48 (1971): 224–226.

Schnell, T. and Sweeny, J. "Sex Role Bias in Basal Readers." *Language Arts* 52 (1975): 737–742.

Sheldon, W. and Lashinger, D. "A Summary of Research Studies Relating to Language Arts in Elementary Education." *Elementary English* 45 (1968): 794–817.

Sheldon, W. and Lashinger, D. "A Summary of Research Studies Relating to Language Arts in Elementary Education." *Elementary English* 46 (1969): 866–885.

Sheldon, W. and Lashinger, D. "A Summary of Research Studies Relating to Language Arts in Elementary Education." *Elementary English* 48 (1971): 243–274.

Sims, R. "Concept Analysis of Primers and Pre-Primers." *Elementary English Review* 15 (1938): 302–305.

Singer, H. "Research That Should Have Made a Difference." *Elementary English* 47 (1970): 27–34.

Singer, H. "Resolving Curricular Conflict in the 1970's." *Language Arts* 54 (1977): 158–163.

Smith, E. "Some High Spots in the Reading Program." *Elementary English Review* 4 (1927): 42–44.

Smith N. "Something Old, Something New in Primary Reading." *Elementary English* 37 (1960): 368–374.

Smith, N. "Prospectives in Reading Instruction Past Perfect? Future Tense? *Elementary Engish* 45 (1968): 440–445.

Smith, N. "Reading Research: Some Notable Findings." *Elementary English* 50 (1973): 259–263.

Smith, R. "The Intermediate Grades Reading Program: Questions Teachers and Principals Ask." *Elementary English* 49 (1972): 364–368.

Smith, R. "Children's Reading Choices and Basic Reader Content." *Elementary English* 39 (1962): 202–209.

Spache, G. "Problems in Primary Book Selection." *Elementary English Review* 18 (1941): 5–12; 52–59; 139–148.

Staiger, R. "How Are Basal Readers Used?" *Elementary English* 35 (1958): 46–49.

Stewart, M. "Workbooks: 1930–1964." *Elementary English* 43 (1966a): 149–153.

Stewart, M. "Workbook: Help or Hinderance?" *Elementary English* 43 (1966b): 477–479.

Stone, D. and Bartschi, V. "A Basic Word List from Basal Readers." *Elementary English* 40 (1963): 420–427.

Strang, R. "Unsolved Problems in Reading." *Elementary English* 31 (1954): 418–421.

Thirty-Sixth Yearbook. "Part 1: The Teaching of Reading." A Second Report of the National Society for the Study of Education. Bloomington, IL: Public School Publishing Co, 1937.

Tierney, R. and LaZansky, J. "The Rights and Responsibilities of Readers and Writers." *Language Arts* 57 (1980): 608–613.

Veatch, J. "Structure in the Reading Program." *Elementary English* 44 (1967): 252–256.

Wiberg, J. and Trost, M. "A Comparison between the Content of First Grade Primers and the Free Choice Library Selections Made by First Grade Students." *Elementary English* 47 (1970): 792–798.

Williams, R. "For the Classroom: Supervised Practice in Reading." *Elementary English* 47 (1970): 397–400.

Wilson, M. "The Teacher's Problem in a Differentiated Reading Program." *Elementary English Review* 24 (1947): 77–85, 118.

Winkeljohann, R. "Queries: How Can Basal Readers Be Used Creatively?" *Language Arts* 57 (1980): 906–907.

Witty, P. "Unsolved Problems in Reading." *Elementary English* 31 (1954): 421–427.

Yoakam, G. "Unsolved Problems in Reading." *Elementary English* 31 (1954): 427–430.

Zirbes, L. "Beginning Reading in America and England." *Elementary English Review* 3 (1926): 126–127.

8. HISTORICAL PERSPECTIVE ON EDUCATIONAL TECHNOLOGY
Patrick Suppes

PAST EDUCATIONAL TECHNOLOGIES

I can identify at least five major technological innovations in the past that are comparable to the current computer revolution.

Written Records

The first is the introduction of written records for teaching purposes in ancient times. We do not know exactly when the use of written records for instructional purposes began but we do have, as early as Plato's Dialogues, written in the fifth century B.C., sophisticated objections to the use of written records.

Today no one would doubt the value of written material in education, but there were very strong and cogent objections to this very earliest innovation in education. The objections were these: a written record is very impersonal; it is very uniform; it does not adapt to the individual student; it does not establish rapport with the student. In other words, Socrates and the ancient Sophists, the tutors of students in ancient Athens, objected to introducing written records and destroying the kind of personal relation between student and tutor that was a part of their main reason for being.

It has become a familiar story in our own time that a technological innovation has side effects that are not always uniformly beneficial. It is important to recognize that this is not a new aspect of innovation but has been with us from the beginning.

Libraries

The second innovation was the founding of libraries in the ancient world, the most important example being the famous Alexandrian Library that was established around 300 B.C. Because of certain democratic traditions, the preeminence of the creative work in philosophy and poetry, it is easy to think of Athens as the intellectual center of the Hellenic world. In fact, that center was really Alexandria. From about 250 B.C. to A.D. 400, not only was Alexandria the most important center of mathematics and astronomy in the ancient world— it was also a major center of literature, especially because of the collection in the Alexandrian Library. The first real beginnings of critical scholarship in the western world in literature, the editing of texts, the analysis of style, the drawing up of bibliographies, took place in the Alexandrian Library. This revolution in education consisted not simply of having in one place a large number of papyrus manuscripts but in the organization of large bodies of learning. Scholars from all over the western world came to Alexandria to study and to talk to others.

Libraries of a substantial nature were to be found in other major cities of the ancient world, not to mention the large collections of learning in China, India, and Korea.

Printing

The third innovation of great historical importance in education was the move from written records to printed books. In the western world we identify the beginning date of this innovation with the printing of the Gutenberg Bible in 1452. It is important to recognize, however, that there was extensive use of block printing in Korea and China three or four hundred years earlier. Nearly half a millennium later it is difficult to have a vivid sense of how important the innovation of printing turned out to be. In the ancient world of the Mediterranean there were only a few major libraries, a number so small that they could be counted on the fingers of one hand. One of the famous aspects of Alexandria, for example, was the wealth and magnitude of its library, and the Alexandrian Library of 100 B.C. had few competitors. The reason is obvious: it was impossible to have large numbers of copies of manuscripts reproduced when all copying had to be done tediously by hand. The introduction of printing in the fifteenth century produced a radical innovation—indeed a revolution—in the distribution of intellectual and educational materials. By the middle of the sixteenth century not only European institutions but wealthy families as well had libraries of serious proportions.

Once again, however, there were definite technological side effects that were not uniformly beneficial. Those who know the art and the beauty of the medieval manuscripts that preceded the introduction of printing can appreciate that mass printing was regarded by some as a degradation of the state of reproduction.

It is also important to have a sense of how slow the impact of a technological innovation can sometimes be. It was not until the end of the eighteenth century that books were used extensively for teaching in schools. In arithmetic, for example, most teachers continued to use oral methods throughout the nineteenth century and it was not until almost the beginning of the present century that appropriate elementary textbooks in mathematics were available. It is certainly my hope that it will not require 500 years to distribute computers into schools, a figure comparable to what it took to distribute arithmetic textbooks into schools. Fortunately, the scale of dissemination in the modern world is of an entirely different order from what it was in the past. Perhaps my favorite example is the estimate that it took over five years for the news of Julius Caesar's assassination to reach the furthest corners of the Roman Empire. Today such an assassination would be known throughout the world in a matter of minutes.

With regard to the pace at which books have been introduced into education, it would be a mistake to think that there was something peculiar about the use of methods of recitation in the elementary school until late in the nineteenth century; stories of a comparable sort also hold at the university level. According to at least one account, the last professor at the University of Cambridge in England who insisted on following the recitative tradition that dates back to the Middle Ages was C. D. Broad. As late as the 1940's he dictated and then repeated each sentence so that students would have adequate time to write each sentence exactly as dictated. I cannot imagine contemporary university students tolerating such methods.

Mass Schooling

The fourth innovation, and again one that we now accept as a complete and natural part of our society, is mass schooling. We have a tendency in talking about our society to put schools and families into the same category of major institutions. But it is extremely important to recognize the great psychological difference between the status of the family and the status of schools. Families are really deep into our blood and our culture. The evidence of families in one form or another being the most important cultural unit goes back thousands of years. Schools are not at all comparable; they are, we might say, very much Johnny-come-lately to our culture. A hundred years ago in 1870, for example, only two percent of young people graduated from high school in the United States. A hundred years before that only a very small percentage even finished third or fourth grade. I cannot give you an exact percentage because our record-keeping, that is, our social statistics, are not much more than a hundred years old and we have no serious idea of how many students were actually in school two hundred years ago, except that we do know that the number was quite small.

Even as short a period as fifty years ago, in most of the world less than one percent of the population completed secondary school. During the recent upheavals connected with the "cultural revolution" in China the elementary schools, not to speak of colleges and secondary schools, were closed for several years. In our society as we now think of it, it is unbelievable to contemplate closing the elementary schools for such a period of time. From a Chinese historical perspective, however, it was not such an important matter, for Chinese culture extends back continuously several thousand years and there is in that cultural tradition no salient place for mass schooling.

In many developing countries of the world today the best that can be hoped is that the majority of the young people will be given four grades of elementary school. Until the population growth is brought in check, it will take all available resources to achieve this much. The position of America as a world leader in education is sometimes not adequately recognized by my fellow Americans, because we accept as so much a part of our culture the concept of all young people completing secondary school and a high percentage going on to college. In fact, our leadership in creating a society with mass education is perhaps one of the most important aspects of American influence in the world.

As recently as the latter part of the nineteenth century the British philosopher, John Stuart Mill, despaired of democracy ever really working anywhere in the world for one reason—it was simply not possible to educate the majority of the population. In his view it was not possible to have a significant percentage of the population able to read and to be informed about political events. As in the case of many such predictions, he was very much in error. The revolution in mass schooling is one of the most striking phenomena of the twentieth century.

Testing

The fifth educational innovation is testing, which is in many ways older than the concept of mass schooling. The great tradition of testing was first established in China; testing there began in the fifth century A.D. and became firmly entrenched by the twelfth century A.D. There is a continuous history from the twelfth century to the end of the nineteenth century in the use of tests for the selection of mandarins—the civil servants who ran the imperial government of China. The civil service positions held by mandarins were regarded as the elite social positions in the society.

The importance of these tests in Chinese society is well attested to by the literature of various periods. If one examines, for example, the literature of the fifteenth or sixteenth century, one is impressed by the concern expressed for performance on tests. A variety of literary tales focused on the question of whether sons would successfully complete the tests and what this would mean for the family. (As you might expect, in those days women had no place in the management of the society and no place as applicants for civil service positions.) The procedures of selection were as rigorous as those found in a contemporary medical school or a graduate school of business in the United States. In many periods fewer than two percent of those who began the tests (which were arranged in a complicated hierarchy) successfully completed the sequence and were put on the list of eligible mandarins.

Although testing has a history that goes back hundreds of years, in many ways it is proper to regard testing as a twentieth-century innovation because it was only in this century that the scientific and technical study of tests began. It is only in this century that there has been a serious effort to understand and to define what constitutes a good test for a given aptitude, a given achievement, or a given skill. Moreover, this intensive study of testing

from a technical standpoint was primarily a focus of American research by such educational psychologists as Edward L. Thorndike. The tradition that Thorndike began has become a major one in our society and is a source of continual controversy in terms of issues of fairness and objectivity. Certainly current speculations as to the reasons for the decline in the verbal and mathematical scores on the Scholastic Aptitude Tests provide an excellent example of the kind of detailed scrutiny we give our tests that is completely uncharacteristic of any tradition of testing, whether in China, Europe or the United States prior to this century.

The five innovations that I have discussed—written records, libraries, printed books, schools, and tests—are the very fabric of our educational system today. It is almost unthinkable to contemplate a modern educational system without each of these innovations playing an important part.

Of these five technologies, none had been in any way adequately forecast or outlined at the time it was introduced. Of course, a few individuals foresaw the consequences and had something to say about those consequences, but certainly the details of the use of any of these five technologies had not been adequately foreseen. I am certain that the same thing will be true of technologies now developing for use in the future, and so I do not want to appear confident that what I say is a correct scenario for the future. But I want to say something about each of the five. First, I have mentioned, and I want to re-emphasize, the very recent and historically very transient character of schools. It is a phenomenon in a general sense of the last hundred years in the most developed parts of the world, and a phenomenon of the last thirty years or so (that is, since World War II) in the underdeveloped parts of the world. Now, an important question for the future is this: In fifty or one hundred years, will we abolish schools? Will we deliver into the home, or into small neighborhood units, by technological means all curriculum and instruction? Further, will the desires or goals of the individual, the family, the parents, or the neighborhood group be such that children will not be in school, but at home or in the neighborhood? The answers to these questions are not easy to predict or to foresee.

The same kind of forecast may be made for books. The importance of books that we have felt for several hundred years, since the beginning of the Renaissance, and that has been associated with the development and education of an informed citizenry, may fade away. I think that all of us, at least those of my age, have seen this already in the case of young students. Some recent studies have indicated that the cultural reference points of the younger generation are no longer to be found in books, or in current novels, but in television and movies.

In the case of tests, I also predict that this classical technology will decrease in importance. I believe that tests will decrease in importance because we will have the technological means to keep a much more satisfactory and much more detailed record of the learning of individual students. Thus inferences about the performance of students and their capabilities for taking next steps will depend upon a much more substantial record, a much better basis of inference than we have in current tests.

As for libraries, they will be totally transformed. I feel more confident of this prediction than of any of the others. Electronic access will be widely available in homes, in offices, and in schools of what other organizational kind we have. There will be libraries but they will be electronic libraries.

Finally, what about the written record? The written record will undoubtedly continue to have importance, but I think that when it comes to teaching, the objections found in Plato's Dialogues to the cold and neutral written word as opposed to the warm and friendly voice of the teacher will once again be heard and perceived as serious objections. What I am saying is that, in starting to think about the future, we can forecast obsolescence or semi-obsolescence for all of the great technologies of the past—and that is proper and appropriate.

ISSUES RAISED BY COMPUTER-ASSISTED INSTRUCTION

The current operational use of computer-assisted instruction in many schools in this country, a use that is well exemplified by the detailed discussion of Alioto and Thornton, raises a number of issues of a broad educational and social kind to which I would now like to turn. I will discuss four rather closely related issues that have had a certain prominence in the discussion of computer-assisted instruction (CAI): 1) individualization of instruction, 2)

standardization of instruction, 3) complexity of instruction, and 4) freedom in education.

Individualization of Instruction

The first issue centers around the claim that the deep use of technology, specifically computer technology, will impose a rigid regime of impersonalized teaching. Perhaps the best image of this issue in the popular press is that of student protest at being represented by computer records in the files of the central school administration.

To those advancing this claim of deep impersonalization, it is important to say that indeed this is a possibility. Computer technology could be used in this way, and in some instances it probably will. This is little different from saying that there are many kinds of teaching and many ways in which the environment of learning and teaching may be debased. The important point to insist upon, however, is that it is certainly not a necessary aspect of the use of the technology.

Indeed, our claim would be that one of the computer's most important potentials is exactly the opposite. Computers can make learning and teaching more personalized rather than less so. Students will be subject to less regimentation and lockstepping, because computer systems will be able to offer highly individualized instruction.

It is important that the remark about individualized instruction not be passed off as sloganeering. For many years, courses in the methodology of teaching have emphasized the importance of teaching according to the needs of individual students and therefore attempting to individualize instruction as much as possible. It is recognized, however, by anyone who has examined the structure of our schools either at the elementary- or secondary-school level that a high degree of individualization is extraordinarily difficult to achieve when the ratio of students to teachers is approximately 25 to 1.

One direct approach is to reduce this ratio to something like 5 or 10 to 1, but the economics of this approach is totally unfeasible in the long run and on a widespread basis. All the evidence points to the fact that the cost of having first-rate teachers in the classroom, training these teachers appropriately, and providing them with the kind of salaries that will be competitive with other technical and professional jobs in our society will simply make it impossible for schools to afford any drastic reduction in the student-teacher ratio. One of the few real opportunities for offering individualized instruction lies in the use of computers as instructional devices.

I do wish to emphasize that I do not envisage replacing teachers entirely, especially at the elementary-school level. It would be my estimate that even under the maximum use of technology only 20 to 30 percent of students' time in the elementary school would be spent at computer terminals. While classes or substantial parts of classes were working at terminals, teachers would be able to work with the remainder. Moreover, they would be able to work intensely with individual students, partly because some of the students would be at the terminals, and equally because routine aspects of teaching would be handled by the computer system.

At the post secondary level, matters are very different. At most colleges and universities, students do not now receive a great deal of individual attention from instructors. Certainly we can all recognize the degree of personal attention is greater in a computer program designed to accommodate itself to individual students' progress than in the lecture course on a general subject that has more than 200 students in daily attendance.

Complex intellectual problems are yet to be solved in offering tutorial computer programs on advanced subjects at the university level. I do believe that the teaching of basic skills ranging from elementary mathematics to foreign-language instruction at the college level can well be performed by computer-assisted courses. . . .

Standardization of Instruction

A second common claim is that the widespread use of computer technology will lead to excessive standardization of education. This claim was raised repeatedly in general discussions with educators and the interested public. In 1968 when I was lecturing on computer-assisted instruction in Australia, exactly this claim was made by one of the senior professors of education in Australia. When he was asked how many different books on Australian history are used in the Australian secondary schools, the reply was that two books are used in over 90 percent of the classes.

To those familiar with current practices in textbook adoption and use in elementary and secondary schools, it is clear that a high degree of standardization already exists in education. It is important to admit at once that a still greater degree of standardization could arise from the widespread use of computers. This is a possibility not to be denied. It is, however, in no sense a necessity. It would technically be possible for a state department of education, for example, to require that at 10:10 in the morning every fourth-grader be adding one-half and one-third, or every junior high school be reciting the amendments to the Constitution. The central danger of the technology is that edicts can be enforced as well as issued, and many persons are rightly concerned at the spector of rigid standardization that could be imposed.

I think we would all agree that the ever-increasing use of books from the sixteenth century to the present has deepened the varieties of educational and intellectual experience generally available. It is not difficult, however, to construct a caricature of present concerns in terms of the horrors it might have been claimed would be introduced with the widespread use of books. It is easy to visualize a certain type of critic arguing that the highly individualized and effective qualities of the individual teacher's voice could be lost in the completely standardized use of the written word and the written text. The individualization of comment, the adaptation of comment to the expression of individual students and to their responsiveness and comprehension, would be lost in the use of books in place of teachers.

Now we all recognize that there is a truth at the heart of this caricature, but it is not a truth that argues for the abolition or suppression of books in education. It argues rather for a wide variety of educational experiences.

There is every reason to believe that the appropriate development of CAI programs will enable us to take a highly significant step beyond the introduction of books and to offer unparalleled variety and depth of curriculum to students of all ages. Indeed, the problem in avoiding standardization is not the limitations of the technology, but our ignorance of how to diversify approaches to learning in meaningful and significant ways.

The basic scientific data on these matters are pitifully small. Opinions can be found in every educational group, but they are opinions. Moreover, from an operational standpoint it is not possible to find any wide diversity of approaches to most of the standard subjects in the curriculum. Do we want an auditory approach to the learning of language for one student and a visual approach to another? Do we want a politically oriented presentation of American history for some students and a socially oriented presentation for others? Do we think that different cognitive styles can be identified in a sufficiently deep way to justify and guide the preparation of vastly different curricula in the same general subject matter?

These questions are not in any way bound to computer technology. These are fundamental questions about the science of curriculum, the art of teaching, and the philosophy of education that reach out to very general questions of social policy. The computer is there to be used in whatever way we choose. Uniform standardization of the curriculum will be the end product only if we are so lacking in imagination as to achieve nothing else.

Complexity of Instruction

The third claim often heard is that the limitations of the technology and the problems that must be overcome in using it will lead to the development of curricula that will almost necessarily be simpleminded in character. There are indeed some unfortunate historical examples in the literature of curriulum efforts, especially curriculum efforts in a technological setting.

In the early days of programmed instruction, for example, a number of texts on elementary mathematics were written by psychologists or educators who did not have adequate training in mathematics. The programmed texts were splattered with "howlers" that received the eager attention of the mathematics educators charged with reviewing the books. Similar kinds of blunders can occur in the case of computer-assisted instruction, but there is nothing special about computers, and it is hard to see that a serious argument can be made to claim that there is any reason why computer-assisted instruction will be worse than other forms of curriculum.

The world is full of textbooks that are obviously bad in many respects. Within mathematics, for example, there are elementary books that are full of mathematical mistakes; there are also elementary books that are mathematically correct, but pedagog-

ically bad beyond belief. No doubt programs exhibiting these two extremes will also be written for computer-assisted instruction in mathematics.

There are reasons, however, for thinking the situation will be more self-corrective in the case of CAI than in the case of ordinary textbook writing. One reason is simply that data can be gathered and authors can be presented in tough-minded fashion with a clear picture of the defects of the materials they have written. For example, in a program in elementary mathematics if a particular sequence of concepts or problems is missed by a high percentage of the students encountering it, the transmission of this information to those who wrote the program is an obvious signal that changes are needed.

Surprising as it may seem, authors of textbooks in elementary mathematics seldom receive such information. They get many good and penetrating criticisms from teachers and other persons concerned with curriculum, but they seldom get hard behavioral data on individual parts of the text. Similarly, the evaluation that compares a given new text with a standard old text by looking at the achievement data for experimental and control groups is almost always far too coarse an evaluation to provide any focus for revising the particular features of the new text. On the other hand, the problems of gathering detailed data about an ordinary textbook are too onerous to be feasible in most cases.

Freedom in Education

The fourth and final issue I wish to discuss is the place of individuality and human freedom in a modern technological society. The crudest form of opposition to widespread use of technology in education and in other parts of society is to claim that we face the real danger of men becoming slaves to machines. This argument is ordinarily made in a romantic and naive fashion by those who seem themselves to have little understanding of science or technology and how it is used in our society. The blatant naiveté of some of these objections is well illustrated by the story of the man who was objecting to all forms of technology in our society and then interrupted his diatribe to say that he has to rush off to telephone about an appointment with his dentist.

No scientifically informed person seriously believes that our society could survive in anything like its present form without the widespread use of technology. It is our problem to understand how to use the technology and to benefit wisely from that use. Indeed, the claim about slavery is just the opposite of the true situation. It is only in this century that widespread use of slavery has been abolished, and it may be claimed by historians of the distant future that mankind could not do without slavery, because just as human slaves are being abolished, within a short time span they will be replaced by machine slaves whose use will not violate our ethical principles and moral sensibilities.

One can indeed imagine a historical text of 2500 to 3000 A.D. asserting that for a short period in the latter part of the twentieth century there was little slavery present on earth, but then it was discovered that machines could be made that could do all the work of human slaves, and so in the twenty-first century the luxury of slaves and the personal service they afforded was brought not to the privileged few as had historically been the case before the twentieth century, but as a standard convenience and luxury for all people on earth.

In our judgment, the threat of human individuality and freedom does not come from technology, but from another source that was well described by John Stuart Mill in his famous essay *On Liberty*. He said,

> The greatest difficulty to be encountered does not lie in the appreciation of means toward an acknowledged end, but in the indifference of persons in general to the end itself. If it were felt that the free development of individuality is one of the leading essentials of well-being; that it is not only a co-ordinate element with all that is designated by the terms civilization, instruction, education, culture, but is itself a necessary part and condition of all those things; there would be no danger that liberty should be undervalued, and the adjustment of the boundaries between it and social control would present no extraordinary difficulty.

Just as books freed serious students from the tyranny of overly simple methods of oral recitation, so computers can free students from the drudgery of doing exactly similar tasks unadjusted and untailored to their individual needs. As in the case of other parts of our society, our new and wondrous technology is there for beneficial use. It is our problem to learn how to use it well.

When a child of six begins to learn in school under the direction of a teacher, he hardly has a concept of a free intelligence able to reach objective knowledge of the world. He depends heavily upon every word and gesture of the teacher to guide his own reactions and responses. This intellectual weaning of children is a complicated process that we do not yet manage or understand very well. There are too many adults among us who are not able to express their own feelings or to reach their own independent judgments. We would claim that the wise use of technology and science, particularly in education, presents a major opportunity and challenge. We do not want to claim that we now know very much about how to realize the full potential of human beings; but we do not doubt that our modern instruments can be used to reduce the personal tyranny of one individual over another, and increase individual freedom.

INTELLECTUAL PROBLEMS OF THE FUTURE

Computers That Talk

Let me break this discussion of future intellectual problems into four parts that will take us back through some of the earlier technologies. The first problem is simply that of talking (oral speech). What does it take to get a computer to talk? The fact is that the technical issues are already pretty well in hand. Perhaps the reader has seen on television "The Forbin Project"—a movie about two large computers in the Soviet Union and the United States getting together to dominate the world. To those who have seen that movie, let me make a casual remark about talking. A technical criticism of the movie is that the two very large and sophisticated computers were conducting only one conversation at a time. Already in our computer system at Stanford, we have eighteen channels of independent simultaneous talk and the computer talks independently and differently to eighteen students at the same time. So you see, we have the capacity for the computer to talk. What we need, however, is better information about what is to be said. For example, when I serve as a tutor, teaching one of you, or even when one of you is teaching me, intuitively and naturally we follow cues and say things to each other without having an explicit theory of how we say what we say. We speak as part of our humanness, instinctively, on the basis of our past experience. But to satisfactorily talk with a computer, we need an explicit theory of talking.

Computers That Listen

The replacement of the written record, the kind of record that was objected to in Plato's *Phaedrus*, can be available to us in the talking computer. The other side of that coin which Socrates also emphasized, or should have emphasized, concerns listening. It is a much more difficult technical problem. The problem of designing a computer that can listen to a student talk is much harder than having a student listen to the computer talk. However, the problem is solvable.

The Use of Knowledge

To have an effective computer-based system of instruction, we must transcend mindless talking and listening and learn to understand and use a large knowledge base. For example, if we were simply to require information retrieval from a knowledge base, it would be relatively simple in the near future to put the entire American Library of Congress in every elementary school. The capacity to store information is increasing so rapidly that we will be able to store much more information than could ever possibly be used.

A different and more difficult question is how to get the student to interact with the sizable knowledge base. As we come to understand how to handle such a knowledge base, the school computer of the future should be able to answer any wayward question that the student might like to ask. Moreover, as we all know, once a student uses such a capability, he will have a strong tendency to pursue still further questions that are more difficult and more idiosyncratic. It will, I think, be wonderful to see how children interact with such a system; in all likelihood, we will see children give to learning the high degree of concentration and the sustained span of attention they now give to commercial television.

There is one related point I want to emphasize. From the very beginning of school, students learn quickly the "law of the land" and know they should not ask questions the teacher cannot answer. This task of diagnosing the limitations of teachers begins early and continues through college and graduate school. So, once we have the capacity for answering out-of-the-way questions, it will be marvelous to see how students will take advantage of the opportunity and test their own capacities with a relentlessness they dare not exhibit now.

Need for Theories of Learning and Instruction

The fourth problem, and in many ways the least-developed feature of this technology, is the development of an adequate theory of learning and instruction. We can make the computer talk, listen, and adequately handle a large knowledge data base, but we still need to develop an explicit theory of learning and instruction. In teaching a student, young or old, a given subject matter or a given skill, a computer-based learning system can keep a record of everything the student does. Such a system can gather an enormous amount of information about the student. The problem is how to use this information wisely, skillfully, and efficiently to teach the student. This is something that the very best human tutor does well, even though he does not understand at all how he does it, just as he does not understand how he talks. None of us understands how we talk and none of us understands how we intuitively interact with someone we are teaching on a one-to-one basis. Still, even though our past and present theories of instruction have not cut very deep, it does not mean that we have not made some progress. First, we at least recognize that there is a scientific problem; that alone is progress. One hundred fifty years ago there was no explicit recognition that there was even a problem. There is not stated in the education literature of 150 years ago any view that it is important to understand in detail the process of learning on the part of the student. Only in the twentieth century do we find any systematic data or any systematic theoretical ideas about the data. What precedes this period is romance and fantasy unsubstantiated by any sophisticated relation to evidence. So at least we can say that we have begun the task.

ALTERNATIVE EDUCATIONAL STRUCTURES

Let me give some examples of changes we can effect in the structure of educational institutions by using appropriately the new technology of computers and television. Because of my own special interest in computers, I shall concentrate on computer possibilities; but it should be understood that television would also be a component for the proposed changes in structure.

High Schools

My first example concerns the organization of high schools. An American phenomenon, much discussed in the history of education in the twentieth century, has been the introducton of the consolidated high school that brings together students from small schools to a centrally located large school that offers a variety of educational opportunities and resources to the students. The American consolidated high school is one of the glories of the history of education. Today, however, many of us feel that the large high school has become one of the most difficult institutions to deal with from a social standpoint. The mass aggregation of adolescents in one spot creates an environment that is on the one hand impersonal, and on the other potentially explosive, partly because of the large numbers of students and supervising adults in close quarters.

The use of our new technology will make possible an alternative structure that will return us to the small schools of the past. The ideal high school of the future may consist of no more than a hundred students and, in many cases, be located close to students' homes; it may be a specialized school, catering to students' particular interests. The variety of curriculum and other educational resources, such as libraries, that has been so important a feature of the consolidated high school, will be made available by computer and television technology. I should say in this connection that the changes that can be brought about through the use of computers are more drastic and more radical than those that can be effected only through television. The difference is the possibility of a high level of interaction between the computer program and the student, the sort of thing that is not possible with a standard televison lecture or laboratory demonstration.

Elementary Schools

My second example concerns alternatives to elementary schools. Through most of the history of civilization, young children have been taught primarily at home, often perhaps in an extended family group. We now have the technical possibility of returning the student to the home or to a small neighborhood group. Although these alternatives have not yet been thoroughly explored, it is important that discussion of their availability begin as early as possible. As far as I know, the new romantics in education have not discussed the radical possibility of dissolving elementary schools entirely and returning the child to the home—or to a neighborhood group of three or four homes—for his education.

In describing this possibility, let me emphasize that I am not maintaining that it is necessarily a wise move. I do, however, think it important that this technical possibility is now available. At the very least, it should be explored experimentally. By proper use of computer technology, the basic skills of reading, mathematics, and language arts can easily be brought to the student in the home or in a cluster of homes. Most of the elementary science curriculum also can be handled by computer. Other parts of the elementary science curriculum, of the social studies program, and much of the work in art and music could be handled by television. I envisage a situatuion in which a master teacher would divide his time among several units. The mothers of the children would assume responsibilities for supervision and some would work as teachers' aides. Such an approach would be completely natural, because of the proximity of the school to their homes. In many urban settings, for example, it would be natural to place classrooms in apartment complexes. In other districts, a small one-room building could be added, or it might even be feasible to pay a small rent to one of the families for the use of space in a home. The main thing to avoid is heavy capital expenditure for physical plants; we have had too much of this in the past.

Higher Education

The third alternative structure deals with higher education. Here the possibilities are perhaps the easiest to implement and may be realized sooner than the others. In the areas surrounding Stanford, several community colleges are already offering courses for credit by television. As we face the costs throughout the world of providing higher education for increasing numbers, the use of computers and television to reduce costs and to decentralize the educational effort seems almost inevitable. One can see terminals available in apartment complexes for students at the community-college level. At a later stage, one can envisage terminals in plants where employees work full-time, but also actively pursue their education. I should mention that in California, for example, a reasonable percentage of students in the state higher educational system are employed full-time, sumultaneously with their enrollment as students. The development of such a delivery system for higher education will also naturally answer demands for continuing education for adults. At a more distant date, one can expect the terminal resources described earlier to be available in the home for the teaching of a wide range of subjects, from foreign languages to advanced technical courses in science and mathematics.

I emphasize, however, that the problems of institutional change of the sort just discussed are poorly understood. There is evidence that universities, for example, are among the most conservative institutions in our society. In any case, the rapid development of alternative structures for education will be neither simple nor easy. On the other hand, the willingness of community colleges, which do not have a long tradition, to consider new methods of instruction and new approaches is encouraging. There are problems of prejudice and entrenchment, but there are also intellectual problems of understanding the kinds of organizaton we want for the future. The technology affords many possibilities, but we have not thought through which of these possibilities we consider the most advantageous, the most interesting, or the most exciting.

The central idea I have been stressing is that through computers we have the means to develop alternative structures that will effectively decentralize the present educational system. The issue of decentralization of services, of places of work, of almost all aspects of our life is gradually coming to the fore as a central social and political problem of the last part of the twentieth century. The issues involved in decentralizing education will be among the most significant of these problems of decentralization. The problems that face us are not really technological: they are conceptual, institutional, and social. I have certainly not made any concrete suggestions for tackling these problems; at most, I have tried to bring them to your attention.

UNIT IV

CLASSROOM TEACHING

1. THE ENVIRONMENT OF INSTRUCTION
The Function of Seatwork in a Commercially Developed Curriculum

Linda Anderson

> There! I didn't understand that, but I got it done.
>
> Donald, age six

In addition to death and taxes, we might include *seatwork* in elementary classrooms as a certainty in life, at least in present-day American schools. Think back to your own elementary school days. Remember the smell of the purple dittos? The excitement of a brand new workbook that would be your very own? The seemingly endless passage to be copied from the front board? They are all still there, although (at least in the author's memory) the ditto ink is now less pungent and the workbooks are more colorful.

A recent study of time use suggested that, in many classrooms, students may spend up to 70 percent of their allocated instructional time doing seatwork: reading or written tasks completed without immediate, direct teacher supervision (Fisher et al. 1978). Although individual products and individual effort are expected with seatwork assignments, such work is usually done in a social setting: that is, other students are doing seatwork at the same time, often working on the same assignment. This social setting affects how (and sometimes if) individual students complete their assignments.

The use of seatwork allows the teacher time to concentrate on face-to-face instruction with small groups and individuals. Another advantage of seatwork (at least when assignments are appropriate) is that students receive individual practice in applying skills and concepts. Thus, the pervasiveness of seatwork can be attributed to valid instructional goals.

The universality, frequency, and rationale of seatwork suggest that it is an appropriate topic for investigation. However, with the exception of studies focusing on "time on task," little research has been done on ways that seatwork affects students' learning. Time-on-task studies suggest that greater achievement on standardized tests occur when students spend more time engaged with tasks at appropriate levels of difficulty (Fisher et al: 1978); that seatwork settings typically yield less time on task than teacher-led small groups (Good and Beckerman 1978); and that teachers' management practices, including accountability for completed seatwork, affect the overall level of engaged time (Emmer and Evertson 1980).

Such findings are important because they confirm the bare minimum conditions that must exist if seatwork is to affect students' learning. Obviously, if students are not attentive to and engaged with their seatwork tasks, those tasks can have little effect.

However, given that students are on task and thus mentally engaged with seatwork, questions may be asked about the quality of that engagement: What mental processes occur while students are doing seatwork? How are these mental processes affected by variations in classroom and task structures? How do these mental processes that occur in response to daily assignments affect cumulative outcomes such as reading fluency?

This paper describes a study that addresses some of these questions about seatwork within the framework of a classroom environment using standard basal text approaches to instruction. While it was not focused on reading comprehension per se, the study *was* conducted during reading periods in

269

primary classrooms and therefore included whatever comprehension instruction occurred there. Because the study was limited in scope and population, it did not provide generalizable statements about relationships, but it did suggest some ways to look at and wonder about children's comprehension of seatwork and the effect of seatwork on cumulative comprehension skills.

BACKGROUND OF THE STUDY

The Student Responses to Classroom Instruction Study examined the "short-term" responses of children to daily classroom tasks, especially seatwork tasks. Some types of short-term responses are attention, initiative to participate, initiative to resolve difficulty, successful completion of tasks, and understanding of how and why to do daily assignments. The rationale for the study was that discrete experiences in response to instruction determine whether and how that instruction contributes to cumulative, or "long-term," outcomes, such as reading achievement (Anderson 1981). Two lines of research were influential in the design of the study. First, Doyle's (1980) work on the student as a mediator of instruction suggested that students' perceptions of classroom tasks (what is the goal, how is it reached, and what is risked in pursuing it) will determine *how* they select and use information from the classroom environment. The second line of work that led to the Student Response Study was teacher effectiveness research, especially investigations of more and less effective classroom managers, where a distinguishing feature was the teachers' apparent sensitivity to the students' attention, involvement, success, and need for information while instruction was proceeding (Anderson, Evertson, and Emmer 1979). More effective managers acted as if they believed that the student was indeed the critical mediator of their teaching, and thus they remained aware of indications that the students were responding in ways that facilitated learning.

SAMPLE

Eight first-grade classrooms in four Title I schools in an urban district were observed. Classrooms were selected on the basis of teacher willingness to participate. Ten teachers were approached, and eight were interested.

In each classroom, four target students (one male and one female high achiever, and one male and one female low achiever) were selected for focused observation from all students whose parents had given permission. During the year, two high-achieving females moved, resulting in a final sample of 30 target students. Achievement classifications were based on the teacher's report of reading group placements, because no entering test scores were available. Thus, the labels "high" and "low" refer to relative position within each classroom, not performance judged on a common scale.

All classrooms were self-contained and taught primarily by one teacher, although aides were present in four classes. In five of the eight classes, reading instruction was presented in small ability-based groups. In the other three classes, little or no group instruction was given, and the teacher met with individuals to hear them read. In all classes, however, students spent some time each day doing reading-related seatwork.

METHODOLOGY

The study produced detailed descriptions of the target students performing seatwork assignments at five different times during the year (usually at one-month intervals). Observations lasted about three hours, during which time an observer alternated her attention between two target students, usually switching from one to the other at ten- or 15-minute intervals. However, this time sampling method was used flexibly in order to see beginnings and endings of certain events. Several instructional settings were observed, but the data collected in seatwork settings are emphasized in this paper.

The observer took notes on what the target child did, what he or she seemed to be attending to, how seatwork was approached, what the student did when he or she encountered a problem, and how successful the student was. The observational record also included as much information as possible about instructional stimuli (teacher's movements, types of materials, role of other students). Copies of the seatwork were obtained or described in detail.

Teacher explanations of assignments were audio-recorded.

After an observation was completed, the observer taped a detailed narrative record of the morning's observation that included times. Also noted were the final performance of the child on assigned work that day and any teacher feedback that occurred while the observer was present.

The resulting data provided a very detailed record of the child's activities on a minute-to-minute basis. For example:

9:51　J. looks back at the board and writes "te" (copying *yesterday*) and then looks around some and then writes "day." all at once, without looking at the board for each letter. Then he glances over toward A, reading, but does not interact with her. (She is reading aloud "to herself," about three feet from J.).

9:52　He goes back to his writing and writes without distraction: "*Matt /ha/d*" (the slashes indicate where he looked up at the board while he was copying) and then looks up at S. (sitting across the table from him) as the teacher is elaborating on a fact in the story that S. has just read.

The observational data was supplemented with informal conversations with students about work done that morning, in order to tap the student's understanding of how and why he or she was doing the work. For example, the child might have been asked to "show me how to do this page" or "how did you know to choose this word instead of that word?" Questions designed to elicit the child's understandings of the purpose of the work were, "What are you learning about when you do this work?" and "Why do you think your teacher wanted you to do this page?"

RESULTS

Qualitative analyses so far have focused on questions about general trends and exceptions to those trends. That is, in what ways were the classrooms and the students similar to one another? In what ways were they different, and could these differences account for some students benefitting from seatwork more than others?

We have found among these eight classes and 30 students some notable similarities in the seatwork done and in the students' apparent understanding of why they are doing seatwork. In fact, these two patterns of similarity may be reflective of one another, as described below.

Despite the similarities across classes and students, significant differences among students were also apparent. There was a group of students whose responses to seatwork frequently were not facilitative of learning. This subgroup included at least one child from each class and sometimes two. In at least a third of their observations, they revealed a lack of understanding of the content or skills featured in the seatwork, and they used strategies that were not likely to strengthen their understanding. In general, they did not seem to "make sense" of their seatwork tasks in ways that might further their learning. Although not all the low achievers fell into this group, all members of the group were originally labeled as low achievers.

Recognizing the prevalence of these "poor responders," our analysis efforts have focused on describing an environment that may create and support such patterns of responses to seatwork. The first step in describing that environment was to look at what all classes and students had in common.

The Nature of the Work: Similarities across Classes

The seatwork used and the ways that it was assigned were similar across the eight classrooms. For example, in all classes, from 30 percent to 60 percent of the students' allocated reading instructional time was spent doing some form of seatwork related to reading. In most of the classes (all but one), there was a strong reliance on commercial workbooks and/or dittos taken from commercial packages. At least 50 percent and in some cases almost 100 percent of seatwork assignments were based on commercial products. In many cases, the workbooks, dittos, and readers were all part of the same basal series.

Most of the reading seatwork from the commercial materials observed in this study emphasized discrete reading skills, with each page emphasizing a single skill. For example, every sentence on a page might include a word that has a soft *g* sound.

In all eight classes, at least part and sometimes

all of the formal reading instruction consisted of moving in order through a reader, a reading workbook, or both. That is, the sequence of the book was important, and one book was completed before another one was begun.

Within each class, certain forms of seatwork assignments became very familiar to the students and were used from two to five times a week, although the classes differed on what forms were used. For example, there might always be a board exercise of the same form, in which students copied sentences with blanks and chose the correct word from several options. In other classes, certain forms of dittos or workbook sheets were used frequently, such as reading a sentence and then choosing one of three pictures that illustrate the meaning of that sentence. Thus, explicit explanations of assignments were not always given since the students had learned the usual procedures for certain forms.

In six of the eight classes, at least half of the seatwork assignments were given to the whole class. That is, all students, regardless of reading level, completed the same assignment.

Thus, the typical pattern revealed by these data shows classrooms where seatwork is a regular and unremarkable occurrence, where workbooks and associated dittos of familiar form are used to provide practice on reading skills, and where there are frequent occasions in which students can compare their progress with one another because of common assignments.

Students' Understanding of Why They Do Work: Similarities across Students

After careful review of all qualitative data, the research team concluded that for most of our target students, both low and high achievers, the most salient aspect of doing their seatwork is simply to get it done.

We began to form this impression as we observed students' behavior while doing seatwork. The following are examples of behavior that, when occurring repeatedly for the same students, indicated to us that they were concerned with getting their work finished:

- Frequent questions to peers about "How far are you?", and frequent statements of "I'm almost done—just two more" or "I'm ahead of you!"

- Upon completing the last item on a page, immediately turning it in or moving on to the next page without any indication of checking or reviewing.
- Completion of work accompanied by expressions of relief (e.g., a long sigh and "There!" as student is stacking papers, or as one student was overheard saying to himself. "There! I didn't understand it, but I got it done").

These behaviors by themselves do not necessarily mean that students are not also attending to the content-related purposes of the work. However, our "on-the-spot" interviews with the students support the behavioral observations.

Some students answered questions about "What are you learning?" in terms of broad skill areas: "I'm learning to read better" or "I'm learning how to write." We seldom received an answer that described specific skills being practiced or specific concepts being applied. This is in spite of the fact that most of the seatwork assignments for reading and math were designed to emphasize a particular skill. For example, one workbook page included five sentences that each included words ending in -ot (e.g., "Look out for the hot pot"). Students were to indicate a picture that illustrates the sentence (e.g., a boiling pot is chosen instead of a steaming pie or a frankfurter being roasted). When asked, "What are you learning about when you do this page?" a student responded, "How to read these sentences and draw circles around the right picture." There was no indication during this conversation that the student recognized the similarity among the sentences (i.e., all featured -ot words) or the specific content-related purpose of the page (i.e., to practice decoding words with -ot.) The few exceptions to this pattern occurred when short and long vowels were introduced. Here students said, "This page is about words with long *a* sounds." Perhaps the analysis of vowel sounds was enough of a novelty that students attended to that content when describing the page.

Taken altogether, the behavioral and student interview data suggested that while doing seatwork, these first-grade students perceive purpose in terms of "doing the work" and progressing through a book rather than understanding the specific content-related purposes of assignments. At this point, we are not saying that this is either desirable or undesirable, simply that this seems to be a prevalent pattern.

We can only speculate about reasons for this pattern of student response. Certainly the age and developmental level of the children should be taken into account, in that one would not expect first graders to give answers suggesting a grand scheme for analyzing reading skills or to have a firm set of concepts for thinking about their own learning processes.

Our observations of the teachers and their presentations of assignments have led us to consider an additional hypothesis. We think that students' perceptions of the purposes of seatwork may be related to the information that they receive from teachers about their work. Unfortunately we cannot test this hyothesis systematically with our present data because there is so little variance for either dependent or independent variables.

Teacher Communications about Seatwork: Similarities across Classes

The following characterized most instances of teacher communication about seatwork:

- Presentation or explanations of assignments seldom included statements about content-related purposes of the work (e.g., references to what will be learned or practiced and how that related to other learning).
- While students were working and teachers commented on their work, most comments concerned looking busy and finishing work rather than actual performance. Many of the teachers seemed to be monitoring student behavior but not student understanding or success while completing the assignment. This is probably because teachers were usually busy with instruction while other students did seatwork. Thus their communication about seatwork while it was being done was influenced by the teacher's immediate goals: to maintain a quiet working environment so that the teacher could concentrate on face-to-face instruction. This was appropriate in many cases (when students could gain from independent practice without constant monitoring), and we do not mean to imply otherwise. The point here is that the teacher's communications emphasized some-

thing other than understanding and accuracy while the work was in progress.

- Teachers very seldom focused on cognitive strategies when presenting seatwork assignments. For example, few statements were heard about ways of checking one's work for accuracy and meaningfulness, identifying areas of difficulty, or applying a general strategy to a particular type of task. Instead, teacher explanations were usually procedural (e.g., "Read the sentence and circle the word that goes in the blank," with no reminders about how to select the appropriate word).
- Most recorded instances of teacher feedback to seatwork included statements about correctness or neatness but seldom included questions or explanations of processes for figuring out the correct answer.

These patterns of teacher communication may have suggested to the students that seatwork is to be done as a routine part of the day, but little thought about it is necessary beyond the self-control needed to stay on task and finish one's work. Certainly the responses of the students reflected this perspective.

It is likely that for some assignments and some students, these kinds of communication are appropriate. If students are working on tasks of familiar form and have a good grasp of necessary cognitive strategies and are doing the assignment to increase speed and fluency, then it would be inefficient to dwell on explicit statements of purpose and strategies. However, students working on new task forms or students who are not at all fluent with a particular skill or concept might benefit from more specific content-related explanations, monitoring and feedback than was typically seen.

This suggestion is based on an anlysis of the subgroup of students whose responses to seatwork often seemed not to contribute to their learning and understanding. Having discussed what was the same about all teachers and students, we turn now to a discussion of the differences between students in their patterns of response.

Students Whose Responses to Seatwork Did Not Contribute to Increased Understanding

In reviewing the narrative records of all 30 students, the researchers were struck by the experiences of some of the low achievers. These students frequently did poorly on their assignments and were often observed to use strategies for deriving answers that allowed them to complete assignments without really understanding what they did (as was stated so explicitly by the child quoted at the beginning). Of special concern to us, especially after talking to the students about their work, was the lack of concern on their part about whether their work "made sense." Like all of the target students, they seemed to define their task in terms of finishing assignments, but because they frequently had difficulty reading and thinking at the level of the assignment, they were placed in a perplexing position: They had to complete the work, but they did not know how to do so in a completely meaningful way.

The students did not give up in frustration. Instead, they adapted to the environmental demands ("Finish your work") by developing and using a variety of strategies that helped them get finished. The major question that arises from these data is how these students' short-term adaptations and use of "getting finished" strategies may affect longer-term learning, especially learning of metacognitive skills such as comprehension monitoring and assessment of difficulty.

Some examples are provided below of students responding to seatwork in ways that did not further understanding. In each case, the student was working under two conditions. First, there was an emphasis on completing one's work on one's own, "keeping busy," and staying on task. Second, the assignment required skills and concepts that the child either lacked or did not understand well enough to use easily. We now believe that when these two conditions occur together, they lead to a pattern of responses that have undesirable long-term consequences.

Sally (a low-achieving target) is working on an assignment that requires her to copy sentences off the board, read them, and draw pictures to illustrate that she understands them (e.g., "The green car is coming down the road"). This is a familiar form of assignment in Sally's class, and all students are to work on it while the teacher meets reading groups. Sally copies a sentence correctly, looking at the board frequently, appearing to copy it letter by letter (rather than in words or phrases, as is usually done by higher achievers). When finished with a sentence, she looks at her neighbor's paper or asks a friend,

"What do we draw here?" The friend answers, "A green car." and Sally draws it. When the observer asked Sally to read the sentences, she could not. However, she was able to complete the paper in this fashion and thus go to lunch and recess (a consequence of not finishing was to stay in the room when the class left for lunch).

Considering the demands of the task as Sally perceived them (i.e., get all sentences copied and some pictures drawn before lunch), her strategy is reasonable. She had mastered letter-by-letter copying and managed to produce an acceptable paper without ever reading, which she did poorly.

Ron (a low-achieving target), along with all other students in his class, is to spend 30 minutes of allotted seatwork time composing a story about "My Family." The teacher has written some words on the board that students might want to use in writing their stories, although she emphasizes that spelling "does not count." Ron writes the following story by himself:

> You can be my brother.
> You can be my puppy.
> I like my pup.
> I like my father.
> I like my mother.
> I am happy.

When the observer asked him to read his story to her, he hesitated on the word *my* (because his *y* was not clearly a *y* and he read it as a *t*). He did not attempt to read the words *brother, puppy, pup, father,* or *mother*; instead he stared at each of them for several seconds and then asked what they were. After they finished reading his story, the observer asked him how he knew to write the word *father* when he wrote it. He pointed to the board and said, "I got it off there."

Ron had used his understanding of sentence structure and functions of various words to create an acceptable product. It was later marked "good" by the teacher, but there was no other feedback given. However, his inability to read what he had written suggested to us that the act of writing the story may have been driven by the need to "get it done" rather than an interest in communicating his thoughts about his family. This is post hoc conjecture, of course, but the incident is consistent with other observations of Ron when he behaved in ways that kept the teacher "off his case" and minimized academic and other contacts with her. His work was frequently difficult for him, but he always got it finished, usually with some incorrect answers. Conversations with him frequently revealed a lack of concepts or skills that were presumably necessary for the work given to him.

Sean (a low-achieving male) is in a class where students do "individualized" work. This means that all students proceed through the same reading and math books, but they "move at their own pace," according to the teacher. The pace seemed to be determined by how long it took each student to get through a page and get the teacher's attention for checking rather than the amount of time spent in instruction. Sean was assigned a page from his reading workbook that emphasized words ending in *-ake* (e.g., cake, make, take). There were six sentences to read and six pictures to match to them. The observer asked Sean to tell her about the page while he was doing it. He readily agreed and began reading aloud. He read most of the *-ake* words as *cake*, and most of his reading did not make sense due to frequent miscalls. However, he did not seem disturbed by the lack of sense of the sentences, and he quickly drew lines to whatever picture he thought went with it. He proceeded through the six sentences, getting three correct despite his misreading, although these correct answers were apparently flukes. For example, the first correct sentence done simply matched the picture closest to the sentence. (On the next assignment, Sean was observed using a similar "proximity" principle to determine the correct choice: Draw the shortest possible line.) The last sentence was done correctly without Sean even attempting to read the sentence because, as he explained, "There's only one picture left, so that's the answer." Coincidentally, it was the right one. Throughout this session, Sean did not indicate that he was aware that he was making errors nor did he demonstrate any concern that what he read was nonsense. As soon as he drew the line between the last sentence and picture, he immediately turned to the next page of his workbook and continued in a similar fashion.

CONCLUSION

Such incidents have led us to hypothesize that one result of a combination of inappropriate (i.e., too difficult) assignments and an emphasis on finishing

work may be that students come to define success on seatwork in terms of completion instead of understanding. This way of defining success may occur for all students, but is more likely to be detrimental to low students. The high achievers, because they were usually working at a higher level of success than were low achievers and thus were probably gaining more from the practice opportunities afforded by seatwork, may have come to expect their reading seatwork to make sense to them because it was more often assimilable (or at their "independent level"). If this pattern continues, it may help them develop adaptive learning-to-learn skills as they continue through school because when something does not make sense or seems confusing, it will be an unusual event. Therefore, it will be salient and likely to trigger action to reduce confusion, add necessary information, or both. This highlighting of unexpected misunderstanding may help further the development of metacognitive skills (which aid in information seeking to reduce confusion), even though formal classroom instruction seldom is focused on the development of such skills. Low achievers, whom we saw more often with assignments that were difficult for them, may be less likely to expect their work to "make sense." Because "sense" is not predictable, a lack of sense (i.e., recognizing that you do not understand) is not unusual. If something is not unusual, then it is not as likely to serve as a signal that something is wrong and needs resolution.

Other elements of classroom life are probably more predictable to low achievers than their assignments making sense. We think that the rewards and sanctions attached to finishing work and covering content are very predictable, at least in the classrooms we have observed. Given unpredictability about how easily assignments can be comprehended, it is not surprising that low achievers may focus their immediate goals while doing seatwork on the predictable elements, such as the need to "get it done" and move on. Over time, this approach may interfere with the development of metacognitive skills that allow students to become better guides of their own learning. Thus, higher achievers are more likely to learn more about how to learn from their assignments as they progress through school, contributing to a widening gap between higher and lower achievers over time. This phenomenon cannot be attributed entirely to the aptitude differences between high and low achievers (although those are influential).

The point here is that the history of a student's experiences with school tasks can influence expectations that assignments, text, activities, and so on can and should make sense, and these expectations in turn will influence a student's responses to instruction. While this has implications for instruction generally, it is particularly relevant to comprehension instruction. If reading is indeed a meaning-getting process, then instruction in comprehension must emphasize sense making. This study suggests that such sense making is not emphasized in classrooms where difficult seatwork comprises a significant amount of some students' instructional time in reading, and where finishing is emphasized as the immediate goal. Such an instructional environment minimizes, rather than expedites, sense making.

REFERENCES

Anderson, L. Short-term student responses to classroom instruction. *Elementary School Journal*, 1981, *82*, 97–108.

Anderson, L., Evertson, C., & Emmer, E. Dimensions of classroom management derived from recent research. *Journal of Curriculum Studies*, 1979.

Doyle, W. *Student mediating responses in teaching effectiveness*. Final Report, National Institute of Education Grant No. NIE-G-76-0099. Denton, Texas: Department of Education, North Texas State University, March 1980.

Emmer, E., & Evertson, C. *Effective management at the beginning of the school year in junior high classes*. R & D Rep. No. 6107. Austin: Research and Development Center for Teacher Education. The University of Texas at Austin, 1980.

Fisher, C., Berliner, D., Filby, N., Marliave, R., Cohen, L., Dishaw, M., & Moore, J. *Teaching and learning in elementary schools: A summary of the beginning teacher evaluation study*. San Francisco: Far West Laboratory for Educational Research and Development, 1978.

Good, T., & Beckerman, T. Time on task: A naturalistic study in sixth-grade classrooms. *Elementary School Journal*, 1978, 78, 193–201.

Publication of this work is sponsored by the Institute for Research on Teaching, College of Education, Michigan State University. The Institute for Research on Teaching is funded primarily by the Program for Teaching and Instruction of the National Institute of Education, United States Department of Education. The opinions expressed in this publication do not necessarily reflect the position, policy, or endorsement of the National Institute of Education. (NIE Contract No. 400-81-0014 and NIE Grant No. 90840.) This work was done in collaboration with Gerald Duffy, Nancy Brubaker, and Janet Alleman-Brooks. Their contributions and participation are gratefully acknowledged.

2. ATTENTION, TASKS AND TIME

Lorin W. Anderson

Every one knows what attention is. It is the taking possession of the mind, in clear and vivid form, of one out of what seem several simultaneously possible objects or trains of thought. Focalization, concentration, of consciousness are of its essence. It implies withdrawal of some things in order to deal effectively with others. (James, 1890, 403–4)

While everyone 'knows what attention is', the importance of attention in classroom instruction and school learning is overlooked from time to time. With the current interest in academically engaged time, or time-on-task, the flame of student attention has been rekindled. Unfortunately, in this rekindling many educators have focused exclusively on *time*

without a complementary focusing on what it means for students to be *engaged* or *on-task*. The purpose of this chapter is to refocus attention on attention. . . .

CLASSROOMS, TASKS AND ATTENTION: A PERSPECTIVE

'Trying to observe instruction in an active first-grade classroom can be a humbling experience. So much is going on and the distractions are so many, the wonder is that teacher and student make any sense of the situation' (Piontkowski and Calfee, 1979, p.

297). The complexity of life in classrooms has been brilliantly documented by Jackson (1968). This complexity stems from two sources: the social psychological aspects of the classroom, and the nature of the learning tasks. Let us consider each in turn.

In 1953 Cherry conducted a study of attention within the framework of what he referred to as the 'cocktail party problem'.

> The cocktail party serves as a fine example of selective attention. We stand in a crowded room with sounds and conversations all about us. Often the conversation to which we are trying to listen is not the one in which we are supposedly taking part. (Norman, 1969, p. 13)

In many ways life in classrooms resembles a cocktail party. . . .

Students 'tune in' to certain classroom events, and then either 'tune in' to other events or literally 'tune in(ward)' to spend some time 'day-dreaming'. A student may listen to a teacher for a period of time, pay attention to a note received from a friend, and then think about the party to which the note invites him or her. Similarly, a student working with one group of students in the classroom may become interested in the discussions taking place in another group of students.

From a social psychological perspective, then, classrooms are extremely complex entities. The number of students, the number of groups, the climate of the classroom, and the variety of remembrances and future plans of the students all combine to produce this complexity. Incredibly, in the midst of all of this social psychological complexity, students are expected to learn something. In more technical terms students are expected to accomplish a set or series of *learning tasks*.

Doyle (1979a, 1979b) defines a task as a goal to be accomplished and a set of operations related to the attainment of that goal. Similarly, Carroll (1963) defines a learning task as the 'the learner's task of going from ignorance of some specified fact or concept to knowledge of it, or of proceeding from incapability of performing some specified act to capability of performing it' (p. 723). A learning task, then, has two parts: (1) a goal, objective, or desired outcome (not already attained or achieved), and (2) a set of mental and/or physical operations which must be performed in order to achieve the goal, objective, or desired outcome.

Several characteristics of a learning task effect its complexity. First the goal can be complex. Learning to memorize pairs of objects (e.g., states-capitals, poems-poets), make appropriate inferences about information contained in prose passages, solve mathematical word problems and write coherent essays are difficult goals for many students to achieve. Secondly, the operations may be difficult to perform. Solving mathematical word problems, for example, becomes even more difficult for students who cannot perform the mental operations necessary to read and understand the material in which the problem is embedded, or have not mastered the required algorithms. Similarly, writing coherent paragraphs becomes increasingly difficult for students who have not mastered the psychomotor activity of cursive writing. Thirdly, the nature of the task itself may not be clear. The student may not understand either what the goal actually is, or how the goal is to be accomplished (that is, the operations that should be performed in order to accomplish the goal).

Finally, the complexity of life in classrooms would appear to be geometrically increased when both sources of complexity (that is, the social psychological aspects of the classroom and the difficulty of the learning task) are in operation at the same time. In an *unruly classroom*, for example, students working at a *difficult learning task* must feel overwhelmed and frustrated. It can come as no surprise that attention is removed from the learning task and shifted to external events (e.g., the causes of the unruliness[)] or internal thoughts and dreams. . . .

AN HISTORICAL PERSPECTIVE ON ATTENTION AND LEARNING

. . . The importance of attention for learning was highlighted in the latter part of the nineteenth century and the early part of the twentieth century. In what is commonly accepted as the first psychology textbook, William James (1890) devoted fully fifty-seven pages to the concept of attention. Concerning the attention-learning relationship James wrote 'my experience is what I agree to attend to. Only those items which I notice shape my mind' (p. 402). Educator Harry Wheat (1931) actually defined learning in terms of attention: 'Learning is the activity of giving attention effectively to the essential phases of a situation' (p. 1). He continued, 'it may be said that, other things being equal, the amount or the quality of learning is in direct proportion to the effectiveness of the attention which the learner is induced to give' (p. 12). Henry Morrison (1926) stated the converse of Wheat's proposition when he wrote: 'perhaps the commonest cause of non-learning is poor attention' (p. 82).

Two general types of attention were differentiated by these early writers: selective attention and sustained attention. Both types are alluded to in the James's quote which began this chapter. In simplest terms, *selective attention involved focalization; sustained attention involved concentration.* In essence, selective attention referred to the focusing of the mind on one object, event, or idea at the expense or exclusion of others. Once a particular object, event, or idea was selected for attention, that attention had to be sustained on the object, event, or idea for sufficient periods of time if adequate learning was to occur. In Morrison's (1926) words, sustained attention extends over a fairly lengthy period of time 'with only occasional and momentary intermissions' (p. 104). . . .

Given the strength of the hypothesized attention-learning relationship, it is not surprising that implications for pedagogy were frequently discussed by writers of this era. In fact, Wheat (1931) defined teaching as 'the activity of *directing* attention effectively to the *essential* phases of a situation' (p. 1) (my italics). Some sixty years earlier Currie (1869) suggested that the

> art of teaching . . . comprehends all of the means by which the teacher *sustains* the attention of his class. By attention, we do not mean the mere absence of noise and trifling[.] . . . The only satisfactory attention is that which is given voluntarily and steadily . . . during instruction. (p. 264) (my italics)

. . . What are some of the means by which teachers could direct and sustain the attention of their students? Currie (1869) suggested that 'attention requires clear and unwavering exposition of the points to be attended to' (p. 92). Wheat (1931)

elaborated on Currie's suggestion. 'It makes little difference how effectively the teacher may direct attention or how effectively the pupil may give his attention; if the attention is fixed upon non-essentials, the intended learning will not take place' (p. 8). . . .

James (1890) suggested a second pedagogical principle:

> The only general pedagogic maxim bearing on attention is that the more interest the child has in advance in the subject, the better he will attend. Induct him therefore in such a way to knit each new thing on to some acquisition already there; and if possible awaken curiosity, so that the new thing shall seem to come as an answer, or part of an answer, to a question pre-existing in his mind. (p. 424)

. . . In addition to the above two principles, Currie (1869) proposed a set of 'motives' for securing attention.

> We can not secure attention by mere compulsion[.] . . . We must gain consent to the effort by suitable motives, and work with the law of habit to strengthen the power. The motives on which we must rely are mainly these: curiosity, love of activity, and sympathy. (p. 90)

. . . Finally,

> [S]ympathy is another guarantee for attention; which will exist in the pupil in proportion to the kind and degree of personal ascendency which the teacher has obtained. If this be well established, the child will make great efforts to enter into the work of the teacher, both from his instinct of imitation, and the happiness he derives from sympathy. (p. 91)

. . . Finally, Morrison (1926) suggested there were, in fact, pedagogical techniques (in addition to pedagogical principles and motives) that were appropriate for securing and holding students' attention. Such pedagogical techniques, which Morrison referred to as 'control techniques', were believed to be necessary because not all learning had its 'own initial appeal' (p. 104). In Morrison's words,

> many of the essential elements of learning are not initially appealing to all pupils, and perhaps some elements lack this quality entirely. It is conceivable that the program of study might be so skillfully arranged and teaching so aptly applied that all normal

pupils would grow from interest to interest and spend their school days in a delightful career of self-motivated studies. Such an ideal school would, however, be useless unless it were the introduction to a self-motivated world. Quite the contrary, the world in which we have to live and find our happiness is full of duties and opportunities which are far from initially interesting, and the individual who has learned to react only to that which is self-motivated becomes a flabby incompetent in the world of realities. (p. 104)

. . . Despite his emphasis on control techniques, Morrison was quick to point out the limits of exclusive reliance on good control techniques in order to produce good learning.

While poor control techniques always mean poor learning, good control technique does not necessarily mean good teaching. The material itself may be unsuitable and even false. It may be wrongly placed in the pupil's program of study[.] . . . Control technique is of primary importance but not necessarily of chief or ultimate importance. (p. 111)

. . . Historically, then, attention has been seen as a necessary condition for learning. More specifically, if learning was to occur learners must first have focused their attention on what they wished (or were expected) to learn. Secondly, that attention must have been sustained for sufficient periods of time. Furthermore, the teacher's role was defined in terms of the learner's role. Put simply, teachers were expected to *direct* and *maintain* the attention of their students.

THE MODERN PERSPECTIVE ON ATTENTION AND LEARNING

Psychologists and psycholinguists have conducted a number of empirical investigations of attention and learning over the past quarter century. Interestingly, the assumptions underlying these studies are similar to the major propositions concerning attention and learning advanced by the early educators and psychologists. What these studies have done is to provide empirical support for the validity of many of these early propositions while at the same time expanding our understanding of the nature of attention and learning as independent constructs in the context of classroom teaching and learning. . . .

As recently as 1979 Piontkowski and Calfee found it necessary to assert that 'attention is critical to learning. If the student isn't paying attention to instruction, he won't profit from it' (p. 317). Similarly, Underwood (1976) suggested that 'unless we attend to a stimulus we are unable to remember and respond to it' (p. 169). Finally, Rothkopf (1970) contended that 'in most instructional situations, what is learned depends largely on the activities of the student' (p. 325). Rothkopf coined the phrase 'mathemagenic behaviours' to refer to such activities, a phrase which emphasizes that these activities or behaviours of the student give 'birth to learning'. In 1976 Rothkopf went a step further in relating attention to learning from written materials.

The most carefully written and edited text will not produce the desired instructional results unless the student acts in a suitable way. The student has complete veto power over the success of written instruction. The student also has the opportunity to extend its scope substantially. (p. 94)

It is somewhat comforting to note that the attention-learning relationship is still strong and essential after all these years.

The concern of teachers for student attention also remains virtually the same as it was in the early 1900s. Consider Jackson's (1968) perspective on what teachers are trying to accomplish in their classrooms.

Certainly no educational goals are more immediate than those that concern the *establishment* and *maintenance* of the students' absorption in the task at hand. Almost all other objectives are dependent for their accomplishment upon the atainment of this basic condition. (p. 85) (my italics)

Then Jackson adds, almost ruefully, 'this fact seems to have been more appreciated in the past than it is today' (p. 85).

In choosing activites and materials for use by students Jackson suggests that teachers seem to be

making some kind of educated guess about what would be a beneficial activity for a student or group of students and then doing whatever is necessary to see that participants remained involved in that activity. The teacher's goal, in other words, is student involvement rather than student learning. It is true, of course, that the teacher hopes the involvement will result in certain beneficial changes in the students, but learning is in this sense a by-product rather than the things about which the teacher is most directly concerned (p. 162).

. . . As can be seen the basic assumptions concerning the attention-learning and the teaching-attention relationships have changed little over the past 75 years. None the less, the modern emphasis on empiricism has lent support to these more philosophically based contentions while at the same time broadening our understanding of the nature of the complex interrelationships among the teaching, attention and learning that occur in school. . . .

While early psychologists and educators had identified *two* phases of attention—selective and sustained—modern theorists and researchers have agreed that there are, in fact, *three* phases of attention. Rothkopf (1970), for example, describes what he terms three forms or classes of mathemagenic activities or behaviours. The first class is *orientation*, which refers to students being in the 'vicinity of instructional objects' (p. 328) and remaining there for suitable periods of time. The second class is *object acquisition*, which refers to 'selecting and procuring appropriate instructional objects' (p. 328). The final class is labelled *translating and processing*, which refers to 'scanning and systematic eye fixations on the instruction objects', 'translation into internal speech or internal representation', and 'discrimination, segmentation, processing, etc.' (p. 328).

Calfee (1981), attempting to synthesize the research of physiological and behavioural psychologists, also identified three phases:

1. Alertness—the general level of awareness and sensitivity to the environment;
2. Selectivity—the scanning of the environment in search of salient and goal-appropriate features;
3. Concentration—the focal act of attention, where selected elements are analyzed in detail. (p. 13)

Depending on the perspective of the particular research or theorist various synonyms exist for each of Calfee's labels. Orientation (Rothkopf, 1970) and arousal (Pribram and McGuiness, 1975) are similar in meaning to alertness. Activation (Pribram and

McGuiness, 1975) is used by the physiological psychologists in place of selectivity. Finally, effort (Pribram and McGuiness, 1975; Kahneman, 1973) and central processing (Posner and Boies, 1971) are virtually identical with concentration. And, of course, *selectivity* is similar to the older concept of *selective attention*, while *concentration* is similar to the older concept of *sustained attention*.

We also have begun to understand more about the nature of these three attentional phases, particularly selectivity or selective attention. We have learned, for example, that 'the human information-processing system can concentrate on only a small number of elements at one point in time. The mind must choose continuously what to think about and how deeply to think about it' (Calfee, 1981, p. 11). . . .

We also have learned that concentration may or may not be necessary. Cognitive psychologists such as Neisser (1967) and physiological psychologists such as Pribram and McGuiness (1975) have proposed two levels of human information processing. While Neisser refers to these levels as preattentive and focal, Pribram and McGuiness refer to them as automatic processing and mental effort. The difference between these two levels has been stated succinctly by Piontkowski and Calfee (1981).

Preattentive or automatic processing occurs when properties of the stimulus are familiar and readily linked to experience, when they are noticed quickly and *without noticeable concentration*[.] . . . On the other hand, focal attention takes time and intellectual effort, and often intrudes on consciousness. Only one or two tasks that require focal attention can be handled simultaneously, and anything else going on at the same time is disregarded. (p. 315) (my italics)

Thus automaticity greatly reduces, or may eliminate entirely, the need for concentration. In fact, LaBerge (1975) defines automaticity in terms of the 'gradual elimination of attention in the processing of informatin' (p. 58). In addition, Norman (1976) suggests that automaticity results from extensive practice. 'A general rule appears to be that when a skill is highly learned—perhaps because it has been practiced for years and years—then it becomes automated, requiring little conscious awareness, little allocation of mental effort' (p. 65). . . .

In many ways the implications for teaching that

can be derived from this conceptualization of attention are simple and straightforward. Teachers need to, first, generate a general level of alertness or arousal on the part of their students. Secondaly, teachers need to direct students' attention to the relevant features or elements of the instructional task, material and learning experiences so as to ensure that students are on-target or on-task. Thirdly, teachers must help or encourage students to put forth the mental effort, when necessary, so that desired learning outcome or product can be acquired by the students.

Fortuntely, some ideas on how teachers can perform these teaching tasks have been generated from fairly recent research studies. Introducing variety into the learning tasks keeps students alert.

> Livening a lecture with humor, posing a cut-and-dried problem in a new way, confronting students with unexpected questions, changing the art work on the walls, introducing variety into the schedule—all these make the classroom situation more interesting, novel, and stimulating (Piontowski and Calfee, 1981, p. 303)

Similarly, providing feedback about task performance maintains student attention. Students pay attention when they are informed periodically of their progress.

Furthermore, as has been indicated earlier, focusing student attention selectively requires that the teacher point out the significant features of instructionally relevant tasks, materials, objects and situations. The teacher can do this in several ways. The teacher can, for example:

1. Emphasize critical features of a stimulus. The different parts of a chart on blood circulation becomes distinct when each is given its own bright color.
2. Eliminate irrelevant features. In Britten's *Young Person's Guide to the Orchestra* each musical instrument has its solo moment in the concerto, when its unique sound is emphasized and all other instruments are muted.
3. Put an old stimulus in a new context. The rubbish in a local stream goes unnoticed normally, but collected and piled at the front of the classroom it becomes impressive. (Piontkowski and Calfee, 1979, p. 307)

Concentration or mental effort appears to be related to the difficulty of the task and the enjoyment in performing the task (Laffey, 1982). As a consequence, tasks should be assigned to students that they (the students) feel able to deal with comfortably and effectively. Similarly, students should enjoy engaging in the assigned tasks. Maintaining student effort or concentration also requires effective monitoring on the part of the teacher. Given the number of internal and external distractions of students in classrooms, teachers should periodically check student attention (via classroom questions and informal observation) and learning (via exercises, homework and formal tests), and redirect student attention back to the relevant features of the task as necessary. Supervising seatwork and effectively managing classrooms are two additional examples of monitoring.

If we examine the recommendations offered by our present educators, researchers and psychologists, and compare them with those offered by the earlier educators and psychologists, the similarities are striking (see Table [1]). The necessity of focusing attention on appropriate tasks and directing attention to the critical features of those tasks is viewed as essential by both early and modern educators. Similarly, the need to make the new learning relevant, yet challenging, is supported by both early and modern educators. Finally, both early and modern educators realize the need to minimize the interference of external factors on the internal state of the learner(s).

The differences between the two groups of educators reside in two general areas. Early educators emphasized the need for the teachers to 'establish personal relationships with students'. Modern educators, on the other hand, realize the need to 'provide feedback (to the students) about task performance'. Thus, early educators advocated more *emotional* linkages between teacher and student; modern educators suggest the use of more *objective* means of enhancing student attention. . . .

TIME-ON-TASK AND STUDENT ENGAGED TIME

During the decade of the 1970s the importance of instructional and learning time was increasingly

TABLE [1].   A Comparison of Recommendations Concerning the Gaining, Directing and Sustaining of Attention

EARLY VIEW	MODERN VIEW
1. Assign tasks that are appropriate to the learner	Assign tasks that students feel able to deal with comfortably and effectively
2. Assign interesting tasks	Introduce variety into learning tasks; assign enjoyable tasks
3. Focus attention on relevant aspects of situation, material, and activities	Point out significant features of instructionally relevant materials, objects, and situations
4. Relate new learning to prior learning	Match new material with already learned material . . .
5. Arouse curiosity	Introduce the ambiguous, unexpected; introduce variety into the schedule
6. Establish personal relationships with students	———
7. Control physical conditions under which learning goes on	———
8. Reduce mechanical detail of class conduct to a minimum	Monitor student behaviour and learning
9. ———	Provide feedback about task performance

emphasized. Beginning with the publication of Carroll's (1963) 'A Model of School Learning', continuing with Bloom's (1974) treatise on 'Time and Learning', and culminating conceptually in Harnischfeger's and Wiley's (1976) expansion of the Carroll model, and empirically with the results of the Beginning Teacher Evaluation Study (Fisher, Filby, Marliave, Cahen, Dishaw, Moore and Berliner, 1978; Denham and Lieberman, 1980), the crucial role of time in learning has come to be accepted by theoreticians, researchers and practitioners alike.

Fortunately, this increased awareness and acceptance has not been without its critics. Gage (1978), for example, referred to academic learning time as a 'psychologically empty quantitative concept' (p. 75). Stallings (1980) indicated the need to move "beyond time on task" (p. 11). Frymier (1981) suggested in the title of his essay that 'learning takes more than time-on-task' (p. 634). Finally, McNamara (1981) contended that advocacy of time-on-task was more ideologically based than research based.

In several respects, most of which were addressed in the earlier sections of this chapter, these critics are correct. Without a concern for, and an understanding of, the attentional processes which occur while students are engaged in learning, student engaged time *is* a 'psychologically empty quantitative concept'. Put simply, the concept of attention gives meaning to the term 'engaged'. It is *engaged time*, not simply *time* that is essential to student learning. This fact, however, was clearly pointed out by Carroll (1963) in his original paper.

> First, it should be understood that 'spending time' means *actually spending time on the act of learning*. 'Time' is therefore not 'elapsed time' but the time which the person is oriented to the learning task and actively engaged in learning. In common parlance, it is the time during which he is 'paying attention' and 'trying to learn' (p. 725) (my italics).

Thus, according to Carroll, the processes or orientation, selectivity, and concentration are critical features of 'spending time'.

Similarly, there must be an academic task to which students are expected to attend, become engaged, and ultimately accomplish if time-on-task is to be meaningful. One of Frymier's (1981) major criticisms of time-on-task is that the materials on which students spend their time are largely unrelated to any meaningful learning outcome.

> What is the task on which the student spends time? Almost always it involves some type of curriculum material: textbook, workbook, filmstrip, ditto sheet, or experiences with materials of various kinds. Almost never are students expected (or even allowed) simply to think, reflect, create, contemplate, or conjure up ideas on their own. One explanation for the generalization that time on task is directly related to achievement may be a function of the fact that, when the task itself requires the learner

to make sense out of meaningless curriculum materials, more time results in more learning (p. 634).

Frymier continues: 'most of us like to believe that teachers specify objectives, select curriculum materials, and then contrive educational experiences for their students, in that order. Nothing could be further from the truth. Most teachers *start* with the curriculum materials' (p. 634). What Frymier stops short of saying is that many teachers who begin with the curriculum materials fail to align the materials and educational experiences with *any* learning objective or with any *specific* learning objective. Without such an alignment, learning tasks as defined by both Carroll (1963) and Doyle (1979a, 1979b) simply *do not exist*. And, if learning tasks do not exist, *students cannot be on-task*.

Doyle (1979a) highlights the need for such an alignment of materials and learning experiences (or activities) with learning goals or objectives when he differentiates time-on-task from time-on-activity. Doyle (1979a) defines activities as 'bounded segments of classroom time, for example, seatwork, tests, small-group discussion, lecture, recitation, reading' (p. 45). Quite clearly the various types of curricular materials identified by Frymier are embedded within these various activities. Doyle makes explicit the relationship between activities and tasks when he states that 'a task gives meaning to an activity by connecting elements within that activity to a purpose' (p. 45). Thus, without proper alignment of goals with activities (and, by association, with curriculum materials), the activities and materials are in fact meaningless, as Frymier suggests. Doyle (1979a) alludes to the importance of the alignment of goals, activities, and curriculum materials in a footnote. 'Most studies of teaching focus on activities rather than tasks[.] . . . As the terms are being used here, it is more appropriate, for example, to speak of "time on activity" than "time on task" ' (p. 46).

Frymier and another critic, McNamara (1981), also maintain that the tasks must be both appropriate for, and comprehensible to, the students. Frymier suggests that

> trying to comprehend the curriculum materials available in many schools today is like trying to read a dictionary, item by item, page by page. The information is technically correct and factually accurate, in the main, but it is basically meaningless because the possibilities for relating what is there to a

learner's past experience are incidental or non-existent (p. 634).

Similarly, McNamara (1981) contends that

> the result of this sort of research [namely, the Beginning Teacher Evaluation Study] is an enervating, *artificial curriculum* in which highly structured, mechanical learning is geared to rigid, formal testing[.] . . . It is important that children learn basic skills and that teachers foster their learning but their education must be more than the narrow, mechanistic, *dull* curriculum implicit and explicit in the time-on-task investigations. (p. 295) (my italics)

Just as the criticism of Gage addresses the need to analyze 'what learning processes go on during academic learning time' (p. 75) (that is, the need to be concerned with the term *engaged* in the phrase 'student-engaged time'), the criticisms of Frymier and McNamara focus on the term *task* in the phrase time-on-task. For time-on-task to make sense there must be clearly defined tasks (that is, alignments of goals, curriculum materials and learning experiences) which must be appropriate for and meaningful to the students. Until there is a task, until the students attention is given or directed to the key features of the task, and until that attention is sustained through the use of the appropriate curriculum materials and learning experiences, both student engaged time and time-on-task are, in fact, psychological and pedagogically 'empty'. In light of this discussion the consistent finding that there *is* a substantial positive relationship between time-on-task and student achievement should be *surprising*, not *expected*. . . .

THE FUTURE OF ATTENTION, TASK AND TIME

The assignment (or selection) of appropriate tasks and the provision of sufficient time in which to accomplish those tasks are two key features of effective classroom instruction. Appropriate attentional processes serve to help learners use time efficiently and enhance the likelihood of task accomplishment. Thus, it behoves teachers to assign appropriate tasks, provide sufficient time for students to learn, and find ways of activating the attentional processes.

Increased understanding of the concept of attention, both from a psychological and pedagogical perspective, is quite likely in the near future. More sophisticated instruments for examining attention and more tightly designed research studies for discovering the nature of attention will very likely emerge in the next two decades to lead to this increased understanding.

In contrast however, the likelihood that *appropriate tasks will be assigned* and that *sufficient time for acquiring the tasks will be allocated* appears small. With regard to the concept of tasks, for example, Carroll (1963) wrote that:

> in actual school practice, the various tasks to be learned are not necessarily *treated as* separate and distinct, and the process of teaching is often organized (*whether rightly so or not*) so that learning will take place 'incidentally' and in the course of other activities. (p. 724) (my italics)

Quite simply, teachers do not think in terms of tasks.

The research on teacher planning (e.g. Clark and Yinger, 1979; Shavelson and Stern, 1981) suggests that the subject-matter content and related instructional activities, *not* instructional objectives, are the basic unit of teaching planning. Frymier's (1981) comment that teachers begin with curriculum materials, not with instructional objectives, coincides with the results of this research. Students will very likely continue to engage in learning experiences and use a variety of curricular materials but precisely *what they are to learn from the experiences and materials will very likely remain unclear to both students and teachers*. Until teachers come to view learning tasks as their primary unit of instructional planning and delivery, little will change.

Furthermore, the provision of sufficient time to ensure excellence in learning also is unlikely. Two reasons can be given for this speculation. First, we know very little about the amount of time that is needed for even the brightest or fastest student to accomplish the goals contained in fairly complex learning tasks (e.g. inferring a main idea of a passage containing several paragraphs). Until we gather information about the amount of time needed to learn (which, by the way, is the denominator of Carroll's (1963) algebraic representation of his model), attempts to provide sufficient time to learn will be arbitrary and futile.

Secondly, the vast majority of schools and teachers appear to be far more concerned with *coverge* of material than *mastery* of specific learning tasks. In view of the fact that the amount of time allocated to schooling has changed very little over the past century (e.g. 180 days per year, 6 hours per day) while the amount of knowledge and number of skills available to be taught to students has increased dramatically, there simply is more to cover than there used to be. Until some order is brought out of the chaos of coverage by establishing priorities among the possible learning tasks, time will continue to be allocated to an increasing number of objectives or content areas, with insufficient time being allocated to any given objective or content area.

Despite this negative view of the future, the concept of time-on-task or student engaged time remains central to the learning of a large number of students in a variety of classrooms. Increased understanding of the concept, wise application of it to classroom practice, and constructive criticism of both the concept and its application should result in the continued inclusion of attention, time, and task in any comprehensive model of school learning.

REFERENCES

Bloom, B. S. (1974) 'Time and Learning', *American Psychologist*, *29*, 682–8

Broadbent, D. E. (1977) 'The Hidden Preattentive Processes', *American Psychologist*, *32*, 109–18

Calfee, R. C. (1981) 'Cognitive Psychology and Educational Practice' in D. C. Berliner (ed.), *Review of Research in Education*, *Volume 9*, Washington: American Educational Research Association

Carroll, J. B. (1963) 'A Model of School Learning', *Teachers College Record*, *64*, 723–33

Cherry, E. C. (1953) 'Some Experiments on the Recognition of Speech, with One and with Two Ears', *Journal of the Acoustical Society of America*, *25*, 975–9

Clark, C. and Yinger, R. (1979) 'Teachers' Thinking' in P. Peterson and H. Walberg (eds.), *Research on Teaching*, Berkeley: McCutchan Publishing

Currie, J. (1869) *The Principles and Practice of Common-school Education*, Edinburgh: Thomas Laurie

Denham, C. and Lieberman, A. (1980) *Time to Learn*, Washington: National Institute of Education

Doyle, W. (1979a) 'Making Managerial Decisions in Classrooms' in D. Duke (ed.), *Classroom Management*, Chicago: University of Chicago Press

——— (1979b) 'Classroom Tasks and Students' Abilities' in P. Peterson and H. Walberg (eds.), *Research on Teaching*, Berkeley: McCutchan Publishing

Fisher, C. W., Filby, N., Marliave, R., Cahen, L., Dishaw, M., Moore, J. and Berliner, D. (1978) *Teaching and Learning in the Elementary School: A Summary of the Beginning Teacher Evaluation Study, Report VII-1*. San Francisco: Far West Laboratory for Educational Research and Development

Frymier, J. (1981) 'Learning Takes More Than Time on Task', *Educational Leadership*, *38*, 634, 649

Gage, N. L. (1978) *The Scientific Basis of the Art of Teaching*, New York: Teachers College Press

Harnischfeger, A. and Wiley, D. E. (1976) 'The Teaching-Learning Process in Elementary Schools: A Synoptic View', *Curriculum Enquiry*, *6*, 5–43

Hecht, L. (1978) 'Measuring Student Behavior during Group Instruction', *Journal of Educational Research*, *71*, 283–90

Hudgins, B. B. (1967) 'Attending and Thinking in the Classroom', *Psychology in the Schools*, *4*, 211–16

Jackson, P. W. (1968) *Life in Classrooms*, New York: Holt, Rinehart & Winston

James, W. (1890) *The Principles of Psychology, Volume 1*, New York: Henry Holt & Co.

Judd, C. H. (1918) *Introduction to the Scientific Study of Education*, Boston: Ginn & Co.

Kahneman, D. (1973) *Attention and Effort*, Englewood Cliffs, NY: Prentice-Hall

LaBerge, D. (1975) 'Acquisition of Automatic Processing in Perceptual and Associative Learning' in P. M. A. Rabbit and S. Dornic (eds.), *Attention and Performance*, London: Academic Press

Laffey, J. M. (1982) 'The Assessment of Involvement with School Work among Urban High School Students', *Journal of Educational Psychology*, *74*, 62–71

McNamara, D. R. (1981) 'Attention, Time-on-Task and Children's Learning: Research or Ideology? *Journal of Education for Teaching*, *7*, 284–97

Merritt, M. (1982) 'Distributing and Directing Attention in Primary Classrooms' in L. C. Wilkerson (ed.), *Communicating in the Classroom*, New York: Academic Press.

Morrison, H. C. (1926) *The Practice of Teaching in the Secondary School*, Chicago: University of Chicago Press

Neisser, U. (1967) *Cognitive Psychology*, New York: Appleton-Century-Crofts

Norman, D. A. (1969) *Memory and Attention: An Introduction to Human Information Processing*, New York: John Wiley & Sons

Piontkowski, D. and Calfee, R. C. (1979) 'Attention in the Classroom' in G. Hale and M. Lewis (eds.), *Attention and Cognitive Development*, New York: Plenum Publishing

Posner, M. J. and Boies, S. J. (1971) 'Components of Attention', *Psychological Review*, *78*, 391–408

Pribram, K. H. and McGuiness, D. (1975) 'Arousal, Activation, and Effort in the Control of Attention', *Psychological Review*, *82*, 116–49

Rothkopf, E. Z. (1970) 'The Concept of Mathemagenic Activities', *Review of Educational Research*, *40*, 325–36

——— (1976) 'Writing to Teach and Reading to Learn: A Perspective on the Psychology of Written Instruction', *The Psychology of Teaching Methods*, Chicago: University of Chicago

Shavelson, R. and Stern, P. (1981) 'Research on Teachers' Pedagogical Thoughts, Judgements, Decisions and Behavior', *Review of Educational Research*, *51*, 455–98

Stallings, J. (1980) 'Allocated Academic Learning Time Revisited, or Beyond Time on Task', *Educational Researcher*, *9*(11), 11–16

Underwood, G. (1976) *Attention and Memory*, Oxford, UK: Pergamon Press

Wheat, H. G. (1931) *The Psychology of the Elementary School*, New York: Silver, Burdette & Co.

3. APPLYING RESEARCH ON TEACHER CLARITY

Donald R. Cruickshank

Much has been written about the need to revamp preservice and inservice curricula to inform educators of recent findings resulting from the study of teaching (see Gage, 1984; Egbert, 1984; and Fenstermacher, 1984). The intention of this article is to present some of what has been learned about one dimension of teaching, that is teacher clarity. Most of the contents presented are extracted from an ongoing review of the literature (Cruickshank and Kennedy, 1985), and the contents are organized around: (a) what we know about clarity, (b) implications of that knowledge base for teacher preparation programming and teaching, and (c) implications for teacher education researchers.

FINDINGS ON TEACHER CLARITY

Teacher clarity is a multidimensional phenomenon. Teachers must do a number of things to be perceived by their students as being clear (Cruickshank, Myers and Moenjak, 1975). They must, according to over one thousand middle and junior high students: orient and prepare students for what is to be taught; communicate content so that students understand; provide illustrations and examples; demonstrate; use a variety of teaching materials; teach things in a related step-by-step manner; repeat and stress directions and difficult points; adjust teaching to the learner and topic; cause students to organize learnings in meaningful ways; provide practice; provide standards and rules for satisfactory performance; and provide students with feedback or knowledge of how well they are doing.

Teacher clarity appears to be stable. Kennedy, Cruickshank, Bush and Myers (1978) found that over 1,300 middle and junior high students in such different settings as Ohio, Tennessee, and Australia are in substantial agreement on the perceived attributes of clear teachers. Further, Hines (1981) noted that university students perceive teacher clarity in much the same way as junior high students. Williams (1983) reported that preservice teacher clarity is stable across time, content taught, and different students. In other words, a clear teacher seemingly is clear regardless of circumstance.

Certain teacher clarity behaviors are more central and important than others. Several investigators (Bush 1976; Bush, Kennedy and Cruickshank, 1977; Kennedy, Cruickshank, Bush and Myers, 1978; and Hines, 1981) reached substantial agreement on clarity behaviors that are most helpful to students. Clear teachers, as opposed to unclear teachers, are consistently concerned that their students understand. They try to ensure understanding by providing students with appropriate opportunities to learn, utilizing abundant illustrations and examples, logically organizing and reviewing the material to be learned, and assessing student learning.

Teacher clarity is related both to student achievement and satisfaction. Frey, Leonard and Beatty (1975), Good and Grouws (1977), and Evans and Guyman (1978) reported substantial relationships between teacher clarity and student achievement. Hines (1981) and Hines, Cruickshank and Kennedy (1985) reported that teacher demonstration of clarity behaviors bears an undeniable, positive, and significant relationship to learning and satisfaction. Williams (1983) noted that teachers who were rated most highly on clarity by observers produced higher student achievement and satisfaction.

Learners judge a teacher's effectiveness in large part on the basis of clarity. French-Lazovik (1974) noted that university students judged to be effective teachers who, among other things, demonstrate clarity of exposition. The clear teacher interprets difficult or abstract ideas clearly, makes good use of examples and illustrations, and presents information in an organized manner.

Teacher clarity can be enhanced through training. Gloeckner (1983) developed a ten-hour training regimen and upon application found that trained preservice teachers demonstrated significantly more clarity behaviors than did a control group.

IMPLICATIONS FOR TEACHER EDUCATION AND TEACHING

Assuming these findings are generalizeable, several implications can be drawn relative to preservice and inservice education.

Preservice

The selection of preservice teachers can be improved by assessing the clarity behavior of applicants. Ishler (1984) reported that education units preparing teachers, when selecting from preservice applicants, are most interested in: (a) whether they have taken some specific number of semester hours (approximately forty-five); (b) whether they can meet a cumulative grade point average (usually between a 2.0–2.5); (c) whether they passed a test of basic skills; and (d) whether they have worked with children. None of these factors has been shown to be closely related to teaching success, and it is logical to assert that criteria for admission should have a reasonably strong, positive relationship to success on the job. If it has been determined through inquiry that effective teachers possess certain attributes or demonstrate certain skills, the selection process should take them into account. If clarity is among those attributes, and it is, the selection process should provide opportunity for prospective majors to demonstrate their present clarity ability.

In practice, this might translate into each applicant's being: assigned a brief teaching task such as a Reflective Teaching Lesson, provided an opportunity to teach the task to a small group of other applicants, and then observed and rated on clarity by trained personnel. Selection processes that assess applicant behaviors which have some predictive validity would go a long way to ensure that we are choosing the right future teachers.

The curriculum for preservice teachers can be improved if it attends to what is known about clarity and provides students with opportunity to practice clarity behaviors. The present curriculum model for teachers described elsewhere (Cruickshank, 1985), which is reflected in the National Council for Accreditation of Teacher Education *Standards* (1982), gives attention to teaching theory or what we know about teaching. Some of that knowledge derives from the increased study of teaching that has taken place over the past fifteen years. It is incumbent on teacher educators to draw from that research base knowledge that will help future teachers enhance pupil learning and satisfaction. If clarity is associated with these teaching outcomes, then related factual information should be presented to undergraduates, and they should have opportunities to learn and practice the clarity behaviors.

In implementation this might mean the development of a new microteaching skill package—one entitled teacher clarity—that provides novices with (a) conceptual knowledge, (b) a visual model of a teacher or teachers demonstrating clarity and (c) an opportunity to teach and reteach the skill in either contrived or natural settings. To the extent that the teacher education curriculum gives attention to and practice in effective teacher behaviors, it will have greater validity.

Instruction of preservice teachers can be improved when faculty members are both knowledgeable of teacher clarity and incorporate clarity-related behaviors in their repertoire of teaching skills. If it is true that teachers tend to model the teaching to which they have been subjected, then teacher educators should be models of effective teaching. Since clarity is an attribute of effective teachers, then teacher educators must know its dimensions and utilize them regularly.

In practice this might mean that there should be staff development opportunities wherein teacher educators, both those on-campus and those involved with field-based activity, would be acquainted with clarity both conceptually and as a skill. To the extent that teacher educators are models of clarity their students will be exposed to one determinant of good teaching.

Inservice

The selection of teachers can be improved by assessing the clarity behavior of applicants. Endicott (1979) reported that school superintendents, when selecting new teachers, give attention to applicants': (a) personal qualities; (b) the nature and extent of professional course work taken; (c) course work related to the teaching specialty; (d) university grade point averages; (e) experience, particularly leadership, in extracurricular activities; and (f) general education background. Again, it should be noted that selection criteria for a profession should bear a reasonably strong relationship to success on the job. If effective teachers are clear, then clarity should be an attribute requisite to obtaining a teaching post.

Translated into practice, this means that applicants for teaching positions could be asked to teach one or more brief lessons at the grade level and in the content field of the position they seek. Observation of clarity by a trained observer would provide significant insight into the extent to which the applicant can contribute to student learning.

Evaluation of teachers can be improved by assessing their clarity. Instruments for use in teacher evaluation or rating are ubiquitous, and they tend to suffer most from criterion contamination and/or criterion deficiency. The first shortcoming refers to the inclusion of criteria that are extraneous or unrelated to good teaching, for example, personality factors. The second refers to the omission or exclusion of pertinent criteria, for example, "uses direct instruction"; that is, the teacher keeps students engaged in learning at a moderate level of difficulty, and makes sure they are covering material on which they later will be evaluated. If effective teachers are clear, then clarity should be a criterion on which their performance is judged.

Teacher evaluations or ratings should take clarity into account. More specifically, if classroom observations are used, clarity should be assessed by observers. School districts do a disservice to themselves and to teachers when they fail to count or to rate effective teaching behaviors when making judgments of teacher competence.

Teacher inservice programs can be improved by providing staff development programs that train teachers to be more clear. Teachers want to be effective, and ample evidence exists that they are willing to undertake staff development programs that they perceive would have a direct and beneficial impact on their classroom teaching. If teachers accept the propositions that clarity is an important dimension of teaching and that its effective practice contributes to both pupil achievement and satisfaction, then they should be amenable to participate in clarity training programs.

In practice this would mean, in perhaps the manner alluded to earlier for preservice teachers, that a training regimen must be made available. School districts that promote the acquisition of essential teaching behaviors can satisfy the professional needs of teachers and relatedly enhance pupil performance.

CLARITY INSTRUMENTS AND TRAINING REGIMENS

To implement these suggestions, at least two things are necessary. First, if clarity is to be observed, then instruments must be available that facilitate its assessment. One or more of the following sources of instrumentation should be considered.

The first instrument was derived from a subjective analysis and synthesis of over 5,000 descriptions of clear teacher behaviors submitted by middle and junior high school students (Cruickshank, Myers and Moenjak, 1975). Reduced to their fewest common denominators, the descriptions comprise an aggregate of twelve behaviors already enumerated under the finding noted earlier, "Teacher clarity is a multidimensional phenomenon."

The second instrument source emerged from studies employing discriminant analyses of a list of 110 clear teaching behaviors from which the earlier noted aggregate of twelve were subjectively deduced (Bush, 1976; Bush, Kennedy and Cruickshank, 1977; Kennedy, Cruickshank, Bush and Myers, 1978). This potential instrument consists of four general categories and numerous specific indicators. The four clarity categories and most discriminating indicators associated with each appear in Figure 1.

A third instrument source was the twenty-eight item "Clear Teacher Checklist" developed by Cruickshank for gleaning *pupil* assessments of clarity and published in Gephart, Strother and Duckett (1981).

The final and probably most noteworthy source for a clarity instrument was Hines' (1981) Teacher Clarity Observation Instrument that has been used by several researchers including Gloeckner (1983) and Williams (1983). With this instrument, observers are asked to assess the frequency of eighteen clarity behaviors and the quality of eleven others, all traceable to the clarity studies preceding Hines' research at Ohio State.

As would be expected, the items contained on the four instrument sources are highly similar since they emerged from the same line of inquiry although at different times.

Secondly, in order to implement certain of the six suggestions made earlier a clarity training regimen is necessary. Successful training regimens have been developed for teaching several skills associated with effective teaching, e.g., enthusiasm (Collins, 1976); first grade reading groups (Anderson, Evertson and Brophy, 1979); arithmetic (Good and Grouws, 1979); and classroom management (Emmer and others, 1981). Based upon these and similar efforts. Gloeckner (1983) devised a regimen successful in training preservice teachers in clarity. The program consisted of an eight hour session during which characteristics of effective teachers were solicited from participants and characteristics of effective teachers were presented from published research. Participants were introduced to the concept of teacher clarity and its multidimensional attributes. Each clarity behavior was then presented operationally. A film in which a teacher demonstrated many of the clarity behaviors was shown, and a clarity rating sheet (Student Observer—Rating Sheet) was

FIGURE 1   Four Factors Contributing to Teacher Clarity and Specific Behavioral Indicators Associated

Factor I. Assesses student learning. The teacher actively attempts to determine if students understand the content or task and as appropriate makes instructional adjustments.

Indicators:
- Tries to find out if learners understand content.
- Gives specific details when teaching.
- Answers questions.
- Asks learners if they know what to do and how to do it.

Factor II. Provides opportunity to learn. The teacher structures classroom activities to allow time for students to think about, respond to, and synthesize what they are learning.

Indicators:
- Teaches at a pace appropriate to the topic and learners.
- Shows pupils how to remember or recall ideas.
- Provides examples and explanations.
- Gives pupils time to think.
- Gives sufficient time for practice.
- Determines level of pupil understanding.
- Stays with the topic. Repeats as necessary.

Factor III. Uses examples. The teacher frequently uses examples, especially on the chalkboard.

Indicators:
- Shows examples of both how to do classwork and homework.
- Gives explanations pupils understand.
- Goes over difficult homework on the chalkboard.
- Stresses difficult points.

Factor IV. Reviews and organizes. The teacher frequently reviews prior work and prepares pupils for up-coming work.

Indicators:
- Prepares pupils for what they will be doing next.
- Describes the work to be done and how to do it.

distributed and discussed. Next, participants viewed previously recorded video tapes of their own as well as their peers' teaching and assessed the performances using the rating sheet. After that the videotapes were replayed and the contents discussed to improve the rating process. Participants then taught a four minute videotaped lesson incorporating as many clarity behaviors as possible. Again tapes were rated, and selected tapes and segments were replayed and discussed. Participants were given a test to determine whether they knew twenty-four clarity indicators, and finally they retaught the pretest lesson. The process proved effective in enhancing participant skill in making reliable observations.

IMPLICATIONS FOR TEACHER EDUCATION RESEARCH

A number of research questions related to clarity continue to warrant attention from the teacher education research community. They include:

1. To what extent have the several dimensions of teacher clarity been properly and fully identified and delineated?
2. How important is the quantity or frequency of clarity behaviors as compared to its appropriateness of usage?
3. What are the related attributes of clear teach-

ers—the antecedents that may contribute to a person's clarity?

4. How diverse are the skills of entering preservice teachers with regard to clarity?
5. How can clarity best be taught?
6. What makes clarity important? How does it trigger achievement and satisfaction?
7. What is the relationship between clarity and vagueness?

DISCUSSION

It is evident that clarity is an important teacher attribute and that it relates, among other things, to learner achievement, learner satisfaction, and learner perception of teacher effectiveness. As such, it seems prudent to use clarity as one criterion for admitting students to preservice programs, to attend to it as both a concept and a skill in the undergraduate professional curriculum, to model the behavior as teacher educators, to use it in school districts as a criterion in teacher hiring and in teacher evaluation, and to train inservice teachers to enhance their clarity.

REFERENCES

Anderson, L., Evertson, C., & Brophy, J. (1979). An experimental study of effective teaching of first grade reading groups. *Elementary School Journal, 79*, 193–223.

Bush, A. (1976). An empirical exploration of teacher clarity. *Dissertation Abstracts International, 37* (05), 2805A. (University Microfilms No. 76-24, 569, 18-46.)

Bush, A., Kennedy, J., & Cruickshank, D. (1977). An empirical investigation of teacher clarity. *Journal of Teacher Education, 28* (2), 53–58.

Collins, M. (1976). *The effects of training for enthusiasm on the enthusiasm displayed by preservice elementary teachers.* Unpublished doctoral dissertation, Syracuse University. (University Microfilm Catalog No. 7709849.)

Cruickshank, D. (1985). *Models for the preparation of America's teachers.* Bloomington, IN: Phi Delta Kappa.

Cruickshank, D., & Kennedy, J. (1985). *Teacher clarity.* Unpublished manuscript. The College of Education, The Ohio State University.

Cruickshank, D., Myers, B., & Moenjak, T. (1975). *Statements of clear teacher behaviors provided by 1,009 students in grades 6–9.* Unpublished manuscript, The College of Education, The Ohio State University.

Egbert, R. (1984). Improving teacher education through the use of research information. *Journal of Teacher Education. 35* (4), 9–10.

Emmer, E., et al. (1982). *The classroom management improvement study: An experiment in elementary school classrooms.* Austin: University of Texas, Development Center for Teacher Education.

Endicott, F. (1979). *Who gets a teaching position in public schools? Teaching opportunities for you.* Madison, WI: Association for School, College, and University Staffing.

Evans, W., & Guyman, R. (1978, March). *Clarity of explanation: A powerful indicator of teacher effectiveness.* Paper presented at the annual meeting of the American Educational Research Association, Toronto, Canada. (ERIC Document Reproduction Service No. ED 151 321.)

Fenstermacher, G. (1984). The preservice improvement project in retrospect. *Journal of Teacher Education, 35* (4), 28–32.

French-Lazovik, G. (1974). Predictability of students' evaluations of college teachers from component ratings. *Journal of Educational Psychology, 66,* 373–385.

Frey, P., Leonard, D., & Beatty, W. (1975). Student ratings of instruction: Validation research. *American Educational Research Journal, 12,* 435–447.

Gephart, W., Strother, D., & Duckett, W. (Eds.). (1981). Instructional clarity. *Practical Applications of Research, 3* (3), 1–4.

Gloeckner, G. (1983). *An investigation into the effectiveness of a preservice teacher clarity training unit in two different experimental settings.* Unpublished doctoral dissertation, The Ohio State University.

Good, T., & Grouws, D. (1979). The Missouri mathematics effectiveness project: An experimental study in fourth grade classrooms. *Journal of Educational Psychology, 71,* 355–362.

Hines, C. (1981). *A further investigation of teacher clarity: The observation of teacher clarity and the relationship between clarity and student achievement and satisfaction.* Unpublished doctoral dissertation, The Ohio State University.

Hines, C., Cruickshank, D., & Kennedy, J. (1985). Teacher clarity and its relationship to student achievement and satisfaction. *American Educational Research Journal, 22* (1).

Ishler, R. (1984). Requirements for admission to and graduation from teacher education. *Phi Delta Kappan, 66* (2), 121–122.

Kennedy, J., Cruickshank, D., Bush, A., & Myers, B. (1978). Additional investigations into the nature of teacher clarity. *Journal of Educational Research, 72* (2), 3–10.

McCaleb, J. (1984). Selecting a measure of oral communication as a predictor of teaching performance. *Journal of Teacher Education, 35* (5), 33–38.

McCaleb, J., & Rosenthal, B. (1984). Relationships in teacher clarity between student perceptions and observer ratings. *Journal of Classroom Interaction, 19,* 15–21.

Medley, D. (1978). Alternative assessment strategies. *Journal of Teacher Education, 29* (2), 38–42.

Schalock, D. (1979). Research on teacher selection. *Review of Research in Education, 7,* 364–417.

Smith, L., & Land, M. (1981). Low inference verbal behaviors related to teacher clarity. *Journal of Classroom Interaction, 17,* 37–41.

Williams, J. (1983). *The stability of teacher clarity in relation to student achievement and satisfaction.* Unpublished doctoral dissertation, The Ohio State University.

REFERENCE NOTE

Support for the use of work samples in screening preservice applicants, in teacher selection, and in evaluation comes from Medley (1978) and Schalock (1979). As Medley notes we (a) must find ways to elicit the specific teacher behaviors, (b) obtain accurate records of them, and (c) score the record with regard to whether or not the behavior was performed appropriately.

4. ACADEMIC WORK
Walter Doyle

The focus of this chapter is on the academic work that the curriculum of elementary and secondary schools requires students to do, how that work is organized and accomplished in classrooms, and what modifications in academic work are likely to increase student achievement. The chapter is divided into two major sections. The first section is devoted to an analysis of the intellectual demands inherent in different forms of academic work. Of special importance to this section is the recent research on the cognitive processes that underlie school tasks. The second section is directed to studies of how academic work is carried out in classroom environments. Particular attention is given in this section to the ways in which the social and the evaluative conditions in classrooms affect students' reactions to work. Both sections contain an analysis of the implications of this research for improving the quality of academic work in classrooms and thus increasing student achievement.

THE INTRINSIC CHARACTER OF ACADEMIC WORK

In broad terms the curriculum of the early elementary grades reflects an emphasis on fundamental operations in reading and mathematics, the so-called basic skills. In addition, pupils are exposed to information about social studies, music, nutrition, art, and physical fitness. The emphasis on basic skills is apparent in the way time is allocated in these grades. In the Beginning Teacher Evaluation Study, for example, it was found that approximately 55 percent of the day in the second- and fifth-grade classes was spent on language arts and mathematics, and these figures are generally consistent with those obtained in earlier studies (see Borg 1980; Rosenshine 1980).

As students progress through the grades, the emphasis gradually shifts from basic skills to the content and the methods of inquiry embodied in academic disciplines. Older students are expected to learn algebra, history, biology, and literature rather than simply to practice reading and computational skills. Also, in the middle school or junior high school years, students begin to develop the capacity for formal operational thought, that is, the ability to think abstractly and use general strategies to analyze and solve problems. Clearly, schoolwork becomes more technical and more demanding over the years.

The Curriculum and Academic Tasks

This brief topical description of the curriculum provides a useful overview of students' work at different grade levels, but it gives little sense of the demands inherent in that work. To explain these demands it is necessary to view the curriculum as a collection of *academic tasks* (see Doyle 1980). The term *task* focuses attention on three aspects of students' work: (a) the products students formulate, such as an original essay or answers to a set of test questions; (b) the operations that are used to generate the product, such as memorizing a list of words or classifying examples of a concept; and (c) the "givens" or resources available to students while they are generating a product, such as a model of a finished essay supplied by the teacher or a fellow student. Academic tasks, in other words, are defined by the answers students are required to produce and the methods that can be used to obtain these answers.

The central point here is that tasks form the basic treatment unit in classrooms. This task perspective can be summarized in two basic propositions:

1. Students' academic work in school is defined by the academic tasks that are embedded in the content they encounter daily. Tasks regulate the selection of information and the choice of strategies for processing that information.
2. Students will learn what a task leads them to do, that is, they will acquire information and operations that are necessary to accomplish the tasks they encounter.

Types of Academic Tasks

Considerable effort has been recently given to defining the cognitive components of "real life" school tasks (see Anderson, Spiro, and Montague 1977). This work is part of a broader movement in psychology toward the analysis of the cognitive processes that underlie various aspects of human aptitude and performance. In this section some of the general concepts and findings emerging from this research will be reviewed to define more fully the character and range of learnings that are contained in the curriculum of elementary and secondary schooling.

General Categories of Academic Tasks. The academic tasks embedded in the curriculum can be differentiated into at least four general categories (Doyle 1980):

1. *Memory tasks* in which students are expected to recognize or reproduce information previously encountered (for example, memorize a list of spelling words or lines from a poem)
2. *Procedural or routine tasks* in which students are expected to apply a standardized and predictable formula or algorithm to generate answers (for example, solve a set of subtraction problems)
3. *Comprehension or understanding tasks* in which students are expected to (a) recognize transformed or paraphrased versions of information previously encountered, (b) apply procedures to new problems or decide from among several procedures those that are applicable to a particular problem (for example, solve "word problems" in mathematics), or (c) draw inferences from previously encountered information or procedures (for example, make predictions about a chemical reaction or devise an alternative formula for squaring a number)
4. *Opinion tasks* in which students are expected to state a preference for something (for example, select a favorite short story)

These categories can be specified more fully by contrasting individual types of tasks.

Memory versus Comprehension. The contrast between memory and comprehension tasks is based on a distinction between surface structure (the exact words printed on a page) and conceptual structure (the underlying network of propositions that define the meaning of a text). Memory tasks direct attention to the surface of a text and to the rote reproduction of words; comprehension tasks direct attention to the ideas embedded in the text and to an understanding of the meaning conveyed by the words and sentences.

Memorizing specific information does not necessarily lead to comprehension of a passage, and reading for comprehension does not necessarily enable the reader to recall words or facts. When a reader focuses primarily on memorizing facts or words, general ideas that are implied but not explicitly stated in the text are often missed. On the other hand, when a reader focuses primarily on the general ideas in a passage, specific facts or words are often forgotten. Thus, preparation for one type of task may not be suitable for the other. It is probably for this reason that students typically adjust study strategies to fit the type of the test they expect to take (McConkie 1977).

Procedural versus Comprehension Tasks. A distinction between procedural tasks and comprehension tasks is especially clear in the field of mathematics. There is a difference between (a) knowing an algorithm, such as the computational steps for adding a column of numbers or multiplying two-digit numbers, and (b) knowing why the procedure works and when it should be used. Procedural tasks, then, are tasks that are accomplished by using a standard routine to produce answers. The work is typically quite predictable because the routines or algorithms consistently generate correct answers if no computational errors are made. Comprehension tasks, with respect to procedures, are tasks that are accomplished by knowing why a procedure works or when to use it.

Learning to use an algorithm does not necessarily enable one to understand it. Similarly, learning to understand why an algorithm works or when it should be used does not necessarily lead to computational proficiency (see Resnick and Ford 1981). It is often argued that extensive drill and practice with computational procedures is a prerequisite for acquiring an understanding of the material. The present analysis suggests, however, that accomplishing one task does not automatically lead to accomplishment of the other. Indeed, memorization, procedural, and comprehension processes may interfere with each other in accomplishing a given task. . . .

Implications for Instructional Policy

Although considerably more basic and applied research in instructional psychology is needed, the way instructional designers conceptualize the task of improving instruction provides some promising directions that warrant consideration.

Direct Instruction in Cognitive Processes. One of the most common reactions to results of research in cognitive science is to recommend direct instruction in the processes used by expert readers, writers, mathematicians, or scientists (see Anderson 1977). For example, several investigators have been working to devise and test methods for teaching children to monitor their own comprehension and make

inferences while reading (Collins and Smith 1980; Pearson and Camperell 1981). In essence, direct instruction means that academic tasks are carefully structured for students, and students are explicitly told how to accomplish these tasks and are systematically guided through a series of exercises that will enable them to master the tasks. Opportunities for directed practice are frequent, as are assessments to determine how well students are progressing and whether corrective feedback is needed. From this perspective, the role of cognitive science is to define the processes underlying subject-matter competency so that programs of direct instruction can be designed to foster these processes in students and thus improve the quality of academic work.

While the research cited above has certainly indicated that direct instruction can be effective for some outcomes, at least three important considerations are relevant to defining the substance of direct instruction and understanding its uses and potential limitations:

1. Direct instruction may not be possible for some areas because the processes that have been identified as necessary for learning tasks in those areas cannot be communicated in terms that are understandable to learners at a particular level of development or ability. We know, for instance, that riding a bicycle requires skill in balancing the equipment, but telling or showing someone how to balance a bicycle is virtually impossible.

2. Many processes that experts use, especially in academic disciplines at the secondary level, have not been identified. Indeed, there are probably certain inherent limits to our ability to specify the components of expertise and thus a limit to the application of direct instruction to foster competence in advanced academic work.

3. Research on performance differences has indicated that without strong guidance novices, young children, and low-ability students often fail to develop the strategies and higher-order executive routines that enable them to understand tasks or construct the goal structures necessary to accomplish tasks. Direct instruction that concentrates on specific operations for accomplishing a task will produce imme-

diate effects, but it is not likely to engender the higher-level knowledge structures or strategies required for the flexible use of these operations. Successful instruction in decoding or vocabulary, for example, does not necessarily lead to proficiency in reading comprehension (see Becker and Gersten 1982).

A series of training studies by Brown and Campione (1977, 1980) has provided especially important insights into the effects of direct instruction. The studies began with a remedial program focusing on teaching young, low-ability children to use memorization strategies. The evidence from several sources had suggested that such learners have a production rather than a capacity deficiency. They are able to use mnemonic strategies, but in contrast to high-ability children, they do not use them spontaneously. With prompting, low-ability children will use mnemonic strategies, but this improvement is temporary and lasts only while the instructional prompts are available. Moreover, they do not use the memorization strategies flexibly to transfer to other memory tasks for which prompts are not supplied. There is, in other words, a "heart-pacer" effect in which performance is maintained only because the instructional program does most of the work for the students. The investigators found that the durability of strategies could be increased through training children in specific memorization strategies, although the amount of training required was much greater than originally expected. In addition, training to achieve durability *reduced* flexibility. The skills became welded to the items used in training and did not transfer to new items. Consistent with the general work in cognitive psychology, these findings suggested that low-ability children have special problems accessing what they know and flexibly using that knowledge. In addition, training that is focused on specific memorization skills does not produce flexibility.

In a redirection of their research, Brown and Campione (1977) produced some promising results for training in higher-level cognitive operations. Little durability was achieved for young children, but some flexibility was evident among older learners. Direct instruction in making inferences in reading (Hansen 1981) and estimating answers in arithmetic (Reys and Bestgen 1981) has had some success. An approach known as "attack strategy training," based on cognitive behavior modification, has been effective in helping low-ability students learn general strategies for solving arithmetic problems of a particular type (see Carnine and Stein 1981). It is important to realize, however, that direct instruction in higher-level processes and knowledge structures will probably take longer and have fewer immediate effects than will direct instruction aimed at lower-order skills.

Indirect Instruction in Cognitive Processes. The push toward higher-level processes and toward meaning or understanding places direct instruction in a territory that is usually occupied by what might be called indirect instruction. Such instruction emphasizes the central role of self-discovery in fostering a sense of meaning and a purpose for learning academic content. From this perspective, students must be given ample opportunities for direct experience with content in order to derive generalizations and invent algorithms on their own. Such opportunities are clearly structured on the basis of what is known about an academic discipline and about human information processing. However, these opportunities are only partially formed in advance; gaps are left that students themselves must fill. In other words, the instructional program does only part of the work for students by opening up opportunities for making choices, decision making, discovery, and invention (for good analyses of the contrast between direct and indirect methods, see Resnick and Ford 1981; Shulman 1970).

An emphasis on invention in learning is certainly consistent with the basic premise in cognitive psychology that knowledge and understanding are constructed by individuals. But, as Resnick and Ford point out, there is less evidence that indirect instruction is the most suitable or efficient way to obtain this outcome deliberately. Two factors seem to limit the applicability to indirect methods. First, the ability level and background of the students are likely to be important influences on the effectiveness of indirect instruction. In a comprehensive review of research on the way the aptitudes of students interact with instructional methods, Cronbach and Snow (1977) found that high-ability students profited from unstructured teaching conditions that gave them choices in organizing and interpreting information. Low-achieving students, on the other hand, did not do well under these unstructured conditions or with indirect methods. One possible explanation for these findings is that low-ability students lack the general understandings and processes that enable them to formulate their own generalizations or procedures necessary to accomplish academic tasks under conditions of indirect instruction. As a result, the "treatment" does not actually occur, that is, they do not have the opportunity to practice higher-level operations.

Second, invention does not automatically lead to usable procedures or an understanding of concepts and principles. Students also invent mistakes as they encounter obstacles in learning. Thus, while increasing the opportunity for invention, indirect teaching also increases the chance for students to develop erroneous strategies for finding solutions and misconceptions of content. Special attention in indirect teaching must therefore be given to monitoring and correcting the inferences students actually make.

Summary

The existing research in cognitive psychology leads to the following general recommendations for improving the quality of academic work:

1. Direct instruction in identified cognitive processes and knowledge structures is probably more appropriate than indirect methods for teaching novices, low-achieving students, and pupils in the early elementary grades.
2. Direct instruction that is focused on specific skills is likely to have few long-term consequences unless combined with instruction, either direct or indirect, in higher-level executive processes and knowledge structures for representing tasks and selecting solution strategies. Thus, instruction in decoding needs to be combined with instruction in comprehension monitoring to foster an ability to read independently. If specific skills are taught in isolation, students can develop either magical thinking or an excessive concern for details, both of which interfere with accomplishment of tasks and learning.
3. Indirect instruction is one way of providing practice in higher-order executive routines and the use of knowledge structures to represent problems. Indeed, even in direct instruction some degree of "unstructuredness" is essential to ascertain whether students really understand

how and when to use their knowledge and skills. In other words, overly explicit signals or programs for solution strategies obviate the need for students to employ executive routines, and thus students are not able to practice these higher-level processes or demonstrate mastery of them. In addition, many operations that are necessary to achieve expertise in academic areas either have not yet been identified or are difficult to formulate into clearly teachable propositions. In such cases, the only alternative is to allow students to experience content so that they can invent procedures and construct knowledge structures on their own. Such experiences obviously need to be structured in ways that seem at least logically related to intended outcomes so that invention will be productive.

4. Resnick and Ford (1981) have observed that "transitions in competence that emerge without direct instruction may be more common in children's educational development than we have thought up to now" (p. 82). That is, students do not simply learn what is taught but invent their own algorithms and conceptions of content whether instruction is direct or indirect. This propensity to invent can have both advantages and disadvantages. As indicated, invention enables students to learn routines and concepts that are difficult to teach directly. At the same time, invention can lead to "buggy" algorithms and misconceptions of content. This possibility underscores the central role of corrective feedback in learning and the need to base that feedback on an understanding of the processes that lead students to make mistakes.
5. Finally, accomplishing academic tasks is not solely a matter of general strategies. Especially in the upper grades, students need domain-specific knowledge in a discipline to do academic work.

ACADEMIC WORK IN CLASSROOMS

In this chapter, academic work has thus far been discussed in isolation from the classroom context within which it is normally carried out. This isolation is clearly artificial, and this artificiality is especially serious if one is interested in understanding and improving classroom practices. To remedy this situation, a brief summary of recent classroom studies is provided (for more information, see Doyle 1983, 1986).

Classroom Complexity and Academic Work

Research on classroom events and processes suggests that academic work is transformed fundamentally when it is placed in the complex social system of a classroom. The character of these transformations can be summarized as follows:

1. Academic tasks organize students' information processing in classrooms. Whether students pay attention to the teacher's questions or participate in a classroom discussion would seem to depend on the relationship of these events to the accomplishment of tasks. Similarly, if the presentation of a procedure in class focuses on understanding how the procedure was derived and why it works, but the assignment is to solve twenty-five computational problems, then attention is likely to be directed to learning the computational steps necessary to produce answers efficiently. In other words, the answers a teacher actually accepts define the real tasks in classrooms.

2. In classrooms, teachers are required to think about more than academic tasks in planning and conducting instruction (see Yinger 1980). Because classrooms are crowded, teachers are faced with the task of organizing students into working units and maintaining this organization across changing conditions for several months. In addition, they must establish and enforce rules, arrange for the orderly distribution of supplies and materials, collect and evaluate students' papers, pace events to fit bell schedules as well as the interests of students, and respond rapidly to a large number of immediate contingencies. And all of these functions must be performed in an environment of considerable complexity and unpredictabilty. In addition to structuring and monitoring academic work, therefore, a teacher must be able to gain and maintain the cooperation of students in activities that fill the available time (Doyle 198[6]).

3. Academic work in classrooms is connected to a reward structure. Students' answers, therefore, are not just evidence of having accomplished academic tasks. They also count as points earned in an accountability system. Accountability, in turn, drives the task system in classrooms. As a result, students are especially sensitive to cues that signal accountability (for example, announcements about tests) or define how tasks are to be accomplished (see Doyle and Carter 1984; King 1980). In addition, students tend to take seriously that work for which they are held accountable. If no answers are required or if any answer is acceptable, then few students will actually attend to the content. In some instances, answering becomes the task in classrooms. That is, student attention is directed to the answering event itself rather than to the content. And it appears that students sometimes invent strategies for producing answers in ways that circumvent the information-processing demands of academic work; students might, for example, copy, offer provisional answers, request that the teacher make instructions more explicit or provide models to follow closely, and so forth.

4. Tasks that involve understanding and higher-level cognitive processes are difficult for teachers and students to accomplish in classrooms (see Doyle and Carter 1984). Such tasks pose high levels of ambiguity and risk for students, who often respond by delaying the start of work or by negotiating to increase either the explicitness of a teacher's instructions or the teacher's generosity in grading final products. Teachers, in turn, face complex management problems resulting from slowdowns in the flow of activity and from the fact that a significant portion of the students may not be able to accomplish the assigned work. As tasks move toward memory or routine algorithms, these problems are reduced substantially. The central point is that the tasks that cognitive psychology suggests have the greatest long-term consequences for improving the quality of academic work are precisely those that are the most difficult to manage in classrooms.

5. Because tasks are administered to groups and

performance on these tasks is often evaluated publicly, teachers are often under pressure to adjust standards and pace to levels suitable for a majority of students (see Arlin and Westbury 1976). To make this adjustment, teachers often avoid comprehension tasks that typically require considerable skill to accomplish. Moreover, prompts given to low-ability students are also available to other students who may not need such help. As a result, some students end up working on tasks that are considerably below their abilities. Finally, it would seem difficult to maintain individual accountability in a group setting. It is always possible that a student can copy answers from peers or slip through the accountability system in other ways.

6. The need to manage group contingencies and evaluate answers often appears to focus the attention of teachers and students on getting work done rather than on the quality or meaning of work (see Anderson 1981). In their analysis of case studies in science education, Stake and Easley (1978), for example, observed that content goals often appeared to have little salience for either students or teachers. Students seemed primarily interested in grades as intrinsically valuable: "They did not think of themselves as mastering a certain body of knowledge, but more as mastering (and of course not mastering) those things being required by the teacher or the test. The knowledge domain was not a reality—it was a great arbitrary abstraction" (chap. 15, p. 29). In addition, several investigators have recently noted that many teachers spend very little time explicitly telling students how to accomplish academic work. Rather, they assign exercises and then monitor students as they work (see Duffy and McIntyre 1982; Durkin 1979).

7. Finally, the classroom makes academic work especially complex for novices, young children, and low-achieving students, that is, those who are likely to find academic tasks difficult to accomplish anyway. Classroom studies also indicate that low-achieving and immature students are often grouped together for instruction, particularly in reading in the early elementary grades. Such groups are

typically difficult for teachers to manage, and the quality of teaching in such groups is frequently low (see a review by Cazden 1981). Any effort to improve the quality of academic work in schools must necessarily address the problem of effectively teaching these students.

Implications for Instructional Policy

Descriptions of classroom realities often evoke the proposal that the classroom system needs to be replaced or fundamentally altered. Such proposals, however, do not seem to have much merit. Replacing classrooms is not likely to happen because there will always be fewer adults than students in schools. Once students are grouped and assigned to teachers for specific periods of time, classrooms are necessary regardless of the format used for activities or the size and shape of rooms. Whatever alternatives are proposed for classrooms, it will still be necessary to manage groups of students through time and space and cope with the ambiguity and risk associated with academic tasks. The central problem is to find ways to make classrooms more productive in the face of the realities of such environments. In this concluding section some possible ways to achieve this goal are reviewed.

Instructional Materials. Studies of classrooms indicate that teachers often rely on instructional materials to carry out the academic tasks system. Students spend a good deal of their time working on exercises and reading passages from textbooks and workbooks. Thus, academic work is defined in large measure by commercially prepared materials. Research also suggests that these materials are often poorly designed and written (Anderson, Armbruster, and Kantor 1980; Beck and McCaslin 1978). As a result, students are sometimes prevented from learning the content because of difficulties inherent in the text rather than in the complexity of the academic discipline or the basic skill being mastered. It is reasonable to propose, therefore, that careful attention be given to academic tasks in the preparation of instructional materials and that more research be conducted to find ways to design such materials and test their efficacy. Some preliminary attempts are being made to design materials in such areas as comprehension monitoring. Efforts are also being made to improve the design of workbooks used in elementary reading (Osborn 1981) and to help students learn to understand the textbooks they read (Adams, Carnine, and Gersten 1982). As more is discovered about the cognitive dimensions of academic work and the processes of learning from texts, the possibility of improving instructional materials should increase substantially.

Training in Managing Tasks. Additional knowledge about academic tasks and how they are carried out in classrooms will increase the possibilities for training teachers to manage academic work more efficiently and effectively. On the basis of present knowledge, at least two areas warrant special attention in teacher preparation. First, accountability appears to be a central component in the academic task system. If answers are not required or any answer is acceptable in a particular area, then students are not likely to take the work seriously, especially in upper elementary and secondary grades. It would seem essential, then, that teachers learn the importance of accountability and explore a variety of ways in which accountability can be handled creatively in classrooms. Second, teachers need to think about curriculum content in cognitive terms and become aware of the various paths students invent to get around task demands in accomplishing academic work, such as delaying, eliciting overly explicit prompts, and so forth. With this awareness, teachers can plan instruction and tests that emphasize understanding rather than the memorization of isolated facts. In addition, they can begin to devise ways to sustain task demands and thus have students use the cognitive processes that are intended for task accomplishment.

It is important to reiterate that the tasks that cognitive science indicates are likely to have long-term consequences, such as those involving higher-level executive routines, are probably the most difficult to manage in classrooms. Tasks that leave room for student judgment are often hard to evaluate and are more likely to evoke attempts by students to circumvent task demands. Special attention needs to be given to managing such tasks if the quality of academic work is to be improved.

In addition to managing academic tasks, teachers also face the larger problem of establishing and maintaining cooperation in classroom activities. Unless skills in this area are well developed, a teacher will have little to think about academic tasks or little freedom to arrange classroom events to sustain a variety of types of tasks. Indeed, without highly developed management skills, a teacher is likely to rely on memory and routine tasks that typically elicit cooperation from more students, especially those who are inclined to disrupt activities. Major progress has been made in recent years in understanding how classroom management is accomplished (Doyle 1985) and in testing procedures for helping teachers learn these processes (Emmer, Sanford, Evertson, Clements, and Martin 1981; Emmer, Evertson, Sanford, Clements, and Worsham 1982). Additional research is needed, however, to extend this work to the management of academic work (see Doyle, Sanford, Clements, French, and Emmer 1983).

Direct and Indirect Instruction. Research on effective teaching has generally indicated that, at least in basic skill areas in elementary and junior high schools, high levels of student engagement are associated with high achievement and that direct instruction in which the teacher actively manages academic work is likely to sustain engagement (Rosenshine 1983). From the perspective of classroom management, direct instruction is efficient. If academic activities are carefully and clearly organized and the teacher has a central role in the classroom, then he or she will usually be in a position to monitor classroom events and intervene early to stop disruptions. In addition, engagement is generally high in teacher-led instruction so that the task of management will be relatively easy. Indirect instruction, on the other hand, is typically more difficult to manage because of resistance from students and because the pace and rhythm of events are inherently slower.

The quality of the time students spend engaged in academic work depends on the tasks they accomplish and the extent to which they understand what they are doing. It is essential, therefore, that direct instruction include explicit attention to meaning and not simply focus on engagement in academic work as an end in itself (see Good 1982). Moreover, some curricular areas, especially in the upper grades, may not lend themselves to direct instruction. It is in these areas that special attention needs to be given to task management.

Finally, emphasis must be placed on the quality of academic work for low-ability and immature students. These students are likely to find academic work difficult, and their problems increase as such work is embedded in a complex classroom environment. Grouping these students together for instruction often increases the complexity of the task environment for the students and creates formidable management problems for teachers. In the end, the quality of teaching suffers. The practices that lead to such grouping need to be examined carefully, and alternatives for working with low-ability students in classrooms need to be explored.

CONCLUSION

The analysis in this chapter suggests that properties of the classroom environment shape academic work in fundamental ways. Classrooms provide a continuity of experience as well as particular resources that can be used to accomplish academic tasks. In addition, accountability by students for their work drives the academic task system in classrooms. If answers are not required or if any answer is acceptable, then the task system is suspended, and little academic work will be accomplished. In turn, the nature of the answers a teacher accepts and the routes a teacher allows for getting answers define the tasks students are required to accomplish. Finally, students invent and use strategies for managing the ambiguity and risk associated with academic tasks when they are embedded in an accountability system, and these strategies also affect the nature and quality of academic work.

Any changes in the classroom system will continue to face these inherent pressures. Major improvements in academic work clearly depend on further inquiry into the event structures of classrooms and how work is accomplished in these environments.

REFERENCES

Adams, Abby; Carnine, Douglas W.; and Gersten, Russell. "Instructional Strategies for Studying Content Area Texts in the Intermediate Grades." *Reading Research Quarterly* 18 (Fall 1982): 27–55.

Anderson, L. M. "Student Responses to Seatwork: Implications for the Study of Students' Cognitive Processing." Paper presented at the annual meeting of the American Educational Research Association, Los Angeles, 1981.

Anderson, Richard C. "The Notion of the Schemata and the Educational Enterprise: General Discussion of the Conference." In *Schooling and the Acquisition of Knowledge,* edited by Richard C. Anderson, Rand J. Spiro, and William E. Montague. Hillsdale, N.J.: Lawrence Erlbaum Associates, 1977.

Anderson, Richard C.; Spiro, Rand J.; and Montague, William E., eds. *Schooling and the Acquisition of Knowledge.* Hillsdale, N.J.: Lawrence Erlbaum Associates, 1977.

Anderson, Thomas H.; Armbruster, Bonnie B.; and Kantor, Robert N. *How Clearly Written Are Children's Textbooks? Or, of Bladderworts and Alpha.* Reading Education Report 16. Urbana: Center for the Study of Reading, University of Illinois, 1980.

Arlin, Marshall N., and Westbury, Ian. "The Leveling Effect of Teacher Pacing of Science Content Mastery." *Journal of Research in Science Teaching* 13 (May 1976): 213–219.

Beck, Isabel L., and McCaslin, Ellen S. *An Analysis of Dimensions That Affect the Development of Codebreaking Ability in Eight Beginning Reading Programs.* Pittsburgh, [Pa.]: Learning Research and Development Center, University of Pittsburgh, 1978.

Becker, Wesley C., and Gersten, Russell. "A Follow-up of Follow Through: The Later Effects of the Direct Instruction Model on Children in Fifth and Sixth Grades." *American Educational Research Journal* 19:1 (1982): 75–92.

Borg, W. R. "Time and School Learning." In *Time to Learn,* edited by Carolyn Denham and Ann Lieberman. Washington, D.C.: National Institute of Education, 1980.

Brown, Ann L., and Campione, Joseph C. *Memory Strategies in Learning: Training Children to Study Strategically.* Tech. Report 22. Urbana: Center for the Study of Reading, University of Illinois, 1977.

Brown, Ann L., and Campione, Joseph C. *Inducing Flexible Thinking: Problem of Access.* Tech. Report 156. Urbana: Center for the Study of Reading, University of Illinois, 1980.

Carnine, Douglas W., and Stein, Marcy. "Organizational Strategies and Practice Procedures for Teaching Basic Facts." *Journal for Research in Mathematics Education* 12 (January 1981): 65–69.

Cazden, Courtney B. "Social Context of Learning to Read." In *Comprehension and Teaching: Research Reviews,* edited by John T. Guthrie. Newark, Del.: International Reading Association, 1981.

Collins, Allan, and Smith, Edward E. *Teaching the Process of Reading Comprehension.* Tech. Report 182. Urbana: Center for the Study of Reading, University of Illinois, 1980.

Cronbach, Lee J., and Snow, Richard E. *Aptitudes and Instructional Methods: Handbook for Research on Interactions.* New York: Irvington, 1977.

Doyle, Walter. *Student Mediating Responses in Teaching Effectiveness.* Final Report, NIE-G-76-0099. Denton: North Texas State University, 1980.

Doyle, Walter. "Academic Work." *Review of Educational Research* 53 (Summer 1983): 159–199.

Doyle, Walter. "Classroom Organization and Management." In *Handbook of Research on Teaching.* 3d ed. Edited by Merle C. Wittrock. New York: Macmillan, 1986.

Doyle, Walter, and Carter, Kathy. "Academic Tasks in Classrooms." *Curriculum Inquiry* 14 (Summer 1984): 129–149.

Doyle, Walter; Sanford, Julie P.; Clements, Barbara S.; French, B. S.; and Emmer, Edmund T. *Managing Academic Tasks: Interim Report of the Junior High School Study.* R&D Report 6189. Austin: Research and Development Center for Teacher Education, University of Texas, 1983.

Duffy, Gerald G., and McIntyre, Lonnie D. "Naturalistic Study of Instructional Assistance in Primary Grade Reading." *Elementary School Journal* 83 (September 1982): 14–23.

Durkin, Dolores. "What Classroom Observations Reveal about Reading Comprehension Instruction." *Reading Research Quarterly* 14:4 (1979): 481–533.

Emmer, Edmund T.; Evertson, Carolyn; Sanford, Julie; Clements, Barbara S.; and Worsham, Murray. *Organizing and Managing the Junior High School Classroom.* R&D Report 6151. Austin: Research and Development Center for Teacher Education, University of Texas, 1982.

Emmer, Edmund; Sanford, Julie; Evertson, Carolyn; Clements, Barbara; and Martin, Jeanne. *The Classroom Management Improvement Study: An Experiment in Elementary School Classrooms.* R&D Report 6050. Austin: Research and Development Center for Teacher Education, University of Texas, 1981.

Good, Thomas. *Classroom Research: What We Know and Need to Know.* R&D Report 9018. Austin: Research and Development Center for Teacher Education, University of Texas, 1982.

Hansen, Jane. "The Effects of Inference Framing and Practice on Young Children's Reading Comprehension." *Reading Research Quarterly* 16 (1981): 391–417.

King, L. H. *Student Thought Processes and the Expectancy Effect.* Research Report 80-1-8. Edmonton, Canada: Center for Research in Teaching, University of Alberta, 1980.

McConkie, George W. "Learning from Text." In *Review of Research in Education.* Vol. 5. Edited by Lee Shulman. Itasca, Ill.: F. E. Peacock, 1977.

Osborn, Jean. *The Purposes, Uses, and Contents of Workbooks and Some Guidelines for Teachers and Publishers.* Reading Education Report 27. Urbana: Center for Study of Reading, University of Illinois. 1981.

Pearson, P. David, and Camperell, Kaybeth. "Comprehension of Text Structures." In *Comprehension and Teaching: Research Reviews,* edited by John T. Guthrie. Newark, Del.: International Reading Association, 1981.

Resnick, Lauren, and Ford, Wendy W. *The Psychology of Mathematics for Instruction.* Hillsdale, N.J.: Lawrence Erlbaum Associates, 1981.

Reys, Robert E., and Bestgen, Barbara J. "Teaching and Assessing Computational Estimation Skills." *Elementary School Journal* 82 (November 1981): 117–127.

Rosenshine, Barak. "How Time is Spent in Elementary Classrooms." In *Time to Learn,* edited by Carolyn Denham and Ann Lieberman. Washington, D.C.: National Institute of Education. 1980.

Rosenshine, Barak. "Teaching Functions in Instructional Programs." *Elementary School Journal* 83 (March 1983): 335–351.

Shulman, Lee S. "Psychology and Mathematics Education." In *Mathematics Education,* edited by Edward G. Begle. Sixty-ninth Yearbook of the National Society for the Study of Education, Part 1. Chicago: University of Chicago Press, 1970.

Stake, Robert E., and Easley, Jack A. *Case Studies in Science Education,* vols. 1 and 2. Urbana: Center for Instructional Research and Curriculum Evaluation and Committee on Culture and Cognition, University of Illinois, 1978.

Yinger, Robert J. "A Study of Teacher Planning." *Elementary School Journal* 80 (January 1980): 107–127.

The author acknowledges the resources made available at the R and D Center for Teacher Education, supported by the National Institute of Education, and the assistance of Oliver Bown in arranging time for this paper to be written. Kathy Carter provided valuable comments and suggestions. The opinions expressed herein do not necessarily reflect the position or policy of the National Commission on Excellence in Education or of the National Institute of Education, and no official endorsement by these offices should be inferred.

An earlier version of this chapter appeared in *Review of Education Research* 53 (Summer 1983): 159–199. Reprinted by permission. © 1983 by the American Educational Research Association.

5. SYNTHESIS OF RESEARCH ON TEACHERS' QUESTIONING
Meredith Gall

The hundreds of questions the typical American teacher asks on a typical day reflect the great popularity of the recitation method. A recitation is basically a series of teacher questions (usually about textbook content), each eliciting a student response and sometimes a teacher reaction to that response.

The prevalence of teaching by recitation has been found in previous reviews of research on teachers' questions, which include studies going back to the turn of the century (Gall, 1970; Hoetker and Ahlbrand, 1969). Recent studies of classroom teaching (Dillon, 1982a: Durkin, 1978; Sirotnik, 1983) confirm that the recitation method is still widely used.

Because questions occur so frequently in classroom teaching, we are led to wonder about their effects on students. Do teachers' questions help students learn the curriculum? Do they promote the development of thinking skills? Are some questioning practices more effective than others? Research prior to 1970 provided few answers to these important questions; since then, however, many relevant investigations have been carried out.

EFFECTS OF FACT AND HIGHER COGNITIVE QUESTIONS

Researchers have developed many systems for classifying teacher questions (Gall, 1970), but they usually simplify their data analyses by classifying all teacher questions into just two categories: fact and higher cognitive. Fact questions require students to recall previously presented information, whereas higher cognitive questions require students to engage in independent thinking.

Do students learn more when teachers emphasize fact questions or when they emphasize higher cognitive questions? When Dunkin and Biddle (1974) and Rosenshine (1971) reviewed early studies on this problem (most of them from the 1960s), they could find no clear trends in the research results. Heath and Nielsen (1974) strongly criticized these studies for their methodological flaws.

Rosenshine (1976) subsequently reviewed a set of three large correlational studies completed in the early 1970s. He interpreted their results as indicating that students learn best when teacher questions "tend to be narrow, pupils are expected to know rather than guess [the] answer, and the teacher immediately reinforces an answer as right or wrong" (p. 365). "Narrow" was Rosenshine's term for a fact question.

In addition to the correlational studies reviewed by Rosenshine, experiments have been conducted on the effects of emphasizing fact or higher cognitive questions in recitations. These experiments were reviewed by Winne (1979), who concluded that "whether teachers use predominantly higher cognitive questions or predominantly fact questions makes little difference in student achievement" (p. 43).

The same set of 18 experiments reviewed by Winne, plus two additional experiments, were subsequently reviewed by Redfield and Rousseau (1981). Instead of using Winne's "voting method" to pool results across experiments, they turned to the more sophisticated method of meta-analysis. Redfield and Rousseau concluded that "predominant use of higher level questions during instruction has a positive effect on student achievement" (p. 241). They did not define "predominate use," but it probably meant a recitation in which at least 75 percent of the questions are at the higher cognitive level. Student achievement in the experiments was measured by tests requiring fact recall and demonstration of thinking skills.

Thus, the Rosenshine review and the Redfield and Rousseau review reached firm but contradictory conclusions about the effectiveness of fact and higher cognitive questions. The contradiction, can be resolved, I think, by analyzing the student populations represented in the two reviews. Each study reviewed by Rosenshine involved disadvantaged primary grade children. The studies reviewed by Redfield and Rousseau involved students representing a much wider range of ability and grade levels. Taking this difference into account, I would conclude that (1) emphasis on fact questions is more effective for promoting young disadvantaged children's achievement, which primarily involves mastery of basic skills; and (2) emphasis on higher cognitive questions is more effective for students of average and high ability, especially as they enter high school, where more independent thinking is required. While *emphasizing* fact questions, teachers of young disadvantaged children should take care to include some higher cognitive questions to stimulate development of their thinking skills.

Additional evidence favoring higher cognitive questions is found in research on the effects of having students answer questions that are inserted every few paragraphs in a textbook passage. Andre (1979) reviewed this research and concluded that higher cognitive questions generally facilitate better textbook learning than do fact questions.

Despite the demonstrated effectiveness of higher cognitive questions, most teachers do not emphasize them in practice. In an earlier research review, I concluded: "About 60 percent of teachers' questions require students to recall facts; about 20 percent require students to think; and the remaining 20 percent are procedural" (Gall, 1970, p. 713). This conclusion continues to be supported by recent observational studies of classroom teaching (Hare and Pulliam, 1980). It appears that teachers emphasize fact questions, whereas research indicates that an emphasis on higher cognitive questions would be more effective.

THE PROCESS OF ANSWERING TEACHER QUESTIONS

The research reviewed above does not explain the process by which fact and higher cognitive questions affect learning. Recent efforts to conceptualize and study this process (Gall, 1983) have shed new light on why questions of a certain type may facilitate learning in some students, but not in others.

The typical teacher question occurs in a recitation after students have been exposed to new curriculum content, usually by reading the textbook. Answering such a question appears to involve five steps.

1. *Attend to the Question.* The first step is to listen to the question as it is asked. Students who are off-task when the question is asked will be unable to generate a response or to profit from listening to another student's response. The need for attending may explain why reserach on young, slow-learning students has found that it is effective

for teachers to ask narrow, easily answered questions *and* to use instructional behaviors that engage students' attention (Rosenshine, 1976).

2. *Decipher the Meaning of the Question.* If the student has attended to the teacher's question, the next step is to decipher its syntax to determine what is being asked. Gullo (1983) found that young children often cannot figure out what the qusetion asks them to do. For example, when the word *what* appeared as the object term of a question, 85 percent of the children in his research sample could answer it correctly. When *what* appeared as the subject term, however, only 21 percent of the children could answer it correctly.

The ways teachers phrase questions can create difficulties for older students, too. Because teachers often generate questions spontaneously, some questions are likely to be poorly phrased. In everyday discourse, we can handle the problem by asking for clarification. In classroom situations, however, students may feel awkward about making such a request because it may be seen as criticsm of the teacher.

3. *Generate a Covert Response.* Students need to think of an answer before they can put it into words. To generate the covert response, students must have relevant information stored in memory or available in curriculum materials; and they must possess appropriate cognitive abilities for manipulating this information.

An indirect measure of students' ability to generate a covert response is the degree of congruence between the cognitive level of the teacher's question and the cognitive level of the student's response. Several studies (Dillon, 1982a; Mills and others, 1980; Willson, 1973) found that only about half of students' responses were at the same cognitive level as the teachers' questions. Of the incongruent responses, Dillon and Willson found that from one-third to one-half were at a lower cognitive level than the teacher's question.

These results run counter to the popular belief, "Ask a higher-level question, get a higher-level answer" (Lamb, 1976). Instead, a higher cognitive question poses a cognitive challenge that the student may or may not be able to meet. Training teachers in questioning techniques has been shown to reduce the incidence of question-answer cognitive incongruity (Klinzing-Eurich and Klinzing, 1982), but the process by which the reduction occurs is unclear.

Cognitive level is just one aspect of the student's response to a question. Gall (1970) and Ryan (1972) identified additional aspects, including whether each assertion contained in the response is clear, plausible, original, supported, and conditional.

The complexity of these response characteristics suggests that teachers should give students sufficient time to think before expecting a verbal response. Rowe (1974) found, however, that most teachers wait only one second for a response before repeating the question, calling on another student, or making a comment. Recent studies (Swift and Gooding, 1983; Tobin and Capie, 1982) found that extending wait time for several seconds has beneficial effects, including improved student engagement and longer verbal responses. In related research, Dillon (1981a) found that length of student responses increased when teachers asked fewer questions per minute.

These research findings argue against the common practice of rapid-fire questioning, which gives students little time to generate a substantial covert response followed by a substantial overt response.

4. *Generate an Overt Response.* Generating a covert response to the teacher's question does not ensure that the student will generate an overt response. A student may compete for "air time" with other students but not be called on to respond. Also, some students maintain a low profile so the teacher won't call on them.

Researchers have investigated whether there is systematic bias in who gives overt responses to teacher questions. Jackson and Cosca (1974) found that teachers of ethnically mixed classes were more likely to address questions to white students than to Mexican-American students. Also, white students responded more often to teacher questions, and more frequently initiated remarks of their own.

Lockheed and Hall (1975) concluded from their review of research that boys are more likely than girls to speak in class discussions. However, recent studies (Dillon, 1982b; Good, Cooper, and Blakey, 1980) have found slight or no differences in boys' and girls' opportunities to respond in class.

The consequences of teacher bias in giving students the opportunity to respond are not well understood. Covert responses evoked by the teacher's questions, or listening to another student's overt response, may be most critical for learning. If so, the student who listens carefully during the recitation

or who answers each question covertly would learn as much information as students who give oral responses. On the other hand, the student's own thoughts may not be fully clarified and developed until put into words.

5. *Revise the Response.* The student may rethink a covert or overt response to the teacher's question depending on what happens next. If the teacher redirects the same question to someone else, some students will revise their response in light of their classmate's contributions. Another option for the teacher is to ask one student probing questions that lead to improving the original response.

Wright and Nuthall (1970) found that teacher redirection of questions was positively correlated with student learning gains, but subsequent experimental research by Hughes (1971) failed to replicate this effect. In other research Riley (1981) found a positive effect for teacher redirection, but my colleagues and I found no effect for teacher redirection used in conjunction with probing questions (Gall and others, 1978).

The reason for these inconsistent findings may lie in how teacher redirection and probing were conducted in each study. That is, these instructional behaviors may have no effect unless they are explicitly focused on improving particular response criteria (for example, clarity, plausibilty, and accuracy).

Redirection and probing do not exhaust the possibilities for teacher response following the student's answer. Duffy (1983) suggested that teachers can facilitate learning by providing explanations that clarify and correct the student's response. Another option is to acknowledge the student's response by accepting and building on it. Researchers have conducted many studies of this technique as it was conceptualized by Flanders (1970). Gage (1978) concluded from his review of this research that teacher acceptance of student ideas is positively correlated with student learning gains.

THE EFFECTIVENESS OF RECITATIONS

Most research on teacher questions over the past two decades has investigated the effectiveness of recitations in which questions vary in cognitive level. A more basic issue, however, is whether recitations, irrespective of cognitive level, are effective. Would students learn as much if teachers did not use the recitation method to help them review a section of the textbook that they have just read?

Few researchers have addressed this question directly. One relevant study (Gall and others, 1978) compared the learning of students who participated in a series of recitations with the learning of other students. Both groups had read the same textbook passages beforehand. The researchers found that students who participated in the recitations performed better than the no-recitation group on various measures of fact and higher cognitive learning.

Research on questions inserted in the text has yielded similar results. Faw and Waller (1976) and Andre (1979) reviewed research on the effectiveness of having the students read textbook passages with and without inserted questions. They concluded that students generally learn more when the passages contain inserted questions.

Questions apparently are *more* effective than no questions, but they are not necessarily the *most* effective instructional alternative. Dillon (1978) strongly criticized the effectiveness of teacher questions and proposed several nonquestioning alternatives such as "declaration of perplexity" and "deliberate silence" (1981b). The effectiveness of these techniques relative to traditional recitation, however, has not been tested.

Why is recitation effective? Analysis of the recitation process suggests four reasons.

Practice and Feedback Effect

Students usually participate in a recitation immediately or soon after reading textbook content. The recitation gives students an opportunity to practice recalling the content and thinking about it. They also receive feedback about the accuracy and quality of their answers. Thus, recitation incorporates two processes, practice and feedback, which are of proven effectiveness in strengthening knowledge and skills.

Cueing Effect

Recitation questions provide cues that may focus students' attention on particular information in the text. Evidence for this function of questions comes from research on intentional and incidental learning.

Intentional learning involves the learning of textbook content that is rehearsed by recitation questions, whereas incidental learning involves the learning of textbook content that is not rehearsed.

Recitations generally have a greater positive effect on students' intentional learning than on their incidental learning (Gall and others, 1978). In other words, students perform better on end-of-unit test items that have been asked previously as recitation questions than they do on test questions they have not heard before. This suggests that when students hear a question during recitation, they are likely to rehearse the answer carefully. Students do this because they develop an expectation, based on experience, that the same question will be included on a subsequent test. Conversely, they devote low study effort, or none at all, to textbook content not covered in the recitation.

The hypothesized cueing effect of questions may explain a perplexing effect obtained in two experiments (Gall and others, 1978; Riley, 1981). In both experiments, students who participated in recitations containing 50 percent higher cognitive questions learned less well than did students whose recitations contained either a much lower or much higher percentage of higher cognitive questions. Since the 50 percent recitations did not emphasize *either* fact or higher cognitive questions, students may have become confused about the recitations' objective—was it to rehearse facts or to think about them? In contrast, students whose recitations emphasized one type of question or the other rehearsed the textbook content without the distraction of having to second-guess the teacher's intent.

Instruction and Test Similarity

The question-and-answer format of recitation parallels closely the conventional test format for determining the amount of student learning at the end of a curriculum unit. This format consists of written test questions requiring a multiple-choice or short-answer response. Thus, the student performance elicited by recitation transfers directly to the performance required on most school tests. The practice provided by recitation certainly appears more relevant to subsequent testing than the practice provided by such instructional methods as lecture and inquiry teaching.

Modality Effect

Researchers have found that elementary school students are more engaged during teacher-led activities than during seatwork activities (Rosenshine, 1980). And they are most engaged when teacher-led activities involve recitations with an academic focus.

One explanation for these findings is that recitations involve speaking and listening, whereas seatwork involves reading and writing. For many students, speaking and listening may be more motivating and less demanding than reading and writing. This explanation is speculative but sufficiently compelling to warrant further research on the effectiveness of recitation and how it can complement instructional methods that emphasize other communication modalities.

IMPLICATIONS OF RESEARCH FOR PRACTICE

The research on teacher questions challenges typical classroom practice in several respects. For example, researchers have found that emphasis on higher cognitive questions generally produces better learning than emphasis on fact questions. There is no lack of books and pamphlets encouraging teachers to ask more higher cognitive questions, but apparently their admonitions have had little influence on classroom instruction. Educators need to search for more effective ways to influence teachers' instructional behavior.

Another challenge for practice comes from research on the question-answering process. The findings demonstrate clearly that teacher questions do not necessarily elicit good student answers. Improving the quality of teachers' questions, then, is not sufficient. Students also need to learn the response requirements of different types of questions. Recent work on this problem has yielded promising results. For example, Raphael and McKinney (1983) found that elementary school students were able to learn several question-answer relationships and use this knowledge to improve their reading comprehension.

Finally, educators need to come to grips with the question posed by Hoetker and Ahlbrand: "If the recitation is a poor pedagogical method, as most teacher educators have long believed, why have they not been able to deter teachers from using it?" (1969, p. 163). Part of the answer may be in the research findings reviewed here: teachers use recitation because it *is* effective in helping students learn the curriculum, which is largely textbook-based. Since there are few signs that this curriculum approach is changing, teachers will continue to use this method. Rather than trying to deter teachers from using recitation, therefore, teacher educators may be better advised to help them learn [to] use it well.

REFERENCES

Andre, T. "Does Answering Higher-Level Questions While Reading Facilitate Productive Learning?" *Review of Educational Research* 49 (1979): 280–318.

Dillon, J. T. "Using Questions to Depress Student Thought." *School Review* 87 (1978): 50–63.

Dillon, J. T. "Duration of Response to Teacher Questions and Statements." *Contemporary Educational Psychology* 6 (1981a): 1–11.

Dillon, J. T. "To Question and Not to Question during Discussions, II. Non-Questioning Techniques." *Journal of Teacher Education* 32 (1981b): 15–20.

Dillon, J. T. "Cognitive Correspondence between Question/Statement and Response." *American Educational Research Journal* 19 (1982a): 540–551.

Dillon, J. T. "Male-Female Similarities in Class Participation." *Journal of Educational Research* 75 (1982b): 350–353.

Duffy, G. G. "From Turn Taking to Sense Making: Broadening the Concept of Reading Teacher Effectiveness." *Journal of Educational Research* 76 (1983): 134–139.

Dunkin, M. J., and Biddle, B. J. *The Study of Teaching.* New York: Holt, Rinehart and Winston, 1974.

Durkin, D. "What Classroom Observations Reveal about Reading Comprehension Instruction." *Reading Research Quarterly* 15 (1978–79): 481–533.

Faw, H. W., and Waller, T. G. "Mathemagenic Behaviors and Efficiency in Learning from Prose Materials: Review, Critique, Recommendations." *Review of Educational Research* 46 (1976): 691–720.

Flanders, N. A. *Analyzing Teaching Behavior.* New York: Addison-Wesley, 1970.

Gage, N. L. *The Scientific Basis of the Art of Teaching.* New York: Teachers College Press, 1978.

Gall, M. D. "The Use of Questions in Teaching," *Review of Educational Research* 40 (1970): 707–721.

Gall, M. D. "Reactions to Recent Research on Questions." Paper presented at the annual meeting of the American Educational Association, Montreal, April 1983.

Gall, M. D.; Ward, B. A.; Berliner, D. C.; Cahen, L. S.; Winne, P. H.; Elashoff, J. D.; and Stanton,

G. C. "Effects of Questioning Techniques and Recitation on Student Learning," *American Educational Research Journal* 15 (1978): 175–199.

Good, T. L.; Cooper, H. M.: and Blakey, S. L. "Classroom Interaction as a Function of Teacher Expectations, Student Sex, and Time of Year," *Journal of Educational Psychology* 72 (1980): 378–385.

Gullo, D. F. "Cognitive Responses to Questioning." Paper presented at the annual meeting of the American Educational Research Association, Montreal, April 1983.

Hare, V. C., and Pulliam, C. A. "Teacher Questioning: A Verification and an Extension." *Journal of Reading Behavior* 12 (1980): 69–72.

Heath, R. W., and Nielson, M. A. "The Research Basis for Performance-based Teacher Education." *Review of Educational Research* 44 (1974): 463–484.

Hoetker, J., and Ahlbrand, W. P., Jr. "The Persistence of the Recitation." *American Educational Research Journal* 6 (1969): 145–167.

Hughes, D. C. "The Effects of Certain Conditions of Pupil Participation and Teacher Reacting on the Achievement of Form 2 Pupils." *Educational Research Newsletter* 4 (1971): 12–14.

Jackson, G., and Cosca, C. "The Inequality of Educational Opportunity in the Southwest: An Observational Study of Ethnically Mixed Classrooms." *American Educational Research Journal* 11 (1974): 219–229.

Klinzing-Eurich, G., and Klinzing, H. G. "Reducing the Incongruities between Teacher Questions and Student Responses: The Effects of a Training Program." Paper presented at the annual meeting of the Australian Association for Research in Teaching, Brisbane, Queensland, Australia, 1982.

Lamb, W. G. "Ask a Higher-Level Question, Get a Higher-Level Answer." *Science Teacher* 43 (1976): 22–23.

Lockheed, M. E., and Hall, K. P. "Sex as a Status Characteristic—the Role of Formal Theory in Developing Leadership Training Strategies." Paper presented at the annual meeting of the American Sociological Association, San Francisco, August 1975.

Mills, S. R.; Rice, C. T.; Berliner, D. C.; and Rousseau, E. W. "The Correspondence between Teacher Questions and Student Answers in Classroom Discourse." *Journal of Experimental Education* 48 (1980): 194–204.

Raphael, T. E., and McKinney, J. "An Examination of Fifth- and Eighth-Grade Children's Question-Answering Behavior: An Instructional Study in Meta-cognition." *Journal of Reading Behavior* 15 (1983): 67–86.

Redfield, D. L., and Rousseau, E. W. "Meta-Analysis of Experimental Research on Teacher Questioning Behavior." *Review of Educational Research* 51 (1981): 237–245.

Riley, J. P. "The Effects of Preservice Teachers' Cognitive Questioning Level and Redirecting on Student Science Achievement." *Journal of Research in Science Teaching* 18 (1981): 303–309.

Rosenshine, B. *Teaching Behaviors and Student Achievement*. Slough, England: National Foundation for Educational Research in England and Wales, 1971.

Rosenshine, B. "Classroom Instruction." In *Psychology of Teaching Methods. The Seventy-fifth Yearbook of the National Society for the Study of Education, Part I*. Edited by N. L. Gage. Chicago: University of Chicago Press, 1976.

Rosenshine, B. V. "How Time Is Spent in Elementary Classrooms." In *Time to Learn*. Edited by Carolyn Denham and Ann Lieberman. Washington, D.C.: U.S. Department of Education and National Institute of Education, 1980.

Rowe, M. B. "Wait-Time and Rewards as Instructional Variables: Their Influence on Language, Logic, and Fate Control. Part I. Wait-Time." *Journal of Research in Science Teaching* 11 (1974): 81–94.

Ryan, F. L. "Analyzing the Questioning Activity of Students and Teachers." *College Student Journal* 6 (1972): 116–123.

Sirotnik K. A. "What You See Is What You Get—Consistency, Persistency, and Mediocrity in Classrooms." *Harvard Educational Review* 53 (1983): 16–31.

Swift, J. N., and Gooding, C. T. "Interaction of Wait Time Feedback and Questioning Instruction on Middle School Science Teaching." *Journal of Research on Science Teaching* 20 (1983): 721–730

Tobin, K. G., and Capie, W. "Relationships between Classroom Process Variables and Middle-School Science Achievement." *Journal of Educational Psychology* 74 (1982): 441–454.

Willson, I. A. "Changes in Mean Levels of Thinking in Grades 1–8 through Use of an Interaction Analysis System Based on Bloom's Taxonomy." *Journal of Educational Research* 66 (1973): 423–429

Winne, P. H. "Experiments Relating Teachers' Use of Higher Cognitive Questions to Student Achievement." *Review of Educational Research* 49 (1979): 13–50.

Wright, C. J., and Nuthall, G. "Relationships between Teacher Behaviors and Pupil Achievement in Three Experimental Elementary Science Lessons." *American Educational Research Journal* 7 (1970): 477–491.

6. RESEARCH ON CLASSROOM TEACHING

Thomas Good

INTRODUCTION

We know considerably more about classroom teaching than we did a decade ago. In 1970 the accumulated knowledge about the effects of classroom processes on student achievement was weak and contradictory. In some curriculum areas at the elementary school level, we now have more information. Within less than a decade, the literature on *basic skills* instruction in reading and mathematics in elementary school has moved from a state of confusion to a point where experimental studies can be designed upon a data base. Although classroom teaching and learning is, and is likely to remain, a problematic activity, the field has developed some important concepts that have rich application value.

Classroom research was an active and productive area in the 1970's. . . . I have chosen to emphasize teacher expectation and teacher effectiveness research, because these were among the most active research areas in [the] 1970's and both topics appear to be related to student performance. Three general goals of this chapter are: (1) to describe the teacher expectation and teacher effectiveness research performed in the 1970's and to suggest why research took the form that it did; (2) to discuss some of the problems associated with this research and to present some recent attempts to improve upon it; and (3) to discuss possible policy implications that are suggested by these inquiries.

Three substantive conclusions based upon the research review will be discussed in this chapter. The first is that teachers can make a measurable difference in students' learning of basic skills. Data collected in the 1970's provide convincing proof that teachers can and do make important differences in student learning. Second, low achievers can benefit from appropriate instruction, and there are now ample data to support this contention. The third conclusion is that we have gained some insight into teaching strategies and teacher beliefs which make a difference in certain instructional settings. In particular, it seems that positive but appropriate teacher expectations for student learning, good man-

agement techniques, and active teaching (teaching that provides conceptual and procedural direction, frequent feedback, and opportunities for student success) are key features of instruction that promote students' mastery of basic · skills. Despite some progress, much more knowledge is needed about classroom phenomena before more optimal learning environments can be designed for students across a variety of learning outcomes. Any advocacy of uniform teaching practices thus seems both premature and doomed to failure. . . .

TEACHER EXPECTATIONS, TEACHER BEHAVIOR, AND STUDENT INFLUENCE

It is beyond the purpose of this paper to review extensively the existing literature on teacher expectation effects. There are several comprehensive reviews, and the interested reader can consult these sources (Brophy, 1982; Braun, 1976; Brophy and Good, 1974; Cooper, 1979; Cooper and Good, in press; Dusek, 1975; Rosenthal, 1974). A good portion of the research conducted in the 1970's was classroom observational research aimed at determining what teachers *do* in their interactions with high- and low-achieving students. Much of this research was organized around the model produced by Brophy and Good (1970). Their conceptual model for examining potential teacher expectation effects included the following steps: (1) the teacher expects specific behavior and achievement from particular students; (2) because of these varied expectations, the teacher behaves differently toward different students; (3) this treatment communicates to the students what behavior and achievement the teacher expects from them and affects their self-concepts, achievement motivation, and levels of aspiration; and (4) if this treatment is consistent over time and if the students do not resist or change it in some way, it will shape their achievement and behavior. High-expectation students will be led to achieve at higher levels, whereas the achievement of low-expectation students will decline; (5) with time, students' achievement and behavior will conform more and more closely to the behavior originally expected of them.

One of the major findings of this extensive literature on how teachers treat high- and low-achieving students in the classroom has been the fact that teachers *vary* greatly in their classroom behavior. There is ample research evidence to show that there are differences in teacher behavior *between* classrooms (for example, some teachers praise a great deal and other teachers praise comparatively little) and *within* classrooms (some students in a particular classroom receive more praise than do other students). The extent to which teachers differentiate in their behavior toward high- and low-achieving students has been found to represent an individual difference variable. Differences toward high and low achievers have been found in both quantitative studies (Brophy and Good, 1970; Cooper and Baron, 1977; Good, Cooper, and Blakey, 1980) and in qualitative studies (Levine and Mann, 1981; McDermott, 1976).

It is not clear whether teachers who differentiate sharply in their behavior toward highs and lows do so because of personality variables (defensiveness, rigidity), school or classroom organizational variables, or characteristics that individual pupils and groups of students bring to the classroom. Although the causes of differential interaction are not definitely established, Brophy and Good (1974) estimated that about ⅓ of the classroom teachers who have been observed in related research have shown patterns of highly differentiated behavior toward high and low achievers. Carew and Lightfoot (1979) reported that teachers who teach at the same grade level in the same school vary more on many instructional dimensions than teachers who teach in different schools. It would thus seem that at least some of the variation in teacher behavior toward high- and low-achieving students can be explained by teachers' personalities and their beliefs about instructional behavior.

Differences in Teacher Behavior toward High- and Low-Achieving Students

Teachers have been found to differentiate their behavior toward students perceived by teachers as high achievers (highs) or low achievers (lows) in a variety of ways. Some of the replicated findings are listed below.

1. Seating slow students farther from the teacher and/or seating lows in a group.
2. Paying less attention to lows in academic situations.
3. Calling on lows less often to answer classroom questions or to make public demonstrations.
4. Waiting less time for lows to answer questions.
5. Not staying with lows in failure situations (providing clues, asking follow-up questions).
6. Criticizing lows more frequently than highs for incorrect public responses.
7. Praising lows less frequently than highs after successful public responses.
8. Praising lows more frequently than highs for marginal or inadequate public responses.
9. Providing low-achieving students with less accurate and less detailed feedback than highs.
10. Failing to provide lows with feedback about their responses more frequently than highs.
11. Demanding less work and effort from lows than from highs.
12. Interrupting the performance of low achievers more frequently than that of high achievers.

The behaviors listed above simply indicate some of the ways in which *some* teachers differentiate in their behavior toward high- and low-achieving students. They do not necessarily represent inappropriate behavior. For example, a teacher who does not call on low students frequently during public participation may still be effective if that teacher is working with low achievers privately and attempting to develop their responding skills so that they can become more active participants later in the year. A single process measure thus *cannot* be used as a sign of effective or ineffective communication. The desirability of a particular teaching behavior depends in part upon the teacher's total instructional plan, the content being taught, and the characteristics of individual students.

Although it is important not to overinterpret differences in teacher behavior that highs and lows receive in the classroom, it is important to question the need for differential treatment when it is identified. Allington (in press) argues that students in low-reading groups often learn less because teachers believe these students have unique needs. He argues that if students in the low group were taught more like students in the high group, they would perform more appropriately. Allington raises a number of questions about the needs of students in high- and low-reading groups, and an examination of his work should challenge teachers and policymakers to consider more fully the assumptions they hold about *how* to instruct students in high- and low-reading groups.

Teacher Expectations and Student Achievement

Most of the research on teacher expectations conducted in the 1970's was correlational in nature and simply examined differences in teacher interaction patterns with high- and low-achieving students. There is thus no firm basis for arguing that certain patterns of teacher behavior *cause* higher (or lower) student performance. Because these studies are correlational, it could be argued that teachers held higher expectations in some instances because students were achieving at higher levels (West and Anderson, 1976). Still, there are consistent data to illustrate that positive teacher expectations are associated with student achievement gains.

McDonald and Elias (1976), in a large study of teacher effectiveness, found a positive relationship between teacher expectations and student achievement. Similarly, Brophy and Evertson (1976) found that teachers who were obtaining the highest achievement from students were teachers who perceived students as capable of learning schoolwork and who viewed themselves as competent in teaching the curriculum. Studies of school effects have found that teachers in high-achievement schools, in contrast to those in less effective schools, appear to believe that students can and will learn (Brookover et al., 1978; Edmonds, 1979; Rutter et al., 1979).

Other research has also demonstrated the *plausibility* of teacher expectation effects. Mary Martin and Sam Kerman sensitized teachers who taught in inner-city schools in Los Angeles to potential ways in which low expectations might be communicated by using the dyadic classroom observation system and related research presented in the book *Looking in Classrooms* (Good and Brophy, 1973). They also helped teachers to develop communication skills for interacting with low-achieving students in effective ways. Their results showed that after training, experimental teachers were able to elicit better student achievement and more favorable attitudes than were control teachers (Martin, 1973). In addition to the expectation training, teachers also had the opportunity to observe other teachers and to be observed themselves by other teachers. The achievement and attitude growth of students in the experimental classes was thus probably due to an increased repertoire of teaching skills as well as to higher expectations. Still, it seems plausible that teachers' increased confidence in their ability to work with low achievers was at least a partial determinant of pupil achievement. Although the data base is not complete, in all naturalistic studies attempting to relate expectations with student achievement, positive correlations have been obtained.

Teaching Dilemma

Clearly, teachers can expect *too much* or *too little* in their instructional interactions with students. This dilemma also has to be addressed by curriculum specialists who write textbooks and by policymakers. There is research evidence that teachers can and do err in making assignments too easy or too difficult. However, in general, existing evidence suggests that teachers are more likely to expect too little from students that they perceive as having limited ability. Inappropriately low performance expectations are often associated with good teacher intentions, but such expectations still have harmful effects. . . .

Explanations for Differential Teacher Behavior

Why is it that some teachers differentiate in their behavior toward high- and low-achieving students in ways that seem inappropriate? One basic reason is that classrooms are very busy and complex environments and it is difficult for teachers to maintain an accurate assessment of the frequency and quality of their interactions with individual students. Philip Jackson (1968) has suggested that elementary school teachers have over 1000 interpersonal exchanges a day. Thus, teachers may interact more or less frequently with certain students because of the speed and complexity with which classroom life unfolds.

A second explanation involves the fact that much classroom behavior has to be *interpreted* before it has meaning. Teachers have to react quickly to student behavior in ongoing classroom settings. When a teacher asks a question and a student raises an eyebrow and makes no response, the teacher has to interpret the student's lack of response and raised eyebrow. Does the raised eyebrow mean that the student is thinking about the response (and hence, the teacher should allow the student more time to respond), or does it mean that the student is hopelessly lost? Some research (for example, a recent ethnographic study by Kathryn Anderson-Levitt, 1981) suggests that teachers may systematically interpret cues in ways that are consistent with their initial expectations. Once a teacher develops an expectation that a student is not capable of learning, the teacher interprets subsequent ambiguous classroom events (and many classroom behaviors are ambiguous) in a way consistent with that original expectation (Good, 1980).

A third reason why teachers show more or less variation in their behavior toward high- and low-achieving students involves the issue of *causality*. Some teachers believe that they can and will influence student learning (for example, see Brophy and Evertson, 1976). Such teachers may interpret student failure as the need for more instruction, more clarification, and eventually, increased opportunity to learn. Other teachers, because they assign blame rather than assume partial responsibility for student failure, may interpret failure as the need to provide less challenge and less opportunity to learn.

Another explanation for differential teacher behavior is student behavior. Students present themselves in different ways to teachers and these self-presentation styles may influence teacher responses. Dee Spencer-Hall (1981) has noted that some students are able to *time* their misbehavior in such a way as to escape teacher attention, whereas other students who misbehave at comparable rates are reprimanded considerably more frequently because the timing of their misbehavior is inappropriate.

Similarly, Carrasco (1979) suggests that students may demonstrate competence in a style that escapes teacher attention. . . .

Variability in Teacher Behavior toward "Low" Students

As noted above, teachers show individual differences in the ways they interact with low-achieving students, and these differences are sometimes very dramatic. Some teachers criticize low achievers more frequently than highs per incorrect answer and praise lows less per correct answer. However, in other classrooms teachers praise marginal or incorrect answers given by low achievers. Good and Brophy (1980) contend that these findings reflect two different types of teachers. Teachers who reward marginal answers are unnecessarily protective of lows. Teachers who criticize lows for incorrect responses seem to be basically intolerant of these pupils and unwilling to deal with failure (and perhaps unwilling to examine their role in the failure process). Both types of teacher behavior will convey to students the idea that effort and class performances are not related. However, such differences in teacher behavior may create *interpretation* difficulties for low achievers and make it difficult for them to understand what is expected of them in their student role (Good, 1981). Consider the implications of variable teacher behavior for a third grade low-achieving student who is called upon frequently and finds teacher acceptance for virtually any verbalization. Upon moving to the fourth grade, however, the student finds that he/she is seldom called upon, seldom praised, and is criticized more frequently than other students. Such discontinuities in teacher expectations and behavior may reduce student effort and, in time, contribute to a *passive* learning style (What is expected of me?). It seems unfortunate that students who have *least adaptive capacity* may be asked to make the *greatest adjustment* as they move from classroom to classroom. It seems probable that low-achieving students receive more varied behavior because teachers agree less about how to respond to students *who do not learn* than about how to react to successful learning experiences (i.e., some teachers react to a poor performance by ignoring it, others by criticizing it, and yet others react to poor performance with gratuitous praise). . . .

Outcomes

One problem in research on teacher expectation effects has been the infrequent measurement of student progress of outcomes (changes in achievement or attitude over time). What measurement of achievement has taken place has tended to occur at the end of the year and there have been few attempts to relate specific outcomes (what students learn during a particular week) to detailed observation of a learning experience (that is, observation during the week in which learning is being measured). Typically, differential teacher behavior collected at one point in time (perhaps collected in October) has been related to student achievement scores at some distant point in time (e.g., in April). If we are to understand *how* teacher expectations and behaviors influence students and how student behavior and expectations influence teachers, we need to examine more immediate outcomes of instruction (Cooper and Good, in press).

We know very little about the effects of expectations and behavior upon immediate classroom events. Fortunately, there is a growing interest in examining this question. More careful attention to immediate classroom outcomes should lead to increased understanding of the relationship between beliefs, behavior, and achievement. Linda Anderson and her colleagues, in ongoing research at Michigan State University (Anderson, 1981), have found that many students, especially low achievers, are often left without adequate information for doing assigned seatwork.

Similar conclusions concerning the lack of attention by teachers to immediate student outcomes have been reached by Confrey and Good (in progress). They observed a secondary English class while the instructor was teaching a unit on paragraph composition. Three times the instructor emphasized that students should use personality descriptors, not physical descriptors, in writing a composition paragraph. During the lesson the instructor wrote a sample paragraph with the students on the board. In part because of the *rapid* nature of the interaction that took place during the writing of the paragraph on the board, the instructor included some physical descriptors in the paragraph. Students then had to decide whether to follow the original instructions (don't use physical descriptors) or to follow the model paragraph on the board. Unfortunately, the instructor did not monitor the work of the students, nor did he talk to individual students once they had started to write their paragraphs. A good opportunity for correcting misunderstandings was thus lost. . . .

Curriculum Research

Although there has been extensive examination of how some teachers vary their behavior toward high- and low-achieving students, few investigations have examined the possibility that students, receive different curriculum assignments. There is a great deal of anecdotal evidence to suggest that high and low achievers in the same classroom receive different curriculum assignments, yet little formal, systematic study of the possibility has taken place (for a discussion of related issues, see Keddie, 1971). Nor has the possibility that a subject area might create expectations which influence teacher and/or student behavior been studied. There is some reason to believe that this will be a fruitful and important line of inquiry. For example, Soltz (1976) has found that teaching behavior is different across curriculum areas. Individual elementary school teachers instruct differently when presenting various subject areas. Jorgenson (1978) has reported that in some classes 85% of the students were required to learn from material that was beyond their reading ability. These potential mismatches between student ability and content would appear to represent an important area of inquiry (and the Jorgenson results suggest that teachers can err on the side of expecting *too much* from students as well as too little). Future research needs to emphasize curriculum variables; however, it should be clear that I am not advocating curriculum research like that which took place in the 1950's, when the behavior and beliefs of teachers and students were ignored. Curriculum variables need to be integrated in the ongoing study of classroom process and into research that concomitantly pays attention to student and teacher beliefs. . . .

TEACHER EFFECTIVENESS RESEARCH

Concern with what teachers actually *do* in the classroom led many researchers to focus on how teachers interacted with high- and low-achieving students. An *incidental outcome* of this research was the demonstration that teachers vary greatly *across* classrooms in their behavior, as well as in how they distribute their time and resources *within* classrooms. Teachers have been found to vary widely in the type and quantity of classroom questions that they ask, in the time that they spend in presenting new material versus review, in the amount of time they spend in general recitation settings versus seatwork settings, and in how they organize classrooms for instruction (whole class, individualized, small groups). The discovery of such variations in structure and behavior led many investigators to become interested in their impact upon student achievement and behavior.

Other pressures and opportunities also directed increased attention to the effect of teaching variables upon students' subject matter mastery. The National Institute of Education's interest and systematic funding of research to study basic skill acquisition in elementary schools created an opportunity for intensive observational work. Because many educational researchers, sociologists, anthropologists, and psychologists were interested in observing and understanding classroom phenomena, support for inquiry to basic skill areas in elementary schools resulted in much research attention to this particular question. As a result of such research, it is now possible to make some statements about the effects of teacher behavior upon students' subject matter acquisition in the elementary school setting. Descriptions of substantive findings and methodological issues associated with teacher effectiveness research can be found elsewhere (Berliner, 1977; Brophy, 1979; Doyle, 1977, 1979; Good, 1979, 1982; Medley, 1979; Rosenshine, 1979; Peterson and Walberg, 1979). . . .

A Case Study

One way to illustrate the potential as well as the problems of effectiveness research is to consider in depth one specific program of research, a program on mathematics learning which Doug Grouws and I coordinated at the University of Missouri. Because it is research that I have helped to conduct, I am both very familiar with it and in some respects I am in a good position to criticize it.

Our initial research on this problem began with a sample of over 100 third- and fourth-grade teachers who taught in a middle-class, urban school district and used the same textbook. To make comparisons across teachers, it was necessary to develop an operational definition of effectiveness. In our research we used student performance on a standardized achievement test in mathmatics as a way of estimating instructional progress. We realized that a standardized achievement score was not a perfect measure of classroom learning and that in some cases the test content did not overlap with the content that classroom teachers actually taught (as a case in point, see Porter et al., 1978).

We nevertheless felt that there was a reasonable consensus among teachers and standardized test developers as to what constituted the mathematics curriculum in the elementary school. However, it is important to realize that initially this was an *assumption* that we made and that by using standardized achievement results as a criterion for effectiveness, we restricted our claims for effectiveness to only those aspects of the teaching role related to producing gains on such tests. Other important teaching behaviors and student outcomes are not covered in our research (and in most other effectiveness research).

Looking at test scores over a 3-year period, we found that teachers varied considerably in their impact on students' learning, despite the fact that they were using the same textbook and in most cases were teaching comparable students (that is, the mean class achievement scores were very similar in the fall). Our initial data were a demonstration of an apparent *teacher effect*. Some teachers produced much more mathematics learning than did other teachers teaching in comparable settings.

Our focus was on observing *stable* teachers because we wanted to identify mathematics teaching strategies which appeared to make a difference in student mastery of basic skill areas. We felt that teachers who had a stable and relatively high or low level of effectiveness would be an excellent basis for estimating the relative effectiveness of different teaching behaviors. Hence, our observational research focused upon teachers who were consistently high and low across several consecutive years in their ability to produce student performance on standardized achievement tests. Interestingly, teachers who had extreme effects on achievement (very high and very low) used a large-group teaching format. Hence, format did not predict achievement.

Since we were interested in observing high and low teachers, our study became an examination of large-group teaching as teachers who used individualized or small-group techniques tended (as a group) to have average effects on student achievement.

We found that stable, high and low large-group teachers differed in their classroom behavior. That is, more and less effective teachers taught in different ways, and some of these differences in teaching behavior were consistent across the two groups of teachers.

Within the constraints of our operational definition, more effective teachers, in contrast to less effective teachers, were found to (1) present information more actively and clearly in the development stage of the lesson (that part of the lesson in which teachers stress the meaning of the material); (2) be task-focused (most of the period was spent on mathematics, not socialization); (3) allow students to initiate more academic questions; (4) be basically nonevaluative and create a relatively relaxed learning environment with comparatively little praise or criticism; (5) express higher achievement expectations (more homework, somewhat faster pace, more alerting); and (6) have fewer behavioral problems.

Although we were pleased with the naturalistic findings in that they provided some clear contrasts between relatively high and low gain classrooms, we were aware of the fact that these were only correlational results and that they did not necessarily imply that these teacher behaviors *caused* student achievement. It could be that behaviors not studied in our observational research were more directly related to achievement (e.g., more effective teachers plan more thoroughly and because of this, they are more task-focused and assign more homework). We felt that it was important to determine whether a more direct association could be established between the behaviors that were identified in our observational, naturalistic study and student achievement.

In particular, we wanted to see if we could instruct teachers to behave in ways consistent with the behavior of "effective" teachers and to determine what, if any, impact such behavior would have on student achievement. Because of the expense involved in field testing the program, we wanted it to be as comprehensive as possible. Thus, in addition to including the contrasts obtained in our earlier naturalistic studies, we tested some of the promising findings from other teacher effectiveness studies, as well as results from previous experimental mathematics studies. Writing the training program resulted in a 45-page manual for teachers. The program, as pointed out elsewhere (Good and Grouws, 1979), is a system of instruction: (1) instructional activity is initiated and reviewed in the context of *meaning*; (2) students are prepared for each lesson stage to enhance involvement and to minimize errors; (3) the principles of distributed and successful practice are built into the program; (4) active teaching is demanded, especially in the developmental portion of the lesson (when the teacher explains the concept being studied, its importance, etc.). An overview of the program is presented in Table [1].

We tested the program in 40 classrooms: about half of the classrooms were assigned to experimental conditions, and the other half to control conditions. Experimental teachers read the manual and were given approximately 2½ hours of training. Several procedures were employed to ensure that the control group was motivated to pursue achievement gains in mathematics, and we feel that a strong control for Hawthorne[1] effects was built into the project (for details, see Good and Grouws, 1979).

One major question was whether teachers would be willing to implement the program. On the basis of observers' records, it was found that the experimental teachers implemented the program very well (with the exception of certain recommendations concerning how to handle the development portion of the lesson). Because experimental teachers did use the program, it was possible to determine how the experimental training and subsequent teaching activity influenced student achievement and attitudes.

Pre- and post-testing with the standardized achievement test indicated that after 2½ months of the program, the performance of students in experimental classrooms was considerably higher than those in control classrooms. It was also found that the experimental students' performance increase continued for at least some time following the treatment. Regular end-of-year testing by the public school system indicated that approximately 3 months after the program had ended, the experimental students were still performing better that the control students. We also constructed a content test that more closely matched the material which teachers

TABLE [1]   Summary of Key Instructional Behaviors*

Daily Review (First 8 minutes except Mondays)
    a. Review the concepts and skills associated with the homework.
    b. Collect and deal with homework assignments.
    c. Ask several mental computation exercises.

Development (About 20 minutes)
    a. Briefly focus on prerequisite skills and concepts.
    b. Focus on meaning and promoting student understanding by using lively explanations, demonstrations, process explanations, illustrations, etc.
    c. Assess student comprehension.
        1. Use process/product questions (active interaction).
        2. Use controlled practice.
    d. Repeat and elaborate on the meaning portion as necessary.

Seatwork (About 15 minutes)
    a. Provide uninterrupted successful practice.
    b. Maintain momentum—keep the ball rolling—get everyone involved, then sustain involvement.
    c. Use alerting—let students know their work will be checked at the end of the period.
    d. Provide accountability—check the students' work.

Homework Assignment
    a. Assign homework on a regular basis at the end of each math class except Fridays.
    b. Homework should involve about 15 minutes of work to be done at home.
    c. Homework should include one or two review problems.

Special Reviews
    a. Weekly Review/Maintenance
        1. Conduct during the first 20 minutes each Monday.
        2. Focus on skills and concepts covered during the previous week.
    b. Monthly Review/Maintenance
        1. Conduct every fourth Monday.
        2. Focus on skills and concepts covered since the last monthly review.

*Definitions of all terms and detailed descriptions of teaching requests are presented in Good, T., Grouws, D., and Ebmeier, H., *Active mathematics teaching: Empirical Research in Elementary and Secondary Classrooms.* New York: Longman, Inc., in press.

were presenting than did the standardized test. The results on this test also showed an advantage for experimental classes, although differences between control and experimental classrooms were not as large as they were on the standardized achievement test (see Good and Grouws, 1979, for additional details and explanations).

We were also interested in knowing if the achievement gains came at the expense of student attitudes toward mathematics. Results of pre- and post-testing on a 10-item attitude scale revealed that experimental students reported significantly more favorable attitudes at the end of the experiment than did control students. Thus, the achievement gains did not appear to come at the expense of students' interest in mathematics. Finally, it is important to note that anonymous feedback from teachers in the project

indicated that they felt the program was practical and that they planned to continue using it in the future. Obviously, if teachers are to continue using the program, they must feel comfortable with it.

Research elsewhere has indicated that teachers have a favorable reaction to the program even when it is presented and discussed without the involvement of the developers (Andros and Freeman, 1981; Keziah, 1980). Also, in research at the junior high level it appears that secondary teachers have implemented the program with positive impact on students' verbal problem-solving ability (Good and Grouws, 1981). Finally, it is important to note that our basic findings have been replicated by others (See Good, Grouws, and Ebmeier, in press).

Our research on mathematics instruction, especially at the elementary school level, has convinced us that teachers do make a *difference* in student learning and that in-service teachers can be trained in such a way that student performance can be increased. The system of instruction that we see as important can be broadly characterized as *active teaching*. It is instructive to note that in our experimental work active teaching was an important difference between teachers who were getting good achievement gains and those who were getting lower-than-expected gains. Teachers whose students made higher gains were much more active in presenting concepts, explaining the meanings of those concepts, providing appropriate practice activities, and monitoring those activities prior to assigning seatwork. The fact that these teachers appeared to look for ways to confirm or disconfirm that their presentations had been comprehended by students was particularly important. They assumed partial responsibility for student learning and appeared to be ready to reteach when necessary.

This difference in active teaching *across* classrooms is comparable to differences found *within* classrooms in teacher expectation research. That is, in the teacher expectation literature, there is evidence that in some classrooms low-achieving students receive less active and less meaningful teaching than high-achieving students. In our effectiveness research in mathematics we have found that some teachers are less active in teaching the *entire* classroom. Active instructional efforts seem to be an important aspect of teaching that is related to achievement gain, at least in basic skill areas.

Several other research efforts were directed at identifying teachers who were consistent in their effects, and this observational research attempted to pinpoint the ways in which more and less effective teachers differed in their classroom behavior. These results have been reviewed by several researchers. For example, Jere Brophy (1979) summarized observational studies of teacher effectiveness in the following way: "In summary, learning gains are most impressive in classrooms in which students receive a great deal of instruction from, and have a great deal of interaction with, the teacher, especially in public lessons and recitations that are briskly paced but conducted at a difficulty level that allows consistent success" (p. 747). Barak Rosenshine (1979) has argued that the following teaching acts are critical aspects of successful instruction in basic

skill areas: (1) a clear focus is kept on academic goals; (2) an effort is made to promote extensive content coverage and high levels of student involvement in classroom tasks; (3) teachers set clear instructional goals and actively monitor student progress toward those goals; (4) learning activities are structured and feedback is immediate and academically oriented; and (5) environments are created that are task-oriented but relaxed.

In addition to the several naturalistic studies of more and less effective teachers, there also have been a few attempts to intervene experimentally in the teaching process to determine whether teacher behavior changes and student achievement could be increased. An especially good review of four of these field experiments has been provided by Gage and Giaconia (1980). Gage and Giaconia note that there is solid evidence which indicates that it is possible to change teaching behaviors in desired directions through relatively inexpensive in-service teacher education programs. They note that changes in teacher behavior have occurred in experiments with random assignment of schools and/or teachers to training conditions and that the results show consistent improvement in student achievement. The reviewers have also noted that these four experiments differ considerably from previous educational experiments. In particular, they were conducted in regular classrooms; the instructional treatment has operated for an extended period of time; the experiments used practicing teachers (not student teachers); and the teaching behaviors manipulated in these experiments were realistic in the sense that other teachers already had been observed exhibiting these behaviors. The experiments thus had ecological validity because they were advocating that teachers perform behaviors which other teachers had been able to exhibit in the ongoing realities of the classroom environment (Good, 1979).

Problems Associated with Teacher Effectiveness Research

Many of the problems associated with teacher effectiveness research parallel those reported earlier in the description of teacher expectation research. It would be possible to repeat most of those criticisms here, emphasizing that much more information is needed about the beliefs that teachers and students have in experimental and control classrooms. These and other criticisms of effectiveness research have been discussed elsewhere (e.g., Doyle, 1979). To illustrate some of the problems associated with this type of research, it will be useful to raise questions about the interpretability of the findings from the Missouri Mathematics Effectiveness Program.

One important consideration is that in a variety of studies using the Missouri Mathematics Program, experimental groups have done better than related control groups. However, the magnitude and importance of the differences are more evident for some teacher and student combinations than others. It is clear that certain combinations of students and teachers together tend to do better using the treatment than do other combinations of students and teachers (Ebmeier and Good, 1979). The effects of the program on some teacher-student combinations have been replicated by Janicki and Peterson (1981). It also seems that the classroom organizational structure interacts with the effects of the instructional treatment (Ebmeier, Good, and Grouws, 1980).

It should be evident that there is *no* single system for presenting mathematics concepts effectively. For example, some of the control teachers in our studies have obtained high levels of student achievement using instructional systems that differ from those presented in the program we have developed. More information about the classroom contexts and particular combinations of teachers and students that make the program more or less effective is needed.

It is satisfying to see that the instructional program we have developed seems to be a viable system which teachers are willing to implement and that it has positive influences upon student achievement. We now need to know much more about *why* some teachers employ the system more fully than do others and the types of local school features (including child characteristics and classroom structure) that lead to greater levels of implementation. In particular, it would seem necessary to study mathematics teachers who use individualized and small-group practices more successfully than do other teachers. Researchers need to study the conditions that lead to success in various organizational settings and to determine which types of students and teachers benefit from these patterns of instruction. . . .

GENERAL POLICY IMPLICATIONS

. . .

Low-Achieving Students Can Learn

Perceptions of low achievers' learning potential are often too low; there is evidence that lows can and do benefit from active teaching. Data collected in the teacher expectation, teacher effectiveness, and students-as-teachers paradigms demonstrate that low-achieving students can benefit from systematic instruction. It is evident that teachers can also err by having too high expectations and by constructing too demanding environments; however, in general low achievers are more likely to suffer from understimulation and underteaching, especially when lows are isolated from other students and taught as a group. Information about the learning potential of lows needs to be disseminated, and active attempts need to be made to develop more constructive ways for teaching these students.

Teachers Make a Difference

Naturalistic studies have found that teachers vary greatly in terms of their active teaching capacity, their classroom managerial abilities, their time allocation decisions, and their use of students as teachers. There are also experimental field studies which show that improvement in these areas can lead to increased student achievement, at least in basic skill subject areas. Such research does not yield rules or guidelines for successful teaching, but it does provide important constructs for the study and potential improvement of instruction, if teachers can adapt this information to the conditions under which they teach. Research results need to be disseminated, but in ways which encourage teachers to adapt creatively the information to their own instructional situations (Good and Brophy, 1978). More qualitative research which intensively studies classroom process and helps to clarify student and teacher behaviors in specified contexts is also needed. In particular, future classroom process research should more intensively examine the motivation and belief systems of teachers and students and the actual content that students and teachers respond to, while continuing the study of what teachers and students do in the classroom.[2] Much research indicates that on occasion the study of only what teachers and students *do* can be misleading. Ultimately, I hope that more comprehensive studies will lead to contextual theories of instruction that help us to understand why certain patterns of instruction appear to be more successful than others under defined circumstances.

Research Funding for Holistic Studies

Research that helps practitioners and researchers to understand and to deal with classrooms in a holistic sense is important. Most research historically has tended to deal with a single aspect of classroom life. Although these studies occasionally provide rich and meaningful concepts, they do not consider the classroom as a complete unit. Holistic research is needed because teachers and students are affected by many classroom variables simultaneously. Recent studies have become much more comprehensive (e.g., Carew and Lightfoot, 1979), but research must become even broader and more ambitious if a more extensive understanding of the holistic nature of classrooms is to emerge. In particular, new studies need to capture the "social" as well as academic aspects of schooling (e.g., see Eder, 1982; Florio, 1979). Such studies will not occur without *systematic funding* that encourages comprehensive, longitudinal inquiry by multidisciplinary terms.

Recent data collected using both quantitative and qualitative methods have demonstrated that classrooms are more complex than many educators thought. Extant literature contains many arguments that quantitative techniques alone are insufficient for understanding classroom life (e.g., Stubbs and Delamont, 1976), as well as illustrations of the weaknesses of the qualitative approach (e.g., McNamara, 1980). If new insights and understandings are to be achieved, I believe they will come through the creative synthesis of both of these general strategies of inquiry. As Power (1977) and Koehler (1978) have contended, both research methods are legitimate and necessary. However, the deployment of these strategies in completely independent ways seems to be an inefficient approach.

Teacher Education

Little is known about the content, beliefs, and skills that teacher education programs communicate to preservice teachers. In particular, information about how teacher education programs help teachers in training to develop translation skills for interpreting research and for adapting what is known about instruction to the contexts in which they will teach is missing. It would appear that many teacher education programs could add important experiences to their curricula in order to improve the observational skills of teachers and their ability to use information gained through observation to adapt instruction to individual students (Amarel, 1981; Good and Brophy, 1978). Recent research evidence has helped to substantiate what classroom teachers have always known—to do an *effective* job in the classroom teachers must possess ability, skills, and work very hard. Given the demands of teaching, teacher education programs should be much more careful in selecting and graduating students than they have in the past. In particular teacher education programs should place more attention on demonstrating that teachers can successfully use principles and concepts in actual classroom situations.

In-Service Teachers

The careful study of multiple ways to involve practitioners in their own self-study and improvement is an important area of inquiry. Teachers seldom have a chance to see other teachers teach and to share ideas about how to improve instruction. Teachers need more opportunities for classroom observation and more skills for taking advantage of those opportunities. It will be increasingly important to develop models which encourage teacher inquiry and bring recent research findings and concepts to teachers' attention.

Theorists and researchers should develop communication models which disseminate information and also help teachers to develop translation skills for adapting new information to their own contexts. Likewise, teachers need to make researchers more aware of the particular constraints under which they teach. Much more information is needed about how (and when) to involve practitioners in conducting and applying research. This question has been addressed by some researchers (Far West Laboratory, San Francisco; Institute for Research on Teaching, Michigan State University), and some useful conceptualization has occurred (e.g., Connelly and Ben-Peretz, 1980). However, at present we are just beginning to learn how researchers and teachers can work collectively and profitably together (Good and Grouws, 1981; Tikunoff, Ward, and Griffin, 1979). If their collaborative roles are to be understood, systematic funding to encourage research in this area must be forthcoming. Such funding would be an important investment in gaining knowledge useful for the formation of social policy.

SOME FINAL THOUGHTS

To describe and/or to understand classroom learning is an enormously complex task. The realization of the complexity of classrooms should cause us to be suspicious of simple models of teaching that offer universal solutions and should encourage us to take divergent approaches to the study of teaching. We know considerably *more* about classrooms now than we did a decade ago. . . .

Concepts that are derived from classroom research provide guidelines or frames of reference that allow teachers to think about, and attempt to alter, their teaching situations. Classroom theories or concepts can be of value in extending the number of dimensions that a teacher, supervisor, or researcher uses to study the classroom, in increasing the number (and range) of hypotheses (alternative strategies) considered, and in increasing awareness of possible consequences of selected actions by all participants (Good and Power, 1976).

Much of the problem and inefficiency of educational reform is due to the frequent acceptance of one fact as a cure-all, only to discard this solution for a new one a few years later. Artley (1981) has reviewed the major methods used to improve reading instruction in the 1900's. He notes that while all the reform programs (different approaches to individualized reading) have had some desirable features, they have not solved the problems of all students. He writes, "In other words, an over-emphasis on certain aspects of a program almost invariably results in neglect of others, and thus change comes about

as a reaction to existing programs." I feel that educators, especially classroom teachers, have to carefully adapt research findings to their own situations. However, I am not advocating a laissez faire decision-making approach. I have argued elsewhere that teachers need to "prove" the validity of their teaching practices by examining the impact of changes in instructional programs on themselves and students (Good and Brophy, 1978; Good and Brophy, 1980). . . .

To reiterate, classrooms are complex environments and it is not easy to describe, to understand, or to improve them. Kepler (1977) and Shulman (1978) have cautioned educators about an overreliance upon the scientific paradigm for the production of simple answers. Research findings do not translate themselves. In order to make research applicable, findings need to be related to the particular characteristics of individual classrooms (Schwab, 1969). . . .

NOTES

1. Hawthorne effect implies that the positive results produced by an experiment are due to increased motivation because subjects realize they are part of an experiment and *not* because of the value of the program. Interestingly, in this project a Hawthorne effect was observed in that control teachers' classrooms exhibited higher achievement than would be expected. However, achievement in experimental classes still far exceeded that in control classrooms. Thus, the mathematics program was found to have an effect that transcended motivational effects.

2. It would be possible, of course, to study students' and teachers' lives outside of schoolrooms as there is reason to believe that what teachers (e.g., Spencer Hall, in press) and students (Medrich et al., 1982) do outside of school influences what occurs inside of school (and vice versa).

REFERENCES

Amarel, M. *Literacy: The personal dimension.* A paper presented at the annual meeting of the American Educational Research Association, Los Angeles, April 1981.

Anderson, L. *Student responses to seatwork: Implications for the study of students' cognitive processing.* A paper presented at the annual meeting of the American Educational Research Association, Los Angeles, April 1981.

Anderson-Levitt, K. *Memory and talk in teachers' interpretations of student behavior.* A paper presented at the annual meeting of the American Educational Research Association, Los Angeles, April 1981.

Artley, A. Individual differences and reading instruction. *Elementary School Journal*, in press.

Berliner, D. Impediments to measuring teacher effectiveness. In G. Borich and K. Fenton (eds.), *The appraisal of teaching: Concepts and process*. Reading, Mass.: Addison-Wesley, 1977.

Braun, C. Teacher expectation: Socio-psychological dynamics. *Review of Educational Research*, 1976, *46*, 185–213.

Brookover, W., Schweitzer, J., Schneider, J., Beady, C., Flood, P., and Wisenbaker, J. Elementary school social climate and school achievement. *American Educational Research Journal*, 1978, *15*, 301–318.

Brophy, J. Teacher behavior and its effects. *Journal of Educational Psychology*, 1979, *71*, 733–750.

Brophy, J. *Research on the self-fulfilling prophecy and teacher expectations*. A paper presented at the annual meeting of the American Educational Research Association, New York City, 1982.

Brophy, J., and Evertson, C. *Learning from teaching: A developmental perspective*. Boston: Allyn & Bacon, 1976.

Brophy, J., and Good, T. Teachers' communication of differential expectations for children's classroom performance: Some behavioral data. *Journal of Educational Psychology*, 1970, *61*, 365–374.

Brophy, J., and Good, T. *Teacher-student relationships: Causes and consequences*. New York: Holt, Rinehart and Winston, 1974.

Carew, J., and Lightfoot, S. *Beyond Bias*. Cambridge: Harvard University Press, 1979.

Carrasco, R. *Expanded awareness of student performance: A case study in applied ethnographic monitoring in a bilingual classroom* (Social Linguistic Working Paper No. 60), Austin, Tex.: Southwest Educational Development Laboratory, April 1979.

Confrey, J., and Good, T. A View from the back of the classroom: Integrating student and teacher perspectives of content with observational and clinical interviews, in progress.

Connelly, F., and Ben-Peretz, M. Teachers' roles in the using and doing of research in curriculum and development. *Journal of Curriculum Studies*, 1980, *12*, 95–107.

Cooper, H. Pygmalion grows up: A model for teacher expectation communication and performance influence. *Review of Educational Research*, 1979, *49*, 389–410.

Cooper, H., and Baron, R. Academic expectations and attributed responsibility as predictors of professional teachers' reinforcement behavior. *Journal of Educational Psychology*, 1977, *69*(4), 409–418.

Cooper, H., and Good, T. *Pygmalion grows up: Studies in the expectation communication process*. New York: Longman, in progress.

Doyle, W. Learning the classroom environment: An ecological analysis. *Journal of Teacher Education*, 1977, *28*, 51–55.

Doyle, W. Classroom tasks and students' abilities. In P. Peterson and H. Walberg (eds.), *Research on teaching: Concepts, findings, and implications*. Berkeley, Calif.: McCutchan Publishing Corporation, 1979.

Dusek, J. Do teachers bias children's learning? *Review of Educational Research*, 1975 *45*, 661–684.

Ebmeier, H., and Good, T. The effects of instructing teachers about good teaching on the mathematics achievement of fourth grade students. *American Educational Research Journal*, 1979, *16*, 1–16.

Ebmeier, H., Good, T., and Grouws, D. *Comparison of ATI findings across two large-scale experimental studies in elementary education*. A paper presented at the American Educational Research Association Annual Conference, Boston, April 1980.

Eder, D. Ability grouping as a self-fulfilling prophecy: A micro-analysis of teacher-student interaction. *Sociology of Education*, 1981, *54*, 151–173.

Edmonds, R. Effective schools for the urban poor. *Educational Leadership*, 1979, *37*, 15–18.

Florio, S. The problem of dead letters: Social perspectives on the teaching of writing, *Elementary School Journal*, 1979, *80*(1), 1–7.

Gage, N., and Giaconia, R. *The causal connection between teaching practices and student achievement: Recent experiments based on correlational findings* (Tech. Rep.). Stanford, Calif.: Stanford University, Center for Educational Research at Stanford, 1980.

Good, T. Teacher effectiveness in the elementary school: What we know about it now. *Journal of Teacher Education*, 1979, *30*, 52–64.

Good, T. Classroom expectations: Teacher-pupil interactions. In J. McMillan (ed.), *The social psychology of school learning*. New York: Academic Press, 1980.

Good, T. A decade of research on teacher expectations. *Journal of Educational Leadership*, 1981, *38*, 415–423.

Good, T. *Classroom research: What we know and what we need to know* (Tech. Rep. No. 9118). Austin: University of Texas, The Research and Development Center for Teacher Education, February 1982.

Good, T., and Brophy, J. *Looking in classrooms* (1st ed.). New York: Harper and Row, 1973.

Good, T., and Brophy, J. *Looking in classrooms* (2nd ed.). New York: Harper and Row, 1978.

Good, T., and Brophy, J. *Educational psychology: A realistic approach* (2nd ed.). New York: Holt, Rinehart and Winston, 1980.

Good, T., Cooper, H., and Blakey, S. Classroom interaction as a function of teacher expectations, student sex, and time of year. *Journal of Teacher Education*, 1978, *29*, 85–90.

Good, T., and Grouws, D. The Missouri Mathematics Effectiveness Project: An experimental study in fourth grade classrooms. *Journal of Educational Psychology*, 1979, *71*, 355–362.

Good, T., and Grouws, D. *Experimental research in secondary mathematics classrooms: Working with teachers* (NIE-G-79-0103 Final Report), May 1981.

Good, T. Grouws, D., and Ebmeier, H. *Active mathematics teaching: Empirical research in elementary and secondary classrooms*. New York: Longman, in press.

Good, T., and Power, C. Designing successful classroom environments for different types of students. *Journal of Curriculum Studies*, 1976, *8*, 45–60.

Jackson, P. *Life in classrooms*. New York: Holt, Rinehart and Winston, 1968.

Janicki, C., and Peterson, P. Aptitude-treatment interaction effects of variations in direct instruction. *American Educational Research Journal*, 1981, *18*, 63–82.

Jorgenson, G. *Student ability—material difficulty matching: Relationship to classroom behavior*. A paper presented at the meeting of the American Educational Research Association, Toronto, March 1978.

Keddie, N. Classroom knowledge. In M. Young (ed.), *Knowledge and control: New directions for the sociology of education*. London: Collier-MacMillan, 1971.

Levine, H., and Mann, K. *The "negotiation" of classroom lessons and its relevance for teachers' decision-making*. Paper read at the annual meeting of the American Educational Research Association, Los Angeles, April 1981.

Martin, M. *Equal opportunity in the classroom* (ESEA, Title III: Session A Report). Los Angeles: County Superintendent of Schools, Division of Compensatory and Intergroup Programs, 1973.

McDermott, R. *Kids made sense: An ethnographic account of the interactional management of success and failure in one first-grade classroom*. Unpublished doctoral dissertation, Stanford University, 1976.

McDonald, F., and Elias, P. *The effects of teaching performance on pupil learning* (Final Report, Vol. 1, Beginning Teacher Evaluation Study, Phase II, 1974–1976). Princeton, N.J.: Educational Testing Service, 1976.

McNamara, B. The outsider's arrogance: The failure of participant observers to understand classroom events. *British Educational Research Journal*, 1980, *6*(2).

Medley, D. The effectiveness of teachers. In P. Peterson and H. Walberg (eds.), *Research on teaching: Concepts, findings, and implications*. Berkeley, Calif.: McCutchan Publishing Corporation, 1979.

Medrich, E., Roizen, J., Rubin, V., and Buckley, S. *The serious business of growing up: A study of children's lives outside school*. Berkeley: University of California Press, 1982.

Peterson, P., and Walberg, H. (eds.), *Research on teaching: Concepts, findings, and implications*. Berkeley, Calif.: McCutchan Publishing Corporation, 1979.

Porter, A., Schmidt, W., Floden, R., and Freeman, D. *Impact on what? The importance of content covered* (Research Series No. 2). East Lansing: Michigan State University, Institute for Research on Teaching, 1978.

Power, C. A critical review of science classroom interaction studies. *Studies in Science Education*, 1977, *4*, 1–30.

Rosenshine, B. Content, time, and direct instruction. In P. Peterson and H. Walberg (eds.), *Research on teaching: Concepts, findings, and implications*. Berkeley, Calif., McCutchan Publishing Corporation, 1979.

Rosenthal, R. *On the social psychology of the self-fulfilling prophecy: Further evidence for Pygmalion effects and their mediating mechanisms*. New York: MSS Modular Publications, 1974.

Rutter, M., Maughan, B., Mortimore, P., Ouston, J., and Smith, A. *Fifteen thousand hours: Secondary schools and their effects on children*. Cambridge: Harvard, 1979.

Soltz, D. *The various teacher: Subject matter, style, and strategy in the primary classroom*. A paper presented at the annual meeting of the American Educational Research Association, San Francisco, April 1976.

Spencer Hall, D. Looking behind the teacher's back. *Elementary School Journal*, 1981, *81*, 281–289.

Stubbs, M., and Delamont, S. (eds.), *Explorations in classroom observation*. London: Wiley, 1976.

Tikunoff, W., Ward, B., and Griffin, G. *Interactive research and development on teaching study* (JR & DT-79-11 Final Report). San Francisco: Far West Laboratory for Education Research and Development, 1979.

West, C., and Anderson, T. The questions of preponderant causation in teacher expectancy research. *Review of Educational Research*, 1976, *46*, 185–213.

7. THE ROLE OF WAIT TIME IN HIGHER COGNITIVE LEVEL LEARNING

Kenneth Tobin

. . . Winne and Marx (1983) stated that classroom researchers should consider internal processes of students and should focus on the student as an information processing learner. They stated that for learning to occur the student must: perceive the instructional stimuli, note their occurrence, understand the cognitive processes that are required, use the processes to create or manipulate information to be stored as learned material, and encode the information for later retrieval. If these criteria are accepted as valid, teaching roles can be defined in terms of maintaining appropriate student task involvement and utilizing cues to stimulate the cognitive processes deemed necessary for learning. In accordance with an information processing model of learning (e.g., Peterson & Swing, 1982; Stahl, 1982; Winne, 1985), the stimuli used to cue learners to particular cognitive processes are important components of a classroom learning environment.

In order for teacher discourse to influence student learning, the information contained in the discourse must be cognitively processed by the learner. As a consequence, the rate at which information is presented should be matched with the cognitive processing capabilities of students. Processing time for cognitively complex discourse is expected to be greater than the time required to process less complex verbal information. Thus, as teachers supply information or establish a cognitive focus through soliciting, sufficient time should be allowed for all students to engage in an appropriate manner. The cognitive processing model formulated by Stahl (1982) highlighted the importance of actively processing stimuli within the first few seconds of receipt. Unless active processing occurs, the stimuli are likely to fade from the storage system and be lost. As a consequence, if learners are to benefit from instruction it is important that sufficient time is provided for cognitive processing. To ensure that adequate time is provided it seems to follow that teachers should consciously manage the duration of pauses after solicitations and provide regular intervals of silence during explanations.

The pauses following student discourse are also of potential importance. As Rowe (1974a) noted, speech is interspersed with pauses ranging from quite short time intervals separating individual words to much longer intervals that occur as a speaker completes a segment of speech and considers what next to say. These time intervals often exceed 3 to 5 seconds. Siegman and Pope (1965) reported that the length of pauses in discourse increased in proportion to the difficulty of the task, whereas Rochester (1973) stated that pauses in speech were related to cognitive processing. Consequently, as a student attempts a complex explanation, greater cognitive activity is called for and longer pauses separate bursts of speech. Longer pauses provide ample opportunity for a teacher to interrupt speech and subsequent cognitive activity by completing the answer for a student or by asking another question. The student is therefore deprived of the opportunity to develop a complete answer to a question or to correct errors that may have been made. Interruptions of this type, having disrupted cognitive activity, could impair learning. If teachers can refrain from speaking until 3 to 5 seconds have elapsed, a student may continue to speak or another student might commence to speak. . . .

METHOD

The papers included in this review are those published on wait time in research journals, research papers presented at professional meetings, and doctoral and masters dissertations. The procedures for identifying relevant papers, books, and dissertations included computer searches of the ERIC, PSYCINFO, and Language and Language Behavior databases. The four keywords used in the computer searches were *wait time, pause time, lapse time,* and *pausing*. Other procedures included use of the Citation Index and manual inspection of the programs for the annual meetings of the American Educational Research Association and the National Association for Research in Science Teaching. In addition, unpublished papers and documents collected over 15 years were included in the review. To avoid repetition, dissertations and unpublished papers were excluded from the review if the same results were subsequently published. . . .

WAIT TIME DEFINITIONS

Rowe (1969) defined two types of wait time: wait time I was defined as the duration of the pause after a teacher utterance; and wait time II was defined as the duration of the pause after a student utterance. An extended or criterion wait time I and II was defined as an average of between 3 and 5 seconds. . . . In most instances wait time I is related to the pause following a teacher question and wait time II is the pause after a student response to a question. In an endeavor to overcome difficulties encountered in implementing extended wait time I and II, Lake (1973) suggested that wait time should be redefined in terms of the period of silence that precedes teacher talk. Lake defined two types of wait time based on which speaker has primary control over the length of the pause. Teacher wait time was defined as the length of the pause preceding teacher talk. Student wait time was similarly defined as the length of the pause preceding student talk. . . . Teacher or student talk can precede the relevant pause in either case.

The conceptualization offered by Lake has been supported empirically in a study by Fowler (1975). In a factor analysis of six time-related variables, Fowler identified two factors he described as student controlled silence and teacher controlled silence. This outcome supports the decision to define wait time in terms of the person having primary control over the length of the silent pause. Fowler defined four types of wait time: teacher reaction wait time, student reaction wait time, teacher initiated wait time, and student initiated wait time. . . . By partitioning wait time in this way a broad range of hypotheses can be tested. The definitions used by Fowler have considerable appeal for research on the manner in which silence is used by teachers and students. The potential for silent pauses to influence student learning quite likely depends on pause duration and the location of the pause with respect to teachers and students.

MAJOR FINDINGS FROM WAIT TIME RESEARCH

This section contains three components. In the first, an historical overview is provided of the seminal work of Mary Budd Rowe and the subsequent directions of research involving wait time. The second component contains a review of studies in which wait time was not manipulated and the final component reviews those studies in which wait time was manipulated.

Historical Overview

Rowe (1969) reported that average wait time I and II values in science classes throughout the United States were less than 3 seconds and usually less than 1 second. These findings were replicated in the United States (e.g., Swift & Gooding, 1983), in other parts of the world (e.g., Tobin, 1986), and in other subject areas (e.g., Fagan, Hassler, & Szabo, 1981). After studying audio-tapes of science lessons in which students displayed high levels of student inquiry behavior, Rowe (1974a) discovered that features of classroom discourse were related to wait time I and II. The studies conducted by Rowe were based on results from intact elementary and high school classes as well as from teachers working with small groups of students. Rowe conducted studies of teachers using wait time with their regular classes, and teachers teaching micro-groups. During most of the studies wait time was manipulated to ascertain the effects of utilizing an average wait time of between 3 and 5 seconds. The results were a synthesis of studies conducted over a 7-year period. Rowe did not report the results of the separate studies that comprised the research program.

The use of an extended wait time changed teacher and student discourse in elementary science classes. Rowe reported that teachers demonstrated greater response flexibility, asked fewer yet more appropriate questions, and developed higher expectations for students previously rated as slow learners. It is possible that these changes in teacher discourse together with more time for thinking contributed to the changes that were observed in student participation.

When the average length of wait time I and II was greater than approximately 3 seconds, Rowe reported an increase in the length of student responses; an increase in the number of unsolicited, but appropriate, student responses; an increase in the number of responses rated as speculative; a decrease in the number of students failing to respond; an increase in the incidence of student-to-student comparisons of data; an increase in the incidence of student inferences supported by evidence; an increase in the number of responses from students rated by the teacher as relatively slow learners; and an increase in the variety of verbal behaviors exhibited by students.

Although the above changes occurred in an environment in which teachers endeavored to increase both types of wait time beyond 3 seconds, Rowe reported that wait time II had greatest effect on the length of student responses, the number of unsolicited but appropriate student responses, and the use of evidence before or after inference statements. When wait time I was extended there was a lower incidence of student failures to respond to teacher solicitations.

Studies in Which Wait Time Was Not Manipulated

Six studies investigated relationships involving wait time in classrooms in which wait time was not manipulated. Wait time I was a dependent variable in each of the studies. . . .

Boeck and Hillenmeyer (1973) investigated the relationship between cognitive level of questioning and wait time I with a sample of 20 preservice teachers in microteaching assignments with groups of four students from grades 6 and 7. The lessons consisted of physical science topics. Wait time was a dependent variable in the study in which two groups of 7 teachers received training to ask higher cognitive level questions. The authors reported that wait times were longer after high cognitive level questions than after low cognitive level questions. Nearly all wait time pauses following higher cognitive level questions exceeded the 3 second criterion. Significantly, the authors reported some instances in which wait time appeared to be related more to the length of response required from students than to the cognitive level of the question.

Arnold, Atwood, and Rogers (1974) utilized 11 teachers of students in grades 1 to 5 to investigate relationships between wait time I and the cognitive level of questioning. Teachers submitted tapes from science, social studies, language arts, and mathematics lessons. Arnold et al. reported that longer pauses followed analysis questions (4.6 seconds) than questions at other levels of Bloom's taxonomy. Further research is warranted, however, as the results were based on only seven questions at the analysis level.

Surprisingly, Gambrell (1983) reported that less time was given for students in third grade reading comprehension classes to consider questions requiring higher cognitive level thinking than questions requiring lower cognitive level thinking. Gambrell concluded that asking inferential questions may be an ineffective reading comprehension strategy unless students are given adequate "think time" to reflect, process, and interrelate necessary information prior to responding to teacher-posed questions.

The results reported by Gambrell do not accord with those reported by Boeck and Hillenmeyer and Arnold et al. The differences highlight a need for additional research with younger children in a range of subject areas. The relatively short wait time provided after a higher cognitive level question might reflect the teacher's expectation that young children are unlikely to respond to questions of this type in reading classes.

Jones (1980) hypothesized that the time required to respond to a question was related to the type and complexity of the question. The type of question was classified as convergent or divergent and complexity was classified in terms of Piagetian level (concrete or formal). The investigation involved 32 eighth-grade students who were studying a unit on projection of shadows. Instruction was administered to the students as a group and questions were posed during interviews with individuals. Student response wait time was used as the unit for analysis. The average time following convergent questions was 2.8 seconds whereas the average time for divergent questions was 6.9 seconds. The time difference between student response wait time following questions classified as concrete and formal was not statistically significant. However, Jones indicated that students were not consistently responding to formal questions in a formal manner. Jones concluded that students being questioned would be better served if the individual asking the question provided time for students to think and then to answer.

In a study of first-year high school Spanish and French classes, Shrum (1985a) reported an average post solicitation wait time, for teachers, of 1.9 seconds and a post response wait time of 0.6 seconds. The post solicitation wait time was almost double that reported in other studies. Shrum stated that this finding suggests that second language teachers do acknowledge the need for students to think before commencing a response. Similar results were obtained for student controlled pauses. The post solicitation wait time for students was 1.5 seconds and the post response wait time for students was 0.7 seconds.

Shrum reported that second language teachers provided significantly longer wait time when solicitations were directed to high and low performers compared to students of average ability. It is possible that an analysis of question types would reveal salient differences in the questions asked of students in each of the three ability groups. For example, the more difficult questions might have been directed to the more able students and less difficult questions might have been asked of the lower ability students. One interpretation of these results is that teachers are prepared to wait for the more able students, as they have an expectation that they can produce a worthwhile answer if they are given the time to formulate a response. Similarly, they are also prepared to wait for lower ability students based on an expectation that such students need more time to think. These interpretations are consistent with the results of research in high school science classes reported by Tobin and Gallagher (in press).

In another report from the same study, Shrum (1985b) found that a shorter wait time was provided after target language solicitations than after native language solicitations. A comparison of the types of questions asked in the target language and those asked in the native language might provide insights into this finding. Shrum raised the possibilty that teachers asked more provocative questions in English than in the target language.

Gore and Roumagoux (1983) investigated the effects of using an extended wait time in fourth-grade mathematics classes. Gender related differences were reported. Three of the five female teachers used a longer wait time when interacting with boys than when they interacted with girls. Boys also were called to respond more frequently than girls. In addition, Gore and Roumagoux reported that high achievers were called to respond more often than low achievers. These results are consistent with those reported by Tobin (1985) in high school science classes and have implications for using an extended wait time when the teacher interacts with the class as a whole.

Studies in Which Wait Time Was Manipulated

Most of the studies reviewed in this section utilized a group of teachers who endeavored to extend wait time beyond 3 seconds and a contrast group who maintained a normal wait time (e.g., DeTure & Miller, 1985; Fagan, Hassler, & Szabo, 1981; Granato, 1983; Swift & Gooding, 1983; Tobin, 1986). In some cases teachers taught their regular classes in the study (e.g., Fagan et al.; Granato; Hoena, 1982; Tobin, 1986); in other cases preservice teachers were assigned to teach microgroups of students (e.g., DeTure & Miller).

Other designs were also used in these wait time studies. For example, Honea (1982) designed a time-series study to investigate the effects of using an extended wait time in a sample of high school social studies activities. The design incorporated five topics that each encompassed two days. The wait time treatment was administered during units two and four. The purpose of the investigation was to determine whether an extended wait time and a slower recitation pace had an effect on characteristics of teacher and student discourse and student attitudes to social studies topics.

In terms of grade level, the studies ranged from kindergarten (Granato, 1983) to high school (Honea, 1982) and included science (DeTure & Miller 1985; Swift & Gooding, 1983), mathematics (Tobin, 1986), language arts (Fagan et al., 1981; Granato; Tobin, 1986) and social studies (Honea). . . .

Changes in teacher behavior. This section contains a review of seven studies in which wait time was a manipulated independent variable. . . .

When teacher wait time was increased to average between 3 and 5 seconds, Tobin (1986) reported that the number of utterances per unit time was reduced in extended wait time classes. This trend was balanced by an increase in the average length of utterances. One possibilty is that teachers and students used the increased time between utterances to consider what they were going to say, and that sufficient time was provided for utterances to be completed. Tobin obtained some support for this assertion with the finding that the number of times teachers interrupted student discourse was reduced in classes in which an extended wait time was implemented.

One change that has been consistently reported under extended wait time conditions is that the number of teacher questions decreased (DeTure & Miller, 1985; Fagan et al., 1981; Honea, 1982). Tobin (1986) noted that the proportion of solicitations (the number of solicitations compared to the total number of verbal moves) was greater in extended wait time classes than in regular wait time classes. At first sight this appears to be contrary to the results of other wait time research. However, it should be noted that in each study the actual number of solicitations per unit time decreased in extended wait time classes. Thus, the consistent pattern that occurred in extended wait time classes was that the actual number of questions asked per unit time decreased, but the proportion of solicitations increased. This situation is explained in terms of the significant reduction in the total number of utterances per unit time in extended wait time classes.

The number of questions was not the only questioning variable to change when an extended wait time was used. Swift and Gooding (1983), and Fagan et al. (1981) found that the cognitive level of teacher questions increased when wait time I and II were increased.

Other research groups looked at the cognitive level of questions in different ways. Swift and Gooding reported a higher occurrence of evaluative questions and less frequent use of chain questions. In a follow-up study, Gooding, Swift, and Swift (1983) reported that the use of an extended wait time was associated with the use of fewer memory level questions, fewer rhetorical questions, fewer management questions, and fewer leading questions. Similarly, DeTure and Miller (1985) found that when the types of questions were examined, there was a reduction in the number of cognitive memory questions and an increase in the number of questions classified as requiring divergent thinking in the extended wait time group.

The specific way in which the questions change is obviously dependent on the content being taught and learned. This point was illustrated in the study conducted by Tobin (1986) in which he compared the use of an extended wait time in mathematics and language arts. In the mathematics lessons, the proportion of questions requiring student application increased and the proportion requiring comprehension decreased. As a consequence, students were provided with more opportunities to engage in application level tasks in extended wait time classes compared to control group classes where solicitations tended to be directed toward assessing student understanding of probabilistic concepts or procedures. A similar situation occurred in the language arts lessons. Teachers in extended wait time classes tended to solicit student understanding of the prose passage, whereas students in control group classes were asked to recall specific facts or information from the piece of prose.

Differences in teacher discourse following a student utterance is evidence that the teacher does use the additional wait time to think about subsequent discourse. DeTure and Miller found that there was a decrease in the number of repeated verbal patterns (i.e., any phrase repeated by the teacher more than five times during an interaction sequence) and in the amount of mimicry in extended wait time classes. Tobin (1986) reported that in the extended wait time classes there was a lower proportion of teacher mimicry and a lower proportion of low level teacher reactions than in control group classes. This trend was associated with a tendency for teachers to probe for additional information or input from students in extended wait time classes. Anshutz (1975) also reported that teachers in an extended wait time group asked more probing questions than teachers in a control group.

Honea described an increase in teacher anxiety when moving from short wait time to long wait time. This finding is important since it has implications for teachers endeavoring to implement an extended wait time. If teachers are to sustain an extended wait time in their classes they may need external support to do so. Increased anxiety might be explained in terms of the significant changes in interaction patterns that quickly occur when an extended wait time is implemented. If teachers become anxious and discouraged it is understandable that they could reject the notion of using an extended wait time in favor of a return to a predictable pattern of classroom interactions.

Changes in student behavior. All studies in which wait time was manipulated reported changes in student variables. . . .

The additional time provided in long wait time classes may have made the lessons more understandable for students. Anderson (1978) reported that students perceived physics content to be less difficult and DeTure and Miller (1985) reported less student confusion in extended wait time classes. Honea (1982) found that students in his class had more confidence in their work and greater group spirit during lessons that utilized an average wait time of more than 3 seconds.

Several findings suggest that students were more involved in classroom discourse in extended wait time classes. The amount of student discourse increased in terms of the actual time the students spoke, the number of words spoken, and the number of student utterances (Granato, 1983; Honea; 1982; Knickerbocker, 1984; Swift & Gooding, 1983; Tobin, 1986; Winterton, 1977). The length of student discourse also increased under extended wait time conditions (Anderson, 1978; Fagan et al., 1981; Granato; Honea; Knickerbocker; Swift & Gooding; Tobin, 1986).

The increased silence and possibly different types of teacher questions appeared to provide a context in which students were able to construct responses that were more complex (DeTure & Miller, 1985; Lake, 1973) and at a higher cognitive level (Doerr, 1984; Fagan et al., 1981). Other evidence of additional student thought was that the number of alternative explanations increased when students in extended wait time classes responded to a teacher question (Fagan et al.; Granato, 1983; Knickerbocker, 1984; Lake).

The research reviewed in the previous section indicated that the number of teacher questions decreased in extended wait time classes. In some circumstances this might not be regarded as a desirable change. However, students in extended wait time classes initiated discourse to a greater extent than students in classes where a normal short wait time was used (Fowler, 1975; Honea, 1982). Similar results were obtained by Marsh (1978) in a study involving museum guides who used a long wait time to increase the number of questions asked by visitors to a public museum. Wait time was defined as the pause separating a visitor response and the subsequent question asked by a museum guide. The number of questions related to meanings and values increased from 1.5 per tour to 11.6 after a long wait time was implemented.

There was also evidence to suggest that extended wait time classes became more conversational. Five studies reported an increase in the number of student to student interactions (Fowler, 1975; Honea, 1982; Knickerbocker, 1984; Lake, 1973; Winterton, 1977). Other indicators of a more relaxed atmosphere in extended wait time classes were longer pauses within conversations (Honea) and a decrease in the number of times that students interrupted one another (Fowler).

A surprising outcome of the Anderson (1978) study was an increased apathy toward physics for students in the increased wait time classes. Females in short wait time classes found the class more formal but also more satisfying than females in long wait time classes. Anderson cautioned that the use of long wait time could lead to decreased satisfaction and increased apathy for pupils conditioned to more rapid question-answer interactions. This is the only wait time study included in the review that utilized student perceptions of the psychosocial learning environment as a dependent variable. The result raises the possibility that student perceptions of the learning environment could decrease on some dimensions in extended wait time classes.

A major problem in reviewing studies involving achievement as a dependent variable is that an unknown number of null results may not be reported. Six studies that reported relationships between wait time and achievement were located. Of these, only one (Anshutz, 1975) reported no differences in achievement between short and long wait time groups. The other five studies, which reported statistically significant findings in favor of the classes receiving extended wait time instruction, are reviewed below.

Samiroden (1983) investigated the relationship between higher cognitive level questions, wait time, and student achievement. Preservice teachers in two experimental groups were trained to use wait times of 1 to 4 seconds or 4 to 7 seconds, respectively. Seventeen preservice teachers each taught a 60-

minute lesson to two 11th-grade biology classes. Only eight preservice teachers achieved the desired wait time lengths. The results indicated that classes receiving the extended wait time treatment achieved at a significantly higher level than those receiving the short wait time treatment.

In an experimental study involving 23 teachers of students in grades 5, 6, and 7 (Tobin, 1980), all teachers taught an introductory science topic to allow their wait time to be calculated and prior measures of student achievement to be obtained. In the experimental phase of approximately 10 weeks, a random sample of teachers endeavored to increase wait time to an average of more than 3 seconds. Post test measures were administered at the end of each of the two instructional units taught during the experimental phase. The outcome measures used in the study consisted of items measuring higher cognitive level science achievement. Class mean achievement was the unit for analysis. When prior differences in achievement were considered, a significant relationship between teacher wait time and science achievement was obtained for the experimental phase of the study.

Tobin and Capie (1982) investigated the effects of increased teacher wait time on student engagement rates and integrated process skill achievement for students in grades 6, 7, and 8 in an experimental study involving 13 teachers. The design of the study allowed for measures of student formal reasoning ability, summative achievement, and retention. The process skill outcomes were all at a higher cognitive level. When student differences in formal reasoning ability were considered, use of a teacher wait time of between 3 and 5 seconds was associated with higher student achievement and retention. Similar results were obtained when the individual student score and the mean class score were used as units of analysis.

In an experimental study involving 20 teachers of students in grade 6 and 7 mathematics classes (Tobin, 1986), the student outcomes were higher cognitive level concepts associated with probabilistic reasoning. The design enabled student formal reasoning ability to be measured for all students participating in the study. Class mean achievement scores were used as the units for analysis. When variation in formal reasoning ability was considered, classes receiving an extended wait time achieved at a higher level than classes receiving a short teacher wait time.

The study also linked student discourse variables to achievement. When between-class variation in formal reasoning ability was statistically removed, a multiple regression analysis indicated that the average length of student discourse and the proportion of student reacting utterances each were related positively to summative mathematics achievement. These results suggest that teachers might concentrate on the average length of student responses and the proportion of student reactions as a possible means of increasing mathematics achievement. Use of a longer wait time appears to be one way of inducing such changes in pupil discourse.

Riley (1986) reported an interaction between wait time I and cognitive level of questioning on achievement for students in grades 1 to 5. A decrease in achievement occurred when wait time was extended from medium to long for low level questions. In contrast, achievement was increased when an average wait time of 3 seconds was used in conjunction with high and mixed cognitive level questioning. Riley suggested that the optimal wait time may be dependent on the cognitive level of questioning and the cognitive level of the outcomes to be achieved. The results reported by Riley raise two important points that need further investigation. First, short wait time may be most appropriate for low cognitive level outcomes second, research on higher cognitive level questioning also should consider wait time when studies are designed and results are interpreted.

IS WAIT TIME A THRESHOLD PHENOMENON?

A problem that sometimes occurs in classroom research is that the level of a variable in naturalistic settings may be below a threshold value that must be exceeded if hypothesized outcomes are to be attained. Wait time appears to be such a variable. Rowe (1974b, 1974c) reported a possible threshold wait time of approximately 3 seconds. When teachers maintained an average wait time above 3 seconds, a range of desirable changes in teacher and student verbal behavior was observed. Because the average wait time in naturalistic settings was approximately

1 second, validation of wait time as a teaching strategy was most unlikely in naturalistic studies.

Results reported by Tobin (1980) in a study conducted in grades 5 through 7 science classes highlight this potential difficulty with naturalistic studies. The study consisted of a naturalistic phase in which teachers were sensitized to wait time and an experimental phase in which wait time was manipulated. In the first phase of the study, all teachers used a normal wait time during instruction. The average teacher wait time was 0.5 seconds. In the second phase, teachers from one group endeavored to extend mean wait time beyond 3 seconds, while another group maintained a wait time between 0.5 and 1.0 seconds. The average teacher wait time in this phase was 2.1 seconds. On the basis of the results of the naturalistic study alone, Tobin would have concluded that teacher wait time and student achievement were not related. In the experimental phase of the study, however, many teachers exceeded the 3 second criterion wait time and a significant relationship was obtained between teacher wait time and student achievement.

Studies reported by Garigliano (1973) and Arnold, Atwood, and Rogers (1973) also reported mean wait times below the 3 second threshold value identified by Rowe. In each study the majority of the findings was found to be nonsignificant. Garigliano conducted a study with 33 volunteer elementary science teachers who taught their regular classes. The study was experimental, however, the extended wait time group was unable to attain mean wait times that exceeded the 3 second criterion. If wait time is a threshold phenomenon, the failure of the teachers to exceed the threshold value could account for the failure to attain statistically significant results in the Garigliano study.

Arnold et al. investigated the influence of lapse-time (a special case of wait time I) on the cognitive levels of questions and answes in 12 elementary classes involved in science and social science. Lapse-time was defined as the interval of silence between the final utterance of a teacher's question and the beginning of an oral response by a student. There was no attempt to vary lapse-time and, as a consequence, the mean lapse-time was less than the 3 second threshold. The relationship between lapse-time and cognitive level of questions was found to be nonsignificant. This nonsignificant result might

be explained in terms of teachers using a uniformly short lapse time that did not take account of the cognitive demands of the question.

MAINTAINING AN ABOVE-THRESHOLD WAIT TIME

A number of studies suggest[s] that teachers appear to have difficulty utilizing a wait time of 3 seconds or more. Accordingly, the identification of procedures to assist teachers to incorporate an extended wait time in their teaching is an important challenge for teacher educators. In a meta-analysis of studies that investigated methods of changing science teacher behavior, Yeany and Padilla (1986) reported a positive effect size for nine different methods. By far the most effective means of changing science teacher behavior was the use of feedback guided by analysis (effect size = 2.3). The least effective of the approaches was analysis of written models (effect size = 0.7). Reasearch on training teachers to implement a longer wait time has been generally consistent with the findings reported by Yeany and Padilla.

Chewprecha, Gardner, and Sapianchai (1980) compared three training methods for modifying wait time I. The study utilized 77 high school chemistry teachers from Bankok, Thailand. Four treatment groups were formed. Three groups participated in a 2-hour orientation on the importance of questioning and wait time; one group was a control. After the orientation, group I teachers studied three different pamphlets each month for a semester; group II teachers listened to three different audio models each month and provided written comments on them; and group III teachers attended a workshop on questioning and undertook a quantitative analysis of an audio tape each month. Wait time I was measured from an audiotape of a chemistry lesson taught at the beginning of semester 2.

The use of instructional pamphlets was found to be more effective than qualitative or quantitative analyscs of audiotapes. However, neither of the analyses involved self-analysis. The Chewprecha et al. study is significant for several reasons. In the first place, the lessons were conducted in the Thai language rather than English; secondly, each treatment group attained an average wait time close to the criterion; and thirdly, the results are probably only generalizable to teacher education in developing countries. The latter point is well illustrated by the authors who noted that the success of the pamphlets was probably due to very limited access to books and articles on education in Thailand. The pamphlets were read with considerable enthusiasm and the ideas were eagerly implemented.

Rice (1977) randomly selected 10 undergraduate elementary education majors enrolled in a science methods course and randomly assigned them to two groups. All 10 teachers prepared six science lessons to be presented to a class of elementary students. Wait time, number of questions, and cognitive level of questioning were determined from an audio tape of the first lesson. After that one group of teachers participated in an instructional treatment that consisted of viewing films and reading articles about aspects of questioning. The wait time component of the instructional treatment consisted of reading an article written by Rowe (1969). The other group of teachers discussed aspects of the presented lesson.

After the instructional treatment the group of five teachers increased their average wait time from 1.3 seconds to 2.1 seconds. However, only two teachers attained the threshold of approximately 3 seconds. One teacher in the instructional treatment group actually decreased wait time from 1.5 seconds to 1.0 seconds. The average wait time for the control group was 1.3 seconds on both occasions.

In an Australian study, Tobin (1983) described the results of a wait time training program in which Australian elementary teachers of grades 1 to 7 were encouraged to increase teacher wait time in all subject areas and provide audio tapes for two lessons each week during a 10-week period. Tapes were submitted for a range of subjects including mathematics, science, social studies, literature, creative writing, English, spelling, reading, and religion. The average teacher wait time for the participants in the program ranged from 0.4 seconds to 3.6 seconds. The results suggested that the average wait time used by teachers did not vary greatly from one subject area to another and that average teacher wait time was approximately the same in all subject areas.

These results contrast with those reported by Swift and Gooding (1983) with a sample of American teachers. Swift and Gooding reported that questioning training based on the use of pamhlets only

marginally increased wait time I and II. Teachers using training pamphlets maintained a mean wait time I of 1.4 seconds and a mean wait time II of 0.7 seconds during a 15 week study. These values were only slightly greater than the average of 1.2 seconds and 0.6 seconds maintained by a control group in the study.

Esquivel, Lashier, and Smith (1978) investigated wait time extension with a group of 92 preservice elementary teachers. Each was assigned to teach science to 6 to 10 elementary students in grades 3 through 5. Each teacher was assigned to their group in pairs so that they could be assisted to maintain an extended wait time. Esquivel et al. reported that feedback on wait time II did not enable teachers to maintain a 3 second average over a sequence of three science lessons. In this study the average wait time II was 1.2 seconds, much below the criterion of 3 seconds, but greater than the 0.5 seconds to 0.9 seconds that is typically reported for wait time II.

Other studies have shown regular feedback to be beneficial. Tobin (1980, 1986) and Tobin and Capie (1982) reported substantial gains in teacher wait time when performace feedback was regularly provided. In these studies teachers receiving feedback maintained an average teacher wait time above the 3 second criterion.

DeTure (1979) used a factorial design to investigate the effects of feedback on the ability of preservice teachers to implement an extended wait time. The subjects were 52 preservice teachers. Each was randomly assigned to one of four treatment groups to microteach a group of four elementary students from grades 4 or 5. The four treatments were: audio model with no feedback, audio model with feedback, video model with no feedback, and video model with feedback. The model consisted of a master teacher and four 5th-grade students discussing a discrepant event while using an average wait time I and II above 3 seconds. The use of a videotape followed by feedback from an advisor enabled teachers to attain a mean wait time II of 3.7 seconds, significantly higher than the mean wait time attained by groups using other training techniques. However, no teachers in the study were able to attain an average wait time I above 1.8 seconds. Since teacher behavior was being modified via the types of feedback given to teachers, the results are most encouraging. As feedback was not provided to students, wait time I was probably reduced by student talk.

Swift and Gooding (1983) used a wait timer to signal a 3-second pause to teachers and students. A voice-activated relay system operated a red light that signalled when an appropriate period of silence had elapsed. The use of the system provided teachers and students with an indication of how long they needed to wait. With the aid of this device teachers and students were able to maintain an average wait time I of 2.6 seconds and an average wait time II of 1.4 seconds. These results indicate that the wait timer was more effective in controlling student discourse than teacher discourse. This may have been attributable to the placement of the device in the classroom. It is possible that students had a good view of the light whereas teachers may have had their backs to it or may have been too preoccupied with teaching to concentrate on the light.

DeTure and Miller (1985) used a written protocol model to change wait time. A written model was read and participants in a training program were required to transcribe a tape of their teaching and to calculate their wait time averages for two or three lessons. The written protocol model required a teaching cycle to be repeated until an average wait time of more than 3 seconds was reached. Feedback also was incorporated into the treatment. Seventy percent of the participants reached a criterion average for wait time I and wait time II after two lessons. The remaining teachers attained criterion after three lessons. However, the teachers in this study were not required to utilize an extended wait time in a sustained manner with a regular class. It is possible that additional training is necessary to enable teachers to maintain an extended wait time in their day-to-day teaching and to use wait time appropriately.

In a follow-up study involving 10 teachers from the Swift and Gooding (1983) study; Swift, Swift, and Gooding (1984) used a supportive intervention technique that was successful in assisting teachers to maintain an extended wait time during their regular teaching assignments. The supportive intervention procedure had many elements in common with coaching (Joyce and Showers, 1983), which has been successful in facilitating sustained teacher change involving the use of other teaching strategies.

The training studies highlighted the need to extend two types of pauses: those that precede teacher talk and those that precede student talk. The results raise questions on the probable effectiveness of teacher education courses in which teachers are requested or urged to try a particular strategy or are simply provided with a handout. The chances of substantially improving the quality of classroom discourse through such methods appears to be remote. The crucial question to be addressed in training studies is how to sustain an extended wait time. In natural settings, most teachers maintain an average wait time of between 0.2 and 0.9 seconds. The main problem appears to be that the magnitude of required change is of the order of 600%. Such a change represents a major departure from normal teaching style; concomitant changes in teacher and student behavior necessitate new approaches to management of classroom interactions. Although Swift, Swift, and Gooding (1983) used positive feedback only, most studies have utilized a form of feedback that involved discussion of positive and negative features of classroom discourse. It is possible that different types of teachers will respond to different forms of feedback. Consequently, research directed toward the most appropriate type of feedback for sustaining wait time is warranted. . . .

CONCLUSION

The proposition that classroom learning environments can be improved substantially by increasing wait time alone is too simplistic. Classroom interactions are complex and differences between teachers and students probably preclude any strategy from being effective in all situations. The predominant use of a whole class interactive activity setting, target students, and a reduced cognitive demand of the academic work are factors that mitigate against an extended wait time improving achievement. Furthermore, there are many classroom contexts in which shorter pauses between speakers can be justified. For example, when rote memorization or recall of facts is required, drill and practice activities might be conducted at a brisk pace using a short wait time. There is little to be gained in providing students and teachers with additional time to think if recall of factual information is required. In fact, if recall or rote learning is the intended outcome of an interaction it may well be better to utilize a short wait time. However, when the purpose of classroom discourse is to stimulate higher cognitive processes, teachers should utilize an average wait time of between 3 and 5 seconds. An extended teacher wait time should be viewed as a necessary but insufficient condition for higher cognitive level achievement. . . .

REFERENCES

Anderson, B. O. (1978). The effects of long wait-time on high school physics pupils' response length, classroom attitudes and achievement. *Dissertation Abstracts International, 39*, 3493A. (University Microfilms No. 78-23, 871)

Anshutz, R. J. (1975). An investigation of wait time and questioning techniques as an instructional variable for science methods students microteaching elementary school children. *Dissertation Abstracts International, 35*, 5978A. (University Microfilms No. 75-06, 131)

Arnold, D. S., Atwood, R. K., & Rogers, V. M. (1973). An investigation of relationships among question level, response level and lapse time. *School Science and Mathematics, 73*, 591–594.

Arnold, D. S., Atwood, R. K., & Rogers, V. M. (1974). Question and response levels and lapse time intervals. *Journal of Experimental Education, 43*(1), 11–15.

Boeck, M. A., & Hillenmeyer, G. P. (1973, March). *Classroom interaction patterns during microteaching: Wait time as an instructional variable*. Paper presented at Annual Meeting of the American Educational Research Asociation, New Orleans. (ERIC Document Reproduction Service No. EDO76574)

Chewprecha, T., Gardner, M., & Sapianchai, N. (1980). Comparison of training methods in modifying questioning and wait-time behaviors of Thai high school chemistry teachers. *Journal of Research in Science Teaching, 17*, 191–200.

DeTure, L. R. (1979). Relative effects of modeling on the acquisition of wait-time by preservice elementary teachers and concomitant changes in dialogue patterns. *Journal of Research in Science Teaching, 16*, 553–562.

DeTure, L. R., & Miller, A. P. (1985). *The effects of a written protocol model on teacher acquisition of extended wait-time*. Paper presented at the annual meeting of the National Science Teachers Association, Cincinnati, OH.

Doerr, S. T. (1984). *Extended wait-time, supportive intervention and Piagetian levels of teacher questions in middle school science classes*. (Unpublished master's thesis, University of New York at Oswego).

Doyle, W. (1983). Academic work. *Review of Educational Research, 53*(2), 159–199.

Esquivel, J. M., Lashier, W. S., & Smith, W. S. (1978). Effect of feedback on questioning of preservice teachers in SCIS microteaching. *Science Education, 62*, 209–214.

Fagan, E. R., Hassler, D. M., & Szabo, M. (1981). Evaluation of questioning strategies in language arts instruction. *Research in the Teaching of English, 15*, 267–273.

Fowler, T. W. (1975, March). *An investigation of the teacher behavior of wait-time during an inquiry science lesson*. Paper presented at the Annual Meeting of the National Association for Research in Science Teaching, Los Angeles. (ERIC Document Reproduction Service No. ED108872)

Gambrell, L. B. (1983). The occurrence of think-time during reading comprehension instruction. *Journal of Educational Research, 77*(2), 77–80.

Garigliano, L. T. (1973). The relation of wait-time to student behaviors in Science Curriculum Improvement Study lessons. *Dissertation Abstracts International, 33*, 4199-A. (University Microfilm No. 73-02595)

Gooding, C. T., Swift, P. R., & Swift, J. N. (1983, April). *An analysis of classroom discussion based on teacher success in observing wait time*. Paper presented at the Annual Conference of the New England Educational Research Organization, Rockport, ME.

Gore, D. A., & Roumagoux, D. V. (1983). Wait time as a variable in sex-related differences during fourth-grade mathematics instruction. *Journal of Educational Research, 76*(5), 273–275.

Granato, J. M. (1983, April). *The effects of wait time on the verbal behavior of kindergarten children*. Paper presented at the Annual Conference of the New England Educational Research Organization, Rockport, ME.

Honea, M. J. (1982). Wait time as an instructional variable: An influence on teacher and student. *Clearinghouse, 56*(4), 167–170.

Jones, N. A. (1980). The effect of type and complexity of teacher questions on student response wait time. (Doctoral dissertation, University of Pittsburgh). *Dissertation Abstracts International, 41*(2), 529-A.

Joyce, B. R., & Showers, B. (1983). *Power in staff development through research on training*. Washingtion, DC: Association for Supervision and Curriculum Development.

Knickerbocker, M. E. (1984). *The effects of wait time on verbal behavior of kindergarten children: A replication*. (Unpublished master's thesis, University of New York at Oswego).

Lake, J. H. (1973). The influence of wait-time on the

verbal dimensions of student inquiry behavior. *Dissertation Abstracts International, 34,* 6476-A. (University Microfilms No. 74-08866)

Marsh, C. A. (1978). Social-psychological influences upon the expression and inhibition of curiosity. (Doctoral dissertation, George Washington University). *Dissertation Abstracts International, 39,* 445-B.

Peterson, P. L., & Swing, S. R. (1982). Beyond time on task: Students' reports of their thought processes during classroom instruction. *Elementary School Journal, 82,* 481–491.

Rice, D. R. (1977). The effect of question-asking instruction on preservice elementary science teachers. *Journal of Research in Science Teaching, 14*(4), 353–359.

Riley, J. P., II. (1986). The effects of teachers' wait-time and knowledge comprehension questioning on pupil science achievement. *Journal of Research in Science Teaching, 23*(4), 335–342.

Rochester, S. R. (1973). The significance of pauses in spontaneous speech. *Journal of Psycholinguistic Research, 2,* 51–81.

Rowe, M. B. (1969). Science, soul and sanctions. *Science and Children, 6*(6), 11–13.

Rowe, M. B. (1974a). Wait time and rewards as instructional variables, their influence in language, logic, and fate control: Part 1. Wait time. *Journal of Research in Science Teaching, 11*(2), 81–94.

Rowe, M. B. (1974b). Reflections on wait-time: Some methodological questions. *Journal of Research in Science Teaching, 11*(3), 263–279.

Rowe, M. B. (1974c). Pausing phenomena: Influence on the quality of instruction. *Journal of Psycholinguistics Research, 3,* 203–223.

Samiroden, W. D. (1983). The effects of higher cognitive level questions wait time ranges by biology student teachers on student achievement and perception of teacher effectiveness. (Doctoral dissertation, Oregon State University). *Dissertation Abstracts International, 43,* 3208-A.

Shrum, J. L. (1985a). Wait time and student performance level in second language classrooms. *Journal of Classroom Interaction, 20*(1), 29–35.

Shrum, J. L. (1985b). Wait-time and the use of target or native languages. *Foreign Language Annals, 18*(4), 305–313.

Siegman, A. W., & Pope, B. (1965). Effects of question specificity and anxiety producing messages on verbal fluency in the initial interview. *Journal of Personality and Social Psychology, 2,* 522–530.

Stahl, R. J. (1982). *How humans process information: A way of viewing how individuals think and learn.* Tempe: Arizona State University.

Swift, J. N., & Gooding, C. T. (1983). Interaction of wait time feedback and questioning instruction on middle school science teaching. *Journal of Research in Science Teaching, 20*(8), 721–730.

Swift, J. N., Swift, P. R., & Gooding, C. T. (1984, April). *Observed changes in classroom behavior utilizing workshop, wait time feedback and immediate supportive intervention.* Paper presented at the Annual Conference of the New England Educational Research Organization, Rockport, ME.

Tobin, K. G. (1980). The effect of an extended wait time on science achievement. *Journal of Research in Science Teaching, 17,* 469–475.

Tobin, K. G. (1983). Management of time in classrooms. In B. J. Fraser (Ed.), *Classroom management* (pp. 22–35). Perth, Australia: WAIT Press.

Tobin, K. G. (1985, April). *Academic work in science classes.* Paper presented at the annual meeting of the American Educational Research Association, Chicago.

Tobin, K. G. (1986). Effects of teacher wait time on discourse characteristics in mathematics and language arts classes. *American Educational Research Journal, 23*(2), 191–200.

Tobin, K. G., & Capie, W. (1982). Relationships between classroom process variables and middle school science achievement. *Journal of Educational Psychology, 14,* 441–454.

Tobin, K. G., & Gallagher, J. J. (in press). Target students in the science classroom. *Journal of Research in Science Teaching.*

Winne, P. H. (1985). Steps toward promoting cognitive achievements. *The Elementary School Journal, 85*(5), 673–693.

Winne, P. H., & Marx, R. W. (1983). *Students cognitive processes while learning from teaching: Summary of findings.* (Occasional paper). Burnaby, Canada: Simon Fraser University, Instructional Psychology Research Group.

Winterton, W. W. (1977). The effect of extended wait-time on selected verbal response characteristics on some Pueblo Indian children. *Dissertation Abstracts International, 38,* 620-A. (University Microfilms, No. 77-16, 130)

Yeany, R. H., & Padilla, M. J. (1986). Training science teachers to utilize better teaching strategies: A research synthesis. *Journal of Research in Science Teaching, 23*(2), 85–95.

UNIT V

ASSESSING AND EVALUATING

1. CLASSROOM ASSESSMENT AND EDUCATIONAL IMPROVEMENT[1]
Peter W. Airasian

Classroom assessment and the decisions which result from it occur at two general levels which are important to distinguish in order to provide a context for my remarks. At one level are assessments such as high school graduation tests, preschool screening procedures, college admission examinations, and tests to allocate remedial funding. These assessments typically are mandated by an authority external to the local school, usually the state school board or legislature. At another level are the assessments individual teachers utilize daily to maintain order, to guide instruction, and to assign grades in their classrooms.

These two types of assessment and the information they provide coexist and interact in the classroom, but are fundamentally different in many regards (Airasian, 1984). For example, externally imposed assessment involves tests, regulations, objectives, and passing scores that are set by an authority external to the local school or classroom. The purpose of such assessment also is external to the local school, and very often has a moral (e.g., to make pupils work harder) or managerial (e.g., to allocate funds) dimension. Furthermore, such externally imposed assessment programs rely heavily upon a single test score and a single cut off point for decision-making. These parameters are quite different from the assessments that teachers carry

out in their own classrooms for purposes which are primarily related to the activities of the classrooms.

At the present time, however, teacher assessments are being all but ignored in the frantic search for educational improvement. The assessments teachers make every minute and every day in their classrooms are simultaneously the most important and yet the most undervalued resource in the quest for the educational excellence our society seeks so desperately. There appears to be a general distrust of school people on the part of legislators, businessmen and many parents and this distrust has resulted in the imposition of varied forms of external testing and accountability schemes in an effort to "raise standards," bring back the basics, and make pupils work harder. Such test focused assessment, which is springing up in varied forms and at varied locales— and which I predict will continue to spring up in the near future—provides a symbolic appeal to its patrons insofar as it is seen as: the only method by which educational standards can be measured; a symbol for traditional educational values; and a set of procedures that will bring increased control, focus, and efficiency to schools (Airasian, 1984; Eraut, 1981).

From the point of view of our discussion, however, the importance of such external assessments is that they have captured the attention of policy makers and parents, and in so doing, have diverted attention away from the less glamorous, less momentous, day to day assessments which teachers make about pupils. These day to day assessments,

---

[1] Keynote Address, "Classroom Assessment: A Key to Educational Excellence." Northwest Regional Educational Laboratory, Portland, Oregon, November 27–8, 1984.

333

in the various and often elusive forms they take, are the lifeline of schooling and the building blocks of excellence in education. We are an impatient society which is more prone to put its faith for social and educational improvement in a grand scheme or the hope for some *deus ex machina*, than in more mundane, particularistic, "spade work" type activities which are usually the basis for successful improvement. In the face of the mandates of federal and state legislators and the exhortations of national commissions on education, we must recognize that improvement in education and in pupil achievement will come about mainly as a result of activities which take place in schools and classrooms, activities which rely heavily upon the assessment practices and resulting decisions of classroom teachers. We cannot make most students learn and achieve simply by acts of fiat, legislation, or exhortation. Attainment will come primarily by the activities and hard work of teachers and pupils in the classroom setting. . . .

ASSESSMENT

Most of us know assessment when we see it, although it must be noted quickly that often we do not see assessment even though it is there. We probably would agree that the general purpose of assessment is to gather meaningful information about a person or an object, usually to aid in decision-making (Anderson, 1981). If we were to compile a list of classroom activities and instruments that are utilized by teachers to provide assessment data, we probably would include most of the following: standardized tests, teacher made tests (both essay and objective), curriculum embedded tests, worksheets, homework, oral responses and performances, checklists and rating forms, work samples, anecdotal records and, of course, formal and informal observations (Guerin and Majer, 1983). Notice that the above list, lengthy though it is, includes only *techniques* for gathering assessment information. A list of the pupil characteristics measured by each of these techniques would be substantially more lengthy.

Upon consideration, this is a fairly motley array of assessment procedures which differ among themselves on a number of dimensions. Some of the procedures are structured and controlled while others are unstructured and spontaneous. Some provide objective data while others provide subjective or impressionistic data. Some measure behavior directly while others measure behavior indirectly. Some occur very often in the course of a school day while others may not occur for weeks or months. Some require the pupils to adapt to the lead of the teacher while others require the teacher to react to the lead of the pupils. Some rely upon paper and pencil assessment, others upon oral responses, and still others upon observation. Some provide information about a single child while others provide information about the class as a whole. What, if any, unifying characteristic can we identify among these various assessment techniques?

Consider a teacher who has just finished teaching her fourth grade class a unit on long division problems without remainders. The teacher wishes to assess pupils' learning. Notice that there can be many reasons *why* the teacher desires an assessment at this time: to grade pupils, to assess her performance, to determine whether the class is ready to go on to the next unit involving long division with remainders, to identify students having difficulty so that additional work can be assigned to them, and so on. Regardless of the *purpose* of the assessment, the nature of the assessment itself is constant. Our teacher has a large number of assessment techniques available to choose from and let us suppose that she decides to construct a paper and pencil test. From all the possible long division problems without remainders that could be presented to her pupils, the teacher selects 10, includes them on her test, and presents the test to pupils.

Consider now another teacher on the first day of school in the Fall. As he watches his class file into the room to begin the day, he notices that one scruffily dressed boy is continually engaged in shoving matches with his classmates and, once seats are assigned, the boy seems unable to sit still or focus on any tasks. Later, in thinking back over the day, the teacher decides that Dominic, the boy, is inattentive, aggressive and likely to be a slow learner who will have to be strongly clamped down on in class and prodded continuously in his school work. This teacher also has made an assessment—unlike the long division test in the prior example, the assessment of Dominic was not a formal assessment but rather an informal one, based primarily upon fleeting, catch as catch can observations. Notice also that the assessment was not confined to Dominic's cognitive behavior, but included his attitudinal and motivational characteristics as well.

What makes both of these situations assessment is that each involves obtaining a sample of a student's behavior and using that sample to make an inference or generalization about similar behaviors which have not been observed. How a pupil performs on the teacher's 10 selected long division problems is used as the basis to make a generalization about how the pupil would have performed on all of the long division problems that could have been but were not included in the test. On the basis of observing only a small sample of Dominic's behavior—a day's worth at most—the teacher made a series of inferences about Dominic's future, unobserved, cognitive and affective behavior.[2] Thus, the two common aspects of all assessment activities are, firstly, collecting information about only a sample of behavior and secondly, using that small sample to make an inference about a larger domain of similar, though unobserved, behavior. By way of preview, it should be evident logically, that the adequacy of any assessment technique is determined by the extent to which it permits one to make accurate inferences about the larger domain of unobserved behavior.

PURPOSES OF CLASSROOM ASSESSMENT

The school and its classrooms are evaluative environments in which assessment and inference making are ubiquitous, integral, and essential aspects. Teachers observe, measure and make inferences about their pupils. Pupils reciprocate. The nature of the assessments and the inferences which result are wide ranging, encompassing not just pupils' academic performace and potential, but their motivation, self-concept, interests, attitudes, values, physical attractiveness, and manners as well. The assessments are made after consideration of many, many aspects of the pupil (Rist, 1970; Jackson, 1968), including,

but not limited to, appearance, cleanliness, interactions with peers and the teacher, language usage, vocabulary, performance of prior siblings, deportment, and, of course, academic performance and interest.

A complete view of the dynamics of classroom assessment is difficult to obtain because they are so complex. Assessments derive from more than one source. The pupil characteristic being assessed varies. The assessment itself may vary in the quality of data it provides and in the reliance teachers place on the information obtained. The purpose of the assessment also may differ. These variations refer only to the observable, descriptive facets of classroom assessment. When implicit, informal assessments are considered, along with the subjective meaning and consequences of assessment, the scenario for classroom assessment becomes quite murky indeed. One point that is crucial to bear in mind, however, is that assessment is inherent in the classroom because the classroom is a social environment, not because of any particular characteristics or proclivities of teachers.

If the present state of knowledge makes it difficult to describe the full complexity of classroom assessment, it does not prevent us from making some generalizations which are useful in focusing concern and providing guideposts for discussion. In spite of a great deal of work which has been done on classroom assessment in recent years, distinctions among the varied purposes of classroom assessment have not always been identified or articulated. As one considers life in classrooms and the many decisions which must necessarily be made by teachers, one can discern three general purposes or classes of decision-making for classroom assessment. Virtually all of the assessments teachers make are directed towards: getting to know or "sizing up" pupils, carrying out required, "official" pupil evaluations, and planning and monitoring the progress of instruction. In addition to purpose, these types of decisions differ also in timing, evidence gathering techniques, pupil characteristics of concern and manner of record keeping. The three types will be considered in turn.

A. "Sizing-up" Assessment

Before the classroom is an academic learning environment, it is a social environment which is

---

[2] Lest one came away thinking that the hypothetical example involving Dominic is artificial, it should be noted that there is substantial and persuasive evidence (Good and Brophy, 1973; Kellaghan, Madaus, and Airasian, 1982; Rist, 1970) that classroom teachers engage in the type of assessment exemplified, use these assessments to form impressions of pupils very early in the school year and, having formed an opinion, alter it reluctantly.

dependent upon certain routines, control mechanisms, and interpersonal relationships. The purpose of "sizing-up" assessment is to initiate and facilitate social communication and control in the classroom by providing teachers with information about the "raw material" they will have to work with during the year. Social interactions are based upon the knowledge each participant possesses about the other. In a very short time, perhaps a week or so (Rist, 1970), most teachers have gathered enough assessment data about their pupils to know that when Simon asks to leave the classroom he is malingering whereas if Greg makes the same request there is a genuine need; or if Suzzane asks a question it is to score what in my day were termed "Brownie points" whereas Lynn's questions are indicative of true puzzlement.

Without the store of perceptions about pupils that a classroom teacher quickly accumulates, social communication and classroom routine would be exceptionally difficult to carry on and maintain. Each new interaction would have to be taken at face value, with each participant's motives, interests, and needs unknown to the other. The situation would be analogous to that faced by a substitute teacher entering a classroom for the first time. Without the store of information about the pupils that the regular classroom teacher has accumulated from "sizing-up" assessments of many types, the substitute is placed in a situation where communication is difficult, motives are suspect, requests to leave the classroom become moral dilemmas, and methods to maintain order are hit and miss.

Consider the following verbatim descriptions about pupils from three first grade teachers (Willis, 1972). About Mary:

> Very, very babyish. She sits and daydreams, looks at other children and does anything she can to entertain herself. Anything except settle down and do her work. She plays with her crayons, plays with her little strap-on bag at her desk. She wants to talk to the other children. This child I think will be a problem all year. Very doubtful if she will settle down. She's very immature in her activities. She doesn't seem to be interested in anything. . . .

About John:

> John is such a pretty boy with big old brown eyes, and he smiles all the time, even his eyes smile.

> Wants to please, well behaved. Really joins in with any activity that is going on, and his work has been nice. I'm expecting him to be one of the better boys.

Most elementary school teachers are capable of making such statements about their pupils, usually with considerable accuracy, because they observe and interact with them every day. Note two aspects of the teachers' descriptions. Firstly, note the range of pupil characteristics that the teachers have attended to: attitudinal, familial, physical, and academic. Secondly, note that these descriptions were obtained from the first grade teachers on the third day of the school year. The children described had not been to kindergarten, had taken no tests, and had had no prior contact with the teachers describing them. . . . "Sizing-up" assessment also takes place at post elementary grades. It is doubtful, however, whether junior or senior high school teachers could provide the breadth and depth of information about . . . pupils in their classes that elementary school teachers can provide. . . .

"Sizing-up" assessment, as its name implies, occurs mainly very early in the school year and becomes a less practiced type of classroom assessment as the year goes on. Although less practiced after the first month or so of the school year, the perceptions and expectations which result from "sizing-up" assessment, remain very important throughout the year and may have an important bearing on other types of assessment. . . . Finally, it is only rarely that the perceptions or expectations that derive from sizing-up assessment are maintained in any formal, written, routinized manner. Rather, teachers keep these perceptions and expectations to themselves for the most part, except for transmitting them verbally to colleagues or parents.

B. Official Assessments

In order to conform to the regulations and procedures of the organization in which they work, teachers are required to engage in certain assessment, decision-making and record keeping activities. In this context, there are many "official" assessments that teachers make, most of them revolving around the academic performance of pupils. One such "official" assessment occurs when teachers gather evidence to help determine what reading group, curriculum track, or course level a pupil ought to be placed in. Assessing for the purpose of assigning grades to pupils is another form of official assessment. A third form of this required assessment is somewhat different from assessments aimed at making placement or grading decisions. As part of his or her official duties, the classroom teacher is expected to serve as a general diagnostician and to identify physical, emotional, behavioral, or academic symptoms of pupils which might require them to need specialized help. The teacher is not expected to provide precise diagnosis or remediation, but the classroom teacher is expected to identify a student who needs glasses or a hearing aid, a student who has severe emotional problems and so on.

With the exception of the diagnostic variety, official asessment, as the name implies, is to a large extent routinized. In most grades it takes place periodically throughout the school year. The main focus for this type of assessment is the individual pupil; rarely are official assessment data collected about a class as a whole. Teacher observation is an important assessment technique for official assessment, as it is for all assessment that transpires in the classroom, but for grading and placement decisions, there is evidence that teachers also rely fairly heavily on teacher made or curriculum embedded tests for more objective performance data. Cognitive skills are the primary behavior domain measured by most official assessments and the results of these assessments are usually maintained in written form.

C. Instructional Assessment

The primary role of the classroom teacher is to guide and foster pupil learning and these tasks cannot be accomplished without assessment. Instruction and planning for instruction occupy the bulk of a teacher's in-school time, and instructional assessment is concerned with all of the decisions a teacher must make about the planning and progress of instruction.

Most attempts to describe instructional assessment have concentrated on what goes on during the teaching process, on the decisions, techniques, and strategies teachers use when they are face to face with a class of pupils. Clearly this is an important aspect of instructional assessment. During instruction, teachers are required to act as traffic cops,

observing innumerable incoming bits of assessment information, distilling them on the spot, and using them to answer questions such as "Should I reteach this concept?"; "Is it time to stop for the day?"; "Do my slow learners understand this?"; "Should I prepare additional worksheets on this topic?"; "Is this point clear?"; "Do I need another example of this point?"; "How can I answer this question so all pupils will understand?"; and so on. These and a multitude of similar questions are the fodder and guidance for teaching, and in terms of sheer number, these usually informal, relatively transitory assessments are the most frequent assessments that teachers make. . . .

Instructional assessment occurs before, during, and after instruction, and since instruction is the predominant activity in the classroom, assessment is both frequent and ongoing throughout the school day and year. The primary object of instructional assessment is groups of pupils, either the class as a whole or a subgroup within the class. When a teacher answers the question "Should I reteach this concept?" or "Are more examples needed?" or "Should I move on to the next topic?" the teacher is usually seeking an answer based upon assessment of some subset of the class. Thus, not all pupils in the class may require reteaching or additional examples, but if a sizable minority of the class does the teacher likely will reteach and find new examples. It would be comforting to think that similar assessment and decision-making occurs for each pupil individually, but rarely is this the case. The main focus of instructional assessment, then, is a group of pupils. Interactive assessment data are obtained from the variety of stimuli which assault teachers during instruction: looks on faces, questions, and responses to questions posed by the teacher. Preactive assessment permits the teacher to consider more types of evidence about pupils, including homework papers, test scores, performances and worksheets. Finally, since instructional assessment occurs so frequently and spontaneously, the transiency of any single decision is often not even remembered by a teacher, let alone written down or formally recorded in some way.

This discussion has considered sizing-up, official, and instructional assessments separately. Although it is beyond the scope of this discussion, it should be borne in mind that data collected to inform one type of decision may also be used to inform some other decision. Perspectives on pupils may meld into a more global view with little sense as to which specific decision need or assessment data contributed most to that view. Thus, for analytic purposes it is useful to distinguish among three types of classroom assessment. However, it may be somewhat artificial to think that teachers consciously impose such distinctions in their decisions about pupils.

Thus far we have seen that assessment is a crucial aspect of instruction and an important factor in attaining educational excellence. We have seen that the key elements of assessment are sampling pupil behaviors and making inferences about the pupil based upon the behaviors sampled and observed. We have seen that classroom assessment has a social and an academic dimension and that a multitude of assessment techniques are available and used widely by teachers. We have seen that there are sizing-up, official, and instructional management purposes to classroom assessment. With this context in mind, we may now consider what is known and not known about the classroom assessment practices and preferences of teachers.

TEACHERS' PRACTICES AND PREFERENCES

Teachers see much and base their assessments on much of what they see (Brophy and Good, 1974). However, perhaps to simplify things for themselves, teachers appear to distinguish two general pupil assessment dimensions (Airasian, Kellaghan and Madaus, 1977; Herbert, 1974; Pedulla, Airasian, and Madaus, 1980). One dimension includes behaviors and characteristics which are fairly directly related to scholastic activities and performance in the classroom. Examples of characteristics in this dimension are participation in class, attention span/concentration, persistence, speech and use of language, working with limited supervision, and test performance. The second dimension includes behaviors . . . which are related to social activities in the classroom. Examples of characteristics assessed in this dimension are general deportment, manners and politeness, getting along with others, personal appearance and dress.

There does not appear to be a difference in the existence of these two dimensions from elementary to high school, although there is a difference in the emphasis accorded the dimensions across grade levels, with high school teachers attending more to the cognitive academic than to the social dimension in both the quantity and perceived importance of assessments. This difference in emphasis is likely due to the fact elementary school teachers tend to express a belief that the goal of elementary school is to develop the whole child, whereas high school teachers, given current organizational patterns, focus greater concern on pupils' academic characteristics (Salmon-Cox, 1980).

A few additional characteristics of teacher assessments are worthy of note. Firstly, the perceptions of and expectations for pupils that teachers form, primarily from sizing-up and initial official assessments, remain quite stable over time. (Rist, 1970; Airasian, Kellaghan and Madaus, 1977). That is to say, not only do teachers use their assessments to form perceptions and expectations early in the school year, but once formed, these perceptions change very little over the course of the year. Little work has been done to examine the extent to which the perceptions formed from "sizing-up" assessment done in the first week of school influence or predetermine succeeding assessments of a pupil by a teacher.

Secondly, it does not take most pupils long to discern their status in the teacher's eye, or their positions in the pecking order of the classroom (Morrison and McIntyre, 1969; Rist, 1970). Moreover, there is some evidence that pupils act in concert with their teacher's expectation for them.

Thirdly, there is substantial evidence to indicate that teachers' perceptions are related to the quality and quantity of interactions that occur between them and pupils (cf. Brophy and Good, 1974). Students perceived to be of higher ability, for example, have been shown to receive more praise (Degroat and Thompson, 1949), greater recitation opportunity (Good, 1970), and more interaction time with teachers (Kranz, Weber and Fishall, 1970) than pupils perceived to be of lower ability. Students teachers like tend to be graded higher than students teachers don't like. Higher grades are also associated with perceived congruence in values between teacher and pupil. Clearly, the assessments teachers make and the perceptions formed from those assessments have clear and practical import for students and their lives in classrooms.

Virtually every recent survey carried out (Herman and Dorr-Bremme, 1984; Kellaghan, Madaus and Airasian, 1982; Salmon-Cox, 1980; Stiggins and Bridgeford, 1984; Yeh, 1978) has indicated that formal and informal observations are reported by teachers to be the most practiced forms of classroom assessment. For elementary school teachers in particular, but for all teachers to some extent, the immediacy of many decisions that must be made precludes more time consuming and disruptive assessment techniques. Secondary school teachers report relying upon observation for decision making (Herman and Dorr-Bremme, 1984), but given the subject matter specialization of high school teaching and the fact that high school teachers see 125–175 pupils per day, the range and depth of their observational assessments are not as great as those of most elementary school teachers and tend to focus upon cognitive and academic behaviors.

In addition to formal and spontaneous observation, teachers rely heavily upon teacher-made and curriculum embedded tests for assessment information. As grade level increases, the weight teachers report giving to teacher-made tests in decision-making increases, although it is almost always less than the weight teachers report giving to teacher observations and teacher opinions in making the same decisions. Relative to observation and teacher-made or curriculum embedded tests, standardized, commercially available tests are reported not to be used extensively by teachers. . . .

There are three points which should be stated in considering this consistent and apparently straightforward finding. Firstly, no studies provide a clear picture of what pieces of data go into forming a teacher's observation/opinion of a pupil. We do not know whether the general category "Teacher observation/opinion" that teachers report relying upon so heavily for decision-making represents a *product* derived from considering all available evidence about a pupil or a *technique*, akin to other assessment techniques. All we know is that teachers report relying heavily upon their own observations/opinions in making official assessments of their pupils.

Secondly, to complicate matters further, we know that teacher ratings of pupils in various academic areas correlate fairly highly, on the order of .6 to

.8, with pupils performance on standardized tests in the same academic areas (Kellaghan, Madaus, and Airasian, 1982). This correlation is manifested even when teachers make their ratings early in the school year and in the absence of any prior standardized test information about the pupils. Thus, teachers most often find their own academic judgments of pupils corroborated by test data which, in turn, may lead them to report according heavier emphasis to their own judgments than to test information[.] . . .

Thirdly, although we know little about the process by which assessment data of various sorts are weighed and synthesized to arrive at a decision involving grades, placement, or grouping, we know considerably less about the processes involved in "sizing-up" and instructional assessments. This state of affairs is not unreasonable or unexpected, given the formality of official decisions vis-à-vis the informality and transiency of "sizing-up" and assessment decisions. However, it is the context and expectations provided by "sizing-up" assessment as well as the feedback-correction process fostered by instructional assessment which have the most direct impact upon student learning. While we should not ignore official assessment, it would behoove us to learn more about the two other general types of assessment. . . .

SUGGESTIONS FOR ACTION

In light of the foregoing scenario, what suggestions for action may be offered in order to improve our understanding and practice of teacher assessment? Firstly, researchers . . . can direct increased energies toward teasing out the processes through which the three general types of assessment purposes identified in this presentation take place, interact, and are used in classroom decision-making. We know that teachers attend to a wide range of student characteristics in making assessments. We have a clear and consistent idea of what assessment devices teachers say they trust and weigh the most in making decisions, although it must be recalled that existing studies have focused primarily upon what we have termed official decisions. We have a sense of the different purposes for which teachers require assessment information in their classrooms. . . .

It will be a substantially more difficult conceptual

and methodological task to turn attention from the whats and whys of teacher assessment practices to the factors which explain how teachers carry out the process of gleaning, weighing, synthesizing and using assessment information. Does information obtained for one assessment purpose, say grading, carry over and become used for other assessment purposes, say evaluating the progress of instruction? Are some forms of assessment based decisions more stable than others? What determines the particular characteristics of a child or a class that a teacher most attends to and is there consistency across children and classes? The answers to these and similar questions will be difficult to obtain because the basis for their answers rests principally upon implicit, often barely conscious, processes that teachers carry out constantly and that leave few external records. Essentially, the teacher is the gatekeeper and storehouse of an enormous amount of information about pupils. We do not know a great deal about how that information is obtained, managed and used to aid teachers in fulfilling their classroom duties.

In addition to raising new questions for researchers, some suggestions are in order for altering the nature of teacher training to include greater emphasis upon assessment techniques in general, and non-test based techniques in particular. At the baccalaureate and inservice levels, teacher training in assessment is either overlooked completely or focuses primarily upon the use and interpretation of standardized test results for assessment and decision-making. Excluding discussion of published and teacher-made tests, various other forms of performance assessment are grossly underrepresented in most of the widely used test and measurement textbooks (Stiggins and Bridgeford, 1984). Yet teachers perceive these non-test forms of assessment as more important than published tests and teachers also rate such non-test assessment techniques as oral questioning, observing work habits, and class discussion as among their most needed areas of training (Gullikson, 1984). Textbooks, college courses and inservice workshops should begin to adopt a broader and more realistic perspective on classroom assessment and on the richness of varied assessment techniques and their uses in classroom decision-making. The applicability of varied assessment forms ought to be presented to teachers and the strengths and weaknesses of each exposed.

My suggestion as regards teacher training is to start small and relatively simply. There is a tendency in the field of education and elsewhere, to take processes that are perceived to be somewhat haphazard, unstandardized and unevenly applied and to try to routinize these into some grand new scheme which practitioners are encouraged to follow slavishly. Such schemes generally destroy the spontaneity and inherent goodness in the original processes and become so logistically cumbersome that they are abandoned quickly. Teacher insight, discretion and judgment will continue to control most of the important assessment that transpires in classrooms because much of that assessment is immediate, informal and can't be planned for. The first step in teacher education is to make teachers aware of the range of uses to which they put varied forms of assessment information every day in their classrooms. Sometimes the immediacy and constancy of activities in the classroom prevent us from garnering a perspective on what we're doing beyond responding to immediate demands.

In addition to information about specific assessment techniques and a general perspective on the whats and whys of classroom assessment, any effort to improve assessment practices should seek to convey some general principles which apply to all forms of assessment. The application of these principles should improve the quality of classroom assessment, the accuracy of information obtained about pupils, and hopefully, pupil learning as well.

Thus, it was noted earlier that assessment involves obtaining a sample of student behavior and making an inference based upon performance on that sample to a larger domain of similar, though unobserved, behavior. The success a student exhibits in solving five long division problems on a paper and pencil test or in giving a five minute prepared speech on the Civil War is taken as an indication of how the pupil would perform on long division problems in general or in giving other prepared speeches. However, because assessment involves only a small portion of pupil behavior, sometimes only a fleeting, momentary sample, it is inappropriate to treat the results of a single assessment as though they were error-free and an infallible indicator of a pupil's characteristics. All assessments contain some error and imprecision, and relying heavily upon any single assessment for decision-making can lead to incorrect decisions.

Therefore a first general principle for classroom assessment is to corroborate assessment data whenever possible before making a decision. Although it will not be possible to corroborate every assessment made, it probably is most important to obtain multiple behavior samples when conducting sizing-up and official assessments, because the decisions made from these two general types of assessment are relatively permanent. . . .

The suggestion that multiple observations and/or strategies be utilized in assessment has an additional concern implicit in it. This concern is for the validity of the assessment, that is, for the extent to which the behavior which is being assessed is indicative of the behavior one wished to assess. The product of assessment is an inference and the main determinant of the adequacy of any assessment technique is the accuracy of the inference it permits one to make. . . . [T]wo simple examples may make clear the importance of assessing with validity. First, many standardized, multiple choice tests try to measure a pupil's spelling ability by having the pupil identify the one out of the four words presented which is misspelled. Recognize that the ability to select misspelled words does not mean that a pupil also has the ability to spell words correctly in his or her own writing. Secondly it has been noted that the predominant way in which many teachers assess the success of their instruction is by observing pupils' facial expressions, enthusiasm, and so forth. One might ask whether facial expressions and enthusiasm are useful indicators of the extent to which pupils are learning. Can one automatically assume that looks on faces and apparent enthusiasm are isomorphic to learning the material being taught? If not, then the assessment evidence being gathered may not be valid to make the desired inference about learning. . . .

A final general suggestion regarding the improvement of the quality of classroom assessment concerns the interpretations that are made about assessment data. We have just seen that some interpretations may not be valid because the behavior assessed does not mirror the behavior about which inferences were desired. A second type of misinterpretation of assessment information occurs when the information is confused with explanations of what caused the behavior that was assessed (Airasian, 1979). Rarely does the behavior assessed in the classroom contain in itself the explanation for what caused that behav-

ior. One must look elsewhere for such explanations. A pupil obtained a low score on a standardized ability test. The score may be attributable to low ability, poor reading, low motivation to perform well, language difficulties, unequal opportunity to learn, transitory physical illness on testing day, or some combination of these and other factors. In order to determine why the pupil's score was low, it is necessary to collect additional assessment data that go beyond the ability test score at hand. The very important "whys" of pupil behavior call for sensitive and complex weighing and interpretation of much assessment data. Too often, however, the initial sizing-up and official assessments which take place in the classroom early in the year are used to produce convenient labels for pupil behavior and to create a closed circle of explanations for that behavior. . . .

CONCLUSION

In the course of this presentation a number of points have been considered, including the nature, status, purposes and techniques of classroom assessment. Suggestions for improving the quality of classroom assessment also have been noted. Underlying the discussion of assessment is the issue of effective schools, schools in which pupils learn. While there are many, many factors which contribute to an effective school (Brookover and Lezotte, 1979; Edmonds, 1979, 1982; Madaus, Airasian, and Kelleghan, 1980; Mackenzie, 1983), one essential ingredient is timely, well-focused assessment.

School effectiveness, if it means anything, means improving pupils' achievement via classroom instruction, or, put another way, how time spent in the classroom is used to promote learning. Recent research in teaching (Denham and Leberman, 1980; Rosenshine and Berliner, 1978) has been devoted to the search for instructional principles that are general, that transcend particular content areas and grade levels, while at the same time recognizing that all teaching is to some extent idiosyncratic and adaptive. Although the search for generalizable instructional techniques and strategies has yet to bear fruit, one point of consensus has emerged clearly in the work that has been done to date. There is wide agreement that effective teaching must incorporate the facets of assessment we have considered. Teachers must know their students, continually diagnose their learning progress, and distribute rewards for their progress in a fair manner. . . .

REFERENCES

Airasian, P. W. A perspective on the uses and misuses of standardized achievement tests. *N.C.M.E. Measurement in Education*, *10*, 3, 1979, pp. 1–12.

Airasian, P. W. Educational testing in public policy: Growth and implications. Paper prepared for "The individual, the environment, and education: A conference in honor of Benjamin S. Bloom." University of Chicago, Chicago, IL, March 2, 1984.

Airasian, P. W., Kellaghan, T., and Madaus, G. F. The stability of teachers' perceptions of pupil characteristics. *The Irish Journal of Education*, *11*, 1 and 2, 1977, pp. 78–84.

Anderson, L. W. *Assessing affective characteristics in the schools*. Boston: Allyn and Bacon, 1981.

Brookover, W. B. and Lezotte, L. W. *Changes in school characteristics coincident with changes in student achievement*. East Lansing, MI: Institute for Research on Teaching, Michigan State University, 1979.

Brophy, J. F. and Good, T. L. *Teacher-student relationships*. New York: Holt, Rinehart and Winston, 1974.

deGroat, A. and Thompson, G. A. A study of the distribution of teacher approval and disapproval among sixth grade pupils. *Journal of Experimental Education*, *18*, 1949, pp. 57–75.

Denham, C. and Lieberman, A. (Eds.). *Time to learn*. Washington, DC: Program on Teaching and Learning, National Institute of Education, 1979.

Edmonds, R. R. Some schools work and more can. *Social Policy*, *9*, 1979, pp. 28–32.

Edmonds, R. R. Programs of school improvement: An overview. *Educational Leadership*, *40*, 1982, pp. 4–11.

Eraut, M. Accountability and evaluation. In Simon, B. and Taylor, W. (Eds.), *Education in the eighties*. London, England: Batsford Academic and Educational, Ltd., 1981, pp. 146–162.

Good, T. L. Which pupils do teachers call on? *Elementary School Journal*, *70*, 1970, pp. 190–198.

Good, T. L. and Brophy, J. F. *Looking in classrooms*. New York: Harper and Row, 1973.

Guerin, G. R. and Maier, A. S. *Informal assessment in education*. Palo Alto, California: Mayfield Publishing Co., 1983.

Gullickson, A. R. Matching teacher training with teacher needs in testing. Paper presented at the annual meeting

of the National Council on Measurement in Education, New Orleans, LA, April, 1984.

Herbert, G. W. Teachers' ratings of classroom behavior: Factorial structure. *British Journal of Educational Psychology*, *44*, 1974, pp. 233–240.

Herman, J. L. and Dorr-Bremme, D. W. Teachers and testing: Implications from a national study. Paper presented at the annual meeting of the American Educational Research Association, New Orleans, LA, April, 1984.

Jackson, P. W. The way teaching is. *NEA Journal*, 1965.

Jackson, P. W. *Life in classrooms*. New York: Holt, Rinehart and Winston, 1968.

Kellaghan, T., Madaus, G. F., and Airasian, P. W. *The effects of standardized testing*. Boston: Kluwer-Nijhoff Publishing, 1982.

Kranz, P., Weber, W., and Fishell, K. The relationships between teacher perceptions of pupils and teacher behavior towards those pupils. Paper presented at the annual meeting of the American Educational Research Association, Minneapolis, MN, April, 1970.

MacKenzie, D. E. Research for school improvement: An appraisal of some recent trends. *Educational Researcher*, *12*, 1983, pp. 5–17.

Madaus, G. F., Airasian, P. W., and Kellaghan, T. *School effectiveness: A reassessment of the evidence*. New York: McGraw-Hill, 1980.

Morrison, A. and McIntyre, D. *Teachers and teaching*. Harmondsworth, Middlesex: Penguin Books, 1969.

Pedulla, J. J., Airasian, P. W., and Madaus, G. F. Do teacher ratings and standardized test results of students yield the same information? *American Educational Research Journal*, *17*, 1980, pp. 303–307.

Rist, R. Student social class and teacher expectations: The self-fulfilling prophecy in ghetto education. *Harvard Educational Review*, *40*, 1970, pp. 411–451.

Rosenshine, B. W. and Berliner, D. C. Academic engaged time. *British Journal of Teacher Education*, *160*, 1978, pp. 38–66.

Salmon-Cox, L. Teachers and tests: What's really happening? Paper presented at the annual meeting of the American Educational Research Association, Boston, MA, April, 1980.

Stiggins, R. J. and Bridgeford, N. J. The use of performance assessment in the classroom, Study Number 4. Report submitted to the National Institute of Education, Contract #400-83-0005, November 30, 1983.

Willis, S. *Formation of teachers' expectations of students' academic performance*. Unpublished doctoral dissertation, The University of Texas at Austin, 1972.

Yeh, J. *Test use in the schools*. Los Angeles, CA: Center for the Study of Evaluation, University of California at Los Angeles, Los Angeles, CA, 1978.

2. TEACHER EVALUATION IN THE ORGANIZATIONAL CONTEXT
A Review of the Literature

Linda Darling-Hammond, Arthur E. Wise, and Sara R. Pease

. . . Over the last decade teacher evaluation has assumed increasing importance. The demand for accountabilty in education has shifted from broad issues of finance and program management to specific concerns about the quality of classroom teaching and teachers. These concerns have led to a resurgence of interest in evaluating teachers and to the development of new systems for teacher evaluation. . . .

POLICY CONTEXT

The public has come to believe that the key to educational improvement lies in upgrading the quality of teachers rather than in changing school structure or curriculum. Improving teacher quality was the most frequent response to the 1979 Gallup poll's question on what public schools could do to earn an "A" grade, beating by large margins such reforms as emphasizing the basics, improving school management, lowering class size, or updating the curriculum (Gallup, 1979). In response to these perceptions, states and local school districts have initiated a wide range of policy changes affecting the certification, evaluation, and tenure of both prospective and currently employed teachers (Gudridge, 1980; Vlaanderen, 1980).

Several states have adopted teacher competency tests, such as the National Teacher Examinations, for teacher certification; others are considering licensure which would include statewide teacher examinations prior to certification along with the establishment of a professional standards and practices board (Lewis 1979; McNeil, 1981; Southern Regional Education board, 1979; Vlaanderen, 1980). Some, like Oklahoma, are adopting comprehensive programs that include higher admission standards for colleges of education, competency tests for certification and recertification, evaluation of performance, and continuing teacher education (Kleine & Wisniewski, 1981). Most states have legislated requirements for teacher performance evaluation (Beckham, 1981), and some of the more recent statutes specify which testing instruments or evaluation procedures are acceptable.

Not surprisingly, teacher evaluation processes increasingly have become the subject of collective bargaining agreements. A Rand Corporation study found that between 1970 and 1975, the percentage of contracts examined that contained teacher evaluation provisions increased from 42 to 65 (McDonnell & Pascal, 1979). Contracts often specify methods of information gathering, frequency of observations and evaluation, processes for communicating evaluation criteria and results, opportunities for teacher response and remediation in the case of negative evaluations, and due process procedures (Strike & Bull, 1981).

Mitchell and Kerchner (1983) argue that because of collective bargaining, teacher evaluation has become an increasingly rule-based process, linked less to judgments of competence than to evidence about whether teachers have adhered to clearly specified minimum work standards. "The objectification of evaluation standards," they state, "has had the effect of discoupling the relationship between teaching performance and the behaviors on which teachers are held subject to discipline and discharge" (pp. 19–20). Their observation reflects the difficulty in using teacher evaluation results for both formative (improvement-oriented) and summative (personnel decisionmaking) purposes.

Although a survey by the American Association of School Administrators (Lewis, 1982) found that few school districts were using evaluation results as the basis for layoff decisions, there is a growing literature on the legal requirements for using evaluation results for dismissal (Beckham, 1981; Peterson & Kauchak, 1982; Strike & Bull, 1981). Courts have generally required that a school system strictly apply an established formal dismissal procedure with due process safeguards. Further, the school authorities must determine minimum acceptable teaching standards in advance, inform the staff of these standards, and, finally, document for the court how a teacher's performance violates these standards (Beckham, 1981). Beckham recommends that to withstand judicial scrutiny an evaluation policy must include: (a) a predetermined standard of teacher knowledge, competencies, and skills; (b) an evaluation system capable of detecting and preventing teacher imcompetencies; and (c) a system for informing teachers of the required standards and according them an opportunity to correct teaching deficiencies.

Each of these criteria poses some problems for the design and implementation of a teacher evaluation system. There are particular difficulties in integrating the requirements of an evaluation policy geared toward job status decisions with those of a policy aimed at improving teaching. The most obvious problem is that developing a predetermined standard of teacher knowledge, competencies, or skills poses nontrivial controversies about the content and specificity of the standards. Furthermore, where standardized tests or performance assessments are used to make job status decisions, courts generally require that they have a demonstrable, direct relationship to effective job performance, that is, they must have proven validity. We explore the difficulties of such a demonstration in a later section of this paper.

Detecting teacher incompetencies involves the development and careful application of reliable, generalizable measures of teaching knowledge or behavior. The state-of-the-art of measurement for teacher evaluation may not be adequate. *Preventing* incompetency implies the development of either a fool-proof approach to teacher training or a teacher-proof approach to instruction; we leave that to utopians. *Correcting* deficiencies seems a more approachable objective; however, this is the point at which research on teaching effectiveness leaves off and where summative and formative evaluation approaches collide.

It is one thing to define and measure teacher competence in a standardized fashion; it is quite another to change teacher performance. Research on individual and organizational behavior suggests that first-order solutions are unlikely to effect change, and, further, that successful approaches involve processes that may be inconsistent with those used to derive summative evaluation judgments. That is, the context-free generalization necessary for implementing a uniform evaluation system may counteract the context-specific processes needed to effect change in individual or organizational behaviors.

Policy Conflicts and Tensions

Many observers have pointed out that public pressures for summative evaluation affecting teacher job status—selection and promotion, dismissal, and reduction in force decisions—may make formative evaluation much more difficult (Knapp, 1982; Peterson & Kauchak, 1982; Feldvebel, 1980). Increasing the prescriptiveness and specificity of evaluation procedures, particularly the need for extensive documentation of all negative findings, generates anxiety among teachers and inhibits the principal's role as instructional leader or staff developer (Munnelly, 1979). Summative evaluation criteria must be more narrowly defined if they are to be applied uniformly, thus limiting their use for formative purposes. Furthermore, constraints on classroom behavior intended to weed out incompetent teachers may prevent good teachers from exercising their talents fully (Darling-Hammond & Wise, 1981). Knapp (1982) concludes

> The net result of these pressures for more careful summative judgements of teachers is to put administrators under particular strain. Though "better" performance evaluation may appear to make the issues explicit and decisions objective, it may also generate as much heat as light, particularly where the various constituents to the design of evaluation do not agree. The pressure to improve teaching performance may foster more elaborate evaluation systems, but with summative thrusts getting in the way of formative efforts. (p. 10)

This tension between evaluation goals is in part a reflection of the differences among evaluation constituencies. These stakeholders have divergent views on the primary purpose of teacher evaluation and, hence, of what constitutes a successful evaluation system. Knapp's (1982) articulation of various stakeholders' perspectives is useful. Teachers have a stake in maintaining their jobs, their self-respect, and their sense of efficacy. They want a teacher evaluation system that encourages self-improvement, appreciates the complexity of their work, and protects their rights. Principals have a stake in maintaining stability in their organizations, allowing them to respond to parental and bureaucratic concerns for accountability while keeping staff morale intact. They want an evaluation system that is objective, not overly time-consuming, and feasible in the organizational context. Parents and public officials have a stake in the "bottom line"—the effects of teaching on student outcomes. They want an evaluation system that relates teacher performance to teacher effectiveness, and that guarantees appropriate treatment of children in classrooms.

These differing views make choices about teacher evaluation processes difficult. They also affect implementation, because even after a policy is adopted, its terms and emphases are renegotiated at every level in the implementation system (Berman & McLaughlin, 1973–1978; Elmore, 1979). This renegotiation may not occur in a formal way, but practices at the school district, school, and classroom levels will be a function of cross pressures that may alter the formal process in important ways.

All these factors argue for understanding teacher evaluation plans in the context of organizational behaviors and processes. In the succeeding sections of this paper we examine the educational and organizational concepts underlying different views of teacher evaluation, we describe the teacher evaluation processes and models currently in use, and we discuss implementation of teacher evaluation in the organizational context.

EDUCATIONAL AND ORGANIZATIONAL CONCEPTS

The newly emerging policy thrusts in the area of teacher evaluation reflect diverse perspectives on the role of teachers in the educational enterprise, the nature of teaching work, the organization and operations of schools, and even the purposes of schooling. Different theories of learning and of the operation of educational organizations are embodied in different models for teacher evaluation, and any attempt to identify the components of "successful" evaluation procedures must explicitly recognize their underlying assumptions.

Perhaps most problematic is the definition of teacher knowledge, skills, and competencies in a fashion useful for a *policy system*. Policies rely on generalizations that can be uniformly applied and administered according to rules. The further away policy development occurs from the implementation level, the more uniformly applicable generalizations and prescriptions for practice must be. They must rely on context-free assumptions linking theory to results.

As Darling-Hammond and Wise (1981) point out, many current policies are "rationalistic"—they seek to rationalize the actions of teachers by specifying curricular objectives, by prescribing instructional methods for attaining the objectives, and by evaluating the extent to which the objectives are attained. They assume a direct link between teacher behavior and student learning, as well as a close match between external goals and classroom activities.

Yet, other theories of education are possible. Various theories differ significantly in their explanations of the nature of teaching and learning, the processes of schooling, and the ways in which educational organizations operate. We cannot here develop a full exposition of the range of educational theories; a few examples must suffice. At the heart of the rationalistic theory stand the policymaker and the administrator who rationalize the operations of the school through deliberate decisionmaking and procedure-setting. In the spontaneous theory, the teacher is the central figure. "The rest of the vast educational enterprise chiefly serves the purpose of permitting the teacher to give spontaneous expression to the educated man he finds within himself—and in so doing, to foster useful intellectual growth in his pupils" (Stephens, 1976, pp. 140–141). The individual child is the focal point for the humanistic theory, and the schooling system revolves around his needs and interests in providing an environment to facilitate his development.

The distinguishing elements of these and other theories of education include differences concerning how goals for education are set (and by whom), what the goals in fact are, how they are to be transmitted among and operationalized by the various actors in the schooling process. The actors are variously viewed as active or passive, deliberate and rational or spontaneous and instinctive. The components of the educational system are variously perceived as autonomous or interdependent tightly or loosely coupled, vertically or horizontally integrated, consensual or individualistic in their perceptions of values, norms, and objectives. De facto power may be perceived as centralized at various hierarchical levels or relatively decentralized.

Depending on which theory of education one subscribes to and which model of the educational process seems most aptly to describe what one observes, the appropriate roles and tasks of policymakers, school administrators, teachers, and students will appear quite different. Certainly if policymakers and practitioners view the reality of schooling in vastly different ways, policies and practices will be dissonant, and intended policy outcomes will be unlikely to occur. Futhermore, whether a particular evaluation approach meets its proximate and ultimate goals will depend on the specific organizational context in which it is used, as well as the implementation processes that take place at each level of the operating system—that is, how the procedures are carried out within the classroom, school district, and, where relevant, the state. . . .

APPROACHES TO TEACHER EVALUATION

The choice of a teacher evaluation process is, as we have observed, associated with views of teaching work and of the school as an organization, although quite often these associations are made only implicitly in evaluation decisionmaking. A more explicit choice factor is the use to which the evaluation results are to be put.

Purposes for Teacher Evaluation

As indicated in Figure 1, teacher evaluation may serve four basic purposes. The figure's cells artificially represent these purposes and levels of decisionmaking as distinct. In fact, teacher evaluation may be directed at small or large groups of teachers (rather than simply individuals or whole schools), and may represent degrees of hybrid improvement and accountability concerns (as when promotion decisions are linked to improvement efforts).

Many teacher evaluation systems are nominally intended to accomplish all four of these purposes, but different processes and methods are better suited

to one or another of these objectives. In particular, improvement and accountability may require different standards of adequacy and of evidence. Focusing on individual or organizational concerns also leads to different processes, for example, bottom-up or top-down approaches to change, unstandardized or standardized remedies for problems identified. Berliner and Fenstermacher illuminate these differences with respect to staff development (our improvement dimension), although their observations are applicable to accountability purposes as well. Their definition of staff development encompasses four scales along which approaches may differ:

> Staff development activities may be [a] internally proposed or externally imposed, in order to [b] effect compliance, remediate deficiencies, or enrich the knowledge and skills of [c] individual teachers or groups of teachers, who [d] may or may not have a choice to participate in the activities. (Fenstermacher & Berliner, in press, p. 6)

They note that as more differentiation occurs between participant roles and organizational levels, the profile of a staff development activity tends to shift from internal to external initiation, from an enrichment to a compliance focus, from participation by individuals or small groups to standardized programs for large groups, and from voluntary to involuntary participation. As the profile of a staff development activity shifts, so does its usefulness for a variety of purposes.

Staff development may be a vehicle for training teachers as technicians to implement policies devised by someone else (Floden & Feiman, 1981). Teacher evaluation in this case would focus on how faithfully the prescribed procedures or curricula are adhered to. This approach is most useful for organizational improvement or accountability purposes. Alterna-

Purpose/Level	Individual	Organizational
Improvement (formative information)	Individual staff development	School improvement
Accountability (summative information)	Individual personnel (job status) decisions	School status (e.g., certification) decisions

FIGURE 1 Four Basic Purposes of Teacher Evaluation

tively, staff development may be viewed as a means for helping teachers move from the acquisition of particular skills to applications of their judgment in order for them to play an analytic role in developing curricula and methods. Or staff development may be designed to help the teacher move to higher developmental stages in order to enable him or her to develop multiple perspectives about teaching and learning, to become more flexible, adaptive, and creative (Floden & Feiman, 1981). Teacher evaluation in these views would focus on teachers' personal stages of development and areas of confidence and would be most suited for individual improvement purposes.

In general, teacher evaluation processes most suited to accountability purposes must be capable of yielding fairly objective, standardized, and externally defensible information about teacher performance. Evaluation processes useful for improvement objectives must yield rich, descriptive information that illuminates sources of difficulty as well as viable courses for change. Teacher evaluation methods designed to inform organizational decisions must be hierarchically administered and controlled to ensure credibility and uniformity. Evaluation methods designed to assist decisionmaking about individuals must consider the context in which individual performance occurs to ensure appropriateness and sufficiency of data.

Although these purposes and the approaches most compatible with them are not necessarily mutually exclusive, an emphasis on one may tend to limit the pursuit of another. Similarly, while multiple methods for evaluating teachers can be used—and many argue, should be used—it is important to consider what purposes are best served by each if teacher evaluation goals and processes are to be consonant. Furthermore, some processes are distinctly inconsistent with others and with some purposes for evaluation. These disjunctures should be recognized before a teacher evaluation system is adopted and put in place.

Teacher Evaluation Processes and Methods

There have been several recent reviews of teacher evaluation processes in which the authors identified from six to twelve general approaches to teacher evaluation (Ellett, Capie, & Johnson, 1980; Haefele,

1980; Lewis, 1982; Millman, 1981a; Peterson & Kauchak, 1982). They reveal that the approaches used to evaluate teachers seek to measure very different aspects of teaching and the teacher. They rely on different conceptions of what demonstrates adequacy and on diverse notions of how to recognize or measure adequacy. Some seek to assess the quality of the *teacher* (teacher competence); others seek to assess the quality of *teaching* (teacher performance). Other approaches claim to assess the teacher or his or her teaching by reference to student outcomes (teacher effectiveness). Medley (1982) offers useful definitions of four terms often treated as synonyms:

- *Teacher competency* refers to any single knowledge, skill, or professional value position, the possession of which is believed to be relevant to the successful practice of teaching. Competencies refer to specific things that teachers know, do, or believe but not to the effects of these attributes on others.
- *Teacher competence* refers to the repertoire of competencies a teacher possesses. Overall competence is a matter of the degree to which a teacher has mastered a set of individual competencies, some of which are more critical to a judgment of overall competence than others.
- *Teacher performance* refers to what the teacher *does* on the job rather than to what she or he *can* do (that is, how competent she or he is). Teacher performance is specific to the job situation; it depends on the competence of the teacher, the context in which the teacher works, and the teacher's ability to apply his or her competencies at any given point in time.
- *Teacher effectiveness* refers to the effect that the teacher's performance has on pupils. Teacher effectiveness depends not only on competence and performace, but also on the responses pupils make. Just as competence cannot predict performance under different situations, teacher performance cannot predict outcomes under different situations.

The tools and processes that are used to assess teacher competence, performance, or effectiveness are based on assumptions about how these qualities are linked to one another, how they may be measured, and how the measurements may be used to make decisions. There is substantial debate on all these questions. . . .

Teacher Evaluation Models

Approaches to teacher evaluation and improvement vary depending on:

- What teacher attributes (e.g., professional training, teaching competencies, etc.) are believed to be important for effective teaching;
- Which aspect of the instructional process the district hopes to affect (e.g., assurance of teacher quality; improved teaching techniques; learning outcomes, etc.); and
- What will be the criteria for evaluating success (e.g., demonstration by the teacher of desired behaviors or competencies, teacher or student test scores, etc.). . . .

Two of the most widely discussed evaluation models[1] are Manatt's (Manatt, Palmer, & Hidlebaugh, 1976) "Mutual Benefit Evaluation" and Redfern's (1980) "Management by Objectives Evaluation." Both models have been implemented in a number of school districts,[2] and both models are characterized by (a) goal-setting, (b) teacher involvement in the evaluation process, and (c) centralized teaching standards and criteria. The major difference between them is the point at which a teacher is brought into the evaluation process.

Manatt describes his model as a system in which teachers, administrators, and the educational program itself may be objectively evaluated (Gudridge, 1980). Although Manatt insists that the model is designed primarily to improve teacher performance rather than to ferret out incompetent teachers, he nevertheless stresses points needed to withstand court scrutiny of resulting dismissals (e.g., evaluation criteria must be "legally" discriminating; must adhere to procedural due process).

There are four steps in the model:

1. The school board and administration (or whoever is responsible for evaluation development) must determine criteria for minimum acceptable teaching standards. For example, Manatt suggests that these might include productive teaching techniques, positive interpersonal relations, organized class management, intellectual stimulation, and out-of-class behavior (Gudridge, 1980, pp. 36–38).
2. A diagnostic evaluation is performed to assess each teacher's present status vis-à-vis the standards. Although Manatt does not prescribe specific measurement instruments, he suggests that evaluation processes should include a preobservation conference with the teacher, a teacher self-evaluation, classroom observations, and postobservation conferences.
3. With the cooperation of the teacher, the evaluator sets job targets (three to five are recommended) for the teacher's performance improvement. Manatt suggests that the targets be specific and objectively measurable.
4. After a specified time, the teacher is reevaluated and new job targets are set.

Redfern borrowed the "management-by-objectives" model from business and applied it to teacher evaluation. Like the Manatt model, a teacher's responsibilities and learning goals are set by the responsible school authority. However, before any evaluation takes place, the evaluator and teacher *jointly* establish individual objectives, an action plan, and measurable progress indicators (Haefele, 1980; Lewis, 1982; Redfern, 1980), the teacher's action plan is monitored through diagnostic rather than summative observations. The observation results are assessed by the evaluators who then meet with the teacher to discuss progress and to set additional objectives. Redfern does not prescribe monitoring or measurement processes because each action plan would call for different methods and tools (Redfern, 1980). The collegial nature of the model makes teacher self-evaluation essential (Iwanicki, 1981).

These models are intended to promote the professional growth of the individual teacher and the integration of individual performance objectives with school board policies. They also establish, with the teacher's participation, a structured set of evaluation

---

[1] We use the word "model" here because it is widely used in the field; we do not use it either in a judgmental sense or in the social science sense of a theoretically based exposition of interrelated assumptions.

[2] Gudridge reported that the Manatt model has been used in five districts in Iowa and Illinois (Gudridge, 1980, p. 42). Between 1975 and 1980, Redfern assisted 16 school districts across the country to develop an "MBO" program (Redfern, 1980, pp. 159–161).

goals intended to reduce uncertainties and misunderstandings between the teacher and evaluator. On the other hand, critics charge that the goal-setting models place too much emphasis on measurable objectives. Further, they argue, to be properly implemented the models may require large investments in time and money (Iwanicki, 1981).

Both models straddle the competency-based and outcomes-based evaluation philosophies. The models are "results-oriented" but allow for various definitions of "results." In some cases, it would appear that results may be measurable increases in learning; in others, a positive result may be the demonstration of a new teaching competency. However, the Redfern model seems to allow more input from the teacher, thus fostering the image of professionalism, while Manatt's model seems to delegate professional decisions to supervisors. . . .

An approach that seems consonant with flexible, multigoal models such as these is the clinical supervision approach, a process often compared to the Manatt and Redfern models (Lewis, 1982, p. 31). While the components are structurally similar, the clinical supervision approach is more informal in setting performance goals and generally involves more one-to-one interaction between the teacher and the evaluator. Ideally, areas of improvement and concern are mutually identified, and professional goals evolve during a systematic plan of classroom observations. As Manatt notes, without specific school board guidelines or evaluation criteria, "supervisor and teacher are both assumed to be instructional experts, with the teacher identifying his concerns and the supervisor assisting . . ." (Lewis, 1982, p. 42). Clinical supervision is highly interactive and may promote professionalism and a sense of efficacy among teachers. However, it is also a time-consuming process, and the data gathered during the observations may be uninterpretable to those outside the supervisor-teacher relationship. Thus, clinical supervision approaches may prove to be of limited use for accountability purposes.

Application of the Models

Most . . . models can be characterized as having a decisionistic orientation (Floden & Weiner, 1978). They reflect a view of evaluation as an activity which functions to inform decisions about the pursuit of stable, consensual programmatic, and instruc-

tional goals. Other models of evaluation, such as [clinical supervision], start from the premise that instructional goals are neither stable nor entirely consensual. Such models include multiple goals for and functions of evaluation, including, for example, conflict resolution and complacency reduction (Floden & Weiner, 1978; Chen & Rossi, 1980), as well as empowerment of the individual teacher.

The application of research-based teacher evaluation models to real-life settings must overcome the gap that exists between technically defensible specifications of criteria or methods and politically viable solutions to organizational problems. There is a growing recognition that any kind of evaluation activity involves value choices—and conflicts—at all levels of the operating system (Rein, 1976; Rossi, Freeman, & Wright, 1979; Sroufe, 1977). Evaluation is political because it serves as a tool in a larger policymaking process and because it is inherently directed at making a judgment of worth about something. Any such judgment ultimately rearranges or reaffirms an existing constellation of stakes that individuals or groups have in what is being evaluated (Englert, Kean, & Scribner, 1977). Furthermore, the *process* of evaluation must be understood as encompassing a continual process of bargaining and goal modification that occurs "because the conditions and effective constituency surrounding goal setting are different from the conditions and effective constituency surrounding implementation" (Stone, 1980, pp. 23–24).

Knapp (1982) describes the divergence existing between many teacher evaluation models and actual practices in terms of the differing standards applied by researchers and practitioners to ultimately political value choices.

Value choices are nowhere more clearly at issue than in decisions about the aspects of the teacher and teaching to be evaluated. Scholars have tended to make these value choices on scientific grounds: in effect, they are arguing that evaluation systems should be focused on whatever can be operationally defined and demonstrated to contribute to student learning. . . . A number of proposals for improved teacher appraisal systems have been advanced, but a "better" system tends to be defined in terms of accuracy and links to an established base of teacher effects research. Such systems rest on an idealized image of school management, that ignores the powerful effects of organizational and contextual forces on management activity. (pp. 4–5)

In actual practice, he finds that schools follow "the lines of least resistance," evaluating aspects of teachers and teaching in more vague terms so as to simultaneously satisfy diverse constituencies. A defensible teacher evaluation process is one that allows them to balance several goals at once:

- Sorting teachers;
- Maintaining staff morale and collegiality;
- Maintaining organizational distance from environmental demands (e.g., for accountability); and
- Devising improvements that require modest, incremental change.

This does not mean that research-based teacher evaluation models cannot succeed in the real world, only that adaptations to the organizational context must be explicitly considered and sought if the processes are to be implemented successfully. . . .

TEACHER EVALUATION IN THE ORGANIZATIONAL CONTEXT

. . . Implementation of any school policy, including a teacher evaluation policy, represents a continuous interplay among diverse policy goals, established rules and procedures (concerning both the policy in question and other aspects of the school's operations), intergroup bargaining and value choices, and the local institutional context. Teacher evaluation procedures, for example, will be influenced by the political climate that exists within a school system, by the relationship of the teachers' organization to district management, by the nature of other educational policies and operating programs in the district, and by the very size and structure of the system and its bureaucracy. These variables and others are equally potent at the school level.

Many organizational theorists have advanced the notion that school systems are loosely coupled. That is, they do not conform to the rational-bureaucratic model, which assumes consensus on organizational goals and technologies, tight links between vertical and horizontal functions and actors, frequent inspection of work tasks, and consistent and unambiguous lines of communication and authority (Deal, Meyer, & Scott, 1974; March, 1976; Weick, 1976).

Weick (1982) goes so far as to suggest that "the task of educating is simply not the kind of task that can be performed in a tightly coupled system" (p. 674). He argues that it is wrong to treat evidence of loose coupling as the result of improper management or indecisiveness. Because of the nature of teaching work, the diversity of school constituencies, and the changing nature of demands on the educational system, tightly coupled, standardized responses to identified problems may reduce the organization's capability to respond to future needs or problems, and may set in motion actions that conflict with other educational and organizational goals.

This perception is supported by research on the effects of implementing performance-based teacher evaluation processes in local school systems. The results of four case studies of the implementation of performance-based staff layoff policies led Johnson (1980) to conclude that the existence of such policies does not guarantee automatic implementation. Furthermore, unintended consequences at the school site call into question the educational worth of top-down implementation processes, which "compromise the autonomy of the local school; alter the role of the principal as protector, provider, and instructional leader; jeopardize the cooperative and collegial relations among staff; and diminish the effectiveness of teacher supervision" (p. 216). The inability of principals to adapt teacher evaluation practices to changing supervisory needs, combined with a decrease in the principal's overall autonomy in shaping school programs, seemed to diminish the principals' capacities to serve as advocates and leaders for their staff, programs, and schools. Ironically, the growing body of "school effects" research suggests that strong leadership from principals is a key component in shaping successful schools (see, e.g., Brookover, 1977). It appears possible that some kinds of tightly coupled teacher evaluation processes may jeopardize the effective functioning of the school organization to the extent that standardization from above inhibits the capacity of the principal for exerting school-level decisionmaking authority. . . .

If these observations are true, as the body of implementation research suggests they may be, we must ask what change strategies can be effective in such a seemingly confused and confusing milieu. Fortunately, organizational theorists do not stop short of suggesting some approaches that are plausible in loosely coupled, nonconsensual organizations like schools.

The first general area for attention concerns the nature and frequency of communications. Weick (1982) contends that one of the most important jobs of administrators in a loosely coupled system is "symbol management"; that is, the articulation of general themes and directions "with eloquence, persistence, and detail" (p. 675). He distinguishes symbols from goals: Symbols tell people what they are doing and why; goals tell people when and how well they are doing it. Because problems, hence goals, change constantly, symbols are the glue that holds the organization together.

> The administrator who manages symbols does not sit in his or her office mouthing clever slogans. Eloquence must be disseminated. And since channels are unpredictable, administrators must get out of the office and spend lots of time one on one—both to remind people of central visions and to assist them in applying these visions to their own activities. The administrator teaches people to interpret what they are doing in a common language. (Weick, 1982, p. 676) . . .

. . . [T]he second area of concern: the development of a sense of efficacy among those at whom improvement efforts are directed. . . . Theories on the exercise of authority in organizations . . . suggest that recognition of task complexity and preservation of some autonomy for personnel encourage a sense of self-efficacy (Dornbusch & Scott, 1975; Thompson, Dornbusch, & Scott, 1975). In addition, motivation by intrinsic incentives through evaluations that allow self-assessment is more powerful than motivation that relies on external assessment and reward (Deci, 1976; Meyer, 1975).

Finally, the nature of decisionmaking and policy formulation processes, which are closely tied to communications and empowerment, is critical to successful implementation of a teacher evaluation system. These processes involve coalitions of stakeholders interacting to define problems and solutions under conditions of ambiguity (Cohen & March, 1974). Resolving ambiguity by attempts at tight coupling may not neccessarily be as productive as indirect change efforts that preserve the ability of smaller units to adapt to local conditions (Deal &

Celotti, 1980; March 1976). As Knapp (1982) comments.

> The process of developing evaluation systems is an occasion for many things in an organization such as the interaction of constituencies, celebration of important values, and the joint recognition of problems. Whether or not performance objectives are met by a specified proportion of a school district's teachers, the *indirect* results of such efforts may have considerable impact on staff enthusiasm, beliefs, or behavior, with ultimate benefits for students. (p. 18)

These propositions lead us to hypothesize four minimal conditions for the successful operation of a teacher evaluation system:

- All actors in the system have a shared understanding of the criteria and processes for teacher evaluation;
- All actors understand how these criteria and processes relate to the dominant symbols of the organization, that is, there is a shared sense that they capture the most important aspects of teaching, that the evaluation system is consonant with educational goals and conceptions of teaching work;
- Teachers perceive that the evaluation procedure enables and motivates them to improve their performance; and principals perceive that the procedure enables them to provide instructional leadership;
- All actors in the system perceive that the evaluation procedure allows them to strike a balance "between adaptation and adaptability, between stability to handle present demands and flexibility to handle unanticipated demands" (Weick, 1982 p. 674); that is, that the procedure achieves a balance between control and autonomy for the various actors in the system.

CONCLUSION

Teacher evaluation is an activity that must satisfy competing individual and organizational needs. The imperative of uniform treatment for personnel decisions may result in standardized definitions of acceptable teaching behavior. However, research on teacher performance and teaching effectiveness does not lead to a stable list of measurable teaching behaviors effective in all teaching contexts. Moreover, research on individual and organizational behavior indicates the need for context-specific strategies for improving teaching rather than system-wide hierarchical efforts. If teacher evaluation is to be a useful tool for teacher improvement, the process must strike a careful balance between standardized, centrally administered performance expectations and teacher-specific approaches to evaluation and professional development.

REFERENCES

Beckham, J. C. *Legal aspects of teacher evaluation.* Topeka, Kans.: National Organization on Legal Problems of Education, 1981.

Berman, P., & McLaughlin, M. W. *Federal programs supporting educational change* (R-1589-HEW). Santa Monica, Calif.: The Rand Corporation, 1973–1978.

Brookover, W. *Schools can make a difference.* East Lansing: College of Urban Development, Michigan State University, 1977.

Chen, H., & Rossi, P. H. The multi-goal, theory-driven approach to evaluation: A model linking basic and applied social science. *Social Forces*, 1980, *59*(1), 106–122.

Cohen, M., & March, J. *Leadership and ambiguity: The American college president.* New York: McGraw-Hill, 1974.

Darling-Hammond, L., & Wise, A. E. *A conceptual framework for examining teachers' views of teaching and educational policies* (N-1668-FF). Santa Monica, Calif.: The Rand Corporation, 1981.

Deal, T. E., & Celotti, L. D. How much influence do (and can) educational administrators have on classrooms? *Phi Delta Kappan*, 1980 *61*(7), 471–473.

Deal, T., Meyer, J., & Scott, R. *Organizational support for innovative instructional programs: District and school levels.* Paper presented at the annual meeting of the American Educational Research Association, Chicago, April 1974.

Deci, E. L. The hidden costs of rewards. *Organizational Dynamics*, 1976, *4*(3), 61–72.

Dornbusch, S. M., & Scott, W. R. *Evaluation and the exercise of authority.* San Francisco: Jossey-Bass. 1975.

Ellett, C. D., Capie, W., & Johnson, C. E. Assessing teaching performance. *Educational Leadership*, 1980, *38*(3), 219–220.

Elmore, R. T. *Complexity and control: What legislators and administrators can do about implementation.* Seattle, Wash.: Institute of Governmental Research, 1979.

Englert, R. M., Kean, M . H., & Scribner, J. D. Politics of program evaluation in large city school districts. *Education and Urban Society*, 1977, *9*, 425–450.

Feldvebel, A. M. Teacher evaluation: Ingredients of a credible model. *Clearing House*, 1980, *53*(9), 415–420.

Floden, R. E., & Feiman, S. *A consumer's guide to teacher development*, East Lansing: Institute for Research on Teaching, Michigan State University, 1981.

Floden, R. E., & Weiner, S. S. Rationality to ritual: The multiple roles of evaluation in governmental process. *Policy Sciences*, 1978, *9*, 9–18.

Gallup, G. H. The eleventh annual Gallup poll of the public's attitudes toward the public schools. *Phi Delta Kappan,* 1979, *60*, 33–45.

Gudridge, B. M. *Teacher competency: Problems and solutions.* Arlington, Va.: American Association of School Administrators, 1980.

Haefele, D. L. How to evaluate thee, teacher—let me count the ways. *Phi Delta Kappan*, 1980, *61*(5), 349–352.

Iwanicki, E. F. Contract plans: A professional growth-oriented approach to evaluating teacher performance. In J. Millman (Ed.), *Handbook of teacher evaluation.* Beverly Hills, Calif.: Sage Publications, 1981.

Johnson, S. M. Performance-based staff layoffs in the public schools: Implementation and outcomes. *Harvard Educational Review*, 1980, *50*(2), 214–233.

Kleine, P. F., & Wisniewski, R. Bill 1706: A forward step for Oklahoma. *Phi Delta Kappan*, 1981, *63*(2), 115–117.

Knapp, M. S. *Toward the study of teacher evaluation as an organizational process: A review of current research and practice.* Menlo Park, Calif.: Educational and Human Services Research Center, SRI International, 1982.

Lewin, K., Dembo, T., Festinger, L., & Sears, P. Level of aspiration. In J. Hunt (Ed.), *Personality and behavioral disorders* (Vol. 2). New York: Ronald Press, 1944.

Lewis, A. *Evaluating educational personnel.* Arlington, Va.: American Association of School Administrators, 1982.

Manatt, R. P., Palmer, K. L., & Hidlebaugh, E. Evaluating teacher performance with improved rating scales. *NASSP Bulletin*, 1976, *60*(401), 21–23.

March J. G. The technology of foolishness. In J. G. March & J. P. Olsen (Eds.), *Ambiguity and choice in organizations.* Bergen, Norway: Universitetsforlaget, 1976.

McDonnell, L., & Pascal, A. *Organized teachers in American schools* (R-2407-NIE). Santa Monica, Calif.: The Rand Corporation, 1979.

McNeil, J. D. The politics of teacher evaluation. In J. Millman (Ed.), *Handbook of teacher evaluation*. Beverly Hills, Calif.: Sage Publications, 1981.

Medley, D. M. *Teacher competency testing and the teacher educator*. Charlottesville: Association of Teacher Educators and the Bureau of Educational Research, University of Virginia, 1982.

Meyer, H. H. The pay-for-performance dilemma. *Organizational Dynamics*, 1975, *3*(3), 39–50.

Millman, J. (Ed.). *Handbook of teacher evaluation*. Beverly Hills, Calif.: Sage Publications, 1981. (a)

Mitchell, D. E., & Kerchner, C. T. *Collective bargaining and teacher policy*. In L. S. Shulman & G. Sykes (Eds.), *Handbook of teaching and policy*. New York: Longman, 1983.

Munnelly, R. J. Dealing with teacher incompetence: Supervision and evaluation in a due process framework. *Contemporary Education*, 1979, *50*(4), 221–225.

Peterson, K., & Kauchak, D. *Teacher evaluation: Perspectives, practices and promises*. Salt Lake City: Center for Educational Practice, University of Utah, 1982.

Redfern, G. B. *Evaluating teachers and administrators: A performance objectives approach*. Boulder, Colo.: Westview Press, 1980.

Rein, M. *Social science and public policy*. New York: Penguin Books, 1976.

Rossi, P. H., Freeman, H. E., & Wright, S. R. *Evaluation: A systematic approach*. Beverly Hills, Calif.: Sage Publications, 1979.

Southern Regional Education Board. *Teacher education and certification: State actions in the South*. Atlanta: Author, 1979.

Sroufe, G. E. Evaluation and politics. In J. Scribner (Ed.), *The politics of education*. Chicago: University of Chicago Press, 1977.

Stephens, J. M. *The process of schooling*. New York: Holt, Rinehart and Winston, 1976.

Stone, C. N. The implementation of social programs: Two perspectives. *Journal of Social Issues*, 1980, *36*(4), 13–34.

Strike, K., & Bull, B. Fairness and the legal context of teacher evaluation. In J. Millman (Ed.), *Handbook of teacher evaluation*. Beverly Hills, Calif.: Sage Publications, 1981.

Thompson, J. E., Dornbusch, S. M., & Scott, W. R. *Failures of communication in the evaluation of teachers by principals* (No. 43). Stanford, Calif.: Stanford Center for Research and Development in Teaching, 1975.

Vlaanderen, R. *Trends in competency-based teacher certification*. Denver, Colo.: Education Commission of the States, 1980.

Weick, K. E. Educational organizations as loosely-coupled systems. *Administrative Science Quarterly*, 1976, *21*, 1–19.

Weick, K. E. Administering education in loosely coupled schools. *Phi Delta Kappan*, 1982, *63*(10), 673–676.

3. FEEDBACK, CORRECTIVES, AND ENRICHMENT

Thomas R. Guskey

. . . Nothing is more central or critical to the implementation of mastery learning than the feedback and corrective process. This is also the aspect of mastery learning that most clearly differentiates it from other more traditional approaches to instruction. Although the feedback and corrective process seldom requires more than a single class period for each learning unit, it is the primary mechanism through which mastery learning becomes truly individualized. Through this process each student receives precise information on his or her learning progress and is directed to specific corrective activities. These correctives are designed to help students overcome their learning errors so that they will acquire the prerequisites for the next learning task. When the feedback and corrective process is handled well, the application of mastery learning is nearly always successful.

THE PURPOSE OF FEEDBACK FOR STUDENTS

The major purpose of providing feedback to students is to help them identify what they have learned well or mastered and what they need to spend more time learning. The primary vehicle for providing this feedback is, of course, the formative test. Regardless of its format, the formative test should help students identify the important elements in the instruction and should give them information about how well they have learned those elements. After taking a formative test, students should be able to tell if their preparations for the class have been adequate or not. They should also be able to tell if their focus in studying is what the teacher wants. For instance, if a student has concentrated on memorizing terms and facts while the teacher is more interested in having students make applications, the disparity should become clear with the results of the formative test. In other words, the feedback provided by a formative test should clarify for students what they are expected to learn and how well they have learned those things.

The nature of the feedback provided will depend in part upon the format of the formative test. For example, if the formative test is a short quiz made up of objective types of items, the feedback it provides may be simply a record of which items were answered correctly and which ones were missed. Knowing that each item is designed to assess learning of a particular concept or objective, students can immediately turn to corrective activities that focus on the concepts or objectives they have not yet mastered. On the other hand, if the formative test includes essay items or a writing sample, students will need a clear and precise description of what was lacking in their response and how it can be improved. In order to provide this description,

specific criteria for evaluating students' responses should be developed, together with ways of communicating these criteria to students. Similarly, if the formative test involves a skill demonstration, criteria for evaluating students' performance are essential if the feedback is to be prescriptive and useful.

THE PURPOSES OF FEEDBACK FOR TEACHERS

The results from a formative test also provide teachers with two very important kinds of feedback. The first is an explicit description of each student's learning progress. With the formative test results, teachers know which students are doing well and which are having problems, and they also know exactly what problems those students are having. The formative test thus provides very precise information about the learning progress of each student, which can then be used to guide corrective activities that focus on those specific learning difficulties.

The second type of feedback is information about the effectiveness of the original instruction. The results from a formative test can help teachers pinpoint what they taught well and what they did not. For example, note the summary chart shown in Figure [1]. Many teachers construct a chart like

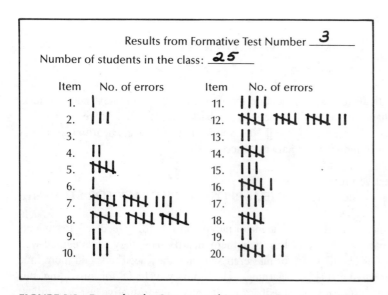

FIGURE [1]   Example of a Summary of Incorrect Responses to Items on a Formative Test

this as soon as they score a formative test. The marks beside each number indicate how many students answered the item incorrectly. If the original instruction were ideally effective, few students would miss any particular item. However, look at items 7, 8, and 12. These items were answered incorrectly by more than half of the students in the class. It is apparent that either these are poor items or that the instruction covering them was not very effective. Perhaps these ideas were explained in a way that was vague or unclear to many students. Perhaps the presentation in the textbook was confusing. Perhaps the questions were inappropriate or ambiguous to most students. Or perhaps there was a mistake in the scoring key. Whatever the reason, this is very important information for the teacher to have. A similar kind of summary can be prepared for writing samples or skill demonstrations by simply listing the criteria used for scoring and then indicating the number of students who did not meet each criterion.

With the feedback from a formative test, teachers know where to concentrate their efforts in improving their teaching. The concepts missed by a large number of students should be reexplained or retaught in a different way. These improvements can be carried over to future presentations, enhancing the overall effectiveness of instruction.

Many teachers gather feedback on their teaching and at the same time provide feedback to students by using a *double answer sheet* with the formative test (see Figure [2]). This kind of answer sheet can be used with most objective tests. Students simply record their answers twice on the answer sheet— that is, they mark both sides of the answer sheet identically. When the test is completed, they tear the answer sheet in half, keep one half, and return the other half to the teacher. In this way, both the student and the teacher have a record of responses to the items on the formative test. Some teachers have students correct both halves of the answer sheet before returning one half. Other teachers ask students to return one half before scoring, generally because they feel that correcting the test allows them to gain a clearer picture of each student's progress. (This procedure also helps avoid the possibility of students changing answers while the test is being corrected.) . . .

Many writing teachers accomplish the same purpose by having students make a carbon copy of their writing samples. The new "carbonless" copies can also be used. This allows the teacher to provide general feedback to students immediately after the test, when the feedback is most effective.

It is important to remember that whatever the format of the formative test, the feedback it provides the teacher is just as useful and as important as the feedback it provides students.

ESSENTIAL CHARACTERISTICS OF CORRECTIVES

Obviously, gaining precise information about students' learning progress is very important. However, if their learning outcomes are really to be improved, that information must be paired with specific activities for remedying the learning difficulties. These activities are generally called *correctives*. In some programs they are referred to as *remedial* activities, while other programs avoid the negative connotations of that word by using such labels as *additional activities* or *additional practice*. Regardless of the label, however, correctives are designed to help remedy the learning difficulties students have experienced during the original instruction.

The most essential characteristic of any corrective activity is that it *teach the same material in a way that is different from the way it was originally taught*. It does little good to repeat the same method or mode of instruction that has already been proven unsuccessful. Hence, corrective activities must provide an alternative pathway to learning the material.

In order for corrective activities to provide this different pathway, they must do at least one of two things. The first is to *present the material differently from the way it was originally presented*. That is, the material must be explained in a different manner or from a different perspective. If a deductive approach (presenting a general concept and then moving to specific examples of the concept) was initially used, an inductive approach (presenting a variety of specific examples and then moving to the general concept) would work well as a corrective. For example, suppose a teacher explained how to compute the area of a rectangle by first presenting the formula: Area = length × width and then moving to specific examples. A corrective approach might have students first cover different rectangles

Answer Sheet

Name _____   Name _____

Formative Test No. _____   Formative Test No. _____

DIRECTIONS: Circle the letter of   DIRECTIONS: Circle the letter of
the correct answer. When necessary, the correct answer. When necessary,
write the answer on the blank   write the answer on the blank
beside the number.   beside the number.

1.	a	b	c	d	e	_____	1.	a	b	c	d	e	_____
2.	a	b	c	d	e	_____	2.	a	b	c	d	e	_____
3.	a	b	c	d	e	_____	3.	a	b	c	d	e	_____
4.	a	b	c	d	e	_____	4.	a	b	c	d	e	_____
5.	a	b	c	d	e	_____	5.	a	b	c	d	e	_____
6.	a	b	c	d	e	_____	6.	a	b	c	d	e	_____
7.	a	b	c	d	e	_____	7.	a	b	c	d	e	_____
8.	a	b	c	d	c	_____	8.	a	b	c	d	e	_____
9.	a	b	c	d	e	_____	9.	a	b	c	d	e	_____
10.	a	b	c	d	e	_____	10.	a	b	c	d	e	_____
11.	a	b	c	d	e	_____	11.	a	b	c	d	e	_____
12.	a	b	c	d	e	_____	12.	a	b	c	d	e	_____
13.	a	b	c	d	e	_____	13.	a	b	c	d	e	_____
14.	a	b	c	d	e	_____	14.	a	b	c	d	e	_____
15.	a	b	c	d	e	_____	15.	a	b	c	d	e	_____
16.	a	b	c	d	e	_____	16.	a	b	c	d	e	_____
17.	a	b	c	d	e	_____	17.	a	b	c	d	e	_____
18.	a	b	c	d	e	_____	18.	a	b	c	d	e	_____
19.	a	b	c	d	e	_____	19.	a	b	c	d	e	_____
20.	a	b	c	d	e	_____	20.	a	b	c	d	e	_____

FIGURE [2] Example of a General Double Answer Sheet for Formative Tests

with unit squares, count how many squares are required to cover each rectangle, and then "derive" the formula. Whatever the approach, some change in format, style, or method of presentation is essential.

The second thing a corrective activity must do is *involve students in learning the material in a way that is different from the way they were initially involved.* If students were originally taught through a visual demonstration, a more detailed auditory presentation or an opportunity to individually manipulate the material tactilely would be helpful. If an individual learning kit was used initially, working with the teacher or another student would be a useful corrective activity. If a group activity was used initially, an individual activity should be used. Again, whatever the alternative, it is important that the student's involvement in the learning be different. The work of R. Dunn and K. Dunn (1975, 1978) on activities for students with varying "learning styles" is very useful when selecting alternative ways to involve students.

There is another essential characteristic of a corrective activity that is equally important but often taken for granted. That is, the corrective should *provide studies with a sucessful learning experience.* Regardless of the format or involvement, if a corrective activity does not help students overcome learning difficulties and experience success in their learning, it is not an effective activity and *should be discarded for another alternative.* Correctives must provide students with the means to be successful in their learning, for that success enables them to be more confident and more motivated for future learning tasks.

TYPES OF CORRECTIVE ACTIVITIES

Corrective activities can range from extremely simple to very complex, depending upon the resources available and the grade level of the students involved. For example, at the high school level a simple and effective corrective activity is to have students carefully reread particular pages in the textbook where a specific concept is discussed. However, the same corrective activity is not effective for second- or third-grade students with limited reading skills.

Many teachers have found it useful to categorize corrective activities into three groups: (1) things to be done *with the teacher*, (2) things to be done *with a friend*, and (3) things to be done *by oneself.* Although any particular activity is likely to fall into more than one of these categories, each can provide students with a difference in presentation and involvement. In addition, providing a variety of corrective activities not only allows students some individual choice, it also accommodates a variety of different learning styles. . . .

Table [1] provides a summary of the various corrective activities and how they might be used. Certainly this list is not complete and other alter-

TABLE [1] The Various Types of Corrective Activities and How They Might Be Used

CORRECTIVE ACTIVITY	WITH THE TEACHER	WITH A FRIEND	BY ONESELF
Reteaching	X		
Course textbook	X	X	X
Alternative textbooks	X	X	X
Alternative materials	X	X	X
Workbooks	X	X	X
Academic games	X	X	
Small group study sessions	X	X	
Individual tutoring	X	X	
Learning kits		X	X
Learning centers or laboratories		X	X
Computer-assisted instruction			X

natives do exist. However, it does provide an idea of the variety of corrective activities that are available.

SPECIFYING CORRECTIVES

One of the most important aspects of the corrective process is deciding the best way to specify the correctives—that is, deciding the best way of letting the students know what the correctives are and how they should be completed. In most instances, the sooner students become involved in corrective activities after taking the formative test, the better for their learning. Therefore the particular corrective activities students need should be clearly specified immediately following the formative test.

There are generally three methods teachers use for specifying correctives to their students, each with particular advantages and limitations. Some teachers even change their method of specifying correctives from one unit to the next. These techniques are described below. . . .

Specifying Correctives on the Formative Test

The correctives that students should complete can be indicated right on the formative test itself. For example, after each item on the test, many teachers list several sources of information on the concept or objective covered by the item. The page numbers in the course textbook where that particular concept is discussed may be listed, together with page numbers from alternative textbooks, workbook activities, and at the high school or college level, even the date of the class lesson in which the concept was explained. This can be done by simply adding a line after each item on the formative test such as:

(Text: pages 56 to 57; Workbook: page 21; Lesson: April 13)

The directions to the test would explain that this means that the concept that item covers is discussed on pages 56 to 57 in the course textbook, on page 21 in the course workbook, and in the class notes from April 13. A student thus has three different sources of information on that particular concept. From this information, students may be asked to prepare a brief paragraph explaining the concept, to

answer several alternative questions, to develop one or two new questions, or to complete any other activity that assures their involvement in the corrective process. . . .

Specifying correctives on the formative test works very well when the correctives are fairly simple. Particularly for upper-grade students, having correctives paired with each item right on the test itself seems to facilitate the corrective process. However, when the correctives are more complex, including them on a formative test can complicate the test and make it unduly long. And whenever correctives are listed on the formative test, students must be able to keep their copy of the test.

Specifying Correctives on the Answer Sheet

Corrective activities can also be listed beside the item numbers on an answer sheet. In this case, the correctives should be very explicit, particularly if students do not keep the test as a reference for the specific concepts or material to be learned.

A double answer sheet can be easily adapted to include a listing of corrective activities. However, such an answer sheet would look somewhat different from the one in Figure [2]. While the half returned to the teacher would need to list only item responses, the half kept by the students would list item responses plus designated corrective activities for each item. (Again, these could be simply page numbers from textbooks or workbooks, or more complex activities.) In addition, while the answer sheet in Figure [2] can be used with any formative test that has twenty or fewer items, listing the correctives on the answer sheet necessitates the use of a different answer sheet with each formative test. . . .

Specifying Correctives on a Separate Sheet

A third way to specify corrective activities is on a sheet separate from both the formative test and the answer sheet. Using a separate "corrective sheet" also requires that the correctives be very explicit, particularly if students do not keep a copy of the formative test. . . .

The use of a separate corrective sheet is most common in applications of mastery learning in early elementary grades. At this level, formative tests typically cover only a few basic skills or objectives.

Thus, corrective activities do not need to be as extensive or as broad in scope as is usually necessary for learning units in more advanced grades. However, because of the limited reading abilities and study skills of these younger students, corrective activities do need to be carefully designed and fairly specific. . . .

MANAGING THE CORRECTIVE WORK

In classes taught by most traditional methods, only the very best students typically engage in corrective work on a regular basis. Therefore involvement in corrective activities is likely to be a new and unfamiliar experience for the majority of students. For this reason, corrective activities need to be carefully managed by the teacher, especially when first implementing mastery learning.

Most mastery learning teachers administer a formative test after about two weeks of instruction. Generally the test is given at the beginning of a class period and usually requires no more than twenty or twenty-five minutes for students to complete. Remember, however, that these are only general guidelines. Some teachers administer a formative test each week while others may spend up to three weeks teaching a particular unit before administering a formative test. Furthermore, some formative tests require only ten or fifteen minutes to complete while others may take thirty or thirty-five minutes, depending upon the content covered and the nature of the test. But although such differences may make some adjustments and modifications necessary, they can usually be accommodated with very little difficulty.

In most cases teachers correct the formative tests in class after students have returned a record of their answers, usually on one-half of the answer sheet. The teacher generally goes over the test with the class, stopping occasionally to reexplain items or concepts that appear to have been troublesome to a majority of students. After the correcting is complete, the mastery score is announced—usually between 80 to 90 percent correct. Most students will already know what the mastery score is since teachers generally explain the standard of mastery when orienting students to the new mastery learning procedures.

At this point the class is typically divided into two groups: those students who attained the mastery score or higher and those who did not. Those who attained the mastery score are either given enrichment activities or asked to serve as peer tutors, while those who did not begin corrective work.

There are two important things for the teacher to remember when dividing the class in this way. The first is to give some recognition or praise to those students who attained mastery. This can be done, for example, with simply a show of hands accompanied by verbal praise from the teacher. Recognizing their achievement is very reinforcing to these students and helps to assure their persistence in future units. The second thing is to express confidence in the abilities of those students who did not attain mastery. These students should be assured that if they work to correct their difficulties, they are likely to attain mastery on the second formative test for the unit, and they will have an excellent chance at mastery on the first test in the next unit. Some teachers convey this confidence as an expectation of students' future performance, assuring students that with hard work, they can certainly reach mastery.

Generally, corrective activities need to be more structured and teacher-directed during early learning units than is necessary later on. As mentioned, this is because of the newness of these procedures for the majority of students. Most teachers require students working alone or with a friend to complete a specific assignment that is returned to the teacher. This assignment may be simply a summary of the corrective work that was done or it may be a more detailed exercise. Once students become accustomed to the corrective process, however, many teachers relax or eliminate this requirement.

In most cases, some class time is required during the first few units to have students become involved in corrective activities. Many teachers administer the formative test, correct the test, and begin corrective activities during the same class period. Corrective work not completed during that class period is then assigned as homework. Some teachers, particularly those in the lower grade levels, allow an entire class period for corrective activities during early learning units. The amount of class time allowed for corrective work is usually reduced in later units, and is sometimes eliminated completely by having students do all of their corrective work as a homework assignment.

Few mastery learning teachers allow more than one complete class period for corrective work between the first and second formative tests. The reason for this limit is the demand for content coverage. Few teachers can afford to spend more than a day or two on corrective work when they are required to cover a given portion of the curriculum within certain time constraints. However, taking some extra time during the early units to familiarize students with the corrective process will help to assure that students continue these activities when the amount of class time allotted for corrective work is reduced.

MOTIVATING STUDENTS TO DO CORRECTIVE WORK

Getting students to become involved in the corrective process and to complete their corrective work is a major challenge to teachers implementing mastery learning. Although there is no way to guarantee that all students will become involved in corrective activities, there are several ways to encourage and to maintain their involvement.

Explaining mastery learning to students in some detail at the beginning of the term or year is particularly important in motivating students to do corrective work. Although the mastery learning process is new, different, and requires some extra work, most students are willing to cooperate if they understand the reasons for each step and can see how they will benefit.

Some teachers explain to students that the corrective process is actually a way to help take the guesswork out of learning. These teachers point out to their students that the formative test shows precisely what is important for them to learn and whether their preparations for the class have been adequate or not. The corrective activities represent simply the additional things that must be done to attain mastery on the unit. There are no tricks, no secrets, and no surprises. Most teachers find that students are less apprehensive and more willing to take risks when they know what is expected of them.

Some teachers stress to students that the corrective process is simply "the one extra step it takes to be successful." Most students see a test or quiz as their one and only chance to be successful—and a great many are not. However, corrective work can be viewed as the extra step that allows all students the opportunity to reach success. In most cases, if students are initially involved in some form of corrective activity and, as a result, see improvement in their scores from the first formative test to the second, motivational problems disappear. Many teachers report that students become anxious to begin corrective assignments in order to have a "second chance" at success. There is little doubt that the experience of success is one of the most powerful of all motivational devices.

Other mastery learning teachers employ still different motivational techniques. Many acquaint parents with the mastery learning process and encourage them to assist their children in doing corrective work. Parents generally appreciate these opportunities to help their children with specific learning problems. Other teachers check corrective assignments and count these in determining the course grade. Regardless of the technique, however, it is imperative that students become involved in corrective activities, especially during early units, if mastery learning is really to improve their learning. . . .

ESSENTIAL CHARACTERISTICS OF ENRICHMENT

Within any class there are likely to be a certain number of fast learners. These are students who have developed very effective learning strategies or those for whom the original instruction was very effective. These students do very well on the first formative test, scoring at the mastery standard or higher. Having demonstrated that they learned the material in the unit quite well, there is no need for them to take part in review, reteaching, or corrective activities. Instead, they should be given opportunities to enrich or extend their learning. This is the primary purpose of enrichment activities in mastery learning.

Enrichment activities provide students with opportunities to broaden and expand their learning. For example, if a student is keenly interested in some aspect of a subject, enrichment activities allow the student to delve into that topic. Unlike most "continuous progress" approaches to instruction, where a student's only option after mastering a unit is to move on to the next sequential unit, enrichment activities in mastery learning are designed to give students the chance to explore a variety of learning options.

There are two essential characteristics of effective student enrichment activities. The first is that *they must be rewarding and exciting learning opportunities*. If enrichment activities are only busy work or simply repetition of previous classroom activities, they present no reward for doing well on the formative test. Enrichment activities need to be designed so that students want to participate in them. When enrichment activities are rewarding and exciting, students become much more highly motivated to attain mastery on the first formative test.

The second essential characteristic of effective enrichment activities is that *they must be challenging to students*. Enrichment activities represent an excellent opportunity to involve students in higher level cognitive tasks such as those involving analysis, synthesis, or evaluation skills. Although these higher level tasks are usually more difficult for students, they are precisely the kind of activities that fast learners find most stimulating and challenging.

Consider, for example, the following problem:

$$\begin{array}{r} D\,O\,N\,A\,L\,D \\ +\ G\,E\,R\,A\,L\,D \\ \hline R\,O\,B\,E\,R\,T \end{array}$$

Hint: D = 5*

This is an addition problem. Each letter represents a unique digit. Note that there are exactly ten different letters and that therefore every digit from 0 through 9 will be used. Solving this problem requires only addition and subtraction skills. Yet it is challenging to even sophisticated college students. Stimulating and challenging problems such as this make excellent enrichment activities for a broad range of students.

An excellent resource for enrichment or extension activities is material designed for gifted and talented students. Most educational systems today have a director or coordinator of gifted education who can recommend a variety of these types of materials. Activities and exercises for gifted students are now available for most grade levels and in a variety of subject areas. The following publications also offer guides to these types of materials:

A. Harnadek, *Critical Thinking Books I & II*. Pacific Grove, Calif.: Midwest Publications, 1976 & 1980.

A. Harnadek, *Mind Benders: Deductive Thinking Skills*. Pacific Grove, Calif.: Midwest Publications, 1978

F. A. Karnes and E. C. Collings, *Handbook of Instructional Resources and References for Teaching the Gifted*. Boston: Allyn & Bacon, 1980.

TYPES OF ENRICHMENT ACTIVITIES

The fast learners who do well on the formative test and qualify for involvement in enrichment activities are usually fairly self-directed. Because of this, enrichment activities typically do not require as much structure as corrective activities do. Also, the rewarding characteristics of enrichment are enhanced by allowing students some degree of choice and flexibility in these activities. Just as it is best to provide a variety of options for students involved in corrective work, it is also advisable to have several kinds of enrichment activities available.

Following is a brief list of some enrichment activities that teachers have found to be very successful. In reviewing this list, keep in mind that enrichment activities should be related to the general subject of a learning unit, but they need not always be specific to the content of that particular unit. Some units simply do not lend themselves to "enriching" experiences. What is important is that the activity be rewarding and challenging.

Peer Tutoring

Helping another student to understand the material in a learning unit can be a very enriching experience for fast learners. As they try to find ways to explain an idea or concept to a classmate, most students discover that they gain a better understanding of the

---

* Solution:
$$\begin{array}{r} 526,485 \\ 197,485\ + \\ \hline 723,970 \end{array}$$

concept themselves. In fact, research studies on peer tutoring indicate that the benefits for the tutor may be even greater than those for the student being tutored (Bloom, S., 1976; Cohen & Kulik, 1981). Peer tutoring also encourages involvement in higher level cognitive skills, such as viewing the idea or concept from a number of different perspectives, thinking of new applications or examples, and analyzing its various components.

Developing Practice Exercises for Fellow Students

Instead of working directly with other students, fast learners can help to create new practice exercises for a particular learning unit. The challenge of trying to come up with new ways of presenting the material can be very exciting. As they struggle with the issues of how to make the material easier to understand and what kind of exercises can be most beneficial, these fast learners also use a variety of higher level cognitive behaviors.

Developing Skill-related Media Materials

Opportunities to construct models, filmstrips, and other types of audiovisual materials, are very exciting to many students. These materials can be in the form of learning kits, academic games, or simply alternative learning resources. They are often very useful to slower learners as corrective activities and, like practice exercises, their development usually involves higher level behaviors.

Special Projects and Reports

One of the most rewarding enrichment activities for many fast learners is simply the opportunity to become involved in a special project or to prepare a special report. This project or report should be on an idea that is particularly interesting to the student and one that is related to the subject. In some cases the project may even extend as enrichment over two or more learning units. This enhances the student's motivation to do well on the first formative test in the next unit in order to return to the project. Although some guidance and direction from the teacher are usually necessary, especially in regard to project specifications, limits, and time lines, fast learners generally welcome these opportunities to

work more or less on their own. In addition, such projects give students the chance to develop their own special talents or to explore a new area of involvement.

More Difficult Games, Problems, and Contests

Many teachers find that fast learners are challenged by more difficult games or problems related to the subject. For instance, mathematics teachers find that many students are intrigued by problems related to geometric reasoning or topography. Exercises in inductive or deductive reasoning are also fascinating to many. . . .

Fast learners in upper elementary grades not only struggle to find solutions to these types of problems and games, but also learn from each other as they compare their problem-solving strategies. Again, books, workbooks, and activities for gifted children are particularly useful resources for these types of games and problems.

Advanced Computer-assisted Lessons

When computers are available, they, too, can serve as an excellent resource for enrichment activities. Many mini- and microcomputers have advanced programs and lessons that can be especially challenging to students. In some cases students can even become involved in developing their own programs to solve problems or create new games. Although some direction and planning on the part of teachers are essential for these kinds of activities, computers can offer a variety of exciting challenges to fast learners. . . .

SUMMARY

Regular and specific feedback on learning progress can help students improve the effectiveness of their learning and can help teachers improve the effectiveness of their teaching. With mastery learning, this feedback is provided to both students and teachers through the results of the formative tests. Students who do not attain the standard of mastery on the formative test are directed to individualized corrective activities. Correctives are designed to provide these students with an alternative approach to learning the material in a given unit by presenting it in a different format or by using a different kind of involvement in learning. Those students who do attain the standard of mastery on the formative test are given opportunities to extend their learning by engaging in enrichment activities that are rewarding, challenging, and usually involve higher level cognitive skills. Feedback, correctives, and enrichment are undoubtedly the most crucial elements in the mastery learning process. . . .

REFERENCES

Bloom, S. (1976). *Peer and cross-age tutoring in the schools*. Washington, D.C.: National Institute of Education.

Cohen, P. A., & Kulik, J. A. (1981). Synthesis of research on the effects of tutoring, *Educational Leadership*, **39** (3), 227–229.

Dunn, R., & Dunn, K. (1975). *Educator's guide to individualizing instructional programs*. West Nyack, N.Y.: Parker.

Dunn, R., & Dunn, K. (1978). *Teaching students through their individual learning styles: A practical approach*. Reston, Va.: Reston Publishing Division of Prentice-Hall.

Guskey, T. R., Englehart, G., Tuttle, K., & Guida, F. (1978). *A report on the pilot project to develop mastery courses for the Chicago Public Schools*. Chicago: Center for Urban Education, Chicago Board of Education.

Guskey, T. R., & Monsaas, J. A. (1979). Mastery learning: A model for academic success in urban junior colleges. *Research in Higher Education*, **11**, 263–274.

Harnadek, A. (1976). *Critical thinking book I*. Pacific Grove, Calif.: Midwest Publishers.

Harnadek, A. (1978). *Mindbenders: Deductive thinking skills*. Pacific Grove, Calif.: Midwest Publishers.

Harnadek, A. (1980). *Critical thinking book II*. Pacific Grove, Calif.: Midwest Publishers.

Karnes, F. A., & Collins, E. C. (1980). *Handbook of instructional resources and references for teaching the gifted*. Boston: Allyn & Bacon.

4. MARKS AND MARKING SYSTEMS

Tom Kubiszyn and Gary Borich

After you have administered your test, you score it and assign a grade to the test. This grade is not what we will be referring to in this chapter. In this chapter we will discuss several issues related to the assignment of *marks*—cumulative grades that reflect academic achievement at the end of a six- or nine-week marking period, semester, or school year.

WHAT IS THE PURPOSE OF A MARK?

Marks are assigned to provide feedback about student achievement. We will reiterate this point several times in this chapter, not because it is so difficult to comprehend, but because it is so often forgotten. All too often marks have been assigned as rewards and punishments. This is not what they are intended for.

WHY BE CONCERNED ABOUT MARKING?

Marks have become an accepted and expected aspect of our culture. Students come to realize very early in their educational careers that they will be graded or marked depending on their performance in school. Parents of students, having been graded themselves, realize that the marks a student receives may well affect their child's educational, occupational, and financial status by opening or closing various opportunities. Parents know that children are compared with each other through their marks. Thus, marks have considerable meaning for both child and parent.

Educators also are strongly influenced by marks, often relegating pupils to faster or slower tracks, depending on their marks. Since marks carry a great deal of importance for many people, it seems sensible that care and objectivity ought to be exercised in assigning marks. Unfortunately, this is often not the case. Rather than being assigned accurately, in hopes of presenting as valid a picture of student achievement as possible, marks are sometimes assigned in haste, or according to nebulous, undefined, and little-understood "marking systems." Different marking systems have different advantages and disadvantages—some of which the average teacher often does not know. We will acquaint you with various marking systems so that you may choose the system that best fits your situation. In general such systems compare students to other students or with established standards of knowledge, or are based on aptitude, effort, and improvement.

WHAT SHOULD A MARK REFLECT?

What a mark should reflect depends on the subject or topic being marked. We generally talk about marks in relation to reading achievement, math achievement, and so on. However, marks are also assigned in areas like conduct, study skills, and responsibility. When marks are related to academic subjects, marks should reflect *academic achievement,* and nothing more!

Marks are assigned to provide feedback about academic achievement in order for students to be compared according to their achievement. If marks reflect *only* academic achievement and are assigned consistently according to a system, such marks may be compared with considerable validity (as long as the system according to which the marks are assigned is made clear). But when a single mark represents a hodgepodge of factors (for example, achievement, attitude, attendance, punctuality, or conduct) or systems (for example, comparisons with other students, comparisons with standards of effort, or improvement), interpretation or comparison of such marks becomes a hopeless task. Unfortunately, the latter case characterizes some marking practices today. Different schools employ different marking systems and weigh various nonachievement factors in assigning marks, making direct and meaningful comparisons of grades from two schools difficult at best.

We are *not* suggesting that information about conduct, punctuality, and so forth should not be reported, or is unimportant. We *are* suggesting that such information should *not* be mixed with test scores and other indicators of academic achievement in a single grade. In other words, don't mix apples with oranges in a single mark for an academic subject. All this may seem perfectly obvious, but strange things happen when marks are assigned. It's all too tempting to use marks as vehicles to reach, or try to reach, other ends. Consider the following dialogue:

PARENT: Mr. Stokes, Jack got a D in reading this six weeks, but he's had A's in reading all year. I don't understand. He seems to be reading better all the time, but I'm no teacher, what can I do to help him?

TEACHER: One thing you can do is tell him to stop looking out the window during oral reading. Some of these fifth-graders seem to think that what is going on outside is more important than reading!

PARENT: Do you mean Jack is being disruptive in class?

TEACHER: Yes, he looks out the window, then the next thing you know another one does, then another——

PARENT: Have you asked him why he's doing it?

TEACHER: Of course, but it's always the same excuse—"I'm bored, listening to the others read aloud what I've already read to myself."

PARENT: I see, but what about his reading ability—has it declined?

TEACHER: Oh no! Jack's one of the top readers in the class—there's nothing he can't read.

PARENT: So he's a top reader, but he got a D in reading for not paying attention—is that it?

TEACHER: Mrs. Burns! What do you think I am? I grade on achievement—not on conduct!

PARENT: Why *did* he get the D then? It sounds as though he was punished for not paying attention.

TEACHER: You've got it wrong. He failed to turn in two homework assignments. That's an automatic D in all my classes. Someone's got to teach these kids responsibility.

PARENT: Mr. Stokes, I know that Sarah Smith failed to turn in two homework assignments, and she got an A.

TEACHER: That's different, she pays attention during oral reading. So, it's obvious that she's getting more out of the class. She also tries harder, even though she's not as smart as Jack.

PARENT: Mr. Stokes, you certainly are an exceptional teacher.

TEACHER: Thank you, Mrs. Burns, but it won't work—Jack's D still stands.

Unfortunately, this type of dialogue is not uncommon. We agree with the teacher in that we feel grades should be based on achievement, not conduct. However, it is quite clear that Jack's D is unrelated to reading achievement. By the teacher's own admission, Jack is reading well, but his classroom *behavior* is not congruent with Mr. Stokes's expectations, and he failed to turn in some homework assignments—another behavioral deficiency that Mr. Stokes equates with poor reading achievement. To what is Mr. Stokes comparing Jack's reading achievement? We can't be sure, although effort and aptitude were mentioned.

It appears that the main function of the marks in this case is punishment. Rather than providing feedback to the student about *reading* achievement, Mr. Stokes is punishing Jack for off-task behavior during class, and for less-than-perfect compliance with his homework expectations. The major problem we see here is that the main function of grades—to provide feedback about achievement—has been lost in Mr. Stokes's zeal to change Jack's behavior. In too many cases, a single grade is used to report achievement, conduct, homework compliance, tardiness, and so on. This would be *less* of a problem, if this were done consistently across schools. However, different schools weight each of these differently. The real point is that as long as grades continue to be based on factors other than achievement, we are robbing ourselves of the effective use of the main purpose of grading—evaluating *achievement*. Let's consider the different marking systems employed in schools.

MARKING SYSTEMS

Various types of marking systems have been used in the schools. They may be considered along two dimensions:

1. Type of comparison involved
2. Type of symbol used

Types of Comparisons

Often the type of symbol a teacher uses is determined at the school or district level—the teacher has little to say about whether an A–F, E–G–S–U, or numerical marking system is employed. However, the classroom teacher often has more flexibility and autonomy in deciding how to assign the marks. That is, teachers often have considerable control over *how* they decide who gets an A or B. As mentioned earlier, marks are based on comparisons, usually from among comparisons of students with:

1. Other students
2. Established standards
3. Aptitude
4. Actual versus potential effort
5. Actual versus potential improvement

Each of these systems has advantages and limitations. Our aim is to acquaint you with these so you may choose wisely. Whichever system you choose to employ, be sure to indicate it on the report card. Remember, the function of marking is to provide feedback on achievement. However, a grade of B based on effort versus a grade of B based on comparisons to established standards can reflect very different absolute levels of achievement. Indicating your marking system will minimize potential misinterpretations of a student's level of achievement.

Comparisons with Other Students. Certainly you have had professors who have graded "on the curve." It almost sounds illegal, shady, or underhanded. It seems at times that this is some mysterious method by which test grades are transformed into semester marks. Basically, all that the expression "grading on the curve" means is that your grade or mark depends on how your achievement compares with the achievement of other students in your class.

. . . [S]uch an approach is also called norm-referenced. Certain proportions of the class are assigned A's, B's, etc., regardless of their absolute level of performance on a test. In such a system a student who misses 50 percent of the items on a test might get an A, F, or any other grade on the test depending on how his or her score of 50 percent compared with the scores of the other students in the class. If his or her score was higher than 95 percent of the students, the student would likely get an A. Sometimes districts or schools encourage grading on the curve by specifying the percentages of students who will be assigned various grades. The distribution below is an example:

Grade	Percent of Students
A	10
B	25
C	40
D	20
F	5

The main advantage of such a system is that it simplifies marking decisions. The student is either in the top 10 percent or he or she doesn't get an A. There is no apparent need for deliberation or agonizing over what cut-off scores should determine if students get this grade or that.

There are several disadvantages in such a system. First, this type of marking system fails to consider differences due to the overall ability level of the class. Imagine the disappointment that would result if such a system were imposed on a class of intellectually gifted students—none of whom had ever earned less than a B. Suddenly 65 percent would be transformed into C through F Students. Regardless of achievement, in such a system some students will always get A's and some will always get F's.

Another problem involves the percentages—why not 5 percent A's, or 15 percent A's? These percentages are rather arbitrarily, set. Furthermore, what does it mean when a student gets an A? Has the student mastered all course content? Or was the student lucky enough to be in with a class of slow learners? Such a system says nothing about *absolute* achievement, which makes comparisons across grades and schools difficult.

Finally, consider the teacher in such a system. No matter how well or poorly the teacher teaches, his or her students always get the same percentage of grades. There is little, if any, reward available through seeing grades on the whole improve following improved teaching. As a result a teacher may not feel quite as motivated to improve teaching.

Comparison with Established Standards. In this marking system, it is possible for all students, or no students to get A's or F's or any other grade in between. How much the rest of the students in the class achieve is irrelevant to a student's grade. All that is relevant is whether a student attains a defined standard of achievement or performance. We label this approach *criterion-referenced*[.] . . . In such a system, letter grades may be assigned based on the percentage of test items answered correctly, as the distribution below illustrates:

Grade	*Percent of items answered correctly*
A	85
B	75
C	65
D	55
F	less than 55

Thus, a student who answers 79 percent of the test items correctly earns a B, regardless of whether the rest of the class did better, poorer, or about the same. Obviously, such a system requires some prior knowledge of what level of achievement or performance is reasonable to expect.

There are several advantages to such a system. First, it is possible, in theory, for all students to obtain high grades if they put forth sufficient effort (assuming the percentage cut-offs are not unreasonably-high). Second, assignment of grades is simplified. A student has either answered 75 percent of the items correctly, or hasn't. As with comparison with other students, there is no apparent need to deliberate or agonize over assigning grades. Finally, assuming that ability levels of incoming students remain fairly constant and that tests remain comparable in validity and difficulty, teachers who work to improve teaching effectiveness should see improvement in grades with the passage of time. Presumably, this would help motivate teachers to continue working to improve their effectiveness.

As you might expect, such a system also has its drawbacks. Establishing a standard is no small task. Just what is reasonable for an A may vary from school to school, and from time to time, as a result of ability levels, societal pressures, and curriculum changes. Furthermore, should the same standards be maintained for a gifted or a special education class as for an average class? Another problem is that the public and administrators often have difficulty "adjusting" to a marking system that potentially allows everyone to make an A. It is a curious fact of life that everyone presses for excellence in education, but many balk at marking systems that make attainment of excellence within everyone's reach.

Comparisons with Aptitude. Aptitude is another name for potential or ability. In such systems students are compared neither to other students nor to established standards. Instead, they are compared to themselves. That is, marks are assigned depending on how closely to his or her potential a student is achieving. Thus, students with high aptitude or potential who are achieving at high levels would get high grades, since they would be achieving at their potential. Those with high aptitude and average achievement would get lower grades since they would be achieving below their potential. But students with average aptitude and average achievement

TABLE [1] The Relationships among Aptitude, Achievement, and Marks in Marking Systems Based on Comparisons of Achievement with Aptitude

APTITUDE LEVEL	ACHIEVEMENT LEVEL	MARKS
High	High	High
	Average	Average
	Low	Low
Average	High	High
	Average	High
	Low	Average
Low	High	High
	Average	High
	Low	High

would get high grades, since they would be considered to be achieving at their potential. Such a system sounds attractive to many educators. However, serious problems exist, as Table [1] shows.

Table [1] illustrates that the concept of assigning grades based on the congruence of a student's achievement with the student's aptitude is quite sensible for high-aptitude students. Look at what happens for the low-aptitude students, however. If a student's aptitude is low enough, the student would have a hard time achieving below his or her potential. Thus the student always would be achieving at or above the expected level. Would this be fair to the moderate- and high-ability students? Perhaps more importantly, can you see how such a system would greatly complicate interpreting grades? For example, a C for a high-aptitude student might indicate 70 percent mastery, while for an average-aptitude student it might indicate 60 percent, and perhaps 50 percent mastery for the low-aptitude student. The same grade may mean very different things in terms of absolute achievement.

Other drawbacks of such a system relate to statistical considerations beyond the scope of this text that affect the reliability of such comparisons. Another is the tendency for the achievement scores of slow learners to increase and the achievement scores of fast learners to decrease when tested again. Technically this phenomena is called the *regression toward the mean* effect—the more extreme an achievement score, the greater it can be expected to "regress" or fall back toward the average or mean of all students at another testing. Finally, such a

system requires more complex record-keeping than the first two systems discussed. Such a system, as appealing as it is at first glance, is not practical.

Comparison of Achievement with Effort. Systems that compare achievement to effort are similar to those that compare achievement to aptitude. Students who get average test scores, but have to work hard to get them, are given high marks. Students who get average scores, but do not have to work hard to get them are given lower grades.

Several problems plague marking systems that are based on effort. First, we have no known measure of effort. Unlike aptitude, for which reliable and valid measures exist, effort is at best estimated by informal procedures. Second, within such a system children are punished for being bright and catching on quickly, while other children are rewarded for taking a long time to master concepts. Third, there is the old problem of the marks not representing academic achievement. Effort may cover up academic attainment, making marks all the more difficult to interpret. Finally, record-keeping is once again complex.

The advantage cited for grading based on effort is that it serves to motivate the slower or turned-off students, but it may also serve to turn-off the brighter students who would quickly see such a system as unfair. Whatever the case, the primary function of marking—to provide feedback about academic achievement—is not well served by such a system.

Comparison of Achievement with Improvement. Such systems compare the amount of improvement between the beginning (pretest) and end (posttest) of instruction. Students who show the most progress get the highest grades. An obvious problem occurs for the student who does well on the pretest. Improvement for such a student is likely to be less overall than for a student who does poorly on the pretest. In fact, bright students have been known to "play dumb" on pretests when such systems are in force. Other shortcomings of such systems include the statistical problems we mentioned above in regard to comparisons with aptitude (that is, unrealiability of such comparisons and regression toward the mean) and unwieldy record-keeping.

Which System Should You Choose?

We have seen that each system has significant drawbacks, as well as advantages. Which should you choose? In our opinion, comparisons with established standards would best suit the primary function of marking—to provide feedback about academic achievement. Once standards are established, comparisons among schools and students may be more easily made. It seems to us that such a system has the best chance of reducing misinterpretation of marks.

In reality, many schools and districts have adopted multiple marking systems, such as assigning separate grades for achievement and effort or achievement, effort, and improvement. As long as the achievement portion of the grade reflects *only* achievement, such systems seem to be reasonable. Two disadvantages of such systems are worth noting, however. First, they double or triple the number of grades to be assigned and interpreted, leading to an increase in record-keeping and interpretation time. Second, unless the purpose of each grade is explained very clearly on the report card, marking systems are often difficult for parents to decipher.

Within marking systems, a variety of symbols has been used. Some of the more common types are discussed in this section.

Letter Grades. Using letter grades is the most common symbol system. . . . 68 percent of American high schools used the letters A–F to report marks in 1972. Often, plus and minus symbols are used to indicate finer distinctions between the letter grades. This system along with its variations (E, G, S, U) has several advantages that have led to its widespread adoption and continuing popularity.

First, the letter system is widely understood. Both students and teachers understand what an A represents and what an F represents. Second, such a system is compact, requiring only one or two spaces to report a summary mark of an entire semester's work. Third, such a system has just about the optimal number of levels of judgment humans can effectively exercise. . . . It can have as few as five or as many as fifteen if plus and minus signs are used.

Limitations of the system are worth considering. First, the specific meaning of letter grades varies from class to class and from school to school. An A in one school may be the equivalent of a C in another. Second, letter grades fail to indicate clearly the student's actual level of mastery. There is often a considerable difference between the achievement

of a "low-B" student and a "high-B" student. Finally, because of this, averaging of letter grades often results in a loss of information or misinterpretation of the student's actual achievement. When averaging letter grades, it is necessary to go back to the actual numerical grades to obtain the "correct" average.

Numerical Grades. . . . [T]he numerical symbol system was used by 16 percent of American high schools in 1972. Such systems usually employ 100 as the highest mark, and report cards often carry letter grade equivalents for the range of numerical grades. For example:

Numerical Grade	Letter Grade
90–100	A
80–89	B
70–79	C
60–69	D
below 60	F

Numerical grades have three main advantages. First, like letter grades, they provide a convenient summary mark for a semester's or year's work. Second, unlike letter grades, numerical grades are easily averaged to obtain the "correct" final marks. Third, they are widely understood—most pupils and parents realize there are substantial differences between a mark of 95 and one of 75.

There are also disadvantages to such a system. First, the discriminations are finer than humans can really make. . . . No one can make 40 reliable distinctions between grades from 61–100. Another way of saying this is that it is not possible to determine the real difference between a grade of 67 and a grade of 68, or a grade of 95 and a grade of 96. Second, as with letter grades, we are never sure just what a grade means since standards may vary considerably from school to school.

Other Symbols. Pass-fail (P–F) grading reached its popularity peak about a decade ago. Few schools employ this approach today because of its many shortcomings, one of which is that such symbols do not provide enough information: P could mean the student exhibited anywhere from exceptional to marginal performance in the class. This makes it difficult for employers and admissions officers to evaluate applicants. Students themselves have complained about the same lack of information—they really do not know how well they did. Finally, students tend to do the minimum necessary to earn a P under such systems.

Checklists. A common adjunct to a letter or numerical symbol system is a checklist. Since both letter and numerical symbol systems fail to define just what a student can or cannot do, many report cards now include skill checklists to go along with their grade symbols for each subject. Checklists are also used to provide information about nonacademic aspects of the child. For example, checklists often are provided to identify problems in the areas of conduct, social skills, responsibility, and organization. Properly utilized checklists represent useful supplements to letter or numerical grades and can

convey much more detailed information about the student without contaminating or confusing the interpretation of a student's overall achievement level.

As mentioned at the beginning of this chapter, districts and schools usually decide which symbol system teachers must use. In such situations you have little choice but to employ the required system. It is more likely though that you will have some say about how the marks are actually assigned (that is, what you will compare student achievement to). Now that you have been exposed to the pros and cons of various systems, you should be able to make better use of any marking or symbol system you are required—or choose—to use. . . .

5. THE MINIMUM CONDITIONS FOR VALID EVALUATION OF TEACHER PERFORMANCE*

Donald Medley, Robert Soar, and Homer Coker

An analysis of the process of performance evaluation indicates that it involves four distinct steps; objective performance evaluation requires that each step be performed with a high degree of objectivity. The four steps, as applied to the evaluation of teacher performance are as follows:

1. Setting, defining, or agreeing upon a *task* to be performed;
2. Making a documentary, quantifiable *record* of the behavior of the teacher while the task is being performed;
3. Quantifying the record, that is, deriving a *score* or set of scores from it; and
4. Comparing the score with a predetermined *standard*.

The presence of all four elements—task, record, score, and standard—is essential; they are the minimum conditions for valid evaluation of teacher performance. Let us examine briefly the purpose

and rationale for each of the four steps and how each fits into the process of evaluation of teacher performance.

STEP 1: DEFINING THE TASK

Since human performance is purposeful human behavior, any sample of teaching performance must have a purpose; and any attempt to evaluate the performance must be done in relationship to that purpose.

Evaluation may be thought of in simple terms as a matter of discriminating "good" from "bad," what is valued from what is not valued. Whether a particular behavior or behavior pattern is "good" or not depends on whether it is appropriate to whatever purpose the performer is supposed to accomplish. Asking a high-order question, praising a pupil response, rebuking a pupil—whether any one of these behaviors is appropriate at any particular time depends on what the teacher is trying to accomplish and, to a less[er] but important extent, on how he or she plans to accomplish it. No action is intrinsically good or bad, appropriate or inappropriate, in

---

* The contents of this article were adapted from a book by the same authors to be published by Longman, Inc. in 1984.

itself. Any action may be bad at one time and good at another. A clear definition of the task that a teacher is trying to perform is important primarily as *a basis for distinguishing between appropriate and inappropriate behaviors*; that is, it makes evaluating the performance possible.

The definition of the task has another critically important function. The task needs to be defined in such a way that while performing it the teacher who is able to do so will display mastery of those competencies (knowledge, skills, attitudes) that characterize the performance of an effective teacher in that situation. A candidate who can perform effectively may fail to do so if he or she misinterprets the task definition and tries to perform some other task, one for which different behaviors are appropriate; and the evaluation will not be valid. The second reason why defining the task is important, then, is *to ensure that any candidate who can do so will perform the task successfully*.

A third reason why defining the task is essential is *to make it possible to compare performances* by ensuring that all teachers will try to perform the same task, or (when that is impractical) comparable tasks. Only then will differences in performances reflect differences in teachers rather than in tasks.

We are aware that some educators regard comparisons as odious. One manifestation of this is the current popularity of "criterion-referenced tests," tests which purport to measure performance in absolute terms wtihout employing inter-individual comparisons. Such "absolute" measurements are useless, however, unless comparisons of some sort are used, consciously or unconsciously. Evaluation has to do with "good" and "bad," two absolute entities that cannot be defined operationally. What can be defined are the relative terms "better" and "worse"; these are the ones that govern decisions in the real world, including these necessary to define performance standards. Decisions based on teacher evaluations are no excepton; defining equivalent tasks is essential if such decisions are to be valid.

To secure a sample of performances of comparable and relevent tasks, and to provide a basis for scoring the performances—these are the reasons why arriving at a clear task definition, a clear agreement between the teacher and the evaluator about the purpose of the performance, is a necessary step in the process of objective and valid evaluation of teacher performance.

STEP 2: OBTAINING THE RECORD

This second step in the objective evaluation of any performance is often overlooked; but unless we have a record of a performance in scorable form it is not possible to *use identical procedures for judging the performances of different teachers*. Any documentary record of a performance can be scored with the same key used to score any other documentary record; without the records it is not possible to be sure that identical performances receive identical scores, or that any effects of bias, ignorance, or caprice on the part of evaluators cannot affect a teacher's score.

How objective an evaluation of teacher performance is depends mainly on how accurate and objective the record is. It is much easier to achieve a high degree of objectivity in records of teacher performance than in records of observer judgments obtained with teacher rating scales. This is so mainly because the observer's personal impression or evaluation of a teacher has much less impact on the observational records then on the ratings. The experience of researchers using systematic observation systems have repeatedly demonstrated that a high level of objectivity and accuracy can be obtained at reasonable cost with such instruments.

Besides providing a basis for scoring the performance, a record of a behavior made with such a system contains *detailed information about the teacher's performance* which has a number of other uses. First, such a record contains detailed diagnostic information which is valuable for planning remedial treatment when performance is unsatisfactory. The record indicates precisely how and where the performance fell short, and how the teacher needs to change her behavior in order to achieve satisfactory performance next time.

Second, a set of observation records can be submitted to item analysis, factor analyses, and other statistical procedures that have been developed to improve the validity of objective measurements.

Third, the details in the record also make it possible to study the structure of performance and design better strategies not only for measuring it but for improving it as well. Changes in teacher performance over time can be measured more precisely by comparing records made "before and after" than by any other means. And, last but not least, if the fairness of an evaluation is challenged in court—if, for example a teacher who fails to be certified sues the certifying agency and accuses it of racial or sexual bias, the documentary record of the performance is available for review. It is possible, for example, to prove from the record that the same criteria were applied to that performance as to those of other teachers who passed, and that the negative evaluation reflects only the performance of the candidate, not some fallible judge's opinion of its quality.

Because the observation schedules or systems which observers making such records use list the behaviors which it is the observer's task to look for and record, they do not require observers to possess any expertise in the teaching process; *no "expert" judgment is involved in recording the behaviors.* The skills the observer needs in order to make accurate records with such a schedule can be acquired during a brief period of training in the use of the system. The skills involved are of such a nature that para-professional or non-professional personnel can usually acquire them as quickly, and become fully as proficient in their use, as professional personnel. By using lower level personnel as observers it is possible to free valuable (or at any rate expensive) time of supervisory, administrative, or other professional staff which they can devote to other duties which capitalize upon their expertise.

The development (or selection) of any instrument for recording behavior requires the user to become very *specific and precise in defining what aspects of teacher performance are relevant* to the quality of the performance s/he wishes to evaluate. In all probability s/he will have to define them more explicitly, operationally, and in greater detail than ever before. This will be a difficult task, but it would seem to be a necessary preliminary to any serious attempt to improve teaching, one which it is all too easy to overlook when a rating scale is used. The experience of making such a detailed specification is likely to have far-reaching (and beneficial) effects on many other activities besides the evaluation of teaching.

STEP 3: SCORING THE RECORD

In order to serve the uses we have just listed, records must be scorable; a video-taped record of a teacher's performance, for example, will not serve. It may be objective, but it is not in scorable form. Most of the observation systems in use today yield records made on mark sensing forms which can be processed mechanically—can be read and scored by machines or clerks. An alternative is provided by the pocket sized and briefcase sized computers which have appeared on the market recently; they are small enough to be carried into the classroom by observers, and records of behavior can be made by keying coded data into them on the spot. Such a computer can be programmed either to score the record on the spot or to store it on cassette tape to be scored later. What is essential and is common to both alternatives is that the record be in a form such that the scoring process can be *mechanized, and therefore completely objective.*

The weights that will be assigned to specific behaviors in deriving a score from a behavior record are of course determined and programmed in advance. This is the point at which expert judgment about the teaching-learning process plays its part—at the point when expert judges determine the weights to be used in scoring the records. Thus each performance is in fact "rated" on the basis of expert judgment; but the same panel of expert judges "rate" every performance—and they do not know who the teacher is. The scoring key never gets tired or careless; it is absolutely insensitive to such things as race or sex, or any teacher quality not visible in the record.

Scoring a behavior record can be designed to yield a profile of scores just as easily as a single one; in either case, the principles and procedures are essentially the same.

STEP 4: EVALUATING THE SCORES

To ensure that the entire process of evaluating teaching is as objective as possible, a standard (or perhaps a set of standards for different purposes) is also specified in advance. The procedure of comparing a candidate's score (or scores) with such a standard can be, and should be, just as objective as any of the other three steps in the evaluation process.

We have listed in the preceding pages four essential steps or elements in the process of performance evaluation; the first three of these define the process of measurement upon which the evaluation is based. The rating scale does not qualify as a device for measuring teacher performance, and, as a result, cannot be scored objectively. The number which is recorded by the rater is not a measurement derived by applying a scoring key to a record but a number subjectively abstracted or inferred from the behavior.

Suppose, for instance, that a rater rates a teacher's instructional skill at point two on a scale from one to five. The number two reflects an inference made by the rater about the teacher's instructional skill that is supposedly based on the teacher's behavior; but there is no record of what the teacher did or did not do which led the rater to rate his or her skill at level two. Nor is there any indication of how the teacher's behavior would need to change so that he or she could get a higher rating next time. Ratings are sometimes referred to as "high inference measures"; this phrase is accurate in implying that a high level of inference is required of the rater; but it is inaccurate in calling ratings measures, which they are not.

A structured observation schedule, on the other hand, is sometimes called a "low inference measure," with equal accuracy. Each item on such a schedule defines a specific behavior (or category of behaviors) that the recorder looks for and records when he or she sees it. The record the observer makes is a record of behaviors; the judgments or "high inferences" that lead to a score are made beforehand and incorporated into a scoring key which is applied to the record after it is complete. The observer using a structured observation schedule responds only to the behaviors specified by the system, and his only task is to recognize these behaviors and record them. Note that the rater may respond to these same behaviors, to other behaviors relevant to the instructional skill of the teacher, or to any other behaviors he or she sees. The rater's task is to infer or judge from whatever he or she chooses what rating the teacher should get.

Imagine three raters supposed to rate a teacher's overall competence. One rater sees the maintenance of order as a major element in teacher competence and looks for evidence of it when s/he rates a teacher. A second rater believes that creating a climate which favors responsible pupil independence is essential and looks for that. A third feels that only the way in which the teacher presents her subject-matter is important.

All three observe in the same classroom at the same time to rate the teacher's overall competence. During the observation one of the pupils gets up, crosses the room to get a book, and returns to his seat. The first rater perceives this as a violation of classroom order; the second sees it as an example of responsibly independent behavior; the third disregards it as irrelevant. Later, in putting together what s/he has seen in preparation for rating the teacher, the first rater weights the behavior [negatively], the second weights it [positively] and the third gives it no weight at all. Finally, each rater compares his or her composite picture of the classroom with his or her own standard and records a rating of the teacher's level of competence.

Three observers using an observation schedule which included this item would all record that it had occurred without regard to its relevance, and the three records would all be scored on the same key so that the teacher's score would be the same no matter who the observer was.

What a rater records on a rating scale depends on at least four extraneous factors: (1) what the rater thought the teacher ought to have been doing, (2) what behaviors the rater took into account, (3) the weight the rater attached to each behavior he or she observed, and (4) the reference standard with which the rater compared what he or she saw in arriving at the rating. None of these is known to anyone else. Since all four of these factors vary from one observer to another, so do the evaluations of teachers who behave in the same way vary according to who the rater is.

A typical scoring key for a structured observation instrument combines the frequencies of a number of different behaviors with different weights to arrive at a composite score. Once data on a sizeable sample of classrooms are available, it becomes possible to use modern techniques to study the relationships among the different items, that is, the internal structure of a scoring key—or set of keys—and to revise the scoring weights to improve the scores. Doing so also yields important insights into the structure of classroom behavior which are impossible to obtain from ratings. Ratings reflect the beliefs of raters about what goes with what; but they do not test the validity of these beliefs. The beliefs upon which a scoring key is based are visible in the weights assigned to the individual items of behavior in the key; and statistical analyses of the items on the key can provide a most valuable empirical test of those beliefs.

Many rating scales, for example, reflect a belief that affective classroom climate is a bipolar dimension with negative affect (hostility and mistrust) at one extreme and positive affect (praise and warmth) at the other. But analyses of objective records of behavior reveal that expressions of negative and positive affect are relatively independent of each other, so that there are four kinds of teachers. One kind expresses both positive and negative affect freely—there is no question how such a teacher feels at any moment. Another type expresses only positive affect, and another expresses primarily negative affect. Finally, there is a fourth kind of teacher who expresses little affect of any kind, whose classroom is a task-focused, smooth-running operation in which most activities are routine and affect seems irrelevant.

How would the first kind of teacher be rated on a bipolar scale of affective climate? The rater would see this teacher express a great deal of both positive and negative affect, of behavior at both ends of the scale. Most probably the rater would put him or her in the middle of the scale, to represent the rater's perception that positive and negative affect are approximately evenly balanced. But how would a rater rate a teacher who expresses little or no affect of either kind? Such a teacher would also fall in the middle of the scale, to indicate that neither extreme occurred in his or her classroom. These are quite different teachers. The fact that both would get the same rating illustrates how inadequate a rating scale based on incorrect beliefs about the structure of teacher behavior can be.

A somewhat more subtle example arises when teachers are rated on the degree to which they ask "broad" questions. There is some evidence that two dimensions are involved here, too. Teachers may ask questions which are broad because they expect pupils to go beyond the information given with or without expecting any evaluation of the ideas produced. Idea production may be the end in view, as in a "brainstorming session." Or teachers may ask questions which encourage pupils to examine their own ideas to see how well they fit reality. The objective here relates to critical thinking, perhaps, and the expectation is that pupils' answers will be

evaluated. A rating scale which asks how often a teacher asks "broad" questions would not recognize this difference (which is manifest in the way the teacher responds), and once again, very different performances would get similar ratings (Soar, 1968-a).

There is also some evidence that teacher control of behavior, of the non-substantive activities of pupils, should be distinguished from teacher control of learning activities, because the two types of controlling behaviors relate differently to learning outcomes (Soar, 1968-b).

We cite these examples as strongly indicating a need for structural analysis of measurements of teacher performance as a basis for testing the assumptions about teacher behavior which underlie any teacher evaluation device, and changing those assumptions if they do not fit the realities of the classroom. Unless and until we do this we cannot hope to develop valid evaluation procedures.

The fact that rating scales cannot readily be improved in this way sharply limits their value. If this limitation is as serious as it sounds, it implies that the validity of rating scales depends almost entirely on the accuracy of the beliefs or assumptions about the nature of competent teacher performance upon which they are based. If the beliefs are accurate, the rating scales may be valid. But if the beliefs are inaccurate, then the rating scales cannot possibly yield valid evaluations, and we have a problem. And the problem is serious, because such ratings are the basis of the vast majority of decisions about teachers made by teacher educators, school administrators, and (in recent years) by those responsible for certifying teachers.

If most or all of these decisions are based on evaluations that lack validity, one would expect that there would be serious consequences for education. An incompetent teacher might be expected to have as good a chance as, or a better chance than, a competent teacher of being certified, hired, given tenure, and even receiving merit pay. There are many critics of education who maintain that this is exactly what is happening, and some of them point to evidence that they are right.

It is curious to note that, despite these signs that all is not well, the validity of rating scales is rarely questioned, and even more rarely tested empirically. The validity of rating scales is defended by demonstrating that the scales faithfully reflect a consensus of the beliefs or assumptions most educators hold about the nature of competent teacher performance; and there is little reason to doubt that the ratings do reflect those beliefs.

But what about the beliefs? Do they correspond with reality? If the beliefs we all hold are even partially false, the validity of the ratings is open to question. Whether pupils learn more from teachers with high ratings than from ones with low ratings; or even whether teachers with high ratings exhibit more behaviors known to relate positively to pupil learning than teachers with low ratings exhibit— these are empirical questions which no one seems to ask. The only thing we can say with confidence is that high-rated teachers make better impressions on us than low-rated teachers. Is that enough? We think not.

A question raised long ago about ratings of any kind is whether a rater might not use each of the different scales on a rating instrument as one more opportunity to express his or her overall impression of how competent the person being rated is. This would account for the high positive correlations generally found between ratings of presumably independent characteristics, and is attributed to the effect of *halo*.

Cooper has summarized data on the halo effect, and makes it clear that it is a problem of current concern:

> Plausible but invalid theories can help us see correlations between categories when there is no correlation . . . if we have minimal reasons to believe categories covary, we are prone to rate as if they did covary in specific cases; uncertain, judgmental settings are situations which such theories are most likely to be used. (Cooper, 1981, p. 225)

Some findings of Dickson and Wiersma (1980) are relevant. In a factor analysis of ratings of a group of student teachers made on the TPAI, the rating scale currently being used to certify teachers in the state of Georgia (Capie *et al.*, 1979), they found that even after rotation, one single factor accounted for most of the variance in the 19 competencies rated. This factor accounted for almost three-fourths of the variance explained by all the factors identified. It loaded on such a variety of characterizations of the teacher that it is difficult to interpret this factor as reflecting anything but halo—

the overall impression that the teacher makes on the rater. The contribution of any specific competency exhibited by the teacher was negligible in comparison.

The validity of teacher rating scales, and of evaluations based on them, is open to serious question, then, because they reflect the beliefs of the rater about the nature of competent teacher performance rather than the actual competence of the performance, which may have little to do with these beliefs. All relevant empirical data indicates that teachers rated high on such instruments are no more effective on the average than teachers rated low.

The nature of ratings makes it difficult if not impossible to discover why any one of a set of ratings may be invalid, both because the halo effect operates to obscure what is actually being rated, and because the behavioral basis of a rating cannot be ascertained by any kind of analysis of data based on the rating itself. Ratings are therefore useless for diagnosis, cannot add to our understanding of the teaching process, and are not valid for evaluating teachers. Ratings of teacher performance tell us only how favorable an impression a teacher makes on the rater, a piece of information that may be useful for some purposes, but which seems to have little or no connection with how competent the teacher is. The misuse of rating scales to evaluate teacher performance may even lead teacher educators to train teachers in ways that decrease their effectiveness instead of increasing it.

That there is a need for a better way of evaluating teachers seems clear. Indeed, the need seems to be urgent. What we have proposed as an alternative approach is to measure teachers performance instead of rating it. In order to measure teacher performance we must first reach a clear understanding with the teacher about the task to be performed, then record the performance objectively, and finally score it with the same objective procedure used to score other teachers' performance of comparable tasks.

REFERENCES

Capie, W., et al. *Teacher performance assessment instruments.* Athens, Georgia. University of Georgia, School of Education, 1979. (ED 182 518).

Cooper, W. H. Ubiquitous halo. *Psychological Bulletin*, 1981, *90*, 218–244.

Dickson, G. E. and Wiersma, W. *Research and evaluation in teacher education: A concern for competent, effective teachers.* Toledo, Ohio: The University of Toledo, May, 1980.

Gage, N. L. (Ed.). *Handbook of research on teaching.* Chicago: Rand McNally, 1963.

Soar, Robert S. "Optimum teacher-pupil interaction for pupil growth." *Educational Leadership Research Supplement*, 1968(a), *1*, 275–280.

Soar, R. S. The study of presage-process-product relationships: Implications for classroom process measurement. Paper presented at American Educational Research Association, Chicago, Ill., February, 1968(b).

6. CLASSROOM ASSESSMENT
A Key to Effective Education

Richard J. Stiggins, Nancy Faires Conklin, and Nancy J. Bridgeford

Scholars in any field of inquiry adopt a set of conventions for research design and concept development to increase their communication efficiency and their research productivity. Those conventions define the dominant paradigm for that field of study:

a paradigm is an implicit, unvoiced and pervasive commitment by a community of scholars to a conceptual framework. In a mature science, only one paradigm can be dominant at a time. It is shared by that community and serves to define proper ways of asking questions . . . [and of identifying] those common "puzzles" that are defined as the tasks of research [in that field]. (Shulman, 1986, p. 4)

What paradigm guides scholarship in educational measurement? Available evidence suggests that the dominant view regards measurement in education as a means of documenting student achievement by using collections of standardized paper and pencil test items for public accountability. Evidence of the dominance of this conceptualization can be found in research reported in scholarly journals, in published standards of accepted professional practice, and in measurement textbooks.

Nearly all major studies of testing in the schools have focused on the role of standardized tests (Airasian, Kellaghan, Madaus, & Pedulla, 1977; Fyans, 1985; Goslin 1967; Kellaghan, Madaus, & Airasian, 1982; Lortie, 1975; Rudman et al., 1980; Salmon-Cox, 1981; Sproul & Zubrow, 1982; Stetz & Beck, 1979; and Tollefson, Tracy, Kaiser, Chen, & Kleinsasser, 1985). . . .

A review of the four most recent volumes of the same journal conducted by Stiggins and Bridgeford (1985) revealed that nearly all reports on achievement measurement dealt with topics relevant to the use of objective paper and pencil tests, and the vast majority of those focused on topics most relevant to large-scale standardized tests.

Further, the only written standards on acceptable testing practice are the *Revised Standards for Educational and Psychological Tests* (American Psychological Association, 1984) that detail the ethical responsibilities of publishers of standardized paper and pencil tests. No such standards exist for teacher-made tests or for tests consisting of non–paper and pencil items. In addition, the primary source of public analysis of educational tests is the *Mental Measurements Yearbook* series, which deals only with published tests.

Finally, the clear dominance of an accountability-oriented measurement paradigm is evident in the textbooks used to train teachers, administrators, and future researchers in measurement methodology. Consider, for instance, the message regarding the purpose of assessment conveyed to teachers and graduate students in these opening sentences from one widely-used introductory measurement textbook:

Educators have always been concerned with measuring and evaluating the progress of their students. As the goals of education have become more complex and with the increasing demand by all parts of our citizenry—pupils, parents, taxpayers and other decision makers—for accountability on the part of educators, these tasks of measurement and evaluation have become more difficult. (Mehrens & Lehmann, 1984, p. v)

. . . The dominance of this measurement paradigm over the past four decades testifies to its utility. As Coffman (1983) and Calfee and Drum (1976) point out, it has afforded education an image of scientific precision and ultimately has fostered a tradition of scientific inquiry in educational research and psychometric theory. Politically, it has given educational measurement a visible role in documenting the effectiveness of schools in our society. The coin of the realm in determining the value of schools is clearly the standardized test score.

However, it is the premise of this paper that the current measurement paradigm is too narrow and restrictive. As the research summarized here will show, the kind of measurement referenced under the dominant paradigm represents only a small fraction of the assessments that take place in schools and that influence the quality of schooling and student learning. Unfortunately, due to the narrow scope of measurement research, we know little about the nature, role, or quality of the preponderance of school assessment: that developed and used by teachers in the classroom. . . .

INSIGHTS FROM RESEARCH ON TESTING

Although research on testing in the schools has tended to concentrate on the role of standardized tests, a few studies provide insights into the nature of the classroom assessment environment. These studies are reviewed in this section, focusing on what they tell us about the nature of classroom assessment, the relative importance of various types of assessment in the classroom, the quality of classroom assessments, and prevailing teacher and student attitudes toward assessment.

The Nature of Assessment Processes

Available research does provide some insight into the nature of classroom assessment. We know that classroom assessment environments are designed and constructed by teachers with little formal training in assessment (Coffman, 1983; Ward, 1982). Many have had no formal coursework and most have had no inservice training in the subject. Further analyses by Stinnet (1969), Woeller (1979), and Burdin (1982) reveal no requirements that teachers be trained in testing to be certified.

Stiggins and Bridgeford (1985) explored the importance teachers attach to different forms of assessment as purpose, grade level and subject matter vary. They concluded that their sample group of teachers were quite consistent in the assessment methods they used across purposes. As purpose varied from diagnosis to grouping to grading, the relative importance teachers attached to different forms of assessment remained quite constant. Further, of the over 200 teachers surveyed, only a very small percentage reported taking any action toward revising their current testing patterns.

However, there is evidence of fundamental differences in the nature of assessment according to grade level. For instance, Herman and Dorr-Bremme (1982) reported that 75% of the tests used by the over 350 high school teachers they surveyed were teacher-developed, and the over 400 elementary teachers relied more heavily on curriculum-embedded tests, for example, tests included in text materials. Stiggins and Bridgeford (1985) also reported that the relative importance of different types assessment changed with grade level: "As grade level increases, the weight given to objective tests and structured performance assessment goes up, while that given to published tests and spontaneous observations and judgments goes down" (p. 10).

Stiggins and Bridgeford (1985) also found differences in the relative importance of different assessment processes as a function of school subject. Math and science teachers tended to rely most on paper and pencil objective tests, whereas teachers focusing on communication skills (writing and speaking) relied more on structured observations and professional judgments. . . .

Three in-depth studies of the characteristics of teacher-made tests have been conducted. Fleming and Chambers (1983) analyzed nearly 400 teacher-developed tests including thousands of test items and drew these conclusions about the qualities of teachers' paper and pencil tests:

- Teachers use short-answer questions most frequently in their test making.
- Teachers, even English teachers, generally avoid essay questions, that represent slightly more than 1% of all test items reviewed.
- Teachers use more matching items than multiple-choice or true-false items.
- Teachers devise more test questions to sample

knowledge of facts than any of the other behavioral categories studied.

- When categories related to knowledge of terms, knowledge of facts, and knowledge of rules and principles are combined, almost 80% of the test questions reviewed focus on these areas.
- Teachers develop few questions to test behaviors that can be classified as ability to make applications.
- Comparison across school levels shows that junior high school teachers use more questions to tap knowledge of terms, knowledge of facts, and knowledge of rules and principles than do elementary or senior high school teachers. Almost 94% of their questions address knowledge categories, versus 69% of the senior high school teachers' questions and 69% of the elementary school teachers' questions. (p. 32)

In another study, Carter (1984) studied the test development skills of 310 high school teachers and reported that teachers had great difficulty recognizing items written to measure specific skills, especially higher order thinking skills. She also reported that teachers learned to write original items at higher skill levels very slowly and felt insecure about their test-making capabilities.

In their research on teachers' use of performance assessment, Stiggins and Bridgeford (1985) explored those assessments in which students are called upon to apply the skills and knowledge they have learned through the completion of a specified task in the context of a real or simulated assessment exercise in which the process or product completed by the examinee is observed and rated by the teacher. Over three quarters of the 228 teachers surveyed reported using this form of assessment, and they described their performance tests to be:

- equally divided between evaluations of processes (students performing as in speaking) and products created by students,
- scored both holistically and analytically, but resulting in a single grade being assigned,
- scored by the teacher rather than by the student or a colleague,
- interpreted in criterion-referenced terms, in terms of a pre-established standard,
- public and preannounced rather than unobtrusive assessments, and

- often used with little attention to assessment quality.

Relative Importance of Assessment Types

Other studies of testing in the schools have shown that teachers rely on their own assessments as the primary source of information on student achievement. This point is illustrated in research by Morine-Dershimer (1979) and Joyce (1979a, 1979b), as summarized by Shulman (1980). The investigation focused on teacher reactions to performance data provided by a state-mandated diagnostic testing program. Test results detailed individual student performance on specific objectives and suggested materials for remediation. After allowing teachers several days to process the results, interviewers contacted the teachers to explore how the information was used. Not one of the 10 teachers in the study had even looked at the results. They already knew the needs of their students and were certain the new tests would not provide new insights.

Studies conducted at the Center for the Study of Evaluation (Herman and Dorr-Bremme, 1982 and Yeh, 1978) suggest that, depending on grade level, one-third to three-quarters of assessments used in classrooms are teacher-developed. Those assessments include far more than collections of paper and pencil test items. For example, Herman and Dorr-Bremme reported that nearly every survey respondent in a national study reported that "my own observations and students' classwork" were crucial or important sources of information.

In another study, Salmon-Cox (1980) concluded that teachers, when talking of how they assess their students, most frequently mention "observation." Clearly, she contends, this favored technique is quite different from the kind of information provided by standardized tests. Further, Kellaghan, Madaus, and Airasian (1982) concluded their international research on use of standardized test information by suggesting that such information is a secondary criterion in teacher judgment. Teachers in their study stated that the most common grouping criteria were the teachers' own observations and tests.

To explore this point, Stiggins and Bridgeford (1985) surveyed teachers to determine preferential use of various asessment types. Each teacher was asked to distribute 100 points across four types of assessment (teacher-made objective tests, standardized tests, structured performance assessments, and spontaneous observations) to convey the relative importance of each type. Although there were some differences as a function of assessment purpose, grade level, and subject, teachers assigned an average 34 points to their own objective tests, 26 points to structured performance assessments (preplanned observation and judgment strategies), 21 points to spontaneous observations and judgments, and 19 points to published tests (including curriculum-embedded and standardized tests). Similarly, Salmon-Cox (1981) found that, of 87 high school teachers she interviewed, 44% reported using their own tests for evaluating students, 30% used interaction, 21% relied on homework, 6% used observation, and one reported using standardized tests.

The Quality of Classroom Assessments

Research on testing in schools has provided very little information concerning the quality of teacher-developed assessments. Further, that which is available is quite narrow in scope. For instance, we can infer that some teacher-developed assessments have validity, since they allow some teachers accurately to predict student performance on standardized achievement tests (Fyans, 1985; Kellaghan et al., 1982). Further, teachers often feel their tests are valid (Farr & Griffin, 1973).

However, there are some indications of problems with quality. For instance, Fleming and Chambers (1983) and Carter (1984) cite a need for teachers to write better test items, particularly items that are less ambiguous and require more of students than the simple recall of facts and information. There is also preliminary evidence that teacher-developed tests are very short, that is, they contain a minimal number of items (Fleming and Chambers). In addition, Stiggins and Bridgeford (1985) reported inattention by some teachers to those procedures likely to promote valid, reliable performance assessment, such as clearly articulating and communicating scoring criteria, defining acceptable levels of performance, repeating observations, keeping written records, and checking judgments against other data (e.g., test scores). However, they did find that attention to quality control increased as grade level increased.

Gullickson's (1982; Gullickson & Ellwein, 1985)

studies of South Dakota teachers' testing strategies provide further evidence of a lack of quality control strategies. For example, few of the teachers he surveyed computed summary statistics needed to evaluate test performance. Most limited test questions to short answer and matching, which test lower cognitive levels. Few teachers took time to improve their tests, and usually reused items without careful item analysis. Overall, Gullickson concluded that teachers have not been taught how to evaluate their test items, take necessary steps to improve quality, or accurately set criterion levels for student performance. Further, they do not value statistical analysis of test items as a helpful strategy in the classroom (Gullickson, 1984a, 1984b).

Attitudes toward Assessment

Although most research on testing in schools has focused on attitudes toward standardized tests, a few studies allow us to draw some conclusions about teacher and student attitudes toward classroom assessment. Some of those attitudes are reflected in the patterns of test use among teachers. Teachers value assessments that provide information relevant to the decisions they may face. Interviews of 35 elementary school teachers conducted by Salmon-Cox (1980) illustrate this point. The teachers judged students even in the absence of formally communicated information. They sometimes gave social and background characteristics greater emphasis than ability. And observation of students was the most frequent mode of assessment for these teachers. Salmon-Cox (1981) concluded that "teacher preference, in effect, is for continuous movies, with sound, while a test score or even a profile of scores, is more akin to a black and white photograph."

Stiggins and Bridgeford (1985) explored teacher attitudes about testing by asking teachers to indicate their concerns about various types of assessment. By far the most frequently expressed concern was uncertainty about how to improve test quality and manage the assessment environment. Although the teachers were not in the midst of changing assessment methods and generally were comfortable with their current procedures, they consistently noted that they were interested in suggestions for improvement.

Student attitudes about standardized tests have been studied to some extent, but again until very recently, researchers have expressed little interest in exploring student perceptions of teacher-developed assessments. A study of standardized tests by Stetz and Beck (1979) included some student-directed questions about classroom assessment. Their results suggest that students are more concerned about teacher-made than standardized tests. Most students thought teacher-made tests are harder, and twice as many got nervous before a teacher-made test. . . .

INSIGHTS FROM RESEARCH ON TEACHING

. . . Recent summaries of research on teaching compiled by Shavelson and Stern (1981), Clark and Peterson (1986), and Shulman (1986) instruct us in two ways. First, by providing a window into teacher decisionmaking processes, they allow us to see the complexity of the teacher's classroom assessment task. Second, by using this window we can explore the nature and role of assessment before, during, and after instruction. From this vantage point we can see the great challenges teachers face in accurately assessing student characteristics.

The Complexity of Classroom Assessment

Research on teaching tells us that assessment is unquestionably one of teachers' most complex and important tasks. Each investigation of the teaching process arises out of a model or conceptualization of teaching and learning. Every model of effective teaching requires that teachers base their instructional decisions on some knowledge of student characteristics. We begin to comprehend the complexity of

classroom assessment as we explore the range and frequency of teachers' decisions and the plethora of student characteristics they must consider in making those decisions.

Factors in Teacher Decisionmaking. Investigations of classroom practices have tended to focus on three major types of decisions, each placing significantly different measurement demands on teachers. These are: preinstructional (preactive, planning) decisions, interactive decisions (made during instruction), and postinstructional decisions. Shavelson and Stern (1981) summarized 30 studies of teacher decisionmaking identifying the type of instuctional decision teachers faced in each and the salient cues those teachers considered in making those decisions. Salient cues represented the specific student characteristics considered. Sixty-six such cues were listed across all studies.

Classifying these cues as representing academic, social, or personality student characteristics, and crossing those with the preinstructional, interactive, and postinstructional categories of group decisions, we can develop a frequency count reflecting (a) the extent to which teachers must be able to measure more than academic achievement, and (b) how factors considered vary as a function of the nature of the decision (see Table 1).

When faced with planning decisions, teachers placed greatest reliance on academic and ability variables. Decisions made during instruction had antecedents in social interaction with academics, and decisions rendered after instruction considered a variety of salient cues. Clearly teachers were measuring more than achievement. Other student characteristics considered by teachers were such social characteristics as disruptiveness, work habits,

TABLE 1 Frequency of Student Characteristics Reported in Research by Type and Decision Context Studies[a]

| CHARACTERISTIC | DECISION CONTEXT | | | |
	PLANNING	DURING INSTRUCTION	AFTER INSTRUCTION	TOTAL
Academic	15	11	2	28
Social	5	15	3	23
Personal	6	4	5	15
Total	26	30	10	66

[a]Summarized from Shavelson and Stern, 1981.

consideration, group mood, and participation. Teachers also considered such personal characteristics as motivation, self-esteem, openness, sense of humor, attentiveness, family background, and attitudes.

From a measurement perspective, perhaps the most important point of these lists of nonacademic student characteristics is that these factors are not considered by teachers just in managing disruptive behavior. They play a role in planning instruction, managing interactive exchanges, and making evaluative judgments about students. Further, when teachers gather information about these factors, they have no published standardized tests or guidelines on which to rely. They are left to their own devices with little support or training.

Interactive Decisionmaking. Most models of interactive decisionmaking posit the teacher observing some form of student behavior or performance and comparing it to a standard to see if it is within tolerance (Clark & Peterson, 1986; Shavelson & Stern, 1981; Yinger, 1977). These decisions occur frequently. For instance, Clark and Peterson synthesized six studies and concluded that teachers make an interactive decision on average every two minutes. To understand the measurement implications of this pace and its importance for learners, consider that in half of these decisions teachers have antecedent thoughts based on concerns about the learner, including comparisons of behavior, knowledge, and so forth, with expectations or standards (Clark and Peterson; Marland, 1977). In this context, the teacher must either assess very rapidly with validity and reliability, or rely on an existing reservoir of valid, reliable information. Surely this is an assessment and information processing task umparalleled in other professions.

Teachers use a wide range of interactional cues to assess their students. However, ethnographic research on classroom interaction suggests that many of these teacher judgements inappropriately incorporate the level of congruence between student behavior and teacher expectation, resulting in potential misdiagnosis of student ability and achievement. Erickson (1977) has described this interactional congruence factor as "assessment of the intellectual competence of children on the basis of social performance" (p. 64), and found that teachers use cues such as the ways children sit, talk, listen,

and respond to instructions to develop a *typology* of the kinds of students in the class. This typology may become a fixed map for interpreting and thus defining subsequent student behavior. The teacher's typological map may be erroneous and, once fixed, inhibit proper assessment of student growth and change. . . .

Teacher Planning. As if interactive decisionmaking were not complex enough, we must also consider the pre- and postinstructional decisions teachers face. In this case, however, the research holds a surprise. Although planning is a complex enterprise for teachers, work conducted by Zaharik (1975), Yinger (1977), and others (summarized by Clark & Peterson, 1986) reveals that teachers tend not to focus on assessments of student characteristics when they plan. Nor do they focus on goals and objectives. The instructional activity is most often the planning unit. Teachers focus on activities and content—what they will do and cover. Shulman (1980) explores the implications of these data for measurement and evaluation:

> For years, those of us in educational research, especially in evaluation and measurement, have been insisting that teachers learn to think straight educationally. By that we mean they have to learn to think of outcomes stated in terms of behavioral objectives. However . . . [t]eachers appear not to evaluate their day-to-day activity in terms of general assessments of achieved outcomes, but rather attend to variations in student *involvement*. When we ask teachers, "What did you achieve today?" they are inclined to say, "Well, we covered three more pages of math, and the kids were really involved." We then become critical and berate teachers for not thinking in terms of objectives—which ones they achieved and which not. I believe we have to treat the teachers' observations as data rather than as sources for blame. That is how teachers evaluate what they do. (p. 70)

When teachers do focus on student characteristics during planning, it is often only early in the year and is done very quickly and efficiently. Calderhead (1983) and Salmon-Cox (1980) point out that experienced teachers become very proficient at using available information to understand their new class almost before it arrives in the classroom. However, these rapid conclusions based on scant data can have detrimental effects. Peterson and Barger (1985) suggest that teachers may become fixed on initial impressions based on unreliable, inaccurate information, and use subsequent data to maintain a consistent picture of the student.

Dealing with Complexity

Given this impressive array of decision contexts and student characteristics, teachers must act decisively to make the assessment task manageable. Research on teaching provides some clues to how they do this. Simon (1957) suggested that, when faced with an overload of information to process, teachers simplify their view of reality to create a manageable task. Teachers find thinking strategies that allow them to process and store information efficiently, often as a reflex action.

For example, teachers sometimes reduce the number of assessments by tapping group rather than individual data. Dahlof and Lundgren (1970) found teachers identifying a "steering group," a subset of students in the class with whom they could check for dependable information on whether to repeat instruction or proceed to the next topic. . . .

As mentioned earlier, it appears that teachers gather information quickly and form it into impressions of student ability very early in the school year (Calderhead, 1983). Once those judgments are made, assessment of ability ceases, leaving those impressions in place and allowing the teacher to move on to other aspects of assessment. There is also evidence that teachers turn to characteristics that are most easily measured, such as social behavior and task completion, that often become as crucial as achievement in classroom assessment (Weiner & Kukla, 1974). And when teachers measure achievement they focus on those levels of achievement most efficiently measured, such as recall of facts (Fleming & Chambers, 1983). . . .

TAKING STOCK

We claimed at the outset that the field of educational measurement has given too little attention to understanding the assessment issues that teachers face daily in classrooms. To illustrate, we have reviewed some of the available research on testing to glean insights into classroom assessment. To supplement them, we turned to emerging research on the teaching and learning process, teacher decisionmaking, and classroom interaction. Still, the composite picture lacks focus.

Summary of Research on Testing

From the body of research on testing in the schools we know a great deal about large-scale standardized testing for accountability. But for the classroom, we know little more than that standardized tests are of secondary importance. We know that nearly all assessments used in the classroom originate with the teacher and that observation and judgment are important tools.

We can say with some confidence that assessment typically is carried out by teachers whose formal training in assessment is minimal and narrow in focus. Some data suggest that assessment methods tend to remain the same for a teacher regardless of the purpose but tend to change with grade and subject matter. Research also suggests that scholastic and social criteria are considered in evaluating students and teachers use such information to form initial, lasting impressions of students. Students and teachers appear sensitive to those impressions and behave accordingly. One analysis indicates that teachers' paper and pencil tests primarily measure recall and are short and objective. Another survey suggests that structured performance assessments are also used as formal assessments in schools.

In general, however, we know little about the quality of these assessments. Two studies suggest that teacher-developed test items are of poor technical quality. Other studies indicate that teachers rarely check the technical quality of their tests.

We are able to draw only preliminary conclusions about attitudes regarding teacher-developed tests. One study found some elementary teachers valuing social and family background characteristics more than ability characteristics in classroom decisionmaking. Another found teachers generally comfortable with the assessments they use, but concerned about improving their quality. A large-scale survey of students revealed that they find teacher-developed tests more difficult than standardized tests and take them more seriously. Finally, there is some evidence that students feel that tests do not help them know what to study, tests generally call for memorization, and tests requiring short rather than extended answers are preferable. . . .

Summary of Research on Teaching

First and foremost , this research gives us a firsthand look at the tremendous complexity of the classroom assessment task. Teachers measure dozens of student variables for a variety of reasons and at an incredible pace. While planning instruction, teachers tend to focus on activities to be accomplished rather than on goals or measured outcomes. They do consider student characteristics, early in the school year while sizing up the class. Those first impressions appear quite stable. During instruction teachers make interactive decisions about every two minutes, in most cases, considering student characteristics as antecedents to those decisions. Decisions are also made after instruction, but the research is surprisingly silent on this phase.

Teachers use a variety of strategies to simplify the information-processing load in the classroom. Some gather information quickly, form impressions, and move on to other tasks. Others focus on a sample of students and generalize. Still others gain efficiency in measurement by attending to easily counted factors such as tasks completed. When measuring achievement, many teachers rely on short, easy-to-score, objective tests of recall. Little is known about the impact of these strategies on the quality of the resulting data. . . .

THE UNMET CHALLENGE

Regardless of the depth of information in these summaries at least one point has become obvious: Teachers trained only in paper and pencil measurement methods face real difficulties in the classroom assessment environment described previously. Both oral questions and performance assessments play key roles in classroom assessment. There are fundamental, far-reachng differences between the science of testing and the assessment demands of the classroom. We have been aware of these differences for decades and have failed to address them.

In 1943, Scates clearly articulated key discrepancies between the science of measurement and classroom assessment. . . .

In the main, science is concerned with abstracting a specific element out of a complex—with isolating a character that is common to a group of objects, and freeing the character from restrictions of immediate circumstance. The teacher's concern is just the opposite. He is working with variable individuals to build a variable product. (p. 3)

The scientist may be satisfied with a series of cross-sectional observations; the teacher must be aware of continuing behavior. The scientist is primarily analytical, seeking the elemental, the universal, the permanent; the teacher is primarily constructive, seeking to produce an artistic whole that is unique and changeful. (p. 4)

The scientist must be striclty uniform, insofar as he can, in his observations. He must have an observational instrument which will reflect the same trait or quality in every instance and in the hands of every observer. . . . The teacher, on the other hand, with much greater tolerance granted him, has no such interest in either objectivity or precision. . . . Impersonal observations may have more universal quality but they are also more barren. . . . [Thus] the things that science wants *out* of its observations the teacher wants *in*. (p[p]. 5–6) . . .

Implications for the Classroom and Schools

One major implication of our failure to meet this challenge and to understand and assist teachers with the task demands of the classroom assessment environment could be the extensive use of unsound measurement procedures in our schools. The result of poor measurement could be poor decisionmaking. At the least, poor decisions mean inefficient instruction, and at worst can lead to failure to learn and an attendant loss of student motivation to participate in the learning process.

A second implication of continuing to ignore classroom assessment will be the continued opinion of laypersons and policymakers that the best or only fair way to measure schooling outcomes is by standardized paper and pencil tests. Despite the failure of these tests to track anywhere near the full range of outcomes we intend schools to achieve, standardized tests represent the complete focus of our attempts to hold schools accountable. Unless and until we document the validity and reliability of classroom assessments and act to correct any deficiencies uncovered in investigating their quality, we remain unable to recommend a broader, more valid set of accountability indicators.

A third implication of our failure to address classroom assessment issues (a corollary of the second) is that because standardized tests have achieved such a strong reputation as the valued measure of educational outcomes, they well continue to be the only criterion variables in currently popular efforts to discover effective teaching practices. This continues despite criticism of these tests as inappropriate, narrow, and insensitive criteria in this research context (Dunkin & Biddle, 1974; Shulman, 1986). Brophy and Good (1986) have reviewed research on the relationship between teacher behavior and school achievement and again have called for an expansion of our definition of achievement to include more than standardized test scores. The measurement community will remain unable to respond to this crucial issue until we conduct the research and training needed to help instill confidence in teacher-developed classroom assessments.

The final and perhaps most compelling implication of our failure to address teachers' classroom assessment needs will be the continued alienation of teachers from systematic assessment and evaluation processes. If teachers oppose standardized testing, it is because they see it as not addressing their needs. If many teacher training programs do not require training in assessment, it is because that training is not perceived as relevant to teaching. Until we understand assessment in the teacher's world in terms relevant to the teacher and translate our concepts into those terms, we will remain unable to alter teachers' perceptions of either the validity or the relevance of those concepts. . . .

Implications for Training

As this research is completed, the demands of the classroom assessment environment will become more clear. In the meantime, it is obvious that current administrator and teacher measurement training priorities must change.

Administrators who are currently trained as accountability agents to report standardized test scores to school boards might also be trained to be instructional leaders and assist and support teachers with their day-to-day measurement of student growth.

Such training in classroom assessment methods might be part of administrator certification programs.

Teachers too should be provided with relevant, focused preservice and inservice training in classroom assessment strategies and useful quality control procedures. At least some of the content of that training is suggested by the research reviewed here. Training priorities include measuring higher order reasoning skills, writing quality paper and pencil test items, integrating assessment and instruction through oral questioning strategies, and designing quality performance assessments based on observation and professional judgment.

This revised training effort should extend beyond the school walls. Legislators, taxpayers, parents, and the public must understand that the mere presence of a testing program does not assure quality education and that more standardized testing will not of itself produce better schools. They must become aware of the full range of complex student characteristics influenced by quality education, and of the many alternatives available for measuring those characteristics equitably. In short, we need an expanded definition of what it means to measure student achievement.

REFERENCES

Airasian, P. W. (1984). *Classroom assessment and educational improvement.* Paper presented at the conference Classroom Assessment: A Key to Educational Excellence, Northwest Regional Educational Laboratory, Portland, OR.

Airasian, P. W., Kellaghan, T., & Madaus, G. F. (1977). The stability of teachers' perceptions of pupil characteristics. *The Irish Journal of Education, 11*(1, 2), 78–84.

Airasian, P. W., Kellaghan, T., Madaus, G. F., & Pedulla, J. (1977). Proportion and direction of teacher rating changes of pupil progress attributable to standardized test information. *Journal of Educational Psychology, 69*(6), 702–709.

American Psychological Association. (1984). *Revised standards for educational and psychological test and manuals.* Washington, DC: Author.

Brophy, J. F., & Good, T. L. (1970). Teachers' communication of differential expectations for children's classroom performance: Some behavioral data. *Journal of Educational Psychology, 61*(5), 365–374.

Brophy, J. F., & Good, T. L. (1974). *Teacher-student relationships*. New York: Holt, Rinehart, & Winston.

Brophy, J. F., & Good, T. L. (1986). Teacher behavior and student achievement. In M. C. Wittrock (Ed.), *Handbook of research on teaching* (3rd ed.) (pp. 328–375). New York: Macmillan.

Burdin, J. L. (1982). Teacher certification. In H. E. Mitzel (Ed.), *Encyclopedia of education research* (5th ed.). New York: Free Press.

Burstein, L. (1983). A word about this issue. *Journal of Educational Measurement, 20*(2), 99–101.

Calderhead, T. (1983). A psychological approach to research on teachers' classroom decision making. *British Educational Research Journal, 7*(1), 51–57.

Calfee, R. C., & Drum, P. A. (1976). *How the researcher can help the reading teacher with classroom assessment*. Unpublished manuscript, Stanford University, Stanford, CA.

Carter, K. (1984). Do teachers understand the principles for writing tests? *Journal of Teacher Education, 35*(6), 57–60.

Clark, C. M., & Peterson, P. L. (1986). Teachers' thought processes. In M. C. Wittrock (Ed.), *Handbook of research on teaching* (3rd ed.) (pp. 255–296). New York: Macmillan.

Coffman, W. E. (1983). *Testing in the schools: A historical perspective*. Paper presented at the Center for the Study of Evaluation Annual Invitational Conference, University of California at Los Angeles.

Cooley, R. E. (1979). Spokes in a wheel: A linguistic and rhetorical analysis of Native American public discourse. *Proceedings of the Fifth Annual Meeting*, 552–558.

Dahlof, U., & Lundgren, V. P. (1970). *Macro and micro approaches combined for curriculum process evaluation: A Swedish field project*. (Research Report.) Gotenberg, Sweden: University of Gotenberg, Institute of Education.

DuMont, R. V., Jr., & Wax, M. L. (1969). Cherokee school society and the intercultural classroom. *Human Organization, 28*(3), 217–227.

Dunkin, M. J., & Biddle, B. J. (1974). *The study of teaching*. New York: Holt, Rinehart, & Winston.

Erickson, F. (1977). some approaches to inquiry in school-community ethnography. *Anthropology and Education Quarterly, 8*(2), 58–69.

Farr, R., & Griffin, M. (1973). Measurement gaps in teacher education. *Journal of Research and Development in Education, 7*, 19–28.

Fleming, M., & Chambers, B. (1983). Teacher-made tests: Windows on the classroom. In W. E. Hathaway (Ed.), *Testing in the schools: New directions for testing and measurement, No. 19* (pp. 29–38). San Francisco: Jossey-Bass.

Fyans, L. J. (1985). *Teachers as test experts: Hidden talent*. Paper presented at the annual meeting of the American Educational Research Association, Chicago.

Gearing, F., & Epstein, P. (1982). Learning to wait: An ethnographic probe into the operations of an item of hidden curriculum. In G. Spindler (Ed.), *Doing the ethnography of schooling: Educational anthropology in action* (pp. 240–267). New York: Holt, Rinehart, & Winston.

Gil, D., & Freeman, D. (1980). *An investigation of the diagnostic and remedial practices of classroom teachers*. (Research Series No. 78). East Lansing: Michigan State University, Institute for Research on Teaching. (ERIC Document Reproduction Service No. ED 192 247)

Good, T. L., & Brophy, J. F. (1978). *Looking in classrooms* (2nd ed.). New York: Harper & Row.

Goslin, D. A. (1967). *Teachers and testing*. New York: Russell Sage.

Gullickson, A. R. (1982). *Survey data collected in survey of South Dakota teachers' attitudes and opinions toward testing*. Vermillon. University of South Dakota.

Gullickson, A. R. (1984a). *Matching teacher training with teacher needs in testing*. Paper presented at the annual meeting of the American Educational Research Association, New Orleans.

Gullickson, A. R. (1984b). Teacher perspectives of their instructional use of tests. *Journal of Educational Research, 77*(4), 224–246.

Gullickson, A. R., & Ellwein, M. C. (1985). Post hoc analysis of teacher-made tests: The goodness-of-fit between prescription and practice. *Educational Measurement: Issues and Practice, 4*(1), 15–18.

Heartel, E., Ferrara, S., Korpi, M., & Prescott, B. (1984). *Testing in secondary schools: Student perspectives*. Paper presented at the annual meeting of the American Educational Research Associaton, New Orleans.

Heath, S. B. (1982). Questioning at home and at school: A comparative study. In G. Spindler (Ed.), *Doing the ethnography of schooling: Educational anthropology in action* (pp. 102–131). New York: Holt, Rinehart, & Winston.

Heath, S. B. (1983). *Ways with words, language, life and work in communities and classrooms*. Cambridge, England: Cambridge University Press.

Herbert, G. W. (1974). Teachers' ratings of classroom behavior: Factorial structure. *British Journal of Educational Psychology, 44*, 233–240.

Herman, J., & Dorr-Bremme, D. W. (1982). *Assessing*

students: Teachers' routine practices and reasoning. Paper presented at the annual meeting of the American Educational Research Association, New York.

Jackson, P. W. (1968). *Life in classrooms.* New York: Holt, Rinehart, & Winston.

Joyce, B. (1979a). *Teachers' thoughts while teaching.* (Research Series No. 58). East Lansing: Michigan State University, Institute for Research on Teaching. (ERIC Document Reproduction Service No. ED 057 016)

Joyce, B. (1979b). *Teaching styles at South Bay School.* (Research Series No. 57). East Lansing: Michigan State University, Institute for Research on Teaching. (ERIC Document Reproduction Service No. ED 187 666)

Kellaghan, T., Madaus, G. F., & Airasian, P. W. (1982). *The effects of standardized testing.* Boston, MA: Kluwer-Nijhoff.

Labov, W. (1970). *The study of nonstandard English.* Urbana, IL: National Council of Teachers of English.

Labov, W. (1972). *Sociolinguistic patterns.* Philadelphia: University of Pennsylvania Press

Lazar-Morris, C., Polin, L., May, R., & Barry, L. (1980). *A review of the literature on test use.* Los Angeles: University of California, Center for the Study of Evaluation. (ERIC Documentation Reproduction Service No. ED 204 411)

Lortie, D. (1975). *School teacher.* Chicago: University of Chicago Press.

Marland, P. N. (1977). *A study of teachers' interactive thoughts.* Unpublished doctoral dissertation, University of Alberta.

Mehan, H. (1979). *Learning lessons: Social organization in the classroom.* Cambridge, MA: Harvard University Press.

Mehan, H. (1980) The competent student. *Anthropology and Education Quarterly, 11*(3), 131–152.

Mehan, H. (1982). The structure of classroom events and their consequences for student performance. In P. Gilmore & A. A. Glatthorn (Eds.), *Children in and out of school* (pp. 59–87). Washington, DC: Center for Applied Linguistics.

Mehrens, W. A., & Lehmann, I. J. (1984). *Measurement and evaluation in education and psychology* (3rd ed.). New York: Holt, Rinehart, & Winston.

Michaels, S., & Cook-Gumperz, J. (1979). A study of sharing time with first grade students: Discourse narratives in the classroom. *Proceedings of the Fifth Annual Meeting* (pp. 647–660). Berkeley, CA: Berkeley Linguistics Society.

Morine-Dershimer, G. (1979). *Teacher conceptions of children.* (Research Series No. 59). East Lansing:

Michigan State University, Institute for Research on Teaching. (ERIC Document Reproduction Service No. ED 180 988)

Morrison, A., & McIntyre, D. (1969). *Teachers and teaching.* Harmondsworth, Middlesex, England: Penguin Books.

Pedulla, J. J., Airasian, P. W., & Madaus, G. F. (1980). Do teacher ratings and standardized test results of students yield the same information? *American Educational Research Journal, 17,* 303–307.

Peterson, P. L., & Barger, S. A. (1985). Attribution theory and teacher expectancy. In J. B. Dasek, V. C. Hall, & W. J. Meyer (Eds.), *Teacher expectancies* (pp. 159–184). Hillsdale, NJ: Laurence Earlbaum.

Philips, S. U. (1972). Participant structures and communicative competence: Warm Springs children in community and classroom. In C. B. Cazden, V. P. John, & D. Hymes (Eds.), *Functions of language in the classroom* (pp. 370–394). New York: Teachers College Press.

Rist, R. (1970). Student social class and teacher expectations: The self-fulfilling prophecy in ghetto education. *Harvard Educational Review, 40,* 411–451.

Rudman, H. E., Kelley, J. L., Wanous, D. S., Mehrens, W. A., Clark, C. M., & Porter, A. C. (1980). *Integrating assessment with instruction: A review (1922–1980).* (Research Series No. 75.) East Lansing: Michigan State University, Institute for Research on Teaching. (ERIC Document Reproduction Services No. ED 189 136)

Salmon-Cox, L. (1980). *Teachers and tests: What's really happening?* Paper presented at the annual meeting of the American Educational Research Association, Boston, MA.

Salmon-Cox, L. (1981). Teachers and standardized achievement tests: What's really happening? *Phi Delta Kappan, 62,* 631–634.

Scates, D. E. (1943). Differences between measurement criteria of pure scientists and of classroom teachers. *Journal of Educational Research, 37,* 1–13.

Schultz, J., & Florio, S. (1979). *Stop and freeze: The negotiation of social and physical space in a kindergarten/first-grade classroom.* (Occasional Paper No. 26.) East Lansing: Michigan State University, Institute for Research on Teaching.

Shavelson, R. J., Cadwell, J., & Izu, T. (1977). Teachers' sensitivity to the reliability of information in making pedagogical decisions. *American Educational Research Journal, 14*(2), 83–97.

Shavelson, R. J., & Stern, P. (1981). Research on teachers' pedagogical thoughts, judgments, decisions, and behavior. *Review of Educational Research, 41*(4), 455–498.

Shulman, L. S. (1980). Test design: A view from practice. In E. L. Baker & E. S. Quellmalz (Eds.), *Educational testing and evaluation* (pp. 63–73). Los Angeles, CA: Sage.

Shulman, L. S. (1986). Paradigms and research programs for the student of teaching: A contemporary perspective. In M. C. Wittrock (Ed.) *Handbook of research on teaching* (3rd ed.) (pp. 3–36). New York: Macmillan.

Simon. H. A. (1957). *Models of man: Social and rational: Mathematical essays.* New York: Wiley.

Sproul, L., & Zubrow, D. (1982). Standardized testing from the administrative perspective. *Phi Delta Kappan, 62*, 628–631.

Stetz, F., & Beck, M. (1979). *Comments from the classroom: Teachers' and students' opinions of achievement tests.* Paper presented at the annual meeting of the American Educational Research Association, San Francisco.

Stiggins, R. J., & Bridgeford, N. J. (1985). The ecology of classroom assessment. *Journal of Educational Measurement, 22*(4), 271–286.

Stinnett, T. M. (1969). Teacher certification. In R. L. Ebel (Ed.), *Encyclopedia of educational research* (4th ed.) (pp. 614–618). New York: Macmillan.

Tollefson, N., Tracy, D. B., Kaiser, J., Chen, J. S., & Kleinsasser, A. (1985). *Teachers' attitudes toward tests.* Paper presented at the annual meeting of the American Educational Research Association, Chicago.

Ward, J. G. (1982). An overview of the AFT's teaching and testing. In S. B. Anderson & L. B. Coburn (Eds.), *Academic testing and the consumer* (pp. 47–52). San Francisco: Jossey-Bass.

Watson-Gegeo, K. A., & Boggs, S. T. (1977). From verbal play to talk story: The role of routines in speech events among Hawaiian children. In S. Ervin-Tripp (Ed.), *Child discourse* (pp. 67–90). New York: Academic Press.

Weiner, B., & Kukla, A. (1974). An attributional analysis of achievement motivation. *Journal of Personality and Social Psychology, 15*, 1–20.

Weinshank, A. B. (1980). *Investigations of the diagnostic reliability of reading specialists, learning disabilities specialists, and classroom teachers: Results and implications.* (Research Series No. 72.) East Lansing: Michigan State University, Institute for Research on Teaching. (ERIC Document Reproduction Services No. ED 189 574)

Whitmer, S. P. (1983). *A descriptive multimethod study of teacher judgment during the marking process.* (Research Series No. 122.) East Lansing: Michigan State University, Institute for Research on Teaching. (ERIC Document Reproduction Services No. ED 234 052)

Woeller, E. H. (1979). *Requirements for certification for elementary school, secondary school and junior college teachers.* Chicago: University of Chicago Press.

Yeh, J. (1978). *Test use in the schools.* Los Angeles, CA: University of California at Los Angeles, Center for the Study of Evaluation.

Yinger, R. (1977). *A study of teacher planning: Description and theory development using ethnographic and informal process methods.* Unpublished doctoral dissertation, Michigan State University, East Lansing.

Zaharik, J. A. (1975). Teachers' planning models. *Educational Leadership, 33*, 134–139.

Support for this review was provided in part by the National Institute for Education (NIE), Department of Education, Contract #400–83–0005. Opinions expressed do not necessarily reflect the position, policy or endorsement of NIE. The authors wish to thank Peter Airasian, William Coffman, Arlen Gullickson, and Bernard McKenna for their review of drafts of this paper.

PERMISSIONS

Unit I: Teachers and Teaching

"How Schools Work"
Rebecca Barr and Robert Dreeben, with Nonglak Wiratchai
From *How Schools Work*, Rebecca Barr and Robert Dreeben, Copyright © 1983 by The University of Chicago. All rights reserved. Published 1983. Reprinted by permission of the publisher.

"The Executive Functions of Teaching"
David C. Berliner
Instructor, September 1983, 43 (2), 28–40. Reprinted by permission of the author.

"Research into Practice: Cautions and Qualifications"
Christopher M. Clark
From *The Contexts of School-Based Literacy*, T. Raphael, ed., 1986, New York: Random House Publishers. Reprinted by permission of the publisher.

"On Knowing How to Teach"
Philip W. Jackson
Reprinted by permission of the publisher from Jackson, Philip W., *The Practice of Teaching*. (New York: Teachers College Press, © 1986 by Teachers College, Columbia University. All rights reserved.) Chapters 1 & 6. (See Unit III.)

"Why Teachers Won't Teach"
Milbrey Wallin McLaughlin, R. Scott Pfeifer, Deborah Swanson-Owens, and Sylvia Yee
Phi Delta Kappan, February 1986, 67 (6), 420–427. Reprinted with permission of the authors.

"Labor Relations and Teacher Policy"
Douglas E. Mitchell and Charles T. Kerchner
From *Handbook of Teaching and Policy*, edited by Lee S. Shulman and Gary Sykes. Copyright © 1983 by Longman Inc. Reprinted by permission.

"Improving the Productivity of America's Schools"
Herbert J. Walberg
Educational Leadership, May 1984, 41 (8), 19–27. Reprinted with permission of the Association for Supervision and Curriculum Development. Copyright © (1984) by the Association for Supervision and Curriculum Development. All rights reserved.

Unit II: Schools and Classrooms

"Synthesis of Research on Classroom Management"
Edmund T. Emmer and Carolyn M. Evertson
Educational Leadership, January 1981, 38 (4), 342–347. Reprinted with permission of the Association for Supervision and Curriculum Development. Copyright © (1981) by the Association for Supervision and Curriculum Development. All rights reserved.

"Classroom Discourse as Improvisation: Relationships between Academic Task Structure and Social Participation Structure in Lessons"
Frederick Erickson
From *Communicating in Classrooms*, L. C. Wilkinson, ed., 1982, New York: Academic Press. Reprinted by permission of the author.

"Cooperative Learning"
David W. Johnson and Roger T. Johnson
Unpublished manuscript 1987. Reprinted by permission of the authors.

"Introduction and Integration of Classroom Routines by Expert Teachers"
Gaea Leinhardt, C. Weidman, and K. M. Hammond
Curriculum Inquiry, Vol. 17, No. 2, Copyright © 1987 The Ontario Institute for Studies in Education. Reprinted by permission of John Wiley & Sons, Inc.

Unit III: Classroom Instruction

"Opportunity to Learn"
Lorin W. Anderson
Reprinted with permission from *The International Encyclopedia of Education*, T. Husen and T. N. Postlethwaite, eds., Copyright 1985, Pergamon Press.

"Tempus Educare"
David C. Berliner
From Penelope L. Peterson and Herbert J. Walberg: *Research on Teaching, Concepts, Findings and Implications*, © 1979 by McCutchan Publishing Corporation, Berkeley, CA 94702. Reprinted with the permission of the publisher.

"Models of the Learner"
Jerome Bruner
Educational Researcher, June/July 1985, 14 (6), 5–8. Reprinted with permission of the American Educational Research Association.

"Reconsidering Research on Learning from Media"
Richard E. Clark
Review of Educational Research, Winter 1983, 53 (4), 445–459. Reprinted by permission of the American Educational Research Association.

"The Mimetic and the Transformative: Alternative Outlooks on Teaching"
Philip W. Jackson
    Reprinted by permission of the publisher from Jackson, Philip W., *The Practice of Teaching*. (New York: Teachers College Press, © 1986 by Teachers College, Columbia University. All rights reserved.) Chapters 1 & 6. (See Unit I.)
"A Retrospective Look at Teachers' Reliance on Commercial Reading Materials"
Patrick Shannon
    Language Arts, November/December 1982, 59 (8), 844–853. Copyright © 1982 by the National Council of Teachers of English. Reprinted by permission of the publisher.
"Historical Perspective on Educational Technology"
Patrick Suppes
    From *Proceedings of the Second Conference of the University/Urban Schools National Task Force: What Works in Urban Schools*, R. M. Bossone, ed., 1982, New York: Center for Advanced Study in Education, City University of New York. Reprinted by permission of the author.

Unit IV: Classroom Teaching

"The Environment of Instruction: The Function of Seatwork in a Commercially Developed Curriculum"
Linda Anderson
    From *Comprehension Instruction* edited by Gerald G. Duffy, Laura R. Robinson and Jana Mason. Copyright © 1984 by Longman Inc. Reprinted by permission.
"Attention, Tasks and Time"
Lorin W. Anderson
    From *Time and School Learning*, Lorin W. Anderson, 1984, London: Croom Helm. Reprinted by permission of the publisher.
"Applying Research on Teacher Clarity"
Donald R. Cruickshank
    Journal of Teacher Education, March/April 1985, 36 (2), 44–48. Reprinted by permission of the American Association of Colleges for Teacher Education.
"Academic Work"
Walter Doyle
    Review of Educational Research, Summer 1983, 53 (2), 159–199. Reprinted by permission of the American Educational Research Association.
"Synthesis of Research on Teachers' Questioning"
Meredith Gall
    Educational Leadership, November 1984, 42 (3), 40–47. Copyright © (1984) by the Association for Supervision and Curriculum Development. All rights reserved. Reprinted with permission of the Association for Supervision and Curriculum Development.
"Research on Classroom Teaching"
Thomas Good
    From *Handbook of Teaching and Policy* edited by Lee S. Shulman and Gary Sykes. Copyright © 1983 by Longman Inc. Reprinted by permission.
"The Role of Wait Time in Higher Cognitive Level Learning"
Kenneth Tobin
    Review of Educational Research, Spring 1987, 57 (1), 69–95. Reprinted by permission of the American Educational Research Association.

Unit V: Assessing and Evaluating

"Classroom Assessment and Educational Improvement"
Peter W. Airasian
    Paper presented at a conference on "Classroom Assessment: A Key to Educational Excellence," 1984, Portland, Ore.: Northwest Regional Educational Laboratory. Reprinted by permission.
"Teacher Evaluation in the Organizational Context: A Review of the Literature"
Linda Darling-Hammond, Arthur E. Wise, and Sara R. Pease
    Review of Educational Research, Fall 1983, 53 (3), 285–328. Reprinted by permission of the American Educational Research Association.
"Feedback, Correctives, and Enrichment"
Thomas R. Guskey
    From *Implementing Master Learning*, 1985, Belmont, Calif.: Wadsworth Publishing Co. Reprinted by permission of the publisher.
"Marks and Marking Systems"
Tom Kubiszyn and Gary Borich
    From *Educational Testing and Measurement* by Tom Kubiszyn and Gary Borich. Copyright © 1984 by Scott, Foresman and Company. Reprinted by permission.
"The Minimum Conditions for Valid Evaluation of Teacher Performance"
Donald Medley, Robert Soar, and Homer Coker
    Journal of Classroom Interaction, Winter 1983, 19 (1), 22–27. Reprinted with permission of the *Journal of Classroom Interaction*.
"Classroom Assessment: A Key to Effective Education"
Richard J. Stiggins, Nancy Faires Conklin, and Nancy J. Bridgeford
    Educational Measurement: Issues and Practice, Summer 1986, 5 (2), 5–17. Reprinted by permission of the National Council on Measurement in Education.